Major Environmental Issues Facing the 21st Century

Mary K. Theodore
Louis Theodore

For book and bookstore information

http://www.prenhall.com

Prentice Hall PTR
Upper Saddle River, NJ 07458

Library of Congress Cataloging-in-Publication Data

Theodore, Louis.
    Major environmental issues facing the 21st century / Louis
   Theodore.
       p. cm.
   Includes index.
   ISBN 0–13–183526–2
    1. Environmental responsibility.   2. Environmental protection.
  3. Environmental sciences.   I. Title.
   GE195.7.T48 1996
   363.7—dc20   95–38019
                                       CIP

Cover design director: Jerry Votta
Acquisitions editor: Bernard Goodwin
Cover designer: Georgeen A. Theodore
Manufacturing buyer: Alexis R. Heydt
Compositor/Production services: Pine Tree Composition, Inc.

 © 1996 by Prentice Hall PTR
Prentice-Hall, Inc.
A Simon & Schuster Company
Upper Saddle River, New Jersey 07458

The publisher offers discounts on this book when ordered in bulk quantities.

For more information contact:
Corporate Sales Department
Prentice Hall PTR
One Lake Street
Upper Saddle River, New Jersey 07458
Phone: 800–382–3419
Fax: 201–236–7141
email: corpsales@cprenhall.com

Printed in the United States of America
10 9 8 7 6 5 4 3 2 1

ISBN 0-13-183526-2

Prentice-Hall International (UK) Limited, *London*
Prentice-Hall of Australia Pty. Limited, *Sydney*
Prentice-Hall Canada, Inc., *Toronto*
Prentice-Hall Hispanoamericana, S.A., *Mexico*
Prentice-Hall of India Private Limited, *New Delhi*
Prentice-Hall of Japan, Inc., *Tokyo*
Simon & Schuster Asia Pte. Ltd., *Singapore*
Editora Prentice Hall do Brasil, Ltda., *Rio de Janeiro*

Contents

IX. OTHER AREAS OF INTEREST 387

X. ETHICS 469

Preface

In the past few decades there has been an increased awareness of a wide range of environmental issues covering all sources: air, land, and water. More and more people are becoming aware of these environmental concerns, and it is important that professional people, many of whom do not possess an understanding of environmental problems, have the proper information available when involved with environmental issues. All professionals should have a basic understanding of the technical and scientific terms related to these issues as well as the regulations involved. In addition to serving the needs of the professional, this book examines how the consumer, or what has come to be defined as the average citizen, can increase his or her awareness of and help solve the environmental problems facing society.

This book is primarily intended for people who do not have a strong technical background. It is presented in simple, understandable terms for lawyers, news media individuals, business personnel, and the consumer (in particular) who need the basic fundamentals of the many environmental issues that exist and will exist in the future. The authors' objective is to provide both background material on numerous environmental issues and information on what each individual can do to help alleviate some of these problems.

This book is divided into ten Parts. Part I provides an overview that includes information on the environmental movement, regulations, and types of pollutants. Part II deals with issues related to air pollution. This section includes material on how air pollution can be controlled and on indoor air quality (which is an issue in many office buildings today). Part III discusses the problems of pollution in water and its control. The focus of Part IV is solid waste management. This section examines the different types of solid waste and how each is handled. Hazardous, medical, and nuclear waste management are also discussed. This part of the book concludes with the Superfund program and the result of its effort to clean up waste sites.

The book then begins to focus on what can be done by the consumer to help solve environmental problems, and introduces the subject of pollution prevention. The three pollution prevention topic areas reviewed include: health, safety, and accident prevention; energy conservation; and waste reduction. Health, safety, and accident prevention is the focus of Part V; energy conservation is the focus for part VI; and pollution prevention the focus of Part VII. Each of these sections of the book examines the issues not only in relationship to industry, but also at the domestic and office level. By presenting it in this manner, the reader is able to recognize his or her part in contributing to the solutions. Since the concern with many of the environmental issues arises because of the risks involved, Part VIII looks at how risks are perceived and communicated, and how individuals can be educated about these risks. Part IX provides information on other areas of interest in the environmental arena. These include many "popular" topics like greenhouse effect, acid rain, and electromagnetic fields. Finally, Part X examines ethical issues as they relate to the environment.

Contributor's List

Nelayne Alvarez
Con Edison
New York, NY

Patricia Brady
SBE Inc.
New York, NY

Elizabeth Butler
Jesuit Volunteer Corps
Syracuse, NY

Elenor Capasso
Applied Technology Services Inc.
New Rochelle, NY

Dorothy Caraher, RN
Long Island Jewish Hospital
New Hyde Park, NY

Ralph Cripino, Environmental Law Candidate
Pace University
Long Island, NY

Peter Damore
Uniroyal Chemical Co., Inc.
Naugatuck, CT

Lorraine Farrell, Dept. of Chemical Engr.
Manhattan College
Bronx, NY

Romeo Fuentebella
Petrochem Development Inc.
New York, NY

Ann Marie Gaynor
Metcalf & Eddy
New York, NY

Kevin Goohs
RTP Environmental
Carle Place, NY

David Gouveia
Boeringer Fugelheim Pharmaceuticals
Ridgefield, CT

Christine Hellwege, Master's Fellow
Manhattan College
Bronx, NY

Christine Jolly, Civil Engr.
Manhattan College
Bronx, NY

Stanley Joseph, Dept. of Chemical Engr.
Manhattan College
Bronx, NY

Pedick Lai, Master's Fellow
Manhattan College
Bronx, NY

Robert Lucas
Exxon Chemicals Inc.
Linden, NJ

James McKenna
ETSI
Roanoke, VA

Megan Reynolds
Air Products & Chemicals
Allentown, PA

Andrew Meier, Doctoral Candidate
Clemson University
Clemson, SC

James Mernin
Roy F. Weston
Edison, NJ

J. Erik Moy
Badger @ Raytheon
Cambridge, MA

Kristina Neuser, Master's Fellow
Manhattan College
Bronx, NY

Domenic Paniccia
ABB Lummus Crest Inc.
Bloomfield, NJ

Christopher Reda, Dept. of Chemical Engr.
Manhattan College
Bronx, NY

Ruth Richardson, Doctoral Candidate
University of California-Berkeley
Berkeley, CA

Julie Shanahan, Environmental Engr.
Manhattan College
Bronx, NY

Jeanmarie Spillane, Environmental Engr.
Manhattan College
Bronx, NY

Georgeen Theodore
Consulting Architect
New York, NY

Molleen K. Theodore
C/NET
San Francisco, CA

Sabrina Tran, Dept. of Environmental Engr.
Manhattan College
Bronx, NY

Brent Wainright
Home Savings of America
Cedarhurst, NY

Part I

Overview

Part I of this book is an overview of the fifty major environmental issues facing the 21st century. Eight chapters comprise Part I. In Chapter 1 a brief review of the early history of environmental issues is presented. Chapter 2 is concerned with the environmental movement in modern times. Information on various environmental groups and organizations is contained in Chapter 3. A critical examination of the United States Environmental Protection Agency is provided in Chapter 4, with no punches being pulled. Chapter 5—the longest and most detailed chapter in the book—focuses on the environmental regulations. Multimedia concerns and approaches are treated in Chapter 6, and Chapter 7 contains the sources and classifications of pollutants. Part I concludes with chapter 8, which addresses the general subject of the effects of pollution.

1

Early History

CONTRIBUTING AUTHOR

Andrew Meier

INTRODUCTION

More than any other time in history, the 21st century will be a turning point for human civilization. Human beings may be facing ecological disasters that could affect their ability to survive. These crises could force them to reexamine the value system that has governed their lives for the past two million years of existence (Gorden & Suzuki, 1991). At some point during its journey human society lost its feeling of connectedness to nature, resulting in a "we can manage the world" attitude. This attitude might ultimately lead to the destruction of this country and the world. How did it come to this? The answer lies in a knowledge of human history, a surprisingly brief chapter in the chronicle of the planet— how brief can be demonstrated by the use of a standard calendar to mark the passage of time on earth. The origin of the earth, estimated at some 4.6 billion years ago, is placed at midnight January 1, 1995, and the present at midnight December 31, 1995. Each calendar day represents approximately 12 million years of actual history. Using this time scheme, dinosaurs arrived about December 10 and disappeared on Christmas day. The first humans can be placed at 11:45 P.M. on December 31. The recorded history of human achievement takes up only the last minutes of the world (Gorden & Suzuki, 1991).

The remainder of this chapter describes the path that led to this dangerous predicament: a path that is now leading a growing number of individuals to unite in a broad social movement called environmentalism—a movement that is building a potential road out of this predicament.

THE FIRST HUMANS

The earliest humans appear to have inhabited a variety of locales within a tropical and semitropical belt stretching from Ethiopia to southern Africa about 1.9 million years ago. These first humans provided for themselves by a combination of gathering food and hunting animals. Humans, for the majority of their two million years' existence, lived in this manner. The steady development and dispersion of these early humans was largely due to an increase in their brain size. This led to the ability to think abstractly, which was vital in the development of technology, and to speak, which lead to cooperation and more elaborate social organization (Ponting, 1991). The ability to use and communicate the technology developed to overcome the hostile environment ultimately lead to the expansion of these first human settlements.

With the use of primitive tools and skins of animals for clothes, the first humans moved outside Africa about one and a half million years ago. The migration lead them into the frostfree zones of the Middle East, India, southern China and parts of Indonesia. The humans at this time could only adapt to those ecosystems found in the semitropical areas that contained a wide variety of vegetable material and small, easily hunted animals to supplement their diet. Despite relatively easy access, Europe was not settled for a long period of time due to the deficient ecosystem, which was later overcome by an increase in technology. The first evidence of human settlement in Europe is dated to about 730,000 years ago. The settlement of America was almost the last stage in the movement of humans across the globe about 20,000 years ago. This was made possible by crossing to Alaska in the last glaciation when the reduced sea levels turned the Bering Strait into a land bridge. Once the first human settlers were able to move south through the passes, they found an enormously rich environment that supplied plenty of food. The human population multiplied rapidly and within a few thousand years had spread to the tip of South America.

By about 10,000 years ago humans had spread over every continent, living in small mobile groups. A minority of these groups lived in close harmony with the environment and did minimal damage. Evidence has been found where groups tried to conserve resources in an attempt to maintain subsistence for a long period of time. In some cases totemic restrictions on hunting a particular species at a certain time of the year or only in a certain area every few years helped to maintain population levels of certain animals (Goudie, 1981). The Cree in Canada used a form of rotational hunting, only returning to an area after a considerable length of time, which allowed animal populations to recover. But the majority of these groups exploited the environment and the animals inhabiting it. In Colorado, bison were often hunted by stampeding them off a cliff, ending up with about 200 corpses, most of which could not be used. On Hawaii, within a thousand years of human settlement, thirty-nine species of land birds had become extinct (Ponting, 1991). In Australia, over the last 100,000 years, 86 percent of the large animals have become extinct. The large numbers of species lost was largely due to the tendency for hunters to concentrate on one species to the exclusion of others. The main reason why these groups avoided further damage to nature was the fact that their numbers were so small that the pressure they exerted on the environment was limited.

THE DEVELOPMENT OF AGRICULTURE

A major shift in human evolution took place between 10,000 and 12,000 years ago. Humans learned how to domesticate animals and cultivate plants and in doing so made a transition from nomadic hunter gatherer to rooted agriculturalist. The global population at this time was about four million people, which was about the maximum that could readily be supported by a gathering and hunting way of life (Ponting, 1991). The increasing difficulty in obtaining food is believed to be a major contributor to this sudden change. The farmer changed the landscape of the planet and was far more destructive then the hunter. While farming fostered the rise of cities and civilizations, it also led to practices that denuded the land of its nutrients and waterholding capacity. Great civilizations flourished and then disappeared as once-fertile land was farmed into desert.

The adoption of agriculture, combined with its two major consequences, settled communities and a steadily rising population, placed an increasing strain on the environment. The strain was localized at first, but as agriculture spread so did its effects. Agriculture involved removing the natural habitat to create an artificial habitat where humans could grow the plants and stock the animals they would need. The natural balance and inherent stability of the original ecosystem were thereby destroyed. Instead of a variety of plants and permanent natural ground cover, a small number of crops made only parttime use of the space available. The soil was exposed to the wind and rain to a far greater extent then before, particularly where fields were left bare for part of the year, leading to more accelerated rates of soil erosion than under natural ecosystems. Nutrient recycling processes were also disrupted and extra inputs in the form of manures and fertilizers were therefore required if soil fertility was to be maintained. The adoption of irrigation was even more disruptive since it created an environment that was even more artificial. Adding large amounts of water to a poor soil would allow the farmer to grow his preferred crop, but it would have catastrophic long term effects. The extra water would drain into the underlying water table, sometimes leading to rising water levels which caused the soil to become waterlogged. This additional water also altered the mineral content of the soil: It increased the amount of salt and would eventually—especially in hot areas with high evaporation rates—produce a thick layer of salt on the surface that made agriculture impossible. The emergence of villages and towns meant that the demand for resources was now more concentrated. These early societies were dependent on the production of a food surplus in order to feed and support the growing number of priests, rulers, bureaucrats, soldiers, and craftsmen. Forests suffered the most as the demand grew for wood to build houses, heat homes, and cook. Local deforestation around settled areas added to the increase of soil erosion. Soil erosion then led to badly damaged landscape, declining crop yields, and eventually an inability to grow a surplus of food. The first signs of widespread damage emerged in Mesopotamia, the area where the most extensive modifications to the natural environment were first made.

Both domestication of animals and the cultivation of plants had dramatic impacts on the environment. The nomadic hunters and gatherers were aware that they shared the earth with other living things. The animals and humans could live in the same area since the hunters and gatherers did not destroy the ecosystem to a great extent. The agriculturalist, on the other hand, deliberately transformed nature in an attempt to simplify the world's ecosystem. As an example, by ploughing and seeding a grassland, a farmer would eliminate a hundred species of native herbs and grasses, which would then be replaced with pure strands of wheat, corn, or alfalfa. This simplification reduced the stability of the ecosystem, making it inhabitable for most animals, and slowly drained it to near nonexistence.

COLONIZATION OF THE NEW WORLD

Only five hundred years, a mere second on the geological clock, have passed since Columbus' discovery opened a fresh and verdant new world to the Europeans—a land with few indications of human occupation except for a few thin plumes of smoke rising from cooking fires in small clearings in the woods. These clearings belonged to the Native Americans, which numbered about four million at this time. Over the centuries these people had created their own complex culture. Their means of sustaining themselves did not rely on scaring or subduing the earth, but on using what it offered. Native American society was not separate from nature but part of it. Geography, as well as history, began to change when Christopher Columbus anchored his little fleet off the island of San Salvador. Like most of those who freely followed, Columbus and his company risked the voyage to the New World for what they could take from it. They came for gold, a trade route to the spices of India and other riches of Asia, land, goods to sell, glory, adventure, religious and personal freedom, and to convert the heathen to Christianity (Shabecoff, 1993). Although the explorers, adventurers, and settlers came to seize whatever riches and opportunities the land had to offer, it was what they brought with them, far from what they took, that changed the face of the continent forever. What they brought was Europe's two thousand or more years of western history, customs, prejudices, and methodology. They brought European technology, philosophy, religion, aesthetics, a market economy, and a talent for political organization. They brought European diseases that decimated the native people. They also brought with them European ideas of what the New World was and visions of what it should be. As a result, the continent, the mountains, the great rivers, and the plains are much as they were in the fifteenth century. But virtually all the landscape has been dramatically altered by human activity.

In the beginning the explorers and first settlers were faced by a dark forbidding line of forest behind which was a vast, unmapped continent, inhabited, they thought, by savages and filled with ferocious wild beasts. Mere survival meant conquering the wilderness. The forest had to be cleared to make living space and to provide wood for shelters and fires (Shabecoff, 1993). Behind the trees lurked the Indians, ready, the settlers suspected, to commit unspeakable atrocities. The forest was filled with wolves, bears, and panthers that would pounce on their children and domestic animals, or so they feared. The greater the destruction of the forest, the greater the safety for the tiny communities clinging to the edge of the hostile continent. Removing the trees also opened land for crops and cattle. Killing the wild animals not only filled the pot with meat but eliminated the deer and other grazing animals that stole the settlers' corn (Shabecoff, 1993).

The European population quickly grew beyond the carrying capacity of the land. Cropland was frequently exhausted by permanent cultivation; cattle, swine, and sheep introduced by immigrants made far heavier demands on field and forest than wild animals. As each new field was harvested, the chemical, mineral, and biological nature of the soil itself was depleted. The Europeans also brought technology that contributed to the heavy impact they had on the land. Horses and oxen enabled the settlers to open and cultivate much broader acres. Plows could dig deeply into the soil, exposing far more loam. With draft animals, the Europeans could harvest heavier loads and transport them to markets. Sailing ships could then transport those loads along the coast or across the ocean.

Whereas the Native Americans would take from the land only what they could consume, the colonist and their successors sought to grow surplus that they could sell for cash or trade for manufactured goods and other commodities. The production of surplus led to the accumulation of capital and the creation of wealthy, largely in the towns that served as marketplaces. That meant clearing more land, cutting more timber, planting more crops, and raising more cattle, all at a rate that could be sustained only at a cost of permanent damage to the land. The deforestation of New England and the disappearance of the beaver in the East are but two dramatic examples of how the demands of the market could deplete abundant resources in short order.

By the time of the American Revolution, the wilderness along the eastern seaboard had been pretty much tamed. While some pockets of forest remained, the thirteen colonies were largely covered with farms, dotted with villages, and punctuated by a few substantial cities, notably Boston, New York, Philadelphia, and Charleston.

THE INDUSTRIAL REVOLUTION

Early in the nineteenth century, an awesome new force was gathering strength in Europe—the term "industrial revolution" was coined by the French as a metaphor of the affinity between technology and the great political revolution of modern times. Soon exported to the United States, the industrial revolution swept away any visions of America being an agrarian society. The steam engine, the railroad, the mechanical thresher, and hundreds of other ingenious artifacts that increased man's ability to transform the natural world and put it to use would soon be puffing and clattering and roaring in all corners of the land. The new machines swiftly accelerated the consumption of raw materials from the nation's farms, forests, and mines.

Lumbering became the nation's most important industry in the late eighteenth century. Wood was the most widely used raw material for heating, houses, barns, and shops; the same can be said for ships, furniture, railroad ties, and for factories and papermaking. The supply seemed inexhaustible since the forest still darkened huge parts of the country. The forest melted away before the axes of the advancing Americans. The settlers never thought of their ax work as deforestation, but as the progress of civilization. Soon after the tree cover was removed, the forest soil began to lose nutrients such as organic matter and materials. The soil began washing away, turning clear streams into slow, muddy ditches, filling lakes, and killing fish.

Meanwhile, the big cities and growing wealth of the East were creating a more rapidly expanding market for wheat, corn, beef, and other cash crops. New roads and canals, the steamboat and the locomotive, made domestic and foreign markets increasingly accessible to farms in the center of the continent. Eli Whitney's cotton gin, Cyrus McCormick's reaper, Benjamin Holt's combine and other ingenious inventions encouraged the development of a highly productive, efficient agriculture that sharply reduced the biological diversity of the land. Mining both preceded and quickly followed settlement of the interior, and left deep and permanent scars on the continent's land and waters. Gold in California, copper in Montana, coal and oil in Pennsylvania, iron ore in Minnesota, and lead in Illinois attracted fortune hunters and job seekers. Reports of a strike would draw thousands of prospectors and workers as well as those who lived off them. Mines operated without care for the surrounding countryside. The picks and shovels, the hoses and dredges, and the smaller fires of the miners created the nation's first widespread pollution and environmental health problems. Mining left behind gutted mountains, dredged-out streams, despoiled vegetation, open pits, polluted creeks, barren hillsides and meadows, a littered landscape, and abandoned camps. Mining contributed to deforestation of the countryside. Woodlands were often cleared for mining operations; enormous amounts of timber were needed for the posts and beams that supported the mine shafts and fueled smelter operations (Shabecoff, 1993).

Steam shovels came into use in the 1880s, enabling the coal operators of Pennsylvania and the iron ore producers of Minnesota to peel away the very crust of the earth to extract raw materials for industry and wealth for themselves. Spoil from the coal started to turn streams more acidic. The discovery of oil in Pennsylvania in 1859 brought drilling rigs that poked into the skyline: Large areas of soil were soaked with black ooze (Shabecoff, 1993). It was in the cities that environmental pollution and its effects were most pervasive. Garbage and filth of every kind were thrown into the streets, covering the surface, filling the gutters, obscuring the sewer culverts that sent forth perennial emanations. In the winter the filth and garbage would accumulate in the streets to the depth of sometimes two or three feet. Most cities were nightmares of primitive sanitation and waste disposal systems. Privies for sewage and private wells for water were still widely used in metropolitan areas until the end of the nineteenth century.

The national government, perhaps, could have done more to protect the land and its resources as well as public health. But for most of the nineteenth century the government was still a weak presence in most areas of the country. There was, moreover, no body of laws with which the government could assert its authority. Laissez-faire was the order of the day. But by the end of the century there was a growing body of information about the harm being done and some new ideas on how to set things straight. Yet, there was no acceptable ethic that would impel people to treat the land, air, and water with wisdom and care. To a large extent the people did not know what they were doing (Shabecoff, 1993). Today, however, the lessons have been learned and there is no excuse.

FUTURE TRENDS

The section on future trends for this chapter is not a particularly easy one to write. However, it has been said that much can be learned from history. Environmental issues are no exception. Much of the early history of the environmental movement described in this chapter did in fact have a significant impact on modern day environmental issues. This impact is discussed in significant detail in the next chapter, "The Environmental Movement." Where this will lead in the future is anybody's guess at this time, but at a minimum, it appears that the environmental movement will continue to move forward "toward a cleaner earth." (Note: "Toward a Cleaner Earth" is the title of a column written by Carol Mouché, former editor, that appeared in the magazine *Environmental Protection*.)

The reader interested in a more detailed and informative presentation on "Early History" is referred to the following two recent outstanding texts, both of which have been referenced earlier in this chapter: Ponting's *A Green History of the World*, Shabecoff's, *A Fierce Green Fire: The American Environmental Movement*.

SUMMARY

1. More than any other time in history, the 1990s are a turning point for human civilization. Human beings are facing ecological disasters that could affect their ability to survive. These crises could force them to reexamine the value system that has governed their lives for the past two million years of existence.

2. From the origin of humans to about 10,000 years ago humans depended on a hunting and gathering lifestyle. At this stage of development they had neither the numbers nor the technological skills to have a very substantial effect on the environment.

3. The agriculturalist deliberately transformed nature in a more destructive way than the early hunters and gatherers, often destroying forest in order to cultivate the land, which eventually lead to infertile land.

4. Although the explorers, adventurers, and settlers came to seize whatever riches and opportunities the land had to offer, it was what they brought with them, far more then what they took, that changed the face of the continent forever.

5. The modern era, especially since the late seventeenth century, has witnessed another major transformation of, or revolution in, culture and technology—the development of major industries. This, like domestication and agriculture, has reduced the space required for sustaining each individual and increased the utilization of resources.

6. Much of the early history of the environmental movement described in this chapter did in fact have a significant impact on current environmental issues.

REFERENCES

Gorden, A., and Suzuki, D. *It's a Matter of Survival.* Cambridge, MA: Harvard University Press, 1991.

Goudie, A. *The Human Impact: Man's Role in Environmental Change.* Cambridge, MA: The MIT Press, 1981.

Ponting, C. *A Green History of the World.* New York: St. Martin's Press, 1991.

Shabecoff, P. *A Fierce Green Fire: The American Environmental Movement.* Harper Collins Canada Ltd, 1993.

2

The Environmental Movement

CONTRIBUTING AUTHOR

Domonic Paniccia

INTRODUCTION

The America discussed in the previous chapter has effectively vanished. Muscle, animal, and steam power have changed to electricity, internal-combustion engines, and nuclear reactors. The horse and locomotive have been replaced with automobiles, jetliners, and supertrains. Industry is not concerned with natural substances—it is primarily concerned with developing synthetic substances. At the same time, industry is consuming natural resources at an incredible rate. The population of the country has more than tripled since 1900. People have become thoroughly urbanized and much of the open countryside has been developed. Production of goods and services has approximately doubled every ten years. All of these events began to escalate, at a dangerous rate, after World War II.

People's concern for nature and its fate began the environmental movement. Artists and writers of the Romantic and Transcendental movements in the first half of the nineteenth century laid a firm foundation of appreciation for America's spectacular natural sights, a sensitivity built upon in the second half by a series of naturalists and activists as different as John Muir (a founder of Sierra Club in 1892) and Gifford Pinchot (first head of the U.S. Forest Service in 1905) (Shabecoff, 1993). The impact on nature from increasing industrialism and commercialism spawned a new theory of conservation and preservation that was the forerunner of environmentalism. However, it was not until after World War II that America began calling for reform of the destruction of nature.

In the late summer of 1962, a marine biologist named Rachel Carson, author of *Silent Spring,* a best-selling book about ocean life, opened the eyes of the world to the dangers of attacking the environment:

As man proceeds toward his announced goal of the conquest of nature, he has written a depressing record of destruction, directed not only against the earth he inhabits but against the life that shares it with him. The history of the recent centuries has its black passage—the slaughter of the buffalo on the western plains, the massacre of the shorebirds by the market gunners, the near-extinction of the egrets for their plumage. Today, man is killing some birds, mammals, fishes, and other forms of wildlife by chemical insecticides indiscriminately sprayed on the land. . . . The question is whether any civilization can wage relentless war on life without destroying itself, and without losing the right to be called civilized. (Carson, 1962)

With words like this, the modern environmental movement began.

For additional literature regarding "The Environmental Movement," the interested reader is referred to the book by Philip Shabecoff, titled *A Fierce Green Fire*. This outstanding book is a "must" for anyone who works in, or has interests with the environment.

THE FOUNDING OF THE MOVEMENT

The first founders of the environmental movement came from everywhere. They were explorers, paleontologists, scientists, sportsmen, writers, and artists. Included are men like John James Audubon, who had a great love and desire for nature. Audubon was a shopkeeper in Louisville, but he was much more interested in painting birds and other wildlife of the country than he was in earning a living for his family (Shabccoff, 1993). Audubon was not a conservationist or environmentalist as defined today. Instead he hunted birds so he could sketch them during his leisure time. His paintings in *The Birds of America* brought the beauty of nature in America to the attention of many people. He was unique in combining a frontiersman's passion for travel and adventure with an almost scientific sense of observation and an artist's appreciation for wildlife. At the time of his search for birds to paint (about 1815), there were also a lot of Americans who wanted to settle in the land Daniel Boone had explored. While he did not condemn the settlement in the west, he did express deep regret over the destruction of the forest. After his great success with the publication of *The Birds of America,* Audubon bought an estate on the Upper West Side of Manhattan in New York. After he died in 1851 his widow, Lucy, subdivided the property, named Audubon Park, and built several houses upon it. It was here that a businessman from Weehawkin, New Jersey named George Blake Grinnell moved his family, including his young son George Bird Grinnell (Shabecoff, 1993).

George Bird Grinnell eventually grew up to study paleontology and became a scientist, a sportsman, and a writer. Grinnell also became publisher of *Forest and Stream* magazine. Having watched the slaughter of the bison on his expeditions in the West, Grinnell wrote frequently of the need to preserve wildlife and to stop the uncalled-for destruction of the nation's forests. In 1886 he wrote an editorial in *Forest and Stream* proposing a society for the protection of the nation's birds, many species of which were in danger of being wiped out by hunters who collected them for their feathers or just for sport. This idea of a society became very popular and was the origin of today's Audubon Societies. He also proposed, in 1887, an organization dedicated to conserving species and joined with a rising young politician named Theodore Roosevelt to form the Boone and Crockett Club, an elite organization that wished to end the relentless, wasteful slaughter of big game animals, including their near extinction (Shabecoff, 1993). Today Grinnell is hardly remembered, even though he was one of the crucial early figures in mainstream American conservation, active and influential even before the term "conservation" came into common use.

By the middle of the nineteenth century, romanticism moved into more populated areas of the United States. Living in the wilderness was no longer thought to be mean and brutish but more fulfilling and desirable than civilization. American writers turned to romanticism, and often used the nation's landscape for inspiration. The idea that nature is inherently more honest, innocent, and virtuous than civilization was welcomed in America (Shabecoff, 1993). The most influential articulation of the importance of nature and the relationship of humans to the natural world came from transcendentalists of New England, particularly from one who was part of the bedrock of American literature and thought. This individual was named Ralph Waldo Emerson.

Emerson's love of nature did not make him dismiss industrialism or technology. He wrote about his visit to England, and how the versatile machinery had earned great wealth for the British. But he also talked about the consequences of dependence on the machine and warned people of abusing technology. He wrote that the night and day were of the same color in the manufacturing towns, as the soot from the factories darkened the day. This blend of reverence for nature and acceptance of technology, provided it is limited and controlled, is reflected in the ideology of today's mainstream environmentalism (Shabecoff, 1993). However, Emerson, like many others in his time, also believed that nature had the ability to heal itself and therefore could recover from the damage caused by humans. Modern environmentalism believes that this is not true and that humans' activity can inflict permanent damage on nature.

As the nineteenth century was drawing to a close, three talented, charismatic, and driven men were making their entrance on the national stage: Gifford Pinchot, John Muir, and Theodore Roosevelt (TR). They would write the first pages of modern environmental history in the United States.

Roosevelt was the first and greatest of the conservation-minded presidents. TR appointed Gifford Pinchot as his chief forester and relied heavily on his counsel to formulate policies to preserve public lands and resources. Pinchot was the leader and chief publicizer of the creed of conservation. Roosevelt was also greatly influenced by John Muir, the naturalist and writer and eloquent spokesman for the preservation of nature and the wilderness. A founder of the Sierra Club in 1892, Muir was the inspiration for much of the present-day effort to preserve wild and open places.

Pinchot, often described as the "father of conservation," was born in 1865 and grew up in Milford, Pennsylvania. Pinchot, like many other environmental activists, was a big outdoorsman. He decided to become a forester, which was not a popular occupation in the United States, so he went to Europe to study scientific forestry and forest management. It was then that he became convinced that government control of the forests was necessary to stop the destruction of trees by those interested in only making money from land. Pinchot believed that the forest should be conserved to serve the future of the nation as well as the present. This would require forestry plans that would make sure only a certain amount of timber is used over the years. The forest should be used, but they should be used wisely. Therefore, he believed, they must be protected from the exploiters and destroyers.

When Roosevelt became president in 1901 after the assassination of William McKinley, he moved conservation to the center of the national agenda. With Pinchot, who had advised him when he was governor of New York State, serving as his righthand man on conservation, Roosevelt moved aggressively to declare public primacy over the nation's resources. Conservation was a major weapon of the progressive movement. This movement was aimed at redressing the social, economic, and political imbalances caused by industrialization, urbanization, and the concentration of economic power within the unrestrained corporations (Shabecoff, 1993).

Many who were getting rich on public resources feared TR's plans. Their fears were soon justified when TR brought the size of the national forest system to nearly its present level. He multiplied the number of national parks. Starting with the tiny Pelican Islands in Florida, he launched the nation's system of wildlife refuges. Following Pinchot's suggestion, he appointed an Inland Waterways Commission to investigate the conditions of the nation's navigable waterways and to recommend measures for their protection and improvement (Shabecoff, 1993). He also persuaded Congress to pass the Reclamation Act of 1902, which helped develop water and power for much of the West. In 1908, he called the governors of all the states to a White House Conference on Conservation. This is regarded as the beginning of a true national conservation movement.

The concern for the wild nature was being effectively sounded by another remarkable man named John Muir. Muir believed that the Creator gave all life an equal right to exist, and to destroy plants and animals was ungodly. He made an ally when, in 1903, he took President Roosevelt camping in the mountains, and discussed the degradation of Yosemite by lumbermen. Three years later, Roosevelt signed a bill making Yosemite a national park.

During the course of the Yosemite campaign, the creation of a permanent society to protect California's natural area was proposed to Muir. At first Muir was skeptical. When a professor of philology at Berkeley approached him in 1892 with a proposal for creating an alpine club, Muir gave him his blessing. Together with California academics, including William D. Armes and Joseph LeConte, who were college teachers, and Warren Olney, a lawyer, they formed the Sierra Club that same year. The goal of the organization was to obtain support from people and the government to preserve the forests and other natural features of the Sierra Nevada Mountains. The Sierra Club came to be one of the most powerful groups that pushed preservation to the front of the environmental movement.

There were great accomplishments at that time in the environmental movement. From John James Audubon to Grinnell, TR, Pinchot, and Muir, to the National Audubon Society and the Sierra Club these people and these two national organizations led the struggle to preserve and protect the land, the resources, the health, and nature upon which life depends. In the next century the dependence on technology, and the energy that fueled it, would present human beings, for the first time, with the ability to make the world potentially uninhabitable for their own species.

KEEPING THE MOVEMENT ALIVE

Progressivism died down with the departure of the energetic TR from the White House and with him the federal leadership of the young conservation movement. Some of the spirit of the movement died with John Muir. Gifford Pinchot soon ran into trouble with President William Howard Taft and his Interior Secretary, Richard A. Ballinger, who went about trying to reverse many of TR's conservation policies. After Pinchot accused Ballinger of attempting to give up government lands to the "power trust," Taft dismissed him as chief of the Forest Service. With the exception of the administration of President Woodrow Wilson, which was distracted by World War I, conservatives, not conservationists, were in control of the federal government. As President Calvin Coolidge noted in 1925, the business of America was business (Shabecoff, 1993). Conserving the nation's lands and resources was not considered an important part of that business by the government and most of the citizens.

The federal government finally got back into the conservation business when Teddy Roosevelt's second cousin Franklin was elected to the White House in 1933. He was born in 1882 and raised on a beautiful, expansive estate overlooking the Hudson River. The young FDR explored the countryside on foot and on horseback, swam in the clean river in the summer, and skated and sailed iceboats on it in winter. Throughout his life he cared deeply about trees and devoted much time to his plantings in Hyde Park, even during government crises. It was his political ideology as much as his love of nature that led Roosevelt to include major conservation projects in his New Deal reforms (Shabecoff, 1993).

The Civilian Conservation Corps (CCC), the Soil Conservation Service, and the Tennessee Valley Authority were among the many New Deal programs designed to serve both the land and the people. The CCC was a public works program that eventually put nearly three million jobless young men to work. The jobs would include planting trees, preventing soil erosion, building roads and structures in national parks, constructing small dams for flood control, and other projects that would heal and improve the land. It was also important that the CCC demonstrated that there should be no conflict between preservation of the environment and the creation of jobs (Shabecoff, 1993). The Soil Conservation Service was born out of the terrible drought and erosion that was tearing the topsoil away from large areas of the Dust Bowl—which included 50 million acres stretching over parts of fifteen Great Plains and southwestern states—and sending it swirling across the skies. The soil from the Dust Bowl darkened the skies across the country. There was also the Taylor Grazing Act of 1934, which, for the first time, set rules on the use of the public land that were intended to limit the abuses that were causing severe degradation of the land.

The Tennessee Valley Authority (TVA) was a government body created to develop resources that had been placed solely in private hands. Many opponents branded this body as socialist or worse. But the neglect brought on by capitalism had turned the Tennessee basin into an ecologically devastated slum. The river and its tributaries were filled with silt and prone to flooding, their potential for hydropower untapped. The region was deforested and badly eroded. Most of its valuable minerals had been taken.

The TVA planned for all of the basin: It changed the rivers into sources of cheap power and made them navigable once more, created jobs, helped restore the soil, and brought agriculture to the area for the first time. It brought hope and prosperity to a despairing people and set an example of government planning for the protection and use of the land and its resources for the benefit of the public instead of a few wealthy and powerful special interests.

The New Deal environmental programs and the nation's attention to conservation were pushed back by World War II. But the conservation ethic introduced as a central feature of federal policy by Theodore Roosevelt was carried forward by his cousin Franklin. For many years, with a few exceptions in this century, efforts to preserve the land and its resources had a low priority on the nation's public agenda until the 1960s.

In the early 1960s the mood of the country with regard to environmental issues was clearly shifting again. A widely noticed television commercial aired by the Advertising Council, which is an arm of the advertising industry, showed a Native American wandering through a landscape littered with garbage, a tear trickling down his cheek. The message was clear: The beautiful land occupied by the Native Americans had been dirtied by consecutive generations and the time had come to start cleaning it up (Shabecoff, 1993).

The growing environmental impulse in this country has many different perspectives, and the consumer is one of them. It is no accident that Ralph Nader, the country's leading consumer advocate, has also been a strong voice for environmental protection. The search for safe automobiles, which made Nader recognized, was also a crusade against pollution. *Unsafe at Any Speed,* the book that attacked the automotive industry, included a chapter on air pollution from motor vehicles. Nader found that the cars were using the atmosphere as septic tanks and not paying for it. The industries, of course, denied any harm.

Nader, born in 1934, grew up in Winstead, Massachusetts, where local industries poured pollution into the air and into the town's two rivers. From his early experiences he concluded that pollution was a form of violence that is different from street violence only because the effects are not immediate. Among the organizations Nader formed, with the help of money he won in a lawsuit against the General Motors Corporation, were state and national Public Interest Research Groups (PIRGs) with goals that included lobbying for environmental protection. Nader, single-mindedly dedicated to the general public, became a symbol of public morality that many Americans believed was lacking in their political and corporate leaders. Nader was an incorruptible voice speaking for the American consumer, and helped bring industrial pollution into the full glare of national attention (Shabecoff, 1993).

For many years, environmentalism was a revolution waiting to explode. A remarkable book written by a remarkable woman finally gave the movement an offensive position. As indicated before, *Silent Spring,* by Rachel Carson is now recognized as one of the truly important books of this century. It changed the way Americans and people around the world looked at the reckless ways individuals live on this planet. Focusing on a specific problem—the poisoning of the earth by chemical pesticides (DDT)—*Silent Spring* was a broad examination of how carelessly applied science and technology were destroying nature and threatening life, including human life. This well-written bestseller affected people emotionally and moved them to act against environmental destruction. It also has been described as the basic book of America's environmental movement.

What Carson did in *Silent Spring* was present the scientific evidence in clear, poetic, and moving talk that demonstrated how the destruction of nature and the threat to human health from pollution were completely interrelated. She showed how all life, including human life, was affected by misguided technology. The book incorporated many of the concerns of the earlier conservationists and preservationists with the new warning from environmentalists who worried about pollution and public health. With *Silent Spring,* Rachel Carson lit the fuse to a bomb—environmentalism in America—ready to explode (Shabecoff, 1993).

THE REVOLUTION

The federal government, which frequently moves at an extremely slow pace when dealing with social problems, responded in the 1970s to the rising concern over the deterioration of the environment when Congress passed a series of environmental laws that can be regarded as one of the great legislative achievements of the nation's history.

On January 1, 1970, President Nixon signed the National Environmental Policy Act, which requires the federal government to analyze and report on the environmental impacts of its activities. A Council on Environmental Quality was created later that year to oversee conformity with the law by federal agencies. The council also would prepare an annual report on the state of the environment and, at least in theory, advise the President on it.

Another agency created by an act of Congress in 1970 was the Occupational Safety and Health Administration, or OSHA, as it is commonly called. This new agency was given authority to ensure that workplaces were safe and healthy, and that employers did not subject workers to toxic chemicals and other dangerous substances such as asbestos and cotton dust or to unsafe machinery and equipment. The new agency gave workers and their unions a powerful tool for protecting themselves from careless or unscrupulous employers. The same legislation that created OSHA established the National Institute of Occupational Safety and Health (NIOSH) to do research into the causes of workplace accidents and illnesses, and to design criteria for lowering risks (Shabecoff, 1993).

The Environmental Protection Agency (EPA), the most powerful and controversial environmental institution in the federal government, was a product of congressional inaction. In December 1970, President Nixon submitted a reorganization plan to Congress, gathering a number of different federal public health and regulatory bureaus and programs into a new organization called the Environmental Protection Agency. Neither house in Congress voted against the reorganization, which would have killed the new agency. The EPA, which was to be the federal government's watchdog, police officer, and chief weapon against all forms of pollution, was thus created without benefit of any statute enacted by Congress (Shabecoff, 1993). It quickly became the nation's hope for cleaning up pollution.

In a very real sense, the EPA had no choice but to hit the turf running. To carry out the Clean Air Act of 1970, it was required to come up with rules for reducing air pollution 120 days after it opened its doors. Congress passed one law after another that added to the agency's mandate. The EPA banned the use of DDT by administrative order, something Congress had not been able to do by legislation. The agency established regional offices and research and testing facilities in a number of states. Its presence was soon felt and usually resented by industry, municipal governments, and even other federal agencies. The role of the EPA was not only to force polluters to obey the laws but also to explain the laws, to provide the laws, to identify the sources of danger within the environment, and to inform, educate, and assist the public on how to protect themselves and the environment.

It is the political pressures of industry, supported by the White House and members of Congress, and the EPA's often excessive bureaucratic approach to dealing with its tasks that have weakened the agency's power (see Chapter 4 for more details on EPA's problems). However, it is still today the single most effective protector of the nation's air, water, and soil.

A number of pieces of environmental legislation were passed during the Nixon, Ford, and Carter administrations. The Federal Water Pollution Control Act was adopted in 1972. Also enacted in 1972 were the Federal Insecticide, Rodenticide, and Fungicide Act; the Noise Control Act; the Coastal Zone Management Act; and the Marine Mammals Protection Act. The Endangered Species Act was passed in 1973 and the Safe Drinking Water Act in 1974. After taking a rest in 1975, Congress produced in 1976 the Toxic Substances Control Act (TSCA) and the Resource Conservation and Recovery Act (RCRA) (both dealing with the control of dangerous materials), the Federal Land Management Act, and the National Forest Management Act the following year. In 1977 the clean air and water laws were strengthened. Finally, in 1980, during the last months of the Carter administration, Congress passed the Comprehensive Environmental Response, Compensation, and Liability Act (CERCLA), or Superfund as it is commonly known, more or less success-fully establishing a well-financed program for cleaning up thc thousands of dangerous abandoned toxic waste sites around the country (Shabecoff, 1993). (Environmental legislation is treated in more detail in Chapter 5).

No part of the public and private sectors have remained untouched by the environmental rev-olution. A new network has been built up to monitor the environment and act to protect it. At the same time, history will undoubtedly mark the landmark environmental statues of the 1970s and the new institutions they started as the most important part of the environmental era. There has been change in government at all levels as well as in science, medicine, education, and mass communi-cation. Because of environmentalism, a society has been transformed.

This was a giant step for the movement. However, it still was only a beginning. The move-ment still had to work for its original tasks. And it would soon become clear that saving the envi-ronment in America would not go on at the same rate as it did in the 1970s for much longer.

THE REAGAN COUNTERREVOLUTION

In the summer of 1980 a document entitled *The Global 2000 Report to the President* was written by the White House Council on Environmental Quality and a task force from the State Department. This was not a comforting report. The dangers facing the world as a result of overpopulation, envi-ronmental abuse, and resource depletion were real and threatening. It also claimed that there was potential for global problems of great proportion by the year 2000. The report was also very un-compromising. The earth's ability to provide resources for human needs was deteriorating, caused by progressive degradation and impoverishment of the earth's natural resource base (Shabecoff, 1993). The report also stated that if the current trends continue, the world in 2000 will be more crowded, more polluted, less stable ecologically, and more vulnerable to both natural and human catastrophes (Sale, 1993).

Six months after *Global 2000,* on January 21, 1981, Ronald Reagan, an actor and former governor of California, was inaugurated as President. The report was effectively transported to the nearest archive. Most of its warnings or its recommendations were apparently not given the slight-est thought. The country that was by itself already the greatest single threat to the environment em-barked on a decade of unchecked speculative economic growth. Just as the magnitude of the envi-ronmental dangers and the need for serious remediation were beginning to be understood, the government of the United States appeared to deny the evidence, ignore the warnings, and live a life of business-as-usual.

The Reagan reaction that began the 1980s was a specific backlash against the environmental innovations of the 1970s. The Office of Management and Budget, created by Nixon to draw fiscal power to the White House, was used by Reagan's men to reorder government finances away from regulatory functions, especially environmental. The Council of Environmental Quality was de-prived of half its budget and most of its staff in a clear case of shooting the messenger with the bad news. Agencies like OSHA and EPA were ripped apart by budget cuts. The EPA lost 29 percent of its budget and a quarter of its staff in the first two Reagan years. The administration also scrapped innovative programs in areas like solar energy and alternative fuels. When such restraints were not enough, the White House let it be known that environmental restrictions for industries such as mining, timber, oil, and automobiles would be operationally ignored or not enforced. When an industry objected to EPA directives, their trade associations were invited to participate in drawing up new regulations on terms they felt were reasonable (Sale, 1993).

This could not last for long. The counterrevolution could not stop the tide of history. Soon there were events even the government could not overlook: The evacuation of dioxins-contaminated Time Beach, Missouri in 1983, the poisoning of several hundred thousand (and some 3000 dead) at the Union Carbide pesticide plant in Bhopal, India in 1984, the discovery of the ozone hole over Antarctica in 1985, and the disastrous explosion of the nuclear plant at Chernobyl in the Ukraine in 1986—were too real, too threatening, to be denied. And the environmental movement, still growing with new organizations and new public support in response to that crisis, was too involved, too necessary, to push aside. In 1985, a Harris poll found that 80 percent of the public, about four times the number that had voted for Reagan, supported current environmental regulations and standards (Sale, 1993).

The irony of the counterrevolution is that the major environmental groups and their colleagues actually benefited from the Reagan assault, which resulted in new support for the environmental movement and its organizations. The Sierra Club showed the most gains in support, going from its 1980 level of 165,000 members to more than 350,000 members by 1985 (Sale, 1993). Many other organizations also grew by mid-decade: the Audubon Society to 450,000; the National Wildlife Federation to 825,000; the Wilderness Society to 100,000; and Friends of the Earth to 25,000 (Sale, 1993).

By the end of the Reagan presidency in 1989, the environmental movement was stronger than it had ever been. It had certainly grown in capital and at the grassroots. Many different types of organizations, with a great diversity of resources and multiplicity of goals, again became a great presence on the national scene. It was, at any rate, strong enough to withstand the power of a popular and persuasive President, and emerged with values, aims, and energies intact.

THE THIRD WAVE OF THE MOVEMENT

With the end of the Reagan administration, the political view seemed to turn back to environmentalism. George Bush, in effect, repudiated his former boss's environmental hostility by promising during his first campaign for the White House to be "the environmental President" (Shabecoff, 1993).

Even the delegates to the Republican National Convention in 1988 focused on environmental issues and overwhelmingly said they would pay higher taxes for a cleaner environment, even though Mr. Bush had pledged not to raise taxes. However, environmentalism had become fashionable for all politicians coast to coast. Political candidates of all kinds paid due respect to environmental issues in their campaigns.

After Bush was elected, the environmentalists personally presented him with a "Blueprint for the Environment." The Bush Administration managed generally to avoid taking action for four years on all except the most pressing issues. In doing so, it raised the art of administrative neglect to a new level. He had his appointees and bureaucrats, often in secrecy, dilute, rewrite, or simply ignore regulation established by Congress and the EPA (Sale, 1993).

Bush was given credit for getting the 1990 Clean Air Act amendments out of Congress where they had been stalled in a legislative logjam for more than a decade, although the White

House succeeded in substantially weakening the restrictions before passing the bill. Bush did agree to accelerate the end of CFC production from the year 2000 to 1996 or sooner. He also got occasional headlines for decisions on a number of painless and low-cost issues: blocking a dam on the Colorado River in 1989, reducing air pollution in the Grand Canyon, granting a ten-year moratorium on most offshore drilling, voting for a UN ban on ocean drift-net fishing, and lowering thresholds on lead poisoning, all in 1991, and extending the Endangered Species list by 50 percent in 1992 (Sale, 1993).

On most other fronts the Bush Administration won no environmental prizes, and its performance became worse as his term went on. On the international front, the Bush Administration refused to sign a treaty on carbon dioxide emissions in the atmosphere, accepted by all the other nations of the world, until it was weakened and meaningless in 1992. A series of administration policies enacted in 1991 and 1992 opened up vast new areas of land, including wilderness, wetlands, and old growth forests to coal, timber, and oil interests (Sale, 1993). Now this land that was once protected could be exploited and used up like all the land. These and other actions raised some concerns that this administration was no better than the early Reagan Administration.

At the end of Bush Administration, there was by no means as much confidence as there had been in the early days of the seventies. The new third-wave approaches as well as the older legislative and electoral strategies clearly had shown their limits, and disappointments and defeats had to be counted along with the important improvements. It may be true that the movement is now stable, efficient, and often effective, and it could claim credit for the passage of hundreds of new laws to protect the landscape and its inhabitants. The movement was responsible for saving millions of acres of lands from rapacious development and hundreds of thousands of wild creatures from extinction. People could point to rivers cleaned, toxics banned, and polluters shut down because of the movement. However, it is also true that half the population of America lives in counties in violation of clean air statutes; at least 170,000 lakes and millions of acres of forest in the United States were acidified; 90 percent of the garbage produced went unrecycled; less than 5 percent of the worse toxic-waste sites in the nation had been treated; and topsoil was being washed away at the rate of 10 billion gallons a year (Sale, 1993). It is obvious that the changes necessary for saving the world had only barely begun. The earth may still be in danger, and seriously so, and the task of the environmental movement seems to have only began.

FUTURE TRENDS

What direction will the environmental movement ultimately take in the future? This is not an easy question to answer at this time. Certainly, the state of the economy and the military situation will have the most profound effect on what has been described in this chapter as the environmental movement. One thing does seem certain: The education and training of the average citizen (consumer) will play a more important role in the future.

Technology transfer regarding environmental issues will allow society to make more intelligent decisions regarding the effects lawyers, politicians, environmental organizations, regulating bodies, and industry can have on environmental issues. In any event, an educated consumer is probably the most cost-effective way of attacking and subsequently solving the environmental problems that face the future.

SUMMARY

1. As the nineteenth century was drawing to a close, three talented, charismatic, and driven men were making their entrance on the national stage. Gifford Pinchot, John Muir, and Theodore Roosevelt were to write the first pages of modern environmental history in the United States.

2. The federal government finally got back into the conservation business in a significant fashion when Teddy Roosevelt's second cousin Franklin entered the White House in 1933. It was his political ideology as much as his love of nature that led Roosevelt to include major conservation projects in his New Deal reforms. The Civilian Conservation Corps, the Soil Conservation Service, and the Tennessee Valley Authority were among the many New Deal programs created to serve both the land and the people.

3. In the 1970s, Congress turned out a series of environmental laws that must be regarded as one of the great legislative achievements of the nation's history.

4. The public reaction to Reagan's policies that began the 1980s was a backlash against the environmental innovations of the 1970s. The irony of the counterrevolution is that the environmental groups and colleagues actually benefited from the Reagan assault.

5. The Bush Administration did not take action on all the most pressing issues, but did provide some significant regulatory reforms.

6. One thing does seem certain: The education and training of the average citizen (consumer) will play a more important role in the future.

REFERENCES

Carson, R. *Silent Spring.* MA: Houghton Mifflin Company, 1962.

Sale, K. *The Green Revolution.* New York: Hill and Wang, 1993.

Shabecoff, P. *A Fierce Green Fire.* New York: Hill and Wang, 1993.

3

Environmental Organizations

CONTRIBUTING AUTHOR

Ann Marie Gaynor

INTRODUCTION

Since the 1972 United Nations Conference on the Human Environment in Stockholm, Sweden, there has been a dramatic increase in the world's awareness of its worsening environmental problems. This is a result of an improved understanding, on the part of citizens of the world, of the importance of natural resources to sustain and continue development. As a result, environmentalism has become a universal phenomenon, which has led to the birth of thousands of environmental organizations. This chapter discusses the activities of some of these governmental, national, and international environmental organizations.

On an international level, many countries do not have national environmental policies, but almost all countries have environmental guidelines or legislation in place. Some of these countries have incorporated environmental protection into their national constitutions. Some third-world countries, such as Jamaica and Haiti, do not have technical, human, and financial resources to enforce their already established environmental regulations. This results in their long-term environmental goals being distracted by other short-term economical objectives. However, there are those countries, such as Canada and the United States, who are able to put more effort and financial resources into the management of their natural resources.

On a national level, there are government organizations such as the United States Environmental Protection Agency (EPA). There are also nongovernmental organizations that have been formed by citizens and independent activists who are motivated by their anxiety over environmental threats not only to the human species but also to other living beings. Some of these groups are very small, but each has had some impact on the environment, particularly with respect to securing and maintaining natural resources and making the world habitable for descendants. However, the ethics of some of these organizations are at times questionable. It is also obvious that the governments and citizens of the world have responded to the environmental challenge at an international (and national level) by establishing different environmental agencies. These organizations deal with issues such as deforestation and reforestation; control of water, air, and soil pollution; sanitation and water supply.

INTERNATIONAL ORGANIZATIONS

There are so many international environmental organizations that it is impossible to list all of them in this short chapter. Some of the more important ones are listed in Table 3–1. Included with each heading is the name, address, and telephone number. A short description of the organization is provided in the text that follows (Tryzyna, 1989).

Beauty Without Cruelty International (BWC) is an animal protection organization, which was founded in 1958 to work against fur farming, animal trapping, testing of cosmetics on animals, and use of certain animal fats and derivatives. Individual members in numerous countries promote the use of synthetic substitutes.

Table 3–1. International Organizations

Beauty Without Cruelty International (BWC) 11 Limehill Road Tunbridge Wells Kent YN1 1LJ, England	International Board for Soil Resources and Management (IBSRAM) P.O. Box 9–109 Bangkhen Bangkok 10900, Thailand Tel: (662) 561-1230
Canada–United States Environmental Council 1244 19th Street, NW Washington, DC, 20037 USA Tel: (202) 659-9510	The Secretariat for the Protection of the Mediterranean Sea Place Lesseps 1 E-08023 Barcelona, Spain Tel: (343) 217-1695
Caribbean Conservation Corporation (CCC) P.O. Box 2866 Gainesville, FL 32602 USA Tel: (904) 373-6441	The United Nations Development Programme (UNDP) 1 United Nations Plaza New York, NY 10017 USA Tel: (212) 906-5000
Clean World International (CWI) c/o Keep Britain Tidy Group Bostel House 37 West Street Brighton BN1 2RE, England Tel: (44) 273-23585	World Environmental Center 605 Third Avenue New York, NY 10158 USA Tel: (212) 986-7200
International Association on Water Pollution Research and Control (IAWPRC) 1 Queen Anne's Gate London SW1 H9BT, England	

The **Canada-United States Environmental Council** was founded in 1971 by a group of major Canadian and U.S. national government organizations to facilitate the exchange of information and cooperative action on issues affecting these two countries.

The **Caribbean Conservation Corporation (CCC)** was founded in 1959 primarily to support research on and conservation of marine turtles in the caribbean and throughout the world .

Clean World International (CWI) was founded in 1975 to unite groups that work for litter prevention, beautification, tidiness, and recycling of resources. The members are national groups in twenty-two countries.

The **International Association on Water Pollution Research and Control (IAWPRC)** was established in 1965, and works to encourage international communication, cooperation, and exchange of information on water pollution and control research and water quality management.

The **International Board for Soil Resources and Management (IBSRAM)** was created in 1983 to promote and test soil management technologies through networks of cooperating national organizations.

The **Secretariat for the Protection of the Mediterranean Sea** was established in 1982 to promote the protection of the Mediterranean Sea and region by facilitating information exchange and action among the concerned municipalities of thirteen Mediterranean countries in Africa, Asia, and Europe.

The **United Nations Development Programme (UNDP)** was established in 1965 to provide grant assistance in over 150 countries, to build skills and develop resources in areas such as agriculture, industry, and health. This organization is also active in the environmental protection in these countries by providing support for large-scale projects that are concerned with combatting various forms of pollution, and projects that are designed to prevent or limit any environmental side-effects caused by any structural development.

The **World Environmental Center** was organized in 1974 at the request of the United Nations Environment Programme (UNEP) and in cooperation with the United Nations Association of the U.S.A. The purpose of this group is to increase the public understanding of international environmental and developmental issues, and how they relate to natural resource management in Canada and the United States.

U.S. NATIONAL GOVERNMENT ORGANIZATIONS

The following government organizations are involved with environmental issues in the United States. Included with each heading in Table 3–2 is the name, address, and telephone number. A short description of the organization follows (Cunningham, Ball, Cooper, Gorham, Hepworth, & Marcus, 1994).

The **Council on Environmental Quality** is responsible for the administration of the National Environmental Policy Act, for the preparation of an annual environmental report, and for advising the President on environmental issues (Baker et al., 1985).

The **Department of Agriculture** provides national leadership in the conservation and wise use of soil, water, and related resources (Baker et al., 1985).

The **Department of Energy** has the job of ensuring that the United States international en-

Table 3–2.   U.S. Government Organizations

Council on Environmental Quality 722 Jackson Place, NW Washington, DC 20006 Tel: (202) 395-5750	Department of the Treasury United States Customs Service 1301 Constitution Avenue, NW Washington, DC 20229 Tel: (202) 566-5104
Department of Agriculture U.S. Forest Service Soil Conservation Service Washington, DC 20250 Tel: (202) 655-4000	National Oceanic and Atmospheric Administration (NOAA) 14th Street, NW Washington, DC 20230 Tel: (202) 377-3567
Department of Energy Washington, DC 20545 Tel: (202) 252-5000	The United States Environmental Protection Agency (EPA) 401 M Street, SW Washington, DC 20460 Tel: (202) 755-2673
Department of Interior Interior Building C Street, between 18th and 19th, NW Washington, DC 20240 Tel: (202) 343-1100	
Department of Justice Land and Natural Resources Division 10th Street and Pennsylvania Avenue, NW Washington, DC 20530 Tel: (202) 633-2701	

ergy policies and programs conform with national goals, legislation, and treaty obligations (Tryzyna, 1983).

The **Department of Interior** is concerned with the development of water and related land resources in the arid, western states (Baker et al., 1985).

The **Land and Natural Resources Division,** Department of Justice, represents the government in the matters relating to public land use and management, and federal environmental protection. This group also provides legal advice and litigation services (Baker et al., 1985).

The **United States Customs Service,** Department of the Treasury, is responsible for the enforcement of the U.S. laws regarding importation and exportation of endangered species (Tryzyna, 1983).

The **National Oceanic and Atmospheric Administration (NOAA)** is mainly concerned with the regulation of marine fisheries, the protection of habitat, the management of the coastal zone and regulation of deep seabed mining (Baker et al., 1985).

The United States Environmental Protection Agency (EPA) was created on December 2, 1970. The main responsibility of the EPA is to control and abate pollution in the areas of water, air, solid waste, noise, radiation, and toxic substances (Cunningham et al., 1994). The EPA does international work through the Office of International Activities, where the EPA participates in the programs of multilateral international organizations to solve common environmental problems (Baker, Basset, & Ellington, 1985).

U.S. NONGOVERNMENTAL ORGANIZATIONS

Some of the nongovernmental environmental organizations, at primarily a national level, are listed in Table 3–3. Each heading contains the name, address, and telephone number. A brief description of each organizations follows.

Under the Endangered Species Act of 1973, federal agencies are required to ensure that their actions are not likely to jeopardize the continued existence of any endangered or threatened species, or result in the destruction of critical habitats. This requirement extends to the protection of migratory species and species outside the United States, if it is covered by the international treaty obligations of the United States (Tryzyna, 1983). The **Endangered Species Committee** is the watchdog for this purpose.

Greenpeace, USA, founded in 1970, is best known for employing nonviolent direct actions to confront environmental abuse. Its projects mainly include an international treaty to ban the testing of nuclear weapons, work to halt dumping of nuclear and other toxic wastes in the oceans, protection of whales, seals, and kangaroos. Its work also includes conferences and dialogues in several countries on the problem of acid rain (Tryzyna, 1983). This organization has come under pressure in the past regarding its modes of operation and true motives.

The **Marine Mammal Commission** was established to ensure that the provisions of the Ma-

Table 3–3.   U.S. Nongovernmental Organizations

Endangered Species Committee Interior Building Room 4160 Washington, DC 20240 Tel: (202) 235-2771	National Wildlife Federation 1412 16th Street, NW Washington, DC 20036 Tel: (202) 797-6800
Greenpeace, U.S.A., Inc. 2007 R Street, NW Washington, DC 20009 Tel: (202) 462-1177	Natural Resources Defense Council (NRDC) Suite 300 1350 New York Avenue, NW Washington, DC 20005 Tel: (202) 783-7800
Marine Mammal Commission 1625 I Street, NW Washington, DC 20006 Tel: (202) 653-6237	Sierra Club 530 Bush Street San Francisco, CA 94108 Tel: (415) 981-8634
National Audubon Society 950 Third Avenue New York, NY 10022 Tel: (212) 832-3200	

rine Mammal Protection Act of 1972 are achieved. This Act set forth a national policy to prevent numbers of marine mammal species such as whales, dolphins, and seals, from diminishing due to human activities (Tryzyna, 1983).

The **National Audubon Society** carries out research, education, and actual programs to preserve wildlife and natural areas, to promote the wise use of land and the efficient use of air and water, and to reduce pollution and human population growth (Baker et al., 1985).

The **National Wildlife Federation** is dedicated to arousing public awareness of the need for wise use, proper management, and conservation of natural resources (Baker et al., 1985).

The main concerns of the **Natural Resources Defense Council (NRDC)** are air and water pollution, nuclear safety, land use, transportation, toxic substance control, resource management, wildlife protection, soil erosion, and forestry (Tryzyna, 1983).

The aim of the **Sierra Club** is to practice and promote the responsible use of the earth's ecosystems and resources (Baker et al., 1985).

FUTURE TRENDS

Environmental organizations, as a group, will continue to survive and prosper because society is concerned about the environment, and justifiably so. However, those radical organizations that continue to conduct business in an unprofessional and unethical manner may not survive into the 21st century. Greenpeace is certainly one of those candidates. It has placed its own survival and prosperity before the best interest of society and the environment (Theodore, private communication, 1994).

The negative impact on public opinion created by the "Greens" on many environmental issues is intellectually dishonest and a public disservice. In the process, they attempt to occupy moral high ground; however, they should be exposed at every opportunity, particularly by the technical community (Santoleri, Lauber, & Theodore, 1993). For some strange reason, many of the Greens feel it is their right to manipulate, distort, and even lie in environmental publications and during presentations. This is something very few technical individuals would do, since such action is deemed not only unprofessional but also unethical (Theodore, private communication, 1994).

The nation's waste management program is a serious subject. Attempts to prevent the use of the proper and best disposal, control, and preventive methods can lead to improper management methods that are not cost-effective. Groups who knowingly and deliberately distort facts and provide false information should be treated the same as those who illegally pollute the environment. Hopefully, society will take action on this in the future (Santoleri et al., 1993).

It is the technical community's responsibility to logically and impassionately select the best processes for waste management for any hope of providing reasonable protection of our health and the environment (Theodore, private communication, 1994).

SUMMARY

1. Ever since the 1972 United Nations Conference on the Human Environment in Stockholm, Sweden there has been a dramatic increase in the world's awareness of its worsening environmental problems.

2. There are many countries that do not have national environmental policies, but almost all countries have environmental guidelines or legislation in place.

3. On a national level, the main environmental government organization is the United States Environmental Protection Agency.

4. Nongovernmental organizations have primarily been formed by citizens and independent activists who are motivated by their anxiety over environmental threats to the human species and other living beings.

5. Those radical organizations that continue to conduct business in an unprofessional and unethical manner may not survive into the 21st century. Greenpeace is certainly one of those candidates. It has placed its own survival and prosperity before the best interest of the society and the environment.

REFERENCES

Baker, M., Basset, L., and Ellington, A. *The World Environmental Handbook.* New York: The World Environmental Center, 1985.

Cunningham, W., Ball, T., Cooper, T., Gorham, E., Hepworth, M., and Marcus, A. *Environmental Encyclopedia.* MI: Gale Research, Inc., 1994.

Santoleri, J., Lauber, J., and Theodore, L., "Facts or Myths: The Burning Issue of Incineration," Paper presented at the Annual Air and Waste Management Appreciation (AWMA) meeting, June 1993. This section is a revised and edited version.

Theodore, L., Private Communication, 1994.

Tryzyna, T. *The United States and Global Environment.* CA: California Institute of Public Affairs, 1983.

Tryzyna, T. *The World Directory of Environmental Organizations,* 3rd ed., CA: California Institute of Public Affairs, 1989.

4

The EPA Dilemma

CONTRIBUTING AUTHOR

Ralph J. Crispino

INTRODUCTION

The problems associated with the regulatory framework of federal environmental management have always been questioned. As with any government-controlled operation, many steps must often be taken before anything meaningful can be accomplished (this appears to apply to many activities, with the exception of war, where the President can exclusively command the armed forces for immediate action).

To implement an environmental regulation, the problem must first be identified (often in an EPA report), then data must be collected and analyzed (usually in another EPA report), and a goal has to be set, ultimately by congressional legislation. Once the law is in effect, it must be enforced by the EPA. The law has often been amended because of unreasonable goals and lax enforcement.

The present problem that exists with the (US)EPA is an intricate one, consisting primarily of four main concerns:

1. Economically efficient measures are seldom, if ever, adopted, causing little progress in achieving environmental goals.
2. Data collection often has limitations, and when insufficient data is used for legislation, an ongoing string of amendments is attached.
3. The legal issues regarding environmental problems have rocketed, brought on mainly by the complex legislation. .
4. The EPA is presently primarily a legal organization that is serving the best interests of the law profession rather than the environment.

The next two sections of the chapter briefly describe the history of the EPA, its functions, and some of the legislation EPA is responsible for enforcing. Much of legislation is examined in more detail in the next chapter. The remainder of the chapter analyzes EPA's accomplishments and performance. Based on this analysis, the last two sections provide suggestions on how the nation, and society in general, can be better served from an environmental point of view.

HISTORY OF THE EPA

1970 was a cornerstone year for modern environmental policy. The National Environmental Policy Act (NEPA), enacted on January 1, 1970, was considered a "political anomaly" by Lenten K. Caldwell, Washington Senator Henry Jackson's chief advisor to the legislation. NEPA was not based on specific legislation; instead it referred in a general manner to environmental and quality of life concerns. The Council for Environmental Quality (CEQ), created by NEPA, was one of the councils mandated to implement legislation. April 22, 1970 brought Earth Day, where thousands of demonstrators gathered all around the nation. NEPA and Earth Day were the beginning of a long, seemingly never ending debate over environmental issues.

As described in the previous two chapters, consumer and public interest movements led by Ralph Nader and growing groups of engineers, scientists, and other environmental experts, including some lawyers, influenced many of the new initiatives on the environmental legislation agenda. Events of the late 1960s, such as the oil burning on the Cuyahoga River in the center of Cleveland and the washing up of dead birds on the oil-slicked shores of Santa Barbara, reflected a sense of crisis and dissatisfaction within society.

In his 1970 State of the Union message and later speeches, President Nixon declared that air pollution and clean water legislation would be the cornerstone of his environmental stance. Nixon's most likely challenger on these issues was Senator Edmund Muskie, the chair of the Senate Committee on Air and Water Pollution. Muskie was the target of some of the new activists, like Nader's groups, for his unwillingness to challenge industry's position on air quality debates and for his tendency to view the environmental problem as a problem of conservation rather than pollution (Gottlieb, 1993). However, environmentalists, government, industry, and society as a whole have come to view Muskie's position in a more favorable light during recent years.

The Nixon Administration became preoccupied with not only trying to pass more extensive environmental legislation, but also implementing the laws. Nixon's White House Commission on Executive Reorganization proposed in the Reorganizational Plan # 3 of 1970 that a single, independent agency be established, separate from the CEQ. The plan was sent to Congress by Nixon on July 9, 1970, and this new U.S. Environmental Protection Agency (EPA) began operation on December 2, 1970.

The EPA was formed by bringing together fifteen components from five executive departments and independent agencies. Air pollution control, solid waste management, radiation control, and the drinking water program were transferred from the Department of Health, Education, and Welfare (now the Department of Health and Human Services). The federal water pollution control program was taken from the Department of the Interior, as was part of a pesticide research program. EPA acquired authority to register pesticides and to regulate their use from the Department of Agriculture, and inherited the responsibility to set tolerance levels for pesticides in food from the Food and Drug Administration. EPA was assigned some responsibility for setting environmental radiation protection standards from the Atomic Energy Commission, and absorbed the duties of the Federal Radiation Council. Unfortunately, these groups were, and today essentially remain, compartmentalized (Holmes, Singh, and Theodore, 1993). The EPA was set up where each office dealt with a specific problem, and new offices were often created sequentially as individual environmental problems were identified and responded to by legislation.

The EPA's first administrator, William Ruckelshaus, initially sought to convey the impression that his agency would aggressively enforce the new policies, and adopted a systems approach by forming two primary program offices to handle the variety of issue areas and legislative mandates under its jurisdiction and several function-oriented divisions designed to be more responsive to White House concerns as well as fulfill certain agencywide objectives, such as enforcement and research. The new agency, however, was quickly overwhelmed by its rapidly expanding regulatory responsibilities, the conflicting signals from the Nixon and later Ford Administrations on how aggressively it should pursue such regulations, and effective industry maneuvering, which used scientific uncertainty in the regulatory process to delay or counter the establishment and enforcement of standards (Gottlieb, 1993).

KEY EPA LEGISLATION

In contemporary environmental policy, the first important legislation, aside from NEPA, was the Clean Air Act of 1970 (CAA). Technology-based standards, along with national standards, became the key. A 1971 report by the CEQ was very optimistic. While the Council mentioned economic incentives, the relevant section regarding command and control indicated: "The Federal quality programs changed dramatically when the Clean Air Amendments became law. They embody recommendations contained in the President's 1970 message on the environment and proposed significant control for new pollution sources and for all facilities emitting hazardous substances. It also establishes a framework for the States to set emission standards for existing sources in order to achieve national air quality standards" (Council on Environmental Quality, 1971).

Congress decided that the driving force for enforcement operations by the EPA was to be control technology, the machinery for cleaning emissions at each source. Once identified, a specific technology, such as "reasonable available control technology" (RACT), was to be the basis of implementation of the legislation. Technology was the object of contracts between the EPA and plant owners. When seeking to prove guilt of environmental trespass, the proof came down to the existence and quality of specific machinery and/or processes. A deadline, June 30, 1975, was set for all air quality regions to meet the national air quality standards. Supporters of this federal movement had visions of numerous monitoring stations all across the US to measure the levels of emissions and assure the delivery of cleaner air. But, as it turned out, when the deadline came, 102 out of 247 regions had not attained the national standards, i. e., they had not achieved attainment (Landau, 1979).

Many other deadlines for specific substances or sources were established in the 1970 CAA. The 1974 and the 1977 CAA amendments extended these deadlines, as well as direct the EPA to study various factors of different pollutants. The 1977 amendments also gave the EPA more power in enforcement by civil penalties.

In addition to air pollution legislation in the 1970s, water pollution was also an important federal concern. The 1972 amendments to the Federal Water Pollution Control Act (FWPCA), better known as the Clean Water Act, set nationally uniform technology-based effluent limitations established by the EPA from major "point sources" of water pollution, with deadlines in 1977 for compliance, according to "best practical control technology." One of the claimed advantages of having geographically uniform regulations is their supposed speed and simplicity; however, this uniformity created other problems. Natural water is by no means uniform; properties such as temperature, toxicity, acidity, alkalinity, natural radioactivity, and the amount of algae and other aquatic life vary, depending on the location (Stewart and Krier, 1978).

Setbacks in FWPCA deadlines, as amended in 1972, required another amendment in 1977, where it became better known as the Clean Water Act (CWA). Here, the deadlines were extended to 1983. The postponement of deadlines, as seen in the CWA and the CAA, demonstrates the overall ineffectiveness, not only in the enforcement of the legislation, but also in creating unrealistic goals.

The Resource Conservation and Recovery Act (RCRA) was created in 1976 to regulate solid and hazardous waste facilities. Provisions for waste recycling had become a major objective. Thousands of new recycling centers were established, not for business purposes, but for environmental consciousness-raising. "Bottle bills," which mandated a deposit or fee for recycled glass containers, were passed in Vermont in 1971 and in Oregon in 1973. They brought conflicts pitting glass industries, retail food industries, and labor groups against mainstream environmental groups and local organizations. "Ultimately, environmental lobbyists were not able to keep the bottle bill provisions in RCRA, but they were able to establish the principle that recovery and management of wastes needed to be developed more systematically at the national level" (Yandle, 1989).

In addition to recycling, RCRA contains regulatory safeguards for operators of landfills and waste sites, which imposed "cradle to grave" rules for generators, carriers, and operators of disposal sites for toxic wastes. Until the 1970s, hazardous waste was treated like any other kind of waste, and the number of new and possible toxic chemicals entering the market each year was creating enormous stresses on this regulatory system. Another toxic related legislation was the Toxic Substance Control Act (TSCA) of 1976, which provided for the federal review of all new chemicals before their production.

In the late 1970s, the public awareness of the toxic waste problem grew with the incident at Love Canal. Even though Hooker Chemical Company knew exactly what was stored in the sealed canal, had taken precautions that would satisfy even today's high standards, gave public warnings of the hazards, and wrote extensive warnings that precluded any use of the land that would threaten human health in the deed of sale, they were sued by the Department of Justice (DOJ) on behalf of the EPA. The land was sold to the Niagara Falls School Board in 1958, where it was developed for a grammar school, and the rest of the land was sold to real estate developers. When sewer lines were developed, the seal of the canal was ruptured and toxic sludge appeared everywhere. Either the developers were not aware of the public records (in the deed of sale from Hooker Chemical), or proper safeguards were not taken. In any event, the school board and the developers were let off the hook (Yandle, 1989).

To deal with Love Canal and the thousands of potentially contaminated sites, Congress passed the Comprehensive Environmental Response, Compensation, and Liability Act (CERCLA) on December 11, 1980, and with it established Superfund. Superfund was set at $1.6 billion and was to receive 87.5 percent of the revenues from taxes on petroleum and forty-two listed chemical feedstocks, and the rest from general tax revenues. To implement Superfund, the EPA had to establish a list of at least 400 sites, and they called on the states to give candidate sites. The 400 sites were to include each state's top priority, but a major problem that emerged was that one state might be filled with toxic sites far worse than another state's worst site.

To many, the Reagan Administration brought a decline to the environmental movement (see Chapter 2). This brought more bureaucratic red tape in the main issue of hazardous waste cleanup. The CWA, CAA, and RCRA were all further amended, with new deadlines. And the acts were getting lengthier—for example, the 1970 CAA had 50 pages, while the 1990 version has 800 (the effects of this will be discussed later in this chapter).

Just as the seventies will be remembered for efforts to clean up hazardous waste, the nineties may be remembered as the decade for pollution prevention. First among pollution-reducing laws is the 1990 Pollution Prevention Act, which requests companies to focus on ways to reduce emissions rather than treat wastes. Among other things, the law establishes a source reduction clearinghouse on pollution prevention information; provides for the development, testing, and disseminating of auditing procedures designed to identify source reduction opportunities; sets up standard methods to measure pollution reduction; expands the toxic release inventory reporting requirements to include questions about source reduction and recycling; and requires EPA to report to Congress on the progress of the reduction programs (Hanson, 1992).

Other laws affecting pollution reduction are the 1990 amendments to the CAA and the TSCA. One such law requires EPA to conduct an engineering research program to develop new technologies for air pollution prevention, and take into consideration process changes or material substitutions when setting emission standards for hazardous chemicals. The idea that EPA could force a facility to change its process or materials to reduce emissions worries some chemical companies (*Journal of Air and Waste Management Association,* 1994).

IS EPA COST-EFFECTIVE?

A major criticism of the present regulatory approach to solving environmental problems (and pollution) is its economic inefficiency. The EPA's proposed budget for 1995 is $7.2 billion, an increase of $500 million from the 1994 budget approved by President Clinton (*Journal of Air and Waste Management Association,* 1994). This budget includes 19,418 workyears (a workyear is equivalent one 40-hour-per-week employee). This represents about a seventh of the staff and a third of the spending of the entire federal regulatory apparatus. The major components of the 1995 EPA budget, called the FY95, are as follows (*Journal of Air and Waste Management Association,* 1994):

1. Over $3 billion and 14,939 workyears for the operating programs
2. $1.5 billion and 4,376 workyears for the Superfund program
3. $77 million and 103 workyears for the Leaking Underground Storage Tank (LUST) program; see Chapter 44 for details on this program
4. $2.6 billion for water infrastructure funding, including resources for a Clean Water State Revolving Fund and for a Drinking Water State Revolving Fund

The EPA's staff has quadrupled since 1970, and the inflation-adjusted spending has increased tenfold. The impact of the EPA on the US economy is considered by many overwhelming. In 1990, the Agency estimated that complying with pollution control regulations was costing Americans $115 billion a year; this is equivalent to 2.1% of the GNP, compared to 0.9% in 1972. And, critics complain that EPA estimates are typically low (Yandle, 1989). In the end, costs are paid by taxpayer in the form of taxes and higher consumer prices. In the 1990s, the EPA projects that compliance costs will total another $1.6 trillion, not including the comprehensive (some in industry have called it radical) 1990 Clean Air Act, which could add another $25 to $40 billion annually.

Much of the early EPA legislation favored older existing plants over new plants. Existing firms could postpone or avoid enforcement actions, while new firms could not. This had the potential to reduce economic growth and strengthen monopolies in affected industries. And, when the CAA was amended in 1975, postponing the deadlines and restricting growth in nonattainment (national ambient air quality standards not met) areas, existing plants in dirty regions were helped more. In addition to the higher costs of control equipment, entry to these nonattainment areas was effectively barred.

A case involving Chevron in California led to a change in the legislation. Chevron wanted to replace two smaller refineries with one large one, with a capacity of 315,000 barrels per day compared to 90,000 for each of the two older plants. Chevron officials agreed to shut down the two plants for the new one, and a deal with the Bay Area Pollution Control District was made. When the new plant was finished, however, Chevron did not shut down the older plants. Chevron argued that the total emissions were less than the 1974 level, so the plants should stay open. Out of controversies such as this, transferable pollution rights were emerging. The EPA responded with the "offset policy," where a new facility could be constructed if emission reductions for the same pollutant from existing polluters were realized in an amount that would more than offset the pollution added by the new source. The "bubble concept" also emerged, where sources would have the opportunity to come forward with alternative abatement strategies that would result in the same air quality impact, but at less expense, by placing relatively more control on emission points with a low marginal cost of control and less on emission points with a high cost (Yandle, 1989). Although condoning this concept of allowing polluters to minimize costs while cleaning the air, EPA quickly added that these rules would not affect clean areas (in attainment), nor would they be allowed for new sources. Through 1986, there have been only 40 air pollution bubbles approved by EPA for the entire country, and an additional 89 bubbles were approved by states. Control cost savings generated total about $435 million. These savings are not trivial, but the number of bubbles established is small considering ten years of establishment (Yandle, 1989).

Another way that EPA creates economic inefficiency for industry is the tendency of regulatory constraints that require equal reduction of pollution from sources whose control costs differ, instead of requiring more pollution control from sources that could reduce emissions at a lower cost. Consider the following example (Stewart and Krier, 1978). Assume two pollution sources, A and B, in a given airshed, each emitting 100 tons of SO_2 or sulfur dioxide with marginal control costs indicated in Figure 4–1. Assume further that it is necessary to reduce total emissions in the airshed by 100 tons in order to achieve compliance with the federal ambient air standards. Under a typical regulatory approach, each source would be required to eliminate 50 tons of pollution, even though source A can eliminate pollution much more cheaply than source B. Total cleanup costs

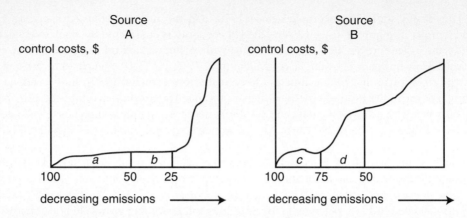

Figure 4–1. Economic Efficiency Comparison. From "Clinton's FY95 Budget for EPA Represents Increase of $500 Million." Adapted from *Journal of Air and Waste Management Association,* March 1994.

will equal the area *a* plus the areas *c* and *d*. However, it would be possible to reduce and indeed minimize costs in order to achieve the ambient standard by apportioning the cleanup burden so that the marginal costs for eliminating the last ton of pollution for source A is the same as for source B. This proposed scenario would be accomplished by requiring source A to eliminate 75 tons and source B, 25 tons, resulting in total cleanup costs equal to the areas of *a, b,* and *c*—a considerable saving over the equal reduction approach. Studies of the Delaware River Basin and of simulated airshed models have indicated that a system of uniform cutback results in abatement costs that can be 300 to 1000 percent greater than under a theoretical least-cost system of disorientated burdens.

In water pollution, economic inefficiencies are just as evident as in air pollution. Consider the example of a large plant with various wastewater streams, each with different levels of toxicity. Common practice is to combine these streams into one and treat everything together. If it is much cheaper to clean the less toxic streams, the costs are increased by combining them all.

Referring to EPA's effluent guidelines for steelmaking, the report noted that the additional cost of removing one unit of the same pollutant was $18,000 in one production process and $2,000 for another. Source-by-source limitations were the basis of the control mechanism, and opportunities for reducing costs existed.

Federal subsidies for the construction of public sewage treatment plants were authorized in the 1972 FWPCA. Also, permission for municipalities to expand their treatment of industrial wastes was granted. Industry near public sewers could simply pipe waste to the local sewage treatment plant, saving themselves money at the taxpayer's expense. Later federal legislation realized this and charged these industries, but these changes rarely covered the full government cost of treating waste.

Probably the biggest example of cost ineffectiveness by the federal government is Superfund (see Chapter 21 for more details). As indicated earlier, CERCLA established a $1.6 billion fund made up of taxes on crude oil and commercial chemicals. At the time, it was expected that this amount would be sufficient. When the EPA began the process of site discovery and evaluation, thousands of supposedly potential hazardous waste sites existed, presenting the nation with some of the most challenging pollution problems ever. In 1986, Congress reauthorized another $8.5 billion to the fund in the Superfund Amendments and Reauthorization Act (SARA). Superfund was again reauthorized by Congress in 1991.

The EPA is trying to make polluters pay for the cleanup. But, this is how EPA goes about it. EPA goes after potentially responsible parties or PRPs, to pay for or to conduct the cleanup of a site. When a PRP refuses to pay, it is sued by the EPA, and EPA may seek "treble damages," where the PRP can pay up to three times the original cost. The major problem with seeking funds from PRPs is that often, when the wastes were dumped, there was no law against it. Also, if more than one party was responsible for damages, the PRP usually becomes the richest company, and leaves further liability questions up to the PRP (the PRP must then sue the smaller companies). This creates endless jobs for lawyers, both for the EPA and for industries.

Even past EPA administrator William Reilly has reportedly described Superfund as the worst piece of legislation ever passed by the U.S. Congress (Brimelow and Spencer, 1992). Congress reacted harshly to the Love Canal incident, and the public is facing the consequences. Superfund has spent billions of tax dollars, yet only 84 of some 1,250 identified sites have been cleaned up. Future estimates of costs paid by consumers and industries range from $125 billion to an astronomical $1.25 trillion, with sometimes up to 85% going to transaction costs like lawyer's fees (Brimelow and Spencer, 1992).

ARE EPA'S DECISIONS JUSTIFIED AND CONSISTENT?

In order to decide what pollutants have adverse effects on human health and environmental well being, extensive research must be done by the EPA. Also, once legislation is passed, the levels of contamination must be measured to assess the outcome. This data collection must be performed by scientists, yet William Reilly admitted in 1991 that "there has been plenty of emotion and politics, but scientific data have not always been featured prominently in environmental efforts and have sometimes been ignored when available" (Samuel and Spencer, 1993).

An EPA-appointed panel supported this view in a March 1992 report, *Safeguarding the Future: Credible Science, Credible Decisions.* The report doubts the quality of science that is used to justify programs within the EPA. Some specific findings are (Samuel and Spencer, 1993):

1. EPA's "science activities to support regulatory development . . . do not always have adequate, credible quality assurance, quality control, or peer review." And although the agency receives "sound advice," it "is not always heeded."
2. The EPA "has not always ensured that contrasting, reputable scientific views are well explored and well-documented from the beginning to the end of the regulatory process." Instead, "studies are frequently carried out without the benefit of peer review or quality assurance. They sometime escalate into regulatory proposals with no further science input, leaving EPA initiatives on shaky scientific ground."
3. The agency "does not scientifically evaluate the impact of its regulations," and "scientists at all levels throughout the EPA believe that the agency does not use their science effectively."

Consider, for example, the issue of asbestos. A ruling of a Federal Circuit Court of Appeals

states that the efforts to ban this substance have not followed scientific evidence, possibly increasing risk to consumers, workers, and schoolchildren. A 1989 ban of asbestos by the EPA in the
TSCA was overturned by the U.S. Court of Appeals by October, 1991. "The EPA lied when it
claimed that its 1989 ban on all asbestos use was prompted by compelling evidence of risk reported by the medical community. No such evidence was ever presented by the medical community" (Moriarty, 1993–1994). The Agency had insufficient evidence to justify a ban, and had failed
to follow the statutory requirement under the TSCA to adopt the least burdensome regulation. In-
termediate regulation, such as warnings and restrictions were rejected by EPA. Also, the court
noted that the EPA failed to consider the potential harm from substitutes, even when they are
known carcinogens. Finally, the court questioned the EPA's pursuit of "zero risk" with regard to
asbestos. The ruling noted, for example, that the proposed ban of three asbestos products would
theoretically save seven lives over a span of thirteen years, at a cost of up to $300 million. The
number of deaths supposedly prevented this way would be roughly half the fatality toll in a similar
period with toothpicks, according to the decision (Samuel and Spencer, 1993). If one considers the
recent surge in automobile and truck accidents attributed to brake failure, because asbestos is no
longer used in many types of brake linings (Moriarty, 1993–1994), the number of lives in danger is
much greater because of not using asbestos in brakes than lung cancer from airborne particulates.
Studies by the EPA itself have shown that removing asbestos created airborne particles that are
more harmful than if asbestos were left alone. The EPA admitted that ripping out the asbestos was
a mistake. The hysteria created by the EPA, as well as some citizens and environmentalists, has
caused this apparent mistake about asbestos to become truth in the eyes of the American public.

The EPA has also made mistakes with radon. There is no question that radon poses health
hazards, particularly lung cancer in miners. However, EPA assumptions, indicating that the number
of deaths caused by radon are between 7,000 and 30,000 a year (a rather wide range), are again
based on uncertain linear models. In the study of the miners, a majority of them smoked. This was
not taken into consideration. There is no evidence that there is any more radon today than there was
thousands of years ago. One may wonder what prompted the EPA's urgent policy. Not one scientific study has proven a statistically significant relationship between indoor radon and lung cancer
(*Garbage,* 1994). Nevertheless, the EPA declares that "virtually all scientists agree that radon
causes thousands of deaths every year." One may wonder if the government is really protecting anyone but themselves and their bureaucratic jobs. The financial costs to EPA and industry are negligible, but homeowners who follow the "national standards" are paying out of their own pockets.

With dioxins, studies of chemical industry workers with 60 times the normal level of dioxin
showed that they had no increase in disease. Still, the EPA has not changed its stance on dioxins.
The safe limit remains a 6 trillionths of a gram per kilogram of body weight per day (tg/kg/d). The
average industrial worker ingests between 1,000 and 10,000 tg/kg/d, or up to 1700 times the safe
limit (Samuel and Spencer, 1993).

Environmental regulations dealing with urban smog are also suspected of lacking good data.
A congressionally mandated and EPA-sponsored report by the National Academy of the Sciences
stated that it is difficult to know how to reduce smog in certain areas or even to know how bad the
problems really are. For example, attempts to measure ozone levels are slowed by a method which
does not account for the role of weather in ozone formation. This has led to EPA qualitative classifications of "serious" or "severe" ozone problems in areas where it is unjustified. A senior scientist
and research manager who served in the EPA says that the EPA intends to enforce all of the "seri-

ous" and "severe" classification strategies, whether they are needed or not. To do this, the agency first delays release of data that show fewer cities fail to meet the smog standard, and then explains that the law cannot be changed anyway—having been set in the CAA of 1990. In other words, the policy regulations in scores of cities, controlling millions of automobiles and other consumer products, is now the law of the land—a law, however, which was based in part on the information EPA supplied to Congress (Samuel and Spencer, 1993). To further complicate the matter, emissions tests for cars have been questioned. For example, the General Accounting Office, examining the effectiveness of the new vehicle inspections, found that 28 percent of the vehicles tested failed an initial test, but passed a second test with no repairs. This raises the question of whether the EPA-mandated test is reliable, and if inaccurate identification could lead to unnecessary repairs.

The problems of the environment need to be examined scientifically. If an environmental concern rises, passing regulations before a good scientific basis and peer review are achieved can result in enormous expenditures in legalities, something that this country is presently burdened with. When environmental legislation is passed, it is often so ambiguous that an array of lawyers is needed to translate them. The main reason for this problem is that amendments are made based on premature or simply ill-defined findings. As mentioned previously, scientific data is not always featured predominately when politics and emotions flare.

In organizing the EPA, members of various environmental movements (see Chapters 2 and 3) received special positions in the agency. Some of these environmental groups receive federal funding, even though they are mostly narrow special interest groups. These groups, even if they felt that certain proposed legislation would be ineffective, do not speak up for fear of losing the funds.

Scientists and engineers in the EPA know of the burdens imposed by legalities. These individuals are now spending more time monitoring contractors since new rules were imposed to combat alleged abuse involving outside research and consulting. EPA scientists are now required to log every interaction with contractors and carefully follow every regulation (Stone, 1993). Now, not only are the scientists responsible for research and data collection, they effectively must do secretarial paperwork.

Complicated legislation passed based on insufficient data is by no means a solution to the environmental problem. Costly control measures are taken, and in some cases, the public's risk is increased. Constant amendments are needed, often doing little to alleviate pollution. Regulations can help only if they are based on sound scientific data. When the legislation is unclear, lawyers are often brought in to "clarify" it. Instead, they complicate the problems further.

CAN THE EPA BE ELIMINATED?

The predictable bureaucratic tendency, which feeds on the professional ambitions of dedicated staff and inevitably generates calls for larger budgets, is reinforced by the high costs of litigation and the long delays associated with the process. This centralizing effect feeds the political machinery to Congress. EPA is the whipping boy, never meeting the impossible deadlines nor doing enough to satisfy the politicians. Industry is the villain, and the flaming emotions of innocent people are fanned by the rhetoric that ensues. Heating hearings, more proposed laws, larger budgets, more lawyers, and limited progress is the result. Political demand continues to outstrip political supply (Yandle, 1989).

When the EPA was formed in 1970, it was—in a very real sense—a technical organization. The Agency was manned primarily with engineers and scientists. Most of these individuals were dedicated to a common cause: correcting the environmental problems facing the nation and improving the environment. The problems these individuals tackled were technical, and there were little or no legal complications or constraints. The EPA was indeed a technical organization, run and operated by technical people, attempting to solve technical problems. Much was accomplished during these early years . . . but something happened on the way to the forum (Theodore, personal notes).

Nearly twenty-five years later, the EPA is no longer a technical organization—it is now a legal organization. The EPA is no longer run by engineers and scientists. It is run and operated by lawyers. And, the EPA is no longer attempting to solve technical problems; it is now stalled in a legal malaise (Theodore, personal notes).

How in the world did this occur? It happened because it served the best interest of the career bureaucrats, in and out of Congress, most of whom are lawyers, and it happened because the technical community did nothing to stop it. The result is that this nation is now paying the price for an environmental organization with nearly 20,000 employees and an annual budget approaching $10 billion that is not serving the best interests of either the nation or the environment (Theodore, personal notes).

Interestingly, all of the administrators to the EPA have been lawyers. Though lawyers are required in every industry for helping to settle disputes over legalities, protecting the environment is generally beyond their scope. In the EPA today, for every three engineers there is one lawyer; it is indeed (as described above) a legal organization, serving the legal profession and not the environment. Actual proposals for regulations and control, based on good scientific data, should be designed by scientists and engineers, or those who have come to be defined as problem solvers. They can analytically break down a problem, initially assess the damages, then fix them (Theodore, personal notes).

Creating problems and not solving them has become the mode of operation for the EPA. One need only look at Superfund (see earlier discussion and Chapter 21) for an example of what the professional bureaucrats have accomplished. When one talks about wasting tax dollars, Superfund is at the top of the list, with nearly $10 billion down the drain.

And to think that the Clinton Administration is still considering raising the EPA to a cabinet level. Recent proposals to elevate EPA to cabinet level and change it to the Department of Environmental Protection, though passed by Senate, were criticized by Congress. The Senate claimed that this would increase the United States' power in international environmental concerns. If the EPA cannot be effective in this country as an agency, how can it be expected to function as a cabinet, and at an international level? It is hoped that Congress' objective for future environmental legislation will focus on easing the financial burden of EPA regulations on industries, private property owners, and state and local governments (Cushman, 1994).

FUTURE TRENDS

Something has gone afoul. In our society, engineers are the problem solvers, but rarely the decision makers. Although the world we know today has been called a product of engineering, engineers play a minor role in important decision making.

By far the most important policy affecting the environmental future of the country, and the planet, is pollution prevention (see Chapters 30 to 34). EPA Administrator, Carol Browner, "has repeatedly claimed that pollution prevention is the organization's top priority. *Nothing can be further from the truth.* Despite near unlimited resources, the EPA has contributed little to furthering the pollution prevention effort. The EPA offices in Washington, Research Triangle Park, and Region II have exhibited a level of bureaucratic indifference that has surpassed even the traditional attitudes of many EPA employees. Pollution prevention efforts have been successful in industry because they have either produced profits, or reduced costs, or both. The driving force for these successes has primarily been economics, and not the EPA" (Theodore and Wainwright, 1993).

Another important way to help solve the environmental problem is training (see Chapter 43). If the public understands the problems scientifically, solving them is much easier. For the future, employees and consumers must be made aware of what causes pollution and must know how to prevent it. Pollution prevention is the future, and it has been used effectively in industry.

Finally, the role played by the consumer, which ultimately can control industry, is very important (see Chapters 32 and 33). If the average consumer purchased environmentally friendly products, such as recycled containers and concentrated products, not only would there be less waste, but industries would have to respond by exclusively offering these products.

The environmental problem is one that developed over many years of civilization by many different sources. To think that the EPA, with its present mode of operation, can solve this problem is ludicrous. However, there is a solution. Dissolve the EPA now! No reorganization will work, since the lawyers and career bureaucrats have a stronghold in the Agency with their ties to Congress and the White House. What is needed is to make the present EPA disappear and start anew. The nation needs an environmental administration that will solve, not create problems (Theodore, personal conversation). The nation needs technically competent people who can lead an organization in making cost-effective decisions based on the public well-being, not politicians whose goal is to get re-elected or lawyers who cost the nation billions of dollars annually proposing and enforcing ill-defined legislation.

SUMMARY

1. The problems associated with the regulatory framework of federal environmental management have always been questioned.

2. The EPA was formed by bringing together many environmental groups primarily to enforce new policies and to research future policies.

3. Though some legislation was technology based, many of the acts and amendments were based on particular incidents (Love Canal), and almost all of it is ambiguous in text.

4. Economics of environmental protection often favored monopolies of older plants.

5. Data collection has proved erroneous in many cases, endangering health, squandering money, and leading to unclear legislation.

6. Nearly twenty-five years after its formation, the EPA is no longer a technical organization—it is now a legal organization, run and operated not by scientists and engineers, but by career bureaucrats and lawyers. The EPA is no longer attempting to solve technical problems; instead, it is stalled in legal deadlocks.

7. Dissolve the EPA now! No reorganization will work, since the lawyers and career bureaucrats have a stronghold in the Agency with their ties to Congress and the White House. The nation needs a new organization that will solve, not create problems.

REFERENCES

Brimelow, P., and Spencer, L. "You can't get there from here," *Forbes* (July 6, 1992).

"Clinton's FY95 Budget for EPA Represents Increase of $500 Million," *Journal of the Air and Waste Management Association* (March 1994).

Council on Environmental Quality. *Environmental Quality.* The second annual report of the CEQ. Washington, DC: Government Printing Office, August, 1971.

Cushman, J. "EPA critics get boost in Congress." *New York Times* (Feb. 7, 1994).

Gottlieb, R. *Forcing the Spring.* Washington, DC: Island Press, 1993.

Hanson, D. "Pollution Prevention Becoming Watchword for Government, Industry." *C & EN* (Jan. 6, 1992): 21–22.

Holmes, G., Singh, B., and Theodore, L. *Handbook of Environmental Management and Technology.* New York: John Wiley and Sons, 1993.

Landau, J. "Who Owns the Air? The Emission Offset Concept and Its Implications." *Environmental Law, 9,*(3) Spring 1979): 578.

Moriarty, M. "Asbestos: The Big Lie." *21st Century Science and Technology* (Winter 1993–1994).

"Radon." *Garbage* (Spring 1994): 24–28.

Samuel, P., and Spencer, P., "Facts catch up with 'Political Science.'" *Consumers' Research* (May 1993): 10–15.

Stewart, R., and Krier, J. *Environmental Law and Policy: Readings, Materials, and Notes,* pp. 514–515, 556. New York: Bobbs-Merrill, 1978.

Stone, R. "New Rules Squeeze EPA Scientists." *Science* (Oct. 29, 1993): 647.

Theodore, L., and Wainwright, B. "Pollution Prevention Overview," Pollution Prevention: Problems and Solutions, Gordon & Breach, Newark, NJ, 1994.

Yandle, B. *The Political Limitiations of Environmental Regulation.* New York: Quorum Books, 1989.

5

Environmental Regulations

CONTRIBUTING AUTHOR

David Gouveia

INTRODUCTION

Environmental regulations are not simply a collection of laws on environmental topics. They are an organized system of statutes, regulations, and guidelines that minimize, prevent, and punish the consequences of damage to the environment. This system requires each individual—whether an engineer, field chemist, attorney, or consumer—to be familiar with its concepts and case-specific interpretations. Environmental regulations deal with the problems of human activities and the environment, and the uncertainties the law associates with them.

With the onset of the industrial revolution, environmental law has increased in popularity due to an interest in public health and safety and the environment. Companies are concerned with exposing themselves to future potentially disastrous liabilities by polluting the environment where their operations are located. Businesses are now taking a proactive approach to environmental compliance. The recent popularity of environmental issues with public and private interest groups has brought about changes in legislation and subsequent advances in technology.

The Environmental Protection Agency's (EPA) authority is increasingly broadening. It is the largest administrative agency in the federal government, and accounts for nearly one-seventh of the capitol budget. The agency has nearly 20,000 employees and churns out more pages of regulation than any other administrative agency. The EPA's comprehensive environmental programs encompass regulations for air pollution, hazardous waste management, solid waste management, drinking water standards, emergency management, and permitting requirements for discharges to the air, land, or waters of the United States and its territories and districts.

Most major environmental statutes stem from dramatic and highly publicized incidents such as: Love Canal, New York where hazardous substances from an abandoned dump site polluted a nearby community in 1970; Union Carbide Corporation's Bhopal, India methyl isocyanate release from a chemical plant in 1984; and the Exxon Valdez oil spill off the coast of Alaska in 1988. The focus on environmental issues seems to be magnified as the official government policies on the environment can be the swing vote in an election year.

Recent legislation, such as the Clean Air Act Amendments of 1990, is requiring members of society to familiarize themselves with its myriad provisions or become lost in the proverbial shuffle. Who would have thought the federal government would be telling us we can't drive our cars to work, wash our cars in our yard, or to retrofit our automobiles with air conditioning units that use a non-chlorofluorocarbon coolant? Even sellers of new homes are required to identify whether there is radon, lead, asbestos, drinking water pollution, or a leaking underground oil storage tank.

This is by far the longest chapter in the book . . . and for good reason. Environmental regulations usually play a key role in any environmental management issue. For this reason, this chapter attempts to explain some of the major topics in environmental regulation (along with its seemingly never-ending list of acronyms!). With society moving toward almost a state of total litigiousness it may pay, by saving exorbitant attorney fees, to examine in more detail than presented here, those environmental regulations that most affect each individual or organization.* As a general rule, based on the author's experience as an environmental professional, using common sense (unfortunately) in environmental regulation does not always render the appropriate choice.

AIR POLLUTION

The American Cancer Society says its a matter of life and breath. On November 15, 1990, President George Bush signed into law the Clean Air Act Amendments (CAAA) of 1990. This section will key on the 1990 amendments. Details regarding the entire amendments are available in 40 Code of Federal Regulations (CFR) 50 through 99. It is the major piece of legislation that today applies to the air. The CAAA build upon the regulatory framework of the earlier Clean Air Acts programs and their amendments and expands their coverage to many more industrial and commercial facilities. The CAAA establish a new permit program, substantially tighten requirements for air pollution emission controls, and dramatically increase the potential civil and criminal liability for noncompliance for individuals and companies. A brief overview of the ten titles of the 1990 CAAA is presented below.

Title I: Provisions for Attainment and Maintenance
of National Ambient Air Quality Standards

This provision of the CAAAs provides a new strategy for controls of urban air pollution problems of tropospheric ozone, carbon monoxide (CO), and particulate matter (PM-10). (The troposphere extends upwards from the surface of the earth to approximately 12 km and is the air we breath.) The new law mandates that the federal government, which in turn empowers the states, to address the problem of urban air pollution by designating geographical locations according to the extent of

---

*Much of the material, including the writing style, has been drawn from the Federal Register.

their contamination of ozone, CO and NO$_x$ (oxides of nitrogen) as "nonattainment" areas, that is, areas that cannot meet specified air quality standards.

The CAAA require states to revise their State Impementation Plans (SIPs) to include more sources of ozone, both mobile and stationary. For the pollutant ozone, nonattainment areas are further categorized as to the severity of the ozone contamination. Each nonattainment area classified, as shown in Table 5–1, by the area's "ozone design value," as either extreme, severe, serious, moderate, or marginal.

States with nonattainment areas have to enact various control measures to reduce these emissions, depending on the classification of the areas. An area that is classified as marginal nonattainment will require less control measure than extreme to bring it into compliance.

CO nonattainment areas are designated as either "moderate" or "serious." Moderate areas are those that have a CO concentration of 9.1 to 16.4 ppm (parts per million). Serious areas are those that have CO concentrations of 16.5 ppm or greater. Moderate areas are to meet milestones for CO reductions by 1995 and serious areas have until 2000 to attain the standard. The statute specifically requires controls for CO by enhanced vehicle inspection and maintenance and clean fuels for fleet vehicles, both mobile source controls.

PM-10 nonattainment areas (PM-10 is particulate matter with an aerodynamic diameter less than or equal to 10 micrometers) are designated as either "moderate" or "serious." Moderate areas had until 1994, while serious areas have until 2001 to meet the standard. States must develop attainment plans that will require implementation of control measures to attain the standard. Depending upon their classifications, PM-10 areas will have to implement reasonably available control measures (RACMs) or best available control measures (BACMs), among other requirements.

Title I also contains provisions for emissions offset requirements at new and modified sources for ozone, PM-10, and CO. Sources will be required to use the lowest achievable control technology (LEAR). Any resulting increase in emissions must be offset by equivalent or greater emissions reductions elsewhere (P.L. 101-549, 1990; 40 CFR, December 10, 1993).

Title II: Provisions Relating to Mobile Sources

Cars and trucks in many nonattainment areas account for over 50 percent of the precursors to ground level ozone (different from stratospheric ozone), volatile organic carbons (VOCs), NO$_x$ and over 90 percent of CO emissions. It has been speculated that this was brought about by an un-

Table 5–1.   Ozone Nonattainment Classifications Specified by the Act

Area Class	Ozone Design Value (ppm)	Number of Metropolitan Areas	Attainment Date
Marginal	0.121–0.138	41	11/15/93
Moderate	0.138–0.160	32	11/15/96
Serious	0.160–0.180	18	11/15/99
Severe	0.180–0.280	8	11/15/2005*
Extreme	>0.280	1	11/15/2010

*11/15/2007 for Chicago, Houston, and New York.

expected growth in motor vehicle emissions. A summary of the major requirements is presented below.

The CAAAs establish emissions standards applicable to heavy- and light-duty trucks and conventional motor vehicles. These standards will help reduce tailpipe emissions of hydrocarbons, CO, NO_x, and PM-10. The EPA will also regulate evaporative emissions from all gasoline-fueled vehicles both during operation and during periods of nonuse. CO emissions from light-duty vehicles may not exceed 10.0 grams per mile when operated at 20 degrees Fahrenheit.

Title II also contain provisions to establish rules for reformulated gasoline in specific nonattainment areas. Methyl tertiary butyl ether (MTBE) is used in some cities. The clean fuel fleet program requires that states revise their SIPs to include a clean fuel program for fleets. The program impacts anyone owning a fleet that is capable of being centrally fueled. Fleet owners and operators who purchase additional new vehicles must do so according to the following schedule (see Table 5–2).

Each of these provisions is aimed at decreasing pollution in nonattainment areas that are in excess of the guideline values. The degree of control placed on industrial sources of CO, VOCs and NOx will depend on reductions of these pollutants achieved through Title II programs (P.L. 101-549, 1990).

Title III: Air Toxics

In its prime, the federal air toxics program, known as the National Emissions Standards for Hazardous Air Pollutants (NESHAP), only encompassed seven toxic air pollutants. Prior to the CAAAs, NESHAP regulated emissions for arsenic, asbestos, beryllium, mercury, radionuclides, benzene, and vinyl chloride. Title III was revamped to give the EPA the authority to establish an elaborate program to regulate emissions of air toxics from sources that emit hazardous air pollutants (HAPs).

The EPA has identified, via an industry-specific list, major sources of HAPs. These industries are categorized by the amount of pollutants they emit. A "major source" is defined as a source that emits 10 tons or more per year of any one of the list of 189 HAPs, or 25 tons per year or more of any combination of HAPs. The regulations also empower the federal government and states to regulate sources that emit less than the aforementioned levels if they are found to pose a "threat of adverse effects to health and the environment." Dry cleaners using perchloroethylene as a cleaning solvent would fall under this category.

Table 5–2.   Clean Fuel Fleet Program

Model Year	Clean Fuel Vehicle Phase-in	
	Light-Duty Vehicles	Heavy-Duty Vehicles
1998	30%	50%
1999	50%	50%
2000	70%	50%

The EPA requires each of these affected sources to comply with maximum achievable control technology (MACT) standards. These technology-based emissions standards are enacted to consider not only emissions control technology that removes pollutants at the point of discharge, but "measures, processes, methods, systems or techniques which:"

1. Reduce or eliminate emissions through process changes, materials substitution or other changes
2. Enclose processes to monitor emissions
3. Are design, equipment, work practice, or operational standards, including operator training and certification

Title III also establishes a new and comprehensive accidental release program modeled in part after New Jersey's Toxic Catastrophic Prevention Act. The Process Safety Management Regulation and the Accidental Release and Emergency Preparedness Regulation respectively are regulations required to be promulgated by the EPA and OSHA under Title III. These new regulations provide for accidental release prevention and define consequences within and external to a facility that has in excess of a threshold quantity of 100 substances that are known to cause, or may be reasonably anticipated to cause, death, injury, or serious adverse health effects to human health and the environment (P.L. 101-549, 1990; 40 CFR, October 20, 1993).

Title IV: Acid Deposition Control

Title IV mandates controls to reduce the deposition of acidic sulfates and nitrates by reducing emissions of sulfur dioxide (SO_2) and nitrogen oxides (NO_x), which are precursors of acid rain. Sulfur emissions are attributed largely to coal burning at electric utilities that contain sulfur as an impurity.

Congress set a two-phased goal for utility emissions reduction. The first phase requires 110 fossil-fuel-fired public power plants to reduce their emissions to a level equivalent to the product of an emissions rate of 2.5 lb of SO_2/MMBtu times the average of their 1985–1987 fuel usage. The second phase requires approximately 2000 utilities to reduce their emissions to a level equivalent to the product of an emissions rate of 1.2 lb of SO_2/MMBtu times the average of their 1985–1987 fuel use.

Title IV also mandates a program in which allowances are created as marketshares, that utilities are allowed to buy and sell in order to meet reductions of emissions. These shares currently have a value of approximately \$2,000. The regulation also contains requirements for reduction of NO_x from tangentially fired boilers and dry bottom wall-fired boilers by 1995 and all other utility boilers by 1997.

Affected sources will be required to perform continuous emissions monitoring, permit their sources, and keep records of their activities. Continuous emissions monitoring devices must be installed on all affected sources. The permit application must include a compliance plan for the source to comply with the requirements of Title IV. Affected sources are also required to pay an annual fee of \$2,000 per ton for emissions in excess of allowance levels (P.L. 101-549, 1990).

Title V: Permits

Under Title V, the EPA has attempted to model the permit requirements from the Clean Water Act (CWA). (See a later section on Water Pollution for additional details on the CWA.) The CWA permitting system is known as the National Pollution Discharge Elimination System (NPDES). The permitting program is enacted to ensure compliance with various portions of the program. States were required to submit a proposed program to the EPA by November 1993 for issuing permits to certain significant sources of air emissions.

The Title V operating permit program requires all affected sources under the CAAAs to submit a permit application to the appropriate permitting authority within one year of the effective date of the state program. The operating permit program applies to the following major sources:

1. Air toxic sources as defined under Title III, with the potential to emit 10 tons per year (tpy) or more of a single HAP or 25 tpy or more of the aggregate of HAPs or a lesser quantity if the Administrator so specifies.

2. Sources emitting more than 100 tons per year, 50 tons per year, 25 tons per year, or 10 tons per year depending on their nonattainment designation; that is, marginal, moderate, severe, or extreme.

3. Sources of air pollutants with the potential to emit 100 tpy or more of any pollutant.

4. Any other source, including an area source, subject to a hazardous air pollutant standard under Title III.

5. Any affected source under the acid rain program under Title IV.

6. Any source required to have a preconstruction permit pursuant to the requirements of the prevention of significant deterioration (PSD) program under Title I, or the nonattainment new source review (NSR) program under Title I.

7. Any other stationary source in a category the EPA designates in whole or in part by regulation after notice and comment.

Once subject to the operating permit program for one pollutant, a major source must submit a permit application including all emissions of all regulated pollutants from all emissions units located at the plant, except that only a generalized list needs to be included for insignificant events or emissions levels. The program applies to all geographic areas within each state, regardless of their attainment status (P.L. 101-549, 1990).

Title VI: Stratospheric Ozone and Global Climate Protection

Title VI requires the EPA to promulgate controls pertaining to the protection of stratospheric ozone. In response to growing evidence that chlorine and bromine could destroy stratospheric ozone on a global basis, many members of the international community concluded that an international agreement to reduce the global production of ozone-depleting substances was needed. Because releases of chlorofluorocarbons (CFCs) from all areas mix in the atmosphere to affect stratospheric ozone globally, efforts to reduce emissions from specific products by only a few nations could quickly be offset by increases in emissions from other nations, leaving the risk to the ozone layer unchanged. In September 1987 the United States and twenty-two other countries signed the Montreal Protocol on Substances that Deplete the Ozone Layer. The Montreal Protocol called for a freeze in the production and consumption of certain CFCs. The Montreal Protocol was the main thrust for Title VI, although in response to recent scientific evidence indicating a hole in the ozone layer, the EPA has adopted a phase-out schedule more aggressive than the Protocol.

The CAAAs established a phase-out schedule as fast as, and in some instances faster than, the 1990 Amendments to the Montreal Protocol. Specifically this title requires the United States to phase out production and consumption of class I substances, that is, CFCs, Halons, carbon tetrachloride, and methyl chloroform by 1996, 1994, 1996, and 1996 respectively. In addition, the CAAA require a freeze in the production of class II chemicals—hydrochlorofluorocarbons (HCFCs)—by the year 2015, and a phase out by 2030. The phase out includes exemptions for certain uses that the administrator of the EPA deems essential, such as CFC as a propellant in metered-dose inhalers (an asthma prescription pharmaceutical). As of January 1, 1994 methyl bromide and hydrobromofluorocarbons (HBFCs) were added to the list of class I chemicals. Recently the EPA has accelerated the phaseout of HCFC-22, HCFC-141b, and HCFC-142b, three relatively heavily-weighted ozone depleters. Production and consumption will be frozen in 2010 with a complete phaseout by 2020.

The Safe New Alternatives Program (SNAP) evaluates the overall effects on human health and the environment of the potential substitutes for ozone-depleting substances. SNAP will render it unlawful to replace an ozone-depleting substance with a substitute chemical or technology that may present adverse effects to human health and the environment if the Administrator determines that some other alternative is commercially available and that this alternative poses a lower overall threat to human health and the environment. The SNAP program is a powerful tool to assure that safe alternatives are developed.

The refrigerant recycling regulations promulgated May 14, 1993 require recycling, emissions reduction, and disposal for ozone-depleting refrigerants. The regulations require technicians servicing and disposing of air-conditioning and refrigeration equipment to observe certain service practices, to be certified by an EPA-approved organization for technicians servicing equipment. They also establish reclaimer certification programs.

Other Title VI provisions require the EPA to promulgate additional controls pertaining to the protection of stratospheric ozone for banning nonessential products, such as party streamers and noise horns, and mandating warning labels for products manufactured with containers of, and products containing, specific ozone-depleting substances (P.L. 101-549, 1990; 40 CFR, December 10, 1993 and February 11, 1993; "Complying with the Refrigerant Recycling Rule," June 1993).

Title VII: Provisions Relating to Enforcement

The 1990 provisions bring with them penalties unlike other environmental laws. Congress has taken several measures in order to make air quality violations felonies or crimes, punishable by jail sentences, where previously they were misdemeanors that were punishable by fines. Under the CAAAs there are now four classes of criminal offenses: negligent; knowing; knowing endangerment; falsification, failure to make required reports and tampering with monitors. Each of these offences is detailed below.

1. Negligent: Anyone who negligently releases any of the 189 hazardous air pollutants designated under section 112, as well as the 360 or so extremely hazardous substances listed under 40 CFR Part 350 into the ambient air is subject to criminal prosecution. In order to be a criminal offense, the negligent release must place another person in imminent danger of death or serious bodily injury. Violators may be imprisoned for up to one year.

2. Knowing Violations: Any knowing violations of a state implementation plan, a nonattainment provision, an air toxics law, and a standard associated with the permits, acid rain, or stratospheric ozone titles, has been upgraded to a felony. These violations are now punishable by a fine and five years imprisonment. The CAAA also increase the maximum fine associated with criminal knowing violations to $250,000 for individuals, and $500,000 for organizations. It is also a criminal offense to knowingly fail to pay any fee owed to the United States under Titles I to VI. Violators may be imprisoned for up to one year and fined.

3. Knowing Endangerment: Anyone who knowingly releases any of the 189 hazardous air pollutants designated under section 112, as well as the 360 or so extremely hazardous substances listed under 40 CFR Part 350 is subject to criminal prosecution. In order to be a criminal offense, the knowing release must place another person in imminent danger of death or serious bodily injury. This is a felony offense punishable by a fine and/or fifteen years in prison. The statute authorizes a $1 million dollar maximum fine for organizations and companies.

4. Falsifications, Failures to Report, and Tampering: Knowing actions to falsify reports, failure to keep necessary monitoring records, and material omissions from such reports and records as well as failures to report or notify as required by the CAAAs or failure to properly install the monitoring equipment are criminal violations. The CAAAs also increase the maximum fine associated with criminal knowing violations to $250,000 for individuals and $500,000 for organizations.

Citizens will be allowed to sue violators for penalties that will go to the U.S. Treasury fund for the EPA in compliance and enforcement activities. Administrative enforcement now includes provisions for issuance of field citations for violations observed in the field (this is like receiving a speeding ticket). These citations may not exceed $5,000 for each day that the violation continues. Administrative penalties are capped at $200,000. The CAAA authorize the EPA to issue administrative compliance orders with compliance schedules of up to one year. The EPA may act in emergency situations to protect public health and the environment. Companies can pay fines of up to $25,000 per day for failure to comply with an emergency order. Knowing violations of an emergency order are punishable by a fine and five years in prison.

The act also includes other titles that are not included here. It is suggested that the interested reader contact his or her specific EPA region for information and literature, call the stratospheric ozone hot line for specific questions, or refer directly to the CAAA (P.L. 101-549, 1990).

HAZARDOUS AND SOLID WASTE

Resource Conservation and Recovery Act

Defining what constitutes "solid waste" and "hazardous waste" requires consideration of both legal and scientific factors. The basic definition is derived from the Resource Conservation and Recovery Act (RCRA) of 1976 and the subsequent Hazardous and Solid Waste Amendments (HSWA) of 1984. Hazardous substances are regulated under the Comprehensive Environmental Response

Compensation and Liability act (CERCLA) of 1980 and the subsequent Superfund Amendments and Reauthorization Act (SARA) of 1986. These two governing bodies regulate management of currently generated hazardous waste and remediation of hazardous waste sites respectively.

The first comprehensive federal effort to deal with the solid-waste problem in general, and hazardous waste specifically, came with the passage of RCRA. The act provides for the development of federal and state programs for otherwise unregulated disposal of waste materials and for the development of resource recovery programs. It regulates anyone engaged in the creation, transportation, treatment, and disposal of "hazardous wastes." It also regulates facilities for the disposal of all solid waste and prohibits the use of open (essentially uncontrolled) dumps for solid wastes in favor of sanitary (essentially controlled) landfills.

The hazardous waste management program identifies specific hazardous wastes either by listing them or identifying characteristics that render them hazardous. Under RCRA, a solid waste that is not excluded as a hazardous waste is a hazardous waste if it exhibits any of the characteristics of reactivity, corrosivity, ignitability, or toxicity under 40 Code of Federal Regulations (CFR) 261.21–261.24, or it is listed hazardous waste under 40 CFR Parts 261.31–261.33. The EPA has established three lists:

1. **"K" Listed Wastes**—These hazardous wastes are from specific sources, that is, those wastes generated in a specific process that is specific to an industry group. Examples include wastewater treatment sludge from the production of chrome yellow and orange pigments and still bottoms from the distillation of benzyl chloride.

2. **"F" Listed Wastes**—These hazardous wastes are from nonspecific sources, that is, those wastes that are generated by a nonspecific industry that are generated from a standard operation that is part of a particular manufacturing process. Examples include spent solvent mixtures and blends used in degreasing containing, before use, a total of 10 percent or more (by volume) of various solvents.

3. **"P" and "U" Listed Wastes**—The third list has been broken into two distinct subsets. The "U" list contains chemicals that are deemed toxic and the "P" list contains chemicals that are deemed acutely hazardous. These hazardous wastes are discarded commercial chemical products, off-specification products, container residues, and spill residues. Examples include beryllium, fluorine, and methyl isocyanate.

As mentioned above, those wastes that are not listed in either the F, K, P, U lists may still be a hazardous waste if they exhibit one or more of the four following characteristics: reactivity, ignitability, corrosivity, or toxicity. These are listed below.

1. Reactivity—The waste will react violently with or release toxic gases or fumes when mixed with water, or is susceptible to explosions or detonations

2. Ignitability—A solid liquid or gas that is easily ignitable

3. Corrosivity—Alkaline or acidic material normally having a pH in the range of less than 2 and greater than 12.5

4. Toxicity—Wastes that have the ability to bioaccumulate in various aquatic species

Facilities generating these wastes are required to notify the EPA of such activity, as well as comply with the standards authorized by RCRA under Subtitle C. Facilities that generate hazardous waste are classified as either large-quantity generators, small-quantity generators, or conditionally exempt small-quantity generators. Large-quantity generators receive this classification if they generate more than 1000 kg, in a calendar month. Small quantity generators receive this classification if they generate less than 1000 kg but more than 100 kg in any calendar month. Both large and small quantity generators are subject to all EPA hazardous waste regulations, except small quantity generators are not required to have formal training programs for employees; an RCRA contingency plan and accumulation time is determined differently. Conditionally exempt small quantity generators, generating no more than 100 kg of hazardous waste in a calendar month, are not subject to EPA regulations, except that all waste(s) generated must be disposed of at a site approved by state or federal authority.

Generators are allowed to accumulate waste on site in two related circumstances. First, the generator is allowed to accumulate up to 55 gallons of a hazardous waste in a satellite accumulation area, provided the waste container is properly marked and compatible with the waste, and is removed to a storage area within three days of reaching the 55-gallon limit. Second, generators may store waste on site for 90 days or less in storage areas and containers that adhere to strict requirements. Small-quantity generators may store waste on site for up to 180 days (270 days if the waste must be transferred 200 miles or more). Conditionally exempt small-quantity generators are conditionally exempt under RCRA but must still meet certain minimum requirements (40 CFR, Part 261, July 1, 1992).

Comprehensive Environmental Response, Compensation, and Liability Act

Congress enacted the Comprehensive Environmental Response, Compensation, and Liability Act of 1980 (CERCLA) commonly known as "Superfund" (see Superfund, Chapter 21 for more details). Superfund establishes two related funds to be used for the immediate removal of hazardous substances released into the environment. Superfund is intended to establish a mechanism of response for the immediate clean-up of hazardous waste contamination from accidental spills and from chronic environmental damage such as associated with abandoned hazardous waste disposal sites. CERCLA works in concert with RCRA to provide full coverage of present and past hazardous waste activities.

A hazardous substance under CERCLA is any substance the EPA has designated for special consideration under the CAA, CWA, Toxic Substance Control Act (TSCA), as well as any hazardous waste under RCRA. Furthermore, the EPA must designate additional substances as hazardous which may present substantial danger to health and the environment. A list of these hazardous substances is found in 40 CFR Part 302.

Under CERCLA, the EPA is empowered to undertake removal and/or remedial action where the pollutant may present an imminent and substantial danger. Potentially Responsible Parties (PRPs) are those private parties that are encouraged by the EPA to clean up sites on the National Priorities List (NPL). Only NPL sites are eligible for fund-financed remedial action. Sites make the list by undergoing evaluation and scoring under the hazard ranking system (HRS), which estimates the degree of risk each suspected site poses to human health and the environment. Factors such as waste volume, toxicity, and potential pathways are evaluated and combined to form a single numbered HRS score. If this HRS score is over 28.5 the site will be included on the NPL.

Spill reporting under CERCLA covers releases to all environmental media: air, surface water, groundwater, and soil. The EPA assigns reportable quantities, that is, the exceeding of the assigned value of a hazardous substance released within any 24-hour period for which the CERCLA reporting requirements are triggered, to all hazardous substances. Immediately after a person in charge of the facility has knowledge of a release in excess of a reportable quantity, that person must immediately contact the National Response Center (NRC) to relay telephone information on the details of the release. Written follow-up information is required for establishing the details of cleanup mitigation efforts.

In response in part to the Bhopal, India tragedy, the Emergency Planning and Community Right to Know Act (EPCRA) was enacted under the Superfund Amendments and Reauthorization Act of 1986. Under EPCRA, state and local governments are required to develop emergency response plans for unanticipated releases of a number of acutely toxic materials known as extremely hazardous substances. EPCRA mandates the formation of State Emergency Response Commissions (SERC) and Local Emergency Planning Committees (LEPC), which are in charge of developing and implementing emergency response plans.

EPCRA also establishes reporting provisions for informing the public of hazardous substances being used, as indicated below.

1. MSDS (Material Safety Data Sheets) Reporting—Facilities for which hazardous chemicals are present in excess of a threshold quantity are required to submit MSDSs to the SERC, LEPC, and local fire departments.
2. Tier I or Tier II Reporting—Facilities for which hazardous substances are present are required to provide information on the annual and daily inventory information on the quantities of those materials and their locations on site. Tier I reports provide the required information on hazardous chemicals grouped by hazard category and Tier II reports provide the information on individual hazardous chemicals. Tier II may be submitted in lieu of Tier I reports.
3. Toxic Release Inventory (TRI)—Facilities that manufacture, process, or otherwise use a toxic chemical in excess of a threshold quantity are required to provide annual reports on the quantities released (40 CFR, Parts 300-372, July 1, 1992; Theodore, Reynolds, & Taylor, 1989).

Solid Waste.   Under RCRA, 40 CFR 261.4(a), a solid waste is defined as any material that is discarded, abandoned, recycled, or inherently waste-like. To gain further insight into the meaning of solid waste, the RCRA Section 1004(27) definition is:

> A solid waste is defined as any garbage, refuse, sludge from a waste treatment plant, water supply treatment plant, or air pollution control facility and other discarded material, including solid liquid, semisolid, or contained gaseous material resulting from industrial, commercial, mining, and agricultural operations and community activities, but does not include solid or dissolved material in domestic sewage (P.L. 80-272, 1965).

A material can be considered a solid waste if it is recycled in a manner constituting disposal. This type of recycling includes materials used to produce products that are applied to the land, burned for energy recovery, or accumulated speculatively before recycling. A material that fits the definition of a solid waste may be regulated as a hazardous waste if it poses a threat to human health or the environment. The definitions of solid waste and hazardous waste interlock, which results in EPA regulating a plethora of materials that may not be commonly thought of as wastes for certain industries.

The following materials are excluded from the definition of solid waste:

1. Domestic sewage
2. Industrial wastewater discharges that are point source discharges subject to regulation under section 402 of the Clean Water Act (This exclusion applies only to point source discharges. It does not exclude industrial wastewaters while they are being collected, stored, or treated before discharge, nor does it exclude sludges that are generated by industrial wastewater treatment.)
3. Irrigation return flows
4. Source, special nuclear, or byproduct material as defined by the Atomic Energy Act
5. Materials subjected to in-situ mining techniques that are not removed from the ground as part of the extraction process
6. Pulping liquors (i.e., black liquor) that are reclaimed in a pulping liquor recovery furnace and then reused in the pulping process, unless it is accumulated speculatively
7. Spent sulfuric acid used to produce virgin sulfuric acid, unless it is accumulated speculatively
8. Secondary materials that are reclaimed and returned to the original process or processes in which they were generated where they are reused in the production process provided (This exemption has limitations stipulating closed processes, reclamation not involving controlled flame combustion, accumulation, use as fuel, and not used in a manner constituting disposal.)

Obviously, solid waste is far less regulated, which, when translated by hazardous waste generators, means a savings on disposal costs. Certain materials are not regulated as a solid waste, when recycled. These include materials shown to be recycled by being:

1. Used or reused as ingredients in an industrial process to make a product, provided the materials are not being reclaimed
2. Used or reused as effective substitutes for commercial products
3. Returned to the original process from which they are being generated, without first being reclaimed. The material must be returned as a substance for raw material feed stock, and the process must use raw materials as principal feed stock.

Certain materials may still be considered solid wastes, that is, RCRA-regulated, even if the recycling involves use, reuse, or return to the original process. This includes:

1. Materials used in a manner constituting disposal, or used to produce products that are applied to the land; or materials burned for energy recovery, used to produce a fuel, or contained in fuels
2. Materials accumulated speculatively
3. Hazardous waste numbers F020, F021 (unless used as an ingredient to make a product at the site of generation), F022, F023, F026, and F028.

It is important to examine the manner of recycling and the material being recycled in determining whether the waste is considered a solid waste.

Once a material is found to be a solid waste, the next question is whether it is a hazardous waste. The EPA automatically exempts certain solid waste from being hazardous waste. A few examples are: household waste; including household waste that has been collected, transported, stored, treated, disposed, recovered (e.g., refuse-derived fuel), or reused; solid waste generated in the growing and harvesting of agricultural crops that is returned to the soil as fertilizer; fly ash waste; bottom ash waste, slag waste; flue gas emissions control waste generated primarily from the combustion of fossil fuels; and cement kiln dust. (Cement kiln dust is under attack by private interest groups to be regulated as a hazardous waste.)

The EPA may also grant a variance from classification as a solid waste on a case-by-case basis. Eligible materials include those that are reclaimed and then reused within the original primary production process in which they were generated, reclaimed partially, but require further processing by being completely recovered, and accumulating speculatively with less than 75 percent of the volume having the potential for recycling (40 CFR, Part 261, July 1, 1992).

WATER POLLUTION CONTROL

Congress put the framework together for water pollution control by enacting the Federal Water Pollution Control Act (FWPCA), the Marine Protection, Research and Sanctuaries Act (MPRSA), the Safe Drinking Water Act (SDWA), and the Oil Pollution Control Act (OPA). Each statute provides a variety of tools that can be used to meet the challenges and complexities of reducing water pollution in the nation. These are discussed below.

Federal Water Pollution Control Act

In 1977, Congress renamed the FWPCA the Clean Water Act and substantially revamped and revised the control of toxic water pollutants. The Act has two basic components: a statement of goals and objectives and a system of regulatory mechanisms calculated to achieve these goals and mechanisms. The objective of the program as outlined in section 101 of the Act is to "restore and maintain the chemical, physical and biological integrity of the nation's waters." To achieve this, the Act provides water quality for protection of fish, shellfish, and wildlife for recreational use and eliminates the discharge of pollutants into the waters of the United States.

The system of achieving these goals and objectives has six basic elements:

1. A two-stage system of technology-based effluent limits establishing base level or minimum treatment required to prevent industries and publicly owned treatment works from discharging pollutants.

2. A program for imposing more stringent limits in permits where such limits are necessary to achieve water quality standards or objectives.

3. A permit program known as the National Pollution Discharge Elimination Program (NPDES). The NPDES permit requires the discharges to disclose the volume and nature of their discharges as well as monitor and report the results to the authorizing agency. The

NPDES permit program authorizes the EPA and citizens enforcement in the case of noncompliance.

4. A set of specific deadlines for compliance or noncompliance with the limitations, with attached enforcement provisions for the EPA and citizens.

5. A set of provisions applicable to certain toxic and other pollutant discharges of particular concern, for example, stormwater and oil spills.

6. A loan program to help fund POTW attainment of the applicable requirements.

Effluent limitations have been established for various categories of point sources which include but are not limited to the chemical, pharmaceutical, paper manufacturing, and pesticide manufacturing industries. The Act is far more than the six-part framework indicates. The reader is referred to 40 CFR Subchapter N, "Effluent Guidelines and Standards" for more information on how a specific industry is regulated (40 CFR, Part 401, July 1, 1992).

Safe Drinking Water Act

The Safe Drinking Water Act (SDWA) was originally passed in 1974 to ensure that public water supplies are maintained at high quality by setting national standards for levels of contaminants in drinking water, by regulating underground injection wells, and by protecting sole source aquifers.

The SDWA requires the EPA to establish Maximum Contamination Level Goals (MCLGs) and National Primary Drinking Water Regulations (NPDWR) for contaminants that, in the judgment of the EPA Administrator, may cause any adverse effect on the health of persons and that are known or anticipated to occur in public water systems. The NPDWRs are to include Maximum Contamination Levels (MCLs) and "criteria and procedures to assure a supply of drinking water which dependably complies" with such MCLs. If it is not feasible to ascertain the level of a contaminant in drinking water, the NPDWRs may require the use of a treatment technique instead of an MCL. The EPA is mandated to establish MCLGs and promulgate NPDWRs for 83 contaminants in public water systems. (The SDWA was amended in 1986 by establishing a list of 83 contaminants for which EPA is to develop MCLGs and NPDWRs). MCLGs and MCLs were to be promulgated simultaneously.

MCLGs do not constitute regulatory requirements that impose any obligation on public water systems. Rather, MCLGs are health goals that are based solely upon consideration of protecting the public from adverse health effects of drinking water contamination. The MCLGs reflect the aspirational health goals of the SDWA that the enforceable requirements of NPDWRs seek to attain. MCLGs are to be set at a level where "no known or anticipated adverse effects on the health of persons occur and which allows an adequate margin of safety."

The House Report on the bill that eventually became the SDWA of 1974 provides congressional guidance on developing MCLGs:

> [T]he recommended maximum contamination level [renamed maximum contamination level goal in the 1986 amendments to the SDWA] must be set to prevent the occurrence of any known or anticipated adverse effect. It must include an adequate margin of safety, unless there is no safe threshold for a contaminant. In such a case, the recommended maximum contamination level would be set at the zero level (40 CFR, Parts 141 and 142, June 7, 1991).

NPDWRs include either MCLs or treatment technique requirements as well as compliance monitoring requirements. The MCL for a contaminant must be set as close to the MCLG as feasible. Feasible means "feasible with the use of the treatment techniques and other means which the Administrator of the EPA finds, after examination for efficacy under field conditions and not solely under laboratory conditions, are available (taking cost into consideration)." A treatment technique must "prevent known or anticipated adverse effects on the health of a person to the extent feasible." A treatment technique requirement can be set only if the EPA Administrator makes a finding that "it is not economically or technically feasible to ascertain the level of the contaminant." Also the SDWA requires the EPA to identify the best available technology (BAT) for meeting the MCL for each contaminant.

EPA sets national secondary drinking water regulations (NSDWRs) to control water color, odor, appearance, and other characteristics affecting consumer acceptance of water. The secondary regulations are not federally enforceable but are considered guidelines for the states (40 CFR, Parts 141 and 142, June 7, 1991).

Oil Pollution Control Act

The Oil Pollution Control Act of 1990 (OPA) was enacted to expand prevention and preparedness activities, improve response capabilities, ensure that shippers and oil companies pay the costs of spills that do occur, and establish and expand research and development programs. This was all in response to the Exxon Valdez oil spill in Prince William Sound in 1989.

The OPA establishes a new Oil Spill Liability Trust Fund, administered by the United States Coast Guard. This fund replaces the fund established under the CWA and other oil pollution funds. The new Act mandates prompt and adequate compensation for those harmed by oil spills, and an effective and consistent system of assigning liability. The Act also strengthens requirements for the proper handling, storage, and transportation of oil and for the full and prompt response in the event discharges occur. The Act does so in part by amending section 311 of the CWA.

There are eight titles codified under the Act, details of which are available in the literature (40 CFR, Part 112, July 1, 1992; 40 CFR, February 17, 1993).

OCCUPATIONAL SAFETY AND HEALTH ACT

The Occupational Safety and Health Act (OSH Act) was enacted by Congress in 1970 and established the Occupational Safety and Health Administration (OSHA), which addressed safety in the workplace; at the same time EPA was created. Both EPA and OSHA are mandated to reduce the exposure of hazardous substances over land, sea, and air. The OSH Act is limited to conditions that exist in the workplace, where its jurisdiction covers both safety and health. Frequently, both agencies regulate the same substances but in a different manner. They are overlapping environmental organizations.

Congress intended that OSHA be enforced through specific standards. Employers would follow these standards in an effort to achieve a safe and healthful working environment. A "general duty clause" was added to attempt to cover those obvious situations that were admitted by all concerned but for which no specific standard existed. The OSHA standards are an extensive compilation of regulations, some that apply to all employers—such as eye and face protection—and some that apply to workers who are engaged in a specific type of work, such as welding or crane operation. Employers are obligated to familiarize themselves with the standards and comply with them at all times.

Health issues, most importantly, contaminants in the workplace, have become OSHA's primary concern. Health hazards are complex and difficult to define. Because of this, OSHA has been slow to implement health standards. To be complete, each standard requires medical surveillance, record keeping, monitoring, and physical reviews. On the other side of the ledger, safety hazards are aspects of the work environment that are expected to cause death or serious physical harm immediately or before the imminence of such danger can be eliminated.

Probably one of the most important safety and health standard ever adopted is the OSHA hazard communication standard, more popularly known as the "right-to-know" laws. The hazard communication standard requires employers to communicate information to the employee on hazardous chemicals that exist within the workplace. The program requires employers to craft a written hazard communication program, keep material safety data sheets (MSDSs) for all hazardous chemicals at the workplace and provide employees with training on those hazardous chemicals, and assure that proper warning labels are in place.

The Hazardous Waste Operations and Emergency Response Regulation enacted in 1989 by OSHA addresses the safety and health of employees involved in cleanup operations at uncontrolled hazardous waste sites being cleaned up under government mandate, and in certain hazardous waste treatment, storage, and disposal operations conducted under RCRA. The standard provides for employee protection during initial site characterization and analysis, monitoring activities, training, and emergency response.

Four major areas are under the scope of the regulation:

1. Cleanup operations at uncontrolled hazardous waste sites that have been identified for cleanup by a government health or environmental agency
2. Routine operations at hazardous waste TSD (Transportation, Storage, and Disposal) facilities or those portions of any facility regulated by 40 CFR Parts 264 and 265
3. Emergency response operations at sites where hazardous substances have or may be released
4. Corrective actions at RCRA sites

The regulation addresses three specific populations of workers at the above operations. First, it regulates hazardous substance response operations under CERCLA, including initial investigations at CERCLA sites before the presence or absence of hazardous substance has been ascertained; corrective actions taken in cleanup operations under RCRA; and those hazardous waste operations at sites that have been designated for cleanup by state or local government authorities. The second worker population to be covered is those employees engaged in operations involving hazardous waste TSD facilities. The third employee population to be covered is those employees engaged in emergency response operations for releases or substantial threat of releases of hazardous substances, and post emergency response operations to such facilities (29 CFR, March 6, 1989; 29 CFR, February 24, 1992).

THE TOXIC SUBSTANCE CONTROL ACT

The Toxic Substance Control Act (TSCA) of 1976 provides EPA with the authority to control the risks of thousands of chemical substances, both new and old, that are not regulated as drugs, food additives, cosmetics, or pesticides. TSCA essentially mandates testing of chemical substances to regulate their uses in industrial, commercial, and consumer products. TSCA fills in the gaps and supplements other laws regulating toxic substances, such as the Clean Air Act, the Occupational Safety and Health Act, and the Federal Water Pollution Control Act. TSCA allows EPA to tailor its regulation to specific sources of risk.

TSCA essentially contains two sections: requirements for information on the substance to identify risks to health and the environment from chemical substances (a premanufacturing notification (PMN)); and regulations on the production and distribution of new chemicals and regulations on the manufacturing, processing, distribution, and use of existing chemicals (recordkeeping and reporting requirements).

TSCA Inventory

No person may manufacture a new chemical substance, or manufacture or process an existing chemical substance for a significant new use, without EPA approval. There are two kinds of chemical substances—"new chemical substances" and "existing chemical substances." A chemical substance that is not on the TSCA inventory (an inventory of existing chemical substances) is a "new chemical substance." Notification is required before a chemical substance can be put to a significant new use.

The TSCA inventory was initially compiled in 1977, but is updated by EPA to include new chemical substances for which manufacturers have filed Notices of Commencement. Every four years, beginning in 1986, manufacturers (and importers) of certain chemicals must submit updated information including chemical identity, plant site, whether the substance is manufactured or imported, whether the substance is distributed offsite for commercial purposes, and production volume on their TSCA-regulated chemicals. Manufacturers of polymers, microorganisms, naturally occurring substances, and inorganics are exempt from inventory updating. Any company that manufactures (or imports) more than 10,000 pounds of any chemical substances (except those excluded) in the latest complete fiscal year preceding a reporting period must submit updated information.

Premanufacturing Notification

Any company that wishes to manufacture (or import) a chemical substance must first determine whether the chemical substance is on the TSCA inventory. If it is not on the inventory, a manufacturer must file a Premanufacturer Notification (PMN) with the EPA. The PMN must be filed 90 days prior to manufacture of the chemical substance. If a PMN is not necessary, EPA will notify the submitter that submissions not necessary. Companies may request a 90-day extension if EPA determines there is good cause to extend the notice.

If the EPA takes no action by the end of the review period, the submitter may begin to manufacture. Within 30 days after the first day of manufacturing the manufacturer must submit a Notice of Commencement (NOC). The NOC essentially places the chemical substance on the TSCA inventory. Companies are exempt from the PMN reporting requirements for the following reasons: The chemical is not a "chemical substance," for example, a nuclear material, tobacco, foods, and drugs; any chemical substance that is manufactured or imported in small quantities solely for research and development, provided certain conditions are met; any chemical substances that will be manufactured or imported solely for test-marketing purposes under an exemption granted pursuant to 40 CFR 720.38; any new chemical substance manufactured solely for export provided certain requirements are met; any new chemical substance that is manufactured or imported under the terms of a rule promulgated under section 5(h) (4) of TSCA, for example, certain chemicals used for instant photographic and peel-apart film articles; any byproduct if its only commercial purpose is for use by public or private organization that burns it as fuel, disposes of it as waste, or extracts chemical substances from it for commercial purposes; certain chemical substances described in 40 CFR 720(h), for example, any impurity or byproduct, provided it is not used or manufactured for commercial purposes; any chemical substance that is manufactured solely for noncommercial research and development purposes.

Recordkeeping and Reporting Requirements

Section 8 of TSCA contains a variety of reporting requirements to fulfill the statute's information-gathering objectives. The scope of chemicals and regulated entities changes between sections. Sections 8(a) and (d) apply only to chemicals listed by regulation. Sections 8(c) and (e) cover the full spectrum of TSCA chemicals. Section 8(a) reporting requirements consist of two reports: the Comprehensive Assessment Information Rule (CAIR) and the Preliminary Assessment Information Rule (PAIR). Manufacturers, importers, and processors must report on each substance such that the EPA can formulate risk assessments and develop regulatory strategies. CAIR requires companies to report on listed substance under 40 CFR 704.200 Subparts C and D. PAIR requires manufacturers and importers to report on each listed substance during the reporting period for that substance as given in the rule (see 40 CFR Part 712). PAIR is to ultimately be replaced by CAIR.

Section 8(c) requires affected companies to maintain records of allegations of significant adverse reactions to health or the environment caused by the substances. Section 8(d) sets forth requirements for the submission of health studies on chemical substances and mixtures selected for priority consideration testing rules under Section 4(a) of TSCA and on other substances on which EPA requires health and safety studies. Section 8(e) requires effected companies to inform the Administrator of the EPA of any chemical substance that presents a substantial risk of injury to health of the environment as soon as this information is discovered.

TSCA also specifically regulates PCBs, CFCs, and asbestos (40 CFR, Parts 700-766, July 1, 1992).

FUTURE TRENDS

The Environmental Protection Agency is under new supervision with the election of the Clinton/Gore tandem. The current labyrinth of environmental statutes and administrative programs is desperately in need of reform (see Chapter 4). Environmental needs are a large budgetary problem for the government and businesses alike. Attempts have even been made to elevate EPA to a cabinet position as the EPA goal is to increase overall power and visibility. As many acts undergo close scrutinization from Congress, the public and private sectors are making a bid to see that their interests are protected.

There is a certain amount of jousting in Congress over risk and cost-benefit analysis. Under this promised legislation EPA would be required to conduct risk assessments and cost-benefit analyses for environmental regulations, as well as an assessment of environmental risks as compared to their daily risks. Risk assessment is an evolving area of science, one that will shape future decision making (see Part VIII, Chapters 35 to 38 for additional details). Comparative risk analysis provides a way to consider and rank many problems at the same time. It is a means for comparing dissimilar environmental risks in a manner that blends public opinion with scientific data and professional judgment. This helps to provide a comprehensive economic analysis analogous to the risk analysis—sort of a bridge between risk assessment and risk management. Comparative risk analysis can lead to short-term economic gains at the expense of leaving long-term environmental problems for future generations.

Most recently the Comprehensive Environmental Response Compensation and Liability Act, Superfund, has been the focus of reform. Remedies, retroactivity, and cleanup cost limitations have dominated the debate over Superfund. Currently, the EPA is endeavoring to set different levels of cleanup standards for contaminated hazardous waste sites, that is, Superfund sites. This proposal would exempt generators and transporters of negligible (de micromis) amounts of waste. Those parties unable to pay their full share of cleanup costs will be permitted to negotiate a settlement with EPA and be protected against third-party lawsuits. Potentially Responsible Parties would be able to settle their disputes by the recommendation of a neutral expert. Additionally, a new environmental insurance fund would be established to settle claims for insurance claims for cleanup costs for wastes disposed before 1986. (This would essentially "grandfather" insurance claims for cleanup costs for wastes disposed before 1986.) The fund would be financed by fees and assessments on insurance companies. To encourage the use of new remedial technology, the federal government will share the risk by paying part of the cost of any additional remedial action should the new remedy fail.

As described above, risk management has become a top priority by industry and federal officials. Future Clean Air Act Amendments will require business to communicate the likelihood and the degree of harm to the public and the environment that could occur during a chemical accident. The detailed risk plans are aimed at reducing chemical accidents. The release mitigation information is geared toward linking data already available to state emergency response commissions and local emergency planning committees. Sharing the worst-case scenarios will lead to a higher state of readiness and keep pressure on government and industry to do a better job. It allows companies to talk openly about chemical accidents and what could happen, giving shareholders the opportunity to explain their emergency response roles.

The EPA's Cabinet Bill is another administrative initiative that has been brought about by the new change in the country's leadership. The move purports to increase efficiency, protect the environment, and raise the visibility of the Council on Environmental Quality (see Chapter 4).

Reauthorization of the Clean Water Act is presently a legislative priority. The following is a set of core issues being considered: an extension of the state revolving loan fund program; control of polluted runoff from a variety of sources, including storm water discharges; preservation of wetlands; and enforcement. Other matters that may be addressed range from further reductions on discharges of toxic chemicals and enhanced pollution prevention incentives to strengthening controls of pollutant runoff from diffuse sources. The EPA continues to update effluent guidelines for various industrial categories.

Hazardous waste identification and recycling schemes are the primary concerns under the

Resource Conservation and Recovery Act. The EPA expects to issue two proposed rules that will reshape the hazardous waste identification and recycling schemes under RCRA. Currently the dialogue group composed of representatives from industry and government has been assigned the duty of revamping the mixture, derived from rules that were recently vacated because the EPA failed to provide adequate notice and comment period when the rules were developed. Hazardous waste recycling would take on a three-tiered scheme. The first tier would require only notification to the agency that certain hazardous wastes are being recycled. The second tier would create a new regulatory recycling scheme that would be less stringent under the current rules. The third tier would require full Subtitle C control over hazardous waste recycling.

Today, the EPA struggles with the difficult task of implementing the 1990 Clean Air Act Amendments. The agency is also under the gun to produce hordes of new regulations. These regulations are complex and comprehensive in nature. Many of these program requirements started taking effect on January 1, 1995. The states are absorbing even a larger share of the burden of implementing the CAAAs. A greater emphasis will be placed on a multimedia approach (see Chapter 6) to regulations. The multimedia regulations, which have been attempted recently in the paper and pulp industry, will regulate both air emissions and water discharges. EPA is also attempting a multimedia approach to inspections and enforcement actions.

SUMMARY

1. Environmental regulation is an organized system of statues, regulations, and guidelines that minimize, prevent, and punish the consequences of damage to the environment. The recent popularity of environmental issues has brought about changes in legislation and subsequent advances in technology.

2. The Clean Air Act Amendments of 1990 build upon the regulatory framework of the Clean Air Act programs and expands their coverage to many more industrial and commercial facilities.

3. Hazardous waste is regulated under the Resource Conservation and Recovery Act for currently generated hazardous waste and under the Comprehensive Environmental, Response, Compensation, and Liability Act for past generation and subsequent remediation at hazardous waste sites.

4. Under the Clean Water Act the permit program known as the National Pollution Discharge Elimination System requires dischargers to disclose the volume and nature of their discharges as well as monitor and report to the authorizing agency the results.

5. The Occupational Safety and Health Act was established to address safety in the workplace, which is limited to conditions that exist within the workplace, where its jurisdiction covers both safety and health.

6. The Toxic Substance Control Act of 1976 provides EPA with the authority to control the risks of thousands of chemical substances, both new and old, that are not regulated as either drugs, food additives, cosmetics, or pesticides.

7. Risk management has become a top priority by industry and federal officials. The Clean Air Act Amendments will require industries to communicate the likelihood and degree of a chemical accident to the public.

REFERENCES

"The Clean Air Act Amendments," Public Law 101-549, 101st Congress, Washington, DC, October 15, 1990

"Complying with the Refrigerant Recycling Rule," EPA Publication, Washington, DC, June 1993.

"General Pretreatment Regulations for Existing and New Sources of Pollution," 40 Code of Federal Regulations, Part 401, pp. 8–54, Washington, DC, July 1, 1992.

"Hazardous Waste Operations and Emergency Response," 29 Code of Federal Regulations, Federal Register, pp. 9294–9336, Washington, DC, March 6, 1989.

"Identification and Listing of Hazardous Waste," 40 Code of Federal Regulations, Part 261, pp. 27–131, Washington, DC, July 1, 1992.

"Maximum Contamination Level Goals and National Primary Drinking Water Regulations for Lead and Copper," 40 CFR 141 and 142, Federal Register, pp. 26460–26564, Washington, DC, June 7, 1991.

"Oil Pollution Prevention," 40 Code of Federal Regulations, Part 112, pp. 18–29, Washington, DC, July 1, 1992.

"Oil Pollution Prevention; Non-Transportation Related Onshore Facilities," 40 Code of Federal Regulations, Federal Register, pp. 8824–8879, Washington, DC, February 17, 1993.

"Process Safety Management of Highly Hazardous Chemicals; Explosives and Blasting Agents," 29 Code of Federal Regulations, Federal Register, pp. 6356–, Washington, DC, February 24, 1992.

"Protection of Stratospheric Ozone," 40 Code of Federal Regulations, Federal Register, pp. 65018–65082, Washington, DC, December 10, 1993.

"Protection of Stratospheric Ozone; Labeling," 40 Code of Federal Regulations, Federal Register, pp. 8136–8169, Washington, DC, February 11, 1993.

"Protection of Stratospheric Ozone; Refrigerant Recycling," 40 Code of Federal Regulations, Federal Register, pp. 28660–28734, May 14, 1993, Washington, DC.

"Risk Management Programs for Chemical Accident Release Prevention," 40 Code of Federal Regulations, Federal Register, pp. 54190–54219, Washington, DC, October 20, 1993.

Solid Waste Disposal Act, Public Law 80–272, 89th Congress, Washington, DC, October 20, 1965.

"Standards Applicable to Generators of Hazardous Waste," 40 Code of Federal Regulations, Part 261, pp. 131–150, Washington, DC, July 1, 1992.

"Subchapter J—Superfund, Emergency Planning, and Community Right-To-Know Programs," 40 Code of Federal Regulations, Parts 300–372, pp. 4–412, Washington, DC, July 1, 1992.

"Subchapter R—Toxic Substances Control Act," 40 Code of Federal Regulations, Parts 700–766, pp. 4–626, Washington, DC, July 1, 1992.

Theodore, L., Reynolds, J.P., and Taylor, F.B. *Accident and Emergency Management.* New York: John Wiley and Sons, 1989.

6

Multimedia Concerns

The current approach to environmental waste management requires some rethinking. A multimedia approach helps integration of air, water, and land pollution controls and seeks solutions that do not violate the laws of nature. The obvious advantage of a multimedia pollution control approach is its ability to manage the transfer of pollutants so they will not continue to cause pollution problems. Among the possible steps in the multimedia approach are understanding the cross-media nature of pollutants, modifying pollution control methods so as not to shift pollutants from one medium to another, applying available waste reduction technologies, and training environmental professionals in a total environmental concept.

A multimedia approach in pollution control is long overdue. As described above, it integrates air, water, and land into a single concern and seeks a solution to pollution that does not endanger society or the environment. The challenges for the future environmental professional include:

1. Conservation of natural resources
2. Control of air-water-land pollution
3. Regulation of toxics and disposal of hazardous wastes
4. Improvement of quality of life

It is now increasingly clear that some treatment technologies (specific technologies will be discussed in later chapters), while solving one pollution problem, have created others. Most contaminants, particularly toxics, present problems in more than one medium. Since nature does not recognize neat jurisdictional compartments, these same contaminants are often transferred across

A significant amount of material in this chapter has been drawn (with permission) from a paper entitled "Educational Aspects of Multimedia Pollution Prevention" by Dr. Thomas Shen that was presented at the International Pollution Prevention Conference in Washington D.C. in 1990.

media. Air pollution control devices and industrial wastewater treatment plants prevent waste from going into the air and water, but the toxic ash and sludge that these systems produce can become hazardous waste problems themselves. For example, removing trace metals from a flue gas usually transfers the products to a liquid or solid phase. Does this exchange an air quality problem for a liquid or solid waste management problem? Waste disposed of on land or in deepwells can contaminate ground water and evaporation from ponds and lagoons can convert solid or liquid waste into air pollution problems (Holmes, Singh, & Theodore, 1993). Other examples include acid deposition, residue management, water reuse, and hazardous waste treatment and/or disposal.

Control of cross-media pollutants cycling in the environment is therefore an important step in the management of environmental quality. Pollutants that do not remain where they are released or where they are deposited move from a source to receptors by many routes, including air, water, and land. Unless information is available on how pollutants are transported, transformed, and accumulated after they enter the environment, they cannot effectively be controlled. A better understanding of the cross-media nature of pollutants and their major environmental processes—physical, chemical, and biological—is required.

HISTORICAL PERSPECTIVE*

The EPA's own single-media offices, often created sequentially as individual environmental problems were identified and responded to in legislation, have played a part in the impeding development of cost-effective multimedia prevention strategies. In the past, innovative cross-media agreements involving or promoting pollution prevention, as well as voluntary arrangements for overall reduction in releases, have not been encouraged. However, new initiatives are characterized by their use of a wide range of tools, including market incentives, public education and information, small business grants, technical assistance, research and technology applications, as well as more traditional regulations and enforcements (see Chapter 5 for additional details).

In the past the responsibility for pollution prevention and/or waste management at the industrial level was delegated to the equivalent of an environmental control department. These individuals were skilled in engineering treatment techniques but, in some instances, had almost no responsibility over what went on in the plant that generated the waste they were supposed to manage. In addition, most engineers are trained to make a product work, not to minimize or prevent pollution. There is still little emphasis (although this is changing) on pollution prevention in the educational arena for engineers. Business school students, the future business managers, also have not had the pollution prevention ethic instilled in them.

The reader should also note that the federal government, through its military arm, is responsible for some major environmental problems. It has further compounded these problems by failing to apply a multimedia or multiagency approach. The following are excerpts from a front-page article by Keith Schneider in the August 5, 1991 edition of the New York Times:

> A new strategic goal for the military is aimed at restoring the environment and reducing pollution at thousands of military and other government military-industrial installations in the United States and abroad . . . the result of the environment contamination on a scale almost unimaginable. The environ-

*The sources for this section are Holmes et al., 1993, and personal notes of L. Theodore.

mental projects are spread through four federal agencies and three military services, and are directed primarily by the deputy assistant secretaries. Many of the military-industry officials interviewed for this article said that the environmental offices are not sharing information well, were suffering at times from duplicate efforts, and might not be supervising research or contractors closely enough. Environmental groups, state agencies, and the Environmental Protection Agency began to raise concerns about the rampant military-industrial contamination in the 1970s, but were largely ignored. The Pentagon, The Energy Department, the National Aeronautics and Space Administration (NASA) and the Coast Guard considered pollution on their property a confidential matter. Leaders feared not the only the embarrassment from public disclosure, but also that solving the problems would divert money from projects they considered more worthwhile. Spending on military-environmental projects is causing private companies, some of them among the largest contractors for the military industry, to establish new divisions to compete for government contracts, many of them worth $100 million to $1 billion.

This lack of communication and/or willingness to cooperate within the federal government has created a multimedia problem that has just begun to surface. The years of indifference and neglect have allowed pollutants/wastes to contaminate the environment significantly beyond what would have occurred had the responsible parties acted sooner.

ENVIRONMENTAL PROBLEMS

Environmental problems result from the release of wastes (gaseous, liquid, and solid) that are generated daily by industrial and commercial establishments as well as households. The lack of consciousness regarding conservation of materials, energy, and water has contributed to the wasteful habits of society. The rate of waste generation has been increasing in accordance with the increase in population and the improvement in living standards. With technological advances and changes in lifestyle, the composition of waste has likewise changed. Chemical compounds and products are being manufactured in new forms with different half-lives (time for half of it to react and/or disappear). It has been difficult to manage such compounds and products once they have been discarded. As a result, these wastes have caused many treatment, storage, and disposal problems. Many environmental problems are caused by products that are either misplaced in use or discarded without proper concern of their environmental impacts. Essentially all products are potential wastes, and it is desirable to develop methods to reduce the waste impacts associated with products or to produce environmentally friendly products. Environmental agencies have been lax in promoting and automating tracking mechanisms that identify sources and fate of new products.

Solving problems, however, can sometimes create problems. For example, implementation of the Clean Air Act and the Clean Water Act has generated billions of tons of sludge, wastewater and residue that could cause soil contamination and underground water pollution problems. The increased concern over cross-media shifts of pollutants has yet to consistently translate into a systematic understanding of pollution problems and viable changes.

As indicated above, environmental protection efforts have emphasized media-specific waste treatment and disposal after the waste has already been created. Many of the pollutants which enter the environment are coming from "area or point sources" such as industrial complexes and land disposal facilities; therefore, they simply cannot be solely controlled by the end-of-pipe solutions.

Furthermore, these end-of-pipe controls that tend to shift pollutants from one medium to another have often caused secondary pollution problems. Therefore, for pollution control purposes, the environment must be perceived as a single integrated system and pollution problems must be viewed holistically. Air quality can hardly be improved if water and land pollution continue to occur. Similarly, water quality cannot be improved if the air and land are polluted.

Many secondary pollution problems today can be traced in part to education, that is, the lack of knowledge and understanding of cross-media principles for the identification and control of pollutants. Neither the Clean Air Act nor the Clean Water Act enacted in the early 1970s adequately addresses the cross-media nature of environmental pollutants. More environmental professionals now realize that pollution legislation is too fragmented and compartmentalized. Only proper education and training will address this situation and hopefully lead to more comprehensive legislation of the total environmental approach.

MULTIMEDIA APPROACH

The environment is the most important component of life support systems. It is comprised of air, water, soil, and biota through which elements and pollutants cycle. This cycle involves the physical, chemical, or biological processing of pollutants in the environment. It may be short, turning hazardous into nonhazardous substances soon after they are released, or it may continue indefinitely with pollutants posing potential health risks over a long period of time. Physical processes associated with pollutant cycling include leaching from the soil into the ground water, volatilization from water or land to air, and deposition from air to land or water. Chemical processes include decomposition and reaction of pollutants to products with properties that are possibly quite different from those of the original pollutants. Biological processes involve microorganisms that can break down pollutants and convert hazardous pollutants into less toxic forms. However, these microorganisms can also increase the toxicity of a pollutant, for instance by changing mercury into methyl-mercury in soil (Shen, 1989).

Although pollutants sometimes remain in one medium for a long time, they are most likely mobile. For example, settled pollutants in river sediments can be dislodged by microorganisms, flooding, or dredging. Displacement such as this earlier constituted the PCB problem in New York's Hudson River. Pollutants placed in landfills have been transferred to air and water through volatilization and leaching. About 200 hazardous chemicals were found in the air, water, and soil at the Love Canal land disposal site in New York State. The advantages of applying multimedia approaches lie in their ability:

1. To manage the transfer of pollutants
2. To avoid duplicating efforts or conflicting activities
3. To save resources by consolidation of environmental regulations, monitoring, database management, risk assessment, permit issuance and fields inspection.

In recent years, the concept and goals of multimedia pollution prevention have been adopted by many regulatory and other governmental agencies, industries, and the public in the

United States and abroad. Multimedia efforts in the United States have been focused on the U.S. Environmental Protection Agency's (EPA) Pollution Prevention Office, which helps coordinate pollution prevention activities across all EPA headquarter offices and regional offices. The current EPA philosophy recognizes that multimedia pollution prevention is best achieved through education and technology transfer rather than through regulatory imposition of mandatory approaches. But the progress of implementing multimedia pollution prevention has been slow (see Chapter 4 and Part VIII, Chapters 30 to 34 for more details on waste reduction/pollution prevention).

Recognition of the need for multimedia pollution prevention approaches has extended from the government, industry, and the public to professional societies. The Air Pollution Control Association (APCA) was renamed as the Air and Waste Management Association (AWMA) to incorporate waste management. The American Society of Civil Engineers (ASCE) has established a multimedia management committee under the Environmental Engineering Division. The American Institute of Chemical Engineers (AIChE) has reorganized its Environmental Division to include a section devoted to pollution prevention. The Water Pollution Control Federation (WPCF) has also adopted a set principle addressing pollution prevention.

MULTIMEDIA APPLICATION*

Perhaps a meaningful understanding of the multimedia approach can be obtained by examining the production and ultimate disposal of a product or service. A flow diagram representing this situation is depicted in Figure 6–1. Note that each of the ten steps in the overall process has potential inputs of mass and energy, and may produce an environmental pollutant and/or a substance or form of energy that may be used in a subsequent or later step. Traditional approaches to environmental management can provide some environmental relief, but a total systems approach is required if optimum improvements—in terms of pollution/waste reduction—are to be achieved.

One should note that a product and/or service is usually conceived to meet a specific market need with little thought given to the manufacturing parameters. At this stage of consideration, it may be possible to avoid some significant waste generation problems in future operations by answering a few simple questions:

1. What raw materials are used to manufacture the product?
2. Are any toxic or hazardous chemicals likely to be generated during manufacturing?
3. What performance regulatory specifications must the new product(s) and/or service(s) meet? Is extreme purity required?
4. How reliable will the delivery manufacturing/distribution process be? Are all steps commercially proven? Does the company have experience with the operations required?
5. What types of waste are likely to be generated? What is their physical and chemical form? Are they hazardous? Does the company currently manage these wastes on-site or off-site?

*The sources for this section are Holmes et al., 1993, and personal notes of L. Theodore.

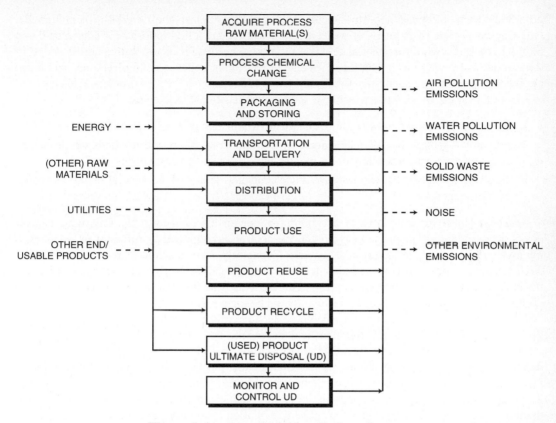

Figure 6–1.   Overall Multimedia flow diagram.

EDUCATION AND TRAINING

The role of environmental professionals in waste management and pollution control has been changing significantly in recent years. Many talented, dedicated environmental professionals in academia, government, industry, research institutions, and private practice need to cope with this change, and extend their knowledge and experience from media-specific, "end-of-pipe," treatment-and-disposal strategies to multimedia pollution prevention management. The importance of this extension and reorientation in education, however, is such that the effort cannot be further delayed. Many air pollution, water pollution, and solid waste supervisors in government agencies spend their entire careers in just one function because environmental quality supervisors usually work in only one of the media functions. Some may be reluctant to accept such activities. This is under-standable given the fact that such a reorientation requires time and energy to learn new concepts and that time is a premium for them. Nevertheless they must support such education and training in order to have well-trained young professionals.

Successful implementation of multimedia pollution prevention programs will require well-trained environmental professionals who are fully prepared in the principles and practices of such programs. These programs need to develop a deep appreciation of the necessity for multimedia pollution prevention in all levels of society, which will require a high priority for educational and training efforts. New instructional materials and tools are needed for incorporating new concepts in the existing curricula of elementary and secondary education, colleges and universities, and training institutions. The use of computerized automation offers much hope. Government agencies need to conduct a variety of activities to achieve three main educational objectives:

1. Ensure an adequate number of high quality environmental professionals
2. Encourage groups to undertake careers in environmental fields and to stimulate all institutions to participate more fully in developing environmental professionals
3. Generate databases that can improve environmental literacy of the general public and especially the media.

These objectives are related to, and reinforce, one another. For example, improving general environmental literacy should help to expand the pool of environmental professionals by increasing awareness of the nature of technical careers. Conversely, steps taken to increase the number of environmental professionals should also help improve the activities of general groups and institutions. Developing an adequate human resource base should be the first priority in education. The training environmental professionals receive should be top quality.

There is significant need to provide graduate students with training and experience in more than one discipline. The most important and interesting environmental scientific/technological questions increasingly require interdisciplinary and/or multidisciplinary approaches. Environmental graduate programs must address this aspect. Most practicing environmental professionals face various types of environmental problems that they have not been taught in the universities. Therefore, continuing education opportunities and cross-disciplinary training must be available for them to understand the importance of multimedia pollution prevention principles and strategies, as well as to carry out such principles and strategies.

The education and training plan of multimedia pollution prevention may be divided into technical and nontechnical areas. Technical areas include:

1. Products—Lifecycle analysis methods, trends-in-use patterns, new products, product lifespan data, product substitution, and product applicability. (A product's lifecycle includes its design, manufacture, use, maintenance and repair, and final disposal.)
2. Processes—Feedstock substitution, waste minimization, assessment procedures, basic unit process data, unit process waste generation assessment methods, materials handling, cleaning, maintenance and repair.
3. Recycling and Reuse—Market availability, infrastructure capabilities, new processes and product technologies, automated equipment and processes, distribution and marketing, management strategies, automation, waste stream segregation, on-site and off-site, reuse opportunities, close-loop methods, waste recapture, and reuse.

Nontechnical areas include:

1. Educational programs and dissemination of information
2. Incentive and disincentives

3. Economic cost and benefits
4. Sociological human behavioral trends
5. Management strategies including coordination with various concerned organizations

Additional details on training can be found in Chapter 43.

FUTURE TRENDS

Environmental quality and natural resources are under extreme stress in many industrialized nations and in virtually every developing nation as well. Environmental pollution is closely related to population density, energy, transportation demand, and land use patterns, as well as industrial and urban development. The main reason for environmental pollution is the increasing rate of waste generation in terms of quantity and toxicity that has exceeded society's ability to properly manage it. Another reason is that the management approach has focused on the media-specific and the end-of-pipe strategies. There is increasing reported evidence of socioeconomic and environmental benefits realized from multimedia pollution prevention (*Chemecology,* 1988, 1990; Schecter & Hunt, 1989). The prevention of environmental pollution in the 21st century is going to require not only enforcement of government regulations and controls, but also changes in manufacturing processes and products as well as in lifestyles and behavior throughout society. Education is key in achieving the vital goal of multimedia pollution prevention.

SUMMARY

1. The current approach to environmental waste management requires some rethinking. A multimedia approach facilitates the integration of air, water, and land pollution controls and seeks solutions that do not violate the laws of nature.

2. The EPA's own single-media offices, often created sequentially as individual problems were identified and responded to in legislation, have played a role in impeding development of cost-effective multimedia prevention strategies.

3. Environmental problems result from the release of wastes (gaseous, liquid and solid) that are generated daily by industrial and commercial establishments as well as households. The lack of consciousness regarding conservation of materials, energy, and water has contributed to the wasteful habits of society.

4. The environment is the most important component of life support systems. It is comprised of air, water, soil, and biota through which elements and pollutants cycle.

5. Traditional partitioned approaches to the environmental management can provide some environmental relief, but a total systems approach is required if optimum improvements—in terms of pollution/waste reduction—are to be achieved.

6. The role of environmental professional in waste management and pollution control has been changing significantly in recent years. Many talented, dedicated environmental professionals in academia, government, industry, research institutions, and private practice need to cope with the change, and extend their knowledge and experience from media specific, "end-of-pipe," treatment-and-disposal strategies to multimedia pollution prevention management.

7. The prevention of environmental pollution in the 21st century is going to require not only enforcement of government regulations and controls but also changes in manufacturing processes and products as well as in lifestyles and behavior throughout society. Education is the key in achieving the vital goal of multimedia pollution prevention.

REFERENCES

Chemecology, 17, (1), 1988; and *19* (2) 1990.

Holmes, G., Singh B., and Theodore, L. *Handbook of Environmental Management and Technology.* New York: Wiley-Interscience, 1993.

Schecter N., and Hunt, G. *Case Summaries of Waste Reduction by Industries in the Southeast.* Raleigh, NC: Waste Reduction Resource Center, 1989.

Shen, T. "The Role of Environmental Engineers in Waste Minimization," Proceedings of the First International Conference on Waste Minimization and Clean Technology, Geneva, Switzerland, 1989.

Theodore, L. personal notes, 1994.

7

Classification and Sources of Pollutants

CONTRIBUTING AUTHOR

Christine Hellwege

INTRODUCTION

Not long ago, the nation's natural resources were exploited indiscriminately. Waterways served as industrial pollution sinks; skies dispersed smoke from factories and powerplants; and the land proved to be a cheap and convenient place to dump industrial and urban wastes. However, society is now more aware of the environment and the need to protect it. The American people have been involved in a great social movement known broadly as "environmentalism." Society has been concerned with the quality of the air one breathes, the water one drinks, and the land on which one lives and works. While economic growth and prosperity are still important goals, opinion polls show overwhelming public support for pollution controls and pronounced willingness to pay for them. This chapter presents the reader with information on pollutants and categorizes their sources by the media they threaten.

AIR POLLUTANTS

Since the Clean Air Act was passed in 1970, the United States has made impressive strides in improving and protecting air quality. As directed by this Act, the EPA set National Ambient Air Quality Standards (NAAQS) for those pollutants commonly found throughout the country that posed the greatest overall threats to air quality. These pollutants, termed "criteria pollutants" under the Act, include: ozone, carbon monoxide, airborne particulates, sulfur dioxide, lead, and nitrogen oxide. Although the EPA has made considerable progress in controlling air pollution, all of the six criteria except lead and nitrogen oxide are currently a major concern in a number of areas in the country. The following subsections focus on a number of the most significant air quality challenges: ozone and carbon monoxide, airborne particulates, airborne toxics, sulfur dioxide, acid deposition, and indoor air pollutants.

Ozone and Carbon Monoxide

Ozone is one of the most intractable and widespread environmental problems. Chemically, ozone is a form of oxygen with three oxygen atoms instead of the two found in regular oxygen. This makes it very reactive, so that it combines with practically every material with which it comes in contact. In the upper atmosphere, where ozone is needed to protect people from ultraviolet radiation, the ozone is being destroyed by manmade chemicals, but at ground level, ozone can be a harmful pollutant.

Ozone is produced in the atmosphere when sunlight triggers chemical reactions between naturally occurring atmospheric gases and pollutants such as volatile organic compounds (VOCs) and nitrogen oxides. The main source of VOCs and nitrogen oxides is combustion sources such as motor vehicle traffic.

Carbon monoxide is an invisible, odorless product of incomplete fuel combustion. As with ozone, motor vehicles are the main contributor to carbon monoxide formation. Other sources include wood-burning stoves, incinerators, and industrial processes. Since auto travel and the number of small sources of VOCs are expected to increase, even strenuous efforts may not sufficiently reduce emissions of ozone and carbon monoxide (Holmes, Singh, & Theodore, 1993).

Airborne Particulates

Particulates in the air include dust, smoke, metals, and aerosols. Major sources include steel mills, power plants, cotton gins, cement plants, smelters, and diesel engines. Other sources are grain storage elevators, industrial haul roads, construction work, and demolition. Wood-burning stoves and fireplaces can also be significant sources of particulates. Urban areas are likely to have wind-blown dust from roads, parking lots, and construction work (Holmes et al., 1993).

Airborne Toxics

Toxic pollutants are one of today's most serious emerging problems are found in all media. Many sources emit toxic chemicals into the atmosphere: industrial and manufacturing processes, solvent use, sewage treatment plants, hazardous waste handling and disposal sites, municipal waste sites, incinerators, and motor vehicles. Smelters, metal refiners, manufacturing processes, and stationary fuel combustion sources emit such toxic metals as cadmium, lead, arsenic, chromium, mercury, and beryllium. Toxic organics, such as vinyl chloride and benzene, are released by a variety of sources, such as plastics and chemical manufacturing plants, and gas stations. Chlorinated dioxins are emitted by some chemical processes and the high-temperature burning of plastics in incinerators (Holmes et al., 1993).

Sulfur Dioxide

Sulfur dioxide can be transported long distances in the atmosphere due its ability to bond to particulates. Usually after traveling, sulfur dioxide combines with water vapor to form acid rain (see Chapter 41, Acid Rain). Sulfur dioxide is released into the air primarily through the burning of coal and fuel oils. Today, two-thirds of all national sulfur dioxide emissions come from electric power plants. Other sources of sulfur dioxide include refiners, pulp and paper mills, smelters, steel and chemical plants, and energy facilities related to oil shale, syn (synthetic) fuels, and oil and gas production. Home furnaces and coal-burning stoves are sources that directly affect residential neighborhoods (Holmes et al., 1993).

Acid Deposition

Acid deposition is a serious environmental concern in many parts of the country. The process of acid deposition begins with the emissions of sulfur dioxide (primarily from coal-burning power plants) and nitrogen oxides (primarily from motor vehicles and coal-burning power plants). As described in the previous sub-section, these pollutants interact with sunlight and water vapor in the upper atmosphere to form acidic compounds. During a storm, these compounds fall to earth as acid rain or snow; the compounds may also join dust or other dry airborne particles and fall as "dry deposition" (EPA, 1988).

INDOOR AIR POLLUTANTS

Indoor air pollution is rapidly becoming a major health issue in the United States. Indoor pollutant levels are quite often higher than outdoors, particularly where buildings are tightly constructed to save energy. Since most people spend 90 percent of their time indoors, exposure to unhealthy concentrations of indoor air pollutants is often inevitable. The degree of risk associated with exposure to indoor pollutants depends on how well buildings are ventilated and the type, mixture, and amounts of pollutants in the building. Indoor air pollutants of special concern are described below. More detailed information on indoor air quality can be found in Chapter 11.

Radon

Radon is a unique environmental problem because it occurs naturally. Radon results from the radioactive decay of radium-226, found in many types of rocks and soils. Most indoor radon comes from the rock and soil around a building and enters structures through cracks or openings in the foundation or basement. Secondary sources of indoor radon are well water and building materials (EPA, 1988).

Environmental Tobacco Smoke

Environmental tobacco smoke is smoke that nonsmokers are exposed to from smokers. This smoke has been judged by the Surgeon General, the National Research Council, and the International Agency for Research on Cancer to pose a risk of lung cancer to non-smokers. Tobacco smoke contains a number of pollutants, including inorganic gases, heavy metals, particulates, VOCs, and products of incomplete burning, such as polynuclear aromatic hydrocarbons (EPA, 1988).

Asbestos

Asbestos has been used in the past in a variety of building materials, including many types of insulation, fireproofing, wallboard, ceiling tiles, and floor tiles. The remodeling or demolition of buildings with asbestos-containing materials frees tiny asbestos fibers in clumps or clouds of dust. Even with normal aging, materials may deteriorate and release asbestos fibers. Once released, these asbestos fibers can be inhaled into the lungs and can accumulate (EPA, 1988). The reader is referred to Chapter 46 for a more expanded discussion of asbestos.

Formaldehyde and Other Volatile Organic Compounds

The EPA has found formaldehyde to be a probable human carcinogen. The use of formaldehyde in furniture, foam insulation, and pressed wood products, such as some plywood, particle board, and fiberboard, makes formaldehyde a major indoor air pollutant.

VOCs commonly found indoors include benzene from tobacco smoke and perchlorethylene emitted by dry-cleaned clothes. Paints and stored chemicals, including certain cleaning compounds, are also major sources of VOCs. VOCs can also be emitted from drinking water; twenty percent of water supply systems have detectable amounts of VOCs (EPA, 1988). (See Drinking Water section of WATER POLLUTANTS later in this chapter.)

Pesticides

Indoor and outdoor use of pesticides, including termiticides and wood preservatives, are another cause of concern. Even when used as directed, pesticides may release VOCs. In addition, there are about 1200 inert ingredients added to pesticide products for a variety of purposes. While not "active" in attacking the particular pest, some inert ingredients are chemically or biologically active and may cause health problems. EPA researchers are presently investigating whether indoor use of insecticides and subsurface soil injection of termiticides can lead to hazardous exposure (EPA, 1988).

WATER POLLUTANTS

The EPA, in partnership with state and local governments, is responsible for improving and maintaining water quality. These efforts are organized around three themes. The first is maintaining the quality of drinking water. This is addressed by monitoring and treating drinking water prior to consumption and by minimizing the contamination of the surface water and protecting against contamination of ground water needed for human consumption. The second is preventing the degradation and destruction of critical aquatic habitats, including wetlands, nearshore coastal waters, oceans, and lakes. The third is reducing the pollution of free-flowing surface waters and protecting their uses. The following is a discussion of various pollutants categorized by these themes.

Drinking Water Pollutants

The most severe and acute public health effects from contaminated drinking water, such as cholera and typhoid, have been eliminated in America. However, some less acute and immediate hazards remain in the nation's tap water. These hazards are associated with a number of specific contaminants in drinking water. Contaminants of special concern to the EPA are lead, radionuclides, microbiological contaminants, and disinfection byproducts.

The primary source of lead in drinking water is corrosion of plumbing materials, such as lead service lines and lead solders, in water distribution systems and in houses and larger buildings. Virtually all public water systems serve households with lead solders of varying ages, and most faucets are made of materials that can contribute some lead to drinking water.

Radionuclides are radioactive isotopes that emit radiation as they decay. The most significant radionuclides in drinking water are radium, uranium, and radon, all of which occur naturally in nature. While radium and uranium enter the body by ingestion, radon is usually inhaled after being released into the air during showers, baths, and other activities, such as washing clothes or dishes. Radionuclides in drinking water occur primarily in those systems that use ground water. Naturally occurring radionuclides seldom are found in surface waters (such as rivers, lakes, and streams).

Water contains many microbes—bacteria, viruses, and protozoa. Although some organisms are harmless, others can cause disease. The Centers for Disease Control reported 112 waterborne disease outbreaks from 1981 to 1983. Microbiological contamination continues to be a national concern because contaminated drinking water systems can rapidly spread disease.

Disinfection byproducts are produced during water treatment by the chemical reactions of disinfectants with naturally occurring or synthetic organic materials present in untreated water. Since these disinfectants are essential to safe drinking water, the EPA is presently looking at ways to minimize the risks from byproducts (EPA, 1988).

Critical Aquatic Habitat Pollutants

Critical aquatic habitats that need special management attention include the nation's wetlands, near coastal waters, oceans, and lakes. In recent years the EPA has been focusing on addressing the special problems of these areas. The following is a discussion of pollutants categorized by the habitats they affect.

Wetlands in urban areas frequently represent the last large tracts of open space and are often a final haven for wildlife. Not surprisingly, as suitable upland development sites become exhausted, urban wetlands are under increasing pressure for residential housing, industry, and commercial facilities.

Increasing evidence exists that our nation's wetlands, in addition to being destroyed by physical threats, also are being degraded by chemical contamination. The problem of wetland contamination received national attention in 1985 due to reports of waterfowl deaths and deformities caused by selenium contamination. Selenium is a trace element that occurs naturally in soil and is needed in small amounts to sustain life. However, for years it was being leached out of the soil and carried in agricultural drainwater used to flood the refuge's wetlands, where it accumulated in dangerously high levels.

Coastal water environments are particularly susceptible to contamination because they act as sinks for the large quantities of pollution discharged from municipal sewage treatment plants, industrial facilities, and hazardous waste disposal sites. In many coastal areas, non-point source runoff from agricultural lands, suburban developments, city streets, and combined sewer and stormwater overflows poses an even more significant problem than point sources. This is due to the difficulty of identifying and then controlling the source of the pollution.

Physical and hydrological modifications from such activities as dredging channels, draining and filling wetlands, constructing dams, and building shorefront houses may further degrade near coastal environments. In addition, growing population pressures will continue to subject these sensitive coastal ecosystems to further stress.

The Great Lakes provide an inevitable resource to the 45 million people living in the surrounding basin. A 1970 study by the International Joint Commission identified nutrients and toxic problems in the lakes. They suffered from eutrophication problems caused by excessive nutrient inputs. Since then the United States and Canada have made joint efforts to reduce nutrient loadings, particularly phosphorus. However, contamination of the water and fish by toxics from pesticide runoff, landfill leachates, and in-place sediments remains a major problem.

Ocean dumping of dredged material, sewage sludge, and industrial wastes is a major source of ocean pollution. Sediments dredged from industrialized urban harbors are often highly contaminated with heavy metals and toxic synthetic organic chemicals like PCBs and petroleum hydrocarbons. Although ocean dumping of dredged material, sludge, and industrial wastes is now less of a threat, persistent disposal of plastics from land and ships at sea have become a serious problem. Debris on beaches from sewer and storm drain overflows, or mismanagement of trash poses public safety and aesthetic concerns (EPA, 1988).

Surface Water Pollutants

Pollutants in waterways come from industries or treatment plants discharging wastewater into streams or from waters running across urban and agricultural areas, carrying the surface pollution with them (non-point sources). The following is a discussion of surface water pollutants categorized by their main sources.

Raw or insufficiently treated wastewater from municipal and industrial treatment plants still threatens water resources in many parts of the country. In addition to harmful nutrients, poorly treated wastewater may contain bacteria and chemicals.

Sludge, the residue left from wastewater treatment plants, is a growing problem. Although some sludges are relatively "clean," or free from toxic substances, other sludges may contain organic, inorganic, or toxic pollutants and pathogens.

An important source of toxic pollution is industrial wastewater discharged directly into waterways or indirectly through municipal wastewater treatment plants. Industrial wastes discharged indirectly are treated to remove toxic pollutants. It is important that those wastes be treated because toxics may end up in sludge, making them harder to dispose of safely.

Non-point sources present continuing problems for achieving national water-quality in many parts of the country. Sediment and nutrients are the two largest contributors to non-point source problems. Non-point sources are also a major source of toxics, among them pesticide runoff from agricultural areas, metals from active or abandoned mines, gasoline, and asbestos from urban areas. In addition, the atmosphere is a source of toxics since many toxics can attach themselves to dust, later to be deposited in surface waters hundreds of miles away through precipitation (EPA, 1988).

LAND POLLUTANTS

Historically, land has been used as the dumping ground for wastes, including those removed from the air and water. Early environmental protection efforts focused on cleaning up air and water pollution. It was not until the 1970s that there was much public concern about pollution of the land. It is now recognized that contamination of the land threatens not only future uses of the land itself, but also the quality of the surrounding air, surface water, and ground water. There are five different forms of land pollutants. These include:

1. Industrial hazardous wastes
2. Municipal wastes
3. Mining wastes
4. Radioactive wastes
5. Underground storage tanks

A short description of each is provided below. More detailed descriptions can be found in separate chapters later in the book.

Industrial Hazardous Wastes

The chemical, petroleum, and transportation industries are major producers of hazardous industrial waste. Ninety-nine percent of the hazardous waste is produced by facilities that generate large quantities (more than 2,200 pounds) of hazardous waste each month.

A much smaller amount of hazardous waste, about one million tons per year, comes from small quantity generators (between 220 and 2,200 pounds of waste each month). These include automotive repair shops, construction firms, laundromats, dry cleaners, printing operations, and equipment repair shops. Over 60 percent of the these wastes are derived from lead batteries. The remainder includes acids, solvents, photographic wastes, and dry cleaning residue (EPA, 1988).

Municipal Wastes

Municipal wastes include household and commercial wastes, demolition materials, and sewage sludge. Solvents and other harmful household and commercial wastes are generally so intermingled with other materials that specific control of each is virtually impossible.

Sewage sludge is the solid, semisolid, or liquid residue produced from treating municipal wastewater. Some sewage sludges contain high levels of disease-carrying microorganisms, toxic metals, or toxic organic chemicals. Because of the large quantities generated, sewage sludge is a major waste management problem in a number of municipalities (EPA, 1988).

Mining Wastes

A large volume of all waste generated in the United States is from mining coal, phosphates, copper, iron, uranium, other minerals, and from ore processing and milling. These wastes consist primarily of overburden, the soil and rock cleared away before mining, and tailings, the material discarded during ore processing. Runoff from these wastes increases the acidity of streams and pollutes them with toxic metals (EPA, 1988).

Radioactive Wastes

Radioactive materials are used in a wide variety of applications, from generating electricity to medical research. The United States has produced large quantities of radioactive wastes that can pose environmental and health problems for many generations (EPA, 1988).

Pollutants from Underground Storage Tanks

Leaking underground storage tanks are another source of land contamination that can contribute to ground water contamination. The majority of these tanks do not store waste, but instead store petroleum products and some hazardous substances. Most of the tanks are bare steel and subject to corrosion. Many are old and near the end of their useful lives. Hundreds of thousands of these tanks are presently thought to be leaking, with more expected to develop leaks in the next few years (EPA, 1988).

HAZARDOUS POLLUTANTS

Before the early 1970s, the nation paid little attention to industrial production and the disposal of the waste it generated, particularly hazardous waste. As a result, billions of dollars must now be spent to clean up disposal sites neglected through years of mismanagement. The EPA often identifies a waste as hazardous if it poses a fire hazard (ignitable); dissolves materials or is acidic (corrosive); is explosive (reactive); or otherwise poses danger to human health or the environment (toxic). Most hazardous waste results from the production of widely used goods such as polyester and other synthetic fibers, kitchen appliances, and plastic milk jugs. A small percentage of hazardous waste (less than one percent) is comprised of the used commercial products themselves, including household cleaning fluids or battery acid.

Definitions of hazardous substances are not as straightforward as they appear. For purposes of regulation, Congress and the EPA have defined terms to describe wastes and other substances that fall under regulation. The definitions below show the complexity of the EPA's regulatory task.

1. Hazardous Substances [Comprehensive Environmental Response, Compensation and Liability Act (CERCLA), or "Superfund"]—Any substance that, when released into the environment, may cause substantial danger to public health, welfare, or the environment. Designation as a hazardous substance grows out of the statutory definitions in several environmental laws: the Comprehensive Environmental Response, Compensation and Liability Act, the Resource Conservation and Recovery Act (RCRA), the Clean Water Act (CWA), the Clean Air Act (CAA), and the Toxic Substances Control Act (TSCA). Currently there are 717 CERCLA hazardous substances.

2. Extremely Hazardous Substance (CERCLA as amended)—Substances that could cause serious, irreversible health effects from a single exposure. For purposes of chemical emergency planning, EPA has designated 366 substances extremely hazardous. If not already so designated, these also will be listed as hazardous substances.

3. Solid Waste (RCRA)—Any garbage, refuse, sludge, or other discarded material. All solid waste is not solid; it can be liquid, semisolid, or contained gaseous material. Solid waste results from industrial, commercial, mining, and agricultural operations from community activities. Solid waste can be either hazardous or nonhazardous. However, it does not include solid or dissolved material in domestic sewage, certain nuclear material, or certain agricultural wastes.

4. Hazardous Waste (RCRA)—Solid waste, or combinations of solid waste, that because of its quantity, concentration, or physical, chemical or infectious characteristics, may pose a hazard to human health or the environment.

5. Nonhazardous Waste (RCRA)—Solid waste, including municipal wastes, household hazardous waste, municipal sludge, and industrial and commercial wastes that are not hazardous (EPA, 1988).

TOXIC POLLUTANTS

Today's high standard of living would not be possible without the thousands of different chemicals produced. Most of these chemicals are not harmful if used properly. Others can be extremely harmful if people are exposed to them even in minute amounts. The following is a discussion of four toxic chemicals under control of the Toxic Substance Control Act of 1976.

Polychlorinated biphenyls (PCBs) provide an example of the problems that toxic substances can present. PCBs were used in many commercial activities, especially in heat transfer fluids in electrical transformers and capacitors. They also were used in hydraulic fluids, lubricants, and dye carriers in carbonless copy paper, and in paints, inks, and dyes. Over time, PCBs accumulated in the environment, either from leaking electrical equipment or from other materials such as inks.

Like PCBs, asbestos was widely used for many purposes, such as fireproofing and pipe and boiler insulation in schools and other buildings. Asbestos was often mixed with a cement-like material and sprayed or plastered on ceilings and other surfaces. Now these materials are deteriorating, releasing the asbestos.

Dioxins refer to a family of chemicals with similar structure, although it is common to refer to the most toxic of these—2,3,7,8-tetrachlorodinitro-p-dioxin or TCDD—as dioxin. Dioxin is an inadvertent contaminant of the chlorinated herbicides 2,4,5-T and silvex, which were used until recently in agriculture, forest management, and lawn care. It is also a contaminant of certain wood preservatives and the defoliant Agent Orange used in Vietnam. Dioxins and the related chemicals known as furans also are formed during the combustion of PCBs.

Several other sources of dioxin contamination have been identified in recent years. These include pulp and paper production, and the burning of municipal wastes containing certain plastics or wood preserved by certain chlorinated chemicals.

In 1978, the use of *chlorofluorocarbons (CFCs)* as a propellent in aerosol cans and other nonessential uses were prohibited by the EPA. The Agency took this action as a result of evidence that CFCs caused a decrease in stratopsheric ozone (EPA, 1988).

SUMMARY

1. All of the criteria pollutants (ozone, carbon monoxide, airborne particulates, sulfur dioxide, lead, nitrogen oxide) except lead and nitrogen oxide are currently a major concern in a number of areas in the country.

2. Indoor air pollutants of special concern include radon, environmental tobacco smoke, asbestos, formaldehyde and other VOCs, and pesticides.

3. The EPA focuses its water pollution control efforts on three themes: maintaining drinking water quality, preventing further degradation and destruction of critical aquatic habitats (wetlands, nearshore coastal waters, oceans, and lakes), and reducing pollution of free-flowing surface waters and protecting their uses.

4. Land pollutants discussed included industrial hazardous wastes, municipal wastes, mining wastes, radioactive wastes, and leaking underground storage tank pollutants.

5. Hazardous pollutants are generally identified as such if they are ignitable, corrosive, reactive, or toxic.

6. Toxic pollutants include PCBs, asbestos, dioxin, and CFCs.

REFERENCES

Holmes, G., Singh, B., and Theodore, L. *Handbook of Environmental Management and Technology.* New York: John Wiley & Sons, 1993.

U.S. EPA, "Environmental Progress and Challenges," *EPA's Update,* August 1988.

8

Effects of Pollutants

CONTRIBUTING AUTHOR

Jeanmarie Spillane

INTRODUCTION

Pollutants are various noxious chemicals and refuse materials that impair the purity of the water, soil, and the atmosphere. The area most affected by pollutants is the atmosphere or air. Air pollution occurs when wastes pollute the air. Artificially or synthetically created wastes are the main sources of air pollution. They can be in the form of gases or particulates, which result from the burning of fuel to power motor vehicles and to heat buildings. More air pollution can be found in densely populated areas. The air over largely populated cities often becomes so filled with pollutants that it not only harms the health of humans, but also plants, animals, and materials of construction.

Water pollution occurs when wastes are dumped into the water. This polluted water can spread typhoid fever and other diseases. In the United States, water supplies are disinfected to kill disease-causing germs. The disinfection, in some instances, does not remove all the chemicals and metals that may cause health problems in the distant future.

Wastes that are dumped into the soil are a form of land pollution, which damages the thin layer of fertile soil that is essential for agriculture. In nature, cycles work to keep soil fertile. Wastes, including dead plants and wastes from animals, form a substance in the soil called humus. Bacteria then decays the humus and breaks it down into nitrates, phosphates, and other nutrients that feed growing plants.

This chapter will review the effects of air pollutants, water pollutants, and land (solid waste) pollutants on:

1. Humans
2. Plants

3. Animals

4. Materials of construction

For reasons hopefully obvious to the reader, the material will key on the effects on humans. It will also primarily focus on air pollutants since this has emerged as the leading environmental issue with the passage of the Clean Air Act Amendments of 1990.

AIR POLLUTION

Humans

Humans are in constant contact with pollutants, whether they are indoors or outdoors. The pollutants, primarily air pollutants, may have negative effects on human health. In some instances humans adapt, and do not realize that they are being affected. For example, people living in smog-covered cities know that smog is bad for their health, but just consider it "normal." There are still some who do not think that there is anything that can be done about it.

Indoors, which includes the home and the workplace, a definite correlation seems to exist between some of the most important indoor activities and the resulting pollutants that are generated. Some examples of these are smoking, the use of personal products, cleaning, cooking, heating, maintenance of hair and facial care, hobbies, and electrical appliances such as washing machines and dryers (Stern, 1977; Parker, 1977). Fumes from these activities can get trapped in the home or workplace, and the buildup of these over time will cause health problems in the short- and long-term future.

When people go outside, they usually say they are going to "get some fresh air." This "fresh air" to them usually means breathing in the air from a different location. Although the common term for the air outside is "fresh air," the air may not necessarily be very "fresh." The outside air can be full of air pollutants that can cause negative effects on the health of humans.

The influence of air pollution on human productivity has not been firmly established. In addition, a number of authorities suspect (and some are convinced) that air pollution is associated with an increasing incidence of lung and respiratory ailments and heart disease (Parker, 1977). Table 8–1 shows some of the health effects of the regulated air pollutants.

"Air toxics" is the term generally used to describe cancer-causing chemicals, radioactive materials, and other toxic chemicals not covered by the National Ambient Air Quality Standards (see Chapter 5) for conventional pollutants. Air toxics result from many activities of modern society, including driving a car, burning fossil fuel, and producing and using industrial chemicals or radioactive materials. The latter is one of the highest health risk problems the EPA is wrestling with (EPA, 1991).

Some major contributors to pollution that affect human health are: sulfur dioxide, carbon monoxide, nitrogen oxides, ozone, carcinogens, fluorides, aeroallergens, radon, smoking, asbestos, and noise. These are treated in separate paragraphs below.

Sulfur dioxide (SO_2) is a source of serious discomfort, and in excessive amounts is a health hazard, especially to people with respiratory ailments. In the United States alone, the estimated amount of SO_2 emitted into the atmosphere is 23 million tons per year. SO_2 causes irritation of the respiratory tract; it damages lung tissue and promotes respiratory diseases; the taste threshold limit

Table 8–1.   Health Effects of the Regulated Air Pollutants

Criteria Pollutants	Health Concerns
Ozone	Respiratory tract problems such as difficult breathing and reduced lung function. Asthma, eye irritation, nasal congestion, reduced resistance to infection, and possibly premature aging of lung tissue.
Particulate Matter	Eye and throat irritation, bronchitis, lung damage, and impaired visibility.
Carbon Monoxide	Ability of blood to carry oxygen impaired, cardiovascular, nervous and pulmonary systems affected.
Sulfur Dioxide	Respiratory tract problems, permanent harm to lung tissue.
Lead	Retardation and brain damage, especially in children.
Nitrogen Dioxide	Respiratory illness and lung damage.
Hazardous Air Pollutants	
Asbestos	A variety of lung diseases, particularly lung cancer.
Beryllium	Primary lung disease, although also affects liver, spleen, kidneys, and lymph glands.
Mercury	Several areas of the brain as well as the kidneys and bowels affected.
Vinyl Chloride	Lung and liver cancer.
Arsenic	Causes cancer.
Radionuclides	Cause cancer.
Benzene	Leukemia.

is 0.3 parts per million (ppm) and SO_2 produces an unpleasant smell at 0.5 ppm concentration. In fact, sulfur dioxides in general have been considered as prime candidates for an air pollution index. Such an index would be a measure reflecting the presence and action of harmful environmental conditions. This would aid in rendering meaningful analyses of the effect of air pollutants on human health, especially since health effects are most probably due to the complementing action of pollutants and meteorological variables. SO_2 is more harmful in a dusty atmosphere. This effect may be explained as follows: The respiratory tract is lined with hair-like cilia, which by means of regular sweeping action force out foreign substances entering the respiratory tract through the mouth. SO_2 and H_2SO_4 (sulfuric acid) molecules paralyze the cilia, rendering it ineffective in rejecting these particulates, causing them to penetrate deeper into the lungs. Alone, these molecules are too small to remain in the lungs; but, some SO_2 molecules are absorbed on larger particles, which penetrate to the lungs and settle there, bringing concentrated amounts of the irritant SO_2 into prolonged contact with the fine lung tissues. SO_2 and the other sulfur dioxide-particulate combinations are serious irritants of the respiratory tract. In high-pollution intervals they can cause death. Their action of severely irritating the respiratory tract may cause heart failure due to the excessive laboring of the heart in its pumping action to circulate oxygen through the body.

   Carbon monoxide (CO) levels have declined in most parts of the United States since 1970, but the standards are still exceeded in many cities throughout the country (Holmes, Singh, & Theodore, 1993). Carbon monoxide pollution is the basic concern in most large cities of the world where traffic is usually congested and heavy. CO cannot be detected by smell or sight, and this adds to its danger. It forms a complex with hemoglobin, called carboxy-hemoglobin (COHb). The formation of this complex reduces the capability of the bloodstream to carry oxygen by interfering with the release of the oxygen carried by remaining hemoglobin. Also, since the affinity of human hemoglobin is 210 times higher for CO than it is for oxygen, a small concentration of CO markedly reduces the capacity of the blood to act as an oxygen carrier. The threshold limit value (TLV), or maximum allowable concentration (MAC), of CO for industrial exposure is 50 ppm; concentrations of CO as low as 10 ppm produce effects on the nervous system and give an equilibrium level of COHb larger than 2 percent. A concentration of 30 ppm produces a level greater than 5 percent COHb, which affects the nervous system and causes impairment of visual acuity, brightness discrimination, and other psychomotor functions. Carbon monoxide concentrations of 50–100 ppm are commonly encountered in the atmosphere of crowded cities, especially at heavy traffic rush hours. Such high concentrations adversely affect driving ability and cause accidents. In addition, an estimate of the average concentration of CO inhaled into the lungs from cigarette smoking is 400 ppm (Shaheen, 1974).

Two major pollutants among *nitrogen oxides* (NO_x) are nitric oxide (NO), and nitrogen dioxide (NO_2). Emissions from stationary sources are estimated to be 16 million tons of NO_x per year. Mobile sources of NO_x pollution are automobiles emitting an estimated average of 10.7 million tons per year. NO is colorless, but it is photochemically converted to nitrogen dioxide, which is one of the components of smog. Nitrogen dioxide also contributes to the formation of aldehydes and ketones through the photochemical reaction with hydrocarbons of the atmosphere. Nitrogen dioxide is an irritant; it damages lung tissues, especially through the formation of nitric acid. Breathing nitrogen dioxide at 25 ppm for eight hours could cause spoilage of lung tissues, while breathing it for one-half hour at 100–150 ppm could produce serious pulmonary edema, or swelling of lung tissues. A few breaths at 200–700 ppm may cause fatal pulmonary edema.

Ozone (O_3) is produced from the activation of sunlight on nitrogen dioxide, pollutants such as volatile organic compounds (VOCs), and atmospheric gases such as oxygen. It is an irritant to the eyes and lungs, penetrating deeper into the lungs than sulfur dioxide. In air it forms complex organic compounds; dominant among these are aldehydes and peroxyacetyl nitrate (PAN), which also causes eye and lung irritation. Rural areas have concentrations of 2–5 parts per hundred million (pphm) of ozone, which is distinguished by an odor of electrical shorting. A few good smells and the individual's sensitivity for this odor disappears. At 5–10 pphm, the odor is unpleasant and pungent. Exposure to ozone for 30 minutes at 10–15 pphm, which is normally encountered in large cities, causes serious irritation of the mucous membranes and reduces their ability to fight infection. At 20–30 pphm it affects vision, and exposure to concentrations of 30 pphm for a few minutes brings a marked respiratory distress with severe fatigue, coughing, and choking. When volunteers were exposed intermittently for two weeks to a 30 pphm ozone atmosphere, they experienced severe headaches, fatigue, wheezing, chest pains, and difficulty in breathing. It reduces the activity of individuals, especially those with previous heart conditions. Even young athletes tire on smoggy days.

Carcinogens, which are often polycyclic hydrocarbons inducing cancer in susceptible individuals, are present in the exhaust emissions of the internal combustion engine, be it diesel or gasoline. Two major carcinogens are benzopyrene, which is a strong cancer-inducing agent, and benzanthracene, which is a weak one. They are essentially nonvolatile organic compounds associated with solids or polymeric substances in the air. These compounds are not very stable, and they are destroyed at varying rates by other air pollutants and by sunlight. However, as a result of industrialization and urbanization, these substances are discharged into the atmosphere in significant quantities, reportedly causing a steady increase in the frequency of human lung cancer in the world (Shaheen, 1974).

Aeroallergens are airborne substances causing allergies. These are predominantly of natural origin, but some are industrial. Allergic reactions in sensitive persons are caused by allergens such as pollens, spores, and rusts. A large percentage of the population is affected by hay fever and asthma each year; ragweed pollen may be the worst offender—it is about 20 microns in diameter, and under normal conditions, nearly all of it will be deposited near the source. Organic allergens come from plants, yeasts, molds, and animal hair, fur, or feathers. Fine industrial materials in the air cause allergies; for example, the powdered material given off in the extraction of oil from castor beans causes bronchial asthma in people living near the factory (Shaheen, 1974).

Radon is a radioactive, colorless, odorless, naturally occurring gas that is found everywhere at very low levels. It seeps through the soil and collects in homes. Radon problems have been identified in every state, and millions of homes throughout the country have elevated radon levels. Radon in high concentrations has been determined to cause lung cancer in humans.

Smoking can be categorized as voluntary pollution. The smokers not only create a health hazard for themselves, but also for the nonsmokers in their company. Cigarette smoke causes lung cancer, and in pregnant women it may cause premature birth and low birthweight in newborns.

Asbestos is a mineral fiber that has been used commonly in a variety of building construction materials for insulation as a fire-retardant. The EPA and other organizations have banned several asbestos products. Manufacturers have also voluntarily limited the use of asbestos. Today asbestos is most commonly found in older homes in pipe and furnace insulation materials, asbestos shingles, millboard, textured paints, and floor tiles. The most dangerous asbestos fibers are too small to see. After the fibers are inhaled, they can remain and accumulate in the lungs. Asbestos can cause lung cancer, cancer of the chest and abdominal linings, and asbestosis (irreversible lung scarring that can be fatal). Symptoms of these diseases do not show up until many years after exposure. Most people with asbestos-related disease were exposed to elevated concentrations on the job, and some developed disease from clothing and equipment brought home from job sites (Holmes et al. 1993). The reader is referred to Chapter 46 for additional details on asbestos.

Noise pollution is not usually placed among the top environmental problems facing the nation; however, it is one of the more frequently encountered sources of pollution in everyday life. Recent scientific evidence shows that relatively continuous exposures to sound exceeding 70 decibels can be harmful to hearing. Noise can also cause stress reactions which include: (1) increases in heart rate, blood pressure, and blood cholesterol levels, and (2) negative effects on the digestive and respiratory systems. With persistent, unrelenting noise exposure, it is possible that these reactions will become chronic stress diseases such as high blood pressure or ulcers (Holmes et al., 1993). Additional details on noise pollution can be found in Chapter 39.

Plants

Pollutants, especially in the air, cover a wide spectrum of particulate and gaseous matter, damaging and effecting the growth of many types of vegetation (Stern, 1977). Whether particulate matter is harmful to vegetation depends upon the type of particulate matter predominating, upon the concentration of particulate matter versus time, the type of vegetation under consideration, climatic conditions, the duration of exposure, and similar factors (Parker, 1977).

Different types of plants are affected differently by pollutants. The three major types of plants are trees, vegetative plants (crops), and flowers. Only a few kinds of trees can live in the polluted air of a big city. Sycamores and Norway maples seem to resist air pollution best. That is why those trees are planted among most city streets. However, air pollution can kill even sycamores and Norway maples. The danger to the trees is greatest at street corners. That is where cars and buses may have to stop and wait for traffic lights to change. While they are waiting, exhaust pours out of their tailpipes, resulting in tree-kills. Pine trees do not resist air pollution as well as sycamores and Norway maples. Air pollutants, even in small amounts, are very harmful to pine trees. For example, the San Bernadino forest was a beautiful forest about sixty miles east of Los Angeles. Most of the trees in the forest were pines. Winds usually blow from west to east. The winds carried polluted air from the streets of L.A. to the San Bernadino forest and harmed the pine trees (Blaustein, Blaustein, & Greenleaf, 1974). Crops and flowers cannot be planted within many miles of industry because they will not grow due to the pollution emitted from the factories. The major contributors to plant pollution are sulfur dioxide, ethylene, acid deposition, smog, ozone, and fluoride.

Metallurgical smelting processes emit substantial quantities of *sulfur dioxide*, and they are in general associated with a good degree of defoliation. Serious damage from sulfur dioxide is usually characterized by loss of chlorophyll and suppression of growth. Leaf and needle tissues are damaged, and die as the time of exposure increases. The attack starts at the edges, moving progressively toward the main body of the leaf or needle. A concentration as low as 2 pphm could suppress growth. Cereal crops, especially barley, are readily damaged at concentrations less than 50 pphm. The presence of soot particles in the air can increase the damage, because sulfur dioxide and sulfuric acid mist are enriched at the surface of particles. It has been determined that pine trees cannot survive the damage when the mean annual concentrations of sulfur dioxide exceed 0.07–0.08 ppm (Shaheen, 1974).

Ethylene in the air causes injury to many flowers, whether they are orchids, lilacs, tulips, or roses. The first symptom of ethylene damage is the drying of the sepals, which are leaf-like formations located at the bottom of the flower bloom. This attack destroys the beauty of the flowers and contributes to extensive economic losses to growers. In addition, accidental escape of ethylene from a polyethylene plant caused 100 percent damage to cotton fields a mile away (Shaheen, 1974).

The process of *acid deposition* begins with emissions of SO_2 and NO_x. These pollutants interact with sunlight and water vapor in the upper atmosphere to form acidic compounds. When it rains (or snows) these compounds fall to the earth. Forests and agriculture may be vulnerable because acid deposition can leach nutrients from the ground, killing nitrogen-fixing microorganisms that nourish plants and release toxic metals.

Smog damage to vegetation is serious, especially in locations such as Los Angeles; the lower leaf surfaces of petunias and spinach become silvery or bronze in color. The most toxic substance of the Los Angeles air has been identified as peroxyacetyl nitrate (PAN), formed by photochemical reactions of hydrocarbons and nitrogen oxides emanating mostly from automobile exhausts (Shaheen, 1974).

Ozone is a major component of the Los Angeles smog; it is phytotoxic at concentrations of 0.2 ppm, even when exposure time is only a few hours. Its effect on spinach is strong and destructive, causing whitening or bleaching of the leaves. Certain tobaccos are damaged by concentrations as small as 5–6 ppm. Ozone hinders plant growth even if bleaching or other distinctive marks are not found.

Fluorides are given off by factories that make aluminum, iron, and fertilizer. Due to these factories, growers have complained about the damage to fruits and leaves of peach, plum, apple, fig, and apricot trees. Fluorides also damage grapes, cherries, and citrus. It has been observed that the average yield of fruit per tree decreases 27 percent for every increase of 50 ppm of fluoride in the leaves (Shaheen, 1974).

Animals

Animals are also affected by pollutants in the air. There are many similarities between the effects on humans and the effects on animals. For example, animals in zoos suffer the same effects of air pollution as humans. They also are beset with lung disease, cancer, and heart disease. Their babies have more birth defects than those of wild animals. Details of each pollutant will not be included in this section, except for the ones that differ from humans: fluorides and insecticides.

Air that is polluted with *fluorides* can be deadly for sheep, cows, and some other animals. However, inhaling the polluted air is not what causes the damage. Some plants that are eaten by the animals store up the fluoride that they have taken from the air, and after a while contain a dangerous amounts of fluoride. Animals become ill and even die after eating these plants (Shaheen, 1974).

The bald eagle is the U.S. national bird, but it is being killed mainly with *insecticides.* The eagles are not killed by breathing the polluted air, but are dying because they cannot reproduce. When an insecticide is sprayed on plants, some of it misses the plants and gets into the air as a pollutant. Certain kinds of insecticides do not change into harmless substances; they are referred to as "persistent" insecticides because they remain harmful for years. Rain washes these insecticides out of the air and into the water. Small animals bioaccumulate the insecticides, and these animals are often eaten by larger animals, who also have absorbed the insecticide, thereby doubling their insecticide intake. Bald eagles eat large animals (fish), and they may store enough insecticide to kill them. Even if they do not die, the insecticide prevents the bird from reproducing. The eggs that the females lay either have very thin shells or no shells at all, causing the inability of baby eagles to hatch (Blaustein et al., 1974).

Materials of Construction

Air pollution has long been a significant source of economic loss in urban areas. Damage to non-living materials may be exhibited in many ways, such as corrosion of metal, rubber cracking, soiling and eroding of building surfaces, deterioration of works of art, and fading of dyed materials and paints.

An example of the deterioration of works of art is Cleopatra's Needle standing in New York City's Central Park. It has deteriorated more in 80 years in the park than in 3,000 years in Egypt. Another example is the Statue of Liberty located on Liberty Island in New York Harbor. When the statue arrived from France in 1884 it was copper, and 100 years later it has turned a greenish color. It was so deteriorated that the internal and external structures had to be renovated. The steady deterioration of the Acropolis in Athens, Greece is yet another example.

WATER POLLUTION

Pollution in waterways impairs or destroys aquatic life, threatens human health, and simply fouls the water such that recreational and aesthetic potential are lost. There are several different types of water pollution and there are several different ways in which water can be polluted. This section will focus on:

1. Drinking water and its sources (ground water and tap water)
2. Critical aquatic habitats (wetlands, near coastal waters, the Great Lakes, and oceans)
3. Surface water (municipal wastes, industrial discharge, and nonpoint sources).

Drinking Water

Half of all Americans and 95 percent of rural Americans use ground water for drinking water. Through testing water in different areas and at different times, pollutants were found in the drinking water. Several public water supplies using ground water exceeded EPA's drinking water standards for inorganic substances (fluorides and nitrates). Major problems were reported from toxic organics in some wells in almost all states east of the Mississippi River. Trichloroethylene, a suspected carcinogen, was the most frequent contaminant found. The EPA's Ground Water Supply Survey showed that 20 percent of all public water supply wells and 29 percent in urban areas had detectable levels of at least one VOC. At least thirteen organic chemicals that are confirmed animal or human carcinogens have been detected in drinking water wells.

The most severe and acute public health effects from contaminated drinking water from the tap, such as cholera and typhoid, have been eliminated in America. However, some less acute and immediate hazards still remain in the nation's tap water. Contaminants of special concern to the EPA are lead, radionuclides, microbiological contaminants, and disinfection byproducts. Each of these is discussed below.

Lead in drinking water is primarily due to the corrosion of plumbing materials. The health effects related to the ingestion of too much lead are very serious and can lead to impaired blood formation, brain damage, increased blood pressure, premature birth, low birth weight and nervous system disorders. Young children are especially at high risk (see Chapter 45 for additional details).

Radionuclides are radioactive isotopes that emit radiation as they decay. The most significant radionuclides in drinking water are radium, uranium, and radon, all of which occur in nature. Ingestion of uranium and radium in drinking water can cause cancer of the bone and kidney. Radon can be ingested and inhaled. The main health risk due to inhalation is lung cancer.

Microbiological contaminants such as bacteria, viruses, and protozoa may be found in water. Although some organisms are harmless, others may cause disease. Microbiological contamination continues to be a national concern because contaminated drinking water systems can rapidly spread disease.

Disinfection byproducts are produced during water treatment by chemical reactions of disinfectants with naturally occurring or synthetic materials. These byproducts may pose health risks and these risks are related to long-term exposure to low levels of contaminants.

Critical Aquatic Habitats

Wetlands are the most productive of all ecosystems, but the United States is slowly losing them. There are many positive effects of wetlands: converting sunlight into plant material or biomass that serve as food for aquatic animals that form the base of the food chain, habitats for fish and wildlife, and spawning grounds; maintains and improves water quality in adjacent water bodies; removes nutrients to prevent eutrophication; filters harmful chemicals; traps suspended sediments; controls floods; prevents shoreline erosion with vegetation; and contributes $20–40 billion annually to the economy.

Coastal waters are home to many ecologically and commercially valuable species of fish, birds, and other wildlife. Coastal waters are susceptible to contamination because they act as sinks for the large quantities of pollution discharged from industry. The effects include toxic contamination, eutrophication, pathogen contamination, habitat loss and alteration, and changes in living resources. Coastal fisheries, wildlife, and bird populations have been declining, with fewer species being represented.

The Great Lakes are all being affected by toxics that are contaminating fish and the water. Lake Ontario and Lake Erie are also being affected by eutrophication.

Oceans are being polluted with sediments dredged from industrialized urban harbors that are often highly contaminated with heavy metals and toxic synthetic organic chemicals. The contaminants can be taken up by marine organisms. In addition, persistent disposal of plastics from land and sea have become serious problems. The most severe effect of the debris floating in the ocean is injury and death of fish, marine animals, and birds. Debris on beaches can affect the public safety, the beauty of the beach, and the economy.

Surface Waters

Municipal wastewater and industrial discharges produce nutrients in sewage that foster excessive growth of algae and other aquatic plants. Plants then die and decay, depleting the dissolved oxygen needed by fish. Wastewater that is poorly treated may contain chemicals harmful to human and aquatic life.

Nonpoint source pollution consists of sediment, nutrients, pesticides, and herbicides. Sediment causes decreased light transmission through water resulting in decreased plant reproduction, interference with feeding and mating patterns, decreased viability of aquatic life, decreased recreational and commercial values, and increased drinking water costs. Nutrients promote the premature aging of lakes and estuaries. Pesticides and herbicides hinder photosynthesis in aquatic plants, affect aquatic reproduction, increase organism susceptibility to environmental stress, accumulate in fish tissues, and present a human health hazard through fish and water consumption.

Humans

Humans are not affected similarly by the presence of water pollution as they may be by the presence of polluted air. Humans are affected by water pollution through consuming contaminated water or animals (fish). Due to contaminated drinking water, lakes, and oceans, humans are inflicted with diseases, impaired blood formation, brain damage, increased blood pressure, premature birth, low birth weight, nervous system disorders, and cancer (bone, kidney, and lung).

Plants

Plants are affected by wastewater, sewage, sediments, pesticides, and herbicides found mainly in surface water. Effects on plants in these areas are:

1. Decreased plant reproduction
2. Hinderance of photosynthesis in aquatic plants
3. Excessive growth of algae and other aquatic plants
4. Ultimate death of plants

Animals

Animals, especially those that live in or near the water, are directly affected by water pollution. Chemical and solid waste disposal in the water can affect animals in many ways, varying from waste/pollutant accumulation to death. Animals such as fish, marine mammals, and birds can be injured or killed due to floating debris in the ocean. Contaminants can be taken up by marine organisms and accumulate there. The accumulations increase as the larger fish consume contaminated smaller fish. This cycle interferes with animals feeding and mating patterns, affects aquatic reproduction, and decreases the viability of aquatic life.

International Effects

In Japan, contamination of seawater with organic mercury became concentrated in fish, and produced a severe human neurologic disorder called Minamata disease. The epidemic occurred in the mid-1950s. Almost ten years passed before it was realized that there was an accompanying epidemic of congenital cerebral palsy due to a transplacental effect, for example, pregnant women who ate contaminated fish gave birth to infants who were severely impaired neurologically (Zoeteman, 1977).

LAND POLLUTION

Land has been used as dumping grounds for wastes. Improper handling, storage, and disposal of chemicals can cause serious problems. Several types of wastes that are placed in the land are:

1. Industrial hazardous wastes
2. Municipal wastes
3. Mining wastes
4. Radioactive wastes
5. Leakage from underground storage tanks.

Humans

Potential health effects in humans range from headaches, nausea, and rashes to acid burns, serious impairment of kidney and liver functions, cancer, and genetic damage. Underground storage tank leaks may contaminate local drinking water systems, or may lead to explosions and fires causing harm and injury to the people in the vicinity (see Chapter 22 for more details).

Plants

Trees are usually not planted around landfills, and if they were they would have difficulty growing due to the contaminated soil in the vicinity of the landfill. Vegetative plants also have difficulty growing around landfills. This is due to the fact that the hazardous wastes from industry are usually dumped in the landfills (see the section on plant effects of air pollution). Flowers also do not normally grow near landfills for similar reasons.

Animals

Animals are essentially affected in the same ways as humans. They may experience the effects of drinking contaminated water, and suffer from acid burns, kidney, liver and genetic damage, and cancer.

FUTURE TRENDS

Pollution prevention has recently become a major environmental concern to everyone, everywhere, and appears to be an issue that will take priority in the future. Since the enactment of the Pollution Prevention Act of 1990, there has been a clear breakthrough in the nation's understanding of environmental problems. The EPA's Pollution Prevention Strategy (see Chapter 30) establishes the EPA's future direction in pollution prevention. The strategy indicates how pollution prevention concepts will be incorporated into the EPA's ongoing environmental protection efforts. The EPA is calling pollution prevention a "national objective" (Holmes et al., 1993). As more people become aware of the dangerous effects of pollutants on themselves, plants, animals, and materials of construction, they will be more conscious of the ways that they may contribute to air, water, and land pollution.

SUMMARY

1. Pollutants are various noxious chemicals and refuse materials that impair the purity of the air, water, and land.

2. Humans and animals are affected in the same way by air pollution. Some sources of pollution affecting them are sulfur dioxide, carbon monoxide, nitrogen oxides, ozone, carcinogens,

fluorides, aeroallergens, radon, cigarette smoke, asbestos, and noise. Those affecting only animals are insecticides. Plants are also affected by air pollutants such as sulfur dioxide, ethylene, acid deposition, smog, ozone, and fluoride.

3. Pollution in waterways impairs or destroys aquatic life, threatens human health, and fouls the water such that recreational and aesthetic potential are lost.

4. Land has been used as dumping grounds for wastes. Improper handling, storage, and disposal of chemicals can cause serious problems.

5. Pollution prevention has recently become a major environmental management issue to everyone and everywhere, and appears to be an issue that will take priority in the future to help reduce the effects of pollutants.

REFERENCES

Blaustein, E., Blaustein, R., Greenleaf, J. *Your Environment and You: Understanding the Pollution Problem.* 1974.

EPA. Environmental Progress and Challenges: EPA's Update, *EPA Journal.* August, 1988.

EPA. "Meeting the Environmental Challenge" EPA's Review of Progress and New Directions in Environmental Protection, Washington D.C., December 1991.

Holmes, G., Singh, B., and Theodore, L. *Handbook of Environmental Management and Technology.* New York: John Wiley and Sons, 1993.

Parker, H. *Air Pollution.* National Research Council, Washington D.C., 1977.

Shaheen, E. *Environmental Pollution: Awareness and Control*, Washington D.C., 1974.

Stern, A. *Air Pollution: The Effects of Air Pollution Vol. II.* New York: Academic Press, 1977.

Zoeteman, B. *Aquatic Pollutants and Biological Effects; With Emphasis on Neoplasia.* New York: New York Academy of Sciences, 1977.

Part II

Air

Part II of this book serves as an introduction to air pollution. Four chapters comprise Part II. In Chapter 9, air pollution control equipment is described for both gaseous and particulate pollutants. Chapter 10 is concerned with atmospheric dispersion, that is, how pollutants are dispersed in the atmosphere. A comprehensive examination of indoor air quality is provided in Chapter 11. Part II concludes with Chapter 12, which addresses the general issue of air toxics.

9

Air Pollution Control Equipment

INTRODUCTION

In solving an air pollution control equipment problem an engineer must first carefully evaluate the system or process in order to select the most appropriate type(s) of collector(s). After making preliminary equipment selection, suitable vendors can be contacted for help in arriving at a final answer. An early and complete definition of the problem can help reduce a poor decision that can lead to wasted pilot trials or costly inadequate installations.

Selecting an air pollution control device for cleaning a process gas stream can be a challenge. Some engineers, after trying to find shortcuts, employ quick estimates for both gas flow and collection efficiency that may be the entire extent of the collector specification. The end result can be an ineffective installation that has to be replaced. Treating a gas stream, especially to control pollution, is usually not a moneymaker, but costs—both capital and operating (see Chapter 40)—can be minimized, not by buying the cheapest collector but by thoroughly engineering the whole system as is normally done in process design areas.

Controlling the emission of pollutants from industrial and domestic sources is important in protecting the quality of air. Air pollutants can exist in the form of particulate matter or gases. Air-cleaning devices have been reducing pollutant emissions from various sources for many years. Originally, air-cleaning equipment was used only if the contaminant was highly toxic or had some recovery value. Now with recent legislation, control technologies have been upgraded and more sources are regulated in order to meet the National Ambient Air Quality Standards (NAAQS). In

This chapter is a condensed, revised, and updated version of material first appearing in the 1981 USEPA Training Manuals titled "Air Pollution Control Equipment of Particulates" and "Control Equipment for Gaseous Pollutants," and the 1993 ETS THEODORE TUTORIAL titled "Air Pollution Control Equipment" by L. Theodore and R. Allen.

addition, state and local air pollution agencies have adopted regulations that are in some cases more stringent that the federal emission standards.

Equipment used to control particulate emissions are gravity settlers (often referred to as settling chambers), mechanical collectors (cyclones), electrostatic precipitators (ESPs), scrubbers (venturi scrubbers), and fabric filters (baghouses). Techniques used to control gaseous emissions are absorption, adsorption, combustion, and condensation. The applicability of a given technique depends on the physical and chemical properties of the pollutant and the exhaust stream. More than one technique may be capable of controlling emissions from a given source. For example, vapors generated from loading gasoline into tank trucks at large bulk terminals are controlled by using any of the above four gaseous control techniques. Most often, however, one control technique is used more frequently that others for a given source-pollutant combination. For example, absorption is commonly used to remove sulfur dioxide (SO_2) from boiler flue gas.

The material presented in this chapter regarding air pollution control equipment contains, at best, an overview of each control device. Equipment diagrams and figures, operation and maintenance procedures, and so on, have not been included in this development. More details, including predictive and design calculational procedures (Theodore & Feldman, 1991; Theodore, Reynolds, & Richman, 1991) are available in the literature.

AIR POLLUTION CONTROL EQUIPMENT FOR PARTICULATES*

As described above, the five major types of particulate air pollution control equipment are:

1. Gravity Settlers
2. Cyclones
3. Electrostatic Precipitators
4. Venturi Scrubbers
5. Baghouses

Each of these devices is briefly described below.

Gravity Settlers

Gravity settlers, or gravity settling chambers, have long been utilized industrially for the removal of solid and liquid waste materials from gaseous streams. Advantages accounting for their use are simple construction, low initial cost and maintenance, low pressure losses, and simple disposal of waste materials. Gravity settlers are usually constructed in the form of a long, horizontal parallel-epipeds with suitable inlet and outlet ports. In its simplest form the settler is an enlargement (large box) in the duct carrying the particle-laden gases: the contaminated gas stream enters at one end, while the cleaned gas exits from the other end. The particles settle toward the collection surface at the bottom of the unit with a velocity at or near their settling velocity. One advantage of this

---

*Information for this section was taken, in part, from Holmes, Singh, and Theodore, 1993.

device is that the external force leading to separation is provided free by nature. Its use in industry is generally limited to the removal of large particles, i.e., those larger than 40 microns (or micrometers).

Cyclones

Centrifugal separators, commonly referred to as cyclones, are widely used in industry for the removal of solid and liquid particles (or particulates) from gas streams. Typical applications are found in mining and metallurgical operations, the cement and plastics industries, pulp and paper mill operations, chemical and pharmaceutical processes, petroleum production (cat-cracking cyclones) and combustion operations (fly ash collection).

Particulates suspended in a moving gas stream possess inertia and momentum and are acted upon by gravity. Should the gas stream be forced to change direction, these properties can be utilized to promote centrifugal forces to act on the particles. In the conventional unit the entire mass of the gas stream with the entrained particles enter the unit tangentially and is forced into a constrained vortex in the cyclindrical portion of the cyclone. Upon entering the unit, a particle develops an angular velocity. Because of its greater inertia, it tends to move across the gas streamlines in a tangential rather than rotary direction; thus, it attains a net outward radial velocity. By virtue of its rotation with the carrier gas around the axis of the tube (main vortex) and its high density with respect to the gas, the entrained particles are forced toward the wall of the unit. Eventually the particle may reach the outer wall, where they are carried by gravity and assisted by the downward movement of the outer vortex and/or secondary eddies toward the dust collector at the bottom of the unit. The flow vortex is reversed in the lower (conical) portion of the unit, leaving most of the entrained particles behind. The cleaned gas then passes up through the center of the unit (inner vortex) and out of the collector.

Multiple-cyclone collectors (multicones) are high efficiency devices that consist of a number of small-diameter cyclones operating in parallel with a common gas inlet and outlet. The flow pattern differs from a conventional cyclone in that instead of bringing the gas in at the side to initiate the swirling action, the gas is brought in at the top of the collecting tube and the swirling action is then imparted by a stationary vane positioned in the path of the incoming gas. The diameters of the collecting tubes usually range from 6 to 24 inches. Properly designed units can be constructed and operated with a collection efficiency as high as 90 percent for particulates in the 5 to 10 micron range. The most serious problems encountered with these systems involve plugging and flow equalization.

Electrostatic Precipitators

Electrostatic precipitators (ESPs) are satisfactory devices for removing small particles from moving gas streams at high collection efficiencies. They have been used almost universally in power plants for removing fly ash from the gases prior to discharge.

Two major types of high-voltage ESP configuration currently used are tubular and plate. Tubular precipitators consist of cylindrical collection tubes with discharge electrodes located along the axis of the cylinder. However, the vast majority of ESPs installed are the plate type. Particles are collected on a flat parallel collection surface spaced 8 to 12 inches apart, with a series of discharge electrodes located along the centerline of the adjacent plates. The gas to be cleaned passes horizontally between the plates (horizontal flow type) or vertically up through the plates (verticle flow type). Collected particles are usually removed by rapping.

Depending on the operating conditions and the required collection efficiency, the gas velocity in an industrial ESP is usually between 2.5 and 8.0 ft/sec. A uniform gas distribution is of prime importance for precipitators, and it should be achieved with a minimum expenditure of pressure drop. This is not always easy, since gas velocities in the duct ahead of the precipitator may be 30 to 100 ft/sec in order to prevent dust buildup. It should be clear that the best operating condition for a precipitator will occur when the velocity distribution is uniform. When significant maldistribution occurs, the higher velocity in one collecting plate area will decrease efficiency more than a lower velocity at another plate area will increase the efficiency of that area.

The maximum voltage at which a given field can be maintained depends on the properties of the gas and the dust being collected. These parameters may vary from one point to another within the precipitator, as well as with time. In order to keep each section working at high efficiency, a high degree of sectionalization is recommended. This means that the many separate power supplies and controls will produce better performance on a precipitator of a given size than if there were only one or two independently controlled sections. This is particularly true if high efficiencies are required.

Venturi Scrubbers

Wet scrubbers have found widespread use in cleaning contaminated gas streams because of their ability to effectively remove both particulate and gaseous pollutants. Specifically, wet scrubbing involves a technique of bringing a contaminated gas stream into intimate contact with a liquid. Wet scrubbers include all the various types of gas absorption equipment (to be discussed later). The term "scrubber" will be restricted to those systems that utilize a liquid, usually water, to achieve or assist in the removal of particulate matter from a gas stream. The use of wet scrubbers to remove gaseous pollutants from contaminated streams is considered in the next section.

Another important design consideration for the venturi scrubber (as well as absorbers) is concerned with suppressing the steam plume. Water-scrubber systems removing pollutants from high-temperature processes (i.e., combustion) can generate a supersaturated water vapor that becomes a visible white plume as it leaves the stack. Although not strictly an air pollution problem, such a plume may be objectionable for aesthetic reasons. Regardless, there are several ways to avoid or eliminate the steam plume. The most obvious way is to specify control equipment that does not use water in contact with the high-temperature gas stream, (i.e., ESP, cyclones or fabric filters). Should this not be possible or practical, a number of suppression methods are available:

1. Mixing with heated and relatively dry air
2. Condensation of moisture by direct contact with water, then mixing with heated ambient air
3. Condensation of moisture by direct contact with water, then reheating the scrubber exhaust gas

Baghouses

The basic filtration process may be conducted in many different types of fabric filters in which the physical arrangement of hardware and the method of removing collected material from the filter media will vary. The essential differences may be related, in general, to:

1. Type of fabric
2. Cleaning mechanism
3. Equipment
4. Mode of operation

Gases to be cleaned can be either pushed or pulled through the baghouse. In the pressure system (push through), the gases may enter through the cleanout hopper in the bottom or through the top of the bags. In the suction type (pull through), the dirty gases are forced through the inside of the bag and exit through the outside.

Baghouse collectors are available for either intermittent or continuous operation. Intermittent operation is employed where the operational schedule of the dust-generating source permits halting the gas cleaning function at periodic intervals (regularly defined by time or by pressure differential) for removal of collected material from the filter media (cleaning). Collectors of this type are primarily utilized for the control of small-volume operations such as grinding and polishing, and for aerosols of a very coarse nature. For most air pollution control installations and major particulate control problems, however, it is desirable to use collectors that allow for continuous operation. This is accomplished by arranging several filter areas in a parallel flow system and cleaning one area at a time according to some preset mode of operation.

Baghouses may also be characterized and identified according to the method used to remove collected material from the bags. Particle removal can be accomplished in a variety of ways, including shaking the bags, blowing a jet of air on the bags, or rapidly expanding the bags by a pulse of compressed air. In general, the various types of bag cleaning methods can be divided into those involving fabric flexing and those involving a reverse flow of clean air. In pressure-jet or pulse-jet cleaning, a momentary burst of compressed air is introduced through a tube or nozzle attached at the top of the bag. A bubble of air flows down the bag, causing the bag walls to collapse behind it.

A wide variety of woven and felted fabrics are used in fabric filters. Clean felted fabrics are more efficient dust collectors than are woven fabrics, but woven materials are capable of giving equal filtration efficiency after a dust layer accumulates on the surface. When a new woven fabric is placed in service, visible penetration of dust within the fabric may occur. This normally takes from a few hours to a few days for industrial applications, depending on the dust loadings and the nature of the particles.

Baghouses are constructed as single units or compartmental units. The single unit is generally used on small processes that are not in continuous operation, such as grinding and paint-spraying processes. Compartmental units consist of more than one baghouse compartment and are used in continuous operating processes with large exhaust volumes such as electric melt steel furnaces and industrial boilers. In both cases, the bags are housed in a shell made of rigid metal material.

AIR POLLUTION CONTROL EQUIPMENT FOR GASEOUS POLLUTANTS*

As described in the Introduction, the four generic types of gaseous control equipment include:

1. Absorption
2. Adsorption
3. Combustion
4. Condensation

Absorption

Absorption is a mass transfer operation in which a gas is dissolved in a liquid. A contaminant (pollutant exhaust stream) contacts a liquid and the contaminant diffuses (is transported) from the gas phase into the liquid phase. The absorption rate is enhanced by (1) high diffusion rates, (2) high solubility of the contaminant, (3) large liquid-gas contact area, and (4) good mixing between liquid and gas phases (turbulence).

     The liquid most often used for absorption is water because it is inexpensive, is readily available, and can dissolve a number of contaminants. Reagents can be added to the absorbing water to increase the removal efficiency of the system. Certain reagents merely increase the solubility of the contaminant in the water. Other reagents chemically react with the contaminat after it is absorbed. In reactive scrubbing the absorption rate is much higher, so in some cases a smaller, economical system can be used. However, the reactions can form precipitates that could cause plugging problems in the absorber or in associated equipment.

     If a gaseous contaminant is very soluble, almost any of the wet scrubbers will adequately remove this contaminant. However, if the contaminant is of low solubility, the packed tower or the plate tower (Theodore & Feldman, 1991; Theodore et al., 1991) is more effective. Both of these devices provide long contact time between phases and have relatively low pressure drops. The packed tower, the most common gas absorption device, consists of an empty shell filled with packing. The liquid flows down over the packing, exposing a large film area to the gas flowing up the packing. Plate towers consist of horizontal plates placed inside the tower. Gas passes up through the orifices in these plates while the liquid flows down across the plate, thereby providing desired contact.

Adsorption

Adsorption is a mass transfer process that involves removing a gaseous contaminant by adhering to the surface of a solid. Adsorption can be classified as physical or chemical. In physical adsorption, a gas molecule adheres to the surface of the solid due to an imbalance of natural forces (electron distribution). In chemisorption, once the gas molecule adheres to the surface, it reacts chemically with it. The major distinction is that physical adsorption is readily reversible whereas chemisorption is not.

     All solids physically adsorb gases to some extent. Certain solids, called adsorbents, have a

*Information in this section is taken, in part, from Holmes et al., 1993.

high attraction for specific gases; they also have a large surface area that provides a high capacity for gas capture. By far the most important adsorbent for air pollution control is activated carbon. Because of its unique surface properties, activated carbon will preferentially adsorb hydrocarbon vapors and odorous organic compounds from an airstream. Most other adsorbents (molecular sieves, silica gel, and activated aluminas) will preferentially adsorb water vapor, which may render them useless to remove other contaminants.

For activated carbon, the amount of hydrocarbon vapors that can be adsorbed depends on the physical and chemical characteristics of the vapors, their concentration in the gas stream, system temperature, system pressure, humidity of the gas stream, and the molecular weight of the vapor. Physical adsorption is a reversible process; the adsorbed vapors can be released (desorbed) by increasing the temperature, decreasing the pressure or using a combination of both. Vapors are normally desorbed by heating the adsorber with steam.

Adsorption can be a very useful removal technique, since it is capable of removing very small quantities (a few parts per million) of vapor from an airstream. The vapors are not destroyed; instead, they are stored on the adsorbent surface until they can be removed by desorption. The desorbed vapor stream is normally highly concentrated. It can be condensed and recycled, or burned as an ultimate disposal technique.

The most common adsorption system is the fixed bed adsorber. These systems consist of two or more adsorber beds operating on a timed adsorbing/desorbing cycle. One or more beds are adsorbing vapors, while the other bed(s) is being regenerated. If particulate matter or liquid droplets are present in the vapor-laden airstream, this stream is sent to pretreatment to remove them. If the temperature of the inlet vapor stream is high (much above 120°F), cooling may also be required. Since all adsorption processes are exothermic, cooling coils in the carbon bed itself may also be needed to prevent excessive heat buildup. Carbon bed depth is usually limited to a maximum of 4 ft, and the vapor velocity through the adsorber is held below 100 ft/min to prevent an excessive pressure drop.

Combustion

Combustion is defined as a rapid, high-temperature gas-phase oxidation. Simply, the contaminant (a carbon-hydrogen substance) is burned with air and converted to carbon dioxide and water vapor. The operation of any combustion source is governed by the three T's of combustion: temperature, turbulence, and time. For complete combustion to occur, each contaminant molecule must come in contact (turbulence) with oxygen at a sufficient temperature, while being maintained at this temperature for an adequate time. These three variables are dependent on each other. For example, if a higher temperature is used, less mixing of the contaminant and combustion air or shorter residence time may be required. If adequate turbulence cannot be provided, a higher temperature or longer residence time may be employed for complete combustion.

Combustion devices can be categorized as flares, thermal incinerators, or catalytic incinerators. Flares are direct combustion devices used to dispose of small quantities or emergency releases of combustible gases. Flares are normally elevated (from 100 to 400 ft) to protect the surroundings from the heat and flames. Flares are often designed for steam injection at the flare tip. The steam provides sufficient turbulence to ensure complete combustion; this prevents smoking. Flares are also very noisy, which can cause problems for adjacent neighborhoods.

Thermal incinerators are also called afterburners, direct flame incinerators, or thermal oxidizers. These are devices in which the contaminant airstream passes around or through a burner and into a refractory-line residence chamber where oxidation occurs. To ensure complete combustion of the contaminant, thermal incinerators are designed to operate at a temperature of 700 to 800°C (1300 to 1500°F) and a residence time of 0.3 to 0.5 sec. Ideally, as much fuel value as possible is supplied by the waste contaminant stream; this reduces the amount of auxiliary fuel needed to maintain the proper temperature.

In catalytic incineration the contaminant-laden stream is heated and passed through a catalyst bed that promotes the oxidation reaction at a lower temperature. Catalytic incinerators normally operate at 370 to 480°C (700 to 900°F). This reduced temperature represents a continuous fuel savings. However, this may be offset by the cost of the catalyst. The catalyst, which is usually platinum, is coated on a cheaper metal or ceramic support base. The support can be arranged to expose a high surface area, which provides sufficient active sites on which the reaction(s) occur. Catalysts are subject to both physical and chemical deterioration. Halogens and sulfur-containing compounds act as catalyst suppressants and decrease the catalyst usefulness. Certain heavy metals such as mercury, arsenic, phosphorous, lead, and zinc are particularly poisonous.

Condensation

Condensation is a process in which the volatile gases are removed from the contaminant stream and changed into a liquid. Condensation is usually achieved by reducing the temperature of a vapor mixture until the partial pressure of the condensable component equals its vapor pressure. Condensation requires low temperatures to liquify most pure contaminant vapors. Condensation is affected by the composition of the contaminant gas stream. The presence of additional gases that do not condense at the same conditions—such as air—hinders condensation.

Condensers are normally used in combination with primary control devices. Condensers can be located upstream of (before) an incinerator, adsorber, or absorber. These condensers reduce the volume of vapors that the more expensive equipment must handle. Therefore, the size and the cost of the primary control device can be reduced. Similarly, condensers can be used to remove water vapors from a process stream with a high moisture content upstream of a control system. A prime example is the use of condensers in rendering plants to remove moisture from the cooker exhaust gas. When used alone, refrigeration is required to achieve the low temperatures required for condensation. Refrigeration units are used to successfully control gasoline vapors at large gasoline dispensing terminals.

Condensers are classified as being either contact condensers or surface condensers. Contact condensers cool the vapor by spraying liquid directly on the vapor stream. These devices resemble a simple spray scrubber. Surface condensers are normally shell-and-tube heat exchangers. Coolant flows through the tubes, while vapor is passed over and condenses on the outside of the tubes. In general, contact condensers are more flexible, simpler, and less expensive than surface condensers. However, surface condensers require much less water and produce nearly twenty times less wastewater that must be treated than do contact condensers. Surface condensers also have an advantage in that they can directly recover valuable contaminant vapors.

HYBRID SYSTEMS

Hybrid systems are defined as those types of control devices that involve combinations of control mechanisms—for example, fabric filtration combined with electrostatic precipitation. Unfortunately, the term hybrid system has come to mean different things to different people. The two most prevalent definitions employed today for hybrid systems are:

1. Two or more different air pollution control equipment connected in series, e.g., a baghouse followed by an absorber.
2. An air pollution control system that utilizes two or more collection mechanisms simultaneously to enhance pollution capture, for example, an ionizing wet scrubber (IWS), that will be discussed shortly.

The two major hybrid systems found in practice today include ionizing wet scrubbers and dry scrubbers. These are briefly described below.

Ionizing Wet Scrubbers

The ionizing wet scrubber (IWS) is a relatively new development in the technology of the removal of particulate matter from a gas stream. These devices have been incorporated in commercial incineration facilities (EPA, 1982; EPA, unpublished). In the IWS, high-voltage ionization in the charge section places a static electric charge on the particles in the gas stream, which then passes through a crossflow packed-bed scrubber. The packing is normally polypropylene in the form of circular-wound spirals and gearlike wheel configurations, providing a large surface area. Particles with sizes of 3 microns or larger are trapped by inertial impaction within the bed. Smaller charged particles pass close to the surface of either the packing material or a scrubbing water droplet. An opposite charge on that surface is induced by the charged particle, which is then attracted to an ion attached to the surface. All collected particles are eventually washed out of the scrubber. The scrubbing water also can function to absorb gaseous pollutants.

According to Celicote (the IWS vendor), the collection effieciency of the two-stage IWS is greater than that of a baghouse or a conventional ESP for particles in the 0.2 to 0.6 micron range. For 0.8 microns and above, the ESP is as effective as the IWS (Holmes et al., 1993). Scrubbing water can include caustic soda or soda ash when needed for efficient adsorbtion of acid gases. Corrosion resistance of the IWS is achieved by fabricating its shell and most internal parts with fiberglass-reinforced plastic (FRP) and thermoplastic materials. Pressure drop through a single-stage IWS is approximately 5 in H_2O (primarily through the wet scrubber section). All internal areas of the ionizer section are periodically deluge-flushed with recycled liquid from the scrubber system.

Dry Scrubbers

The success of fabric filters in removing fine particles from flue gas streams has encouraged the use of combined dry scrubbing/fabric filter systems for the dual purpose of removing both particulates and acid gases simultaneously. Dry scrubbers offer potential advantages over their wet counterparts, especially in the areas of energy savings and capital costs. Futhermore, the dry-scrubbing process design is relatively simple, and the product is a dry waste rather than a wet sludge.

There are two major types of so-called dry scrubber systems: spray drying and dry injection. The first process is often referred to as a wet-dry system. When compared to the conventional wet scrubber, it uses significantly less liquid. The second process has been referred to as a dry-dry system because no liquid scrubbing is involved. The spray-drying system is predominately used in utility and industrial applications.

The method of operation of the spray dryer is relatively simple, requiring only two major items: a spray dryer similar to those used in the chemical food-processing and mineral-preparation industries, and a baghouse or ESP to collect the fly ash and entrained solids. In the spray dryer, the sorbent solution, or slurry, is atomized into the incoming flue gas stream to increase the liquid-gas interface and to promote the mass transfer of the SO_2 from the gas to the slurry droplets where it is absorbed. Simultaneously, the thermal energy of the gas evaporates the water in the droplets to produce a dry powdered mixture of sulfite-sulfate and some unreacted alkali. Because the flue gas is not saturated and contains no liquid carryover, potentially troublesome mist eliminators are not required. After leaving the spray dryer, the solids-bearings gas passes through a fabric filter (or ESP), where the dry product is collected and where a percentage of unreacted alkali reacts with the SO_2 for further removal. The cleaned gas is then discharged through the fabric-filter plenum to an induced draft (ID) fan and to the stack.

Among the inherent advantages that the spray dryer enjoys over the wet scrubbers are:

1. Lower capital cost
2. Lower draft losses
3. Reduced auxiliary power
4. Reduced water consumption
5. Continuous, two-stage operation, from liquid feed to dry product

The sorbent of choice for most spray-dryer systems is a lime slurry.

Dry-injection processes generally involve pneumatic introduction of a dry, powdery alkaline material, usually a sodium-base sorbent, into the flue gas stream with subsequent fabric filter collection. The injection point in such processes can vary from the boiler-furnace area all the way to the flue gas entrance to the baghouse, depending on operating conditions and design criteria.

FACTORS IN CONTROL EQUIPMENT SELECTION

There are a number of factors to be considered prior to selecting a particular piece of air pollution control hardware (ETS, 1989). In general, they can be grouped into three categories: environmental, engineering, and economic. These are detailed below.

Environmental

1. Equipment location
2. Available space
3. Ambient conditions

4. Availability of adequate utilities (i.e., power, water, etc.) and ancillary system facilities (i.e., waste treatment and disposal, etc.)

5. Maximum allowable emissions (air pollution regulations)

6. Aesthetic considerations (i.e., visible steam or water vapor plume, impact on scenic vistas, etc.)

7. Contribution of air pollution control system to wastewater and solid waste

8. Contribution of air pollution control system to plant noise levels

Engineering

1. Contaminant characteristics (i.e., physical and chemical properties, concentration, particulate shape and size distribution, etc.; in the case of particulates, chemical reactivity, corrosivity, abrasiveness, toxicity, etc.)

2. Gas stream characteristics (i.e., volume flow rate, temperature, pressure, humidity, composition, viscosity, density, reactivity, combustibility, corrosivity, toxicity, etc.)

3. Design and performance characteristics of the particular control system (i.e., size and weight, fractional efficiency curves, mass transfer and/or contaminant destruction capability, pressure drop, reliability and dependability, turndown capability, power requirements, utility requirements, temperature limitations, maintenance requirements, flexibility toward complying with more stringent air pollution regulations, etc.)

Economic

1. Capital cost (equipment, installation, engineering, etc.)

2. Operating cost (utilties, maintenance, etc.)

3. Expected equipment lifetime and salvage value

Proper selection of a particular system for a specific application can be extremely difficult and complicated. In view of the multitude of complex and often ambiguous pollution regulations, it is in the best interest of the prospective user to work closely with regulatory officials as early in the process as possible. Finally, previous experience on a similar application cannot be overemphasized.

COMPARING CONTROL EQUIPMENT ALTERNATIVES

The final choice in equipment selection is usually dictated by that equipment capable of achieving compliance with the regulatory codes at the lowest uniform annual cost (amortized capital investment plus operation and maintenance costs). The reader is referred to Chapter 47 for details on the general subjects of economics. In order to compare specific control equipment alternatives, knowledge of the particular application and site is essential. A preliminary screening, however, may be performed by reviewing the advantages and disadvantages of each type of air pollution control equipment. For example, if water or a waste stream treatment is not availiable at the site, this may preclude use of a wet scrubber system and instead focus on particulate removal by dry systems, such as cyclones or baghouses and/or ESP. If auxiliary fuel is unavailable on a continuous basis, it may not be possible to combust organic pollutant vapors in an incineration system. If the particle-size distribution in the gas stream is relatively fine, cyclone collectors would probably not be considered. If the pollutant vapors can be reused in the process, control efforts may be directed to adsorption systems. There are many more situations where the knowledge of the capabilities of the various control options, combined with common sense will simplify the selection procedure. General advantages and disadvantages of the most popular types of air pollution control equipment for gases and particulates are too detailed to present here but are available in literature (ETS, 1989; Theodore & Buonicore, 1992).

FUTURE TRENDS

The basic design of air pollution control equipment has remained relatively unchanged since first used in the early part of the twentieth century. Some modest equipment changes and new types of devices have appeared in the last twenty years, but all have essentially employed the same capture mechanisms used in the past. One area that has recently received some attention is hybrid systems (see earlier section)—equipment that can in some cases operate at higher efficiency more economically than conventional devices. Tighter regulations and a greater concern for environmental control by society has placed increased emphasis on the development and application of these systems. The future will unquestionably see more activity in this area.

Recent advances in this field have been primarily involved in the treatment of metals. A dry scrubber followed by a wet scrubber has been employed in the United States to improve the collection of fine particulate metals in hazardous-waste incinerators; the dry scrubber captures metals that condense at the operating temperature of the unit and the wet scrubber captures residue metals (particularly mercury) and dioxin/furan compounds. Another recent application in Europe involves the injection of powdered activated carbon into a flue gas stream from an hazardous waste incinerator at a location between the spray dryer (the dry scrubber) and the baghouse (or electrostatic precipitator). The carbon mixing with the lime particulates from the dry scrubbing system and the gas stream itself adsorb the mercury vapors and residual dioxin/furan compounds and are separated from the gas stream by a particulate control device. More widespread use of these types of systems is anticipated in the future.

SUMMARY

1. Controlling the emission of pollutants from industrial and domestic sources is important in protecting the quality of air. Air pollutants can exist in the form of particulate matter or as gases.

2. Equipment used to control particulate emissions are gravity settlers (often referred to as settling chambers), mechanical collectors (cyclones), electrostatic precipitators (ESPs), scrubbers (venturi scrubbers), and fabric filters (baghouses).

3. Techniques used to control gaseous emissions are absorption, adsorption, combustion, and condensation.

4. Hybrid systems are defined as those types of control devices that involve combinations of control mechanisms—for example, fabric filtration combined with electrostatic precipitation. Two of the major hybrid systems found in practice today include ionizing wet scrubbers and dry scrubbers.

5. There are a number of factors to be considered prior to selecting a particular piece of air pollution control hardware. In general, they can be grouped into three categories: environmental, engineering, and economic.

6. The final choice in the equipment selection is usually dictated by that equipment capable of achieving compliance with regulatory codes at the lowest uniform annual cost (amortized capital investment plus operation and maintenance costs).

7. One area that has recently received some attention is hybrid systems, equipment that can in some cases operate at higher efficiency more economically than conventional devices.

REFERENCES

EPA. *Engineering Handbook for Hazardous Waste Incineration,* Dayton, OH: Monsanto Research Corporation, EPA Contract No. 68–03–3025, September 1982.

EPA. *Revised U.S. EPA Engineering Handbook for Hazardous Waste Incineration,* unpublished.

ETS. Assorted technical literature, Roanoke, VA: Author unknown, 1989.

Holmes, G., Singh B., and Theodore, L. *Handbook of Environmental Management and Technology.* New York: Wiley-Interscience, 1993.

Theodore, L., and Buonicore, A. J. *Industrial Air Pollution Control Equipment for Particulates.* Roanoke, VA: ETS International, 1992.

Theodore, L., and Feldman, P. *Air Pollution Control Equipment for Particulates.* A Theodore Tutorial, Research-Cottrell, Bound Brook, NJ, 1991.

Theodore, L., Reynolds, J., and Richman, R. *Air Pollution Control Equipment for Gaseous Pollutants.* A Theodore Tutorial, Research-Cottrell, Bound Brook, NJ, 1991.

10

Atmospheric Dispersion Modeling

INTRODUCTION

Stacks discharging to the atmosphere have long been one of the methods available to industry for disposing waste gases. The concentration to which humans, plants, animals, and structures are exposed at ground level can be reduced significantly by emitting the waste gases from a process at great heights. This permits the gaseous pollutants to be dispersed over a much larger area and will be referred to as control by dilution. Although tall stacks may be effective in lowering the ground-level concentration of pollutants, they still do not in themselves reduce the amount of pollutants released into the atmosphere. However, in certain situations, tall stacks can be the most practical and economical way of dealing with an air pollution problem.

Atmospheric contamination arises primarily from the exhausts generated by industrial plants, power plants, refuse disposal plants, domestic activities, commercial heating, and transportation. These pollutants—which are in the form of particulates, smog, odors, and others—arise mostly from combustion processes and also contain varying amounts of undesirable gases such as oxides of sulfur, oxides of nitrogen, hydrocarbons, and carbon monoxide. The expanding needs of society for more energy and advanced transportation technology, coupled with the rapid growth of urban areas, has led to ever-increasing amounts and concentrations of pollutants in the atmosphere.

Just as a river or stream is able to absorb a certain amount of pollution without the production of undesirable conditions, the atmosphere can also absorb a certain amount of contamination

This chapter is a condensed, revised, and updated version of the chapter Design of Stacks appearing in the 1975 CRC Press text titled *Industrial Control Equipment for Gaseous Pollutants, Vol. II,* by L. Theodore and A. J. Buoniocore, and the chapter Atmospheric Dispersion from the 1994 Lewis Publishers text titled, *Handbook of Air Pollution Control Technology,* by J. Mycock, J. McKenna, and L. Theodore (chapter contributing authors: R. Lucas and A. Tseng).

without "bad" effects. The self-purification of a stream is primarily the result of biological action and dilution. Dilution of air contaminants in the atmosphere is also of prime importance in the prevention of undesirable levels of pollution. In addition to dilution, several self-purification mechanisms are at work in the atmosphere, such as sedimentation of particulate matter, washing action of precipitation, photochemical reactions, and absorption by vegetation and soil.

This chapter focuses on some of the practical considerations of the dispersion of pollutants in the atmosphere. Both continuous and instantaneous discharges are of concern to individuals involved with environmental management. However, the bulk of the material here has been presented for continuous emissions from point sources—for example, a stack. This has traditionally been an area of much concern in the air pollution field because stacks have long been one of the more common industrial methods of disposing waste gases.

NATURE OF DISPERSION

The release of pollutants into the atmosphere is a traditional technique for disposing of them. Although gaseous emissions may be controlled by various sorption processes (or by combustion) and particulates (either solid or aerosol) by mechanical collection, filtration, electrostatic precipitators, or wet scrubbers, the effluent from the control device must still be dispersed into the atmosphere. Fortunately, one of the important properties of the atmosphere is its ability to disperse such streams of gaseous pollutants. Of course, the atmosphere's ability to disperse such streams is not infinite and varies from quite good to quite poor, depending on the local meteorological and geographical conditions. Therefore, the ability to model atmospheric dispersion and to predict pollutant concentrations from a source are important parts of air pollution engineering.

A continuous stream of pollutants released into a steady wind in an open atmosphere will first rise (usually), then bend over and travel with the mean wind, which will dilute the pollutants and carry them away from the source. This plume of pollutants will also spread out or disperse both in the horizontal and vertical directions from its centerline (Cooper & Alley, 1986). In doing so, the concentration of the gaseous pollutant is now contained within a larger volume. This natural process of high concentration spreading out to lower concentration is the process of dispersion. Atmospheric dispersion is primarily accomplished by the wind movement of pollutants, but the character of the source of pollution requires that this action of the wind be taken into account in different ways.

The dilution of air contaminants is also a direct result of atmospheric turbulence and molecular diffusion. However, the rate of turbulent mixing is so many thousand times greater than the rate of molecular diffusion that the latter effect can be neglected in the atmospheric diffusion analysis. Atmospheric turbulence and, hence, atmospheric diffusion vary widely with the weather conditions and topography. Taking all these factors into account, a four-step procedure is recommended for performing dispersion health effect studies:

1. Estimate the rate, duration and location of the release into the environment
2. Select the best available model to perform the calculations
3. Perform the calculations and generate downwind concentrations resulting from the source emission(s)

4. Determine what effect, if any, the resulting discharge has on the environment, including humans, animals, vegetation, and materials of construction.

METEOROLOGICAL CONCERNS

The atmosphere has been labeled the dumping ground for air pollution. Industrial society can be thankful that the atmosphere cleanses itself (up to a point) by natural phenomena. Atmospheric dilution occurs when the wind moves because of wind circulation or atmospheric turbulence caused by local sun intensity. As described earlier, pollution is removed from the atmosphere by precipitation and by other reactions (both physical and chemical) as well as by gravitational fallout.

The atmosphere is the medium in which air pollution is carried away from its source and diffuses. Meteorological factors have a considerable influence over the frequency, length of time, and concentrations of effluents to which the general public may be exposed. The variables that affect the severity of an air pollution problem at a given time and location are wind speed and direction, insolation (amount of sunlight), lapse rate (temperature variation with height), mixing depth, and precipitation. Unceasing change is the predominant characteristic of the atmosphere; for example, temperatures and winds vary widely with latitude, season, and surrounding topography (Hesketh, 1972; Gilpin, 1963).

Atmospheric dispersion depends primarily on horizontal and vertical transport. Horizontal transport depends on the turbulent structure of the wind field. As the wind velocity increases, the degree of dispersion increases with a corresponding decrease in the ground level concentration of the contaminant at the receptor site. This is a result of the emissions being mixed into a larger volume of air. The dilute effluents may, depending on the wind direction, be carried out into essentially unoccupied terrain away from any receptors. Under different atmospheric conditions, the wind may funnel the diluted effluent down a river valley or between mountain ranges. If an inversion (temperature increases with height) is present aloft that would prevent vertical transport, the pollutant concentration may build up continually.

One can define atmospheric turbulence as those vertical and horizontal convection currents or eddies that mix process effluents with the surrounding air. Several generalizations can be made regarding the effect of atmospheric turbulence on the effluent dispersion. Turbulence increases with increasing wind speed and causes a corresponding increase in horizontal dispersion. Mechanical turbulence is caused by changes in wind speed and wind shear at different altitudes. Either of these conditions can lead to significant changes in concentration of the effluent at different elevations.

Topography can also have a considerable influence on the horizontal transport and thus pollutant dispersion. The degree of horizontal mixing can be influenced by sea and land breezes. It can also be influenced by manmade and natural terrain features such as mountains, valleys, or even a small ridge or a row of hills. Low spots in the terrain or natural bowls can act as sites where pollutants tend to settle and accumulate because of the lack of horizontal transport in the land depressions. Other topographical features that can affect horizontal transport are city canyons and isolated buildings. City canyons occur when the buildings on both sides of a street are fairly close together and are relatively tall. Such situations can cause funneling of emissions from one location to another. Isolated buildings or the presence of a highrise building in a relatively low area can cause redirection of dispersion patterns and route emissions into an area in which many receptors live.

Dispersion of air contaminants is strongly dependent on the local meteorology of the atmosphere into which the pollutants are emitted. The mathematical formulation for the design of pollutant dispersal is associated with the open-ground terrain free of obstructions. Either natural or manmade obstructions alter the atmospheric circulation and with it the dispersion of pollutants. Particularly well cited are the effects of mountain valley terrain, hills, lakes, shorelines, and buildings.

PLUME RISE

A plume of hot gases emitted vertically has both a momentum and a buoyancy. As the plume moves away from the stack, it quickly loses its vertical momentum (owing to drag by and entrainment of the surrounding air). As the vertical momentum declines, the plume bends over in the direction of the mean wind. However, quite often the effect of buoyancy is still significant, and the plume continues to rise for a long time after bending over. The buoyancy term is due to the less-than-atmospheric density of the stack gases and may be temperature or composition induced. In either case, as the plume spreads out in the air (all the time mixing with the surrounding air), it becomes diluted by the air.

Modeling the rise of the plume of gases emitted from a stack into a horizontal wind is a complex mathematical problem. Plume rise depends not only on such stack gas parameters as temperature, molecular weight, and exit velocity, but also on such atmospheric parameters as wind speed, ambient temperature, and stability conditions (Cooper & Alley, 1986).

The behavior of plumes emitted from any stack depends on localized air stability. Effluents from tall stacks are often injected at an effective height of several hundred feet to several thousand feet above the ground because of the added effects of buoyancy and velocity on the plume rise. Other factors affecting the plume behavior are the diurnal variations in the atmospheric stability and the long term variations that occur with changing seasons (Bethea, 1978).

EFFECTIVE STACK HEIGHT

Reliance on atmospheric dispersion as a means of reducing ground-level concentrations is not foolproof. Inversions can occur with a rapid increase in ground-level pollutant concentrations. One solution to such situations is the tall stack concept. The goal is quite simple: Inject the effluent above any normally expected inversion layer. This approach is used for exceptionally difficult or expensive treatment situations because tall stacks are quite expensive. To be effective, they must reach above the inversion layer so as to avoid local plume fallout. The stack itself does not have to penetrate the inversion layer if the emissions have adequate buoyancy and velocity. In such cases, the effective stack height will be considerably greater than the actual stack height (Gilpin, 1963). The effective stack height (equivalent to the effective height of emission) is usually considered the sum of the actual stack height, the plume rise due to velocity (momentum) of the issuing gases, and the buoyancy rise, which is a function of the temperature of the gases being emitted and the atmospheric conditions.

The effective stack height depends on a number of factors. The emission factors include the gas flow rate, the temperature of the effluent at the top of the stack and the diameter of the stack opening. The meteorological factors influencing plume rise are wind speed, air temperature, shear of the wind speed with height, and the atmospheric stability. No theory on plume rise presently takes into account all these variables, and it appears that the number of equations for calculating plume rise varies inversely with one's understanding of the process involved. Even if such a theory was available, measurements of all of the parameters would seldom be available. Most of the equations that have been formulated for computing the effective height of an emission stack are semi-empirical in nature. When considering any of these plume rise equations, it is important to evaluate each in terms of assumptions made and the circumstances existing at the time the particular correlation was formulated. Depending on the circumstances, some equations may definitely be more applicable than others.

The effective height of an emission rarely corresponds to the physical height of the source or the stack. If the plume is caught in the turbulent wake of the stack or of buildings in the vicinity of the source or stack, the effluent will be mixed rapidly downward toward the ground. If the plume is emitted free of these turbulent zones, a number of emission factors and meteorological factors will influence the rise of the plume. The influence of mechanical turbulence around a building or stack can significantly alter the effective stack height. This is especially true with high winds when the beneficial effect of the high stack gas velocity is at a minimum and the plume is emitted nearly horizontally.

Details regarding a host of plume rise models and calculation procedures are available in literature (Theodore and Allen, 1994; Theodore, Reynolds, and Taylor, 1989).

ATMOSPHERIC DISPERSION MODELS (TURNER, 1970)

The initial use of dispersion modeling occurred in military applications during World War I. Both sides of the conflict made extensive use of poison gases as a weapon of war. The British organized the Chemical Defense Research Establishment at Porton Downs during the war. Research at this institute dominated the field of dispersion modeling for more than thirty years through the end of World War II.

With the advent of the potential use of nuclear energy to generate electrical power, the United States Atomic Energy Commission invested heavily in understanding the nature of atmospheric transport and diffusion processes. Since about 1950 the United States has dominated researching the field. The U.S. Army and Air Force have also studied atmospheric processes to understand the potential effects of chemical and biological weapons.

The Pasquill-Gifford model has been the basis of many models developed and accepted today (Pasquill, 1961; Gifford, 1961; Cota, 1984). This model has served as an atmospheric dispersion formula from which the path downwind of emissions can be estimated after obtaining the effective stack height. There are many other dispersion equations (models) presently available, most of them semi-empirical in nature. Calculation details regarding the use of this equation are available in the literature (Theodore et al., 1994; Theodore et al., 1989).

The problem of having several models is that various different predictions can be obtained. In order to establish some reference, a standard was sought by the government. The *Guideline on Air Quality Models* (U.S. EPA, 1978; 1986) is used by the EPA, by the states, and by private industry in reviewing and preparing prevention of significant deterioration (PSD) permits and in state implementation plans (SIP) revisions. The guideline serves as a means by which consistency is maintained in air quality analyses. On September 9, 1986 (51 FR 32180), EPA proposed to include four different changes to this guideline: (1) addition of specific version of the Rough Terrain Diffusion Model (RTDM) as a screening model, (2) modification of the downwash algorithm in the Industrial Source Complex (ISC) model, (3) addition of the Offshore and Coastal Dispersion (OCD) model to EPA's list of preferred models, and (4) addition of the AVACTA II model as an alternative model in the guideline. In industry today, the ISC models are the preferred models for permitting and therefore are used in many applications involving normal or "after the fact" releases, depending on which regulatory agency must be answered to.

The ISC model is available as part of UNAMAP (Version 6). The computer code is available on magnetic tape from the National Technical Information Service (NTIS) or via modem through their Bulletin Board Services (BBS). It can account for the following: settling and dry deposition of particulates; downwash; area, line and volume sources; plume rise as a function of downwind distance; separation of point sources; and limited terrain adjustment.

In order to prepare for and prevent the worst, screen models are applied in order to simulate the worse-case scenario. One difference between the screening models and the refined models mentioned earlier is that certain variables are set that are estimated to be values to give the worst conditions. In order to use these screen models, the parameters of the model must be fully grasped.

In short, these models are necessary to somewhat predict the behavior of the atmospheric dispersions. These predictions may not necessarily be correct; in fact, they are rarely completely accurate. In order to choose the most effective model for the behavior of an emission, the source and the models have to be well understood.

STACK DESIGN

As experience in designing stack has accumulated over the years, several guidelines have evolved:

1. Stack heights should be at least 2.5 times the height of any surrounding buildings or obstacles so that significant turbulence is not introduced by these factors.
2. The stack gas exit velocity should be greater than 60 ft/sec so that stack gases will escape the turbulent wake of the stack. In many cases, it is good practice to have the gas exit velocity on the order of 90 or 100 ft/sec.
3. A stack located on a building should be set in a position that will assure that the exhaust escapes the wakes of nearby structures,
4. Gases from the stacks with diameters less than 5 ft and heights less than 200 ft will hit the ground part of the time, and the ground concentration will be excessive. In this case, the plume becomes unpredictable.
5. The maximum ground concentration of stack gases subjected to atmospheric dispersion occurs about five to ten effective stack heights downwind from the point of emission.
6. When stack gases are subjected to atmospheric diffusion and building turbulence is not a fac-

tor, ground-level concentrations on the order of 0.001 to 1 percent of the stack concentration are possible for a properly designed stack.

7. Ground concentrations can be reduced by the use of higher stacks. The ground concentration varies inversely as the square of the effective stack height.

8. Average concentrations of a contaminant downwind from a stack are directly proportional to the discharge rate. An increase in discharge rate by a given factor increases ground-level concentrations at all points by the same factor.

9. In general, increasing the dilution of stack gases by the addition of excess air in the stack does not effect ground-level concentrations appreciably. Practical stack dilutions are usually insignificant in comparison to the later atmospheric dilution by plume diffusion. Addition of diluting will increase the effective stack height, however, by increasing the stack exit velocity. This effect may be important at low wind speeds. On the other hand, if the stack temperature is decreased appreciably by the dilution, the effective stack height may be reduced. Stack dilution will have an appreciable effect on the concentration in the plume close to the stack.

These nine guidelines represent the basic design elements of a pollution control system. An engineering approach suggests that each element be evaluated independently and as part of the whole control system. However, the engineering design and evaluation must be an integrated part of the complete pollution control program.

SUMMARY

1. Stacks discharging to the atmosphere have long been one of the methods available to industry for disposing waste gases. The concentration to which humans, plants, animals, and structures are exposed at ground level can be reduced significantly by emitting the waste gases from a process at great heights.

2. A four-step procedure is recommended for performing dispersion health effect studies:
a. Estimate the rate, duration and location of the release into the environment.
b. Select the best available model to perform the calculations.
c. Perform the calculations and generate downstream concentrations resulting from the source emission(s).
d. Determine what effect, if any, the resulting discharge has on the environment, including humans, animals, vegetation, and materials of construction.

3. Major meteorological concerns include: horizontal transport, vertical transport, topography, wind speed and direction, and temperature and humidity.

4. The effective stack height is usually considered the sum of the actual stack height, the plume rise due to velocity of the issuing gases and the buoyancy rise, which is a function of the temperature of the gases being emitted and the atmospheric conditions.

5. The Pasquill-Gifford model has been the basis of most models developed and accepted today (Pasquill, 1961; Gifford, 1961; Cota, 1984). This model has served as an atmospheric dispersion formula from which the path downwind of emissions can be estimated after obtaining the effective stack height.

6. There are numerous design suggestions for stacks. One of the key recommendations is that stack heights should be at least 2.5 times the height of any surrounding building or obstacles so that significant turbulence is not introduced by these factors.

REFERENCES

Bethea, R. M. *Air Pollution Control Technology* (pp. 39–59). New York: Van Nostrand Reinhold, 1978.

Cooper, C. D., and Alley, F. C. *Air Pollution Control: A Design Approach* (pp. 493–515, 519–552). Prospect Heights, IL, Waveland Press, 1986.

Cota, H. *Journal of the Air Pollution Control Association, 31,* (8) (1984): 253.

Gifford, F. A. *Nuclear Safety, 2* (4) (1961): 47.

Gilpin, A. *Control of Air Pollution* (pp. 326–333). New York: Butterworth, 1963.

Hesketh, H. E. *Understanding and Controlling Air Pollution* (pp. 33–70). Ann Arbor Science Publishers, 1972.

Pasquill, F. *Meteorology Magazine, 90* (33) (1961): 1063.

Theodore, L., and Allen, R. "Air Pollution Control Equipment," an ETS Theodore Tutorial. Roanoke, VA: ETS International, 1994.

Theodore, L., Reynolds, J., and Taylor, F. *Accident and Emergency Management.* New York: Wiley, 1989.

Turner, D. B. *Workbook of Atmospheric Dispersion Estimates* (EPA Publication No. AP-26). Research Triangle Park, NC: Environmental Protection Agency, 1970 (revised).

U.S. EPA. *Guideline on Air Quality Models,* Publication No. EPA-450/2-78-027. Research Triangle Park, NC: August 1978 (OAQPS No. 1.2-08).

U.S. EPA. *Industrial Source Complex (ISC) Dispersion Model User's Guide,* 2nd ed., Vols. 1 and 2, Publication Nos. EPA-450/4-86-005a and EPA-450/4-86-005b. Research Triangle Park, NC: Author unknown, 1986 (NRTIS PB 86 234259 and 23467).

11

Indoor Air Quality

CONTRIBUTING AUTHOR

Christopher Reda

INTRODUCTION

Indoor air pollution is rapidly becoming a major worldwide health issue. Although research efforts are still underway to better define the nature and extent of the health implications for the general population, recent studies have shown significant amounts of harmful pollutants in the indoor environment. The serious concern over pollutants in indoor air is due largely to the fact that indoor pollutants are not easily dispersed or diluted as are pollutants outdoors. Thus, indoor pollutant levels are frequently higher than outdoors, particularly where buildings are tightly constructed to save energy. In some cases, these indoor levels exceed the Environmental Protection Agency (EPA) standards already established for outdoors. Research by the EPA in this area, called the Total Exposure Assessment Methodology (TEAM) studies, has documented the fact that levels indoors for some pollutants may exceed outdoor levels by 200 to 500 percent (EPA, 1988).

Since most people spend 90 percent of their time indoors, many may be exposed to unhealthy concentrations of pollutants. People most susceptible to the risks of pollution—the aged, the ill, and the very young—spend nearly all of their time indoors. These indoor environments include such places as homes, offices, hotels, stores, restaurants, warehouses, factories, government buildings, and even vehicles. In these environments, people are exposed to pollutants emanating from a wide array of sources.

Some common indoor air contaminants are:

1. Radon
2. Formaldehyde
3. Volatile Organic Compounds (VOCs)
4. Combustion gases

5. Particulates

6. Biological contaminants

In addition to air contaminants, other factors need to be observed in Indoor Air Quality (IAQ) monitoring programs to fully understand the significance of contaminant measurements. Important factors to be considered in IAQ studies include:

1. Air exchange rates

2. Building design and ventilation characteristics

3. Indoor contaminant sources and sinks

4. Air movement and mixing

5. Temperature

6. Relative humidity

7. Outdoor contaminant concentrations and meteorological conditions

Designers, builders, and homeowners must make crucial decisions about the kinds and potential levels of existing indoor air pollutants at proposed house sites. Building structure design, construction, operation, and household furnishings, all rely on specific design parameters being set down to handle the reduction of these pollutants at their sources.

The health effects associated with IAQ can be either short- or long-term. Immediate effects experienced after a single exposure or repeated exposures include irritation of the eyes, nose, and throat; headaches; dizziness; and fatigue. These short-term effects are usually treatable by some means, oftentimes by eliminating the person's exposure to the source of pollution.

The likelihood of an individual developing immediate reactions to indoor air pollutants depends on several factors, including age and pre-existing medical conditions. Also, individual sensitivity to a reactant varies tremendously. Some people can become sensitized to biological pollutants after repeated exposures, and it appears that some people can become sensitized to chemical pollutants as well. Other health effects may show up either years after exposure has occurred, or only after long or repeated periods of exposure. These effects range from impairment of the nervous system to cancer; emphysema and other respiratory diseases; and heart disease, which can be severely debilitating or fatal. Certain symptoms are similar to those of other viral diseases and difficult to determine if it is a result of IA pollution. Therefore, special attention should be paid to the time and place symptoms occur.

Further research is needed to better understand which health effects can arise after exposure to the average pollutant concentrations found in homes. These can arise from the higher concentrations that occur for short periods of time. Yet, both the amount of pollutant, called the dose, and the length of time of exposure are important in assessing health effects. The effects of simultaneous exposure to several pollutants are even more uncertain. Indoor air quality can be severely debilitating or even fatal. Indoor air pollutants of special concern are described below in separate sections.

It is not possible to provide estimates of typical mixtures of pollutants found in residences. This is because the levels of pollutants found in homes vary significantly depending on location, use of combustion devices, existing building materials, and use of certain household products. Also, emissions of pollutants into the indoor air may be sporadic, as in the case of aerosols or organic vapors that are released during specific household activities or when woodstoves or fire-places are in use. Another important consideration regarding indoor pollutant concentrations is the interaction among pollutants. Pollutants often tend to attach themselves to airborne particles that get caught more easily in the lungs. In addition, certain organic compounds released indoors could react with each other to form highly toxic substances.

The data provided in this chapter consists of approximate ranges of indoor pollutants based on studies conducted around the United States. These provide an overview of several major pollutants that have been measured in residences at levels that may cause health problems ranging from minor irritations or allergies to potentially debilitating diseases.

RADON

Radon is a unique environmental problem because it occurs naturally. Radon results from the radioactive decay sequence of uranium-238, a long-lived precursor to radon. The isotope of most concern, radon-222, has a half-life (time for half to disappear) of 3.8 days. Radon itself decays and produces a series of short-lived decay products called radon progeny or daughters. Polonium-218 and polonium-214 are the most harmful because they emit charged alpha particles more dangerous than x-rays or gamma rays (Taylor, 1987). They also tend to adhere to other particles (attachment) or surfaces (plate out). These larger particles are more susceptible to becoming lodged in the lungs when inhaled and cause irreparable damage to surrounding lung tissue (which may lead to lung cancer).

Radon is a colorless, odorless gas that is found everywhere at very low levels. Radon becomes a cause for concern when it is trapped in buildings and concentrations build up. In contrast, indoor air has approximately two to ten times higher concentrations of radon than outdoor air. Primary sources of radon are from soil, well water supplies, and building materials.

Most indoor radon comes from the rock and soil around a building and enters structures through cracks or openings in the foundation or basement. High concentrations of radon are also found in wells, where storage, or hold-up time, is too short to allow time for radon decay. Building materials, such as phosphate slag (a component of concrete used in an estimated 74,000 U.S. homes) has been found to be high in radium content (Mueller Associates, 1987). Studies have shown concrete to have the highest radon content when compared to all other building materials, with wood having the least.

It is becoming increasingly apparent that local geological factors play a dominant role in determining the distribution of indoor radon concentrations in a given area. To date, no indoor radon standard has been promulgated for all residential housing in the United States. However, various organizations have proposed ranges of guidelines and standards.

Data taken from various states suggest an average indoor radon-222 concentration of 1.5 pCi/L (picoCuries per liter, a concentration of radiation term), and approximately 1 million homes with concentrations exceeding 8 pCi/L (Mueller Associates, 1987). One curie is equal to a quantity of a material with 37 billion radioactive decays per second. One trillionth of a curie is a pCi. Assuming residents in these homes spend close to 80 percent of their time indoors, their radon exposure would come close to the level for recommended remedial action set by the U.S. National Council on Radiation Protection and Measurements. The EPA believes that up to 8 million homes may have radon levels exceeding 4 pCi/L air, the level at which the EPA recommends corrective action. In comparison, the maximum level of radon set for miners by the U.S. Mine Safety and Health Administration is as high as 16 pCi/L.

Radon may be the leading cause of lung cancer among nonsmokers. Several radiation protection groups have approximated the number of annual lung cancer deaths attributable to indoor radon. The EPA estimates that radon may be responsible for 5,000 to 20,000 lung cancer deaths among nonsmokers. Also, scientific evidence indicates that smoking, coupled with the effects of exposure to radon, increases the risk of cancer by ten times that of nonsmokers (EPA, 1988).

A variety of measures can be employed to help control indoor concentrations of radon and/or radon progeny. Mitigation methods for existing homes include placing barriers between the source material and living space itself using several techniques, such as:

1. Covering exposed soil inside a structure with cement
2. Eliminating and sealing any cracks in the floors or walls
3. Adding traps to underfloor drains
4. Filling concrete block walls

Soil ventilation prevents radon from entering the home by drawing the gas away before it can enter the home. Pipes are inserted into the stone aggregate under basement floors or onto the hollow portion of concrete walls to ventilate radon gas accumulating in these locations. Pipes can also be attached to underground drain tile systems drawing the radon gas away from the house. Fans are often attached to the system to improve ventilation. Crawl space ventilation is also generally regarded as an effective and cheap method of source reduction. This allows for exchange of outdoor air by placing a number of openings in the crawl space walls.

Home ventilation involves increasing a home's air exchange rate—the rate at which incoming outdoor air completely replaces indoor air—either naturally (by opening windows or vents) or mechanically (through the use of fans). This method works best when applied to houses with low initial exchange rates. However, when indoor air pressure is reduced, pressure-driven radon entry is induced, increasing levels in the home instead of decreasing them. The benefits of increased ventilation can be achieved without raising radon exposure by opening windows evenly on all sides of the home.

Mechanical devices can also be used to help rid indoor air of radon progeny. Air cleaning systems use high efficiency filters or electronic devices to collect dust and other airborne particles, some with radon products attached to them. These devices decrease the concentration of airborne particles, but do not decrease the concentration of smaller unattached radon decay products, which can result in a higher radiation dose when inhaled.

FORMALDEHYDE

Formaldehyde is a colorless, water-soluble gas that has a pungent, irritating odor noticeable at less than 1 ppm. It is an inexpensive chemical with excellent bonding characteristics that is produced in high volume throughout the world. A major use is in the fabrication of urea-formaldehyde (UF) resins used primarily as adhesives when making plywood, particleboard, and fiberboard. Formaldehyde is also a component of UF foam insulation, injected into sidewalls primarily during the 1970s. Many common household cleaning agents contain formaldehyde. Other minor sources in the residential environment include cigarette smoke and other combustion sources such as gas stoves, woodstoves, and unvented gas space heaters. Formaldehyde can also be found in paper products such as facial tissues, paper towels, and grocery bags, as well as stiffeners and wrinkle resisters (Taylor, 1987).

Although information regarding emission rates is limited, in general, the rate of formaldehyde release has been shown to increase with temperature, wood moisture content, humidity, and with decreased formaldehyde concentration in the air.

UF foam was used as a thermal insulation in the sidewalls of many buildings. It was injected directly into wall cavities through small holes that were then sealed. When improperly installed, UF foam emits significant amounts of formaldehyde. The Consumer Product Safety Commission (CPSC) measured values as high as 4 ppm and imposed a nationwide ban on UF foam, but it was later overturned.

The superior bonding properties and low cost of formaldehyde polymers make them the resins of choice for the production of building materials. Plywood is composed of several thin sheets of wood glued together with UF resin. Particleboard (compressed wood shavings mixed with UF resin at high temperatures), can emit formaldehyde continuously for a long time, from several months to several years. Medium density fiberboard was found to be the highest emitter of formaldehyde.

Indoor monitoring data on formaldehyde concentrations are variable because of the wide range of products that may be present in the home. However, elevated levels are more likely to be found in mobile homes and new homes with pressed-wood construction materials. Indoor concentrations also vary with home age since emissions decrease as products containing formaldehyde age and cure. In general, indoor formaldehyde concentration exceed levels found outdoors.

Although individual sensitivity to formaldehyde varies, about 10 to 20 percent of the population appears to be highly sensitive to even low concentrations. Its principal effect is irritation of the eyes, nose, and throat, as well as asthma-like symptoms. Allergic dermatitis may possibly occur from skin contact. Exposure to higher concentrations may cause nausea, headache, coughing, constriction of the chest, and rapid heartbeat (EPA, 1988).

One of the most promising techniques for reducing indoor formaldehyde concentrations is to modify the source materials to reduce emission rates. This can be accomplished by measures performed during manufacture or after installation. A variety of production changes, that is, changes in raw materials, processing times, and temperatures, are promising methods for reducing emission rates. Applying vinyl wallpaper or nonpermeable paint to interior walls, venting exterior walls, and increased ventilation are other methods employed after installation.

VOLATILE ORGANIC COMPOUNDS (VOCs)

In addition to formaldehyde, many other organic compounds may be present in the indoor environment. More than 800 different compounds can be attributed to volatile vapors alone. Common sources in the home are building materials, furnishings, pesticides, gas or wood burning devices, and consumer products (cleaners, aerosols, deodorizers). In addition, occupant activities such as smoking, cooking, or arts and crafts activities can contribute to indoor pollutant levels.

Organic contaminants in the home are usually present as complex mixtures of many compounds at low concentrations. Thus, it is very difficult to provide estimates of typical indoor concentrations or associated health risks. It is likely, however, that organic compounds may be responsible for health-related complaints registered by residents where formaldehyde and other indoor pollutants are found to be low or undetectable. The sources of three major types of organic contaminants include solvents, polymer components, and pesticides.

Volatile organic solvents commonly pollute air. Exposure occurs when occupants use spot removers, paint removers, cleaning products, paint adhesives, aerosols, fuels, lacquers and varnishes, glues, cosmetics, and numerous other household products. Halogenated hydrocarbons such as methyl chloroform and methylene chloride are widely used in a variety of home products. Aromatic hydrocarbons such as toluene have been found to be present in more than 50 percent of samples taken on indoor air (Mueller Associates, 1987). Alcohols, ketones, ethers, and esters are also present in organic solvents. Some of them, especially esters, emit pleasant odors and are used in flavors and perfumes, yet are still potentially harmful.

Polymer components are found in clothes, furniture, packages, and cookware. Many are used for medical purposes—for example, in blood transfusion bags and disposable syringes. Fortunately, most polymers are relatively nontoxic. However, polymers contain unreacted monomers, plasticizers, stabilizers, fillers, colorants, and antistatic agents, some of which are toxic. These chemicals diffuse from the polymers into air. Certain monomers (acrylic acid esters, toluene-diisocynate, and epichlorohydrin) used to produce plastics, polyurethane, and epoxy resins in tile floors, are all toxic.

Most American households use pesticides in the home, garden, or lawn, and many people become ill after using these chemicals. According to an EPA survey, nine out of ten U.S. households use pesticides and another study suggests that 80 to 90 percent of most people's exposure to pesticides has been found in the air inside homes. Pesticides used in and around the home include products to control insects, termites, rodents, and fungi. Chlordane, one of the most harmful active ingredients in pesticides, has been found in structures up to twenty years after its application. In addition to the active ingredient, pesticides are also made up of inerts that are used to carry the active agent. These inerts may not be toxic to the targeted post, but are capable of causing health problems. Methylene chloride, discussed earlier as an organic pollutant, is used as an inert (EPA, 1988).

Human beings can also be significant sources of organic emissions. Human breath contains trace amounts of acetone and ethanol at 20°C and 1 atmosphere. Measurements taken in schoolrooms while people were present averaged almost twice the amount of acetone and ethanol present in unoccupied rooms. At least part of this increase for ethanol was presumed to be due to perfume and deodorant, in addition to breath emissions (Taylor, 1987).

As mentioned earlier, large numbers of organic compounds have been identified in residences. Studies have shown that of the forty most common organics, nearly all were found at much higher concentrations indoors than outdoors. Another EPA study identified eleven chemicals present in more than half of all samples taken nationwide. Although individual compounds are usually present in low concentrations, which are well below outdoor air quality standards, the average total hydrocarbon concentration can exceed both outdoor concentrations and ambient air quality standards (Mueller Associates, 1987).

Little is known of the short- and long-term health effects of many organic compounds at the low levels of exposure occurring in nonindustrial environments. Yet cumulative effects of various compounds found indoors have been associated with a number of symptoms, such as headache, drowsiness, irritation of the eyes and mucous membranes, irritation of the respiratory system, and general malaise. In general, volatile organic compounds are lipid soluble and easily absorbed through the lungs. Their ability to cross the blood-brain barrier may induce depression of the central nervous system and cardiac functions. Some known and suspected human and animal carcinogens found indoors are benzene, trichloroethane, tetrachloroethylene, vinyl chloride, and dioxane.

One of the best methods to reduce health risks from exposure to organic compounds is for residents or consumers to increase their awareness of the types of toxic chemicals present in household products. Attention to warnings and instructions for storage and use are important, especially regarding ventilation conditions. In some instances, substitution of less hazardous products is possible, as in use of a liquid or dry form of a product rather than an aerosol spray. Consumers should also be wary of the simultaneous use of various products containing organic compounds, since chemical reactions may occur if products are mixed, and adverse health effects may result from the synergism between/among components.

COMBUSTION GASES

Combustion gases, such as carbon monoxide, nitrogen oxides, and sulfur dioxide, can be introduced into the indoor environment by a variety of sources. These sources frequently depend on occupant activities or lifestyles and include the use of gas stoves, kerosene and unvented gas space heaters, woodstoves, and fireplaces. In addition, tobacco smoke is a combustion product that contributes to the contamination of indoor air. More than 2,000 gaseous compounds have been identified in cigarette smoke, and carbon monoxide and nitrogen oxide are among them (EPA, 1988).

This section focuses on nitrogen oxides (primarily nitrogen dioxide) and carbon monoxide because they are frequently occurring products of combustion often found at higher indoor concentrations than outdoors. Other combustion products such as sulfur dioxide, hydrocarbons, formaldehyde, and carbon dioxide are produced by combustion sources to a lesser degree or only under unusual or infrequent circumstances.

Unvented kerosene and gas space heaters can provide an additional source of heat for homes in cold climates or can serve as a primary heating source when needed for homes in warm climates. There are several basic types of unvented kerosene and gas space heaters which can be classified by the type of burner and type of fuel. Unvented gas space heaters can be convective or infrared and can be fueled by natural gas or propane. Kerosene heaters can be convective, radiant, two-stage, and wickless. A recent study found that emission rates from the various types of heaters fall into three distinct groups. The two-stage kerosene heaters emitted the least CO and the least NO_2. The radiant/infrared heater group emitted the most CO under well-tuned conditions; and the convective group emitted the most NO_2. Many studies have also noted that some heaters have significantly higher emission rates than heaters of other brands or than models of the same type. Older or improperly used heaters will also increase emission rates.

The kitchen stove is one of the few modern gas appliances that emit combustion products directly into the home. It is estimated that natural gas is used in over 45 percent of all U.S. homes, and studies show that most of these homes do not vent the combustion-produced emissions to the outside. Combustion gas emissions vary considerably and are dependent upon factors such as the fuel consumption rate, combustion efficiency, age of burner, and burner design, as well as the usage pattern of the appliance. An improperly adjusted gas stove is likely to have a yellow-tipped flame rather than a blue-tipped flame, which can result in increased pollutant emissions (mostly NO_2 and CO).

Increasing energy costs, consumer concerns about fuel availability, and desire for self-reliance, are some of the factors that have brought about an upswing in the use of solid fuels for residential heating. These devices include woodburning stoves, furnaces, and fireplaces. Although woodstoves and fireplaces are vented to the outdoors, a number of circumstances can cause combustion products to be emitted to the indoor air: improper installation (such as insufficient stack height), cracks or leaks in stovepipes, negative air pressure indoors, downdrafts, refueling, and accidents (as when a log rolls out of a fireplace). The type and amount of wood burned also influences pollutant emissions, which vary from home to home. Although elevated levels of CO and NO_2 have been reported, the major impact of woodburning appears to be on indoor respirable suspended particles.

The term nitrogen oxides (NO_x) refers to a number of compounds, all of which have the potential to affect humans. NO_2 and NO have been studied extensively as outdoor pollutants, yet cannot be ignored in the indoor environment. There is evidence that suggests these oxides may be harmful at levels of exposure that can occur indoors. Both NO and NO_2 combine with hemoglobin in the blood, forming methemoglobin, which reduces the oxygen-carrying capacity of the blood. It is about four times more effective than CO in reducing the oxygen-carrying capacity of the blood. NO_2 produces respiratory illnesses that range from slight burning and pain in the throat and chest to shortness of breath and violent coughing. It places stress on the cardiovascular system and causes short-term and long-term damage to the lungs. Concentrations typically found in kitchens with gas stoves do not appear to cause chronic respiratory diseases, but may affect sensory perception and produce eye irritation.

Carbon monoxide (CO) is a poisonous gas that causes tissue hypoxia (oxygen starvation) by binding with blood hemoglobin and blocking its ability to transport oxygen. CO has in excess of 200 times more binding affinity for hemoglobin than oxygen does. The product, carboxyhemoglobin, is an indicator of reduction in oxygen-carrying capacity. A small amount of CO is even produced naturally in the body, producing a concentration in unexposed persons of about 0.5 percent CO-bound hemoglobin. Under chronic exposure (for example, cigarette smoking), the body compensates somewhat by increasing the concentration of red blood cells and the total amount of hemoglobin available for oxygen transport. The central nervous system, cardiovascular system, and liver are most sensitive to CO-induced hypoxia. Hypoxia of the central nervous system causes a wide range of effects in the exposure range of 5 to 15 percent carboxyhemoglobin. These include loss of alertness and impaired perception, loss of normal dexterity, reduced learning ability, sleep disruption, drowsiness, confusion, and at very high concentrations, coma and death. Health effects related to hypoxia of the cardiovascular system include decrease in exercise time required to produce angina pectoris (chest pain); increase in incidences of myocardosis (degeneration of heart muscle); and a general increase in the probability of heart failure among susceptible individuals (Mueller Associates, 1987).

Population groups at special risk of detrimental effects of CO exposure include fetuses, persons with existing health impairments (especially heart disease), persons under the influence of drugs, and those not adapted to high altitudes who are exposed to both CO and high altitudes.

Proper installation, operation, and maintenance of combustion devices can significantly reduce the health risks associated with these appliances. Manufacturers' instructions regarding the proper size space heater in relation to room size, ventilation conditions, and tuning should be observed. This includes using vented range hoods when operating gas stoves. Studies have indicated reductions in CO, CO_2, and NO_2 levels as high as 60 to 87 percent with the use of range hoods during gas stove operation. Unvented forced draft and unvented range hoods with charcoal filters can be effective for removing grease, odors, and other molecules, but cannot be considered a reliable control for CO and other small molecules. Fireplace flues and chimneys should be inspected and cleaned frequently, and opened completely when in use (Taylor, 1987).

PARTICULATES

Environmental tobacco smoke, ETS (smoke that nonsmokers are exposed to from smokers), has been judged by the Surgeon General, the National Research Council, and the International Agency for Research on Cancer to pose a risk of lung cancer to nonsmokers. Nonsmokers' exposure to environmental tobacco smoke is called "passive smoking," "second-hand smoking," and "involuntary smoking." Tobacco smoke contains a number of pollutants, including inorganic gases, heavy metals, particulates, VOCs, and products of incomplete burning, such as polynuclear aromatic hydrocarbons. Smoke can also yield a number of organic compounds. Including both gases and particles, tobacco smoke is a complex mixture of over 4700 compounds (EPA, 1988).

There are two components of tobacco smoke: (1) mainstream smoke, which is the smoke drawn through the tobacco during inhalation, (2) sidestream smoke, which arises from the smoldering tobacco. Sidestream smoke accounts for 96% of gases and particles produced (Taylor, 1987).

Studies indicate that exposure to tobacco smoke may increase the risk of lung cancer by an average of 30 percent in the nonsmoking spouses of smokers. Published risk estimates of lung cancer deaths among nonsmokers exposed to tobacco smoke conclude that ETS is responsible for 3,000 deaths each year (Cox, & Miro, 1993). It also seriously affects the respiratory health of hundreds of thousands of children. Very young children exposed to smoking at home are more likely to be hospitalized for bronchitis and pneumonia. Recent studies suggest that environmental tobacco smoke can also cause other diseases, including other cancers and heart disease in healthy nonsmokers (EPA, 1988).

The best way to reduce exposure to cigarette smoke in the house is to quit smoking and discourage smoking indoors. Ventilation is the most common method of reducing exposure to these pollutants, but it will not eliminate it altogether. Smoking produces such large amounts of pollutants that neither natural nor mechanical methods can remove them from the air as quickly as they build up. In addition, ventilation practices sometimes lead to increased energy costs.

Respirable suspended particles (RSP) are particles or fibers in the air that are small enough to be inhaled. Particles can exist in either solid or liquid phase or in a combination. Where these particles are deposited and how long they are retained depends on their size, chemical composition, and density. Respirable suspended particles (generally less than 10 micrometers in diameter), can settle on the tissues of the upper respiratory tract, with the smallest particles (those less than 2.5 micrometers) penetrating the alveoli, the small air sacs in the lungs.

Particulate matter is a broad class of chemically and physically diverse substances that present risks to health. These effects can be attributed to either the intrinsic toxic chemical or physical characteristics, as in the case of lead and asbestos, or to the particles acting as a carrier of adsorbed toxic substances, as in the case of attachment of radon daughters. Carbon particles, such as those created by combustion processes, are efficient adsorbers of many organic compounds and are able to carry toxic gases such as sulfur dioxide into the lungs.

Asbestos is a mineral fiber used mostly before the mid-seventies in a variety of construction materials. Home exposure to asbestos is usually due to aging, cracking, or physical disruption of insulated pipes or asbestos-containing ceiling tiles and spackling compounds. Apartments and school buildings may have an asbestos compound sprayed on certain structural components as a fire retardant. Exposure occurs when asbestos materials are disturbed and the fibers are released into the air and inhaled. Consumer exposure to asbestos has been reduced considerably since the mid-seventies, when use of asbestos was either prohibited or stopped voluntarily in sprayed-on insulation, fire protection, soundproofing, artificial logs, patching compounds, and handheld hair dryers. Today, asbestos is most commonly found in older homes in pipe and furnace insulation materials, asbestos shingles, millboard, textured paints and other coating materials, and floor tiles. Elevated concentrations of airborne asbestos can occur after asbestos-containing materials are disturbed by cutting, sanding, or other remodeling activities. Improper attempts to remove these materials can release asbestos fibers into the air in homes, thereby increasing asbestos levels and endangering the people living in those homes. The most dangerous asbestos fibers are too small to be visible. After they are inhaled, they can remain and accumulate in the lungs. Asbestos can cause lung cancer, mesothelioma (a cancer of the chest and abdominal linings), and asbestosis (irreversible lung scarring that can be fatal). Symptoms of these diseases do not show up until many years after exposure began. A more detailed presentation on asbestos can be found in Chapter 46.

Lead has long been recognized as a harmful environmental pollutant. There are many ways in which humans are exposed to lead, including air, drinking water, food, and contaminated soil and dust. Airborne lead enters the body when an individual breathes lead particles or swallows lead dust once it has settled. Until recently, the most important airborne source of lead was automobile exhaust. Lead-based paint has long been recognized as a hazard to children who eat lead-contained paint chips. A 1988 National Institute of Building Sciences Task Force report found that harmful exposures to lead can be created when lead-based paint is removed from surfaces by sanding or open-flame burning. High concentrations of airborne lead particles in homes can also result from the lead dust from outdoor sources, contaminated soil tracked inside, and use of lead in activities such as soldering, electronics repair, and stained-glass artwork. Lead is toxic to many organs within the body at both low and high concentrations. Lead is capable of causing serious damage to the brain, kidneys, peripheral nervous system (the sense organs and nerves controlling the body), and red blood cells. Even low levels of lead may increase high blood pressure in adults. Fetuses, infants, and children are more vulnerable to lead exposure than are adults because lead is more easily absorbed into growing bodies, and the tissues of small children are more sensitive to the damaging effects of lead. The effects of lead exposure on fetuses and young children include delays in physical and mental development, lower IQ levels, shortened attention spans, and increased behavioral problems. Additional details on lead, as well as other metals, can be found in Chapter 45.

Particles present a risk to health out of proportion to their concentration in the atmosphere because they deliver a high-concentration package of potentially harmful substances. So, while few cells may be affected at any one time, those few that are can be badly damaged. Whereas larger particles deposited in the upper respiratory portion of the respiratory system are continuously cleared away, smaller particles deposited deep in the lung may cause adverse health effects. Particle sizes vary over a broad range, depending on source characteristics.

Major effects of concern attributed to particle exposure are impairment of respiratory mechanics, aggravation of existing respiratory and cardiovascular disease, and reduction in particle clearance and other host defense mechanisms. Respiratory effects can range from mild transient changes of little direct health significance to incapacitating impairment of breathing.

One method of reducing RSP concentrations is to properly design, install, and operate combustion sources. One should make sure there are no existing leaks or cracks in stovepipes, and that these appliances are always vented to the outdoors.

Also available are particulate air cleaners, which can be separated into mechanical filters and electrostatic filters. Mechanical filtration is generally accomplished by passing the air through a fibrous media (wire, hemp, glass, etc.). These filters are capable of removing almost any sized particles. Electrostatic filtration operates on the principle of attraction between opposite electrical charges. Ion generators, electrostatic precipitators, and electric filters use this principle for removing particles from the air.

The ability of these various types of air-cleaning devices to remove respirable particles varies widely. High efficiency particulate air (HEPA) filters can capture over 99 percent of particles, and are advantageous in that filters only need changing every three to five years, but costs can reach $500 to $800. It is also important to note the location of air-cleaning device inlets in relation to the contaminant sources as an important factor influencing removal efficiencies.

BIOLOGICAL CONTAMINANTS

Heating, ventilation, and air conditioning systems and humidifiers can be breeding grounds for biological contaminants when they are not properly cleaned and maintained. They can also bring biological contaminants indoors and circulate them. Biological contaminants include bacteria, mold and mildew, viruses, animal dander and cat saliva, mites, cockroaches, and pollen. There are many sources for these pollutants. For example, pollens originate from plants; viruses are transmitted by people and animals; bacteria are carried by people, animals, and soil and plant debris; and household pets are sources of saliva, hair, and dead skin (known as dander).

Available evidence indicates that a number of viruses that infect humans can be transmitted via the air. Among them are the most common infections of mankind. Airborne contagion is the mechanism of transmission of most acute respiratory infections, and these are the greatest of all causes of morbidity.

The primary source of bacteria indoors is the human body. Although the major source is the respiratory tract, it has been shown that 7 million skin scales are shed per minute per person, with an average of 4 viable bacteria per scale (Mueller Associates, 1987). Airborne transmission of bacteria is facilitated by the prompt dispersion of particles. Infectious contact requires proximity in time and space between host and contact, and is also related to air filtration and air exchange rate.

Although many important allergens—such as pollen, fungi, insects, and algae—enter buildings from outdoors, several airborne allergens originate predominately in homes and office buildings. House dust mites, one of the most powerful biologicals in triggering allergic reactions, can grow in any damp, warm environment. Allergic reactions can occur on the skin, nose, airways, and alveoli.

The most common respiratory diseases attributable to these allergens are rhinitis, affecting about 15 percent of the population, and asthma, affecting about 3 to 5 percent (Mueller Associates, 1987). These diseases are most common among children and young adults, but can occur at any age. Research has shown that asthma occurs four times more often among poor, inner-city families than in other families. Among the suspected causes are mouse urine antigens, cockroach feces antigens, and a type of fungus called Alternia.

Hypersensitivity pneumonitis (HP), characterized by shortness of breathe, fever, and cough, is a much less common disease, but is dangerous if not diagnosed and treated early. HP is most commonly caused by contaminated forced-air heating systems, humidifiers, and flooding disasters. It can also be caused by inhalation of microbial aerosols from saunas, home tap water, and even automobile air conditioners. Humidifiers with reservoirs containing stagnant water may be important sources of allergens in both residential and public buildings.

Some biological contaminants trigger allergic reactions, while others transmit infectious illnesses, such as influenza, measles, and chicken pox. Certain molds and mildews release disease-causing toxins. Symptoms of health problems caused by biologicals include sneezing, watery eyes, coughing, shortness of breathe, dizziness, lethargy, fever, and digestive problems.

Attempts to control airborne viral disease have included quarantine, vaccination, and inactivation or removal of the viral aerosol. Infiltration and ventilation play a large role in the routes of transmission. Because many contaminants originate outdoors, attempts to reduce the ventilation rate might lower indoor pollutant concentrations. However, any reduction in fresh air exchange should be supplemented by a carefully filtered air source.

Central electrostatic filtration (as part of a home's forced-air system) has proven effective in reducing indoor mold problems. Careful cleaning, vacuuming, and air filtration are effective ways to reduce dust levels in a home. Ventilation of attic and crawl spaces help prevent moisture buildup, keeping humidity levels between 30 to 50 percent (Holmes, Singh, & Theodore, 1993). Also, when using cool mist or ultrasonic humidifiers, one should remember to clean and refill water trays often, since these areas often become breeding grounds for biological contaminants.

MONITORING METHODS

Methods and instrumentation for measuring indoor air quality vary in their levels of sensitivity (what levels of pollutant they can detect) and accuracy (how close they can come to measuring the true concentration). Instruments that can measure low levels of pollutant very accurately are likely to be expensive and require special expertise to use. Some level of sensitivity and accuracy is required, however, to ensure that data collected are useful in assessing levels of exposure and risk.

In choosing methods for monitoring indoor air quality, a tradeoff must be made between cost and the levels of sensitivity, accuracy, and precision achieved in a monitoring program. Required levels for each pollutant are based on ranges found in residential buildings. In providing detailed information concerning specific methods or instruments, emphasis is placed on those that are readily available, easy to use, reasonably priced, and that provide the required levels of sensitivity and accuracy.

Methods to monitor indoor air fall into several broad categories. Sampling instruments may be fixed-location, portable, or small personal monitors designed to be carried by an individual. These samplers may act in an active or passive mode. Active samplers require a pump to draw in air. Passive samplers rely on diffusion or permeation.

Monitors may be either analytical instruments that provide a direct reading of pollutant concentration, or collectors that must be sent to a laboratory for analysis. Instruments may also be categorized according to the time period over which they sample. These include grab samplers, continuous samplers, and time-integrated samplers, each of which is briefly described below.

1. Grab sampler: Collects samples of air in a bag, tube, or bottle, providing a short-term average
2. Continuous sampling: Allows sampling of real-time concentration of pollutants, providing data on peak short-term concentrations and average concentrations over the sampling period
3. Time-integrated sampling: Measures an average air concentration over some period of time (active or passive), using collector monitors that must be sent out for analysis; cannot determine peak concentrations.

More details regarding monitoring methods for specific indoor air pollutants can be found in the IAQ Handbook (Mueller Associates, 1987).

CosaTron is just one example of a company that produces mechanical air cleaning devices. The patented CosaTron system has been handling IAQ successfully in thousands of installations for over twenty-five years. CosaTron is not a filter that ionizes air. It cleans the air electronically, causing the submicron particles of smoke, odor, dirt and gases to collide and adhere to each other until they become larger and airborne and are easily carried out of the conditioned space by the system air flow to be exhausted or captured in the filter. Mechanical air devices such as this one improve IAQ so much that outside air requirements can be reduced significantly (Ashrae, 1993).

FUTURE TRENDS

In recent years, the EPA has increased efforts to address IAQ problems through a building systems approach. EPA hopes to bolster awareness of the importance of prevention and encourage a whole systems perspective to resolve indoor air problems. The EPA Office of Research and Development is also conducting a multidisciplinary IAQ research program that encompasses studies of the health effects associated with indoor air pollution exposure, assessments of indoor air pollution sources and control approaches, building studies and investigation methods, risk assessments of indoor air pollutants, and a recently initiated program on biocontaminants.

Federal research on air quality issues is driven in part by the increasing attention that IAQ has attracted from journalists as well as scientists and engineers. EPA has performed comparitive studies that have consistently ranked indoor air pollution among the top five environmental risks to public health. In analyzing over 500 IAQ investigations conducted through the end of 1988, the National Institute for Occupational Safety and Health (NIOSH) categorized its findings into seven broad sources of poor indoor air quality: inadequate ventilation (53%), inside contamination (15%), outside contamination (13%), microbiological contamination (5%), building materials contamination (4%), and unknown sources (13%) (Cox & Miro, 1993). Since then, ventilation has been the primary focus of most EPA programs.

Requirements for clean air are still changing rapidly and most buildings will need to be refitted with different filters to meet with these new standards and guidelines. EPA's research will continue in these and other areas to try to ensure comfortable and clean air conditions for the indoor environment.

SUMMARY

1. Indoor air quality is rapidly becoming a major environmental concern since levels of indoor air pollutants are often higher than levels outdoors and a significant amount of people spend the majority of their time indoors.

2. Radon is a naturally occuring, colorless, odorless gas that can be found almost anywhere at very low levels. Radon may be the leading cause of lung cancer among nonsmokers.

3. Formaldehyde is a colorless, water soluble gas with a pungent odor that can be found in a variety of household products as well as building materials.

4. A wide variety of organic compounds is associated with the use of various household cleaners, pesticides, and painting materials.

5. More than 2,000 gaseous compounds have been identified in cigarette smoke. Among them are carbon monoxide and nitrogen oxide, which significantly reduce the oxygen carrying capacity of the blood.

6. Heating, ventilation, air condition systems, and humidifiers can be breeding grounds for biological contaminants when they are not properly cleaned and maintained.

7. Basic strategies to improve indoor air quality include source control, ventilation, and mechanical devices.

8. Recent studies have focused on improving ventilation techniques and proper air quality control.

REFERENCES

Cox, J. E., and Miro, C. R. "EPA, DOE, and NIOSH Address IAQ Problems." *Ashrae Journal,* July 1993, 10.

EPA. "Environmental Progress and Challenges." *EPA's Update,* August 1988.

"Four Proven Solutions for IAQ!" *Ashrae Journal,* March 1993, 2.

Holmes, G., Singh, B., and Theodore, L. *Handbook of Environmental Management and Technology.* New York: John Wiley and Sons, 1993.

Mueller Associates, Inc. *Indoor Air Quality Environmental Information Handbook: Building System Characteristics*, Baltimore, MD: Author, 1987.

Taylor, J. *Sampling and Calibration for Atmospheric Measurements*. Philadelphia, PA: ASTM Publication, 1987.

12

Air Toxics

CONTRIBUTING AUTHOR

Lorraine Farrell

INTRODUCTION

Although air is generally considered as approximately 20 percent oxygen and 80 percent nitrogen (by mole or volume), other substances get into the air, and some of these are referred to as pollutants. Some of the pollutants that have the potential to adversely affect human health at certain concentrations are known as toxic air pollutants (TAPs), or air toxics. The dimensions of toxic exposure are staggering. Not until well after World War II was public attention drawn to toxic exposure. Not until the 1970s did the United States begin to address toxic contamination resulting from the common use of synthetic chemicals that also affected water and food. Incidents, such as Love Canal, in which a major toxic waste dump was discovered beneath a residential community, and Bhopal, India, in which methyl isocyanate was accidentally released into the atmosphere, have sounded a warning. Contaminated communities, or residential areas that are located within the boundaries of a known exposure to some form of pollution are causing a gradual deterioration of the relationship between humans and the ecosystem (Belmonte & Theodore, in preparation). An increased awareness of the implications of toxic pollution has led society to confront a new type of threat, that of toxic exposure. The need for information on the toxicity of environmental pollutants is based on the need to protect human health. Toxic exposure may now be considered to be "the plague of our time" (Edelstein, 1988).

CLASSIFICATION OF AIR TOXICS

There are three major criteria for a compound to be included under the heading of "toxic air pollutant":

131

1. It is measurable in the air.
2. It is for the most part produced by the activities of man.
3. It is not a primary air quality pollutant as currently defined by the United States Environmental Protection Agency (EPA).

There are literally over a thousand candidate TAP chemicals that fit the above categories that are used commercially in the United States and emitted into the atmosphere. An estimated 70,000 chemicals are in regular use in the United States and another thousand are added every year. This includes one billion pounds of pesticides, herbicides, and fungicides that are used everyday in the United States. Beyond the toxic exposure due to the manufacture, transportation, storage, and use of these materials, this country generates between 255 million and 275 million metric tons of hazardous waste annually, of which as much as 90 percent may be improperly disposed of. Some facts about the causes of residential toxic exposure are provided below (Edelstein, 1988).

1. There are some 600,000 contaminated sites in the country.
2. There are some 400,000 municipal landfills.
3. There are more than 100,000 liquid waste impoundments.
4. There are millions of septic tanks.
5. There are hundreds of thousands of deep-well injection sites.
6. Some 300,000 leaking underground storage tanks threaten groundwater.

Toxic air pollutants need to be prioritized based on risk analysis, so that those posing the greatest threats to health can be regulated. A risk analysis is the scientific activity of evaluating the toxic properties of a chemical and the conditions of human exposure to it in order to determine the extent to which exposed humans will be adversely affected, and to characterize the nature of the effects that they may experience (Holmes, Singh, & Theodore, 1993). The risk analysis may contain some or all of the following four steps:

1. Hazard identification—The determination of whether a particular chemical is or is not casually linked to particular health effects.
2. Dose response assessment—The determination of the relation between the magnitude of exposure and the profitability of occurrence of the health effects in question.
3. Exposure assessment—The determination of the extent of human exposure.
4. Risk characterization—The description of the nature and often the magnitude of human risk.

Once completed, the risk analysis should be a significant aid in determining the potential risks associated with TAPs. A more detailed presentation on risk analysis can be found in Chapter 35.

CAUSES OF TOXIC AIR POLLUTION

Industrial success commonly results in relatively high population density and has produced the problems of air, water, and soil pollution. Petrochemical facilities, motor vehicles, metal processing industries, and home space heaters are just a few of the many pollution sources that have led to contamination in the environment. Toxic organic compound emission sources can be categorized into seven major source groupings:

1. Process sources (chemical production)
2. Fugitive sources—All on-site emissions resulting from leaks in pumps, valves, flanges, and similar connections
3. Storage tanks
4. Transport—Usually by railcars or trucks
5. Surface coating—Paints and coatings
6. Other solvent use—Degreasing, dry cleaning, and printing
7. Nonindustrial sources—Motor vehicles

There are three types of TAP emissions: continuous, intermittent, and accidental. Both routine emissions associated with a batch process or a continuous process that is operated only occasionally can be intermittent sources. An example of an accidental emission was the release of methyl isocyanate in Bhopal, India.

Many of the modern industrial and commercial processes utilized by society involve the application of organic solvents. Through the transport, storage, transfer, and use of these materials, releases can occur into the atmosphere. In addition, the use of liquid fuels by motor vehicles can also result in evaporative and tailpipe losses of organic substances to the air environment. A significant quantity of the organic materials emitted into the atmosphere as solvents or through the use of liquid fuels can be classified as volatile organic compounds (VOCs). VOCs are widely used in industrial and commercial operations, and they play an important role in the formation of ozone and smog aerosols. Ozone (O_3) is the most powerful oxidizing agent among common pollutant gases and is known to be highly toxic.

The atmosphere is the medium by which air pollutants are transported away from their sources of emission. The most important parameter in the movement of pollutants by the atmosphere is the wind. Meteorological conditions will affect the levels of pollutants accumulated in the atmosphere. The greater the wind speed, the greater the turbulence and the more rapid and complete is the dispersion of pollutants in the atmosphere. Atmospheric dispersion, however, does not remove air pollution, but merely dilutes it through an increasing volume (McKenna, Mycock, & Theodore) (see also Chapter 10).

Polluted air environments, community or industrial, usually contain complex and ever-changing mixtures of contaminants, not all of which can be monitored adequately. The elimination of, or large reductions in, air pollution can only be accomplished by controlling the sources of emission. When a potential emission is suspected of being extremely toxic or containing a cancer-suspect material, exceptional measures are needed in the control strategy. Hazardous and toxic chemicals may require removal down to levels of a few ppmv (parts per million by volume). Two basic approaches are available for removing hazardous and volatile organics from vent streams. The pollutant may be recovered in concentrated form for use in the process or used for process heat. The other approach is to destroy the toxic material before it reaches the atmosphere. Five control methods make up the most common methods for controlling hazardous pollutants: absorption, adsorption, condensation, chemical reaction, and incineration. It is possible to combine two or more of these methods to achieve a desired goal. The selection of the best method will depend on effluent quantity, pollutant concentration, required efficiency, desired ultimate disposal, economic factors, and chemical and physical characteristics of the stream.

IMPACTS OF TOXIC AIR POLLUTION

Basic air pollutant toxicology, or the science that treats the origins of toxics, must be considered in terms of entering the body through inhalation. This makes the respiratory tract the first site of attack. Among the primary air pollutants, only lead and carbon monoxide exert their major effects beyond the lung. The more reactive a compound, the less likely it is to penetrate the lung. However, many individuals breathe a mixture of air contaminants, and many of the TAP compounds are known to cause cancer. The total nationwide cancer incidence due to outdoor concentrations of air toxics in the United States was estimated to range from approximately 1700 to 2700 excess cancer cases per year. This is roughly equivalent to between 7 and 11 annual cancer cases per million population (data obtained from a 1986 population of 240 million). The EPA initiated a broad "scoping" study with a goal of gaining a better understanding of the size and causes of the health problems caused by outdoor exposure to air toxics. This broad scoping study was referred to as the Six-Month Study. The objective was to assess the magnitude and nature of the air toxics problem by developing quantitative estimates of the cancer risks posed by selected air pollutants and their sources from a national and regional perspective. The main conclusion of the Six-Month Study was that the air toxics problem is widely thought to be related to the elevated cancer mortality. Table 12–1 provides a summary of the estimated annual cancer cases by pollutant (EPA, 1990).

Table 12–1.   Summary of Estimated Annual Cancer Cases by Pollutant

Pollutant	EPA Classification[a]	Estimated Annual Cancer Cases
1. Acrylonitrile	B	113
2. Arsenic	A	68
3. Asbestos	A	88
4. Benzene	A	181
5. 1,3-Butadiene	B	2266
6. Cadmium	B	110
7. Carbon tetrachloride	B	241
8. Chloroform	B	2115
9. Chromium (hexavalent)	A	147–265
10. Coke oven emissions	A	7
11. Dioxin	B	22–125
12. Ethylene dibromide	B	268
13. Ethyl dichloride	B	245
14. Ethlene oxide	B	1–26
15. Formaldehyde	B	1124
16. Gasoline vapors	B	219–276
17. Hexachlorobutadiene	C	9
18. Hydrazine	B	26
19. Methylene chloride	B	25

20. Perchloroethylene	B	26
21. PIC[b]		438–1120
22. Radionuclides	A	3
23. Radon[c]	A	2
24. Trichloroethylene	B	27
25. Vinyl chloride	A	25
26. Vinylidene chloride	C	10
27. Miscellaneous[d]		15
Totals		1726–2706

[a]For a discussion of how EPA evaluates suspect carcinogens and more information on these classifications, refer to "Guidelines for Carcinogen Risk Assessment" (51 Federal Register 33992).
[b]EPA has not developed a classification for the group of pollutants that compose products of incomplete combustion (PIC), although EPA has developed a classification for some components, such as benzo(a)pyrene (BaP), which is a B2 pollutant.
[c]From sources emitting significant amounts of radionuclides (and radon) to outdoor air. Does not include exposure to indoor concentrations of radon due to radon in soil gases entering homes through foundations and cellars.
[d]Includes approximately 68 other individual pollutants, primarily from the TSDF study and the Sewage Sludge Incinerator study.

The EPA classifications used in this report are: A = proven human carcinogen; B = probable human carcinogen (B1 indicates limited evidence from human studies and sufficient evidence from animal studies; B2 indicates sufficient evidence from animal studies, but inadequate evidence from human studies); C = possible human carcinogen.

Toxic exposures during a disaster, such as Love Canal, or Bhopal, India, can occur in three stages:

1. Predisaster stages: origin and incubation—During the incubation stage, the community is unaware that the disaster is developing. Therefore, there are no preparations.
2. Disaster stages: discovery, acceptance, community action—The community, defined by the pollution boundaries, becomes isolated from its surroundings.
3. Postdisaster stages: mitigation and lasting impacts—Toxic exposure may be chronic and indefinite. A site may be contaminated so that it will remain unsafe for generations due to the persistence of the toxic hazard. Recovery is difficult.

RESPONSE TO TOXIC EXPOSURE

With the discovery and announcement of contamination, toxic victims suddenly find themselves in a complicated institutional complex made up of the various local, state, and federal agencies having control over their contamination incident. Their lives are, in a sense, captured by agencies upon which they become dependent for clarification and assistance.

As a result of the accident at Bhopal, the U.S. Congress created Title III, a free-standing statute included in the Superfund Amendments and Reauthorization Act (SARA) of 1986. Title III provides a mechanism by which the public can be informed of the existence, quantities, and releases of toxic substances, and requires the states to develop plans to respond to accidental releases of these substances. Further, it requires anyone releasing specific toxic chemicals above a certain threshold amount to annually submit a toxic chemical release inventory (TRI) form to the EPA. At present, there are 308 specific chemicals subject to Title III regulation.

In the 1970 Clean Air Act (CAA) Amendments, the U.S. Congress established a program that was to regulate a category of pollutants that it considered to be more hazardous or more toxic than those regulated by the application of air quality standards. The hazardous air pollutant (HAP) concept recognized a need to regulate pollutants that were unique because of the nature of their toxic or hazardous properties and the localized contamination problems they posed. The 1970 CAA required that the EPA provide an ample margin of safety to protect against hazardous air pollutants by establishing national emissions standards for hazardous air pollutants (NESHAP). However, in actual practice, the designation and subsequent regulation of hazardous pollutants has been very slow. Initially three pollutants (asbestos, mercury, and beryllium) were designated and regulated in the 1970s. After a considerable pause, the EPA assigned regulations for vinyl chloride, benzene, radioactive isotopes, and arsenic. From 1970 to 1990, over fifty chemicals were considered for designation as hazardous air pollutants, but the EPA's review process was completed for only twenty-eight chemicals. In a period of twenty years, the EPA was only able to designate and regulate NESHAPs for a total of eight substances: beryllium, mercury, vinyl chloride, asbestos, benzene, radionuclides, inorganic arsenic, and coke oven emissions.

Because the EPA was so slow in setting standards for hazardous air pollutants, many states had gone their own ways in regulating air toxics. States developed and implemented their own TAP control programs. Such programs, as well as the pollutants they regulate, differ widely from state to state. Up until 1990, state agencies had established some type of emission standard for over 800 toxic chemicals. The slow federal pace in regulating air toxics was in part due to the fact that the EPA, under NESHAP provisions, was required, in setting emission standards, to provide an ample margin of safety. Because many air toxics are carcinogenic, the EPA has at various times interpreted the statutory language of the 1970 CAA amendments as requiring an emission standard of zero for carcinogens. It was therefore reluctant to regulate emissions of economically important substances that are potentially carcinogenic in humans because such regulation could have required a total ban on their production (Godish, 1991).

The 1990 CAA amendments deal with the problem of hazardous air pollutants or air toxics in a substantial way. Congress lists approximately 190 toxic pollutants for which the EPA is to designate emission standards by enforcing maximum achievable control technologies (MACT). The amendments mandate that the EPA issue MACT standards for all sources of the 190 substances in phased stages by the year 2000. These are pollutants that are known to be, or reasonably anticipated to be, carcinogenic, mutagenic, teratogenic, neurotoxic, cause reproductive dysfunctions, or are acutely or chronically toxic. In addition, the EPA must determine the risk remaining after MACT is in place and develop health-based standards that would limit the cancer risk to one case in one million exposures. Emission standards are intended to achieve maximum reduction taking into account the cost of control measures. The benchmark for gaseous air toxics is a 90 percent average reduction.

FUTURE TRENDS

The use of solvents that are integral to many chemical process industry operations are changing. Industry and regulatory players are rethinking solvent processes, compounds, and equipment. Regulations are targeting industries such as food processing, wastewater treatment, electronics manufacturing, and forest products processing. New adsorbents, catalysts, and recovery systems have been added to the arsenal of control technologies for these hazardous solvents. New and redesigned systems are promising even more less expensive choices in the years ahead. Volatiles can be burned in order to provide extra energy or they can be recycled for resale. In the case of halogenated organics, the use of catalytic systems is allowing for safer incineration of these compounds. Over the last decade and in the decades to come, regulations and economics will continue to drive the increased use of technology to control toxic pollutants.

In addition to improved control technologies, the future is certain to find widespread use of pollution prevention principles (see Part VII) for managing air toxics. These include:

1. Retrofit, don't change, a process—Many units can be retrofitted to reduce emissions and solvent use.
2. Reuse waste solvents—High-quality solvents are used once for precision cleaning and are then disposed of. They can often be reused, untreated, for applications that require lower standards of purity, such as general purpose cleaning.
3. Use replacement solvents.
4. Make a process solventless.

SUMMARY

1. Pollutants that have some potential to adversely affect human health at certain concentrations are known as toxic air pollutants (TAPs), or air toxics.

2. There are three major criteria for a compound to be included under the heading of toxic air pollutant and over a thousand candidate TAP chemicals that fit these criteria.

3. Industrial success has mainly produced the problems of air, water, and soil pollution. Toxic organic compound emission sources can be categorized into seven major source groupings with three types of TAP emissions.

4. Many of the TAP compounds are known to cause cancer. The air toxics problem is widely thought to be related to the elevated cancer mortality.

5. Toxic victims suddenly find themselves in a complex institutional context made up of the various local, state, and federal agencies having control over their contamination incident.

6. The use of solvents that are integral to many chemical process industries are changing. New and redesigned systems are promising less expensive choices in the years ahead.

REFERENCES

Belmonte, P., and Theodore, L. *Introduction to Air Toxics,* in preparation.

Edelstein, M. *Contaminated Communities.* London: Westview Press, 1988.

EPA. *Cancer Risk from Outdoor Exposure to Air Toxics.* Washington, DC: Author unknown, 1990.

EPA, Air Pollution Training Institute. *Introduction to Air Toxics—Reference Manual,* Research Triangle Park, NC, 1981.

Godish, T. *Air Quality,* 2nd ed., Boca Raton, FL: Lewis Publishers, 1991.

Holmes, G., Singh, B., and Theodore, L. *Handbook of Environmental Management and Technology.* New York: John Wiley & Sons, 1993.

McKenna, J., Mycock, J., Theodore, L. *Handbook of Air Pollution Control Technology.* Boca Raton, FL: Lewis Publishers, 1995.

Part III

Water

Part III of this book serves as an introduction to water pollution. Three chapters comprise Part III. Chapter 13 is concerned with industrial water pollution control equipment. A reasonably comprehensive examination of municipal water pollution control equipment is provided in Chapter 14. Part III concludes with Chapter 15, which addresses the general subject of dispersion modeling in water systems.

13

Industrial Wastewater Management

INTRODUCTION

Clean water is a resource that has been taken for granted. Pure water is often necessary for growing food, manufacturing goods, disposing of wastes, and for consumption. Water conservation is most frequently thought of as a measure to protect against water shortages. While protecting water supplies is an excellent reason to practice conservation, there is another important benefit of water conservation—improved water quality.

The link between water use and water pollution may not be immediately apparent, yet water use is a considerable source of pollution to waste systems. When water is used for household, industrial, agricultural, or other purposes, it is almost always degraded and polluted in the process. Called wastewater, this byproduct of human and industrial activities may carry nutrients, biological and chemical contaminants, floating wastes, or other pollutants. Upon discharge, wastewater ultimately finds its way into groundwater or surface waters, contributing to their pollution.

Every day United States industry discharges billions of gallons of wastewater generated by industrial processes. This liquid waste stream often contains many toxic metals and organic pollutants. Unfortunately, the discharge point for a large portion of these industries is frequently a municipal sewer system that leads to a publicly owned treatment works (POTW). It is estimated that roughly 60 percent of the total toxic metals and organics discharged by industry winds up at municipal treatment plants.

This flood of toxic wastewater described above varies from day to day, and from region to region. Its principal pollutants are toxic metals and organic chemicals. Some important toxic metals are lead, zinc, copper, chromium, cadmium, mercury, and nickel. Toxic organics include benzene, toluene, and trichloroethylene. Each of these substances, to a greater or lesser degree, is known to be harmful to human health. Many are toxic to aquatic life as well.

The consequences of these wastewater discharges have been severe. It is estimated that 14,000 miles of stream in thirty-nine states have been polluted by toxic substances. It is also estimated that over a half million acres of lakes in sixteen states and nearly 1,000 square miles of estuaries in eight states have been adversely affected.

Industries that send their wastes to POTWs are known as "indirect dischargers;" that is because their discharges enter America's surface waters by an indirect route via municipal sewage treatment works. Direct dischargers, on the other hand, are industries that release their treated wastewater directly to surface waters.

Another area of concern is groundwater pollution. A few years ago this was almost an unknown problem. Today, groundwater is one of the major environmental areas of concern. Some of the reasons are detailed in the next three paragraphs.

Groundwater is that part of the underground water that is below the water table. Groundwater is in the zone of saturation within which all the pore spaces of rock materials are filled with water. The United States has approximately 15 quadrillion gallons of water stored in its groundwater systems within one half mile of the surface.

Annual groundwater withdrawals in the United States are on the order of 90 billion gallons per day, which is only a fraction of the total estimated water in storage. This represents about a threefold increase in American groundwater usage since 1950. Most of this is replenished through rainfall and offsets the hydraulic effects of pumpage, except in some heavily pumped, arid regions of the Southwest. American groundwater use is expected to rise in the future. Public drinking water accounts for 14 percent of groundwater use. Agricultural uses, such as irrigation (67 percent) and water for rural households and livestock (6 percent), account for 73 percent of groundwater usage. Self-supplied industrial water accounts for the remaining U.S. groundwater use. Approximately 50 percent of all Americans obtain all or part of their drinking water from groundwater sources.

The richest reserves of American groundwater are in the mid-Atlantic coastal region, the Gulf Coast states, the Great Plains, and the Great Valley of California. The Ogallala aquifer, which extends from the southern edge of North Dakota southwestward to the Texas and New Mexico border, is the single largest American aquifer in terms of geographical area. The most important American aquifer in agricultural terms is the large unconsolidated aquifer underlying the Great Valley of California. The most important groundwater sources of public drinking water are the aquifers of Long Island, New York, which have the highest per capita usage concentration in the United States.

Six areas of interest need to be addressed in order to obtain a clear picture of industrial wastewater management objectives and solutions. These include:

Regulations
Sources of industrial wastewater pollution
Industrial wastewater characterization
Nonpoint source water pollution
Wastewater treatment technologies
Future trends

These areas of concern will serve as the major focus for this chapter. Details of municipal wastewater management can be found in the next chapter. Some overlap exists because of the complimentary nature of the two chapters.

REGULATIONS

Beginning in the 1970s, several pieces of legislation were designed to address the increasing wastewater crisis. The EPA was given the authority to promulgate and enforce the various regulations that were derived from: the Federal Water Pollution Control Act, as amended (1972); The Clean Water Act Amendments (1977); the Resource Conservation and Recovery Act (1976), and; the Toxic Substances Control Act (1977). Specific industry pretreatment regulations were also promulgated by the EPA in the early 1980s that limited the discharge concentrations of targeted pollutant parameters (Holmes, Singh, & Theodore, 1993).

Congress enacted the Clean Water Act to "restore and maintain the chemical, physical, and biological integrity of the Nation's waters." Section 404, one of the key sections of the Clean Water Act, regulates the discharge of dredged and fill material into waters of the United States, and establishes a permit program to ensure that such discharges comply with environmental requirements. The Section 404 program is administered at the federal level by the United States Army Corps of Engineers (Corps) and the EPA. The United States Fish and Wildlife Service (FWS) and the National Marine Fisheries Service (NMFS) have important advisory roles. The Corps has the primary responsibility for the permit program and is authorized, after notice and opportunity for a public hearing, to issue permits for the discharge of dredged or fill material. States can assume a portion of the permitting program from the federal government (for some waters only), but there has been limited interest by the states. EPA has primary roles in several aspects of the Section 404 program including development of the environmental guidelines by which permit applications must be evaluated; review of proposed permits; prohibition of discharges with unacceptable adverse impacts; approval and oversight of state assumption of the program; establishment of jurisdictional scope of waters of the United States; and interpretation of Section 404 exemptions. Enforcement authority is shared between EPA and the Corps.

Waters of the United States protected by the Clean Water Act include rivers, streams, estuaries, the territorial seas, and most ponds, lakes and wetlands. The term wetlands includes swamps, marshes, bogs, and similar areas. Wetlands are a particularly important and sensitive segment of the nation's waters, and, therefore, have merited special attention. Wetlands provide a critical habitat for many important species of fish and wildlife, and export plant particles (called detritus) that serve as food for aquatic organism in adjacent waters. Peak floodwaters are absorbed by wetlands, reducing damage to downstream property—often farms and municipalities. Water quality is improved as a result of a number of natural processes that remove pollutants from water flowing through wetlands. In addition, aesthetic, recreational, scientific, and educational values are provided by these natural aquatic areas.

At the time of the writing of this chapter, revisions to the Safe Drinking Water Act recently approved by the Senate marked a significant change in at least one branch of Congress' reaction to environmental problems. The bill, S. 2019, would give the EPA and state governments more flexibility in addressing water contamination problems as opposed to the usual response of mandating ever more specific criteria for solving them (*Chemical and Engineering News,* 1994).

SOURCES OF INDUSTRIAL WASTEWATER POLLUTION

There are literally thousands of industrial sources that contribute to the wastewater pollution problem. Some of the major industrial wastewater contributors are listed as follows:

Textile	Tannery
Laundry	Cannery
Dairy	Brewery, Distillery, and Winery
Pharmaceutical	Meat Packing, Rendering, and Poultry
Beet Sugar	Food Processing
Wood Fiber	Metal
Liquid Material	Chemical
Energy	Nuclear Power

The reader should note that within each industry listed above, a variety of wastes are generated. For example, the chemical industry produces the following wastes:

Acids	Phosphates
Soaps and detergents	Explosives
Formaldehyde	Pesticides
Plastics and resins	Fertilizers
Toxic chemicals	Mortuary science wastes
Hospital and laboratory wastes	Polychlorinated biphenyls
Chloralkali wastes	Organic chemicals (in general)

Extensive details regarding the types and levels of pollutants discharged from these industries are available in the literature (Nemerow & Dasgupta, 1991).

INDUSTRIAL WASTEWATER CHARACTERIZATION

The characteristics of wastewater having readily definable effects on water systems and treatment plants can be classified as follows:

1. Biochemical oxygen demand (BOD)
2. Suspended solids
3. Floating and colored materials
4. Volume
5. Other harmful constituents

Biochemical oxygen demand is defined as the amount of oxygen required by living organisms engaged in the utilization and stabilization of the organic matter present. Standard tests are conducted at 20°C with a five-day incubation period. BOD is usually exerted by dissolved and colloidal organic matter and imposes a load on the biological units of the treatment plant. Oxygen must be provided so that bacteria can grow and oxidize the organic matter. An added BOD load, caused by an increase in organic waste, requires more bacterial activity, more oxygen, and greater biological-unit capacity for its treatment. Two other tests are generally used to estimate waste organic content: total organic carbon (TOC) and chemical oxygen demand (COD). TOC and COD are primary measures of total organic content, a portion of which may not be removed by biological treatment means.

Suspended solids are found in considerable quantity in many industrial wastes, such as cannery and paper mill effluents. They are screened and/or settled out of the sewage at the disposal plant. Solids removed by settling and separated from the flowing sewage are called sludge. Suspended solids settle to the bottom or wash up on the banks and decompose, causing odors and depleting oxygen in the river water. Fish often die because of a sudden lowering of the oxygen content of a stream, and solids that settle to the bottom will cover their spawning grounds and inhibit propagation. Visible sludge creates unsightly conditions and destroys the use of a river for recreational purposes.

Floating solids and liquids include oils, greases, and other materials that float on the surface; they not only make the river unsightly but also obstruct passage of light through the water, retarding the growth of vital plant food.

Color—contributed by textile and paper mills, tanneries, slaughterhouses and other industries—is an indicator of pollution. Compounds present in wastewaters absorb certain wavelengths of light and reflect the remainder, a fact generally conceded to account for color development of streams. Color interferes with the transmission of sunlight into the stream and therefore lessens photosynthetic actions (Nemerow & Dasgupta, 1991).

A sewage plant can handle a large volume of flow if its units are sufficiently designed. Unfortunately, most sewage plants are already in operation when a request comes to accept the flow of waste from some new industrial concern.

Finally, other harmful constituents in industrial wastes can cause problems. Some problem areas and corresponding effects are:

1. Toxic metal ions that interfere with biological oxidation.
2. Feathers that clog nozzles, overload digesters, and impede proper pump operation.
3. Rags that clog pumps and valves and interfere with proper operation.
4. Acids and alkalis that may corrode pipes, pumps, and treatment units, interfere with settling, upset the biological purification of sewage, release odors, and intensify color.
5. Flammables that cause fires and may lead to explosions.
6. Pieces of fat that clog nozzles and pumps and overload digesters.
7. Noxious gases that present a direct danger to workers.
8. Detergents that cause foaming.
9. Phenols and other toxic organic material.

NONPOINT SOURCE WATER POLLUTION*

In this period of public skepticism over government's ability to solve problems, the results of the Clean Water Act stand as a refreshing counterpoint. By many indicators, this legislation—and the programs it has generated—must be counted as a major success.

Gross pollution of the nation's rivers, lakes, and coastal waters by sewage and industrial wastes is largely a thing of the past. Fish have returned to waters that were once depleted of life-giving oxygen. Swimming and other water-contact sports are again permitted in rivers, in lakes, and at ocean beaches that once were closed by health officials. This success, however, is at best only a partial one. Water pollution remains a serious problem in most parts of the country. Sediment, nutrients, pathogenic organisms, and toxics still find their way into the nation's waters, where they degrade the ecosystem, pose health hazards, and impair the full use of water resources.

It is clear that this success in combatting the gross pollution of yesteryear—however incomplete—is largely the result of tackling the easy things first. This approach has, in large part, brought under control the so-called point sources of pollution. These include municipal and industrial outfalls and other sources that are clearly identified with a well-defined location or place. Government, by requiring permits to operate such facilities, has created a mechanism whereby control technology—such as a waste treatment plant—can be mandated, and the effect of such technology can be monitored.

It is equally clear that to continue the progress made over the past two decades, efforts must now focus on "nonpoint-source" (NPS) pollution. The task of controlling NPS pollution is in many respects more difficult than controlling pollution from point sources, and requires different control strategies.

Nonpoint-source pollution—unlike pollution from point sources—is quite diffuse, both in terms of its origin and in the manner in which it enters ground and surface waters. It results from a variety of human activities that take place over a wide geographic area, perhaps many hundreds or even thousands of acres. Unlike pollutants from point sources—which enter the environment at well-defined locations and in a relatively even, continuous discharge—pollutants from nonpoint sources usually find their way into surface and groundwaters in sudden surges, often in large quantities, and are associated with rainfall, thunderstorms, or snowmelt. Seven of the most significant sources of NPS pollution are described below (*EPA Journal*, 1991)

1. Agriculture: From 50 to 70 percent of impaired or threatened surface waters are affected by NPS pollution from agricultural activities. Pollutants include sediments from eroded croplands and overgrazed pastures; fertilizers or nutrients, which promote excessive growth of aquatic plants and contamination of ground water by nitrate; animal waste from confined animal facilities, which contains nutrients and bacteria that can cause shellfish bed closures and fish kills; and pesticides, which can be toxic to aquatic life as well as to humans.

2. Urban runoff: Pollutants carried by runoff from such urban artifacts as streets and roadways, commercial and industrial sites, and parking lots affect between 5 to 15 percent of surface waters. Urban runoff contains salts and oily residues from road surfaces and may include a variety

*Information for this section was taken from the *EPA Journal*, November/December 1991.

of nutrients and toxics as well. Elevated temperatures—which are typical of urban runoff—can result in "thermal pollution," contributing to higher-than-normal temperatures in nearby streams, reservoirs, or lakes.

3. Hydromodification: Engineering projects, such as reservoir or dam construction, stream channelization, and flood prevention will inevitably result in changes in water flow patterns. When such changes occur, there is often an increase in sediment deposits. By modifying habitat, such projects may adversely affect aquatic life. Between 5 and 15 percent of surface waters in the United States are estimated to be affected by hydromodification.

4. Abandoned mines and other past resource-extraction operations: Up to 10 percent of surface waters are adversely affected by acid drainage from abandoned mines, pollution from mill tailings and mining waste piles, and pollution from improperly sealed oil and gas wells.

5. Silviculture: Pollution associated with commercial timber cutting and other forestry operations affects up to 5 percent of surface waters. Erosion from deforested lands, and particularly debris from eroded surfaces of logging roads, produces large amounts of sediment that ultimately finds its way into streams and lakes. Habitat altered by logging can adversely affect a wide range of plant and animal species.

6. Construction: New building and major land development projects, including highway construction, produce sediment and toxic materials that have been estimated to degrade up to 5 percent of the nation's surface waters.

7. Land disposal: Between 1 and 5 percent of the nation's surface waters are affected by disposal of waste on land—largely leakage from septic tanks and the spreading of sewage sludge.

WASTEWATER TREATMENT TECHNOLOGIES

Numerous technologies exist for treating industrial wastewater. These technologies range from simple clarification in a settling pond to a complex system of advanced technologies requiring sophisticated equipment and skilled operators. Finding the proper technology or combination of technologies to treat a particular wastewater to meet federal and local requirements and still be cost effective can be a challenging task (Holmes et al., 1993; Jeris, 1992).

Treatment technologies can be divided into three broad categories: physical, chemical, and biological. Many treatment processes combine two or all three categories to provide the most economical treatment. There are a multitude of treatment technologies for each of these categories. Although the technologies selected for discussion below are among the most widespread employed for industrial wastewater treatment, they represent only a fraction of the available technologies.

Two physical treatment processes are clarification or sedimentation and flotation. When an industrial wastewater containing a suspension of solid particles that have a higher specific gravity than the transporting liquid is in a relatively calm state, the particles will settle out because of the effects of gravity. This process of separating the settleable solids from the liquid is called clarification or sedimentation. In some treatment systems employing two or more stages of treatment and clarification, the terms primary, secondary, and final clarification are used. Primary clarification is the term normally used for the first clarification process in the system. This process is used to remove the readily settleable solids prior to subsequent treatment processes, particularly biological treatment. This treatment step results in significantly lower pollutant loadings to downstream processes and is appropriate for industrial wastewaters containing a high suspended solids content. Flotation, as opposed to clarification, which separates suspended particles from liquids by gravitational forces, accomplishes this operation because of their density difference by the introduction of air into the system. Fine bubbles adhere to, or are absorbed by, the solids, which are then lifted to the surface (Holmes et al., 1993; Jeris, 1992).

Two chemical treatment processes include coagulation-precipitation and neutralization. Often the nature of an industrial wastewater is such that the conventional physical treatment methods described in the previous paragraph will not provide an adequate level of treatment. Particularly, ordinary settling or flotation processes will not remove ultrafine colloidal particles and metal ions. Therefore, to adequately treat these particles in industrial wastewaters, coagulation-precipitation may be warranted. Rapid mixing is employed to ensure that the chemicals are thoroughly dispersed throughout the wastewater flow for uniform treatment. The wastewater then undergoes flocculation which provides for particle contact, so that the particles can agglomerate to a size large enough for removal. The final part of this technology involves precipitation. This is effectively the same as settling and thus can be performed in a unit similar to a clarifier. Neutralization is often required because coagulation-precipitation is capable of removing pollutants such as BOD, COD, and TSS from industrial wastewater. In addition, depending upon the specifics of the wastewater being treated, coagulation-precipitation can remove additional pollutants such as phosphorus, nitrogen compounds, and metals. This technology is attractive to industry because a high degree of classifiable and toxic pollutants removal can be combined in one treatment process. A disadvantage of this process is the substantial quantity of sludge generated, which presents a sludge disposal problem.

Highly acidic or basic wastewaters are undesirable. They can adversely impact the aquatic life in receiving waters. In addition, they might significantly affect the performance of downstream treatment processes at the plant site or at a publicly owned treatment works. Therefore, in order to rectify these potential problems, one of the most fundamental treatment technologies, neutralization, is employed at industrial facilities. Neutralization involves adding an acid or a base to a wastewater to offset or neutralize the effects of its counterpart in the wastewater flow, namely, adding acids to alkaline wastewaters and bases to acidic wastewaters (Jeris, 1992).

The most appropriate industrial treatment technology for removing oxygen-demanding pollutants is biological treatment. Biological treatment processes frequently used in the industrial field include: aerobic suspended growth processes (activated sludge), aerobic contact processes, aerated lagoons (stabilization ponds), and anaerobic lagoons. An aerobic suspended growth process (activated sludge) is one in which the biological growth products (micro-organisms) are kept in suspension in a turbulent liquid medium consisting of entrapped and suspended colloidal and dissolved organic and inorganic materials. This biological process uses the metabolic reactions of the microorganisms to attain an acceptable effluent quality by removing those substances exerting an oxygen demand. An aerobic attached growth process is one in which the biological growth products (microorganisms) are attached to some type of medium (i.e., rock, plastic sheets, plastic rings, etc.), and where either the wastewater trickles over the surface or the medium is rotated through the wastewater. The process is related to the aerobic suspended growth process in that both depend upon biochemical oxidation of organic matter in the wastewater to carbon dioxide, with a portion oxidized for energy to sustain and promote the growth of microorganisms (Jeris, 1992). Aerobic lagoons (stabilization ponds) are large, shallow earthen basins that are used for wastewater treatment by utilizing natural processes involving both algae and bacteria. The objective is microbial conversion of organic wastes into algae. Aerobic conditions prevail throughout the process. Finally, anaerobic lagoons are earthen ponds built with a small surface area and a deep liquid depth of eight to twenty feet. Usually these lagoons are anaerobic throughout their depth, except for an extremely shallow surface zone.

The development of advanced treatment technologies, along with an increasing scarcity of fresh water, has led to marked changes in effluent management. Numerous strategies for purified wastewater reuse are presently being employed in ways appropriate to the particular industrial operation. The combination of scarcity of water with increasingly stiff regulations has made effluent disposal into natural receiving bodies the option of last resort (Holmes et al., 1993).

FUTURE TRENDS

Today, considerable effort is being expended toward investigating and cleaning up some of the past mistakes, especially those involving hazardous wastes, that have led to the contamination of water supplies. These activities, however, must be matched in the future by the equally important effort of preventing water pollution in the first place. Because of the diverse nature of sources of contamination and their widespread occurrence, much of the responsibility for protecting water resources must be left to state and local agencies. This is especially true because programs to protect water quality will not be successful unless they reflect the close relationship of the land, groundwater, and surface water.

Society is still learning more and more each year about the impact that various sources of contamination can have on water. In fact, the emphasis on which source or area to concentrate regulatory efforts has changed drastically over the past two decades. Thus, there is a critical need to give water resource protection the high national priority that it deserves and to encourage federal, state and local agencies to develop the required strategies and programs to carry out this effort.

SUMMARY

1. Clean water is a resource that has been taken for granted. Pure water is necessary for growing food, manufacturing goods, disposing of wastes, and for consumption.

2. Congress enacted the Clean Water Act to "restore and maintain the chemical, physical, and biological integrity of the Nation's waters." Waters of the United States protected by the Clean Water Act include rivers, streams, estuaries, the territorial seas, and most ponds, lakes, and wetlands.

3. There are literally thousands of industrial sources that contribute to the wastewater pollution problem.

4. The characteristics of wastewater having readily definable effects on water systems and treatment plants can be classified as follows:

    a. biochemical oxygen demand (BOD)

    b. suspended solids

    c. floating and colored materials

    d. volume

    e. other harmful constituents

5. Unlike pollutants from point sources—which enter the environment at well-defined locations and in relatively even, continuous discharges—pollutants from nonpoint sources usually find their way into surface and groundwaters in sudden surges, often in large quantities, and are associated with rainfall, thunderstorms, or snowmelt.

6. Treatment technologies can be divided into three broad categories: physical, chemical, and biological. Many treatment processes combine two or all three categories to provide the most economical treatment.

7. Society is still learning more and more each year about the various sources of contamination can have on water.

REFERENCES

Chemical and Engineering News. "Senate! Drinking Water Act Revisions Take New Tack on Environmental Issues," June 6, 1994, 21.

EPA Journal, "NPS Pollution," 22k-1005, 17 (5), November/December, 1991.

Holmes, G., Singh, B., and Theodore, L. *Handbook of Environmental Management and Technology.* New York: Wiley-Interscience, 1993.

Lecture notes: Dr. Johnny Jeris, Manhattan College, 1992.

Nemerow, N., and Dasgupta, A. *Industrial and Hazardous Waste Treatment.* New York: Van Nostrand Reinhold, 1991.

14

Municipal Wastewater Treatment

CONTRIBUTING AUTHORS

Kevin J. Goohs and Sabrina Tran

INTRODUCTION

The portion of liquid waste produced by the human intervention with the hydologic cycle is known as wastewater. Such interventions can be the use of water for washing dishes, clothes, and automobiles; the provision of a recreational pool for public use; or the use of water by a local factory to maintain proper temperatures within their machinery. The use of water is important in each community's daily events in order to function normally and comfortably. In each case, the wastewater must be treated and disposed of, or discharged, into a naturally occurring water source (lakes, rivers, bays, etc.). Therefore, the use and disposal of water can be considered as an artificial water cycle. Wastewater is that which can be generated by the liquid wastes removed from residential, municipal, and industrial areas requiring collection, treatment, and disposal in accordance with local, state, and federal standards. However, municipal wastewater is the general term applied to the liquid collected in sanitary sewers and treated in a municipal plant and will be the focus of this chapter.

In the late 1800s, the United States gave little attention to the treatment and disposal of wastewater from communities. Large, fresh sources of potable water (suitable for human consumption) were available without any threat to human health. The impact upon the public and on the water quality from the discharge of untreated wastewater into adjacent water bodies was considered to be a minor issue. Additionally, large areas of land and water were available for all waste disposal purposes. However, during the early 1900s, parallelled by a large influx of immigrants, decreasing health conditions were attributed to the concentrated increase of raw wastewater being disposed into surrounding water bodies and the lack of fresh water used to dilute the wastewater before discharge. This led to the demand for a more effective means of wastewater management. Ultimately, the planning, design, construction, and operation of high-level wastewater treatment facilities, sanitary sewer systems, and fresh water collection systems was initiated.

Untreated wastewater is collected in sewer systems and transported underground to a treatment plant prior to disposal. Wastewater has three major characteristics of concern to a community and its surrounding environment: biological, chemical, and physical characteristics. These are discussed in the next three paragraphs.

If wastewater is allowed to accumulate, there are numerous pathogenic, disease-causing microorganisms contained within the waste that can cause outbreaks of intestinal infections within humans. Typical notified infectious diseases are cholera, typhoid, paratyphoid fever, balantiasis (dysentery), salmonellosis, and shigellosis (Holmes, Singh, & Theodore, 1993). During the writing of this chapter, 20,000 people had died of cholera in Rwanda, Africa within the time span of one week. This was due to the lack of a fresh water supply and mostly the nonexistent treatment for their waste. Shortly after this misfortune, mobile treatment facilities were made available.

The chemical characteristics that are of interest are toxic metals (cadmium, chromium, lead, and mercury) and nutrients (nitrogen, phosphorus, and carbon) being discharged into the water. Toxic metals and/or chemical compounds can cause large fish kills or can lead to the consumption of contaminated fish by humans and other mammals. The discharge of nutrients into a water body at first seems to be beneficial to the local ecology due to the production of algae and its supplement to the food chain. However, too many nutrients will produce gross masses of algae. Eventually the algae will die off and sink to the bottom of the water column forming a layer of biomass. As the algae decays (use of oxygen), the deficit of dissolved oxygen will suffocate the bottom-dwelling fish and shellfish.

The physical characteristics that are of concern to the water environment can basically be described as any organic matter entering a water source. The decomposition (biodegradation) of organic materials (suspended solids, oils, greases, and fats) in local waters occurs by using oxygen. If proper dilution of these waters is not available to accommodate decaying organic matter, the production of offensive odors and gases can occur, indicating a low to zero value for the dissolved oxygen needed for fish to survive in the water body.

For the above reasons, the treatment and disposal of wastewater from each source of generation, is imperative to satisfy those conditions that are beneficial to maintaining a healthy water supply, recreation, harvesting of fish, and future considerations. In order to assure that all oceans, lakes, rivers, bays, harbors, streams, estuaries, and so on are maintained properly, laws have been established with short- and long-term goals that provide standards for every point source of wastewater discharging into a body of water and standards for the overall quality of that water body. This maintains a watch on the quality of the water body and the quality of the treated wastewater being discharged by a municipal wastewater treatment plant. Standards are to be met in order to be given a permit to operate, otherwise each source generating wastewater will have to be upgraded before any permit is approved to operate the facility. Any delay in operation is a potential loss of tax dollars or private funds, depending upon the location.

REGULATIONS

The first water-quality standards were established in 1914 for drinking water. Surface-water standards for the control of wastewater treatment and disposal practices were not introduced until years later. With population growth and dramatic industrial expansion, the untreated wastewater discharges began to exceed the renewal capacity of the natural water body systems. Refractory compounds were often identified with the industrial and municipal waste streams. These compounds could not be removed by simple chemical treatment. As the quality of the drinking water supply became poorer, public complaints forced new legislation in the early 1960s. Initially the surface-water quality standards were established along with drinking-water standards. This was followed by the discharge limits set for those substances that were known to be dangerous to human and aquatic life.

From about the 1900s to the early 1970s, treatment objectives were concerned with:

1. The removal of suspended and floatable material
2. The removal of biodegradable organics
3. The removal of pathogenic organisms

Unfortunately, these objectives were not uniformly met throughout the United States. Perhaps the most important piece of wastewater management regulations was the Federal Water Pollution Control Act of 1972, often referred to as the Clean Water Act (CWA). It established levels of treatment, deadlines for meeting these levels, and penalties for violators. It also marked a change in water pollution control philosophy. No longer was the classification of the receiving stream of ultimate importance as it had been before. The quality of the nation's waters was to be improved by the imposition of specific effluent limitations. A National Pollution Discharge Elimination System (NPDES) program was established at that time based on uniform technological minimums with which each point source discharger had to comply (Hegewald, 1988). The permit program governs the discharge into navigable waters. The current definition of secondary treatment includes three major effluent parameters: 5-day BOD (to be discussed later), suspended solids and pH, and is reported in Table 14–1 (40 CFR, Part 133, July 1, 1988 & January 27, 1989). The secondary treatment regulations were amended further in 1989 to clarify the percent removal requirements during dry periods for treatment facilities served by combined sewers.

The Clean Water Act of 1977 contains two major provisions for the wastewater solids removed during treatment. It intended to set limits on the quantity and kind of toxic materials reaching the general public. The Resource Conservation and Recovery Act (RCRA) of 1976 requires that solid wastes be utilized or disposed of in a safe and environmentally acceptable manner. The Marine Protection, Research and Sanctuaries Act 1977 amendments prohibited disposal of sewage sludge by ocean barge dumping after December 31, 1981 (Holmes et al., 1993).

Table 14–1.   Minimum National Standards for Secondary Treatment

Characteristic of Discharge	Unit of Measurement	Average 30-Day Concentration	Average 7-Day Concentration
BOD_5	mg/L	30	45
Suspended solids	mg/L	30	45
pH	pH	6–9	6–9
Fecal coliform bacteria	mg/L	200	400

mg = microgram/Liter; L = liter

Congress also enacted the Water Quality Act of 1987 (WQA); this was the first major revision to the Clean Water Act. Its goals were to eliminate the discharge of pollutants into the nation's waters and to attain water quality capable of supporting recreation and protecting aquatic life and wildlife. Important provisions of the WQA are:

1. The strengthening of federal water quality regulations by providing changes in permitting and adding substantial penalties for permit violations.
2. Emphasizing the identification and regulation of toxic pollutants in sludge.
3. Providing funding for EPA and state studies on nonpoint toxic sources of pollution.
4. Establishing new deadlines for compliance of priorities for stormwater.

At the time of writing this chapter, the United States Senate was set to work on legislation to rewrite the Clean Water Act. Many of the lobbying groups that have a stake in clean water believe that currently proposed legislation does not meet their requirements. However, the regulated community, as any discharging industry, is concerned for its ability to maintain businesses that supply employment and provide equity for the country. The new legislation would expand the NPDES permit program to also require permits for discharges into the ground or groundwater. Although the expansion of the permit program is essentially aimed at industry and water quality standards, there is also the threat of the inability to, again, maintain a business. Many believe the new proposed legislation to be redundant. However, the more significant impact is to those operating the municipal treatment facilities. Choices about where to allocate limited funds are being forced, certainly at a cost to public health. Additional regulatory details are available in the literature (Henrichs, 1988; Office of Technology Assessment, 1987; EPA 1984).

CHARACTERISTICS OF MUNICIPAL WASTEWATER

Municipal wastewater is composed of a mixture of dissolved and particulate organic and inorganic materials and infectious disease-causing bacteria. The total amount of each parameter accumulated in wastewater is referred to as the mass loading and is given the units of pounds per day (lbs/day). The concentration, given in pounds per gallon of water (lbs/gal) of any individual component entering a wastewater treatment plant can change as a result of the activities that are producing this waste. The units used to express any concentration, lbs/gal, can also be converted into other nomenclature, such as pounds per liter of water (lbs/L), milligrams per liter of water (mg/L), or even micrograms per cubic meter of water ($\mu g/m^3$). The concentration of each individual component while in the treatment plant is usually reduced significantly by the time it reaches the end of the plant, prior to discharge.

Wastewater characteristics depend largely on the mass loading rates flowing from the various sources in the collection system. The flow in sanitary sewers is a composite of domestic and industrial wastewaters, infiltration into the sewer from cracks and leaks in the system, and intercepted flow from combined sewers. During wet weather, the addition of rainfall collected from the combined sewer system and the storm drain collection system (combined sewer overflow systems) can significantly change the characteristics of wastewater and the increased demand of how much water is to be carried by the sewer to the treatment plant. The peak flow rate can be two to three times the average dry (or sunny) weather flow rate. The mass loading rate into the plant also varies cyclically throughout the day. The impact of flow rate is an important determining factor in the design and operation of wastewater treatment plant facilities. The records kept by the treatment plant should include the minimum, average, and maximum flow values (gallons per unit time) on a hourly, daily, weekly, and monthly basis for both wet and dry weather conditions. A moving 7-day daily average flow and mass loading rate entering the plant and at various locations throughout the plant can then be computed from the record. This intricate form of recordkeeping of all factors affecting a wastewater treatment plant must be considered to assess the wastewater flow and variations of wastewater strength in order to operate a facility correctly. The parameters used to indicate the total mass loading in the wastewater entering the treatment plant are the measurements of total suspended solids (TSS), suspended solids (SS), and total dissolved solids (TDS) (Holmes, Singh, & Theodore, 1993). The parameters used to indicate the organic and inorganic chemical concentration in the wastewater are the measurements of the biological oxygen demand (BOD) and the chemical oxygen demand (COD). Both BOD and COD are discussed in more detail later in this section. Additionally, the total nutrients (carbon, nitrogen, and phosphorus), any toxic chemicals, and trace metals are also characterized prior to the wastewater entering the treatment plant so that the plant operators may adjust their treatment techniques to accommodate the varying waste loads.

Before proceeding to more technical details, some definitions and concerns in the wastewater management field are presented below.

Suspended Solids: Matter that is retained through a filter. Suspended solids can lead to the development of sludge deposits and anaerobic conditions (zero dissolved oxygen) when untreated wastewater is discharged in the aquatic environment.

Biodegradable organics: Composed principally of proteins, carbohydrates, and fats. Biodegradable organics are measured most commonly in terms of BOD and COD. If discharged untreated to the environment, their biological stabilization can lead to the depletion of natural oxygen resources and to the development of septic conditions. As indicated earlier, additional details on BOD and COD are provided later.

Pathogens: Pathogenic organisms that can transmit communicable diseases via wastewater. Typical notified infectious disease reported are cholera, typhoid, paratyphoid fever, salmonellosis, and shigellosis.

Nutrients: Both nitrogen and phosphorus, along with carbon. When discharged to the receiving water, these nutrients can lead to the growth of undesirable aquatic life. When discharged in excessive amounts on land, they can also lead to the pollution of groundwater.

Priority pollutants: Organic and inorganic compounds selected on the basis of their known or suspected carcinogenicity, mutagenicity, or high acute toxicity. Many of these compounds are found in wastewater.

Heavy metals: Heavy metals are usually added to wastewater from commercial and industrial activities and may have to be removed if the wastewater is to be reused.

Municipal wastewater normally contains approximately 99.9 percent water. The remaining materials (as described earlier) include suspended and dissolved organic and inorganic matter as well as microorganisms. These materials make up the physical, chemical, and biological qualities that are characteristic of residential and industrial waters. Each of these three qualities are briefly described in the subsections below.

Physical Quality

The physical quality of municipal wastewater is generally reported in terms of temperature, color, odor, and turbidity and is an important parameter because of its effect upon aquatic life and the amount of oxygen available for aquatic respiration. Water temperature varies slightly with the seasons, normally higher than air temperature during most of the year and lower only during the hot summer months. The color of a wastewater is usually indicative of age. Fresh wastewater is usually gray; septic wastes impart a black appearance. Odors in wastewater are caused by the decomposition of organic matter that produces offensive smelling gases such as hydrogen sulfide. Turbidity in wastewater is caused by a wide variety of suspended solids. Suspended solids are defined and can be measured as solid matter, which can be removed from water by filtration through a 1-micron pore filter paper. Volatile suspended solids for the most part represent the biodegradable organics. Suspended solids may cause undesirable conditions of increased turbidity and silt load in the receiving water. In general, stronger wastewater has higher a turbidity (Holmes et al., 1993).

Chemical Quality

The principal groups of organic substances found in municipal wastewater are proteins (30 to 40%), carbohydrates (40 to 60%), and fats and oils (15 to 25%). Carbohydrates and proteins are easily biodegradable, whereas fats and oils are more stable and require a longer exposure time to be decomposed by microorganisms. In addition, wastewater may also contain small fractions of phenolic compounds, pesticides, PCBs, dioxins, and herbicides. These compounds are usually industrial wastes, depending on their concentration and may create problems such as nonbiodegradability and carcinogenicity.

Biochemical oxygen demand (BOD) measurement is very important parameter indicating the organic (e.g., fats and oils) pollution concentration in both wastewater and surface discharge. The 5-day BOD test (BOD_5) measured at 20 °C is the most commonly used test for calculating the amount of total organic matter requiring oxygen for its decomposition. The decomposition or biodegradation is accomplished by microorganisms (bacteria and protozoa) that breathe the oxygen in the water while feeding on the amount of organic matter available to them. The BOD_5 value reflects the original organic concentration by observing a depletion of oxygen. The higher BOD content in the wastewater would result in a higher depletion of the oxygen concentration in that wastewater. Dissolved oxygen in the receiving water must be maintained at a level of 4 to 5 mg/l for the survival of aquatic life. Therefore, it is important to remove the organic matter or to decrease the BOD prior to discharge.

BOD testing is used as the sole basis to determine the efficiency of the treatment plant. There are two basic types of BOD: carbonaceous-BOD (CBOD) from the oxidation of the organic carbon sources, and nitrogenous-BOD (NBOD) from the oxidation of the organic nitrogen (nitrification). The addition of CBOD and NBOD is given the term ultimate BOD (BOD_U) and it usually takes 20 to 30 days to complete a measurement. BOD_5 is a 5-day measurement that indicates how much CBOD is utilizing a nitrification inhibitor to inhibit the oxidation of NBOD. By inhibiting one type of BOD's ability to oxidize, one may measure the other directly.

The chemical oxygen demand (COD) test is a measurement of organic matter in wastewater. It is similar to the BOD test in concept but different in the analytical procedure. It is the measurement of the amount of oxygen depleted during the chemical oxidation process, without the use of microorganisms. COD analysis is a more reproducible and less time-consuming test, approximately three hours. The COD test measures the nonbiodegradable as well as the ultimate biodegradable organics. The COD test and BOD test can be correlated and used as a controlling factor in the treatment of waste. A change in the biodegradable to nonbiodegradable organic ratio affects this correlation, and is therefore waste specific.

The most frequently found inorganic compounds in wastewater are chloride salts; acids, hydrogen ions and alkalinity-causing compounds; bases and heavy metals (cadmium, copper, lead, mercury and zinc); and nutrients for the growth of the organism in addition to the required food substrate, such as ammonia, sulfur, carbon, nitrogen and phosphorous (Holmes et al., 1993). A trace amount of metals can be toxic to the organisms in the receiving water. Excessive nutrients of nitrogen and phosphorous discharged to the receiving water can cause eutrophication, causing excessive growth of aquatic plants. As indicated earlier, aged aquatic plants later become the source of particular organic matter that settle to the bottom of the receiving water and indirectly exert an excessive demand of oxygen by their decomposition and deplete the oxygen source for other aquatic life and fish.

Gases commonly found in raw wastewater include nitrogen, oxygen, carbon dioxide, hydrogen sulfide, ammonia, and methane. Of all these gases mentioned, the ones that are most considered in the design of a treatment facility are oxygen and hydrogen sulfide. Oxygen is required for all aerobic life forms either within the treatment facility (microorganisms) or in the receiving water (aquatic life). During the absence of aerobic conditions (extreme low dissolved oxygen levels), oxidation is brought about by the reduction of inorganic salts such as sulfates or through the action of methane-forming bacteria in a treatment process known as sludge thickening. The end products are often very malodorous. To avoid such conditions it is important that an aerobic state be maintained or odor equipment be used. Additional odor control has received major consideration in recent large sized wastewater treatment facilities. Large capital investments have been made in resolving this offensive smelling issue and complaints from the neighboring residential area of the wastewater treatment plant.

Biological Quality

Within the treatment facility, the wastewater provides the perfect medium for good microbial growth, whether it be aerobic or anaerobic. Bacteria and protozoa are the keys to the biological treatment process used at most treatment facilities. In the presence of sufficient dissolved oxygen, bacteria convert the soluble organic matter into new cells and inorganic elements. This causes a reduction of organic loading through the buildup of more complex organisms (Holmes et al., 1993). The location of such microbial proliferation is the aeration tank or the activated sludge system. Although the treatment facility utilizes bacteria and protozoa to perform the breakdown of wastewater loads, these are not necessarily the same bacteria, or pathogens, mentioned earlier that cause intestinal (enteric) disease.

Water quality in a receiving body of water is strongly influenced by the biological interactions that take place. The discharged effluent to the receiving waters becomes a normal part of the biological cycle and its effect on aquatic organisms is the ultimate consideration of treatment plant operation. Typically, the species and organisms found in biological examination of the receiving waters include zooplankton, phytoplankton, peryphyton, macro-invertebrates, and fish. The quality and species of micro- and macroscopic plants and animals that make up the biological characteristics in a receiving body of water may be considered as the final test of wastewater treatment effectiveness. Because of the increasing awareness that enteric viruses can be waterborne, attempts have been made to identify and quantify virus contributions to receiving waters via wastewater treatment plants.

WASTEWATER TREATMENT PROCESSES

Wastewater treatment plants utilize a number of individual or unit operations and processes to achieve the desired degree of treatment. The collective treatment schematic is called a flow scheme, a flow diagram, or a flow sheet. Many different flow schemes can be developed from various processes for the desired level of treatment. Processes are grouped together to provide what is known as primary, secondary, and tertiary (or advanced) treatment. The term primary refers to physical unit operations. Secondary treatment refers to chemical and biological unit processes. Tertiary treatment refers to combinations of all three; this is discussed in the next section.

   Treatment methods in which the application of physical process predominate are known as physical unit operations. These were the first methods to be used for wastewater treatment. Screening, mixing, flocculation, sedimentation, flotation and thickening, and filtration are typical processes. Each of these processes removes the initial solid or total suspended solids (TSS) from the raw sewage entering the facility.

   Treatment methods in which the removal or conversion of contaminants is brought about by the addition of chemicals or by other chemical reactions are known as chemical unit processes. Precipitation, adsorption, and disinfection are the most common examples used in wastewater treatment. The first two of these processes will form a solid particle for easier removal and the subsequent is to rid the discharge of any bacteria.

   Treatment methods in which the removal of contaminants is brought about by biological activity are known as biological unit processes. Biological treatment is used primarily to remove and convert the biodegradable organic substances, colloidal or dissolved in wastewater, into gases that can escape to the atmosphere. The well-fed organisms are sequentially removed by allowing them to settle in a quiescent pond. Biological treatment can also be utilized to remove the nutrients in wastewater.

SLUDGE CHARACTERISTICS

Sludge arises when solids in the raw sewage settle prior to treatment. It can also be generated from filtration, aeration treatment, and chemical-addition sedimentation enhancement processes. The characteristics are greatly dependent on the type of treatment to which they have been subjected. Sludge typically consists of 1 to 7 percent of solids with the rest 93 to 99 percent wastewater. There are two basic types of sludge. They are settleable sludges and biological/chemical sludges. These are reviewed in the next two paragraphs.

   Settleable sludge is removed during the primary sedimentation in the primary settling tanks. It is fairly easy to manage and can be readily thickened or reduced of its water content by gravity, or can be rapidly dewatered. A higher solids capture and better dry sludge cake can be obtained with primary settleable sludge. Primary sludge production can be estimated by computing the quantity of total suspended solids (TSS) entering the primary sedimentation tanks, assuming a typical 70 percent efficiency of removal (Holmes et al., 1993). It normally is within the range of 800 to 2500 pounds per million gallons (100 to 300 mg/l) of wastewater.

The biological and chemical sludges are produced in the advanced or secondary stages of treatment, such as the activated sludge process from the aeration tanks. These sludges are more difficult to thicken; therefore, a portion of the sludge is recycled back into the activated sludge tank (aeration tank) in order to maintain a good population of microorganisms.

The quantity and nature of sludge generated relates to the characteristics of the raw wastewater and the type of process used to settle out the sludge. The operating expenses related to sludge handling can amount to one-third of the total investment of the treatment plant. Due to the high costs related to sludge operations and handling, new innovative technologies have been incorporated into producing fertilizer pellets for farming, addition to compost for the production of rich soils, and the formation of bricks for construction purposes.

FUTURE TRENDS

Advanced wastewater treatment, known as tertiary treatment, is designed to remove those constituents that may not be adequately removed by secondary treatment. This includes removal of nitrogen, phosphorus, and heavy metals.

Biological nutrient removal has received considerable attention in recent years in the inorganic constituents in the wastewater for the reasons explained above. Excessive nutrients of nitrogen and phosphorus discharge to the receiving water can lead to eutrophication, causing excessive growth of aquatic plants, and indirectly depleting oxygen sources from the aquatic life and fish. There are also other beneficial reasons for biological nutrient removal that include monetary saving through reduced aeration capacity and reduced expense of chemical treatment. This area will see more activity in the future.

Part of the tertiary treatment of a municipal treatment plant is the disinfection. Currently there are controversial issues as to what type of disinfection techniques should be employed. Historically, chlorine was the choice of many facilities. However, it has come to the point that disinfection byproducts (of chlorides and bromides) that are being formed are toxic to the water environment. New techniques that will be seen are ozonation and ultraviolet processes.

SUMMARY

1. The ultimate goal of wastewater treatment is the protection of the environment in a manner commensurate with economic, social, and political concerns.

2. The Federal Water Pollution Control Amendments of 1972 and 1990 require municipalities to prevent, reduce, or eliminate pollution of surface waters and groundwater. The planning and design of a wastewater treatment plant must achieve these criteria. Presently, municipal wastewater plants are being upgraded and expanded to meet all government regulations.

3. Biochemical oxygen demand is the sole basis for determining the efficiency of the treatment plant. Secondary treatment typically utilizes a biological process to further remove the organic content and BOD from the effluent of the primary sedimentation tank. Above 90 percent BOD removal can be achieved in the aeration biological process tank.

4. Sludge is produced as a waste product during the wastewater treatment process. Sludge management and disposal issues are currently being tackled to provide a safer and cleaner environment. Composting and stabilization of sludge into a recyclable soil conditioning product is widely selected as the final disposal method of the sludge.

5. Primary treatment is used mainly for the removal (approximately 70 percent) of settleable total suspended solids in the primary sedimentation tank. Paper, rags, sand, coffee grounds, and other solid waste materials are removed at this stage of the process.

6. Advanced wastewater treatment, known as tertiary treatment, is designed to remove those constituents that may not be adequately removed by secondary treatment. This includes removal of nitrogen, phosphorus, and heavy metals.

REFERENCES

EPA. *Study of the Future Federal Role in Municipal Wastewater Treatment.* Washington, DC: Author. December, 1984.

Federal Register. "Amendment to the Secondary Treatment Regulations: Percent Removal Requirements During Dry Weather Periods for Treatment Works Served by Combined Sewers." 40 CFR Part 133, January 27, 1989.

Federal Register. "Secondary Treatment Regulation." 40 CFR Part 133, July 1, 1988.

Hegewald, M. "Setting the Water Quality Agenda: 1988 and Beyond," *Journal WPCF,* 60 (5), 1988.

Henrichs, R. "Law, Literature Review." *Journal WPCF,* 60 (6), 1988.

Holmes, G., Singh, B., and Theodore, L. *Handbook of Environmental Management and Technology.* New York: Wiley-Interscience, 1993.

U.S. Congress, Office of Technology Assessment, "Wastes in the Marine Environment," 07A-0334. Washington, DC: U.S. GPO, April, 1987.

15

Dispersion Modeling in Water Systems

CONTRIBUTING AUTHOR

Kristina M. Neuser

INTRODUCTION

Four distinct periods can be distinguished in the development of mathematical models (Novotny, 1986):

1. The precomputer age (1900–1950). During this time, the focus was entirely on water quality with little concern for the environmental aspects.

2. The transition period of the 1950s. Data collection was accelerated but the analysis was slow and costly.

3. The early years of computer use. During the 1960s, the first computer models were developed, and many models were developed during the 1970s due to greater computer access.

4. The mid-1970s to date. Because of the development of inexpensive microcomputers, models can now be used for routine evaluations.

Models are classified by the number of dimensions modeled and by the type of model employed. These can be described as follows (Rau & Wooten, 1980):

1. One-dimensional models. The only direction modeled is that of the direction of flow. This is a valid model for flowing streams, where the concentration of pollutants is taken to be constant with stream cross-section.

2. Two-dimensional models. This is used in wide rivers where concentration may not be uniform across the entire width. The model is a function of both width and flow direction. For deep, narrow rivers, lakes, or estuaries, the horizontal and vertical dimensions are modeled, while the lateral dimension is held constant.

3. Three-dimensional models. The assumption here is that concentration can vary with length, width and depth. Of the three models, this is the most accurate model. It is also, however, both tedious and time consuming. The potential accuracy is greater, but the development and running costs are also greater.

There is also a zero-dimensional model that takes none of the lateral, vertical, or longitudinal motion into consideration. In this model, a segment of stream is treated as a completely mixed reactor (Dortch & Martin, 1988). The chemical engineer often refers to this type of model as a CSTR, that is, a continuous stirred tank reactor.

The model referred to above is an assembly of concepts in the form of one or more mathematical equations that approximates the behavior of a natural system or phenomenon (ASTM, 1983). Rather than focus on the water systems themselves, however, this chapter will examine the individual pollutants and components that are modeled. These include microorganisms, dissolved oxygen, eutrophication, and toxic chemicals. Within each of these areas, specific types of contaminants as well as the different water systems that are affected will be explored.

MATHEMATICAL MODELS

There are mass (componential) and flow (overall mass) balance equations for rivers and streams. They are as follows (Holmes, Singh, & Theodore, 1993):

Mass Balance

$$\begin{array}{c}\text{Mass rate of}\\\text{substance upstream}\end{array} + \begin{array}{c}\text{Mass rate added}\\\text{by outfall}\end{array} = \begin{array}{c}\text{Mass rate of substance}\\\text{immediately downstream}\\\text{from outfall assuming}\\\text{complete mixing}\end{array} \qquad (15\text{--}1)$$

Flow Balance

$$\begin{array}{c}\text{Flow rate}\\\text{upstream}\end{array} + \begin{array}{c}\text{Flow rate added}\\\text{by outfall}\end{array} = \begin{array}{c}\text{Flow rate immediately}\\\text{downstream from outfall}\end{array} \qquad (15\text{--}2)$$

The physical characteristics of lakes set them apart from other water systems in modeling for micro-organisms, as well as for the other contributors to water quality. These characteristics include evaporation due to a large surface area, and temperature stratification due to poor mixing within the lake. Therefore, these differences must be taken into account in the balance equation (Thomann & Mueller, 1987).

$$\begin{array}{c}\text{Net flow into and}\\\text{out of the lake due to}\\\text{river and/or}\\\text{groundwater flow}\end{array} + \begin{array}{c}\text{Precipitation}\\\text{directly onto}\\\text{the lake}\end{array} - \text{Evaporation} = \begin{array}{c}\text{Change in the}\\\text{lake volume}\\\text{with time}\end{array} \qquad (15\text{--}3)$$

The last, and most complicated water system that will be examined is the estuary. Unlike lakes and rivers, there are no simple balance equations that can be written for estuaries. Estuaries are coastal water bodies where freshwater meets the sea. They are traditionally defined as semi-enclosed bodies of water having a free connection with the open sea and within which sea water is measurably diluted with fresh water entering from land drainage (Pritchard, 1967).

The seaward end of an estuary is easily defined because it is connected to the sea. The landward end, however, is not that well defined. Generally, tidal influence in a river system extends further inward than salt intrusion. That is, the water close to the fall line of the estuary may not be saline, but it may still be tidal. Thus, the estuary is limited by the requirement that both salt and freshwater be measurably present. The exact location of the salt intrusion depends on the freshwater flow rate, which can vary substantially from one season to another (Mills, Procella, Ungs, Gherini, Summers, Mok, Rupp, & Bowie, 1985).

The variations in an estuary throughout the year, together with the fact that each estuary is different, makes modeling rather difficult. Some simplifications can, however, be made that provide some remarkably useful results in estimating the distribution of estuarine water quality. The simplifications can be summarized through the following assumptions:

1. The estuary is one-dimensional.
2. Water quality is described as a type of average condition over a number of tidal cycles.
3. Area, flow, and reaction rates are constant with distance.
4. The estuary is in a steady-state condition.

A water body is considered to be a one-dimensional estuary when it is subjected to tidal reversals (i.e., reversals in direction of the water velocity) and where only the longitudinal gradient of a particular water quality parameter is dominant (Thomann & Mueller, 1987).

MICROORGANISMS

The transmission of waterborne diseases (e.g., gastroenteritis, amoebic dysentery, cholera, and typhoid) has been a matter of concern for many years. The impact of high concentrations of disease-producing organisms on water uses can be significant. Bathing beaches may be closed permanently or intermittently during rainfall conditions when high concentrations of pathogenic bacteria are discharged from urban runoff and combined sewer overflows. Disease associated with drinking water continue to occur (Thomann & Mueller, 1987).

There are four types of organisms that can affect water quality. The first are indicator bacteria, which may reflect the presence of pathogens. In the past they were used as a measure of health hazard. Pathogenic bacteria are the cause of such diseases as salmonella, cholera, and dysentery, and continue to be a problem worldwide. Viruses are submicroscopic, inert particles that are unable to replicate or adapt to environmental conditions outside a living host (National Academy of Sciences, 1977), and if ingested, they can cause hepatitis. And finally, pathogenic protozoa are parasitic, but able to reproduce, and are responsible for amoebic dysentery. Table 15–1 lists examples of communicable disease indicators and organisms.

Table 15–1. Examples of Communicable Disease Indicators and Organisms

Indicators	Viruses
Bacteria	Hepatitis A
Total coliform	Enteroviruses
Fecal coliform	Polioviruses
Fecal streptococci	Echoviruses
Obligate anaerobes	Coxsackieviruses
Bacteriophages (bacterial viruses)	

Pathogenic Bacteria	Pathogenic protozoa and helminths
Vibrio cholerae	*Giardia lambia*
Salmonella	*Entamoeba hystolytica*
Shigella	Facultatively parasitic ameobae
	Nematodes

Source: Thomann, R.V. and J.A. Mueller. *Principles of Surface Water Quality Modeling and Control,* 1987

The factors that can affect the survival or extinction of these microorganisms are (Thomann & Mueller, 1987):

1. Sunlight
2. Temperature
3. Salinity
4. Predation
5. Nutrient deficiencies
6. Toxic substances
7. Settling of organism population after discharge
8. Resuspension of particulates
9. Growth of organisms within the body of water

The overall decay rate equation for microorganisms is given as:

$$K_B = K_{B1} + K_{BI} +/- K_{Bs} - K_a \qquad (15\text{–}4)$$

where K_B is the overall rate of decay, K_{B1} is the death rate due to temperature, salinity and predation, K_{BI} is the death rate due to sunlight, K_{Bs} is the net loss or gain due to settling or resuspension, and K_a is the aftergrowth rate (Thomann & Mueller, 1987).

One describing equation for the downstream distribution of bacteria in rivers and streams is given as

$$N = N_0 \exp(-K_B t^{*)} \qquad (15\text{–}5)$$

where N is the concentration of an organism, N_0 is the concentration of the organism at the outfall, K_B is the overall net rate of decay as given previously, and t* is the time it takes to travel a downstream distance x at a water velocity U (Thomann & Mueller, 1987). As the equation states, the organism will decay exponentially with time. (Thus a classical first order chemical equation takes the form of reaction.)

DISSOLVED OXYGEN

The problems of dissolved oxygen (DO) in surface waters have been recognized for over a century. The impact of low DO concentrations or of anaerobic conditions was reflected in an unbalanced ecosystem, fish mortality, odors, and other aesthetic nuisances. While coliform was a surrogate variable for communicable disease and public health, DO is a surrogate variable for the general health of the aquatic ecosystem (Thomann & Mueller, 1987).

The variations in dissolved oxygen levels are caused by sources and sinks. The sources include: reaeration from the atmosphere, which is dependent upon turbulence, temperature, and surface films; photosynthetic oxygen production where plants react CO_2 and H_2O to form glucose and oxygen; and incoming DO from tributaries (streams that feed a larger stream or a lake) or effluents. The sinks of DO are: oxidation of carbonaceous (CBOD) and nitrogenous (NBOD) waste materials, oxygen demand of the sediments of the water body, and the use of oxygen for respiration by aquatic plants (Thomann & Mueller, 1987).

With these inputs, sources and sinks, the following general mass balance equation for DO in a segmented volume can be written as:

$$
\begin{array}{l}
\text{Rearation} + (\text{Photosynthesis} - \text{respiration}) - \begin{array}{l}\text{Oxidation} \\ \text{of CBOD} \\ \text{NBOD}\end{array} - \begin{array}{l}\text{Sediment} \\ \text{oxygen} \\ \text{demand}\end{array}
\end{array}
$$

$$(15\text{–}6)$$

$$
+ \begin{array}{l}\text{Oxygen} \\ \text{input}\end{array} +/- \begin{array}{l}\text{Oxygen transport} \\ \text{(into or out} \\ \text{of segment)}\end{array} = \begin{array}{l}\text{Change with time of} \\ \text{dissolved oxygen in a} \\ \text{specific volume of water}\end{array}
$$

This equation can be applied to a specific water body where the transport, sources and sinks are unique to that aquatic system (Holmes et al., 1993).

The discharge of municipal and industrial waste, and urban and other nonpoint source runoff will necessitate a continuing effort in understanding the DO resources of surface waters. The DO problem can thus be summarized as the discharge of organic and inorganic oxidizable residues into a body of water, which, during the processes of ultimate stabilization of the oxidizable material (in the water or sediments), and through interaction of aquatic plant life, results in the decrease of DO to concentrations that interfere with desirable water uses (Thomann & Mueller, 1987). The balance equations that can be applied to the various water systems, namely rivers and lakes, are the same as described in the previous section.

EUTROPHICATION

Even the most casual observer of water quality has probably had the dubious opportunity of walking along the shores of a lake that has turned into a sickly green pea soup. Or perhaps, one has walked the shores of a slow-moving estuary or bay and had to step gingerly to avoid rows of rotting, matted, stringy aquatic plants. These problems have been grouped under a general term called eutrophication. The unraveling of the causes of eutrophication, the analysis of the impact of human activities on the problem, and the potential engineering controls that can be exercised to alleviate the condition have been a matter of special interest for the past several decades.

Eutrophication is the excessive growth of aquatic plants, both attached and planktonic (those that are free-swimming), to levels that are considered to be an interference with desirable water uses. One of the principal stimulants is an excessive level of nutrients such as nitrogen and phosphorus. In recent years, this problem has been increasingly acute due to the discharge of such nutrients by municipal and industrial sources, as well as agricultural and urban runoff. It has often been observed that there is an increasing tendency for some water bodies to exhibit increases in the severity and frequency of phytoplankton blooms and growth of aquatic weeds apparently as a result of elevated levels of nutrients (Thomann & Mueller, 1987).

The principal variables of importance in the analysis of eutrophication are (Thomann & Mueller, 1987):

1. Solar radiation at the surface and with depth
2. Geometry of water body; surface area, bottom area, depth, volume
3. Flow, velocity, dispersion
4. Water temperature
5. Nutrients
   a. Phosphorus
   b. Nitrogen
   c. Silica
6. Phytoplankton

The nonorganic products that result from oxidation are referred to as nutrients. They include nitrogen found in the form of ammonia, nitrite, and nitrate, and phosphorus, which occurs in the form of phosphates. A third nutrient, silicon in the form of silicate, enters the system through the weathering of soils and rocks. These nutrients, along with carbon dioxide, "feed" the process of photosynthesis, which creates the beginning components of the biological cycle—phytoplankton, the microscopic plants that drift around in the water, diatoms (which need silicon for their shells), flagellates (organisms possessing one or more whip-like appendages often used for locomotion), and green and blue-green algae among them. Some of these nutrients will go into producing a complementary pool of rooted aquatic plants. Figure 15–1 shows the basic biological cycle in lakes and estuaries. A critical portion of the cycle is the phytoplankton pool. Increased nutrient availability can lead to unsightly plankton blooms and to anoxic conditions as the available oxygen is used up in the plankton decay (Officer & Page, 1993).

Other processes related to algal growth and nutrient recycling are sorption and desorption of inorganic material, settling and deposition of phytoplankton, uptake of nutrients and growth of phytoplankton, death of phytoplankton, mineralization of organic nutrients, and nutrient generation from the sediment (Lung, 1993).

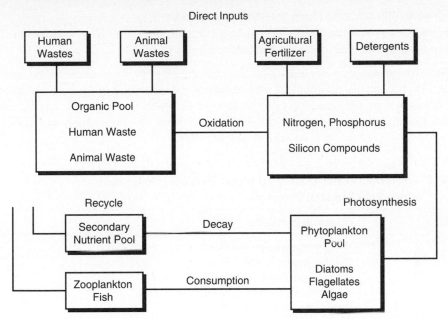

Figure 15–1.   Anthropogenic Inputs (Source: Charles Officer, and Jake Page, *Tales of the Earth,* 1993)

TOXIC SUBSTANCES

The issue of the release of chemicals into the environment at a level of toxic concentration is an area of intense concern in water quality and ecosystem analyses. Passage of the Toxic Substances Control Act (TSCA) of 1976 in the United States, unprecedented fines, and continual development of data on lethal and sublethal effects attest to the expansion of control on the production and discharge of such substances. However, as illustrated by pesticides, the ever-present potential for insect and pest infestations with attendant effects on humans and livestock results in a continuing demand for product development. As a result of these competing goals, considerable effort has been devoted in recent years to the development of predictive schemes that would permit an a priori judgment of the fate and effects of a chemical in the environment (Thomann & Mueller, 1987).

Table 15–2 summarizes a few specific chemicals that are of special interest in evaluating water quality, with brief descriptions of the problems that they may cause. Note especially the differences in the effects on water quality caused by various chemical forms of the same element, for example, sulfur. This illustrates the importance, sometimes, of assaying specific ions or molecules instead of merely total content of the element itself (Lamb, 1989).

The uniqueness of the toxic substances problem lies in the potential transfer of a chemical to humans with possible attendant public health impacts. This transfer occurs primarily through two principle routes:

1. Ingestion of the chemical from the drinking water supply.
2. Ingestion of the chemical from contaminated aquatic foodstuffs (e.g., fish and shellfish) or from food sources that utilize aquatic foodstuffs as a feed.

The toxic substances water quality problem can therefore be summarized as the discharge of chemicals into the aquatic environment. This results in concentrations in the water or aquatic food chain at levels that are determined to be toxic, in a public health sense or to the aquatic ecosystem itself, and thus may interfere with the use of the water body for water supply or fishing or contribute to ecosystem instability (Thomann & Mueller, 1987).

Table 15–2. Potential Water Quality Problems That May Be Caused by a Few Selected Chemicals

Chemical	Potential Problems
Arsenic	Toxicity to humans
	Toxicity to aquatic life
Chlorine	Organic reactions form trihalomethanes
	Toxicity to fish and other aquatic life
Calcium	Causes "hardness" in water
	May result in scale formation in pipes
Iron	Causes stains in laundry and on fixtures
	May kill fish by clogging their gills
Nitrogen: ammonia	May accelerate eutrophication in lakes
	May improve productivity of the water
	May be toxic to aquatic life
Nitrogen: nitrates	May be toxic to babies
	May accelerate eutrophication in lakes
	May improve productivity of the water
Oxygen, dissolved	Low concentrations harmful to fish
	Low concentrations may cause odor problems
	High concentrations accelerate metal corrosion
	Low or zero concentration may allow sulfide formation and concrete corrosion
Phenolics	Tastes and odors in drinking water
	Can cause tainting of fish flesh
	May be toxic to aquatic life
Sulfur: sulfides	Objectionable odors in and near water
	May be toxic to aquatic life
	May corrode concrete through acid formation
	Oxidation of sulfide to sulfate exerts an oxygen demand
Sulfur: sulfites	React with DO and exert oxygen demand
Sulfur: sulfates	Increase water corrosiveness to metals
	Decompose anaerobically to form sulfides
	Salty taste and laxative effects

Source: Lamb, James C., III, Water Quality and Its Control, 1985

SUMMARY

1. A model is an assembly of concepts in the form of one or more mathematical equations that approximates the behavior of a natural system or phenomena.

2. There exist mass balance equations for both rivers and lakes, but a simple equation for estuaries does not exist due to their complexity.

3. The levels of microorganisms in a water system depend on sunlight, temperature, salinity, predation, nutrients, toxic substances, settling of the organic population, resuspension of particulates, and growth within the body of water.

4. The impact of dissolved oxygen concentrations or of anaerobic conditions is reflected in an unbalanced ecosystem.

5. Eutrophication is the excessive growth of aquatic plants, both attached and planktonic, to levels that are considered to interfere with desirable water uses.

6. With toxic substances, it is as important to look at the effects of individual ions or molecules as it is to look at the total content of the element itself.

REFERENCES

American Society of Testing and Materials (ASTM). *Standard Practice for Evaluating Environmental Fate Models for Chemicals,* proposed standard, Subcommittee E-47.06 on Environmental Fate, Committee E-47 on Biological Effects and Environmental Fate, 1983.

Dortch, M., and Martin, J. *Alternatives in Regulated Flow Management.* Boca Raton, FL: CRC Press, 1988.

Holmes, G., Singh, B., and Theodore L. *Handbook of Environmental Management and Technology,* New York: John Wiley & Sons, 1993.

Lamb, J., III. *Water Quality and Its Control.* New York: John Wiley & Sons, 1989.

Lung, W. "Application to Estuaries." *Water Quality Modeling, Vol. III.* Boca Raton, FL: CRC Press, 1993.

Mills, W., Porcella, D., Ungs, M., Gherini, S., Summers, K., Mok, L., Rupp, G., and Bowie, G. "Water Quality Assessment: A Screening Procedure for Toxic and Conventional Pollutants," Part II, EPA/600/6-85/002b, 1985.

National Academy of Sciences. "Drinking Water and Health," Washington, DC: Safe Drinking Water Committee, Natural Resources Council, 1977.

Novotny, V. "Agricultural Nonpoint Source Pollution, Model Selection and Application," *Dev. Environ. Model,* 10, 1986.

Officer, C., and Page, J. *Tales of the Earth.* New York: Oxford University Press, 1993.

Pritchard, D. "What Is an Estuary?" *Estuaries,* American Association for the Advancement of Sciences, 83(2), 1967.

Rau, J., and Wooten, D. *Environmental Impact Analysis Handbook.* New York: McGraw-Hill, 1980.

Thomann, R., and Mueller, J. *Principles of Surface Water Quality Modeling and Control.* New York: Harper & Row, 1987.

Part IV

Solid Waste

Part IV of this book, comprised of six chapters, serves as an introduction to solid waste, since today's industries are faced with the major technological challenge of identifying ways to manage solid waste effectively. In Chapter 16, the general subject of solid waste management is examined. Chapter 17 is specifically concerned with industrial waste management, while Chapter 18 is concerned with municipal waste management. A comprehensive examination of the hospital waste problem and the various waste management options available is provided in Chapter 19; Chapter 20 focuses on the highly sensitive issue of nuclear wastes. Part IV concludes with Chapter 21, which addresses Superfund and all of its ramifications.

16

Solid Waste Management

CONTRIBUTING AUTHOR

Peter Damore

INTRODUCTION

Solid wastes encompass all of the wastes arising from human and animal activities that are normally solid, and that are discarded as unwanted or useless. The term solid waste is all-inclusive of the heterogeneous mass of throwaways from urban areas, as well as the more homogeneous accumulation of agricultural, industrial, and mineral wastes. In urban communities especially, the accumulation of solid wastes is a direct and primary consequence of life. This accumulation adds up to approximately 4 pounds of solid waste per person every day in the United States. That is equal to one billion pounds of waste requiring disposal every day. Properly dealing with this huge amount of waste is what solid waste management is all about. This chapter is concerned with a variety of topics in this area, including past and future trends, legislative impacts, and current practices.

HISTORY

From the days of primitive society, humans and animals have used this planet's resources to live and dispose of wastes. In early times, the disposal of these wastes did not cause a significant problem because populations were small and the amount of land available for assimilation of wastes was large. Problems with solid waste disposal began developing, though, when humans first began to congregate in communities and the accumulation of wastes became a consequence of life (see also Chapters 1 and 2).

An example of the early consequences of improper, or more appropriately, nonexistent solid waste management can be seen in 14th-century Europe. The practice of throwing solid wastes into the unpaved roads and vacant land in medieval towns led to the breeding of rats, with their fleas carrying the bubonic plague. Thus, the lack of any plan for the management of solid wastes led to the Black Death, which killed half of the population of Europe.

It was not until the last century that public health control measures became a vital issue to public officials, who finally realized that solid wastes had to be collected and disposed of in a sanitary manner in order to control the spread of disease (Tchobanoglous, Theisen, & Vigil, 1993). In the United States, at the turn of the century, the most common methods for the final disposal of solid wastes were dumping on land, dumping in water, plowing into the soil, feeding to hogs, reduction, and incineration. These methods, though a good start, were for the most part unregulated and inefficient. In many cases they wound up causing other types of pollution problems. Recent solid waste management practices, with emphasis on sanitary landfilling, began in the 1940s in this country. Standards and guidelines were established for municipal sanitary landfills. However, municipalities did not follow these programs with consistency. By 1965, there were still major problems with solid waste disposal. As a result, the government, in that year, passed the first in a series of solid waste legislation designed to ensure proper solid wastes practices, as well as to protect the environment. This event thus marked the beginning of solid waste management as we know it today. In addition to sanitary landfilling, modern day practices include pollution prevention, i.e., source reduction and recycling/reuse (see Part VII, Chapters 30–34) (Tchobanoglous et al., 1993).

MAJOR LEGISLATION

As previously mentioned, the first major modern solid waste legislation was passed in 1965 by Congress and was called the Solid Waste Disposal Act of 1965. The purpose of this act was to:

1. Promote the demonstration, construction, and application of solid waste management and resource and recovery systems that preserve and enhance the quality of air, water, and land resources.

2. Provide technical and financial assistance to state and local governments in the planning and development of resource recovery and solid waste disposal programs.

3. Promote a national research and development program for improved solid waste management techniques, more effective organizational arrangements, and the environmentally safe disposal of nonrecoverable residues.

4. Provide for creation of guidelines for solid waste collection, transport, separation, recovery, and disposal systems.

5. Provide for training grants in occupations involving the design, operation, and maintenance of solid waste disposal systems (Masters, 1991).

Four years later, the National Governmental Policy Act was passed. It is an all-encompassing congressional law, since it impacts on all projects that have any federal funding or that come under the regulation of federal agencies. This act specified the creation of the Council of Environmental Quality. This body has the power to force every federal agency to submit to the council an Environmental Impact Statement (EIS) on every activity or project over which it has jurisdiction. Basically, an EIS is a study of every conceivable effect on the environment that a project could have. It is a legal document, and may have to be defended in court (Tchobanoglous et al., 1993).

The Solid Waste Disposal Act of 1965 was amended by the Resource Recovery Act of 1970. It directed that the emphasis of the national solid waste management program should be shifted from disposal, as its primary objective, to recycling and reuse of recoverable materials in solid wastes, or to the conversion of wastes to energy. Also, it was shortly after the passage of this act that the U.S. EPA was formed (Holmes, Singh, & Theodore, 1993).

Progress under the aforementioned act caused Congress to pass the Resource Conservation and Recovery Act of 1976 (RCRA). This legislation had a profound effect on solid waste management. The RCRA gave the legal basis for implementation of guidelines and standards for solid waste storage, treatment, and disposal (Holmes et al., 1993).

The Comprehensive Environmental Response, Compensation and Liability Act of 1980, also known as Superfund, was created to provide a means of directly responding, and funding the activities of response, to problems at uncontrolled hazardous waste disposal sites. This included uncontrolled municipal solid waste landfills that were demonstrated to contain hazardous wastes (Holmes et al., 1993).

Finally, the Public Utility Regulation and Policy Act of 1981 directed public and private utilities to purchase power from waste-to-energy facilities. The intent was to establish a consistent method of reporting utility costs by all public utilities in the country. This legislation has been very effective in advancing the use of solid waste as a fuel in generating electricity (Tchobanoglous et al., 1993).

ELEMENTS OF A SOLID WASTE MANAGEMENT SYSTEM

There are six main elements associated with the management of solid wastes from the point of generation to final disposal. They are:

1. Waste generation
2. Waste handling and separation
3. Collection
4. Separation, processing and transformation of solid wastes
5. Transfer and transport
6. Disposal (Tchobanoglous et al., 1993)

Waste generation includes activities in which materials are identified as no longer being of value and are either thrown away or gathered together for disposal. In a typical community, solid waste is generated by many sources including residential, commercial, industrial, agricultural, and municipal services.

Waste handling and separation involves the management of wastes until they are placed in storage containers for collection. This includes the separation of waste materials for reuse and recycling, as well as the movement of loaded containers to the point of collection.

The collection of solid wastes includes the gathering of solid wastes and recyclable materials, as well as the transport of these materials to their destination. This destination may be a materials-processing facility, a transfer station, or a landfill site. In addition, transport of the waste becomes a problem in large cities where long hauling distances can make disposal costly.

Next comes the separation, processing, and transformation of solid waste materials. The activities included in this element occur in locations away from the source of waste generation. Processing includes: the separation of waste components by size using screens, manual separation of waste components, size reduction by shredding, separation of ferrous metals using magnets, compaction, and combustion. Transformation of solid wastes to reduce volume and weight is achieved using one of two types of processes: chemical or biological. The most common form of chemical transformation is combustion, while the most common form of biological transformation is aerobic composting. The transfer and transport of solid wastes involves two steps: (1) the transfer of wastes from the smaller collection vehicle to larger transport equipment, and (2) the subsequent transport of the wastes over long distances to a disposal site. The transfer usually takes place at a transfer station.

The last element in the solid waste management system is disposal. The disposal of solid wastes by landfilling or land spreading is the ultimate fate for most solid wastes. This includes wastes transported directly to the site, processed wastes, residue(s) from the combustion of solid waste, and compost.

HIERARCHY OF SOLID WASTE MANAGEMENT

A hierarchy is often employed in waste management to rank actions in implementing programs in the community. This hierarchy was adopted by the EPA (often referred to as the pollution prevention hierarchy, as described in Chapter 30), and is composed of four elements: source reduction, recycling, waste transformation, and ultimate disposal (Tchobanoglous et al., 1993).

The highest ranking element in the solid waste management hierarchy, source reduction, involves reducing the amount and/or toxicity of the wastes that are now generated. It is obviously the most effective way to reduce the quantity of waste, the cost of handling it, and its impact on the environment. Waste reduction may occur through the design, manufacture, and packaging of products with minimum toxic content, minimum volume of material, and a longer useful life. It can also occur at the residential or commercial level through selective buying patterns and the reuse of materials and products.

The second element in the hierarchy is recycling. It involves:

1. The separation and collection of waste materials.
2. The preparation of these materials for reuse, reprocessing, and remanufacture.
3. The actual reuse, reprocessing, and remanufacture of these materials.

Recycling plays an important part in helping to reduce the demand on resources and the amount of waste that ends up in landfills.

The third ranking element is waste transformation. It deals with the physical, chemical, or biological alteration of wastes. This is performed to improve the efficiency of solid waste management operation, to convert waste(s) to reusable and recyclable materials, and to recover heat and useful combustible gases. In addition, waste transformation ultimately results in the reduced use of landfill capacity.

Ultimate disposal, which usually involves landfilling, is the least desirable means of dealing with society's wastes. It is used for the solid wastes that cannot be recycled and are of no further use, the residual matter left after separation of solid wastes at a materials recovery facility, and the residual matter remaining after the recovery of conversion products or energy. Landfilling involves the controlled disposal of wastes into the land, and is the most common method of ultimate disposal for waste residuals.

IMPLEMENTATION AND OPERATION OF OPTIONS

In implementing a solid waste management plan, several areas need to be considered: the proper mix of alternatives and technologies, flexibility in meeting future changes, and the need for monitoring and evaluation (Tchobanoglous et al., 1993).

A wide variety of alternative programs and technologies now exists for the management of solid wastes. This has led to confusion as to what is the proper mix between the amount of waste separated for reuse and recycling, the amount of waste that is composted, the amount of waste that is combusted, and the amount of waste to be placed in landfills. This decision is further complicated by the wide range of people involved in the decision-making process (including regulatory individuals) for the implementation of solid waste management options.

The ability to be flexible in meeting future changes is of great importance in the development of a solid waste management system. Some important factors to consider include changes in the quantities in composition of the waste stream, changes in the specifications and markets for recyclable materials, and rapid developments in technology. By studying the possible outcomes related to these factors, it is possible for a local community to be protected from unexpected changes in local, regional, and national conditions.

Solid waste management is an ongoing process that requires continual monitoring and evaluation to determine if program objectives and goals are being met. Thus, timely adjustments can be made to the system that reflect changes in waste characteristics, changing specifications, and markets for recovered materials, and new and improved waste management technologies.

In the actual operation of a solid waste management system, a number of other management issues must also be considered. Workable but protective regulatory standards must be set. They can neither be so lax nor so strict that they cause the failure of the whole process. Next, there must be more improved scientific methods for interpretation of data as well as in the way in which this data is presented to the public. Third, household hazardous wastes should be removed from the garbage can for disposal in smaller, highly controlled waste management units. The reasoning behind this is that the accumulation of household hazardous wastes at a municipal landfill could eventually contaminate it. Another issue is whether land disposal units should be placed near or at large urban centers. Concern here centers on the transportation cost to a faraway landfill versus the "not in my back yard" (NIMBY) syndrome of the local urban residents. Finally, due to the increasing quantity and complexity of solid waste management units, more qualified managers must be trained and maintained in order to operate them (Tchobanoglous et al., 1993).

FUTURE TRENDS

There are several challenges facing society, including methods for improving the handling of solid wastes. The first is to change consumption habits that have been established over many years as a result of advertising pressure that has stressed increased consumption. Next, efforts must be made to reduce the quantity of materials used in the packaging of goods, and begin the process of recycling at the source. In this way, fewer materials will become part of the disposable solid wastes of a community. Thirdly, landfills must be made safer. Every effort should be made to reduce the toxicity of wastes ending up there. Also, the design of landfills must be improved to provide the safest possible locations for the long-term storage of waste materials. Finally, the development of new technologies that not only conserve natural resources but also are cost effective, is necessary for the future.

There are several trends that will affect solid waste management in the future. First, the cost of solid waste management will almost certainly continue to increase as a result of increased waste generation coupled with more restrictive regulations. Next, solid waste management will be more balanced between source reduction, recycling, energy recovery, and land disposal—as opposed to today where landfills are the most predominant waste management unit. Finally, education and training will be expanded in the future to provide competent people who will be better prepared to manage solid wastes.

SUMMARY

1. Solid wastes encompass all of the wastes arising from human and animal activities that are normally solid, and that are discarded as unwanted or useless. The term solid waste is all-inclusive of the heterogeneous mass of throwaways from urban areas, as well as the more homogeneous accumulation of agricultural, industrial, and mineral wastes.

2. Problems with solid waste disposal have faced society since early times, and have led to major epidemics such as the bubonic plague in 14th-century Europe.

3. The first major modern solid waste legislation in the United States was the Solid Waste Disposal Act of 1965. It started a series of laws that have become the framework of solid waste management today.

4. The major elements in a solid waste management system are waste generation, waste handling and separation, collection, separation, processing and transformation of wastes, transfer and transport, and disposal.

5. The hierarchy of solid waste management, in order of decreasing importance, is source reduction, recyling, waste transformation, and ultimate disposal.

6. When implementing a solid waste management plan, several facts need to be considered: the proper mix of alternatives and technologies, flexibility in meeting future changes, and the need for monitoring and evaluation.

7. Challenges facing society in the future regarding solid waste management include: changing consumption habits, to reducing the volume of waste at the source, making landfills safer, and to developing new technologies. Future trends in solid waste management include better managing costs, more balanced disposal options, and expanded education and training.

REFERENCES

Holmes, G., Singh, B., and Theodore, L. *Handbook of Environmental Management and Technology,* New York: John Wiley & Sons, 1993.

Masters, G. *Introduction to Environmental Engineering and Science.* Englewood Cliffs, NJ: Prentice Hall, 1991.

Tchobanoglous, G., Theisen, H., and Vigil, S. *Integrated Solid Waste Management,* New York: McGraw-Hill, 1993.

17

Industrial Waste Management

CONTRIBUTING AUTHOR

Romeo G. Fuentebella

INTRODUCTION

Pollution has grown to proportions where a reasonable solution to the total problem is almost unfathomable, but not necessarily unattainable. One of the human problems has always been the proper disposal of refuse. Upon the discovery that diseases and illnesses develop as the result of inadequate and unsanitary disposal of wastes, demand for sanitary systems grew. Industrial pollution then started to become intolerable to society.

It is established that the chemical process industries contribute only a small part of the total pollution problem; however, they now expend and will continue to expend in the future a large portion of the resources for corrective methods (Ross, 1968). Sometimes, pollution from process industries poses problems more complex than pollution from other areas. The magnitude of air pollution from automotive exhaust and central power stations, and nonindustrial water pollution from raw sewage dumped into streams, lakes, and oceans surpass the pollution generated by the chemical industry.

Large processing plants may have a multitude of different individual waste problems, each requiring a separate solution to meet air, water, and solid waste pollution standards. The solutions to these problems may range from the very simple to the very complex. In developing solutions, it is of primary importance to know the characteristics of the waste. Learning as much as possible about the various management tools that are available is secondary.

The composition of industrial wastes varies not only with the type of industry but with the processes used within the same industry. They may be classified according to composition in many ways, but in general, the wastes may be classified as wastes that may be utilized, and as wastes that require treatment. Industry continues to recognize the importance of saving and making use of all available resources from certain wastes. The wastes that require treatment should attract more attention. These wastes are usually of a form that contains waste materials in a more or less dilute solution or suspension. Since any materials of value are present in small quantities in a dilute solution, they cannot be economically recovered by known processes. In turn, these wastes that require treatment can be divided into three classes of wastes. There are those where organic compounds predominate and constitute the undesirable components, those that contain poisonous substances, and those that contain certain inert materials in such concentrations as to have undesirable features.

This chapter will review a wide range of industries and their respective wastes. In discussing these wastes, both liquid and solid wastes are treated together since it is difficult, if not impossible, to compartmentalize each phase/class of waste in any presentation. Each particular waste requires a different method of handling and treatment. In general, the predominating compounds in a waste usually determine the treatment process that will be required for that distinctive waste.

FOOD PROCESSING

Food-processing industries are industries whose main concern is the production of edible goods for human or animal consumption. The production processes usually consist of the cleaning, the removal of inedible portions, the preparation, and the packaging of the raw material. The generated wastes are the spoiled raw material or the spoiled manufactured product, the liquid or water used (rinsing, washing, condensing, cooling, transporting, and processing), the cleaning liquids of the equipment, the drainage of the product, the overflow from tanks, and the unused portions of the product.

The wastes that result from food processing usually contain varying degrees of concentrations of organic matter. To provide the proper environmental conditions for the micro-organisms upon which biological treatment depends, additional adjustments such as continuous feeding, temperature control, pH adjustment, mixing, supplementary nutrients, and microorganism population adaptation are necessary.

The major and more effective methods of aerobic or anaerobic biological treatments make use of activated sludge, biological filtration, anaerobic digestion, oxidation ponds, and spray irrigation (see Chapter 14 for additional details about their treatment methods). Since many of the wastes contain high concentrations of organic matter, the loadings of the biological units must be maintained with care. Most often, long periods of aeration or high-rate two-stage biofiltration (a biological control process) is required to produce an acceptable effluent.

The selection of the type of treatment depends on the degree of treatment required, the nature and phase of the organic waste, the concentration of organic matter, the variation in waste flow (if applicable), the volume of the waste, and the capital and operating costs.

CANNERY WASTES

Cannery wastes are classified according to the product being processed, its growth season, and its geographic location. Many canneries are designed to process more than one product because vegetables, fruits, and citrus fruits have short harvesting and processing periods. The wastes from these plants are primarily organic. These wastes are the result of the trimming, juicing, blanching, and pasteurizing of raw materials; the cleaning of the processing equipment; and the cooling of the finished product. The most common and effective methods of treatment for the bulk of these wastes are discharging to a municipal treatment plant, lagooning with the addition of chemical stabilizers, soil absorption or spray irrigation, and anaerobic digestion.

The vegetables that produce strong wastes when processed for canning are peas, beets, carrots, corn, squash, pumpkins, and beans. The origin of all vegetable wastes is analogous since the canning procedures are alike even though the processing preparations differ for each vegetable. The wastes that result from food processing consist of the wash liquid; the solids from sorting, peeling, and coring operations; the spillage from filling and sealing the machines; and the wash liquid from cleaning the facilities.

The fruits that present the most common problems in the discharge of waste after processing are peaches, tomatoes, cherries, apples, pears, and grapes. Their wastes come from lye peeling, spray washing, sorting, grading, slicing and canning, removing condensates, cooling of cans, and plant cleanup.

The main citrus fruits (oranges, lemons, and grapefruit) are usually processed in one plant to make canned citrus juices, concentrates, citrus oils, dried meal, molasses, and other byproducts. The wastes come from cooling waters, pectin wastes, pulp-press liquors, processing-plant wastes, and floor washings. The canning solid waste is a mixture of peel, rag, and seeds of the fruits, surplus juices, and blemished fruits.

The selection of the most suitable type of treatment of cannery wastes involves the review of the volume, phase, and treatment involved in the process and the unique conditions of the packaging periods. Cannery wastes are most efficiently treated by screening, chemical precipitation, lagooning, and spray irrigation (digestion and biological filtration are also used, but to a lesser extent).

The preliminary step of screening is designed to remove large solids prior to the final treatment or discharge of the waste to a receiving stream or municipal waste-water system. Only slight reductions in BOD (biological oxygen demand) are accomplished by screening. The machines either rotate or vibrate, and have loads ranging from 40 to 50 pounds per 1000 gallons of waste water. The wastes retained on the screens are disposed of by being spread on the ground, used as sanitary fill, dried and burned, or used as animal food supplement.

To reduce the concentration of solids in the wastes, chemical precipitation is used to adjust the pH. This method is quite effective for treating apple, tomato, and cherry wastes. Ferric salts or aluminate and lime have produced 40 to 50 percent BOD reductions (Nemerow, 1971). The product of this procedure is normally dried on sand beds without producing an odor for a week.

Treatment in lagoons involves biological action, sedimentation, soil absorption, evaporation, and dilution. When adequate land is available, lagooning may be the only practical and economical treatment of cannery wastes. $NaNO_3$ (sodium nitrite) is used to eliminate odors produced by lagoons with unmaintained aerobic conditions. However, the use of these treated lagoons for complete treatment may be costly because of the large volumes of wastes involved. Surface sprays are used to reduce the flies and other insect nuisances that breed around these lagoons.

Whenever the cannery waste is nonpathogenic and nontoxic to plants, spray irrigation is the preferred economical method to use. Ridge-and-furrow irrigation beads are used on soils of relatively high water-absorbing capacity. In general, wastes should be screened before spraying, although comminution alone has been used successfully in conjunction with spray irrigation.

Oxygen-demanding materials in cannery wastes can be removed by biological oxidation. When the operation is limited by seasonal conditions, it is difficult to justify capital investment for bio-oxidation facilities. However, in many instances cannery wastes can be combined with domestic sewage, and then, bio-oxidation processes provide a practical and economic solution.

DAIRY WASTES

Most dairy wastes are made up of various dilutions of whole milk, separated milk, butter-milk, and whey. They result from accidental or intentional spills, drippings, and washings. Dairy wastes are largely neutral or slightly alkaline, but have a tendency to become acid quite rapidly because of the fermentation of milk sugar to lactic acid. Lactose in milk wastes may be converted to lactic acid when streams become lacking of oxygen, and the resulting lowered pH may cause precipitation of casein. Because of the presence of whey, cheese-plant waste is decidedly acid. Milk wastes have very little suspended material and their pollution effects are almost entirely due to the oxygen demand that they impose on the receiving stream. Decomposing casein causes heavy black sludge and strong butyric-acid odors that characterize milk-waste pollution.

There is a considerable variation in the size of the dairy plants and in the type of products they manufacture. The disposal or treatment of milk waste may be done through irrigation on land, hauling, biological filtration on either the standard or the recirculating filter, biochemical treatment, or the oxidized sludge process. Milk-plant wastes have a tendency to ferment and become anaerobic and odorous because they are composed mostly of soluble organic materials. This characteristic enables them to respond ideally to treatment by biological methods. The selection of a treatment method hinges on the location and size of the plant. The most effective conventional methods of treatment are aeration, trickling filtration, activated sludge, irrigation, lagooning, and anaerobic digestion.

There is a wide variation in the flow rates and strength of milk wastes, and through holding and equalization, a desirable uniform waste could be achieved. Aeration for one day often results in 50 percent BOD reduction and eliminates odors during conversion of the lactose to lactic acid. Some two-stage filters yield greater than 90 percent BOD reduction, while single-stage filters yield about 75 to 80 percent BOD reduction (Nemerow, 1971).

A successful method for the complete treatment of milk wastes is the activated-sludge process. It uses aeration to cause the accumulation of an adapted sludge. When supplied with sufficient air, the flora and fauna in the active sludge oxidize the dissolved organic solids in the waste. Excess sludge is settled out and subsequently returned to the aeration units. Properly designed plants that provide ample air for handling the raw waste and returned sludge are not easily upset, nor is the control procedure difficult.

The amount of milk and milk products lost in waste water from factories depends very much on the degree of control and attention to detail in the operation of the plants. The first and most important step in reducing pollution from milk factories is to make sure that whole whey and butter-milk are never discharged with the wastewater. Also, churns in which the milk is delivered should be adequately drained. The effects of whey and buttermilk on the environment are intense if neglected; besides, they have high food values and can be used as food or in the preparation of foods.

FERMENTATION AND PHARMACEUTICAL INDUSTRIES

The fermentation industries range from breweries and distilleries to some parts of the pharmaceutical industry (the producers of antibiotics); the pharmaceutical industry is treated later in this section. To produce alcohol or alcoholic products, starchy materials (barley, oats, rye, wheat, corn, rice, potatoes) and materials containing sugars (blackstrap and high-sugar molasses, fruits, sugar beets) are used. The process of converting these raw materials to alcohol depends upon the desired alcoholic product. Beer manufacturers focus on taste, while distillers are concerned about alcohol yield.

The brewing of beer has two stages. The first stage involves the malting of the barley and the second involves the brewing the beer from the malt. Both these operations occur at the same plant. The two major wastes produced by the malting process come from the steep tank after grain has been removed, and those remaining in the germinating drum after the green malt has been removed. A considerable amount of water is required for cooling purposes in the actual brewing process. Brewery wastes are composed mainly of liquor pressed from the wet grain, liquor from yeast recovery, and wash water from the various departments. The residue remaining after the distillation process is referred to as "distillery slops," "beer slops," or "still bottoms."

In a distillery, there are several sources of wastes. The dealcoholized still residue and evaporator condensate are major concerns. Minor wastes include redistillation residue and equipment washes. In the manufacture of compressed yeast seed, yeast is planted in a nutrient solution and allowed to grow under aerobic conditions until maximum cell multiplication is attained. The yeast is then separated from the spent nutrient solution, compressed, and finally packaged. The yeast-plant effluent consists of filter residues resulting from the preparation of the nutrient solutions, spent nutrients, wash water, filter-press effluent, and cooling and condenser waters or liquid.

Pharmaceutical wastes come primarily from spent liquors from the fermentation process, with the addition of the floor washings and laboratory wastes. Wastes from pharmaceutical plants producing antibiotics and biologicals can be categorized as strong fermentation beers, inorganic solids, washing of floors and equipment, chemical waste, and barometric condenser water from evaporation. The wastes from pharmaceutical plants that produce penicillin and similar antibiotics are strong and generally should not be treated with domestic sewage, unless the extra load is considered in the design and operation of the treatment plant.

Stillage is the principal pollution load from a distillery; it is the residual grain mash from distillation columns. Industry attempts to recover as much of this as possible as a byproduct to manufacture animal feed or for conversion to chemical products. Centrifuging has also been used to concentrate distillery slops.

MEAT INDUSTRY

The three main sources of waste in the meat industry are stockyards, slaughterhouses, and packinghouses. The stockyard is where the animals are kept until they are killed. The actual killing, dressing, and some byproduct processing are carried out in the slaughterhouse. Packinghouse operations include the manufacture of sausages, canning of meat, rendering of edible fats into lard and edible tallow, cleaning of casings, drying of hog's hair, and some rendering of inedible fats into grease and inedible tallow. Packinghouse wastes are generated from various operations on the killing floor, during carcass dressing, rendering, bag-hair removal and processing, casing, and cleaning. Stockyard wastes contain both liquid and solid excretions. The amount and strength of the wastes vary widely, depending on the presence or absence of cattle horns, the thoroughness and frequency of manure removal, the frequency of washing, and so on.

Blood should be recovered as completely as possible, even in small plants. Blood is a rich source of protein and is more economical to recover for large plants. Small plants do not have the equipment nor the conditions necessary to profit from the sales of the blood. Paunch manure should be recovered and used for fertilizer purposes. There is little reason for this material to enter the waste system except as washings from the floor. Grease recovery or removal should be common practice in all packing houses and even in smaller slaughterhouses. Grease removal is accomplished through the use of baffled tanks or grease traps. Cleanup by water from high-pressure hoses has been and continues to be the general practice in the meat-packing industry. The use of dry cleanup prior to wet cleanup reduces pollution loads substantially; although it reduces wastewater volume, it does increase solid waste volume.

Slaughterhouse processes are centered about the killing floor. Meat plant wastes are similar to domestic sewage in regard to their composition and effects on receiving bodies of water. The total organic contents of these wastes are considerably higher than those of domestic sewage. Without adequate dilution, the principal detrimental effects of meat plant wastes are oxygen depletion, sludge deposits, discoloration, and general nuisance conditions. The total liquid waste from the poultry-dressing process contains varying amounts of blood, feathers, fleshings, fats, washings from evisceration, digested and undigested foods, manure, and dirt. The largest amount of pollution from the process is contributed by the manure from receiving and feeding stations and blood from the killing and sticking operations.

The treatment processes adapted to slaughterhouse and packing plant wastes depend on the size of the industry. The most common methods used for treatment are fine screening, sedimentation, chemical precipitation, trickling filters, and activated sludge. Biological filtration is perhaps the most dependable process for the medium- and larger-sized plants.

Poultry-plant wastes should and do respond readily to biological treatment; it is attainable if troublesome materials such as feathers, feet, heads, and so on are removed beforehand. Treatment facilities include stationary screens in pits, septic tanks, and lagoons.

The small packinghouse or slaughterhouse requires a process of treatment that is dependable and simple to operate. Small plants operate sporadically resulting in an undesirable operation conditions for biological processes. Biological processes are much more easily upset by careless treatment or large variations in waste content than are chemical processes.

TEXTILE INDUSTRY

The textile industry has been one of the largest of users and polluters of water, and unfortunately, there has been little success in the development of the low-cost treatment methods needed by the industry to lessen the pollution that is discharged into streams. The operations of textile mills consist of waving, dyeing, printing, and finishing. Many processes involve several steps, each contributing a particular type of waste, like sizing of the fibers, kiering (alkaline cooking at elevated temperature), desizing the woven cloth, bleaching, mercerizing, dyeing, and printing. Textile wastes are generally colored, highly alkaline, high in BOD and suspended solids, and high in temperature. Manufacturing synthetic fiber generates wastes that resemble chemical-manufacturing wastes, and their treatment depends on the chemical process used. Equalization and holding are generally preliminary steps to the treatment of those wastes because of their varying compositions. Additional methods are chemical precipitation, trickling, filtration, and, more recently, biological treatment and aeration.

FUTURE TRENDS

Often it is not necessary for the producer of the waste to reprocess the material internally. Many companies, through the ingenious application of sound engineering practices, have been able to sell waste products, particularly solid waste products, as raw materials to other processors. Numerous small companies have geared their business towards the sale of reprocessed waste materials. In the evaluation of any waste disposal program, the possible reuse or sale of the waste or its components is certain to receive more attention in the future. Successful strategies will take into account both short-term waste disposal costs and long-term site treatment liabilities. The total cost of waste management consists of the disposal costs, which include taxes and fees, transportation costs, administration costs and present value for future liability costs. Disposal and transportation costs are usually the only ones considered. The time spent by personnel in handling the wastes on-site to off-site approvals, to conduct analytical testing, and to fill out any state, federal, or industry association reports are costly. Long-term costs can include the costs to clean up misused sites. This obligation is due to the presence of substances identified as hazardous under the Comprehensive Environmental Response, Compensation, and Liability Act (CERCLA, which established Superfund), which is the basis for most site remediation actions (Rice, 1991).

An important factor for waste management planning in the future is the rise in the costs of disposal. Costs vary depending on the type of the waste, the quantity (bulk), its containment, and its method of disposal. Landfills close to the location of the waste generation are rapidly shrinking in capacity. The trend toward incineration, led extensively by land disposal restrictions, may also increase incinerations costs in the near future.

As older sites close, the newer containment sites will refuse to take wastes or at least seriously cut back levels (Brown, 1991). The ideal option will be the development of successful waste minimization programs so that there is no longer the need for disposal. Unfortunately, this attractive situation will take some time. Another option is having the companies take on the responsibility of waste treatment themselves, but not every company wants, or is able, to treat its own wastes on site.

For some companies, hiring a contractor to do the treatment is a better option than building their own treatment plant. The amount of waste generated may not even justify the amount spent for the facility. Naturally, there are additional costs for running the plant and for the personnel to run the plant. Also, if the amount the products being produced changes from time to time, then the amount of waste treatment/management would change accordingly. There could be a large disparity between the quantities generated, and the plant may not be able to comply with that range, thereby making contracting a preferred option.

Waste management issues must be combined with realistic company factors to develop practical, attainable strategies in the future. Capital planning will influence the decision of whether to invest in new production that can use existing waste-handling equipment or to add new equipment that may not be justified. The business plan of the company is essential to estimate the future generation of waste.

The solution to industrial waste problems normally do not present themselves directly, but rather, some ingenuity and practicality must be employed so that the management of these waste can be carried out safely and efficiently. The methods, strategies, and equipment to be employed in the future will vary according to the situation and the type of waste. Regarding industry and manufacturers, the major factors that determine the way wastes are dealt with will continue to be cost and necessity.

SUMMARY

1. The predominating compounds in a waste usually determine the treatment processes that will be required for that particular waste.

2. The wastes that result from food processing usually contain varying degrees of concentration of organic matter. To provide the proper environmental conditions for the micro-organisms upon which biological treatment depends, additional adjustments such as continuous feeding, temperature control, pH adjustment, mixing, supplementary nutrients, and micro-organism population adaptation are necessary.

3. The selection of the most suitable type of treatment for cannery waste is concerned with a review of the volume, character, and treatment involved in the process and the unique conditions of the packaging periods.

4. Milk wastes have very little suspended material and their pollution effects are almost entirely due to the oxygen demand that they impose on the receiving stream.

5. Pharmaceutical wastes come primarily from spent liquors from the fermentation process, with the addition of the floor washings and laboratory wastes.

6. The three main sources of waste in the meat industry are stockyards, slaughterhouses, and packinghouses.

7. The textile industry has been one of the largest of users and pollutants of water, and unfortunately, there has been little success in the development of the low-cost treatment methods that the industry needs in order to lessen the pollution that is discharged into the environment.

8. An important factor for waste management planning in the future is the rise in the costs of disposal. Costs vary depending on the type of the waste, the quantity (bulk), its containment, and its method of disposal.

REFERENCES

Brown, S. "Washing Your Hands of Waste Water Disposal." *Process Engineering*, 34–35, July 1991.

Nemerow, N. *Liquid Waste of Industry: Theories and Treatment*, New York: Syracuse University, 1971.

Rice, S. "Waste Managenment: The Long View." *Chemical Technology*, 543–546, Sept 1991.

Ross, R. *Industrial Waste Disposal*, New York: Reinhold Book Corporation, 1968.

18

Municipal Solid Waste Management

INTRODUCTION*

It's not news that many communities in America are faced with a garbage disposal problem. In 1990, Americans generated over 195 million tons of municipal solid waste, and the annual amount is expected to increase to more than 220 million tons by 2000. Since over two-thirds of municipal solid waste is sent to landfills, this chapter will primarily key on landfilling—the solid waste management option that simply will not go away. However, some landfills are closing and the siting of new landfills has become increasingly difficult because of public opposition. Past problems sometimes associated with older landfills might have contributed to this situation. Landfills that were poorly designed, that were located in geologically unsound areas, or that might have accepted toxic materials without proper safeguards have contaminated some groundwater sources. Many communities use groundwater for drinking, and people living where contamination has occurred understandably worry about its threat to their health and the cost of cleaning it up. Communities where new landfills are needed share these concerns. Consequently, at a time when more are needed, there is increasing resistance to building new landfills.

To ease these worries and to make waste management work better, federal, state, Native American tribal, and local governments have adopted an integrated approach to waste management. This approach involves a mix of three waste management techniques:

1. Decreasing the amount and/or toxicity of waste that must be disposed of by producing less waste to begin with (source reduction)

*Information for this section was primarily drawn from the EPA document "Safer Disposal for Solid Waste," March 1993.

2. Increasing recycling of materials such as paper, glass, steel, plastics, and aluminum, thus recovering these materials rather than discarding them

3. Providing safer disposal capacity by improving the design and management of incinerators and landfills

The EPA has defined a number of activities that need to be carried out in order to help solve the municipal solid waste problem. These management options include increased source reduction, increased recycle/reuse, and improving the design and operation of both incinerators and landfills. The remainder of the chapter addresses the following topic areas: regulations, source reduction and recycle/reuse, incineration and landfilling.

REGULATIONS*

In a general sense, the regulations attempt to establish a cost-effective and practical system for managing the nation's waste by:

1. Encouraging source reduction and recycling to maximize landfill life.
2. Specifying safe design and management practices that will prevent releases of contaminants into groundwater.
3. Specifying operating practices that will protect human health.
4. Protecting future generations by requiring careful closure procedures, including monitoring of landfill conditions and the effects of landfills on the surrounding environment.

The federal government sets minimum national standards applicable to municipal solid waste disposal, but state, tribal, and local governments are responsible for actually implementing and enforcing waste programs. States are required to develop their own programs based on the federal regulations. The EPA is offering the same opportunity to tribes. The EPA's role is to evaluate states' and tribes' programs and decide if they are adequate to ensure safe disposal of municipal solid waste.

States and tribes that apply for and receive EPA approval of their programs have the opportunity to provide significant flexibility in implementing the regulations. This added flexibility allows states and tribes to take local conditions and needs into account, and can make the costs of municipal solid waste management more affordable. States and tribes also may establish requirements that are more stringent than those set by the federal government.

Private citizens have a role, too. Individuals can help ensure that adequate landfill capacity exists for their wastes by supporting the siting and development of facilities that comply with the regulations. Individuals can exercise their responsibilities through grassroots activities, such as participating in public meetings regarding landfill or incinerator siting, by taking part in permitting processes, and by working closely with the responsible state or tribal officials. Citizens also have the right to sue landfillowners/operators who are not in compliance with the federal regulations.

*Information for this section was drawn from "Safer Disposal for Solid Waste," EPA, March 1993 and personal lecture notes of L. Theodore.

Under the regulations, a municipal solid waste landfill (MSWLF) is defined as a discrete area of land or an excavation that receives household waste, and that is not a land application unit, surface impoundment, injection well, or waste pile, as those terms are defined in the law. Household waste includes any solid waste, including garbage, trash, and septic tank waste, derived from houses, apartments, hotels, motels, campgrounds, and picnic grounds. An MSWLF unit also may receive other types of wastes as defined under Subtitle D of the Resource Conservation and Recovery Act (RCRA), such as commercial solid waste, nonhazardous sludge, small quantity generator waste, and industrial solid waste. Such a landfill may be publicly or privately owned. An MSWLF unit can be a new unit, and existing unit, or a lateral expansion. An existing unit is defined as a municipal solid waste landfill unit that received solid waste as of October 9, 1993. Waste placement in existing units must be consistent with past operating practices or modified practices to ensure good management. A new unit is any municipal solid waste landfill unit that did not receive waste prior to October 9, 1993. A landfill serving a community that disposes of less than 20 tons of municipal solid waste per day, averaged yearly, is referred to as a small landfill.

SOURCE REDUCTION AND RECYCLE/REUSE*

The general subject area of source reduction and recycle/reuse is treated extensively in the pollution prevention sections (Parts, V, VI, and VII) of this text. Specific details on waste reduction in the home, office, and other areas are examined in Chapters 32, 33, and 34, respectively. The interested reader should review these chapters to obtain a better understanding of the problems associated with all the management options available for municipal solid waste.

To increase recycling nationwide, the EPA has undertaken a number of efforts to stimulate markets for secondary materials and to promote increased separation, collection, processing, and recycling of waste. The EPA also funded the establishment of a National Recycling Institute, composed of high-level representatives from business and industry, to identify and resolve issues in recycling.

Composting is another process commonly associated with recycling. Composting is the microbiological decay of organic materials in an aerobic environment. Materials that potentially could be composted include agricultural waste, grass clippings, leaves and other yard waste, food waste, and paper products. Many municipalities have implemented leaf composting programs.

One of the problems with the implementation of any recycling program is the public perception of associated costs. Many people believe that recycling is free or, at the very least, inexpensive. However, in most instances, that is not the case. Costs are associated with every aspect of the program, including collection of the materials, processing of the materials, and disposing of any residues. Purchase of new equipment or the retrofitting of existing equipment that is used to separate or recycle materials, or incorporating recycled materials into a process, is often very expensive. Direct operational costs include labor and utilities. With the exceptions of glass and aluminum, it is unfortunately usually more cost effective to use virgin materials rather than recycled materials in manufacturing processes. Many times markets are not available for sorted materials.

*Information in this section was taken from personal lecture notes of L. Theodore; Holmes, Singh, and Theodore, 1993; and Theodore and McGuinn, 1992.

The plastics industry is representative of this problem. Although much research has gone into plastics recycling in the past few years, markets for both the segregated material and the end products are very limited. The public needs to realize that recycling is not cheap; and, many times the cost of recycling is only offset by the avoided cost of disposal rather than by any profits generated (Theodore, lecture notes; Holmes et al., 1993).

INCINERATION*

Incineration is not a new technology and has been commonly used for treating wastes for many years in Europe and the United States. The major benefits of incineration are that the process actually destroys most of the waste rather than just disposing of or storing it; it can be used for a variety of specific wastes; and it is reasonably competitive in cost compared to other disposal methods.

Municipal solid waste incineration involves the application of combustion processes under controlled conditions to convert wastes containing hazardous materials to inert mineral residues and gases. Four parameters influence the mechanisms of incineration:

1. Adequate free oxygen must always be available in the combustion zone.
2. Turbulence, the constant mixing of waste and oxygen, must exist.
3. Combustion temperatures must be maintained; the combustion process must provide enough heat to raise the burning mixture to a sufficient temperature to destroy all organic components.
4. Elapsed time of exposure to combustion temperatures must be adequately long in duration to ensure that even the slowest combustion reaction has gone to completion. In other words, transport of the burning mixture through the high temperature region must occur over a sufficient period of time.

Municipal solid waste can be combusted in bulk form or in reduced form. Shredding, pulverizing, or any other size reduction method that can be used before incineration decreases the amount of residual ash due to better contact of the waste material with oxygen during the combustion process (Geiger, 1991). Shredded waste used as fuel is generally referred to as refuse-derived fuel (RDF) and is sometimes combined with other fuel types. Table 17–1 lists the American Society of Testing and Materials (ASTM) classification for RDF(8).

The types of incinerators used in municipal waste combustion include fluidized bed incinerators, rotary waterwall combustors, reciprocating grate systems, and modular incinerators. The basic variations in the design of these systems are related to the waste feed system, the air delivery system, and the movement of the material through the system. Specific details are available in the literature (Theodore & Reynolds, 1988; Theodore & May, 1994).

*Information in this section was taken from personal lecture notes of L. Theodore; Theodore and McGuinn, 1992; and Shen, McGuinn, and Theodore, 1986.

Table 17–1.   ASTM Classifications for Refuse-Derived Fuel (RDF)

ASTM RDF	RDF Classification	Nomenclature Description
RDF1	Raw	Solid waste used as a fuel as discarded form, without oversize bulky waste.
RDF2	Coarse	Solid waste processed to a coarse particle size, with or without ferrous metal extraction, such that 95% by weight passes through a 6-inch, 2-mesh screen.
RDF3	Fine or fluff	Solid waste processed to a particle size such that 95% by weight passes through a 2-inch, 2-mesh screen, and from which the majority of metals, glass, and other inorganics have been extracted.
RDF4	Powder	Solid waste processed into a powdered form such that 95% by weight passes through a 10-mesh screen and from which most metals, glass, and other inorganics have been extracted.
RDF5	Densified	Solid waste that has been processed and densified into the form of pellets, slugs, cubettes, or briquettes.
RDF6	Liquefied	Solid waste that has been processed into a liquid fuel.
RDF7	Gaseous	Solid waste that has been processed into a gaseous fuel.

LANDFILLING*

As indicated earlier, approximately two-thirds of the nation's municipal solid waste is landfilled. This is due to the fact that it is not possible to reuse, recycle, or incinerate the entire solid waste stream; therefore, a significant portion of the waste must be landfilled. Landfills have been a common means of waste disposal for centuries. A process that originally was nothing more than open piles of waste has now evolved into sophisticated facilities. Perhaps the best approach to both describe and discuss the solid waste management option is to examine the federal regulations pertaining to landfills. The federal regulations for municipal solid waste landfills cover the following six basic areas:

1. Location
2. Operation
3. Design
4. Groundwater monitoring and corrective action
5. Closure and postclosure care
6. Financial assurance

The following material presents the applicable regulations in some detail. However, states and tribes with EPA-approaved programs have the opportunity to exercise flexibility in imple-

*Information for the section is taken from "Safer Disposal for Solid Waste," EPA, March 1993 and from personal lecture notes of L. Theodore.

menting these regulations. Some of the exceptions described below are only available in states and tribes with EPA-approved programs.

Location

Because landfills can attract birds that can interfere with aircraft operation, owners/operators of sites near airports must show that birds are not a danger to aircraft. This restriction applies to new, existing, and laterally expanding landfills. Landfills may not be located in areas that are prone to flooding unless the owner/operator can prove the landfill is designed to withstand flooding and prevent the waste from washing out. This restriction also applies to new, existing, and laterally expanding landfills. Since wetlands are important ecological resources, new landfills and laterally expanding ones may not be built in wetlands unless the landfill is in a state or on tribal lands with an EPA-approved program, and the owner/operator can show that it will not pollute the area. The owner/operator must also show that no alternative site is available. This restriction does not apply to existing landfills. To prevent pollution that could be caused by earthquakes or other kinds of earth movement, new and laterally expanding landfills may not be built in areas prone to them. This restrictions does not apply to existing landfills. Finally, landfills cannot be located in areas that are subject to landslides, mudslides, or sinkholes; this restriction applies to new, existing, and laterally expanding landfills.

Operation

The EPA and the states have developed regulations specifically covering the disposal of hazardous wastes in special landfills. Owners/operators of municipal landfills must develop programs to keep these regulated hazardous wastes out of their units. In general, each day's waste must be covered to prevent the spread of disease by rats, flies, mosquitoes, birds, and other animals that are naturally attracted to landfills. Methane gas, which occurs naturally at landfills, must be monitored routinely. If emission levels at the landfill exceed a certain limit, the proper authorities must be notified and a plan must be developed to solve the problem. Owners/operators must restrict access to their landfills to prevent illegal dumping and other unauthorized activities. So that no pollutants are swept into lakes, rivers, or streams, landfills must be built with ditches and levees to keep storm water from flooding their active areas and to collect and control stormwater runoff. Landfills cannot accept liquid waste from tank trucks or in 55-gallon drums. This restriction helps reduce both the amount of leachate (liquids that have passed through the landfill) and the concentrations of contaminants in the leachate. Finally, landfills must be operated so they do not violate state and federal clean air laws and regulations. This means, among other things, that the burning of waste is prohibited at landfills, except under certain conditions.

Design

New and expanding landfills must be designed for groundwater protection by making sure that levels of contaminants do not exceed federal limits for safe drinking water. In states and tribes with EPA-approved programs, landfill owners/operators have flexibility in designing their units to suit local circumstances, providing the state or tribal program director approves the design. This allows owners/operators to ensure environmental protection at the lowest possible cost to citizens served by the landfill. This flexibility means, for example, that the use of a liner, and the nature and thickness of the liner system, may vary from state to state, and perhaps from site to site. In states and tribal areas without EPA-approved programs, owners/operators must build their landfills according to a design developed by EPA, or seek a waiver. The EPA design lays out specific requirements for liners and leachate collection systems. Liners must be composite, that is, a synthetic material over a 2-foot layer of clay. This system forms a barrier that prevents leachate from escaping from the landfill into groundwater. The design also requires leachate collection systems that allow the leachate to be captured and treated.

Groundwater Monitoring and Corrective Action

Generally, landfill owners/operators must install monitoring systems to detect groundwater contamination. Sampling and analysis must be conducted twice a year. States and tribes with EPA-approved programs have the flexibility to tailor facility requirements to specific local conditions. For example, they may specify different frequencies for sampling ground water for contaminants, or phase in the deadline for complying with the federal groundwater monitoring requirements.

If the groundwater becomes contaminated, owners/operators in approved states and tribal areas must clean it up to levels specified by the state or tribal director. In states and tribes without EPA-approved programs, the federal regulations specify that contaminants must be reduced below the federal limits for safe drinking water.

Closure and Post Closure Care

When a landfill owner/operator stops accepting waste, the landfill must be closed in a way that will prevent problems later. The final cover must be designed to keep liquid away from the buried waste. For 30 years after closure, the owner/operator must continue to maintain the final cover, monitor groundwater to ensure the unit is not leaking, collect and monitor landfill gas, and perform other maintenance activities. (States and tribes with approved programs may vary this period based on local conditions.)

Financial Assurance

To ensure that monies are available to correct possible environmental problems, landfill owners/operators are now required to show that they have the financial means to cover expenses for site closure, postclosure maintenance, and cleanups. The regulations spell out ways to meet this requirement, including (but not limited to) surety bonds, insurance, and letters of credit.

FUTURE TRENDS

As described earlier, there is significant public opposition to the siting of any type of municipal solid waste management facility. In the future, the public needs to be educated and informed so that these facilities can be properly located. Most of these facilities are found in commercial and/or industrial zones, and away from restricted areas.

The effects of the facilities on health and safety have not been measured at this time. However, even with proper management, wastes containing contaminated materials and dangerous chemicals are potential hazards to millions of people. The health of an entire community can be jeopardized if these wastes are temporarily but inadequately and or improperly managed. The whole health risk assessment area needs to be addressed in the future.

The future is also certain to bring a reduced dependence on landfilling of municipal solid waste. Source reduction and recycle/reuse options will be emphasized. And, although incineration has come under pressure recently with the Clinton Administration, it too may very well gain favor if the authorities and the public are educated as to the inherent advantages of this solid waste management option (Theodore, personal lecture notes).

SUMMARY

1. In 1990, Americans generated over 195 million tons of municipal solid waste; this annual amount is expected increase to more than 220 million tons by 2000.

2. The federal government sets minimum national standards applicable to municipal solid waste disposal, but state, tribal, and local governments are responsible for actually implementing and enforcing waste programs. States are required to develop their own programs based on the federal regulations.

3. To increase recycling nationwide, the EPA has undertaken a number of efforts to stimulate markets for secondary materials and to promote increased separation, collection, processing, and recycling of waste.

4. Incineration is not a new technology and has been commonly used for treating wastes for many years in Europe and the United States. The major benefits of incineration are that the process actually destroys most of the waste rather than just disposing of or storing it; it can be used for a variety of specific wastes and is reasonably competitive in cost compared to other disposal methods.

5. The federal regulations for municipal solid waste landfills cover the following six basic areas: location, operation, design, groundwater monitoring and corrective action, closure and post-closure care, and financial assurance.

6. There is significant public opposition to the siting of any type of municipal solid waste management facility. In the future, the public needs to be educated and informed so that these facilities can be properly located.

REFERENCES

EPA. "Safer Disposal for Solid Waste," Document EPA/530SW91092, March, 1993.

Geiger, G. "Incineration of Municipal and Hazardous Waste." *Natl. Environ. J.* 1(2), Nov/Dec 1991.

Holmes, G., Singh, B., and Theodore, L. *Handbook of Environmental Management and Technology*. New York: Wiley Interscience, 1993.

Shen, T., McGuinn, Y., and Theodore, L. "Hazardous Waste Incineration: Student Manual," USEPA APTI, RTP, NC, 1986.

Theodore, L. Personal lecture notes.

Theodore, L. and McGuinn, Y. *Pollution Prevention*. New York: Van Nostrand Reinhold, 1992.

Theodore, L., and Moy, E. "Hazardous Waste Incineration," An ETS THEODORE TUTORIAL, Roanoke, VA: ETS International, 1994.

Theodore, L., and Reynolds, J. *Introduction to Hazardous Waste Incineration*. New York: Wiley Interscience, 1988.

19

Hospital Waste Management

CONTRIBUTING AUTHOR

Dorothy Caraher, RN

INTRODUCTION

Virtually all of the 6,600 hospitals in the United States house X-ray equipment, laboratories, kitchens, pharmacies, and waste disposal stations. More than half also have diagnostic radioisotope facilities, CT scanners, and ultrasound equipment. The environmental impact of the waste is considerable. All of these substances are subject either to the Environmental Protection Agency (EPA) and/or the Occupational Safety and Health Administration (OSHA) rules and regulations on the environment and worker exposure (see Chapter 5). OSHA has numerous regulations pertaining specifically to workers in health-care settings.

Medical wastes are not only generated by hospitals but also by laboratories, animal research facilities, and by other institutional sources. The term "biomedical waste" is coming into usage to replace what had been referred to as pathological waste or infectious wastes. Hospitals, however, are generating more and more medical waste with their increasing use of disposable products as well as their increasing service to the community. Hence, the focus of this chapter will be on the issue of hospital waste management.

Progress has been made in methods and equipment for the care of hospital patients. Hundreds of single-service items have been marketed to reduce the possibility of hospital-acquired infections. Yet hospitals generally have been slow to improve their techniques for the handling and disposing of the waste materials, which are increasing in quantity as a result of more patients and higher per-patient waste loads.

Some of the material in this chapter is an edited, revised, and updated version of several chapters from the Garland STPM Press textbook *Air Pollution Control for Hospitals and Other Medical Facilities,* where copyright is owned by L. Theodore.

Medical waste comes in a wide variety of forms. These forms include packaging, such as wrappers from bandages and catheters; disposable items, such as tongue depressors and thermometer covers; and infectious wastes, such as blood, tissue, sharps, cultures, and stocks of infectious agents.

The location of these wastes include laboratories, X ray facilities, surgical departments, pharmacies, emergency rooms, offices, and service areas.

There is an equally wide variety of sources. While hospitals, clinics, and health-care facilities may generate the vast majority of medical waste, both infectious and noninfectious waste is also generated by private practices, home health care, veterinary clinics, and blood banks. In New York and New Jersey alone, there are approximately 150,000 sources producing nearly 250 million pounds a year.

The beach closures along costal New Jersey in 1987 and along the south shore of Long Island in 1988 have focused attention on medical wastes. Their volume is relatively small (probably less than 1 percent of the total), but as with sewage wastes, concern centers around the issue of public health. Why these wastes are appearing more frequently is not certain. However, there are several possible contributing factors. The three major factors include:

1. A marked increase in disposable medical care materials.
2. An increase in the use of medically associated equipment on the streets as drug paraphernalia.
3. An increase in illegal disposal of medical wastes as a consequence of the increased costs of disposal.

MEDICAL WASTE REGULATIONS AND DEFINITIONS

On March 24, 1989, the EPA published regulations in the Federal Register as required under the Medical Waste Tracking Act of 1988. The term "medical waste" was defined as any solid waste that is generated in the diagnosis, treatment, or immunization of human beings or animals, in research pertaining thereto, or in the production or testing of biologicals. Medical waste can be either infectious or noninfectious. The term medical waste does not include any hazardous or household waste, defined in regulations under Subtitle C of the Act.

Infectious waste is waste that contains pathogenic micro-organisms. In order for a disease to be transmitted, the waste must contain sufficient quantity of the pathogen that causes the disease. There must also be a method of transmitting the disease from the waste material to the recipient.

Medical waste that has not been specifically excluded in the EPA provisions (for example, household waste) and is either a listed medical waste or a mixture of a listed medical waste and a solid under the demonstration program of the act is known as "regulated medical waste." Seven classes of listed wastes are defined by the EPA as regulated medical waste. Details on these seven classes are provided below.

1. Cultures and stocks. Cultures and stocks of infectious agents and associated biologicals, including: cultures and stocks of infectious agents from research and industrial laboratories; wastes from the production of biologicals; discarded live and attenuated vaccines; and culture dishes and devices used to transfer, inoculate, and mix cultures.

2. Pathological waste. Human pathological wastes, including (a) tissues, organs, body parts, and body fluids that are removed during surgery, autopsy, or other medical procedures, and (b) specimens of body fluids and their containers.

3. Human blood and blood products. Products here include: liquid waste human blood; products of blood; items saturated and/or dripping with human blood that are now caked with dried human blood including serum, plasma, and other components; and containers that were used or intended for use in either patient care, testing, laboratory analysis, or the development of pharmaceuticals (intravenous bags are also included in this category).

4. Sharps. The category includes sharps that have been used in animal or human patient care or treatment, in medical research, or in industrial laboratories, including hypodermic needles, syringes (with or without the attached needles), pasteur pipettes, scalpel blades, blood vials, needles with attached tubing, and culture dishes (regardless of presence of infectious agents).

5. Animal waste. Contaminated animal carcasses, body parts, and bedding of animals that were known to have been exposed to infectious agents during research, production of biologicals, or testing in pharmaceuticals.

6. Isolation wastes. Biological waste and discarded materials contaminated with blood, excretions, or secretions from humans known to be infected with certain highly communicable diseases.

7. Unused sharps. These included hypodermic needles, suture needles, syringes, and scalpel blades.

WASTE STORAGE AND HANDLING

Hospital wastes are stored in many kinds of receptacles: wastepaper baskets, garbage cans, empty oil drums, laundry hampers, carts, buckets, and even on the floor. Plastic containers are coming into widespread use. They are easier to lift and clean than metal containers, and the bases and sides are impermeable to insects, since they do not rust, bend, or dent.

Most hospitals segregate their medical wastes prior to treatment and disposal. However, most hospitals do not segregate all medical waste categories from one another, although certain wastes, most often sharps, cultures and stock, are segregated from other medical wastes prior to treatment or disposal. Most hospitals carefully segregate sharps in rigid plastic sharps containers. Medical wastes are usually segregated from the general trash (e.g., office and cafeteria wastes). Medical waste is almost always separated into red, orange, or biohazard marked bags, and general waste is usually placed in clear, white, or brown bags.

In some hospitals a sharps container is mounted on the wall of every patient room. In other hospitals, the sharps containers are placed in central collection areas on the patient floors, in other areas as necessary (operating room, emergency room, laboratory), and on the carts themselves.

Red bags are almost always used in the laboratory, operating rooms (OR), emergency rooms (ER), and isolation rooms, In some cases, red bags also appear in patient rooms. As an alternative to redbagging all waste from patient rooms, some hospitals place red bags and sharps containers on patient care carts. In this fashion, medical wastes are segregated from other discarded wastes.

Medical waste from the "floors" (as patient wings are called) are sometimes stored in "soiled utility rooms" on the patient floors until carried to central storage rooms for incineration or transport. The housekeeping staff is often responsible for gathering the waste and carting it to the storage area. In some cases, general trash is collected in the same cart with red bag wastes.

Suctioned fluids are more commonly discharged into a sanitary sewer rather than containerized or incinerated. However, some hospitals use disposable suction containers and place the entire container in red bags. Other fluids—from the laboratory, for example—are often contained and then redbagged. In some cases, fluids are poured into red bags.

Sharps, other than needles and syringes (such as discarded slides and test tubes), often are placed in the red plastic bags without first being placed in a punctureproof container. Some of these are then placed in cardboard boxes to avoid punctures. The boxes also provide support for heavier sharps such as glassware, slides, and tubes of blood.

An unusual feature of hospital waste management is that wastes are generated continuously around the clock, but they are collected at fixed intervals during the day shift. The housekeeping department usually has the primary responsibility for collection within the hospitals, although a number of other departments have regular responsibility for other facets of waste collection. Generally, only minimal qualifications are required for individuals collecting wastes.

Hospitals often use manually propelled carts of some variety to collect waste materials. Hospital carts are frequently constructed in such a way that sanitizing them is impossible, thus providing surfaces where bacteria can multiply. The routing of carts into and through areas where freedom from contamination is critical increases the probability of contamination from wastes. In addition, individuals collecting wastes are repeatedly exposed to chemical and microbiological contamination and other hazards, but usually have minimal knowledge, skill, or equipment to protect themselves.

Gravity chutes are a simple and inexpensive means of transferring wastes vertically. However, the chutes are seldom constructed with mechanical exhausts, interlocking charging doors, or other systems for preventing the spread of microbiological contamination. In several instances, linen chutes are reserved for conveying solid wastes during certain times of the day thus providing another potential way of spreading contamination. Chute usage has additional drawbacks: fire hazards, spilling of wastes during loading, blockages, difficulties in cleaning, and odors. Proper design and construction can help to prevent some of these, especially the fire hazard and cleaning problems. Others can be avoided by excluding certain wastes, especially grossly contaminated articles, and by exercising more care in the use of chutes.

WASTE PROCESSING AND DISPOSAL

Hospital wastes are disposed of in a number of ways, usually by the hospital's maintenance or engineering department. Eventually, almost two-thirds of the wastes leave the hospitals and go out

Table 19–1.   Approximate Percent of Hospitals Using Treatment/Disposal Methods for Each Waste Type

Type of Waste	Incineration	Sanitary Landfill	Steam Sterilization	Sewer
Blood and Blood Products	58%	12%	25%	23%
Body Fluids and Wastes	58%	32%	11%	6%
Lab Wastes	61%	16%	33%	3%
Pathological Wastes	92%	4%	4%	2%
Sharps	79%	16%	14%	0
Animal Wastes	81%	2%	2%	0
Disposable Materials	29%	54%	4%	6%

into the community for disposal. Approximately 35 percent by weight, principally combustible rubbish and biological materials, are disposed of in hospital incinerators. Noncombustibles are usually separated and, along with the incinerator residue, leave the hospital to be disposed of on land.

Waste management methods include incineration, autoclaving, sanitary landfilling, sewer systems, chemical disinfection, thermal inactivation, ionizing radiation, gas vapor sterilization, segregation, and bagging (Doucet, 1991). Table 19–1 lists typical treatment/disposal methods for each waste type. This table reveals that only 55 percent of hospitals that segregate infectious from noninfectious waste incinerate their infectious waste. Eighteen percent treat infectious waste by steam serialization and then incinerate or landfill the waste. Three percent of hospitals dispose of infectious waste in sanitary landfills without prior treatment (U.S. Environmental Protection Medical Waste Meeting, 1988).

WASTE MANAGEMENT PROGRAMS

The large amounts of potentially contaminated wastes generated by hospitals raise the possibility that they are a concentrated source of environment health problems. Many hospital solid wastes are indeed contributing to occupational injuries, environmental pollution, and insect and rodent infestation. Some remedial steps that can be taken include the following:

1. Seal as many wastes as possible in disposable bags at the point of generation, or enclose them in such a way as to prevent or minimize contamination of the hospital environment.

2. Construct carts and other equipment used to handle waste so they are easy to keep in sanitary condition.

3. Construct and operate chutes in such a way as to prevent or minimize microbiological contamination of air, linen, and various areas of the hospital.

4. Reduce the danger to personnel handling wastes. Provide preventive health services such as immunization, as well as protective equipment such as gloves and uniforms. In the future, introduce equipment and systems that require less manpower.

5. Require higher qualifications for those handling wastes. Provide them with training on the hazards associated with hospital wastes and the means of protecting not only themselves but others in the hospital and the community.

6. Improve operation of incinerators by training operators to keep loads within incinerator capacity and to maintain temperatures high enough for proper combustion.

7. Provide for safe management of hazardous wastes within the hospital so that they cannot pose a danger to the community.

Most hospitals have comprehensive and sound policies on solid waste management, including specific directives on segregation and special handling of hazardous materials. But, in practice, the policies break down. Employees fail to make the right judgments consistently, and stricter supervision is needed to ensure that employees maintain proper handling and disposal of pathological and sharp wastes, separate disposable wastes from reusable wastes such as dinnerware and linens, bag materials properly, and deposit chute materials promptly. In addition, storage, processing, and disposal areas should be supervised closely and security maintained so that unauthorized personnel cannot gain access.

INFECTIOUS WASTE MANAGEMENT PROGRAMS

A waste management plan for an institution should be a comprehensive written plan that includes all aspects of management for different types of waste, including infectious, radioactive, chemical, and general wastes as well as wastes with multiple hazards (e.g., infectious and radioactive, infectious and toxic, infectious and radioactive and carcinogenic). In addition, it is appropriate for each laboratory or department to have specific detailed, written instructions for the management of the types of waste that are generated in that unit. The waste management section would probably constitute one part of a general, more comprehensive document that also addresses other policies and procedures. Many such documents that include sections on the management of infectious waste have been prepared by various institutions and government agencies. (U.S. Department of Health and Human Services, CDC, 1978; U.S. Army Medical Research Institute of Infectious Diseases, 1978).

An infectious waste management system should include the following elements:

1. Designation of infectious wastes
2. Handling of infectious wastes, including:
   a. Segregation
   b. Packaging
   c. Storage
   d. Transport and handling
   e. Treatment techniques
   f. Disposal of treated waste
3. Contingency planning
4. Staff training

Various options are available for the development of an infectious waste management system. Management options for an individual facility should be selected on the basis of what is most appropriate for the particular facility. Factors such as location, size, and budget should be taken into consideration. The selected options should be incorporated into a documented infectious waste management plan. An infectious waste management system cannot be effective unless it is fully implemented. Therefore, a specific individual at the generating facility should be responsible for implementation of the plan. This person should have the responsibility as well as the authority to make sure that the provisions of the management plan are being followed.

There are a number of areas in which alternative options are available in an infectious waste management system. (e.g., treatment techniques for the various types of infectious waste, types of treatment equipment, treatment sites, and various waste handling practices). The selection of available options at a facility depends upon a number of factors, such as the nature of the infectious waste, the quantity of infectious waste generated, the availability of equipment for treatment on-site and off-site, regulatory constraints, and cost considerations. These factors are presented here in order to provide assistance in the development of an infectious waste management program.

Since treatment methods vary with waste type, the waste must be evaluated and categorized with regard to its potential to cause disease. Such characteristics as chemical content, density, water content, bulk, etc., are known to influence waste treatment decisions. For example, many facilities use a combination of treatment techniques for the different components of the infectious waste stream, for example, steam sterilization for laboratory cultures and incineration for pathological waste.

The quantity of each category of infectious waste generated at the facility may also influence the method of treatment. Decisions should be made on the basis of the major components of the infectious waste stream. Generally, it would be desirable and efficient to handle all infectious waste in the same manner. However, if a selected option is not suitable for treatment of all wastes, then other options must be included in the infectious waste management plan.

Another important factor in the selection of options for infectious waste management is the availability of on-site and off-site treatment. On-site treatment of infectious waste provides the advantage of a single facility or generator maintaining control of the waste. For some facilities, however, off-site treatment may offer the most cost-effective option. Off-site treatment alternatives include such options as morticians (for pathological wastes), a shared treatment unit at another institution, and commercial or community treatment facilities. With off-site treatment, precautions should be taken in packaging and transporting to ensure containment of the infectious waste. In addition, generators should comply with all state and local regulations pertaining to the transport of regulated medical waste, and ensure that the waste is being handled and treated properly at the off-site treatment facility.

It is also important to consider prevailing community attitudes in such matters as site selection for off-site treatment facilities. These include local laws, ordinances, and zoning restrictions as well as unofficial public attitudes that may result in changes in local laws.

Cost considerations are also important in the selection of infectious waste management options. Cost factors include personnel, equipment cost (capital expense, annual operating and maintenance expenses—see Chapter 47 for more details), hauling costs (for infectious waste and the residue from treatment), and, if applicable, service fees for the offsite treatment option.

As indicated earlier, the EPA recommends that each facility establish an infectious waste management plan. A responsible individual at the facility should prepare a comprehensive document that outlines policies and procedures for the management of infectious waste (including infectious wastes with multiple hazards). This recommendation is consistent with the standard of the Joint Commission on Accreditation of Hospitals (JCAH), which specifies a system "to safely manage hazardous materials and wastes" (Doucet, 1991).

FUTURE TRENDS

Hopefully, the infectious waste management plans in the future that deal with health and safety will include a contingency plan to provide for emergency situations. It is important that these measures be selected in a timely manner so that they can be implemented quickly when needed. This plan should include, but not be limited to, procedures to be used under the following circumstances:

1. Spills of liquid infectious waste, cleanup procedures, protection of personnel, and disposal of spill residue.
2. Rupture of plastic bags (or other loss of containment), cleanup procedures, protection of personnel, and repackaging of waste.
3. Equipment failure, alternative arrangements for waste storage and treatment (e.g., off-site treatment).

Facilities that generate waste should provide employees with waste management training. This training should include an explanation of the waste management plan and assignment of roles and responsibilities for implementation of the plan. Such education is important for all employees who generate or handle wastes regardless of the employee's role (i.e., supervisor or supervised) or type of work (i.e., technical/scientific or housekeeping/maintenance).

Training programs should be implemented when:

1. The infectious waste management plans are first developed and instituted.
2. New employees are hired.
3. Waste management practices are changed.

Continuing education is also an important part of staff training, including refresher training aids in maintaining personnel awareness of the potential hazards posed by wastes. Training also serves to reinforce waste management policies and procedures that are detailed in the waste management plan. The reader is referred to Chapter 43 for more detailed discussion or training.

Many hospitals are beginning to address the issues raised in this chapter on a comprehensive basis. Developing environmental management health and safety programs does more than meet the letter of the law. They can cut costs, reduce liability, and ensure that the hospital's primary mission of delivering health care is not jeopardized by a fine or an incident that requires shutting down a facility. On average, though, most hospitals still have attained only partial compliance. That will surely change in the future (Lundy, 1994).

SUMMARY

1. Medical wastes are not only generated by hospitals, but also by laboratories, animal research facilities, and by other institutional sources.

2. On March 24, 1989, the EPA published regulations in the Federal Register as required under the Medical Waste Tracking Act of 1988. The term "medical waste" was defined as any solid waste that is generated in the diagnosis, treatment, or immunization of human beings or animals, in research pertaining thereto, or in the production of testing of biologicals.

3. Most hospitals segregate their medical wastes prior to treatment and disposal. However, most hospitals do not segregate all medical waste categories from one another, although certain wastes, most often sharps, cultures and stock, are segregated from other medical wastes prior to treatment or disposal.

4. Hospital wastes are disposed of in a number of ways, usually by the hospital's maintenance or engineering department. Eventually, almost two-thirds of the wastes leave the hospitals and go out into the community for disposal.

5. Most hospitals have comprehensive and sound policies on solid waste management, including specific directives on segregation and special handling of hazardous materials.

6. A waste management plan for an institution should be a comprehensive written plan that includes all aspects of management for different types of waste, including infectious, radioactive, chemical, and general wastes as well as wastes with multiple hazards (e.g., infectious and radioactive, infectious and toxic, infectious and radioactive and carcinogenic).

7. Future trends in hospital waste management are certain to more carefully address accident/emergency situations.

REFERENCES

Doucet, L. "Update of Alternative and Emerging Medical Waste Treatment Technologies, AHA Technical Document Series, 1991.

EPA. *Draft Manual for Infectious Waste Management,* SW957. Washington, DC: Author. August 1982.

Lundy, K. "It's Enough to Make You Sick." *Resources,* February, 1994.

U.S. Department of the Army, U.S. Army Medical Research Institute of Infectious Diseases (USAMRIID): "Hot" Suite Operations: Standard Operating Procedure. Fort Dietrick, Frederick, MD, USAMRIID, 30 November, 1978.

United States Environmental Protection Medical Waste Meeting: November 14–16, 1988.

20

Nuclear Waste Management

CONTRIBUTING AUTHOR

James B. Mernin

INTRODUCTION

As with many other types of waste disposal, radioactive waste disposal is no longer a function of technical feasibility but rather a question of social or political acceptability. The placement of facilities for the permanent disposal of municipal solid waste, hazardous chemical waste, and nuclear wastes alike has become an increasingly large part of waste management. Today a large percentage of the money required to build a radioactive waste facility will be spent on the siting and licensing of the facility.

Nuclear or radioactive waste can be loosely defined as something that is no longer useful and that contains radioactive isotopes in varying concentrations and forms. Radioactive waste is then further broken down into categories that classify the waste by activity, by generation process, by molecular weight, and by volume.

Radioactive isotopes emit energy as they decay to more stable elements. The energy is emitted in the form of alpha particles, beta particles, neutrons, and gamma rays. The amount of energy that a particular radioactive isotope emits, the timeframe over which it emits that energy, and the type of contact with humans all help determine the hazard it poses to the environment. The major categories of radioactive waste that exist are highlevel waste (HLW), lowlevel waste (LLW), transuranic waste (TRU), uranium mine and mill tailings, mixed wastes, and naturally occurring radioactive materials.

CURRENT STATUS OF NUCLEAR WASTE MANAGEMENT

Nuclear or radioactive materials are used in many applications throughout today's society. Radioactive materials are used to generate power in nuclear power stations, and are used to treat patients in hospitals (see previous chapter). The generators of radioactive waste in today's society are primarily the federal government, electrical utilities, private industry, hospitals and universities. Although, each of these generators uses radioactive materials, the waste that is generated by each of them may be very different and must be handled accordingly. Any material that contains radioactive isotopes in measurable quantities is considered nuclear or radioactive waste. For the purposes of this chapter, the terms nuclear waste and radioactive waste will be considered synonymous.

Waste management is a field that involves the reduction, stabilization, and ultimate disposal of waste. Waste reduction is the practice of minimizing the amount of material that requires disposal. Some of the common ways in which waste reduction is accomplished are incineration, compaction, and dewatering. The object of waste disposal is to isolate the material from the biosphere, and in the case of radioactive waste allow it time to decay to sufficiently safe levels. Table 20–1 is a chronology of the laws that have affected radioactive waste management practices over the last fifty years.

The federal government has mandated that individual states or interstate compacts, which are formed and dissolved by Congress, be responsible for the disposal of the LLW generated within their boundaries. Originally, these states were to bring the disposal capacity online by 1993. Although access to the few remaining facilities is drawing to an end, none of the states or compacts have a facility available to accept waste. Some states are making progress, but none of the proposed facilities is currently in the construction phase.

Both the high level waste (HLW) and the transuranic (TRU) waste programs have sites defined for their respective facilities at Yucca Mountain, and at the Waste Isolation Pilot Plant

Table 20–1.   Chronology of Major Events Affecting Nuclear Waste Management (Berlin & Stanton, 1989)

Year	Event
1954	The Atomic Energy Act is passed.
1963	First commercial disposal of LLW.
1967	DOE facilities begins to store TRU wastes retrievably.
1970	National Environmental Policy Act becomes effective; Environmental Protection Agency is formed.
1974	Atomic Energy Commission divides into the Nuclear Regulatory Commission (NRC) and the Energy Research and Development Administration (ERDA).
1975	WIPP proposed as unlicensed defense TRU disposal facility; West Valley, New York low level disposal facility closed.
1977	President Carter deferred reprocessing, pending the review of the proliferation implications of alternative fuel cycles.
1979	Three Mile Island, Unit #2 accident; report to the President of the Interagency Review Group on Radioactive Waste Management.
1980	Low Level Waste Policy Act is passed; all commercial disposal of TRU wastes ends.
1982	Nuclear Waste Policy Act is passed; 10 CFR Part 61 issued as final regulation for LLW.
1985	Low Level Radioactive Waste Policy Act Amendments.
1986	The reactor explosion at Chernobyl.
1987	Nuclear Waste Policy Act Amendments provide for the characterization of the proposed HLW repository at Yucca Mountain, Nevada.

(WIPP) in Carlsbad, New Mexico. The WIPP facility is a Department of Energy (DOE) research and development facility that has been designed to accept 6 million ft^3 of contact-handled TRU waste, as well as 25,000 ft^3 of remote-handled TRU waste. The facility will accept defense-generated waste and place it into a retrievable geologic repository. A geologic repository is in this instance the salt formations located near Carlsbad. The facility has a design-based lifetime of twenty-five years.

RAMIFICATIONS OF NUCLEAR ACCIDENTS

The three largest radiological accidents of the last twenty years are the explosion at Chernobyl, the partial core meltdown at Three Mile Island Unit #2, and the mishandling of a radioactive source in Brazil. The least publicized, but perhaps the most appropriate of these accidents, with respect to waste management, was the situation in Brazil.

The uncontrolled radiotherapy source was overlooked in an abandoned medical clinic, and was eventually discarded as scrap. The stainless steel jacket and the platinum capsule surrounding the radioactive cesium were compromised by scavengers in a junkyard. The cesium was distributed among the people for use as "carnival glitter," because of its luminescent properties. The material was spread directly onto individuals' skin and face, as well as their clothing. Severe illness was immediately evident to most of the exposed victims. Four people died from exposure by the spring of 1988, and it was estimated that an additional five persons would die over the next five years. Over 40 tons of material, including clothing, shoes, and housing materials, were contaminated from the release of less than 1 gram of radioactive cesium.

Biological Effects of Radiation

Although much still remains to be learned about the interaction between ionizing radiation and living matter, more is known about the mechanism of radiation damage on the molecular, cellular, and organ system level than most other environmental hazards. The radioactive materials warning sign is shown in Figure 20–1. A vast amount of quantitative dose-response data has been accumulated throughout years of studying the different applications of radionuclides. This information has allowed the nuclear technology industry to continue at risks that are no greater than any other technology. The following subsections will provide a brief description of the different types of ionizing radiation and the effects that may occur upon overexposure to radioactive materials.

Radioactive Transformations

Radioactive transformations are accomplished by several different mechanisms, most importantly alpha particle, beta particle, and gamma ray emissions. Each of these mechanisms are spontaneous nuclear transformations. The result of these transformations is the formation of different more stable elements. The kind of transformation that will take place for any given radioactive element is a function of the type of nuclear instability as well as the mass/energy relationship. The nuclear instability is dependent on the ratio of neutrons to protons; a different type of decay will occur to allow for a more stable daughter product. The mass/energy relationship states that for any radioac-

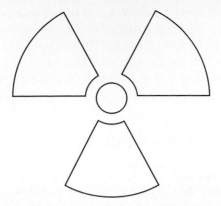

FIGURE 20–1.   Radioactive materials warning sign.

tive transformations the laws of conservation of mass and the conservation of energy must be followed.

An alpha particle is an energetic helium nucleus. The alpha particle is released from a radioactive element with a neutron to proton ratio that is too low. The helium nucleus consists of two protons and two neutrons. The alpha particle differs from a helium atom in that it is emitted without any electrons. The resulting daughter product from this type of transformation has an atomic number that is two less than its parent and an atomic mass number that is four less. Below is an example of alpha decay using polonium (Po); polonium has an atomic mass number (protons and neutrons) and atomic number of 210 and 84, respectively.

$$^{210}_{84}Po \rightarrow ^{4}_{2}He + ^{206}_{82}Pb \tag{20–1}$$

The terms He and Pb represent helium and lead, respectively.

This is a useful example because the lead daughter product is stable and will not decay further. The neutron to proton ratio changed from 1.5 to 1.51, just enough to result in a stable element. Alpha particles are known as having a high LET or linear energy transfer. The alphas will only travel a short distance while releasing energy. A piece of paper or the top layer of skin will stop an alpha particle. So, alpha particles are not external hazards, but can be extremely hazardous if inhaled or ingested.

Beta particle emission occurs when an ordinary electron is ejected from the nucleus of an atom. The electron (e), appears when a neutron (n) is transformed into a proton within the nucleus.

$$^{1}_{0}n \rightarrow ^{1}_{1}H + ^{0}_{(-1)}e \tag{20–2}$$

Note that the proton is shown as a hydrogen (H) nucleus. This transformation must conserve the overall charge of each of the resulting particles. Contrary to alpha emission, beta emission occurs in elements that contain a surplus of neutrons. The daughter product of a beta emitter remains at the same atomic mass number, but is one atomic number higher than its parent. Many elements that decay by beta emission also release a gamma ray at the same instant. These elements are known as betagamma emitters. Strong beta radiation is an external hazard, because of its ability to penetrate body tissue.

Similar to beta decay is positron emission, where the parent emits a positively charged electron. Positron emission is commonly called betapositive decay. This decay scheme occurs when the neutron to proton ratio is too low and alpha emission is not energetically possible. The positively charged electron, or positron, will travel at high speeds until it interacts with an electron. Upon contact, each of the particles will disappear and two gamma rays will result. When two gamma rays are formed in this manner it is called annihilation radiation.

Unlike alpha and beta radiation, gamma radiation is an electromagnetic wave with a specified range of wavelengths. Gamma rays cannot be completely shielded against, but can only be reduced in intensity with increased shielding. Gamma rays typically interact with matter through the photoelectric effect, Compton scattering, pair production, or direct interactions with the nucleus.

Dose Response

The response of humans to varying doses of radiation is a field that has been widely studied. The observed radiation effects can be categorized as stochastic or nonstochastic effects, depending upon the dose received and the time period over which such dose was received. Contrary to most biological effects, effects from radiation usually fall under the category of stochastic effects. The nonstochastic effects can be noted as having three qualities: A minimum dose or threshold dose must be received before the particular effect is observed; the magnitude of the effect increases as the size of the dose increases; and a clear causal relationship can be determined between the dose and the subsequent effects. Cember (1992) uses the analogy between drinking an alcoholic beverage and exposure to a noxious agent. For example, a person must exceed a certain amount of alcohol before he or she shows signs of drinking. After that, the effect of the alcohol will increase as the person continues to drink. Finally, if he or she exhibits drunken behavior, there is no doubt that this is a result of his or her drinking.

Stochastic effects, on the other hand, occur by chance. Stochastic effects will be present in a fraction of the exposed population as well as in a fraction of the unexposed population. Therefore, stochastic effects are not unequivocally related to a noxious agent as the above example implies. Stochastic effects have no threshold, any exposure will increase the risk of an effect, but will not wholly determine if any effect will arise. Cancer and genetic effects are the two most common effects linked with exposure to radiation. Cancer can be caused by the damaging of a somatic cell, while genetic effects are caused when damage occurs to a germ cell that results in a pregnancy.

SOURCES OF NUCLEAR WASTE

Naturally Occurring Radioactive Materials*

Naturally occurring radioactive materials, or NORM, are present in the earth's crust in varying concentrations. The major naturally occurring radionuclides of concern are radon, radium, and ura-

*Information in this section is taken from "Diffuse NORM Wastes Characterization and Risk Assessment," EPA, May 1991.

nium. These radionuclides have been found to concentrate in water treatment plant sludges, petroleum scale, and phosphate fertilizers.

In United States an estimated 40 billion gallons of water are distributed, through public water supplies, daily. Since water comes from different sources, streams, lakes, reservoirs, and aquifers, it contains varying levels of naturally occurring radioactivity. Radioactivity is leached into ground or surface water while in contact with uranium- and thorium-bearing geologic materials. The predominant radionuclides found in water are radium, uranium, and radon, as well as their decay products.

For reasons of public health, water is generally treated to ensure its quality before consumption by the public. Water treatment includes passing the water through various filters and devices that rely on chemicals to remove any impurities and organisms. If water with elevated radioactivity is treated by one or more of these systems, there exists the possibility of generating waste sludges or brines with elevated levels of radioactive materials. These wastes may be generated even if the original intention of the treatment process was not to remove radionuclides.

Mining of phosphate rock (phosphorite) is the fifth largest mining industry in the United States in terms of quantity of material mined. The southeastern United States is the center of the domestic phosphate rock industry, with Florida, North Carolina, and Tennessee having over 90 percent of the domestic rock production capacity.

Phosphate rock is processed to produce phosphoric acid and elemental phosphorus. These two products are then combined with other materials to produce phosphate fertilizers, detergents, animal feeds, other food products, and phosphorus-containing materials. The most important use of phosphate rock is the production of fertilizer, which accounts for 80 percent of the phosporite in the United States.

Uranium in phosphate ores found in the United States ranges from 20 to 300 parts per million (ppm), or about 7 to 100 pCi/g. Thorium occurs at a lower concentration between 1 and 5 ppm, or about 0.1 to 0.6 pCi/g. The unit picocuries per gram (pCi/g) represents a concentration of each radionuclide based on the activity of that radionuclide. The units of curies represent a fixed number of radioactive transformations in a second. Phosphogypsum is the principal waste byproduct generated during the phosphoric acid production process. Phosphate slag is the principle waste byproduct generated from the production of elemental phoshorous. Elevated levels of both uranium and thorium as well as their decay products are known to exist at elevated levels in these wastes. Since large quantities of phosphate industry wastes are produced, there is a concern that these materials may present a potential radiological risk to individuals that are exposed to these materials if distributed in the environment.

Fertilizers are spread over large areas of agricultural land. The major crops that are routinely treated with phosphate-based fertilizer include coarse grains, wheat, corn, soybeans, and cotton. Since large quantities of fertilizer are used in agricultural applications, phosphate fertilizers are included as a NORM material. The continued use of phosphate fertilizers could eventually lead to an increase in radioactivity in the environment and in the food chain.

Currently, there are no federal regulations pertaining directly to NORM containing wastes. The volume of wastes produced is sufficiently large that disposal in a low-level waste facility is generally not feasible. A cost effective solution must be implemented to both guard industry against large disposal costs and ensure the safety and health of the public.

Low Level Radioactive Waste

Low level radioactive waste (LLRW) is produced by a number of processes and is the broadest category of radioactive waste. Low level waste is frequently defined for what it is not rather than for what it is. According to the Low Level Waste Policy Act of 1980, LLRW is defined as: "radioactive waste not classified as highlevel radioactive waste, transuranic waste, spent nuclear fuel, or byproduct material as defined in Section 11(e)(2) of the Atomic Energy Act of 1954."

This definition excludes high-level waste and spent nuclear fuel because of its extremely high activity. Transuranic wastes (those containing elements heavier than uranium) are excluded because of the amount of time needed for them to decay to acceptable levels. Finally, byproduct material or mill tailings are excluded because of the very low concentrations of radioactivity in comparison to the extreme volume of waste that is present.

The generators of low level waste include nuclear power plants, medical and academic institutions, industry, and the government. Low level waste can be generated from any process in which radionuclides are used. A list of the different waste streams and the possible generators of each is presented in Table 20–2.

Each of the aforementioned generators produce wastes that fall into the category of low-level waste. The waste streams identified in Table 20–2 are categorized by generation process, but may also, in some instances, be identified by the type of generating facility.

The disposal of low level waste is accomplished through shallow land burial. This process usually involves the packaging of individual waste containers in large concrete overpacks. The overpack is designed to reduce the amount of water that may come into contact with the waste. Another function of the overpack is to guard against intruders coming into contact with the waste once institutional control of the facility is lost. When waste is delivered to the facility in drums, boxes, or in HDPE liners, they are placed in an overpack and sealed with cement before being buried in the landfill.

Table 20–2.   Typical Waste Streams by Generator Category (EG & G Idaho, Inc., 1985)

Waste Stream	Power Reactors	Medical & Academic	Industrial	Government
Compacted Trash or Solids	X	X	X	X
Dry Active Waste	X			
Dewatered Ion Exchange Resins	X			
Contaminated Bulk	X		X	X
Contaminated Plant Hardware	X		X	X
Liquid Scintillation Fluids		X	X	X
Biological Wastes		X		
Absorbed Liquids		X	X	X
Animal Carcasses		X		
Depleted Uranium MgF_2			X	

High Level Radioactive Waste

High level waste (HLW) consists of spent nuclear fuel, liquid wastes resulting from the reprocessing of irradiated reactor fuel, and solid waste that results from the solidification of liquid high level waste. Spent reactor fuel is the fuel that has been used to generate power in a reactor. The spent fuel may be owned by a government reactor, a public utility reactor, or a commercial reactor. The wastes resulting from fuel reprocessing are either governmentally or commercially generated. Only a small fraction of the liquid HLW has been generated commercially. Approximately 600,000 gallons of waste were produced in the nation's only commercial fuel reprocessing facility in West Valley, New York. The remainder of the HLW present in the United States today has been generated by the government in weapon facilities.

Spent nuclear fuel is removed from a reactor and stored in a pool of water on the site. The water in the spent fuel storage pools shields the workers and the environment from the fission products, as well as provides cooling to the fuel. The residual heat from a fuel assembly is quantified as approximately 6 percent of the operating power level of the reactor. Failure to provide additional cooling after the fission reaction has stopped was the reason for the fuel damage at Three Mile Island. Once a geologic repository is constructed, the spent fuel assemblies will be placed in a sealed canister and disposed of.

Most of the liquid high level waste is stored in underground storage tanks. Many of these tanks are getting old and the availability of a geologic repository in the near future is doubtful. Many methods of solidifying the wastes for transport and ultimate disposal have been investigated. Plans are under way to store HLW in one central location in the United States. The chosen location is Yucca Mountain, Nevada.

Transuranic Waste

Transuranic wastes are those wastes containing isotopes that are heavier than uranium, U. Generally, transuranic isotopes are not found in nature. These isotopes are manmade, produced by the irradiation of heavy elements, such as uranium and thorium. Transuranic wastes are

$$^{238}_{92}U + {}^{1}_{0}n \rightarrow {}^{239}_{93}Np + {}^{0}_{(-1)}e \leftarrow {}^{239}_{93}Np \rightarrow {}^{239}_{94}Pu + {}^{0}_{(-1)}e \qquad (20\text{--}3)$$

where Np and Pu represent neptunium and plutonium, respectively. They are normally generated by the government, particularly from weapons testing. The transuranic waste is now being stored at a number of DOE facilities across the country, awaiting permanent disposal at WIPP in Carlsbad, New Mexico.

RADIOACTIVE WASTE TREATMENT AND DISPOSAL

Many treatment processes can be employed to reduce the volume, or increase the stability, of waste that must ultimately be permanently disposed. Landfill fees for radioactive waste is assessed largely on the volume of the waste to be disposed. Current trends in the rising cost of waste disposal have led to the generators' implementing one or a number of waste minimization techniques.

The physical form of the waste is a critical factor in determining the probability that the waste will remain isolated from the biosphere.

Compacting is a method of directly reducing the volume and increasing the specific weight of the resulting waste. Materials such as glass vials, protective clothing, and filter media can be compacted to reduce the volume. Compacting does not reduce the environmental hazard of the waste stream—its purpose is purely waste minimization.

Incineration of waste both reduces the volume and provides a more stable waste stream. Many biological wastes, including animal carcasses, are incinerated. The storage of animal carcasses in drums is generally not cost effective because of the gas generation of the materials as they decay biologically. A drum packed with animal carcasses must be filled with absorbent material so that the pressure inside the drum does not rise to unsafe levels. Incineration is a very cost-effective waste reduction technique for large generators of combustible materials.

Dewatering or evaporation is another waste minimization and stabilization technique that is practiced by waste generators. Evaporating sludges or slurries can greatly reduce the volume of the waste stream and stabilize the waste prior to disposal.

FUTURE TRENDS

Current regulations call for each individual state or interstate compact to store and dispose of all of the LLW generated within its boundaries. An interstate compact consist of a group of states that have joined together to dispose of LLW. Interstate compacts can only be formed and dissolved by Congress. Many regulatory milestones have passed, leaving most states with restricted access to Barnwell, South Carolina. Barnwell is the only remaining LLW disposal facility for such wastes. It is most certain that the Barnwell facility will close before most states have centralized storage capacity on line. Some states, like New York, have unsuccessfully attempted to sue the federal government, arguing that it is unconstitutional to mandate that states dispose of radioactive waste within their boundaries. Without the individual states or compacts taking immediate action to site and construct a permanent disposal facility or temporary centralized storage facility, generators of waste will be forced to either store radioactive materials on-site or stop generating radioactive wastes by ceasing all operations that utilize radioactive materials. While these two options may seem appropriate, neither of them will solve the problem of waste disposal for any extended period of time. Many radioactive waste generators, like hospitals, do not have the storage space allocated to handle on-site storage for periods exceeding one or two years. Much of the waste generated at hospitals is directly related to patient care, and it is unacceptable to assume that all processes, like chemotherapy, that produce radioactive waste will be stopped.

Both the HLW and TRU programs are limping along because of public concern for the areas surrounding the proposed facilities. The WIPP facility has performed some waste emplacement, but this has only been accomplished as a research and development activity. The HLW program has met drastic public opposition because of the amount of time that the waste will remain extremely hazardous. This time period is in the order of thousands of years. Opponents to this facility are arguing that the ability to properly label the disposal facility and guard against future intruders is lacking. Many symbols, such as thorns or unhappy faces, have been proposed.

The public at large will continue to oppose most activities involving nuclear waste until they are made aware of the unwanted characteristics of current more acceptable technologies as well as the extreme benefits that radioactive materials have made to society.

SUMMARY

1. After an individual state or an interstate compact is denied access to the current nation-wide disposal facilities, the generators of the state will be forced to store LLW on site. The only other alternative is to stop generating waste until such time as the state or compact develops and constructs an appropriate disposal or storage facility. Neither of these options constitutes an appropriate choice for generators such as hospitals that offer nuclear medical services.

2. The interaction between ionizing radiation and living matter is one of the most understood environmental hazards. Radioactive isotopes are transformed into more stable elements through the mechanisms of alpha, beta, gamma, and neutron emission.

3. Naturally occurring radioactive materials may be concentrated by many industrial and municipal processes. The individual states and interstate compacts now have the responsibility to site and construct facilities to dispose of low level waste. Both high level waste and transuranic waste is being stored on the site of generation until the respective geologic repositories begin to accept waste for disposal.

4. Waste disposal fees are assessed primarily on the volume of waste. Generators have invested in treatment technologies because of the rising cost of disposal. Many of the treatment technologies also improve the stability of the waste.

5. Generators of radioactive wastes will be forced to store all generated materials on-site until the next generation of disposal facilities comes on line.

REFERENCES

Berlin, R., and Stanton, C. *Radioactive Waste Management*. New York: John Wiley & Sons, 1989.

Cember, H. *Introduction to Health Physics*. New York: McGraw Hill, 1992.

EG&G Idaho, Inc. *The State by State Assessment of LowLevel Radioactive Wastes Shipped to Commercial Disposal Sites*, DOE/LLW50T, December 1985.

EPA, *Draft: Diffuse NORM Wastes Waste Characterization and Risk Assessment*, May 1991.

Faw, R., and Shultis, J. *Radiological Assessment Sources and Exposures*. Englwood Cliffs, NJ: Prentice Hall, 1993.

21

Superfund

CONTRIBUTING AUTHOR
Christine Jolly

INTRODUCTION

During the 1970s, people started to realize that the planet Earth and its environment had reached a critical point and pollution could cause potential health risks. If one examines the environmental laws passed during these times, one can see how the need for Superfund arose out of the public's concern for the environment.

The environmental problem became a major national issue of public concern because of a number of reasons. People were unable to fish or swim in some of the waterways and the air quality was poor. The health effects of smog and industrial air pollution alarmed the people and environmental concern initially moved towards clean air. In order to improve the nation's air quality, Congress passed the Clean Air Act in 1970, which was recently amended in 1990. This act reduced the pollutants being released into the air by forcing emission standards and regulations on individuals and private industry. Congress then responded in 1977 to the public's concern for clean water by passing the Clean Water Act. This act regulated safe drinking water by requiring secondary treatment on all wastewater facilities. The second provision of the Clean Water Act required previously polluted natural water bodies to become suitable for animal life. In 1976, Congress passed the Resources Conservation and Recovery Act (RCRA), which was one of the first laws to regulate solid and hazardous waste. Landfills had become a big problem since swampland, which was otherwise useless, was utilized for dumping waste. This led to groundwater contamination and other problems. RCRA addressed the issue of landfill sites and led to the issuance of permits for dumping hazardous waste.

During the late 1970s, the press and the American people's attention focused on hazardous waste sites like Love Canal and Times Beach. Love Canal is a hazardous waste site located in up-state New York, which at one time, was merely an unfinished canal. As it was never completed, this large hole remained until a chemical company bought the property, used it as a landfill, and buried tons of hazardous waste chemicals. Once the dumping stopped, the land was covered with fill. The land was later used as a residential area where houses and a school were built. The people living in the houses became ill, and they soon realized that their illness was caused by the dumping that had taken place twenty-five years earlier. The media began to publicize the story and stir up social concern as the public began to see the health risks of pollution. Because of this concern about hazardous waste sites, Congress passed the first law in 1980 to deal with the nation's hazardous waste sites. This law is called the Comprehensive Environmental Response, Compensation, and Liability Act (CERCLA), now commonly known as Superfund. In 1980, Superfund was given $1.6 billion dollars by Congress to clean up the nation's highest risk hazardous waste sites. A method was sought to determine the worst sites. The act required every individual state to compile a list of the worst sites in their state and submit it to the Environmental Protection Agency. From this list, each site was evaluated and ranked on its risk to public health and to the environment. The sites were then placed in risk order from highest to lowest. This method of ranking sites was known as the National Priorities List (NPL). Congress initially had no idea how big the hazardous waste site problem was, and Superfund was not given enough money to clean up many of the sites now on the NPL. Congress extended Superfund in 1986 for five more years by passing the Superfund Amendments and Reauthorization Act (SARA). This gave Superfund $8.5 billion dollars more in order to clean up hazardous waste sites. SARA also set up an infrastructure to run daily transactions and provided other means to obtain money for Superfund.

This chapter will examine the following topics:

1. Funding and legal considerations.
2. The ranking systems.
3. The clean-up process.
4. The role of the private sector.
5. The progress up to date.
6. Future trends.

THE FUNDING OF SUPERFUND AND LEGAL CONSIDERATIONS

When CERCLA was first passed in 1980, the law set up a trust fund of $1.6 billion dollars, commonly known as Superfund. Congress initially obtained the money to fund the trust from taxes on crude oil and some commercial chemicals. Once this money ran out, Superfund was reauthorized by SARA in 1986, and Congress was again faced with the problem of how to fund the law. Congress decided that "these monies are to be made available to the Superfund directly from excise taxes on petroleum and feedstock chemicals, a tax on certain imported chemical derivatives, environmental tax on corporations, appropriations made by Congress from general tax revenues, and any monies recovered or collected from parties responsible for site contamination" (EPA, 1991).

CERCLA has three concepts that make it an unusual law. These are ex post facto, innocent landowner liability, and joint and several liability. These are discussed below.

Ex post facto means that after the fact, a party can be liable for what was once legal, but now is illegal. For example, a party could have legally disposed of waste at the time of disposal. However, they could later be found liable under CERCLA for whatever that waste was and legally responsible for its clean up. Since it is necessary to obtain money for the clean up of a sight, it is very important that the EPA find the parties responsible for the hazardous site. The Potentially Responsible Party (PRP) under Section 107(a) of CERCLA is defined as:

1. The current owner or operator of the site that contains hazardous substances.
2. Any person who owned or operated the site at the time when hazardous substances were disposed.
3. Any person who arranged for the treatment, storage, or disposal of the hazardous substances at the site.
4. Any generator who disposed of hazardous substances at the site.
5. Any transporter who transported hazardous substances to the site.

The persons listed above are liable for:

1. All costs of removal or remedial action incurred by the government.
2. Any other necessary costs of response incurred by any other person consistent with the National Contingency Plan (NCP).
3. Damages for injury to, destruction of, or loss of natural resources, including the reasonable costs for assessing them.
4. The costs of any health assessment or health effects study carried out under Section 104(i).

The second unique part of CERCLA is the innocent landowner liability. This states that anyone who buys property that is contaminated with a hazardous substance may be liable for the cost of cleanup even if they did not know the site was contaminated. The only way they might avoid liability is if they made an "all appropriate inquiry" before purchase and found nothing. The following factors are to be examined to see if an "all appropriate inquiry" was made:

1. Any specialized knowledge or experience on the part of the defendant.
2. Commonly known or reasonably ascertainable information about the property.
3. Relationship of the purchase price to the value of the property if uncontaminated.
4. Obviousness of the presence or likely presence of contamination at the property.
5. Ability to detect such contamination by appropriate inspection (Wagner, 1991).

A third unique part of the law is the joint and several liability clause. This simply means that liability for a site can be shared between several PRPs or just one. "Each party could be liable for the same amount or one party may be liable for the entire amount even though the parties did not dispose of equal amounts" (Wagner, 1991). Joint and several liability makes the enforcement side of CERCLA easier because the EPA can sue only one PRP and get all the money. In turn, that PRP can then sue the other contributors for their part. This saves the EPA money in legal fees. Under section 107(b) of CERCLA, there are only four legal defenses to avoid liability for hazardous site contamination. They are:

1. An act of God

2. An act of war

3. An act of omission of a third party

4. Any combination of the foregoing (Wagner, 1991)

Enforcement and liability go hand in hand when cleaning up a Superfund site. Some of Superfund's goals are to encourage potentially responsible parties to finance and conduct the necessary response action and to recover the costs for response action(s) that were financed using the fund's money. The EPA has several enforcement options. Of the several options, the EPA usually seeks voluntary compliance. An enforcement agreement could be one of two options. The first is a judicial consent decree, which "is a legal document that specifies an entity's obligations when that entity enters into a settlement with the government" (Wagner, 1991). The second is an administrative order which is a mutual agreement between the PRP and the EPA outside of court. If the PRP does not chose to reach an agreement with the EPA, then the EPA can issue a unilateral administrative order forcing the PRP to take charge. If the PRP still refuses, then the EPA can file a lawsuit. If the EPA wins, they may recover treble (triple) damages, which means that an uncooperative PRP could be charged three times what it cost the government to clean up the site. This is done to encourage the PRP to take responsibility early on in the clean up process.

RANKING OF HAZARDOUS WASTE SITES

When Superfund first began, every state was told to compile a list of their worst hazardous waste sites to be evaluated by the EPA for cleanup. It was soon realized that the number of sites were too large for federal action, so the government decided to rank the sites in order from the highest to the lowest risk to human health and the environment. This ranking system list is known as the national priorities list (NPL). If a site makes the NPL, it is then eligible for federal money through the Superfund program. In order to be placed on the NPL, the site must meet at least one of the following three criteria:

1. Receive a health advisory from the Agency for Toxic Substances and Disease Registry (ATSDR) recommending that people be relocated away from the site.

2. Score 28.5 or higher in the Hazard Ranking System (HRS), which is the method that the EPA uses to assess the relative threat from a release, or potential release, of hazardous substances; HRS is the scoring system used to enhance the process for identifying the most hazardous and threatening sites for Superfund cleanup.

3. Be selected as the state top priority (EPA, 1991).

As risk is a very difficult quantity to measure, the HRS score was used to reflect the potential harm to human health and the environment from the migration of hazardous substances. In order to understand how waste can be ranked, it is necessary to look at the different types of hazardous wastes, and how they end up in the environment. The three media in which hazardous wastes can enter the environment are air, water, and soil. Hazardous wastes may leach, percolate, wash into ground or surface water, evaporate, explode, or they may get carried with the wind or rain into any media. Hazardous waste can bioaccumulate and end up in the food chain or water supply. The risk assessment looks at the waste quantity, where it is, who or what is near it, and relates these to its potential effects on the public health and the environment.

In 1990, the National Contingency Plan (NCP) was created to implement the response authorities and responsibilities created by Superfund and the Clean Water Act. The NCP outlines the steps that the federal government must follow in responding to situations in which hazardous substances are released or are likely to be released into the environment. The four basic components of the hazardous substance response provisions of the NCP are:

1. Methods for discovering sites at which hazardous substances have been disposed.
2. Methods for evaluating and remedying releases that pose substantial danger to public health and the environment.
3. Methods and criteria for determining the appropriate extent of cleanup.
4. Means of assuring that remedial action measures are cost effective (Wagner, 1991).

In order to understand how Superfund works it is necessary to look at the structure of the Superfund program. The EPA was given responsibility as the designated manager of the trust fund by CERCLA. The policies Superfund follows comes from the EPA headquarters. However, the EPA has ten offices in different regional cities throughout the country. They have more control of the

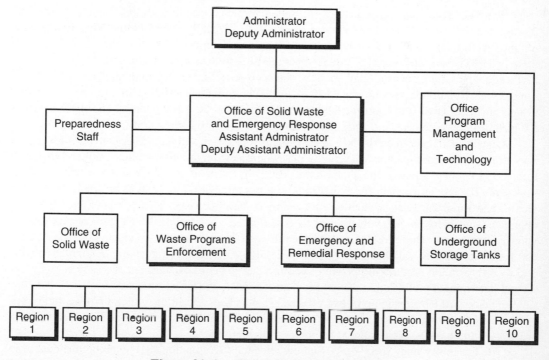

Figure 21–1. EPA Superfund organization.

day-to-day program decisions and operations. This makes it easier to keep a closer eye on what is going on at any particular site. Figure 21–1 shows the political structure of Superfund.

THE CLEAN UP PROCESS

The purpose of Superfund is to eliminate the short- and long-term effects of a hazardous waste. There are ten basic steps in the cleanup process, and they are:

1. Site discovery
2. Preliminary assessment
3. Site inspection
4. Hazard ranking analysis (HRS)
5. National Priorities List determination (NPL)
6. Remedial investigation and feasibility study (RI/FS)
7. Remedy selection/record of decision (ROD)
8. Remedial design (RD)
9. Remedial action (RA)
10. Project closeout

The first five steps have been discussed in previous sections of this chapter. Steps six through ten will be discussed here. Once a site has been officially placed on the NPL, it is eligible for money from the fund. It first becomes necessary to determine which is the Lead agency. If there is a PRP, then fund money is not used but the EPA follows up on the progress of the site. If a PRP cannot be found, or cannot pay, then the site becomes a State Lead, Federal Agency Lead, or a Fund Lead. Regardless of who the lead is, the EPA's regional office will provide a remedial project manager (RPM) to coordinate between the EPA and the Lead agency. The RPM oversees the technical, enforcement, and financial aspects at the site until completion.

Once a site is placed on the NPL a remedial investigation and feasibility study (RI/FS) report is performed. In order to choose a remedy that would best protect the public health and the environment, a detailed study of the site is done. The RI consists of sampling to determine a risk assessment. The risk assessment for a Superfund site has three different parts. The first is the Human Health and Environmental Evaluation that examines baseline risks. This part measures levels of chemicals and helps in the evaluation of the site characteristics and the selection of possible response alternatives. The second part is the Health Assessment, which is conducted by The Agency for Toxic Substances and Disease Registry (ATSDR). ATSDR looks at risk in a qualitative way, and its effect on the neighboring people. The third part is the Endangerment Assessment, which is a legal determination of risk and the requirements to satisfy the RI/FS process.

The overall RI is made up of two phases: (1) site characterization, which involves field sampling and laboratory analyses, and (2) treatability investigations that examine how treatable the wastes are and the possible treatment technology alternatives.

The feasibility study (FS) works with the remedial investigation (RI) by taking the data from the RI and developing and screening different treatment alternatives for a given site. Once the FS is started, the RI continues as more sampling may be needed to make a determination. It then becomes necessary to look at the RI/FS and choose a remedy. This is done by a record of decision (ROD), which is a written report of the alternatives found in the RI/FS and reasons for the selection of a treatment technology. In the ROD, a remedy is proposed for the site and then it goes out for public evaluation. The comments are studied and then a final selection is made. In the ROD, there is a decision summary that explains the site characteristics and the determination of the method chosen for that site.

The next step in the treatment process is the Remedial Design (RD) phase. This is when the remedy selected in the ROD is engineered to meet the specifications and cleanup levels specified by law and the ROD. Detailed engineering plans are drawn up to implement the selected remedy and then the site enters the next phase, which is Remedial Action (RA). The RA phase is when the construction on the site begins and the treatment, removal, and other tasks are undertaken.

The last stage of cleanup is project closeout and deletion from the NPL.

Project closeout is divided into three phases: NPL deletion, operation and maintenance, and final project closeout. For a site to be eligible for deletion, at least one of the following three criteria must be met:

1. EPA, in consultation with the state, must have determined that responsible or other parties have implemented all appropriate response actions.
2. All appropriate fund-financed responses must have been implemented, and EPA, in consultation with the state, must have determined that no further response is appropriate.
3. Based on a remedial investigation, EPA, in consultation with the state, must have determined that no further response is appropriate (Wagner, 1991).

The EPA has recently created a new way to declare a site complete even if all the cleanup standards have not been met. It is called construction completion of a superfund site and it would occur after the RD/RA and before the actual deletion of the site from the NPL. A site may be declared construction complete if the entire RD/RA process is finished and the remedy has taken effect and has been proven to be working. The site may, however, need operations and maintenance (O&M) of the equipment, and an extended period of time to reach the cleanup levels. For example, a site that has contaminated groundwater could take years of pumping and treatment to actually clean it up to the standards specified in the ROD. All other procedures may be met and the treatment plant may be functioning, but the site is not eligible for deletion from the NPL until it reaches the specified cleanup levels. Declaring the site construction complete makes it possible for the site to be counted as complete as far as the public progress reports are concerned.

ROLE OF THE PRIVATE SECTOR

Superfund follows the policy that the public has a right to know what happens at a site. The EPA needs the public's help for many aspects of Superfund cleanups. Often, it is the private citizens of a community that report hazardous waste dumping. Superfund is mandated by law to involve the public in all aspects of a site except PRP legal activities. The public is given an information and comment period whenever a site makes it on to the NPL. Public concerns are analyzed and sometimes influence the decision toward an alternative remedy. Also, people in a town where a site is located are often helpful in locating a PRP. In this way, the public can help with liability and enforcement issues by assisting the EPA in finding a PRP.

In order to inform the public the EPA creates a community relations plan where they outline activities that they will use to inform the public of what is going on at a site. Once a plan is made, the EPA has a general informational meeting to explain to the public what will happen at the site. The EPA collects any comments and includes them in the ROD, as part of the considerations for selecting a remedy. The EPA then establishes an information repository, which contains the site updates, news releases, and phone numbers to call for questions or concerns about the site. Here are some of the things citizens can do:

1. Report hazardous waste dumping: Call the National Response Center at 1-(800) -424–8802.
2. Individual or organizations that suspect they are or may be affected by a hazardous waste release may petition the EPA to preform a Preliminary Assessment. Contact ATSDR at 1600 Clifton Road NE, Atlanta, GA 30333.
3. Find out when cleanup investigators will arrive and share information with them.
4. Get information from the EPA or state Superfund office.
5. Learn about the EPA's Community Involvement Programs.
6. Write the EPA for information on the status of any site (EPA, 1991).

PROGRESS TO DATE

Superfund often deals with dangerous contaminated sites that can have serious effects on the public health and the environment. There are nearly 1,300 sites now on the NPL and of those sites over 200 have made it through the entire cleanup process discussed early in this chapter. One of the common questions often asked is what kind of progress is the EPA making on every site to deal with such a serious problem. First, the Superfund program is required to evaluate, stabilize, treat, or otherwise take actions to make dangerous sites safe (EPA, 1991). This is accomplished through emergency response action tailored to specific sites. After any emergency responses have been completed a site goes through the ten phases of cleanup discussed in the earlier sections of this chapter.

Regarding progress, the EPA has reported:

> The net results of the work done at the NPL sites has been to reduce the potential risks from hazardous waste for an estimated 23.5 million people who live within 4 miles of these sites. Other results are to bring technology to bear by increased use of permanent treatment remedies at NPL sites, to remove contamination from the environment, and control the sources of contamination (EPA, 1991).

The reader is referred to Chapter 3, The EPA Problem, for an alternative view of the progress to date.

FUTURE TRENDS

The Superfund program has come under fire with the Clinton Administration. Critics feel that Superfund has not been efficient in cleaning up the nation's hazardous waste sites. A large portion of the money in Superfund goes to "transaction costs," which are lawyer and consultant fees. Since enforcement is a very large part of the Superfund program, much money gets spent on legal considerations instead of on actual site clean up. The future of Superfund lies in improving the existing system. Some argue that Superfund cannot be abolished because it is still needed. Many hazardous sites that pose threats to public health and the environment still exist. The Clinton Administration has suggested two ideas that may improve Superfund. The first would cause remedies for cleaning toxic sites to be based partly on "probable future use," and the second would reduce wasteful transaction costs (Cushman, 1994). The idea of "probable future use" means that a hazardous waste site will be cleaned up to a certain level depending on what the site will be used for after the cleanup. For example, sites that will be used as parking lots will be cleaned to different specifications than will sites that are to become hospitals. The second suggestion for reducing wasteful transaction costs involves engaging a "neutral professional," such as a judge, to be an arbitrator between the potentially responsible party (PRP) and government. This idea would reduce the legal costs incurred by Superfund, because it expedites a decision in payment responsibility. These two changes in the future of Superfund may improve the program. However, based on past history, the EPA continues to move towards a legally based rather than a technology-driven agency.

SUMMARY

1. Because of concern about hazardous waste sites, Congress passed a law in 1980 to deal with the nation's hazardous waste sites. This law is called the Comprehensive Environmental Response, Compensation, and Liability Act (CERCLA), now commonly known as Superfund.

2. CERCLA has three concepts that make it an unusual law. These are ex post facto, innocent landowner liability, and joint and several liability.

3. The national priorities list (NPL) is a government list that ranks hazardous sites in order from the highest to the lowest risk to human health and the environment.

4. There are ten basic steps in the cleanup process: site discovery, preliminary assessment, site inspection, hazard ranking analysis (HRS), National Priorities List determination (NPL), remedial investigation and feasibility study (RI/FS), remedy selection/record of decision (ROD), remedial design (RD), remedial action (RA), and project closeout.

5. Superfund maintains a policy that the public has a right to know what happens at a site.

6. There are over 1,300 sites now on the NPL and of those sites, over 200 have made it through the entire cleanup process.

7. Two ideas to improve Superfund are to base remedies for cleaning toxic sites on "probable future use," and to reduce wasteful transaction costs. However, based on past history, the EPA continues to move towards a legally based rather than a technology-driven agency.

REFERENCES

Cushman, J., Jr. "Not So Superfund." *New York Times,* National section, Monday, February 7, 1994, p. A1 & A15.

EPA. "Focusing on the Nation at Large." *EPA's Update,* EPA/540/8–91/016, September 1991.

Wagner, T. *The Complete Guide to the Hazardous Waste Regulation,* 2nd ed. New York: Van Nostrand Reinhold, 1991.

Part V

Health, Safety and Accident Management

The next three parts of the book—Parts V, VI and VII—serve to introduce the reader to the general subject of pollution prevention and the three major elements in the pollution prevention field. Part V of this book serves as an introduction to health, safety, and accident management issues. Development of plans for handling accidents and emergencies must precede the actual occurrence of these events. Four chapters comprise Part V. Chapter 22 is concerned with industrial safety applications, since in recent years incidents related to the chemical, petrochemical, and refinery industries have caused particular concern to safety. The remaining three chapters cover what the authors have defined as domestic issues. A comprehensive examination of health, safety, and accident issues at home is provided in Chapter 23. Chapter 24 focuses on the same issues in the workplace. Part V concludes with Chapter 25, which addresses health, safety, and accident issues during leisure time, and in other circumstances not covered in the home or the workplace.

22

Industrial Applications

CONTRIBUTING AUTHOR

Megan Reynolds

INTRODUCTION

Accidents happen. They are a fact of life. No matter how well planned, or how carefully a project is carried out, there is always room for human error or other calamities. This is especially true for industrial applications, where everything, including accidents, is present on a grand scale. However, careful planning and stringent safety procedures can significantly lower the potential risk that an accident will occur. Furthermore, when something does go wrong, knowledgeable workers with access to emergency equipment can keep an incident from turning into a disaster.

Industry is constantly progressing, making it possible to build equipment and plants that are bigger, run faster, operate more effectively, but are more complex than previous models. These constant technological improvements require continuously updated safety regulations.

In addition to preventing accidents, industry must be concerned with the increasing amount of hazardous waste being produced. The United States Environmental Protection Agency (EPA) estimates that approximately 57 million tons of hazardous waste are being produced each year in the United States. These wastes must be treated and stored, or disposed of in a matter that protects the environment from the adverse affects of the various constituents of those wastes. In response to the need to protect human health and the environment from improper disposal of hazardous wastes, anyone working in a hazardous or unsafe environment must receive health and safety training. This is normally accomplished through OSHA, the Occupational Safety and Health Administration.

Training and knowledge are crucial to accident prevention, as well as proper handling of potentially dangerous circumstances. Many serious catastrophes were either caused, in part or compounded by human error and misjudgment. For example, in 1979, at the Three Mile Island nuclear power plant, a routine problem became catastrophic because of misinterpretation by the operators of the signs of danger. The fault of this incident lies not merely with the operators, but equally as much with the managers who had not seen to it that their workers were properly trained. The response the operators gave to the original problem showed they lacked a basic understanding of the actual events that were taking place, and therefore could not make proper judgments on how to correct the matter.

This chapter will deal with the dangers posed not only by hazardous substances, but will also examine the general subject of health, safety, and accident prevention. In addition, the laws and legislation passed to protect workers, the public, and the environment from the effects of these chemicals are also reviewed. The chapter will discuss the regulations with particular emphasis on emergency planning and the training of personnel.

EXPOSURE TO TOXIC SUBSTANCES

It has only been in the latter half of this century that there has been a recognition of the threats posed by toxic chemicals. In fact, until 1962, the ever-increasing production and use of chemical substances went unchallenged. The general public made the naive assumption that these chemicals were safe based on the facts that "billions of dollars were being expended in manufacturing facilities and that governments did not disapprove of chemical use." Today, the public, now far more mistrusting, demands fact-based information on what occurs inside the industrial plants and what substances are being released into the atmosphere. This attitude is reflected in such legislation as the federal right-to-know standard, which will be discussed later in the chapter.

Recently, there has been growing concern over the toxicity of new chemicals. This concern has been escalated due to a number of well-publicized incidents in which toxic substances caused injury to or loss of human life. At the incidence in Bhopal, India, a tremendous gas leak of methyl isocyanate (MIC) from a Union Carbide factory sent a toxic cloud into the atmosphere and the city surrounding the factory. The effect was devastating—thousands of people were sent fleeing blindly through the streets, choking and vomiting. In the end, it is estimated that more than 2500 people lost their lives on that December night in 1984, and many more, possibly 200,000, have been physically scarred from the release of the toxin.

Toxic and chemically active substances, including radioactive materials and biological agents, present a special concern because they can be readily inhaled or ingested, or can be absorbed through the skin. This fact makes any toxic gas leak hard to contain, because once the toxin becomes airborne, it can spread rapidly and affect an untold number of people, as well as present adverse effects to the atmosphere and water supply. Liquids or sludges present problems, not only because they can be splashed on the skin and cause damage, but because they can leak into the soil and affect vegetation and the water supply. The severity of danger of these substances can vary significantly. If ingested or inhaled, a substance may cause no apparent illness, or the results can be fatal. When spilled on the skin, one chemical may incur a slight rash or no reaction at all, or, as in the case of liquid mercury, may be absorbed through it, leading to systemic toxic effects.

Two general types of potential exposure exist. These are classified as:

1. *Acute:* Exposures occur for relatively short periods of time, generally minutes to one to two days. Concentration of toxic air contaminants are usually high relative to their protection criteria. In addition to inhalation, airborne substances might directly contact the skin, or liquids and sludges may be splashed on the skin or into the eyes, leading to toxic effects.

2. *Chronic:* Continuous exposure occurs over longer periods of time, generally several months to years. Concentrations of inhaled toxic contaminants are usually relatively low. Direct skin contact by immersion, by splash, or by contaminated air involves contact with substances exhibiting low dermal activity.

In general, acute exposures to chemicals in air are more typical in either transportation accidents and fires, or releases at chemical manufacturing or storage facilities. High concentrations of contaminants in air usually do not persist for long periods of time. Acute skin exposure may occur when workers come in close contact with the substances in order to control a release—for example, while patching a tank car, offloading a corrosive material, uprighting a drum, or while containing and treating a spilled material.

Chronic exposures, on the other hand, are usually associated with longer-term removal and remedial operations. Contaminated soil and debris from emergency operations may be involved, soil and groundwater may be polluted, or temporary impoundment systems may contain diluted chemicals. Abandoned waste sites typically represent chronic exposure problems. As activities start at these sites, personnel engaged in certain operations such as sampling, handling containers, or bulking compatible liquids, face an increased risk of acute exposures. These exposures stem from splashes of liquids, or from the release of vapors, gases, or particulates that might be generated.

In any specific incident, the hazardous properties of the materials may only represent a potential risk. For example, if a tank car containing liquefied natural gas is involved in an accident but remains intact, the risk from fire and explosion is low. In other incidents, the risk to response personnel are high. As, for instance, when toxic or flammable vapors are released from a ruptured tank truck. The continued health and safety of response personnel requires that the risks, both real and potential, at an accident be assessed, and appropriate measures instituted to reduce or eliminate the threat to response personnel.

Specific chemicals and chemical groups affect different parts of the body. One chemical, such as an acid or base, may affect the skin, whereas another, such as carbon tetrachloride, attacks the liver. Some chemicals will affect more than one organ or system. When this occurs, the organ or system being attacked is referred to as the *target organ*. The damage done to a target organ can differ in severity depending on chemical composition, length of exposure, and the concentration of the chemical.

When two different chemicals simultaneously enter the body, the result can be intensified or compounded. The *synergistic effect*, as it is referred to, results when one substance intensifies the damage done by the other. Synergism complicates almost any exposure due to a lack of toxological information. For just one chemical, it may typically take a toxological research facility approximately two years of studies to generate valid data. The data produced in that two-year timeframe applies only to the effect of that one chemical acting alone. With the addition of another chemical, the original chemical may have a totally different effect on the body. This fact results in a great many unknowns when dealing with toxic substances, and therefore increases risk due to lack of dependable information.

The National Institute of Occupational Safety and Health (NIOSH) recommends standards for industrial exposure that the Occupational Safety Hazard Administration (OSHA) uses in its regulations. The NIOSH packet guide to chemical hazards contains a wealth of information on specific chemicals such as:

1. Chemical name, formula and structure
2. Trade names and synonyms
3. Chemical and physical properties
4. Time-weighted average threshold limit values (TLVs)
5. Exposure limits
6. Lower explosive limit (LEL)
7. "Immediately dangerous to life and health" concentrations (IDLHs)
8. Measurement methods
9. Personal protection and sanitation guidelines
10. Health hazards information

As discussed above, there are many different dangers resulting from the toxicity of reactive substances. It therefore becomes evident that a knowledge of the specific hazards is important, as are detailed regulations on how to handle situations arising from the use of these chemicals.

SAFETY AND ACCIDENTS

As discussed in the first section of this chapter, accidents can occur in many ways. Unlike the next three chapters, which examine nonindustrial and nontechnical issues, this section solely addresses industrial accidents and the companion topic of safety.

In the chemical industry, there is a high risk of accidents due to the nature of the processes and the materials used. Although precautions are taken to ensure that all processes run smoothly, there is always (unfortunately) room for error, and accidents will occur. This is especially true for highly technical and complicated operations, as well as processes under extreme conditions such as high temperatures and pressures. In general, accidents occur due to one or more of the following primary causes:

1. Equipment breakdown
2. Human error
3. Fire exposure and explosions
4. Control system failure
5. Natural causes
6. Utilities and ancillary system outage
7. Faulty siting and plant layout

These causes are usually at the root of most industrial accidents. Although there is no way to guarantee that these problems will not arise, steps can be taken to minimize the number, as well as the severity, of incidents. In an effort to reduce occupational accidents, measures should be taken in the following areas (Theodore, Reynolds, & Taylor, 1989):

1. *Training*: All personnel should be properly trained in the use of equipment and made to understand the consequences of misuse. In addition, operators should be rehearsed in the procedures to take should something go wrong.

2. *Design*: Equipment should only be used for the purposes for which it was designed. All equipment should be periodically checked for damage or errors inherent in the design.

3. *Human performance*: Personnel should be closely monitored to ensure that proper procedures are followed. Also, working conditions should be such that the performance of workers is improved, thereby simultaneously reducing the chance of accidents. Periodic medical examinations should be provided to assure that workers are in good health, and that the environment of the workplace is not causing undue physical stress. Finally, under certain conditions, it may be advisable to test for the use of alcohol or drugs—conditions that severely handicap judgment, and therefore make workers accident-prone.

EMERGENCY PLANNING AND RESPONSE

The extent of the need for emergency planning is significant, and continues to expand as new regulations on safety are introduced. Planning for emergency must begin at the very start, when the plant itself is still being planned. The new plant will have to pass all safety measures and OSHA standards. This is emphasized by Piero Armenante, author of *Contingency Planning for Industrial Emergencies* (1991), "The first line of defense against industrial accidents begins at the design stage. It should be obvious that it is much easier to prevent an accident rather than to try to rectify the situation once an accident has occurred."

Successful emergency planning begins with a thorough understanding of the event or potential disaster being planned for. The impacts on public health and the environment must also be estimated. Some of the types of emergencies that should be included in the plan are:

1. Natural disasters such as earthquakes, tornados, hurricanes, and floods
2. Explosions and fires
3. Hazardous chemical leaks
4. Power or utility failures
5. Radiation accidents
6. Transportation accidents

In order to estimate the impact on the public or the environment, the affected area or emergency zone must be studied in depth. A hazardous gas leak, fire, or explosion may cause a toxic cloud to spread over a great distance, as it did in Bhopal. An estimate of the minimum affected area, and thus the area to be evacuated, should be performed based on an atmospheric dispersion model. There are various models that can be used. While the more difficult models produce the most realistic results, simpler models are faster to use and usually still provide adequate data and information for planning purposes. The main objective for any plan should be to prepare a procedure to make maximum use of the combined resources of the community in order to accomplish the following:

1. Safeguard people during emergencies
2. Minimize damage to property and the environment
3. Initially contain and ultimately bring the incident under control

4. Effect the rescue and treatment of casualties

5. Provide authoritative information to the news media who will communicate the facts to the public

6. Secure the safe rehabilitation of the affected area

REGULATIONS

Each company must develop a health and safety program for its workers. OSHA has regulations governing employee health and safety at hazardous waste operations and during emergency responses to hazardous substance releases. These regulations (29 CFR 1910.120) contain general requirements for:

1. Safety and health programs

2. Training and informational programs

3. Work practices along with personal protective equipment

4. Site characterization and analysis

5. Site control and evacuation

6. Engineering controls

7. Exposure monitoring and medical surveillance

8. Material handling and decontamination

9. Emergency procedures

10. Illumination

11. Sanitation

The EPA's Standard Operating Safety Guides supplement these regulations. However, for specific legal requirements for industry, OSHA's regulations must be used. Other OSHA regulations pertain to employees working with hazardous materials or working at hazardous waste sites. These, as well as state and local regulations, must also be considered when developing worker health and safety programs (EPA, 1988).

The OSHA Hazard Communication Standard was first promulgated on November 25, 1983, and can be formed in 29 CFR Part 1910.120. The standard was developed to inform workers who are exposed to hazardous chemicals of the risk associated with those specific chemicals. The purpose of the standard is to ensure that the hazards of all chemicals produced or imported are evaluated, and information concerning chemical hazards is conveyed to employers and employees.

Information on chemical hazards must be dispatched from manufacturers to employers via material safety data sheets (MSDSs) and container labels. This data must then be communicated to employees by means of comprehensive hazard communication programs, which include training programs, as well as the MSDSs and container labels.

The basic requirements of the Hazardous Communication Standard are as follows:

1. There must be an MSDS on file for every hazardous chemical present or used in the workplace.

2. MSDSs must be readily available during each work shift, and all employees must be informed how to obtain the information. If employees travel on the shift, the MSDSs may be kept in a central location at the primary job site, as long as the necessary information is immediately available in the event of an emergency.

3. It must be ensured that every container holding hazardous chemicals in the workplace is clearly and properly labeled and includes appropriate hazard warnings.

4. Labels of incoming hazardous chemical containers must not be removed or defaced in any way.

5. Prior to initial assignments, employees must be informed of the requirements of the standard operations in their work area where hazardous chemicals are present.

6. Employers must train employees how to identify and protect themselves from chemical hazards in the work area, as well as how to obtain the employer's written hazard communication program and hazard information.

7. Employers must develop, implement, and maintain a written communication program for each workplace that describes how material safety data sheets, labeling, and employee information and training requirements will be met. This written program must also include a list of hazardous chemicals present in the workplace and the methods that will be used to inform employees of the hazards associated performing non-routine tasks.

Companies with multiemployer workplaces must include with the material safety data sheets methods the employer will use for contractors at the facility. These employers must also describe how they will inform the subcontractors' employees about the precautions which must be followed and the specific labeling system used in the workplace.

The Superfund Amendments and Reauthorization Act (SARA) of 1986 renewed the national commitment to correcting problems arising from previous mismanagement of hazardous wastes. Title III of SARA, specifically known as the Emergency Planning and Community Right-To-Know Act, forever changed the concept of environmental management. Planning for emergencies became law. While SARA was similar in many respects to the original law, it also contained new approaches to the program's operation. The 1986 Superfund legislation accomplished the following:

1. Reauthorization of the original program for five more years, dramatically increasing the cleanup fund from $1.6 to 8.5 billion.
2. Setting of specific goals and standards, stressing permanent solutions.
3. Expansion of state and local involvement in decision-making policies.
4. Provision for new enforcement authorities and responsibilities.
5. Strengthened the focus on human health issues caused by hazardous waste sites.

This law was more specific than the original statute with regard to such things as remedies to be used at Superfund sites, public participation, and accomplishment of cleanup activities.

The Emergency Planning and Community Right-To-Know Act is undeniably the most important part of SARA when it comes to public acceptance and support. Title III addresses the most important issues regarding community awareness and participation in the event of a chemical release. Title III establishes requirements for emergency planning, hazardous emissions reporting, emergency notification, and "community right-to-know." For instance, it is now law that companies release any data that a local or community planning committee needs in order to develop and implement its emergency plan (Lees, 1989). The objectives of Title III are to improve local chemical emergency response capabilities, primarily through improved emergency planning and notification, and to provide citizens and local governments with access to information about chemicals in their area. Title III has four major sections that aid in the development of contingency plans. They are as follows:

1. Emergency Planning (Sections 301–03)
2. Emergency Notification (Section 304)
3. Community Right-to-Know Reporting Requirements (Sections 311–12)
4. Toxic Chemicals Release Reporting—Emissions Inventory (Section 313)

Title III has also developed timeframes for the implementation of the Emergency Planning and Community Right-to-Know Act of 1986.

TRAINING

Safety and health training must be an integral part of a total health, safety, and accident prevention program. Safety training must be frequent and up-to-date for response personnel to maintain their proficiency in the use of equipment and their knowledge of safety requirements. Personnel must also be familiar with the substances they are dealing with in order to respond appropriately. The consequences of improper response can be devastating. For example, in Canning, Nova Scotia in 1986, a fire broke out in a warehouse. The firefighters responding to the blaze assumed it was a "normal" fire, and went in with fire hoses to spray it down. However, the building housed pesticides and other agricultural products. The chemicals mixed with the tons of water and escaped through run-off streams into the streets and finally into a nearby river. All vegetation and animals in the path of the deadly streams were killed. Although, fortunately, no human lives were lost, the community had to be evacuated, and could not safely return for weeks. If the firefighters had known about the chemicals, they would have been better off to let the warehouse burn, and merely contained the blaze to keep it from spreading. This would have prevented the escape of the toxins to a greater extent. Fighting the blaze in the normal manner only compounded the problem (Côté, 1991).

All personnel involved in responding to environmental incidents, and who could be exposed to hazardous substances, health hazards, or safety hazards, must receive safety training prior to carrying out their response functions. Health and safety training must, as a minimum, include:

1. Use of personal protective equipment (i.e., respiratory protective apparatus and protective clothing)

2. Safe work practices, engineering controls, and standard operating safety procedures

3. Hazard recognition and evaluation

4. Medical surveillance requirements, symptoms that might indicate medical problems, and first aid

5. Site safety plans and plan development

6. Site control and decontamination

7. Use of monitoring equipment, if applicable

Training must be as practical as possible and include hands-on use of equipment and exercises designed to demonstrate and practice classroom instruction. Formal training should be followed by at least three days of on-the-job experience working under the guidance of an experienced, trained supervisor. All employers should, as a minimum, complete an 8-hour safety refresher course annually. Health and safety training must comply with OSHA's training requirements as defined in 29 CFR 1910.120.

The personnel at an industrial plant, particularly the operators, are trained in the operation of the plant. These people are critical to proper emergency response. They must be taught to recognize abnormalities in operations and report them immediately. Plant operators should also be taught how to respond to various types of accidents. Emergency squads at plants can also be trained to contain an emergency until outside help arrives, or, if possible, to terminate the emergency. Shutdown and evacuation procedures are especially important when training plant personnel.

Training is important for the emergency teams to ensure that their roles are clearly understood, and that accidents can be reacted to safely and properly without delay. The emergency teams include police, firefighters, medical people, and volunteers who will be required to take action during an emergency. These people must be knowledgeable about the potential hazards. For example, specific antidotes for different types of medical problems must be known by medical personnel. The entire emergency team must also be taught the use of personal protective equipment.

FUTURE TRENDS

As evident in the lessons from past accidents, it is essential for industry to abide by stringent safety procedures. The more knowledgeable the personnel, from the management to the operators of a plant, and the more information that is available to them, the less likely a serious incident will occur. The new regulations, and especially Title III of 1986, help to insure that safety practices are up to standard. However, these regulations should only provide a minimum standard. It should be up to the companies, and specifically the plants, to see that every possible measure is taken to insure the safety and well-being of the community and the environment in the surrounding area. It is also up to the community itself, under Title III, to be aware of what goes on inside local industry, and to prepare for any problems that might arise.

The future promises to bring more attention to the topics discussed in the above paragraph. In addition, it appears that there will be more research in the area of risk assessment, including fault-tree, event-tree, and cause-consequence analysis. Details on these topics are beyond the scope of this book, but are available in the literature (Theodore et al., 1989).

SUMMARY

1. Toxic and chemically active substances present special concern because they can be dangerous when inhaled, ingested, or absorbed through the skin.

2. Although accidents cannot be completely prevented, careful planning and stringent safety procedures can significantly lower the potential risk that an accident will occur.

3. Emergency planning is essential in preventing a potential disaster, and in foreseeing what possible incidents might occur.

4. The Occupational Safety Hazard Administration has guidelines and regulations for the safe operation of industrial plants and the handling of emergencies.

5. Safety and health training for personnel is essential in preventing accidents. Workers must know what they are dealing with, and understand the consequences.

6. In the future, more stringent regulations and hopefully better safety techniques will help minimize industrial accidents.

REFERENCES

Armenante, P. *Contingency Planning for Industrial Emergencies*. New York: Van Nostrand Reinhold, 1991.

Côté, R. *Controlling Chemical Hazards*. London: Unwin Hyman, 1991.

EPA Office of Emergency and Remedial Response Division. *Standard Operating Safety Guides*, July 1988.

Lees, F. *Safety Cases within the Control of Industrial Major Accidents Hazards Regulations 1984*. London: Butterworths and Co., Ltd., 1989.

Theodore, L., Reynolds, J., and Taylor, F. *Accident and Emergency Management*, New York: Wiley-Interscience, 1989.

23

At Home

INTRODUCTION

This chapter examines the general subject of health, safety, and accident prevention in the home, or what one might describe as a domestic setting. For the authors' purpose, the word "home" refers to the living quarters where a person or family dwells, be it a house, apartment, or room. Contrary to popular belief, the home is *not* the safest place in the world. In fact, most industrial (including chemical) plants have records that indicate it is not safer to be at home. Top management of many chemical companies now require that new and/or proposed plants, or changes to existing plants, require a work environment that is *safer* than that at home.

Accidents at home take the lives of more than 20 thousand Americans each year. These occurrences are the number one cause of the death of young children; two-thirds of these accidents involve boys. Accidents claim the lives of more children aged one to fourteen than do the leading diseases combined (Holmes, Singh, & Theodore, 1993).

Often after an accident has occurred, one sadly realizes that if simple safety practices had been followed in a timely manner, the accident could have been prevented. Yet each year, more accidents and injuries take place in the home than anywhere else. Injuries and deaths from fires, burns, and falls lead the list of home accidents. Many accidents are automobile-related. In competition for this infamous list is the gun-related accident category, which now has the potential to surpass automobile-related fatalities. There are also an estimated 5 million plus home fires in the United States each year. Building fires claim over 5 thousand lives a year, and most of these victims die in their own homes (Holmes et al., 1993).

This chapter is a condensed, revised, and updated version of an unpublished (but copyrighted) 1992 text prepared by M. K. Theodore and L. Theodore titled *A Citizen's Guide to Pollution Prevention.*

The remainder of this chapter provides suggestions and tips that one can apply at the domestic level to make the home a safer place. This information is provided in the next three sections and has been divided into the following topic areas:

1. Health concerns
2. Safety precautions
3. Accident prevention

The suggestions for each of the above areas are detailed in numerical rather than essay form. The reader should also note the overlapping nature of the three topics. For this reason, suggestions regarding health concerns address the well-being of the residents of the home from a health perspective. Dividing safety precautions and accident prevention was not as simple. However, a decision was made to primarily include those overlapping topics that involve both health concerns and accident prevention in the safety precautions section. The accident prevention section was then left to contain accident preventive suggestions that do not directly impact on health.

HEALTH CONCERNS*

Suggestions regarding health concerns in a domestic environment are provided below.

1. When choosing a house, carefully consider the neighborhood in terms of proximity to power plants, dumps and exposure to electromagnetic waves, automobile traffic and pollution, and air traffic patterns. Visit the area after heavy rain or snow melt to observe the presence of flooding and drainage problems.

2. Maintain a proper environment with particular attention to cleanliness, lighting, temperature, and nourishment of family members.

3. Efficient maintenance of the heating/cooling system insures more healthful air in the house. Consider the addition of an air purifying system. Also investigate the benefits of installing a water purifying system. Testing of water for lead and other properties is wise; additionally, further testing for asbestos, radon, and carbon monoxide levels is suggested.

4. The chimneys should be cleaned according to the frequency of use of the fireplace. The furnace chimneys should be checked and maintained by a professional.

5. Enforce a smoke-free house. Do not smoke or allow others to smoke in the house. Emphasize the danger of second-hand inhalation as well as the danger of a fire as a result of smoking.

6. Doors and windows should operate smoothly. The house should be caulked properly to prevent water damage and offset unhealthy growth of mold. However, it should not be so tight as to not allow some exchange of inside and outside air.

7. Refrigerators should run efficiently, keeping food at a safe temperature for consumption.

*Information for the next three sections was taken from Holmes et al., 1993; "79 Tips to Make Your House Safer"; and "Be a Firesafe Neighbor," NFPA, 1988.

Refrigerator thermometers are available and are an inexpensive way to monitor the inside temperature. Oven thermometers are available as well.

8. The long range effect of radiation on health has not been determined. As a precaution, do not stand in front of the microwave so as to avoid radiation exposure. Precaution should be observed also by keeping the electric alarm clocks on the far corner of the nightstand instead of immediately at the head of the bed. Also, curtailing the use of an electric blanket is recommended; try to use it just to warm the bed when retiring and then switch the power off.

9. Annual medical checkups for family members should be encouraged with records conscientiously maintained with respect to medical history—citing potential problems, allergies, vaccination data, and so on.

10. It is recommended that identifying medical tags or bracelets be worn by individuals suffering particular medical problems to alert and assist personnel should an emergency occur.

11. There should be a common emergency station, perhaps by the telephone in the kitchen wherein vital emergency information is kept. In this file, the following are suggested: emergency numbers for fire, police, or medical assistance; location of house, for example, the house is located in the northeast quadrant of the village; medical history of family members, particularly allergies to medication, vaccination data, and other applicable information. Practice emergency drills so that when an real emergency occurs members of the household will be prepared.

12. At the emergency station, a First Aid kit should be available. A complete First Aid kit may be purchased. However, with some planning, one can customize a kit more completely using higher quality supplies that better meets individual needs. It should contain: a handbook of First Aid instruction; cold pack (almost anything from the freezer could be used in an emergency), thermometer, tweezers, scissors, adhesive strips and tape, butterfly bandages, cotton balls, gauze, safety pins, syrup of ipecac, antihistamine, acetaminophen, aspirin, antibiotic cream, antiseptic, hydrogen peroxide, rubbing alcohol, liquid soap, and eye wash. A flashlight with extra batteries, a candle and dry matches, a radio with extra batteries and bottled water should be on hand. A duplicate kit should be carried in the car. This kit should contain additional automotive necessities such as liquid tire inflators, extra fuses, road torches, and a blanket (Williston Times, 1994)

13. The elderly as well as young children should be given special consideration, such as, instructions in large print to compensate for failing eyesight or preprogrammed emergency telephone numbers to promote confidence in emergency situations.

14. Safeguard health of pets. When an animal is outside, it should have a collar carrying an identification tag.

SAFETY PRECAUTIONS

Safety suggestions that one can adopt at home are provided below. This section addresses the well-being of the residents of the house from a safety perspective. As described earlier, dividing safety precautions and accident prevention was problematic and a decision was made to include primarily those overlapping topics that involve both health concerns and accident prevention in this section.

1. House alarm systems that are monitored by a central office offer reassurance to the home-owner and will give speedy response to a call for assistance. When leaving the home for an extended period, ask a neighbor to pick up mail and newspapers. Ask someone to move cars in the driveway. To further protect the home from intrusion, light-timers operating in different rooms, and pro-grammed randomly, give the appearance of an occupied home. When returning to the home, be ob-servant. One may have been targeted for harm. If one suspects that one is being followed, go to a po-lice or fire station. If a car phone is available, use it to call for assistance. Upon arriving home safely, electric-eye-controlled outside lights are another good device. These devices offer light when needed and also signal a warning when an intruder steps in its path. When arriving home, if anything seems amiss, do not enter to investigate, leave immediately, go to a neighbor, and call police.

2. Parents should talk to their children about safety but experts maintain there are ways to do so without terrifying young children. Some of their tips are (a) always tailor your talk to the age of the child and to what your child will understand. Dr. Michael Jellinek, the chief of the child-psychiatry service at Massachusetts General Hospital in Boston, indicates that most parents should start talking to their children about safety issues when they are old enough (about four or five) to wander from a parent's line of sight for a period of time; (b) parents should refer to the potential for danger but stress that such incidents are rare; (c) in any discussion, parents should first try to find out what their children already understand; (d) parents and children can rehearse in a matter-of-fact way what to do if children are separated from parents or followed by strangers; and (e) talk about common enticements. Mr. Kenneth Wooden of Child Lures Community Plan describes en-ticements such as a stranger asking a child to help find a lost puppy or a stranger in a car asking for directions. He also recommends that parents not put name tags on a child's garments where they might be visible to a passing observer. "This allows offenders to engage children in conversation, thus disarming them," he says (Chira, 1994).

3. Laminated cards with picture, fingerprints and description have been made of children through the cooperation of the Police Department and school administrators. These cards are help-ful if a child is missing or lost. Family members should be aware, on a daily basis, of the clothing a child is wearing so that a description can be given if necessary. These precautions should also be made for the elderly or anyone who may be in need of assistance or identification.

4. Entrances and stairways to the home should be well lighted and free of clutter. Stairway mishaps are among the most dangerous and are more likely to result in serious injury or death.

5. Each year, approximately 84 thousand individuals receive hospital emergency treatment for injuries involving floors and flooring materials. Most of these injuries are the result of falls. More than 9 thousand people die each year as the result of falls.

6. Accidents associated with ladders, as reported by the U.S. Consumer Product Safety Commission, which resulted in a trip to the hospital emergency room, amounted to over 65 thou-sand cases in a one-year period. Ladders should be stored properly to prohibit access by a child or an intruder.

7. Excessively hot tap water caused over 5 thousand burns and serious scald injuries annu-ally, mostly to the elderly and the very young. As many as 32 thousand injuries could be prevented each year if water heaters were set at a safer temperature.

8. Automatic garage doors must have an electric eye that reverses the door direction when it comes in contact with an object. Similarly, electric car windows should have the same safety feature.

9. To avoid "backing up" types of car accidents, park facing out of a driveway or garage. Always walk around the back of the car before getting in to ensure that the path is clear. A small child or object may not be visible from the driver's seat vantage point.

10. Never leave children alone in a car while it is running or not. A child can engage the shift or disengage the brake causing the car to roll into danger. During warm weather, there is the danger of heat prostration.

11. Wear eye protection such as goggles or shields while operating power tool equipment. Never leave power tools operational or allow a child to "play" with such equipment.

12. Follow directions carefully when using chemicals. Wear protective gloves to avoid skin irritation and/or absorption through the skin. Ensure proper ventilation to prevent inhalation of harmful chemicals.

13. Keep drugs and harmful chemicals out of the reach of children. Use chemicals only when natural alternatives are not feasible.

14. When purchasing children's apparel, keep in mind that long scarfs, ties, and so on have the potential of getting caught in doors, machinery, bike wheels, or other such hazards. Likewise, buttons can catch on mesh playpens.

15. Children's clothing should be fire retardant.

16. Toys should be age appropriate and given a safety check by an adult before a child plays with it.

17. Latchkey children should be observant on entering the house of anything amiss and instructed as to their next step, such as, do not enter, go to a neighbor, and so on.

18. In the kitchen, care should be taken with the operation of appliances: Tie hair back, do not stick spoons or fingers near a moving blade, shut the appliance off to stir contents, and other such precautions.

19. When cooking on the stove, the kitchen should not be left unattended. Handles of pots should always be turned in so that they do not stick out over the edge to tempt a child or to be inadvertently knocked over. Never put anything on or near the stove that could catch fire. Use protective, fire-retardant potholders. Be careful about igniting clothing when working around stoves, barbecues, or any open flame. Keep sand, baking soda, a fire extinguisher, or a nonflammable cover readily available in case of a fire emergency.

20. Certain safety precautions should be observed during microwave use. Use microwave-safe cookware. When checking the progress of food, avoid the steam that escapes when uncovering the dish. Let microwaved food stand the recommended amount of time, allowing it to return to a safe temperature for consumption. An example would be a baby bottle in which the outside is comfortable to the touch while the temperature of the contents might be high enough to burn the child's mouth.

ACCIDENT PREVENTION

Suggestions that can help reduce and/or prevent accidents at home are provided below.

1. Insure that entrances and stairways are well-lighted and in good repair. Steps, coverings, and handrails should be sturdy and secure. Stairways should be free of clutter. Childproof gates should be installed at the top of stairs. Extra precaution should be considered for the elderly, since they are particularly vulnerable to a mishap on the stairs, especially at night.

2. Floors and floor covering should be well maintained to eliminate and/or reduce the possibility of tripping or falling.

3. Ladders should be checked for loose rungs or signs of disrepair. Use good sense in the operation of a ladder, and store properly and promptly after use so that a child or an intruder does not have access to it. It should, however, be accessible in case of emergency.

4. Clotheslines and tree branches should be above head level. Roots that could cause a fall should be removed. The yard should be free of debris. Outdoor furniture and play equipment should be oiled and checked periodically for loose or protruding screws.

5. Garage doors should be properly maintained. Automatic doors should have an electric eye and other safety features.

6. Bathtubs and showers should be equipped with nonskid mats or strips to help prevent falls. Grab bars can facilitate getting in and out of the tub safely; these are a must for the elderly.

7. Hot water temperatures should be maintained at a safe temperature to prevent accidental scalding. A temperature of 120 degrees Fahrenheit is ideal for dishwasher sanitizing, clothes washing and comfortable showering. This temperature will not scald and is energy efficient (see Chapter 27).

8. Ovens, stovetops, and microwaves should operate safely. Children should be instructed as to proper use and danger or misuse of any appliance. Use of such devices should be age appropriate.

9. Never store tools or sharp objects overhead. It has been recorded that 1800 accidents a year have taken place when a child or adult has attempted to remove a tool box from an overhead position. The tool accounting for the most household accidents has been the hammer.

10. Use a special compartment, tray, or utensil block to store sharp knives. Each year, more than 100 thousand people are treated in the hospital emergency room for cuts on fingers, hands, and arms which might have been avoided.

11. Use the specified light bulb in an overhead or ceiling fixture. The wrong bulb or wattage can lead to overheating and fire.

12. Most local fire departments will instruct residents on the use of carbon monoxide and smoke detectors. The fire department will also provide stickers to be placed on the windows of rooms that contain children or the infirm. Make sure at least one smoke detector is placed on every floor of the home. Locate the detectors on the ceiling away from air vents and near bedrooms. Test the detectors every month to ensure they are working properly. One might check the unit on the first day of each month or assign the responsibility to a child to encourage fire safety awareness in the family.

13. Develop an emergency exit plan for the home in case of a fire. Practice the plan to make sure everyone can escape quickly and safely. Designate a meeting place. Practice at least once in the dark. Focus on these four elements in a fire safety plan: (a) prevention, (b) detection, (c) escape planning and practice, and (d) fire department notification.

14. Every year, over 400 children drown in backyard pool accidents. Approximately 236 are children under the age of five, and 65 percent are male. Almost 5000 children under the age of five are treated in hospital emergency rooms for submersion accidents. Do not rely on fencing to keep young children safe from drowning accidents. Educate children about safety procedures, and never leave them unsupervised by the pool. Rescue floatation devices should be in place and ready for use at all times. Parents, guardians, and baby sitters should know how to initiate water rescue, cardiopulmonary resuscitation (CPR), or mouth-to-mouth resuscitation immediately while awaiting the arrival of emergency personnel. A telephone along with emergency numbers and procedures should be poolside. Install ground fault circuit interrupters (GFCIs) near pool (or any high-risk area).

15. Appliances and electric equipment should not be operated near a filled sink or bathtub.

16. Do not overload electric outlets or tamper with safety features of same. Use outlet covers to safeguard children and pets.

17. Store flammable liquids, such as gasoline, paints, and solvents, away from heating sources. Do not store them in the house or car. Vapors from flammable liquids can ignite even at temperatures below zero. Some chemicals give off deadly gases when combined. Certain combinations are flammable when mixed. Be aware of the possibility of spontaneous combustion and dispose of rags according to instructions. All products should be kept in their original containers and should be clearly marked as to their use, expiration, possible hazards, antidotes, and proper disposal.

18. When leaving the home for an extended period of time, unplug solid state appliances, such as TVs, as an added fire safety tactic. Turn the water heater off. During cold weather, do not turn the furnace off but adjust the thermostat setting to 55 degrees Fahrenheit. This will prevent damage such as frozen water pipes, which could occur when the temperature in the house drops below freezing.

SUMMARY

1. Contrary to popular belief, the home is *not* the safest place in the world. In fact, most industrial (including chemical) plants have records that indicate that it is "safer" to be at work than at home.

2. Some key health concerns at home include:

a. form a healthful environment by encouraging family members to practice cleanliness and safety;

b. maintain the heating/cooling/water system ecologically;

c. encourage annual medical care and institute First Aid and emergency procedures.

3. Some key safety concerns at home include:

a. Insure that entrances, stairways, floors, and coverings are maintained free of clutter and well lighted;

b. practice safety in the kitchen while cooking;

c. recommend installation of carbon monoxide and smoke detectors and design and practice a fire escape plan.

4. Some key accident prevention measures at home include:

a. develop an emergency exit plan for the home in case of a fire;

b. maintain hot water temperature at level below scalding;

c. use dangerous chemicals prudently by wearing protective clothing and following ventilation recommendations.

REFERENCES

"79 Tips to Make Your House Safer," Long Island Lighting Company, Nassau County, NY, undated.

Chira, S. "Taking Old-Fashioned Precautions," *The New York Times,* February 17, 1994, C6.

"Health First Network Magazine," *Williston Times,* 52 (6), February 11, 1994.

Holmes, G., Singh, R., Theodore, L. *Handbook of Environmental Management and Technology.* New York: Wiley-Interscience, 1993.

N. F. P. A., "Be a Firesafe Neighbor." B. R.-5, 1988.

24

At Work

INTRODUCTION

The previous chapter provided suggestions in the health, safety, and accident prevention areas in a domestic setting. Individual sections were devoted to each of these topic areas. This chapter will also, in turn, provide similar information, but for a work setting, with particular emphasis on an office environment.

The reader should note that due to the overlapping nature of the material presented in the previous chapter, In the Home, and the next chapter, Other Health, Safety and Accident Management Areas, there is duplication of some material. This has occurred because of a decision to write each chapter in a stand-alone manner. It is hoped that this approach will not inconvenience the majority of the reading audience.

Once again, the sections to follow provide suggestions or tips that can be employed in a work/office setting for each of the following topics:

1. Health Concerns
2. Safety Precautions
3. Accident Prevention

The suggestions for each of the above areas is detailed in numerical rather than essay form. The reader should also note the overlapping nature of the three topics. For this reason, suggestions regarding health concerns address the well-being of the personnel at work from a health perspec-

This chapter is a condensed, revised, and updated version of an unpublished (but copyrighted) 1992 text prepared by M. K. Theodore and L. Theodore titled *A Citizen's Guide to Pollution Prevention*.

tive. Dividing safety precautions and accident prevention was not as simple. However, a decision was made to primarily include those overlapping topics that involve both health concerns and accident prevention in the safety precautions section. The accident prevention section was then left to contain accident preventive suggestions that do not directly impact on health.

HEALTH CONCERNS*

Sixteen suggestions regarding health concerns in the work/office environment are provided below.

1. Ideally, choose a vocation that you enjoy and where the work environment would be pollution free, operated safely, require reasonable hours, a fair commute, and just compensation. Consideration should also be given to the long-term impact with respect to health plan benefits, educational incentives, advancement possibilities and pension plans. Unfortunately, for the vast majority of the work force, all these conditions are often not options.

2. Avoid locating the workplace near power plants, dumps, contaminating chemical runoffs, exposure to radiation, electromagnetic waves, air pollution, and the like.

3. The workplace should be clean and well lighted.

4. The heating/cooling system in the workplace should be maintained efficiently. The environment should be tested for asbestos, radon, and carbon monoxide. An air purifying system should be installed if needed.

5. Bottled water should be available if tap water contains contaminants.

6. Encourage a smoke-free workplace. Do not smoke, and encourage others to refrain. Ask smokers to do so outside so that others are not exposed to second-hand smoke. Smoking also increases the possibility of fire.

7. Participation in physical exercise should be encouraged. Offering health club privileges, advocating biking or walking to and from work, using stairs instead of elevators, participating in corporate runs, and supporting team sports, intensify health consciousness. Records indicate that this type of activity raises productivity.

8. As part of a medical package, annual medical checkups should be encouraged. Employees should be encouraged to seek medical advice when needed and not come to work when sick or disabled.

9. Avoid back and neck problems. Orthopedic chairs should be utilized where needed. Computers and other office equipment should be set up to avoid strain. Take periodic breaks from sedentary positions to improve circulation.

10. Good hygiene, in a general sense, should be maintained.

11. A First Aid kit should be available.

*Information in the next three sections was taken from Holmes, Singh, and Theodore, 1993; "79 Tips to Make Your House Safer"; "Be a Firesafe Neighbor," NFPA, 1988; and Theodore, Reynolds, and Taylor, 1989.

12. The office personnel should have a emergency evacuation plan that should be practiced periodically.

13. A handbook covering employer/employee expectations should be given to each worker. This guide could be used as a bible for the office and perhaps prevent health problems.

14. A suggestion box can be utilized for improvements and new ideas as well as to air grievances. If a suggestion is implemented, a reward might be considered.

15. An office newsletter containing announcements of promotions, lateral moves, births, graduations, and other events gives fellow employees another dimension of each other's lives.

16. Mental health counseling should be available.

SAFETY PRECAUTIONS

Safety suggestions that one can adapt in a work/office setting are provided below. This section addresses the well-being of the worker from a safety perspective. Dividing safety precautions and accident prevention was problematic and a decision was made to include primarily those overlapping topics that involve both health concerns and accident prevention in this section.

1. The office should comply with all city, state, and federal safety measures.

2. A company manual containing safety material should be available and followed. Updated or new procedures should be posted in a common area. The safety officer should insure that this takes place.

3. A fire warden should be selected. This person must insure that fire and safety drills are practiced on a regular basis and that all fire safety laws are adhered to.

4. Fire alarm locations, fire extinguisher locations, and exits should be clearly marked and brought to the attention of all.

5. A sprinkler system should be operational.

6. Emergency numbers should be stickered on each phone or entered on memory buttons for quick access.

7. A security system connected to a central monitoring station should be considered.

8. Dress appropriately for one's situation at the workplace. Wear a lab coat, safety goggles, or other protective gear when needed. Wear gloves to prevent absorption of chemicals.

9. Follow safety rules when using machinery. Make sure hair is securely tied or under a hat. Sleeves, ties, necklaces, and rings should be removed when operating machinery.

10. Personal hygiene is expected. It is a must where food is handled. If the consequences of consumption of contaminated food are understood, these problems could be avoided. The worker should be encouraged to be his or her own watchdog.

11. Avoid exposure to radiation by following safety procedures.

12. Proper ventilation should be maintained with periodic checks to insure the air is safe.

13. When working with chemicals, fans should remove contaminants so that harmful vapors are not inhaled.

14. Restrooms should be locked and monitored by video camera or personnel.

15. Parking garages, entrances, and exits should be secure with any entry monitored.

16. The buddy system should be encouraged when working off-hours.

17. When traveling to and from work on public transportation, keep personal safety in mind. Avoid desolate or darkened bus or train stops. On trains, sit in car occupied by the conductor. Change one's seat immediately if concern for safety arises; and do not hesitate to seek help.

18. If traveling by personal car, consider car pooling.

19. Obey traffic laws and speed limits. Safe driving courses could be given during or after work hours. Insurance companies encourage clients to do this by reducing premiums after proof of completion of the course. Cars equipped with air bags and an antilock brake system (ABS) also receive a reduction from insurance companies.

20. The company car as well as the worker's personal car must be kept in top working condition. Regular maintenance prolongs the life of the car and protects the driver and passengers.

21. Every car should have its manual, a jack, an emergency repair kit and a First Aid kit. A car phone is a plus in an emergency situation.

22. Passengers always wear a seat belt. The supplemental restraint system (SRS) airbag affords the driver additional protection in a frontal collision. This system is designed to supplement the protection provided by the seat belt (Fuji Industries, 1992). Twenty percent of serious injuries result when unbelted people collide. The chances of being fatally injured are twenty-five times greater for someone who is thrown from a car. If one survives being thrown from or through the car, the additional peril of striking an object or being hit by a moving vehicle is enhanced.

23. The unexpected action of another vehicle cannot be predicted or controlled. This is particularly problematic when alcohol is present. Alcohol accounts for more than half of all automobile-related highway fatalities. Thus, alcohol is the largest contributing factor in fatal motor vehicle accidents. There are approximately two million alcohol related accidents annually that produce approximately 25,000 fatalities and 300,000 seriously injured victims (M&M Protection Consultants, n.d.).

24. Be particularly aware of being followed on pay day or when using automated teller machines (ATMs). Use ATMs during regular business hours when more people are present. After withdrawals, remain at the machine to secure your money. Try to use drive-up ATMs, but when using an ATM in a vestibule, do not enter if someone else is already there. Be especially observant of obstacles near the ATM, like bushes, where a thief could hide. In a large majority of ATM robberies, police indicated that the suspects hide behind some kind of obstacle and jump out when their victim is in the middle of or concluding a transaction ("Avoiding a Robbery," 1994).

25. When using phone credit cards or when punching in any type of secured code, be aware that there could be someone observing this process in order to sell the numbers for a quick profit. Keep this in mind when storing or passing information through the computer. Change passwords frequently.

ACCIDENT PREVENTION

Suggestions that can help reduce and/or eliminate accidents in the office or while at work are provided below.

1. Maintain entrances and stairways in good repair. Steps, coverings, and handrails should be sturdy and secure. Stairways should be free of clutter. They should also be well lighted.

2. Floors and floor covering should be well maintained to eliminate and/or reduce the possibility of tripping or falling.

3. Elevators and escalators should comply with state and local safety standards. Entrances and exits of same should be designed according to safety recommendations. Personnel should be aware of emergency procedures if an elevator or escalator is disabled.

4. If chemicals are spilled, emergency showers and eyewashes should be available. Proper cleanup should be initiated.

5. Tools and machinery should be stored properly and used only by trained personnel. Take periodic breaks when operating machinery to prevent loss of concentration.

6. Do not abuse machinery and compromise safety by subjecting machinery to conditions for which it is not rated or for which it was not intended.

7. Do not overload electric outlets or tamper with safety devices. Make repairs in a timely manner.

8. Be aware of fire exits. Practice fire and emergency evacuation drills periodically.

9. Sponsor a First Aid course. Encourage employees to learn cardiopulmonary resuscitation (CPR) and initiate treatment while waiting for medical personnel to arrive.

SUMMARY

1. There are many health, safety and accident prevention precautions that can be taken in an office setting.

2. Some key suggestions regarding health concerns include:

a. the heating/cooling system in the workplace should be maintained efficiently. The environment should be tested for asbestos, radon, and carbon monoxide;

b. encourage a smoke-free workplace. Do not smoke, and encourage others to refrain. Ask smokers to do so outside so that others are not exposed to second-hand smoke;

c. participation in physical exercise should be encouraged. Offering health club privileges, advocating biking or walking to and from work, using stairs instead of elevators, involvement in corporate runs, supporting team sports, etc., intensify health consciousness.

3. Some key suggestions regarding safety concern include:

a. a company manual containing safety material should be available and followed. Updated or new procedures should be posted in a common area;

b. fire alarm locations, fire extinguisher locations, and exits should be clearly marked and brought to the attention of all;

c. when traveling to and from work on public transportation, keep personal safety in mind. Avoid desolate or darkened bus or train stops. On trains, sit in car occupied by the conductor. Change one's seat immediately if concern for safety arises; and, do not hesitate to seek help.

4. Some key suggestions regarding accident prevention include:

a. maintain entrances and stairways in good repair. Steps, coverings, and handrails should be sturdy and secure. Stairways should be free of clutter;

b. floors and floor covering should be well maintained to eliminate and/or reduce the possibility of tripping or falling;

c. tools and machinery should be stored properly and used only by trained personnel. Take periodic breaks when operating machinery to prevent loss of concentration.

REFERENCES

"79 Tips to Make Your House Safer," Long Island Lighting Company, Nassau County, New York, undated.

"Avoiding a Robbery," *Newsday,* February 17, 1994, 35.

Holmes, G., Singh, R., and Theodore, L. *Handbook of Environmental Management and Technology.* New York: Wiley-Interscience, 1993.

M&M Protection Consultants. "Let's Slip Into Something Comfortable . . . ," SB 4-87-3.0, undated.

N. F. P. A., "Be a Firesafe Neighbor," B. R.-5, 1988.

"Owner's Manual," Fuji Heavy Industries Ltd., Tokyo, Japan, 1992.

Theodore, L., Reynolds, J., and Taylor, F. *Accident and Emergency Management.* New York: Wiley-Interscience, 1989.

25

Other Health, Safety, and Accident Management Areas

INTRODUCTION

As noted in the previous three chapters, accidents have occurred since the birth of civilization and were just as damaging in early times as they are today. Anyone who crosses a street or swims in a pool runs the risk of injury through carelessness, poor judgment, ignorance, or other circumstances. This has not changed through history. This introductory section examines a number of accidents and disasters that took place before the advances of modern technology.

Catastrophic explosions have been reported as early as 1769, when one-sixth of the city of Frescia, Italy, was destroyed by the explosion of 100 tons of gunpowder stored in the state arsenal. More than 3,000 people were killed in this, the second deadliest explosion in history (Theodore, Reynolds, & Taylor, 1989).

The worst explosion in history occurred in 1856 on the Greek island of Rhodes. A church, which had gunpowder stored in its vaults, was struck by lightning. The resulting blast is estimated to have killed 4,000 people. This remains the highest death toll for a single explosion (Holmes, Singh, & Theodore, 1993).

One of the most legendary disasters occurred in Chicago in October 1871. The "Great Chicago Fire," as it is now known, is alleged to have started in a barn owned by Patrick O'Leary, when one of his cows overturned a lantern. The O'Leary house escaped unharmed, since it was upwind of the blaze, but the barn was destroyed, as well as 2,124 acres of Chicago real estate.

Four persons died and eight others were injured on March 26, 1976, when two gondola cars fell more than 100 feet down the slopes of Vail Mountain in Vail, Colorado. The accident occurred

This chapter is a condensed, revised, and updated version of an unpublished (but copyrighted) 1992 text prepared by M. K. Theodore and L. Theodore titled *A Citizen's Guide to Pollution Prevention.*

because an automatic shutoff mechanism failed to respond to the partial derailment of a car ahead of the two that crashed. The cause was traced to five strands of steel sheath encasing the cable. The strands had begun to unravel at a point about two-thirds of the way up the mountain. The frayed cable caused the cars bearing the victims to derail and jam up, which should have activated an electrical overload switch designed to shut down the gondola. There is no explanation of why this safety device did not function ("79 Tips to Make Your House Safer," n.d.).

In Caracas, Venezuela on April 9, 1952, a large crowd gathered at a church at the beginning of Holy Week. Apparently a pickpocket, wishing to create confusion, shouted "Fire!", whereupon the worshippers rushed toward exits at the rear of the church. Many people fell and were trampled by their fellow parishioners who were rushing to escape the imaginary fire. Fifty-three people were killed, nearly half of whom were small children and infants ("Be a Firesafe Neighbor," NFPA, 1988).

On January 2, 1971, at the Ibrox soccer stadium in Glasgow, Scotland, sixty-six persons were killed and 145 injured when a reinforced steel barrier collapsed under the weight of a surging crowd. The tragedy came after 8,000 spectators had thronged the exits near the end of a hotly contested game between the Glasgow Rangers and the Glasgow Celtics, traditional rivals. A group of Rangers supporters at an exit stairway reportedly attempted to reenter the stadium when they heard that their team had scored to tie the game at 1-1. A massive human pileup was created, causing the loss of many lives ("79 Tips to Make Your House Safer," n.d.).

On June 27, 1978, a freak accident at a fountain pool on Hilton Head Island, South Carolina, claimed four victims. A young man and woman apparently broke one of the lights illuminating the fountain as they jumped into it at 8:00 PM, sending several hundred volts through the water. The woman's roommate entered the pool, either unaware of the danger or attempting to save the pair. A neighbor then jumped in to attempt a rescue. All four were electrocuted ("79 Tips to Make Your House Safer," n.d.).

On March 20, 1980 a regional seismic network operated by the U.S. Geological Survey and University of Washington recorded an earthquake of Richter magnitude 4.0 from a point north of the summit of Mount St. Helens, a dormant volcano that had last erupted in 1857. Two days later, the intensity of the seismic activity increased. Geologists suspected that magma, or melted rock, was moving up inside the mountain. The activity continued to increase. On March 27 a plume of steam and ash was emitted from Mount St. Helens and rose about 66 thousand feet above the mountain. At a point one mile north of the summit crater, a large bulge was observed to be forming in the mountain's side. By early May, this bulge had grown to a length of one mile and a width of six-tenths of a mile. Volcanologists watched this bulge for signs that it might split open, extruding magma. On May 18, without any warning, Mount St. Helens suddenly exploded.

Apparently triggered by an earthquake of Richter magnitude 5.0, the entire north slope burst open along the upper edge of the bulge, releasing the bottled up gases and magma. Up to three cubic kilometers of rock and ash were blown away from the mountain laterally. The blast spewed over one and a third billion cubic yards of material into the atmosphere. Almost everything within five miles of the volcano was destroyed. Tons of choking ash and dust were dropped on central and eastern Washington, northern Oregon, and Idaho, and even parts of western Montana. The volcano continued to erupt during the remainder of 1980 and throughout the summer and fall of 1981. The death toll was confirmed in 1981 as 34, and 27 remain missing. Wildlife officials estimate that approximately 10,000 wild and domestic animals may also have been killed.

Eight "less significant" incidents are described below ("79 Tips to Make Your House Safer," n.d.):

1. Kandy, Ceylon, August 19, 1959. An elephant ran amok at a religious festival, killing 14 persons and injuring many others.

2. Bombay, India, September 20, 1959. A crush created at the scene of a religious "miracle" is reported to have killed 75 persons.

3. Kumaon Hills, India, February 13, 1970. A man-eating tiger, roaming a hilly area 50 miles northeast of New Delhi, was reported to have killed 48 persons.

4. Baltimore, Maryland, August 2, 1970. State health authorities reported that an outbreak of salmonella food poisoning at a city nursing home caused the deaths of 12 elderly patients; 60 others who were stricken recovered.

5. Sallen, France, May 15, 1971. The floorboards of a rented hall gave way at the close of a wedding reception, plunging the guests into a well beneath the floor; 13 persons perished.

6. Mozambique, November 1973. A large quantity of methyl alcohol washed ashore in drums and was mistakenly consumed as whiskey; 58 deaths were confirmed, but hundreds were believed to have died.

7. Near Jaipur, India, September 7, 1977. The roof of a village class room collapsed under the weight of a troop of baboons; 15 schoolgirls were killed instantly.

8. Harrisburg, Pennsylvania, June 13, 1978. An attempt by 2,200 students and teachers to set a world record for tug-of-war ended with 70 persons injured when the 2,000-foot nylon rope they were using broke. Four persons had parts of their hands and fingers ripped off.

The remainder of this chapter provides suggestions that can help reduce accidents and improve health and safety in the following areas:

1. Building a house
2. In the garden
3. While traveling and vacationing
4. While shopping
5. While dining and entertaining

No introductory comments are included with each of these five sections; rather, the reader is provided with specific suggestion for the topic in question. Despite the obvious overlap in some of the sections, each is treated on a stand-alone basis.

BUILDING A HOUSE*

1. Consider site in terms of proximity to plants, dumps, contaminating chemical runoffs, exposure to radiation, electromagnetic waves, noise, air pollution, and traffic.

---

*Information for this section was drawn from Theodore et al., 1989; "79 Tips to Make Your House Safer," n.d.; and NFPA, 1988.

2. Consider location in terms of direction of sun, natural protection from trees, elevation and exposure to the elements, such as wind and rain.

3. Investigate credentials of architect, builder, plumber, electrician, and any other subcontractors. Ask for references and visit their clients, if possible, to insure reliability and satisfaction with construction and contractors.

4. Comply with city, state, and federal construction codes.

5. Construction materials should comply with fire and safety regulations. Material should be environmentally safe. Use fire resistant construction material wherever possible. This should also be considered when purchasing furniture.

6. Minimize both direct and indirect uses of CFCs; for example, foam materials, air conditioning, and fire extinguishers.

7. Care should be exercised when working or inspecting the site. Proper clothing, such as hard hats, steel-toed shoes, safety glasses, protective gloves, and hearing protection should be worn as necessary.

8. Use extreme caution around excavations or while walking on or under scaffolding. Cautionary signs should be displayed.

9. The construction site should be secure so that children are prevented access as well as to prevent theft and vandalism.

10. Construction debris should be handled according to city, state, and federal regulations. Disposal should be environmentally safe.

11. Heating and cooling of the house should be energy efficient and environmentally safe. Air and water purifiers should be considered. Safeguards against radon and other contamination should be taken.

12. Energy-efficient windows and doors should be installed. Efficient and safe insulation should be used. Proper ventilation for exchange of air should also be insured.

13. To avoid the inhalation of carbon monoxide, the garage should be detached. If attached, avoid using the space above it as a bedroom.

14. Use specified electrical wiring honoring all safety codes.

15. Install ground fault circuit interrupters (GFCIs) where appropriate; for example, near a sink or pool area.

16. Have ample electrical outlets and circuit breakers. Allowance should be made for installing additional outlets at a future time as the need arises.

17. Consider a generator for emergency power failure.

18. Consider alternatives to lead piping such as brass or PVC piping.

19. Install an alarm system to warn of intruders and fire.

20. Install smoke detectors throughout the house.

21. Install a sprinkler system as part of the fire alarm system.

22. Install fire escapes where necessary.

23. Use fireproof doors, particularly between floors or near high risk areas such as the heating system.

24. Provide for emergency exits within the house in case of fire.

25. Consider bathroom and kitchen fixtures that are designed with the safety of the user in mind. In the bathroom, for ease of entry into shower or tub, consider non-skid surfaces and hand rails; design and position of knobs on doors and water fixtures contribute greatly to safety.

26. Specifically designed features for the handicapped, such as wheelchair accessibility, customized door and drawer handles, height of counters, and other options are available.

27. Stair rails should be sturdy.

28. The electric garage door should be equipped with electric eye safety feature.

IN THE GARDEN*

1. Trees in the garden not only add to the beauty of the property, but, properly placed, will insulate the house from cold winds in the winter and provide welcome shade in the summer.

2. Shrubs will help provide protection from soil erosion.

3. Trees and shrubs should never be allowed to overgrow to the point that windows or entrances are hidden, thus providing a place for intruders to hide.

4. Investigate developing a habitat that encourages natural control of insects, that is, make an effort to attract and protect birds. Insects form a large part of avian sustenance and birds are most numerous and active just at those times when harmful insects are at their height. Birds also consume large quantities of weed seeds. Furthermore, small rodents that are troublesome in the garden form a large part of the diet of birds of prey (Seymour, 1970).

5. Attract beneficial insects to the garden to feed upon plant-destructive insects. One of the most important helpful insects is the ladybug who feeds on aphids and mealy bugs that infest many garden plants (Seymour, 1970).

6. Avoid chemical pesticides. Children and pets play on treated lawns. While at school, children may be exposed to toxic chemicals daily. A study by the Natural Resources Defense Council found that some toxins damage growing and developing tissue more readily than mature tissues. According to the National Academy of Sciences, exposures to pesticides early in life can lead to greater risks of cancer as well as immunity and neurological problems. Other studies report that

---

*Information in this section was drawn from Holmes et al., 1993; "79 Tips to Make Your House Safer," n.d.; NFPA, 1988; and Seymour, 1970.

children retain toxins longer than adults, and one study linked pesticide exposure to childhood leukemia (Penenberg, 1994). There are natural alternatives to use against pests in the garden. To control aphids, spray plants with dish suds or soapy water. Rinse off when insects are dead. To control snails and slugs, fill a shallow pan with stale beer and place in the garden. Instead of a herbicide, use live nematodes to combat the Japanese beetle. These pests are attracted to the beer and drown in the liquid.

7. Cultivate a vegetable garden and fruit trees. Superior varieties may be grown in a home garden. The products can always be freshly gathered at their peak of perfection. The products are not contaminated by chemicals either in the growth process or sprayed for shelf life unless the home gardener makes the decision to do so.

8. If chemicals or fertilizers are used, store properly and dispose safely.

9. For the safety and well-being of children and pets, teach children which plants are poisonous.

10. Wear protective clothing while gardening. When operating machinery, wear safety goggles, hearing protection, tie hair back, and avoid wearing clothing that could get caught in moving parts.

11. Always read the manual for the machine being used and do not abuse a piece of machinery by subjecting it to use for which it is not intended.

12. When purchasing equipment, do not overbuy. Some commercial machines may be too complicated, powerful, or heavy for the average gardener.

13. Power machines should have a safety cutoff.

14. Never use an electric machine when dampness is present or at any time when the threat of electrocution might be enhanced.

15. When using power machines, rest when you become fatigued.

16. When operating machinery, children and pets should not be underfoot.

17. All garden tools should be maintained properly to prolong their life and assure safe use.

18. Tools should be stored safely, particularly those that have sharp or pointed pieces. A carelessly placed tool can fall and maim, can be tripped over, or end up in a child's hands, resulting in dangerous consequences.

19. Tree cutting should be handled by an expert.

20. Keep firewood away from the house to prevent infestation by carpenter ants and other pests.

21. Maintaining good sanitation in and around the outside of the house is the best defense against infestation of many pests, since it reduces their food and water supply (Dunn, 1994).

22. Outdoor lighting showcases landscaping and enhances safety.

WHILE TRAVELING AND VACATIONING*

The reader should note that many of the health, safety, and accident prevention measures provided below can also be applied to other modes of land travel as well as sea or air travel.

1. If traveling by personal car, it should be in maximum operating condition. Before embarking on a long trip, the car should be given a thorough inspection by a competent mechanic. The destination, the weather, and varied type of terrain should be taken into consideration.

2. The car should contain the car manual, insurance card, spare tire and jack, emergency repair kit, and First Aid kit. A car phone is an added plus. The condition of these should be checked before the trip and replacements made, where necessary.

3. A trip well planned is usually a trip enjoyed. Preparation will pay dividends in enjoyment, efficient use of available hours, as well as other factors. Experienced travelers allow two and one-half hours for each 100 miles. This provides reasonable allowance for driving time, meals, gasoline, and rest stops (AAA Tour Book, 1993).

4. Maps should be thoroughly studied before leaving for the trip. Have a magnifying glass and flashlight available for reading in the car, if needed.

5. Pack the car sensibly but travel as lightly as possible. An overloaded car is dangerous for many reasons. It is more difficult to drive and adds stress to the car and the driver. Occupants are uncomfortable, which also contributes to stress. An overloaded car can inhibit vision, sudden stops can dislodge objects causing injury, and the contents of the car can invite the attention of thieves. If a repair has to be made, the car may have to be unloaded.

6. When traveling with children, have appropriate safety seats. Give thought to games that are geared to car travel. Take along favorite toys and security blankets, for example. Allow extra time for breaks for children to run around.

7. Give a copy of your travel plans to a responsible person. Contact this person periodically.

8. Carry a driver's license, car registration, a medical history card containing vital information such as any major health problem, blood type, medical insurance card, and emergency contact numbers.

9. Good driving is the result of sound techniques executed with courtesy and common sense. Observe posted speed limits, and pay strict attention to road signs and traffic lights. Pass only when you are certain of ample clear space ahead. Signal your intentions always. Most important, the way you drive should be appropriate for the prevailing road, traffic and weather conditions. Be certain that your vehicle can negotiate the road you plan to take.

10. Should your car become disabled, pull as far onto the shoulder of the road as you can. Activate the four-way flashers or place warning devices to warn other drivers. If visibility is poor,

---

*Information for the next three sections was drawn from Holmes et al., 1993; "79 Tips to Make Your House Safer," n.d.; and NFPA, 1988.

do both, keeping alert for oncoming traffic. A raised hood or trunk lid or a white cloth tied to an antenna or left door handle should signal emergency crews. Use a car phone, if available. Stay with your car until assistance arrives.

11. If you observe a disabled car, do not stop but note the location and notify the police to give assistance.

12. Never pick up hitchhikers.

13. Be aware of car-jacking and avoid placing yourself in a victimizing position.

14. When traveling on public transportation, plan ahead. Avoid traveling alone or at night. Avoid waiting in desolate areas. When traveling by rail, sit near the conductor. Avoid sleeping, if possible.

15. Leave valuables at home and keep money out of sight. Use traveler's checks as much as possible.

16. When planning a visit out of the country, obtain passport, visas, shots, and prescriptions, in a timely manner.

17. In a foreign country, keep your passport with you at all times. Make copies of the passport and visas, and give a copy to a responsible person. A lost passport is easier to replace when a photocopy is available.

18. In a foreign country, respect the customs of that country.

19. When considering a hotel or motel, check for fire safety. Ask at the desk what type of fire alarm is used and how it sounds. In your room, read the fire evacuation plan carefully. Find the two exits nearest your room and check to be sure they are unlocked and unblocked. Count the doors between your room and the exits. This will help you find the exits if the corridor is unlighted or filled with smoke. If the fire is in your room, get out immediately and close the door. If the fire is not in your room, leave if possible. Touch the door to test it for heat. If it is cool, brace your shoulder against it and open slowly. Be ready to close it immediately if there are flames on the other side. Crawl low in the smoke to the exit; fresher air will be near the floor. If your room door is hot, do not open it. Instead, seal the door with wet towels or sheets. Turn off any fans and air conditioners. Call the fire department, even if you can see firefighters outside, and give your exact location. Signal at your window. Leave your window closed if you can see smoke outside, since smoke and fire may enter through it. If there is smoke inside your room and it is clear outside, try opening the window. Be ready to close it if more smoke enters your room. Fire exits and stairwells are your best escape routes. Never use an elevator during a fire since the elevator could stop at the fire floor.

20. When considering a hotel or motel, observe security features. Check if entry can be made from outside without a key. When in room, look for security of windows, doors and adjoining room(s). See if the telephone has a hot line for emergency assistance. Do not open the door without checking the peephole. Call the front desk, if suspicious. Keep valuables in the hotel safe. If leaving and returning at odd hours, check the security of the parking lot and ask a parking attendant to accompany you if needed.

WHILE SHOPPING

1. Make a list of items/materials to be purchased. This will organize the outing in the most efficient way.

2. Never leave a child alone or in a car to save time while running into a store or to avoid waking a sleeping child. The consequences are not worth the minutes one might save.

3. When parking the car, make note of the location so that it will not be a problem finding it when the shopping excursion is over and to avoid, perhaps, searching in the dark.

4. Never leave a child unattended in a shopping cart.

5. A child should never be left alone to play in a store while adults shop.

6. Instruct the child as to what to do if he or she finds him- or herself lost or in danger. The child should know that if he or she feels threatened or even uncomfortable he or she should react strongly. A polite or timid child may be reluctant to disobey a threatening adult. If a child is missing, notify authorities immediately so that safety measures can be put into place. Store personnel will lock doors and alert occupants that a child might be in danger.

7. Do not wear expensive jewelry or display money while shopping. The safest way to carry a bag is football style in front of you. If it is worn strapped around the neck, it could be used against the owner.

8. Be alert and aware of people and sorroundings when walking. Victims are chosen by their vulnerability.

9. Hold onto children when riding an escalator. Be aware of items that could get caught in moving parts and cause injury. Know where the emergency stop button is located.

10. Complain to management about unsafe or unsanitary conditions that are noticed. Do not patronize stores that leave these uncorrected.

11. When food shopping, make note of unhealthy food practices, such as cold foods not maintained at the proper temperature, employees not maintaining hygiene or following the sanitary code while handling food, or failure to remove food with an expired date.

12. When returning to the car, look ahead for anything suspicious. If a problem is suspected, return immediately to the store. Be particularly wary if a van or pickup truck is parked next to the car. These vehicles offer a suspect a place to hide in wait for a victim. Check the car, front and back, before entering. Be alert while loading purchases into the car. Get into car with children. Then secure children in safety devices. Lock the doors immediately after entrance.

WHILE DINING AND ENTERTAINING

1. When planning to entertain, consider the space available and the number that can be safely accommodated. Safety becomes more complicated as the numbers increase. Insure that all safety and fire codes are enforced. See that exits are not blocked and that the area is well ventilated.

2. When planning an event, consider whether the site is appropriate for the participants in terms of child proofing, accessibility for the elderly and handicapped, and any other factors. Within reason, the menu should be varied enough to allow for dietary restrictions in terms of the medical or religious history of those attending, as well as for personal preferences.

3. Young children should be supervised at all times, but particularly at a large gathering or in an unfamiliar setting.

4. When preparing and serving food, good hygiene and sanitary procedures must be followed. If the food is to be catered, check the reputation of the company you are dealing with.

5. When planning a party at home or elsewhere, nonalcoholic beverages should be available and easily attainable. Food should be served in a timely fashion so that alcohol is not consumed on an empty stomach, which intensifies the effect of the alcohol. Refrain from serving alcohol at least one hour before the end of a party to allow the effects of alcohol to wear off. Transportation should be provided for those who may have overimbibed.

6. When serving or consuming food at a buffet table where food is standing out for a prolonged period, insure that it is maintained safely. Food that is to be served cold should be kept very cold, and hot food should be kept very hot. Avoid or remove food that has reached room temperature, since this could lead to food spoilage.

SUMMARY

1. Accidents have occurred since the birth of civilization and were just as damaging in early times as they are today. Anyone who crosses a street or swims in a pool runs the risk of injury through carelessness, poor judgment, ignorance, or other circumstances. This has not changed through history.

2. Three health, safety, and accident prevention measures concerned with building a house include:

a. investigate the credentials of architect, builder, plumber, electrician, etc. Request references and visit clients, if possible, to insure reliability and satisfaction with the construction and contractors;

b. comply with city, state, and federal construction codes;

c. heating and cooling of the house should be energy efficient and environmentally safe. Air and water purifiers should be considered. Safeguards against radon and other contamination should be taken.

3. Three health, safety, and accident prevention measures recommended for the garden include:

a. trees in the garden not only add to the beauty of the property but, properly placed, will insulate the house from cold winds in the winter and provide welcome shade in the summer;

b. attract beneficial insects to the garden to feed upon plant-destructive insects. One of the most important helpful insects is the ladybug who feeds on aphids and mealy bugs that infest many garden plants;

c. wear protective clothing while gardening. When operating machinery, wear safety goggles, hearing protection, tie hair back, and avoid wearing clothing that could get caught in moving parts.

4. Three health, safety and accident prevention measures to be taken while traveling and vacationing include:

a. if traveling by personal car, it should be in maximum operating condition. Before embarking on a long trip, the car should be given a thorough inspection by a competent mechanic. The destination, the weather, and varied type of terrain should be taken into consideration;

b. a trip well planned is usually a trip enjoyed. Preparation will pay dividends in enjoyment and efficient use of available hours. Experienced travelers allow two and one-half hours for each 100 miles. This provides reasonable allowance for driving time, meals, gasoline, and rest stops;

c. when traveling with children, have appropriate safety seats. Give thought to games that are geared to car travel. Take along favorite toys and security blankets. Allow extra time for breaks for children to run around.

5. Three health, safety and accident prevention measures to be taken while shopping include:

a. never leave a child alone or in a car while you run into a store. The consequences are not worth the minute you might save;

b. do not wear expensive jewelry or display money while shopping. The safest way to carry a bag is football style in front of the body. If it is worn with the strap around the neck, it could be used against the wearer and cause injury;

c. when food shopping, make note of unhealthy food practices, such as cold foods not maintained at the proper temperature, employees not maintaining hygiene or following the sanitary code while handling food, and the failure to remove food which has an expired date.

6. Three health, safety and accident prevention measures to be taken while dining and entertaining include:

a. when planning to entertain, consider the space available and the number you can safely accommodate. Safety becomes more complicated as the numbers increase. Insure that all safety and fire codes are enforced. See that exits are not blocked and that the area is well ventilated;

b. young children should be supervised at all times, but particularly at a large gathering or in an unfamiliar setting;

c. when preparing and serving food, good hygiene and sanitary procedures must be followed. If the food is to be catered, check the reputation of the company you are dealing with.

REFERENCES

"79 Tips to Make Your House Safer," Long Island Lighting Company, Nassau County, New York, undated.

AAA Tour Book, February 1993.

Dunn, A. "War on the Roaches," *The New York Times,* April 24, 1994, Section 14, 1.

Holmes, G., Singh, R., and Theodore, L. *Handbook of Environmental Management and Technology.* New York: Wiley-Interscience, 1993.

N. F. P. A., "Be a Firesafe Neighbor," B. R.-5, 1988.

Penenberg, A. "Parents Pressuring Schools for Alternatives to Pesticides," *The New York Times,* January 30, 1994, 1C.

Seymour, E. L. D. (ed.). *The Wise Garden Encyclopedia.* New York: Grosset & Dunlap, 1970.

Theodore, L., Reynolds, J., and Taylor, F. *Accident and Emergency Management.* New York: Wiley-Interscience, 1989.

Part VI

Energy Conservation

The pollution prevention sequence continues here. Part VI, comprised of four chapters, serves as an introduction to energy conservation. Chapter 26 is concerned solely with industrial applications. The remaining three chapters discuss what the authors have defined as domestic issues. A comprehensive examination of energy conservation at home is provided in Chapter 27. Chapter 28 focuses on energy conservation in the office. Part VI concludes with Chapter 29, which addresses energy conservation issues during leisure activities or in other circumstances not covered in the home or the workplace.

26

Industrial Applications

CONTRIBUTING AUTHOR

Robert D. Lucas

INTRODUCTION

Energy is the keystone of American life and prosperity as well as a vital component of environmental rehabilitation. The environment must be protected and the quality of life improved but, at the same time, economic stability must also be maintained. These two objectives will be prime factors in determining domestic and foreign policies for years to come. Since energy consumption is a major contributor to environmental pollution, decisions regarding energy policy alternatives require comprehensive environmental analysis. Environmental impact data must be developed for all aspects of an energy system and/or conservation program and must not be limited to separate components.

Because energy has been relatively cheap and plentiful in the past, many energy-wasting practices have been allowed to develop and continue in all sectors of the economy. Industries have wasted energy by discharging hot process water instead of recovering the heat, and by wasting the energy discharged from power plant stacks. Waste hydrocarbons have been discharged or combusted with little consideration for recovering their energy value. There are many more examples, too numerous to mention. Elimination of these practices will, at least temporarily, reduce the rate of increase in energy demand. If conservation can reduce energy demand, it can reduce the associated pollution.

The most dramatic environmental improvements can be developed by conservation in the industrial sector of the economy. Industry accounts for approximately 40 percent of the energy con-

This chapter is a condensed, revised, and updated version of the chapter "Plant Design" appearing in the 1992 text entitled *Pollution Prevention,* by L. Theodore and Y. McGuinn and the chapter "Energy Conservation" from the 1993 Wiley-Interscience text entitled *Handbook of Environmental Management and Technology,* by G. Holmes, R. Singh, and L. Theodore.

sumed in this country. Also, industry might be considered more dynamic, progressive, and strongly motivated by the economic incentives offered by conservation than the other energy-user sectors (residential, commercial, and transportation).

The environmental impacts of energy conservation and consumption are far-reaching, affecting air, water, and land quality as well as public health. (These are discussed in the next section.) Combustion of coal, oil, and natural gas is responsible for air pollution in urban areas, acid rain that is damaging lakes and forests, and some of the nitrogen pollution that is harming estuaries. Although data show that for the period from 1977–1989 annual average ambient levels of all criteria air pollutants were down nationwide, 96 major metropolitan areas still exceeded the national health-based standard for ozone, and 41 metropolitan areas exceeded the standard for carbon monoxide.

Energy consumption also appears to be the primary manmade contribution to global warming, often referred to as the greenhouse effect (see Chapter 42 for more details). The EPA has concluded that energy use—through the formation of carbon dioxide during combustion processes—has contributed approximately 50 percent to the global warming that has occurred in the last 10 years. Although the scientific community is not unanimous in regard to the causes of global warming, most individuals and groups have indicated that a "reasonable" chance of climatic change exists and have already begun to define the potential implications of such changes, many of which are catastrophic. In light of this situation, the Alliance to Save Energy has challenged Congress to pass meaningful legislation to promote and achieve energy efficiency.

ENVIRONMENTAL IMPACTS OF VARIOUS CONVENTIONAL ENERGY SOURCES

At present, there are two major industrial energy sources in use: fossil fuel and nuclear energy. Fossil fuel may be subdivided according to the various raw fuels such as coal, oil, natural gas, liquefied petroleum gas, wood, smoke, coke, refining gas, blast furnace gas, and byproduct fuels. This section covers only the three major fossil fuels: coal, oil, and natural gas.

The fossil fuel energy picture has changed drastically since the 1973 oil crisis. The current national energy policy aims toward energy independence through conservation and promotes increased coal utilization, due to increasingly severe shortages of domestic oil and natural gas. However, an increase of coal consumption would produce more pollutants which are carried through the environment affecting individual organisms and ecosystems. Therefore, emphasis is placed on the impacts of fossil fuel cycles on the physical environment.

ENVIRONMENTAL IMPLICATIONS OF ALTERNATE ENERGY SOURCES

There has been considerable controversy in recent years concerning the roles that various forms of energy production should assume in the nation's energy supply. As discussed in the previous section, the air pollution impacts of coal combustion, the fears of radiation from nuclear accidents and/or wastes, and the dependence on foreign oil have raised numerous questions about conventional supplies. A shift towards alternate energy sources (i.e., those that do not currently contribute significantly to the nation's energy supply) has long been suggested.

Many of the alternate sources have been termed "soft" or "benign," and their relative costs, risks, and other points have been debated in the literature. The risk to human health from nonconventional sources can be as high as, or even higher than, that of conventional sources. One of the principal problems in comparing conventional and alternate energy systems is that alternate sources will not be independent of conventional systems, at least in the short term. Analyses must therefore proceed by comparing various mixes of source types, rather than direct comparisons. This limitation holds for environmental comparisons as well.

While the balance may eventually favor alternate sources, the very real environmental impacts of these systems should not be ignored. Some of the major alternate energy sources are listed below.

1. Oil shale
2. Geothermal systems
3. Solar energy
4. Hydrogen
5. Wind power
6. Tar sands
7. Ocean thermal energy

Extensive details regarding environmental impacts are available in the literature (Raufer & Yates, 1979).

The American people appear to be overwhelmingly in favor of alternate energy sources. They favor cooperation between industry and the government to develop alternate fuel sources. However, public support for the environment is also high. In any event, the overwhelmingly popular support for alternate sources should not be allowed to mask the public's support for environmental protection; the environmental impacts outlined earlier must still be taken into account.

GENERAL CONSERVATION PRACTICES IN INDUSTRY

There are numerous general energy conservation practices that can be instituted at plants. Ten of the simpler ones are detailed below.

1. Lubricate fans
2. Lubricate pumps
3. Lubricate compressors
4. Repair steam and compressed air leaks
5. Insulate bare steam lines
6. Inspect and repair steam traps
7. Increase condensate return
8. Minimize boiler blowdown

 9. Maintain and inspect temperature measuring devices

10. Maintain and inspect pressure measuring devices

Providing details on fans, pumps, compressors, and steam lines is beyond the scope of this text. Descriptive information (Theodore & Reynolds, 1987) and calculational procedures (Kauffman, 1992) are available in the literature.

Some energy conservation practices applicable to specific chemical operations are also provided below.

 1. Recover energy from hot gases

 2. Recover energy from hot liquids

 3. Reduce reflux ratios in distillation columns

 4. Reuse hot wash water

 5. Add effects to existing evaporators

 6. Use liquefied gases as refrigerants

 7. Recompress vapor for low-pressure steam

 8. Generate low-pressure steam from flash operations

 9. Use waste heat for absorption

10. Cover tanks of heated liquid to reduce heat loss

Providing details on distillation columns, evaporators, and refrigerators is beyond the scope of this text. Descriptive information (Theodore & Reynolds, 1987) and calculational procedures (Kauffman, 1992) are available in the literature.

For the purposes of implementing an energy conservation strategy, process changes and/or design can be divided into four phases, each presenting different opportunities for implementing energy conservation measures. These include:

 1. Product conception

 2. Laboratory research

 3. Process development (pilot plant)

 4. Mechanical (physical) design

Energy conservation training measures that can be taken in the chemical process and other industries include:

 1. Implementing a sound operation, maintenance, and inspection (OM&I) program

 2. Implementing a pollution prevention program (see Chapter 31)

 3. Instituting a formal training program for all employees (see Chapter 43)

It should be obvious to the reader that a multimedia approach that includes energy conservation considerations requires a total systems approach (see Chapter 6). Much of the environmental engineering work in future years will focus on this area, since it appears to be the most cost-effective way of solving many energy problems. This is discussed in more detail in the last section.

Energy efficiency is a cornerstone of EPA's pollution prevention strategy. If less electricity is used to deliver an energy service—such as lighting—the power plant that produces the electricity burns less fuel and thus generates less pollution.

Lighting accounts for 20 to 25% of all electricity sold in the United States. Lighting for industry, stores, offices, and warehouses represents 80 to 90% of total lighting electricity use, so the use of energy-efficient lighting has a direct effect on pollution prevention. Every kilowatt-hour of lighting electricity not used prevents emissions of approximately 1.5 pounds of carbon dioxide, 5.8 grams of sulfur dioxide, and 2.5 grams of nitrogen oxides. If energy-efficient lighting were used where profitable, the nation's demand for electricity would be cut by more than 10 percent. This would result in annual reductions of 200 million metric tons of carbon dioxide—the equivalent of taking 44 million cars off the road; 1.3 metric tons of sulfur dioxide; and 600,000 metric tons of nitrogen oxides. These reductions represent 12 percent of U.S. utility emissions. These goals may not be fully achievable, but EPA's Green Lights program seeks to capture as much of the efficiency "bonus" as possible.

Lighting is not typically a high priority for the vast majority of U.S. institutions. Often the responsibility of facility management, lighting is viewed as an overhead item. Because of this, most facilities are equipped with the lowest first-cost (rather than the lowest lifecycle-cost) lighting systems, and profitable opportunities to upgrade the systems are ignored or passed over in favor of higher-visibility projects. As a result, institutions pay needless overhead every year, reducing their own competitiveness and that of the country. And, wasteful electricity use becomes a particularly senseless source of pollution.

By signing the Green Lights Memorandum of Understanding (part of program), senior management makes it clear that energy-efficient lighting is now one of the organization's highest priorities. Authority is granted, budgets are approved, procedures are streamlined, and staff is assigned to make the upgrades happen. The commitment to maximize energy savings by upgrading an organization's facilities often requires a change in the way an organization does business. Management will have to take a fresh look at how the organization maintains and upgrades its facilities, ensures environmental responsibility, and plans for maximum workforce production. For some organizations, this change will require significant planning and coordination among several different sectors of the organization. In addition, partners and allies agree to provide annual documentation of the lighting upgrades they complete. To simplify this process, EPA asks them to submit a 1-page form for each facility—the Green Lights Implementation Report—to report their progress.

The Green Lights approach to lighting upgrades defines as "profitable" those projects that—in combination and on a facility aggregate basis—maximize energy savings while providing an annualized internal rate of return (IRR) that is at least equivalent to the prime interest rate plus six percentage points. Projects that maximize energy savings while providing internal rates of return higher than the prime interest rate plus six percentage points meet the Green Lights profitability criterion. The typical Green Lights upgrade yields a posttax IRR of 20 to 40%.

FUTURE TRENDS

Nuclear fusion, solar energy, wind energy, biomass, energy produced as a result of thermal gradients in the earth or the oceans, tidal energy, and advanced chemical energy systems show promise as potential power sources in the future with minimum environmental damage. Controlled thermonuclear fusion is receiving increasing research and development funds. It would make use of light-element fuels that are sufficiently abundant to supply power needs almost indefinitely. Solar energy is also receiving increasing attention as a virtually pollution-free and inexhaustible source of energy. The renewed interest in tidal power systems stems from their environmental advantages. They produce no harmful wastes, cause minor scenic and ecological disturbances, and are inexhaustible. Although not economically feasible at this time, tidal energy is another future source that could reduce the environmental consequences of power generation.

Energy conservation will reduce the environmental damage from the various energy systems. Conservation will also enhance the reliability of future energy supplies. By slowing the rate of growth of energy demand, the longevity of energy supplies may be extended, allowing more flexibility in developing systems for meeting long-term needs. For too long a time, energy has been considered a limitless commodity. Energy was continuously wasted because it was abundant and cheap. This situation is now reversed. No longer will industry refuse and other solid wastes that are potential sources of energy be discarded. Instead, they will be used to supplement fuel supplies. No longer will reusable items be discarded. Recycling, which inherently will extend the lifetime of many natural resources, in many instances will be found profitable and compatible with environmental goals.

There is also tremendous potential for conservation in the energy production and consumption stages. On the average, only 30 percent of the oil in a reservoir is being extracted from onshore wells; offshore extraction is somewhat more efficient. As the price of crude oil rises, more extensive use of secondary recovery techniques, such as water flooding and thermal stimulation, will become evident. In the deep mining of coal, less than 60 percent of the resource in place is recovered, and over 10 percent of the energy in coal can be lost in cleaning. The pillar method of mining coal limits primary coal recovery to 30 to 60%. Secondary coal recovery techniques, such as the "robbing the pillars" method, will become economical and increase the amount of recoverable coal from a mine.

For electric power systems, a major source of inefficiency is the power plant itself. Thermionic or magnetohydrodynamic topping of electric power plants and the use of combined cycles show promise in increasing power plant efficiency. This will significantly reduce the thermal discharge to the environment and conserve fuel resources, and the constructive use of the waste heat will benefit the environment. Waste heat from power plants is a rich source of energy for plant growth. Already there have been very successful applications of warm water irrigation to increase yields. There is a great deal to be learned about aquaculture, but it appears that clams, shrimp, and scallops are adaptable to this procedure.

Energy systems in industry must be evaluated in light of their impact on the total environment in all aspects of their respective production methods and uses. As more and more air and water pollution control devices are being employed, air and water emissions have been reduced considerably, but increasing amounts of solid waste have been generated. More land is needed for the disposal of this waste and this will reduce the net effects of reclamation of mined out areas. Although the damages from air and water pollution are much less severe with controls, the need to avoid unintentionally shifting environmental problems from one medium or location to another must be recognized (see Chapter 6).

SUMMARY

1. Environmental consumption is a major contributor to environmental pollution; thus, decisions regarding energy policy alternatives require comprehensive environmental analysis. Environmental impact data must be developed for all aspects of an energy system and/or conservation program and must not be limited to their separate components.

2. At present, there are two major industrial energy sources in use: fossil fuel and nuclear energy. The fossil fuel may be subdivided according to the various raw fuels such as coal, oil, natural gas, liquefied petroleum gas, wood, coke refining gas, blast furnace gas, and byproduct fuels.

3. The American people appear to be overwhelmingly in favor of alternate energy sources. They favor cooperation between industry and the government to develop alternate fuel sources. However, public support for the environment is also high.

4. For the purposes of implementing an energy conservation strategy, process changes and/or design can be divided into four phases, each presenting different opportunities for implementing energy conservation measures. These include product conception, laboratory research, process development, and mechanical design.

5. Nuclear fusion, solar energy, wind energy, biomass, energy produced as a result of thermal gradients in the earth or the oceans, tidal energy, and advanced chemical energy systems show promise as potential power sources in the future with minimum environmental damage.

REFERENCES

Kauffman, D. "Process and Plant Design," an ETS Theodore Tutorial. Roanoke, VA: ETS International Inc., 1992.

Raufer, R., and Yates, J. "Alternate Energy Sources: An Environmental Perspective," Proceedings of the Fifth National Conference on Energy and the Environment, D. Nichols, R. Servais, and E. Rolinski, (eds.) AIChE, 1979.

Theodore, L., and Reynolds, J. *Introduction to Hazardous Waste Incineration.* New York: Wiley-Interscience, 1987.

27

At Home

INTRODUCTION

Action by Congress and state legislatures, rulings by courts, pronouncements by important people, or wishing alone cannot conserve energy. Individual efforts by everyone can make things happen and win the battle against wasting energy. Each is an important combatant in this campaign. Here are suggestions that can be used to make a difference. Individuals working alone or cooperating with their neighbors, with schools and colleges, with industry, with government, and with some nonprofit organizations can make a difference.

Domestic applications involving energy conservation have been divided into six topic areas. These include:

1. Cooling
2. Heating
3. Hot water
4. Cooking
5. Lighting
6. New appliances

Specific suggestions are provided in the sections that follow ("Conserving Energy," n.d.).

This chapter is a condensed, revised, and updated version of an unpublished (but copyrighted) 1992 text prepared by M. K. Theodore and L. Theodore titled *A Citizen's Guide to Pollution Prevention,* and the chapter Energy Conservation from the 1993 Wiley-Interscience text titled *Handbook of Environmental Management and Technology,* by G. Holmes, R. Singh, and L. Theodore.

COOLING*

For most people, summertime comfort means room temperatures ranging from 72 to 78 degrees and relative humidity ranging from 25 to 55 percent. There are a variety of ways to achieve this comfort zone. Unfortunately, air-conditioning carries a very high economic and environmental cost. Even the most efficient air-conditioners use prodigious amounts of electricity.

1. Before purchasing an air conditioner, determine how much cooling capacity is needed. Worksheets are available from several sources, including the Association of Home Appliances, *Consumer Reports,* and appliance stores, that will enable one to estimate the correct size. Too large a model tends to cycle on and off so much that it might not properly dehumidify the room. Too small a unit would not keep the room cool enough.

2. Every air conditioner must carry a bright yellow Energy Guide label that displays the unit's EER, or energy efficiency rating, a measure of how much it costs to operate. In most cases, the higher the EER, the lower the unit's energy costs.

3. If the air conditioner is to be operated at night, the location of the unit itself is not crucial. However, if it is to be operated during the day, try to locate it on the north, east, or best-shaded side of the home. If the unit is exposed to direct sunlight, consider an awning over it. However, do not block vents or inhibit the exchange of air around the unit.

4. After installing a window or wall unit, caulk any openings around the unit.

5. Consult the owner's guide and follow maintenance recommendations for washing filters and vacuuming coils. Public utilities estimate regular changing of filters can save up to 20 percent in energy costs (Christman, 1994).

6. Central air-conditioning is found in three of every four new houses, as well as in many existing homes and can enhance the resale value of a house. Central air-conditioning is an expensive kind of cooling but one can significantly reduce annual operating costs simply by raising the thermostat setting two or three degrees—from 74 to 76 degrees Fahrenheit.

7. A ceiling fan can generate enough of a breeze to make one feel cooler. This wind-chill effect can make a room that is 82 degrees Fahrenheit feel like 75 degrees Fahrenheit. Even an air-conditioned room will seem cooler if a ceiling fan stirs the air. That allows the air conditioner's thermostat to be set higher, for a small but modest saving on utility bills. Models tested by *Consumer Reports* drew between 50 and 115 watts at high speed and as little as 5 watts on low. At the national average of 8.25 cents per kilowatt-hour, it would cost less than 8 cents to run any fan for eight hours a day at its highest speed. By contrast, the most efficient small-capacity room air-conditioner would consume 36 cents of electricity for every eight hours of operation.

8. A whole-house fan can quickly pull large amounts of fresh air through the entire house. At night, this type of fan can draw in cool air from outside, reducing the inside temperature enough to allow some occupants to run an air conditioner less often. Under the right conditions, a

*Information for this section was taken from "Conserving Energy" n.d.; "A Guide to an Energy Efficient Home," n.d.; and *Consumer Reports,* 1993.

whole-house fan can ventilate an entire house on the electricity an air conditioner would use to cool one room.

9. Try to keep warm air from accumulating in the attic and increasing the need to run fans or an air conditioner. Vents in the gable ends, the eaves, and along the roof ridge help let out the heat. Adequate insulation will slow heat buildup, though it may not reduce overall cooling costs. A radiant barrier (reflective foil on the attic floor) can help slow the flow of heat to the rooms below.

10. Shades or blinds can reduce the amount of sunlight entering the house, thus reducing the need for cooling.

11. Small things can add to the amount of heat in a house and create more demand for cooling. Incandescent lights release heat and changing to fluorescent lighting can help.

12. Awnings or leafy trees to shade east and west windows contribute to keeping the house cool.

13. A green belt of lawn or shrubs between driveways or sidewalks and the house reduce heat and glare from the pavement.

14. Minimize the use of lights and heat-emitting appliances during the day when cooling loads are the highest. Run the appliances at night whenever possible. Rates are usually lower at off-peak hours when demand drops.

15. During hot weather, cooking, cleaning, or any exercise should be done in the early morning or in the evening.

16. Using the microwave instead of the oven will reduce heat in the kitchen.

17. Barbecue outdoors to avoid raising the temperature in the kitchen by using the oven or stove.

18. Light-colored clothing of natural fibers, such as cottons and linens, will make the wearer feel more comfortable during hot weather.

HEATING*

1. Heating, in most areas, is the single biggest energy user in the house. A well-maintained heating system will hold down fuel costs and provide reliable comfort. The system should be checked periodically by a professional to assure efficiency.

2. During the winter, keep the thermostat at 70 degrees Fahrenheit during the day, lowering it when the family retires. For every degree over 70, one can expect to use 3 percent more heating energy. Installing a timer is energy efficient and convenient. Thermostats for different levels or areas are also energy conscious.

*Information in the next five sections was taken from "Conserving Energy," n.d.

3. Storm windows and doors are big energy and money savers. They can reduce heating costs by as much as 15 percent by preventing warm air from escaping to the outside. Double glazed and thermopane windows or even clear plastic across windows can minimize heat escape.

4. Proper insulation in walls, ceilings, and floors also significantly reduces the loss of heat to the outdoors. Insulation will pay for itself in fuel cost savings and home comfort.

5. The many small openings in a house can add up to big heat losses. Caulking and weather-stripping cracks in walls and floors, windows, and doors will save fuel and money.

6. Cover large openings and keep doors between rooms closed so that the heat does not escape.

7. Minimize the use of the fireplace. Although a fireplace provides a cozy atmosphere on a cold night, the costly heat in the house is also going up the chimney with the smoke. Keeping the fireplace damper closed tightly when not in use will also result in heating conservation.

8. When drying laundry, consider hanging wash to dry instead of using the dryer. During cold weather, hang wash near the furnace but do not create a fire hazard. The heat from the furnace will dry the laundry satisfactorily and with great energy conservation. In warmer weather, solar energy is naturally available.

9. When using the dryer, dry wash loads consecutively; the heat left over from the previous cycle will increase the efficiency of the dryer. It is important to clean the lint trap on the dryer prior to each use. Separate heavy and light fabrics to keep drying time to a minimum. Mixing different weight fabrics causes the dryer to run longer than necessary.

10. Let sunlight in by opening curtains, blinds, and shades over windows which face the sun; this will help keep the house warm and reduce heating needs. At night or when the sky is overcast, keeping drapes and curtains closed to help keep the warmth indoors.

11. Since dry air makes one feel colder than moist air at the same temperature, maintaining home humidity will produce personal comfort at a lower thermostat setting and save money. Shallow pans of water on radiator tops or near warm air vents, or a room humidifier, will help raise humidity levels.

12. Dress in layers to keep warmer.

HOT WATER

1. The hot water heater is the second largest energy consumer in the home. Using it efficiently can add up to big savings. One can save up to 10 percent on water heating costs by simply wrapping a fiberglass blanket around the water heater and securing it with duct tape, or by installing a ready-made insulation kit. Most new heaters are already insulated and do not need additional fiberglass blankets.

2. Proper maintenance assures the heater's efficiency. Drain a few gallons of water from the heater every six months to remove sediment that accumulates and reduces the heater's efficiency. Consult the owner's guide for other maintenance recommendations.

3. If the house will be vacant for two or more days, lower the temperature of the water heater.

4. For families with an automatic dishwasher, the hot water heater setting can safely be lowered to 130 to 140 degrees Fahrenheit. Without a dishwasher, the setting can be lowered to 110 to 120 degrees Fahrenheit.

5. A dishwasher conserves water and energy. More hot water is wasted when dishes are hand washed. If dishes must be rinsed or scrubbed beforehand, use a pot filled with water for this purpose.

6. Run the dishwasher when it has a full load. Since 80 percent of the energy used by automatic dishwashers goes toward heating water, one can save energy by running the dishwasher only when it is full.

7. If the dishwasher does not have the energy-saver option, open the dishwasher door after the rinse cycle to allow the dishes to air dry.

8. Run the dishwasher during off peak hours when it is more cost efficient and energy conscious. Follow this rule with washers and dryers as well.

9. Use hot water sparingly when washing. Since 90 percent of the energy the washer consumes goes toward heating water, one can save by using hot water only for heavily soiled laundry. Most laundry can be washed in warm or cold water with very good results.

10. Install low-flow showerheads in the shower to limit the flow of water to about two gallons per minute. Once installed, these devices reduce hot water use by one-third without affecting water pressure.

11. When showering, turn off the water while soaping up or shampooing.

COOKING

1. A microwave oven is an energy efficient alternative to a conventional oven. It cooks food more quickly and it uses 70 to 80 percent less electricity than a regular oven.

2. When cooking on top of the stove, use pots and pans that are properly sized to fit the burners. Using a small pot on a large burner or a large pot on a small burner wastes energy.

3. When using a conventional oven, try to avoid "peeking" by opening the oven door. Each "peek" can lower the oven temperature by 25 degrees.

4. Although often recommended, it is not necessary to preheat the oven for foods with a cooking time of over one hour. Also, using glass pans allows one to set the oven 25 degrees lower since glass retains heat.

5. Certain dishes can be prepared in quantity at an energy savings. An example would be sauce. Making a large batch at one time and then freezing several packets for future use is more energy efficient. Preparing one dinner serving and heating it on top of the stove takes almost the same amount of energy as a large batch requires.

6. If possible, before baking frozen dishes, allow them to defrost in the refrigerator to cut down on the length of time it would take to heat them to the proper temperature in the oven.

7. When preparing a meal in the oven, try to use foods that are cooked at about the same temperature. This way, the oven can heat several dishes at the same time and will not waste valuable energy and dollars.

8. Use a toaster-oven type appliance for small baking needs, thus avoiding the bigger energy demands of the larger oven.

LIGHTING

1. Lighting accounts for about 15 percent of a house's electric use. New screw-in fluorescent bulbs can replace the incandescent ones most individuals use. Fluorescent bulbs are more expensive, but they last ten times longer and use 75 percent less electricity.

2. One can save energy by turning off incandescent lights when leaving the room. In using fluorescent lighting, however, turn them off only if one will be gone longer than 15 minutes. Fluorescent lights use as much energy in starting as they use during 15 minutes of operation, so it is not energy efficient to turn them off for brief periods.

3. If one prefers incandescent bulbs, try to use "energy-saver" bulbs. These bulbs use halogen gases that allow the filament to burn brighter while consuming less electricity.

4. Significant energy can be saved by matching, as closely as possible, light bulb wattage to lighting needs. As an example, a high wattage reading light in a hallway or alcove, is not energy efficient.

5. Lighting controls or "timers" can help save energy dollars. Timers can be set to turn lights on or off at predetermined times while photocell controls are sensitive to light and turn lamps on and off at sundown and sunrise. Dimmers can vary the level of illumination according to how much light is needed in a given situation.

6. Consider using task lighting (lighting directed at a specific area) instead of overhead or general lighting, which may light unused areas of the room. By limiting lighting only to areas where it is needed, savings in the cost of bulbs and energy can be made.

7. By keeping lights and fixtures clean, lighting efficiency can be improved. As much as 20 percent of the light generated can be lost to hazing dusts. Also, take advantage of reflected light by keeping portable fixtures as close as possible to light-colored walls or other surfaces. These easy steps may reduce the number and wattage of bulbs.

8. Arrange furniture to take advantage of natural light.

NEW APPLIANCES

1. When shopping for a new appliance, check for the yellow Energy Guide label that indicates the unit's energy efficiency. This is particularly important for appliances that use a lot of electricity, such as air conditioners and refrigerators.

2. For air conditioners, the Energy Guide provides an energy efficiency rating or EER. The higher the EER, the more efficient the air conditioner; thus, the more money and energy saved. Many utilities recommend an EER of 10 or higher.

3. For refrigerators and other appliances, the Energy Guide label provides the estimated yearly energy cost for operating the appliance based on an average national utility rate.

4. With any appliance, it is helpful to compare units in the same size range when trying to determine which model has the lowest annual operating cost.

5. Although very efficient appliances may cost more to buy, they pay for themselves through lower energy bills. For example, by purchasing a very efficient refrigerator, one could save up to $1,200 over its life ("A Guide to an Energy Efficient Home," n.d.)

SUMMARY

1. Action by Congress and state legislatures, rulings by courts, pronouncements by important people, or wishing alone cannot conserve energy. Individual efforts by everyone can make things happen and win the battle against wasting energy.

2. Some key cooling suggestions include:
a. Before purchasing an air conditioner, determine how much cooling capacity is needed.
b. Consult the owner's guide and follow maintenance recommendations for washing filters and vacuuming coils.
c. A whole-house fan can quickly pull large amounts of fresh air through the entire house. At night, this type of fan can draw in cool air from outside reducing the inside temperature enough to allow some occupants to run an air conditioner less often.

3. Some key suggestions regarding heating include:
a. Heating is the single biggest energy user in the house. A well-maintained heating system will hold down fuel costs and provide reliable comfort. The system should be checked periodically by a professional to assure efficiency.
b. When using the dryer, dry wash loads consecutively; the heat left over from the previous cycle will increase the efficiency of the dryer. It is important to clean the lint trap on the dryer prior to each use.
c. Let sunlight in by opening curtains, blinds, and shades over windows which face the sun to help keep the house warm and reduce heating needs. At night or when the sky is overcast, keep drapes and curtains closed to help keep the warmth indoors.

4. Some key suggestions regarding hot water include:

a. Proper maintenance assures the hot water heater's efficiency. Drain a few gallons of water from the heater every six months to remove sediment that accumulates and reduces the heater's efficiency. Consult the owner's guide for other maintenance recommendations.

b. For families with an automatic dishwasher, the hot water heater setting can safely be lowered to 130 to 140 degrees Fahrenheit. Without a dishwasher, the setting can be lowered to 110 to 120 degrees.

c. Install low-flow showerheads in the shower to limit the flow of water to about two gallons per minute. Once installed, these devices reduce hot water use by one-third without affecting water pressure.

5. Some key suggestions regarding cooking include:

a. A microwave oven is an energy efficient alternative to a conventional oven. It cooks food more quickly and it uses 70 to 80 percent less electricity than a regular oven.

b. When cooking on top of the range, use pots and pans that are properly sized to fit the burners. A small pot on a large burner wastes energy.

c. When using a conventional oven, avoid "peeking" by opening the oven door. Each "peek" can lower the oven temperature by 25 degrees.

6. Some key suggestions regarding lighting include:

a. If one prefers incandescent bulbs, try to use "energy saver" bulbs. These bulbs use halogen gases that allow the filament to burn brighter while consuming less electricity.

b. Lighting controls or "timers" can help save energy dollars.

c. Consider using task lighting (lighting directed at a specific area) instead of overhead or general lighting, which may light unused areas of the room.

7. Some key suggestions regarding new appliances include:

a. When shopping for a new appliance, check for the yellow Energy Guide label that indicates the unit's energy efficiency.

b. For refrigerators and other appliances, the Energy Guide label provides the estimated yearly energy cost for operating the appliance based on an average national utility rate.

c. With any appliance, it is helpful to compare units in the same size range when trying to determine which model has the lowest annual operating cost.

REFERENCES

Christman, L. "Air Conditioners Need Spring Service," *Newsday,* May 26, 1994.

Adapted from, "Conserving Energy," Long Island Lighting Company, Long Island, not dated.

Consumer Reports, published by Consumers Union, June, 1993.

Adapted from, "A Guide to an Energy Efficient Home," Long Island Lighting Company, New York, not dated.

28

At Work

INTRODUCTION

As described earlier in the text, there is a significant amount of overlap of environmental measures that can be implemented at both the domestic level and in a work/office setting. This is particularly true regarding energy conservation measures. Notwithstanding this, this chapter has been prepared on a stand-alone basis and emphasizes measures in an office environment.

Before providing specific energy conservation recommendations and suggestions at the work/office level, a short description of the United States Environmental Protection Agency's (EPA) Energy Star Computers Program is presented. It is an example of how some simple, yet creative, thinking can result in significant energy savings in society, particularly regarding office computer usage (Kressner, 1994, private communication).

The EPA Energy Star Computers Program is a partnership effort with the computer industry to promote the introduction of energy-efficient personal computers, monitors, or printers and reduce air pollution caused by power generation. These new products will save enough electricity to power Maine, New Hampshire, and Vermont each year, saving ratepayers nearly two billion dollars in annual electricity bills.

Office equipment is the fastest growing electricity load in the commercial sector. Computer systems alone are believed to account for five percent of commercial electricity consumption, and potentially ten percent by the year 2000. Research shows that the vast majority of time the nation's 30 to 35 million personal computers are turned on, they are not actively in use—and 30 to 40 percent are left running at night and on weekends.

This chapter is a condensed, revised, and updated version of part of an unpublished (but copyrighted) 1992 text prepared by M. K. Theodore and L. Theodore titled *A Citizen's Guide to Pollution Prevention*.

President Clinton recently announced that the federal government—the largest buyer of computers in the world—is committed to purchasing only Energy Star compliant products. Clinton's executive order directs United States agencies to acquire only desktop computers, monitors, and printers that meet EPA Energy Star requirements, provided that they are commercially available and meet the agencies' performance needs. The order took effect in October 1993.

Through corporate purchasing efforts modeled after EPA's Green Lights program, EPA will encourage consumers to buy computers bearing the Energy Star trademark logo wherever possible. Under agreements signed with EPA through Green Lights, over 1,200 organizations and government agencies have been committed to energy-efficient lighting upgrades.

By the year 2000, Energy Star Computers and other campaigns to promote energy efficient computer equipment will lead to an estimated savings of 26 billion kilowatt-hours of electricity annually, reduced from an estimated consumption of 70 billion kilowatt-hours per year. These savings will reduce emissions of the primary greenhouse gas (see Chapter 42), carbon dioxide, by 20 million tons—the equivalent of 5 million automobiles. Also reduced will be emissions of 140 thousand tons of sulfur dioxide and 75 thousand tons of nitrogen oxide, the two pollutants most responsible for acid rain (see Chapter 21).

Purchasing decisions for office equipment usually depend on such characteristics as price, speed, reliability and quality. Many corporate equipment purchasers fail to account for the costs of the electricity to operate office equipment, and the energy and equipment costs of removing the heat this equipment creates in an office or building (Ledbetter & Smith, 1993). This new innovative program should provide some major energy conservation results if properly applied across-the-board to all office equipment and procedures.

Office/work applications involving energy conservation have been divided into four topic areas for this chapter. These include:

1. Cooling and heating
2. Lighting
3. Automobile use
4. Electricity use

Specific suggestions are provided in the sections that follow.

COOLING AND HEATING

1. The location of an office site should be considered in terms of exposure to the sun and other elements as well as proximity to public transportation since these factors have an impact on energy conservation.

2. The material used in the construction of the office also has an impact on energy conservation. Selection of concrete, steel, wood, plastic, insulation, number of openings, doors, windows, etc., all affect energy conservation and must be investigated.

3. The heating and cooling system must be maintained properly. A well-maintained system is more efficient, provides savings in energy use, and can safeguard the health and comfort of the worker. This results in higher productivity and less time lost to sickness.

4. When the heating system is used, keep the thermostat at a maximum of 70 degrees Fahrenheit during the day. Dress in layers rather than raising the thermostat. Overheating the office not only raises energy costs but can lower the energy level of the worker, causing lethargy and dehydration.

5. During warm weather, most people are comfortable at room temperatures ranging from 72 to 78 degrees Fahrenheit and at a relative humidity ranging from 25 to 55 percent. Central air-conditioning is an expensive kind of cooling, but annual operating costs can be significantly reduced by raising the thermostat setting two or three degrees, for example, from 74 to 76 degrees Fahrenheit.

6. If room units are used, it is important to know how much cooling capacity is needed. It depends mainly on the size of the space to be cooled, the number of windows, and the local climate. An undersized unit will not cool a big room, while an oversized one will cycle off before it wrings enough humidity out of the air. For a precise cooling-capacity estimate, organizations such as Consumers Union will provide a detailed worksheet, adapted from one published by the Association of Home Appliance Manufacturers (*Consumer Reports,* 1994).

7. Every air conditioner must carry a bright yellow Energy Guide label that displays the unit's EER, or energy efficiency rating. It represents a measure of how much it costs to operate. In most cases, the higher the EER, the lower the unit's energy costs.

8. Install water flow reduction devices in the employee washroom and showers. Faucet aerators are small flow control devices that easily fit in bathroom faucets. Once installed, they reduce hot water use by one-third without affecting water pressure.

9. Consider banning smoking since it increases the temperature of the room during hot weather and pollutes the air (often requiring air conditioning as opposed to air cooling).

10. Plumbing problems should be reported and repairs made promptly.

11. Cleaning the filter is an important maintenance task since filters clogged with dust from recirculating room air reduce efficiency and increase energy consumption. The filter should be inspected every week or so during the cooling season and washed or vacuumed according to manufacturer's instructions.

12. A ceiling fan can work up enough of a breeze to make one feel cooler. This wind-chill effect can make a room that is 82 degrees feel like 75 degrees Fahrenheit. Even an air-conditioned room will seem cooler if a ceiling fan stirs the air. That allows the air-conditioner's thermostat to be set higher and result in a small but modest saving on utility bills.

13. A small individual fan at a workstation has a cooling effect.

14. Shades or blinds can reduce the amount of sunlight entering the office, thus reducing the need for cooling. In cooler weather, sunlight can be used for its warming effects.

15. Awnings or leafy trees that shade east and west windows can contribute to keeping the office cool.

16. Lawn or shrubs between walkways and parking lots reduce heat and glare from the pavement.

17. Institute summer hours where possible. Start shifts at an earlier hour to take advantage of cooler morning hours. Where feasible, minimize the use of lights and heat-emitting appliances during the day when cooling loads are the highest. Operate heavy machinery at night if possible. In addition, rates are usually lower at off-peak hours when demand drops.

18. Light-colored clothing of natural fibers, such as cottons and linens, will make the wearer feel more comfortable during hot weather.

19. Encourage employee participation in energy conservation by recognizing or rewarding employee suggestions that result in energy savings.

LIGHTING

1. Furniture should be arranged to take advantage of natural light. When planning the office lighting, keep in mind the function of the lighting for a particular situation.

2. Use durable fluorescent bulbs. Fluorescent bulbs are more expensive, but last ten times longer and use approximately 75 percent less electricity than incandescent ones.

3. Lighting controls or "timers" can help save energy dollars. Timers can be set to turn lights on or off at predetermined times while photocell controls are sensitive to light and turn lamps on and off at sundown and sunrise.

4. Consider using task lighting (lighting directed at a specific area) instead of overhead or general lighting that may light unused areas of the office. By limiting lighting only to areas where it is needed, savings in the cost of both the bulbs and energy can be made.

5. Lighting efficiency can be maintained by keeping office lights and fixtures clean. As much as 20 percent of the light generated can be lost to hazing dusts.

6. Light-colored walls reflect light, which can reduce the number and wattage of bulbs.

7. Save energy by turning off lights when leaving the room. With fluorescent lighting, turn off lights only if one will be gone longer than 15 minutes. A fluorescent bulb's lifespan is affected by the number of times it is turned on and off.

8. Employees should realize that energy waste is factored into their paycheck so that conserving energy is in their best interest. Reward or recognize employee participation in energy conservation.

AUTOMOBILE USE

1. Walk, bike, or use public transportation as an alternative to automobile use.

2. If an automobile must be used, arrange an office shuttle service.

3. Encourage car pooling.

4. If feasible, arrange shifts to avoid traveling to and from work during rush hours.

5. The company fleet should be well maintained. A well-tuned car is an energy efficient machine.

6. The personal car should be well maintained.

7. Travel should be well planned so as to be as energy conscious as possible.

8. Recognize or reward employee effort to conserve energy use.

ELECTRICITY USE

1. Use automatic timers where it is energy efficient. Timers can be set to turn equipment on or off at predetermined times while photocell controls are sensitive to light and turn lamps on and off at sundown and sunrise. Cooling and heating systems can utilize timers as well as certain office machines.

2. Think before automatically turning on an appliance that requires electricity.

3. When purchasing new equipment for the office, check for the yellow Energy Guide label that indicates the unit's energy efficiency.

4. Post energy conservation instructions for equipment that use energy.

5. Educate employees on ways to conserve energy.

6. Organize the work day, taking into consideration which and when machines should be turned on or off. Certain equipment use a significant amount of energy powering up. If feasible, schedule a time slot for use of these machines.

7. Have the power utility make a study of energy use and make changes appropriately.

8. Get employees involved in energy conservation. Recognize or reward employee suggestions that are implemented and result in savings.

SUMMARY

1. The EPA Energy Star Computers Program is a partnership effort with the computer industry to promote the introduction of energy-efficient personal computers, monitors, or printers.

2. Some key suggestions for energy conservation at work with respect to cooling and heating are:
    a. The heating and cooling system must be maintained properly.
    b. When the heating system is used, keep the thermostat at a maximum of 70 degrees Fahrenheit during the day.
    c. Shades or blinds can reduce the amount of sunlight entering the office, thus reducing the need for cooling. In cooler weather, sunlight can be used for its warming effects.

3. Some key suggestions for energy conservation at work with respect to lighting are:

a. Furniture should be arranged to take advantage of natural light. When planning the office lighting, keep in mind the function of the lighting for a particular situation.

b. Use durable fluorescent bulbs. Fluorescent bulbs are more expensive, but last ten times longer and use 75 percent less electricity than incandescent ones.

c. Consider using task lighting (lighting directed at a specific area) instead of overhead or general lighting that may light unused areas of the office.

4. Some key suggestions for energy conservation at work with respect to automobile use are:

a. Walk, bike, or use public transportation as an alternative to automobile use.

b. Encourage car pooling.

c. Travel should be well planned so as to be as energy conscious as possible.

5. Some key suggestions for energy conservation at work with respect to the use of electricity are:

a. Use automatic timers where it is energy efficient. Timers can be set to turn equipment on or off at predetermined times while photocell controls are sensitive to light and turn lamps on and off at sunrise and sundown, respectively.

b. Think before automatically turning on an appliance that requires electricity.

c. When purchasing new equipment for the office, check for the yellow Energy Guide label that indicates the unit's energy efficiency.

REFERENCES

Consumer Reports, published by Consumers Union, June 1994.

Kressner, A. Private communication, Con Edison of New York, 1994.

Ledbetter, M., and Smith, L. "Guide to Energy-Efficient Office Equipment," EPRI Publication No. TR-102545, EPRI, Pleasant Hill, CA., 1993.

29

Other Energy Conservation Areas

INTRODUCTION

The outline and form of presentation for this chapter is similar to that provided in Chapters 25 and 34. It provides suggestions regarding energy conservation measures that can be employed in the following areas:

1. Building a house
2. In the garden
3. Traveling and vacationing
4. Shopping
5. Dining and entertaining

A separate section is provided for each of the above topic areas. In addition to the reference cited at the start of this chapter, some material has also been drawn from other sources in the literature (M. K.Theodore & L. Theodore, personal notes; Theodore & McGuinn, 1992; Holmes, Singh, & Theodore, 1993). Although some overlap exists between the sections to follow and the two previous chapters, each section below has been written on a stand-alone basis.

BUILDING A HOUSE

1. The construction, operation, and demolition of buildings in the United States account for approximately one-third of the energy consumed in this country. Care should be exercised in conserving energy in this area.

This chapter is a condensed, revised, and updated version of an unpublished (but copyrighted) 1992 text prepared by M. K. Theodore and L. Theodore titled *A Citizen's Guide to Pollution Prevention.*

2. The energy crisis of the mid-1970s forced government officials, builders, and home-owners to find ways to cut the consumption of expensive energy. Building codes were changed to make new houses more energy efficient.

3. The location of the house can enhance the use of natural sources of energy, thus conserving other energy use. The direction of the sun on the house, prevailing winds, shade and shelter from trees, and terrain must be considered by the architect.

4. The design and type of materials used in the construction of the house have an impact on energy conservation. Selection of concrete, steel, wood, plastic, insulation, number of openings, doors, and windows must be made with future energy conservation in mind.

5. Consider the use of recycled material for construction.

6. Consider a steel-framed house. With the shortage and high price of quality lumber, it is predicted that twenty-five percent of all houses built between now and the year 2000 will have steel frames. Steel-framed houses use recycled steel. Steel wall framing can be placed on four- or eight-foot centers instead of the sixteen-inch centers common with standard wood framing. This reduces the thermal bridges, or gaps, in the wall insulation. The steel framing also provides room for nine inches of wall insulation, providing an insulation level of better than R-30. Another energy advantage of steel framing is that steel settles very little over time. Therefore, the house should remain airtight over its life, and windows and doors should continue to fit and operate smoothly (Dulley, 1994).

7. All new residential-sized furnaces are required by federal law to carry an Annual Fuel Utilization Efficiency rating, or AFUE, and to achieve an AFUE of at least 78 percent. New furnaces with an AFUE up to 85 percent are often called mid-efficiency. Furnaces that condense some of the water vapor in the flue gas and have an AFUE of 90 percent or more are termed high-efficiency. However, high-efficiency units are more complicated and may require more frequent repair than other furnaces.

8. Zone thermostats can help save energy by allowing the homeowner to adjust heating or cooling demands for different sections of the house. An automatic setback thermostat offers comfort and convenience since it allows the user to program different comfort and setback periods for each day of the week.

9. Central air conditioning is found in three of every four new houses. It adds little to the overall cost of new construction and can enhance the resale value of a house. But central air conditioning is an expensive kind of cooling, even though government standards have made the equipment much more energy-efficient than in years past. The homeowner can compare competing brands for efficiency by checking the Seasonal Energy Efficiency Rating (SEER).

10. A good contractor will use a recognized set of duct-installation guidelines. The material used for the ducts, as well as how firmly the sections are connected, is an energy concern. Cold air leaking from seams or migrating through the duct walls can drastically increase overall operating costs.

11. Under the right conditions, a whole-house fan can ventilate an entire house on the electricity an air conditioner would use to cool one room.

12. A ceiling fan can work up enough of a breeze to make one feel cooler. This wind-chill effect can make a room that is 82 degrees feel like 75 degrees Fahrenheit. Even an air-conditioned room will seem cooler if a ceiling fan stirs the air. That allows the air conditioner's thermostat to be set higher and result in a small but modest saving on utility bills.

13. Vents in the gable ends, the eaves, and along the roof ridge help let out the heat. Adequate insulation will slow heat buildup, though it may not reduce overall cooling costs. A radiant barrier (reflective foil on the attic floor) can help slow the flow of heat to the rooms below.

14. When choosing windows, the frame has a significant effect on a window's thermal performance, price, and upkeep. Wood frames, plain or clad in vinyl or aluminum, tend to be more expensive than all vinyl. Aluminum is a good heat conductor. In a temperate climate, an aluminum frame may be a practical choice but it will not offer the best thermal protection in cold New England winters.

15. The glass you choose also affects a window's price and performance. Single glazed are best reserved for garages and other spaces that do not require heating or cooling. Most new houses have double-pane. In a regular double-glazed window, air fills the gap between the panes. A step up in thermal performance and price are windows filled with an inert gas, usually argon. Low emissivity (low-e) glass has a coating that helps reduce heat loss in the winter and heat gain in the summer by blocking nearly all the long-wave infrared rays. Some low-e coatings, designed for hot climates or southern exposures, reduce the buildup of heat from the sun. Other low-e coatings, meant for cold climates, allow more of the sun's warmth into the house.

16. Weather stripping, which blocks drafts around doors and windows, will not save much energy. Recent studies have shown that such drafts actually contribute little to overall heat loss. Still, weather stripping will do a lot to make the house feel more comfortable. That may save some energy indirectly since the homeowner may not feel the necessity to turn up the thermostat as much if the room is not drafty.

17. When choosing an appliance, consult the bright yellow Energy Guide label that displays the unit's energy efficiency rating (EER). It represents a measure of how much it costs to operate. In most cases, the higher the EER, the lower the unit's energy costs.

18. The United States Department of Energy has required all refrigerators made after January 1, 1993 to use about 30 percent less electricity than previously. Further tightening of the standard is expected for 1998.

19. Choose a refrigerator that has a low amount of chloroflurocarbons (CFCs). Most refrigerators of this type will be phased out by 1996.

20. Take care not to place the refrigerator right next to the range, or where sunlight will fall on it; otherwise, it will have to work harder to stay cool (*Consumer Reports,* 1994).

21. Bathrooms should be equipped with energy conservation in mind. Install water flow reduction devices in the showers. Faucet aerators should be used. These devices reduce hot water use by one-third without affecting water pressure.

22. Lighting controls or "timers" can help save energy dollars. Timers can be set to run lights on or off at predetermined times while photocell controls are sensitive to light and turn lamps on and off at sundown and sunrise.

23. Consider using task lighting (lighting directed at a specific area) instead of overhead or general lighting that may light unused areas. By limiting lighting only to areas where it is needed, savings in the cost of both the bulbs and energy can be made.

24. Light-colored walls reflect light, which can reduce the number and wattage of bulbs.

25. Ask the local utility to do a walk through and provide suggestions on ways to conserve energy in the house.

IN THE GARDEN

1. Landscaping is an important component in energy conservation. The direction of the sun, prevailing winds, shade and shelter from trees, and terrain play a part.

2. Select shrubs and trees not only for their beauty but for the year-round effect they have on energy needs of the house.

3. Deciduous trees (those that shed their leaves in winter) provide a great deal of shade during the summer months. This cooling effect decreases the need for air conditioning. In the winter months when these trees lose their leaves, sunlight is allowed to pass through, thus providing the house with solar warmth.

4. A natural shelter of shrubs at an entrance doorway can divert and minimize the effect of chilling winter winds and reduce the amount of heat loss.

5. Plant shrubs that curtail soil erosion, particularly at the foundation of the house. The soil protects the foundation and allows the structure to be more effectively maintained using less energy.

6. Allow shrubs to grow in their natural shapes rather than sculpturing to decrease the amount of energy used for maintenance.

7. Develop a habitat that encourages natural control of insects rather than resort to energy users such an electronic zappers. Make an effort to attract and protect birds. Insects form a large part of avian sustenance. Interestingly, birds are most numerous and active just at those times when harmful insects are at their height of activity (Seymour, 1970).

8. Birds consume large quantities of weed seeds. Furthermore, small rodents that are troublesome in the garden form a large part of the diet of birds of prey. This control by nature should be encouraged as opposed to a control measure that requires energy.

9. Cultivate a vegetable garden and fruit trees. Superior varieties may be grown in a home garden. The products can be freshly gathered at their peak of perfection. The homeowner will produce food energy for his family and expend only his energy in the physical labor of planting and caring for the produce. The energy expended at the plant store is much less than that spent while shopping at the supermarket for the same yield, and is often far more satisfying.

10. Use a manual lawnmower and hand tools when possible.

11. When shopping for garden machinery or tools, check the bright yellow Energy Guide label that displays the unit's EER, or energy efficiency rating. It represents a measure of how much it costs to operate. In most cases, the higher the EER, the lower the unit's energy costs.

12. Consider whether the use of electric rather than gas powered machines and tools are more energy efficient.

13. Machinery and tools should be maintained according to their guidebooks to ensure efficient and energy conscious operation and at the same time prolong the life of the appliance.

14. Energy conservation measures can be shown to include conserving water. This and other suggestions are related to this measure. Giving the lawn or garden too much water wastes water and money and does not help the plants. Position sprinkler and hoses carefully. Sidewalks need not be dampened.

15. Water early or late in the day, avoiding full sun, to minimize evaporation.

16. Apply water slowly to prevent runoff. In a garden, consider using a soaker hose. For a large plant or shrub, create a "catch basin" around its trunk.

17. Put in ground cover and plants that can survive on moderate amounts of water. Contact a local nursery or the Cooperative Extension Service to learn more about water-saving vegetation suited to a particular area (*Consumer Reports,* 1993).

18. Set out a rain barrel to create a reservoir when needed or to fill a watering can or wash a car.

19. Use mulch to help retain moisture, prevent erosion and inhibit weeds.

TRAVELING AND VACATIONING

1. Walk, bike or use public transportation when possible.

2. A trip well planned is usually a trip enjoyed. Preparation will pay dividends in enjoyment and efficient use of available hours and energy.

3. If traveling by personal car, it should be in maximum operating condition. Before embarking on a long trip, the car should be given a thorough inspection by a competent mechanic. The destination, the weather, and varied type of terrain should be taken into consideration.

4. Allowing two and one-half hours for each 100 miles provides reasonable allowance for driving time, meals, gasoline, rest stops, and has been shown to conserve energy (as well as lives).

5. Pack the car sensibly but travel as lightly as possible. An overloaded car consumes more energy and is dangerous for many reasons. It is more difficult to drive and adds stress to the car and the driver. Occupants are uncomfortable, which contributes to stress. In warm weather, the overcrowding also generates more heat requiring more air conditioning. Further, if a repair has to be made, the car may have to be unloaded.

6. When the air conditioner is first turned on, leave the car windows open so that the hot air is blown out. The air conditioner will have less overheated air to cool.

7. Conserve fuel and brakes by using smart driving techniques. Avoid jackrabbit starts and do not accelerate up to a stop.

8. Underinflated car tires can worsen fuel economy, degrade handling and accelerate tire wear. Overinflated tires harshen the ride, wear unevenly, and sometimes contribute to blowouts. Consumers Union recommends that tires be checked at least once a month.

9. Travel during off-peak time. It is more energy conscious for many reasons. Since there is less volume, there is less time and energy wasted waiting in line, on the road, in train stations, airports, or restaurants. Airlines and hotels often offer incentives to travel during off-peak hours in an effort to increase capacity and offset losses at these times.

10. Carry a beverage container for coffee or soda that can be refilled rather than using a disposable container each time.

11. Coordinate trips to conserve energy. Avoid situations such as two cars traveling to the same destination when a carpool could have been utilized.

12. When staying at a hotel, do not allow housekeeping to replace and rewash towels that were not used or soap that may have been used only once.

13. When staying at a hotel, turn off lights when leaving the room.

14. When staying at a hotel, keep the temperature at 68 degrees Fahrenheit, lowering the thermostat when you leave or retire for the night. Practice the same energy conservation with the air conditioning during the summer months, keeping the thermostat around 74 degrees Fahrenheit.

SHOPPING

1. Make a list. This will organize the outing in the most efficient way.
2. Only buy items which are needed.
3. Shop during off-peak hours whenever possible.
4. Walk, bike, or take public transportation whenever possible.
5. Coordinate shopping with friends and carpool to save energy.
6. Shop by catalog.
7. Take advantage of the telephone to comparison shop.
8. When shopping for a new appliance, look for the yellow Energy Guide label that indicates the unit's energy efficiency.
9. Buy products that are packaged with energy conservation in mind.
10. Since energy is required to produce nearly any product, buy products that make use of recycled material.
11. Carry a reusable tote rather than taking a new bag.

DINING AND ENTERTAINING

1. Arrange furniture to take advantage of natural light.

2. Use candles for low lighting if safety permits.

3. Entertain outdoors when weather permits.

4. Use fans to assist and supplement air conditioning.

5. Consult recipes so that ingredients can be organized. For instance, if some ingredients will be used in several dishes, they can be chopped or minced ahead of time, divided up, even frozen, and ready when needed.

6. Use the oven efficiently. Organize baking so that the oven is not heated and reheated unnecessarily.

7. Do not "peek" in the oven. Every time the door is opened, the temperature drops approximately 25 degrees Fahrenheit and the oven has to use more energy to raise the temperature to its original setting.

8. It is not necessary to preheat the oven when cooking dishes that require more than an hour.

9. Certain dishes can be prepared in quantity at an energy savings.

10. If quality is not affected, allow frozen dishes to defrost in the refrigerator before baking to reduce the length of time it would take to heat the dish from a frozen state to the proper temperature in the oven.

11. Use oven to table serving dishes rather than separate dishes when possible.

12. Conserve energy with a microwave. It defrosts, cooks, and reheats food more rapidly and uses seventy to eighty percent less electricity than a regular oven.

13. Conserve water with a dishwasher. More water is wasted when dishes are hand-washed. If dishes must be rinsed or scrubbed beforehand, use a dishpan filled with water for this purpose.

14. Run a full dishwasher and save energy. Eighty percent of the energy used in automatic dishwashers goes toward heating water.

15. If the dishwasher does not have the energy-saver option, open the dishwasher door after the rinse cycle to allow the dishes to air dry.

16. Encourage guests to carpool.

SUMMARY

1. In addition to the home and office, energy conservation measures can be employed in the following areas: building a house, in the garden, traveling and vacationing, shopping, and dining and entertaining.

2. Some key energy conservation measures that can be employed while building a house include:

    a. The location of the house can enhance the use of natural sources of energy, thus conserving other energy use. The direction of the sun on the house, prevailing winds, shade and shelter from trees, and terrain must be considered by the architect.

    b. Consider the use of recycled material for construction.

    c. Under the right conditions, a whole-house fan can ventilate an entire house on the electricity an air conditioner would use to cool one room.

3. Some key energy conservation measures that can be employed in the garden include:

    a. Cultivate a vegetable garden and fruit trees. Superior varieties may be grown in a home garden. The products can be freshly gathered at their peak of perfection. The homeowner will produce food energy for his family and expend only his energy in the physical labor of planting and caring for the produce.

    b. Use a manual lawnmower and hand tools when possible.

    c. Machinery and tools should be maintained according to their guidebooks to ensure efficient and energy conscious operation and at the same time prolong the life of the appliance.

4. Some key energy conservation measures that can be employed while traveling and vacationing include:

    a. Walk, bike, or use public transportation when possible.

    b. If traveling by personal car, it should be in maximum operating condition. Before embarking on a long trip, the car should be given a thorough inspection by a competent mechanic. The destination, the weather and varied type of terrain should be taken into consideration.

    c. When staying at a hotel, do not allow housekeeping to replace and rewash towels that were not used, or soap that may have been used only once.

5. Some key energy conservation measures that can be employed while shopping include:

    a. Shop during off-peak hours whenever possible.

    b. When shopping for a new appliance, look for the yellow Energy Guide label which indicates the unit's energy efficiency.

    c. Buy products which are packaged with energy conservation in mind.

6. Some key energy conservation measures that can be employed while dining and entertaining include:

    a. Entertain outdoors when weather permits.

    b. Do not "peek" in the oven. Every time the door is opened, the termperature drops approximately 25 degrees Fahrenheit and the oven has to use more energy to raise the temperature to its original setting.

    c. Encourage guests to car pool.

REFERENCES

Consumers Reports, February, 1994.

Consumers Reports, May, 1993.

Dulley, J. "Steel Yourself for Big Task of Building Your Own House," *Newsday,* May 28, 1994, C7.

Holmes, G., Singh, R., and Theodore, L. *Handbook of Environmental Management and Technology.* New York: Wiley-Interscience, 1993.

Seymour, E. L. D. (ed.) *The Wise Garden Encyclopedia,* New York: Grosset & Dunlap, 1970.

Theodore, L., McGuinn, Y. *Pollution Prevention.* New York: Van Nostrand Reinhold, 1992.

Theodore, M. K., and Theodore, L. Personal notes, 1991.

Part VII

Pollution Prevention

The pollution prevention sequence concludes with Part VII, which serves as an introduction to pollution prevention through waste reduction. Five chapters comprise Part VII. Chapter 30 introduces the general concept of waste reduction, particularly at the industrial level. Numerous companies have already established formal pollution prevention programs and reported successes in reducing the amount of waste they produce. Chapter 31 is concerned solely with industrial applications where it is demonstrated that the best alternative today for companies is to produce less waste in the first place. The remaining three chapters cover what the authors have defined as domestic issues. A comprehensive examination of waste reduction at home is provided in Chapter 32; Chapter 33 focuses on waste reduction in the office setting. Part VII concludes with Chapter 34, which addresses waste reduction issues during leisure activities and in other circumstances not covered in the home or the workplace.

30

The Pollution Prevention Concept

CONTRIBUTING AUTHOR

Brent D. Wainwright

INTRODUCTION

The amount of waste generated in the United States has reached staggering proportions; according to the United States Environmental Protection Agency (EPA), 250 million tons of solid waste alone are generated annually. Although both the Resource Conservation and Recovery Act (RCRA) and the Hazardous and Solid Waste Act (HSWA) encourage businesses to minimize the wastes they generate, the majority of current environmental protection efforts are centered around treatment and pollution cleanup.

The passage of the Pollution Prevention Act of 1990 has redirected industry's approach to environmental management; pollution prevention has now become the environmental option of this decade and the 21st century. Whereas typical waste management strategies concentrate on "end-of-pipe" pollution control, pollution prevention attempts to handle waste at the source (i.e., source reduction). As waste handling and disposal costs increase, the application of pollution prevention measures is becoming more attractive than ever before. Industry is currently exploring the advantages of multimedia waste reduction and developing agendas to *strengthen* environmental design while *lessening* production costs.

There are profound opportunities for both the individual and industry to prevent the generation of waste; indeed, pollution prevention is today primarily stimulated by economics, legislation, liability concerns, and the enhanced environmental benefit of managing waste at the source. The EPA's Pollution Prevention Act of 1990 has established pollution prevention as a national policy declaring "waste should be prevented or reduced at the source wherever feasible, while pollution that cannot be prevented should be recycled in an environmentally safe manner" (EPA, 1991). The EPA's policy establishes the following hierarchy of waste management:

Table 30–1.   Waste Management Timetable

Timeframe	Control
Prior to 1945	No Control
1945–1960	Little Control
1960–1970	Some Control
1970–1975	Greater Control (EPA Founded)
1975–1980	More Sophisticated Control
1980–1985	Beginning of Waste Reduction Management
1985–1990	Waste Reduction Management
1990–1995	(Pollution Prevention Act)
1995–	???

1. Source reduction
2. Recycling/reuse
3. Treatment
4. Ultimate disposal

The hierarchy's categories are prioritized so as to promote the examination of each individual alternative prior to the investigation of subsequent options (i.e., the most preferable alternative should be thoroughly evaluated before consideration is given to a less accepted option.) Practices that decrease, avoid, or eliminate the generation of waste are considered source reduction and can include the implementation of procedures as simple and economical as good housekeeping. Recycling is the use, reuse, or reclamation of wastes and/or materials and may involve the incorporation of waste recovery techniques (e.g., distillation, filtration). Recycling can be performed at the facility (i.e., on-site), or at an off-site reclamation facility. Treatment involves the destruction or detoxification of wastes into nontoxic or less toxic materials by chemical, biological or physical methods, or any combination of these methods. Disposal has been included in the hierarchy because it is recognized that residual wastes will exist; the EPA's so-called "ultimate disposal" options include landfilling, land farming, ocean dumping and deep-well injection. However, the term "ultimate disposal" is a misnomer, but is included here because of its adaptation by the EPA. Table 30–1 provides a rough timetable demonstrating the national approach to waste management. Note how waste management has begun to shift from pollution *control* to pollution *prevention*.

POLLUTION PREVENTION HIERARCHY

As discussed in the Introduction, the hierarchy set forth by the EPA in the Pollution Prevention Act establishes an order in which waste management activities should be employed to reduce the quantity of waste generated. The preferred method is source reduction, as indicated in Figure 30–1. This approach actually precedes traditional waste management by addressing the source of the problem prior to its occurrence.

    Although the EPA's policy does not consider recycling or treatment as actual pollution pre-

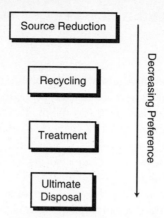

Figure 30–1. Pollution Prevention Hierarchy

vention methods per se, these methods present an opportunity to reduce the amount of waste that might otherwise be discharged into the environment. Clearly, the definition of pollution prevention and its synonyms (e.g., waste minimization) must be understood to fully appreciate and apply these techniques.

Waste minimization generally considers all of the methods in the EPA hierarchy (except for disposal) appropriate to reduce the volume or quantity of waste requiring disposal (e.g., source reduction). The definition of source reduction as applied in the Pollution Prevention Act, however, is "any practice which reduces the amount of any hazardous substance, pollutant or contaminant entering any waste stream or otherwise released into the environment . . . prior to recycling, treatment or disposal" (EPA, 1991). Source reduction reduces the amount of waste generated; it is therefore considered true pollution prevention and has the highest priority in the EPA hierarchy.

Recycling (reuse, reclamation) refers to the use or reuse of materials that would otherwise be disposed of or treated as a waste product. Wastes that cannot be directly reused may often be recovered on-site through methods such as distillation. When on-site recovery or reuse is not feasible due to quality specifications or the inability to perform recovery on-site, off-site recovery at a permitted commercial recovery facility is often a possibility. Such management techniques are considered secondary to source reduction and should only be used when pollution can not be prevented.

The treatment of waste is the third element of the hierarchy and should be utilized only in the absence of feasible source reduction or recycling opportunities. Waste treatment involves the use of chemical, biological, or physical processes to reduce or eliminate waste material. The incineration of wastes is included in this category and is considered "preferable to other treatment methods (i.e., chemical, biological, and physical) because incineration can permanently destroy the hazardous components in waste materials" (Theodore & McGuinn, 1992).

Of course, many of these pollution prevention elements are used by industry in combination to achieve the greatest waste reduction. Residual wastes that cannot be prevented or otherwise managed are then disposed of only as a last resort.

MULTIMEDIA ANALYSIS AND LIFECYCLE COST ANALYSIS

Multimedia Analysis

In order to properly design and then implement a pollution prevention program, sources of all wastes must be fully understood and evaluated. A multimedia analysis involves a multifaceted approach. It must not only consider one waste stream but all potentially contaminant media (e.g., air, water, land). Past waste management practices have been concerned primarily with treatment. All to often, such methods solve one waste problem by transferring a contaminant from one medium to another (e.g., air-stripping); such waste shifting is *not* pollution prevention or waste reduction.

Pollution prevention techniques must be evaluated through a thorough consideration of all media, hence the term multimedia. This approach is a clear departure from previous pollution treatment or control techniques where it was acceptable to transfer a pollutant from one source to another in order to solve a waste problem. Such strategies merely provide short-term solutions to an ever-increasing problem. As an example, air pollution control equipment prevents or reduces the discharge of waste into the air but at the same time can produce a solid hazardous waste problem. (See Chapter 6 for additional details on multimedia analyses.)

Lifecycle Analysis

The aforementioned multimedia approach to evaluating a product's waste stream(s) aims to ensure that the treatment of one waste stream does not result in the generation or increase in an additional waste output. Clearly, impacts resulting during the production of a product must be evaluated over its entire history or lifecycle.

A lifecycle analysis, or "Total Systems Approach," (Theodore, personal notes), is crucial to identifying opportunities for improvement. This type of evaluation identifies "energy use, material inputs, and wastes generated during a product's life: from extraction and processing of raw materials, to manufacture and transport of a product to the marketplace, and, finally, to use and dispose of the product" (World Wildlife Fund, 1991).

During a forum convened by the World Wildlife Fund and the Conservation Foundation in May 1990, various steering committees recommended that a three-part lifecycle model be adopted. This model consists of the following:

1. An inventory of materials and energy used, and environmental releases from all stages in the life of a product or process.
2. An analysis of potential environmental effects related to energy use and material resources and environmental releases.
3. An analysis of the changes needed to bring about environmental improvements for the product or process under evaluation.

Traditional cost analysis often fails to include factors relevant to future damage claims resulting from litigation, the depletion of natural resources, the effects of energy use, and so on. Therefore, waste management options such as treatment and disposal may appear preferential if an overall lifecycle cost analysis is not performed. It is evident that environmental costs from "cradle-to-grave" have to be evaluated together with more conventional production costs to accurately ascertain genuine production costs. In the future, a total systems approach will most likely involve a more careful evaluation of pollution, energy, and safety issues. For example, if one was to compare the benefits of coal versus oil as a fuel source for an electric power plant, the use of coal might be considered economically favorable. In addition to the cost issues, however, one must be concerned with the environmental effects of coal mining, transportation, and storage prior to use as a fuel. Many have a tendency to overlook the fact that there are serious health and safety matters (e.g., miner exposure) that must be considered, along with the effects of fugitive emissions. When these effects are weighed alongside of standard economic factors, the cost benefits of coal usage may no longer appear valid. Thus, many of the economic benefits associated with pollution prevention are often unrecognized due to inappropriate cost accounting methods. For this reason, economic considerations are detailed in the next chapter.

POLLUTION PREVENTION ASSESSMENT PROCEDURES

The first step in establishing a pollution prevention program is the obtainment of management commitment. Management commitment is necessary given the inherent need for project structure and control. Management will determine the amount of funding allotted for the program as well as specific program goals. The data collected during the actual evaluation is then used to develop options for reducing the types and amounts of waste generated. Figure 30–2 depicts a systematic approach that can be used during the procedure. After a particular waste stream or area of concern is identified, feasibility studies are performed involving both economic and technical considerations. Finally, preferred alternatives are implemented. The four phases of the assessment (i.e., planning and organization, assessment, feasibility, and implementation) are introduced in the following subsections. Sources of additional information, as well as information on industrial programs is also provided in this section.

Planning and Organization

The purpose of this phase is to obtain management commitment, define and develop program goals, and to assemble a project team. Proper planning and organization are crucial to the successful performance of the pollution prevention assessment. Both managers and facility staff play important roles in the assessment procedure by providing the necessary commitment and familiarity with the facility, its processes, and current waste management operations. The benefits of the program, including economic advantages, liability reduction, regulatory compliance and improved public image, often lead to management support.

Once management has made a commitment to the program and goals have been set, a program task force is established. The selection of a team leader will be dependent upon many factors including his or her ability to effectively interface with both the assessment team and management staff.

The task force must be capable of identifying pollution reduction alternatives, as well as be cognizant of inherent obstacles to the process. Barriers frequently arise from the anxiety associated with the belief that the program will negatively affect product quality or result in production losses.

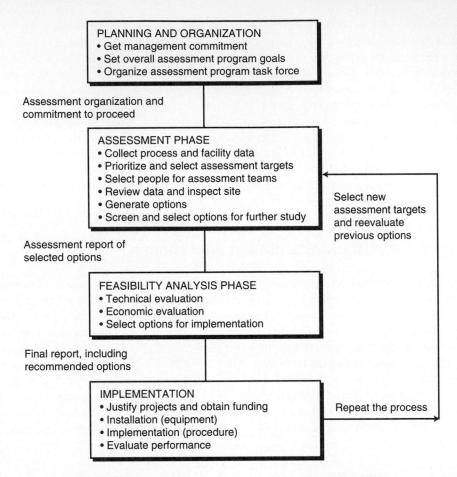

Figure 30–2.   Pollution Prevention Assessment Procedures

According to an EPA survey, 30 percent of industry comments responded that they were concerned that product quality would decline if waste minimization techniques were implemented (EPA, 1990). Thus, the assessment team, and the team leader in particular, must be ready to react to these and other concerns (Theodore, personal notes).

Assessment Phase

The assessment phase aims to collect data needed to identify and analyze pollution prevention opportunities. Assessment of the facility's waste reduction needs includes the examination of hazardous waste streams, process operations, and the identification of techniques that often promise the reduction of waste generation. Information is often derived from observations made during a facility walk-through, interviews with employees (e.g., operators, line workers), and review of site or regulatory records. The American Society of Testing and Materials (ASTM) suggests the following information sources be reviewed, as available (ASTM, 1992).

1. Product design criteria.

2. Process flow diagrams for all solid waste, wastewater, and air emissions sources.

3. Site maps showing the location of all pertinent units (e.g., pollution control devices, points of discharge).

4. Environmental documentation, including: Material Safety Data Sheets (MSDS), military specification data, permits (e.g., NPDES, POTW, RCRA), SARA Title III reports, waste manifests, and any pending permits or application information.

5. Economic data, including: cost of raw material management; cost of air, wastewater, and hazardous waste treatment; waste management operating and maintenance costs; and, waste disposal costs.

6. Managerial information: environmental policies and procedures; prioritization of waste management concerns; automated or computerized waste management systems; inventory and distribution procedures; maintenance scheduling practices; planned modifications or revisions to existing operations that would impact waste generation activities; and the basis of source reduction decisions and policies.

The use of process flow diagrams and material balances are worthwhile methods to "quantify losses or emissions, and provide essential data to estimate the size and cost of additional equipment, data to evaluate economic performance, and a baseline for tracking the progress of minimization efforts" (Theodore, personal notes). Material balances should be applied to individual waste streams or processes, and then utilized to construct an overall balance for the facility. Details on these calculations are available in the literature (Theodore & Allen, 1993). In addition, an introduction to this subject is provided in the next section.

The data collected is then used to prioritize waste streams and operations for assessment. Each waste stream is assigned a priority based on corporate pollution prevention goals and objectives. Once waste origins are identified and ranked, potential methods to reduce the waste stream are evaluated. The identification of alternatives is generally based on discussions with the facility staff, review of technical literature, and contacts with suppliers, trade organizations, and regulatory agencies.

Alternatives identified during this phase of the assessment are evaluated using screening procedures so as to reduce the number of alternatives requiring further exploration during the feasibility analysis phase. The criteria used during this screening procedure include: cost-effectiveness; implementation time; economic, compliance, safety, and liability concerns; waste reduction potential; and, whether the technology is proven (Theodore, personal notes; Theodore & Allen, 1993). Options which meet established criteria are then examined further during the feasibility analysis.

Feasibility Analysis

Preferred alternative selection is performed by an evaluation of technical and economic considerations. The technical evaluation determines whether a given option will work as planned. Some typical considerations follow:

1. Safety concerns
2. Product quality impacts or production delays during implementation
3. Labor and/or training requirements
4. Creation of new environmental concerns
5. Waste reduction potential
6. Utility and budget requirements
7. Space and compatibility concerns

If an option proves to be technically ineffective or inappropriate, it is deleted from the list of potential alternatives. Either following or concurrent with the technical evaluation, an economic study is performed weighing standard measures of profitability such as payback period, investment returns, and net present value. Many of these costs (or more appropriately, cost savings) may be substantial yet are difficult to quantify.

Implementation

The findings of the overall assessment are used to demonstrate the technical and economic worthiness of program implementation. Once appropriate funding is obtained, the program is implemented not unlike any other project requiring new procedures or equipment. When preferred waste pollution prevention techniques are identified, they are implemented, and should become part of the facility's day-to-day management and operation. Subsequent to the program's execution, its performance should be evaluated in order to demonstrate effectiveness, generate data to further refine and augment waste reduction procedures, and maintain management support.

It should be noted that waste reduction, energy conservation, and safety issues are interrelated and often complementary to each other. For example, the reduction in the amount of energy a facility consumes results in reduced emissions associated with the generation of power. Energy expenditures associated with the treatment and transport of waste are similarly reduced when the amount of waste generated is lessened; at the same time worker safety is elevated due to reduced exposure to hazardous materials.

SOURCES OF INFORMATION

The successful development and implementation of any pollution prevention program is not only dependent on a thorough understanding of the facility's operations but also requires an intimate knowledge of current opportunities and advances in the field. In fact, 32 percent of industry respondents to an EPA survey identified the lack of technical information as a major factor delaying or preventing the implementation of a waste minimization program (EPA, 1991). Fortunately, the EPA has developed a national Pollution Prevention Information Clearinghouse (PPIC) and the Pollution Prevention Information Exchange System (PIES) to facilitate the exchange of information needed to promote pollution prevention through efficient information transfer (EPA, 1991).

PPIC is operated by the EPA's Office of Research and Development and the Office of Pollution Prevention. The clearinghouse is comprised of four elements:

1. *Repository:* including a hard copy reference library and collection center and an on-line information retrieval and ordering system.

2. *PIES:* a computerized conduit to databases and document ordering, accessible via modem and personal computer—(703) 506–1025.

3. *Hotline:* PPIC uses the RCRA/Superfund and Small Business Ombudsman Hotlines as well as a PPIC technical assistance line to answer pollution prevention questions, access information in the PPIC, and assist in document ordering and searches. To access PPIC by telephone, call:

RCRA/Superfund Hotline (800) 242–9346

Small Business Ombudsman Hotline (800) 368–5888

PPIC Technical Assistance (703) 821–4800

4. *Networking and Outreach:* PPIC compiles and disseminates information packets and bulletins, and initiates networking efforts with other national and international organizations.

Additionally, the EPA publishes a newsletter entitled *Pollution Prevention News,* which contains information including EPA news, technologies, program updates, and case studies. The EPA's Risk Reduction Engineering Laboratory and the Center for Environmental Research Information has published several guidance documents, developed in cooperation with the California Department of Health Services. The manuals supplement generic waste reduction information presented in the EPA's *Waste Minimization Opportunity Assessment Manual* (EPA, 1988). Additional information is available through PPIC.

Pollution prevention or waste minimization programs have been established at the State level and as such are good sources of information. Both Federal and State agencies are working with universities and research centers and may also provide assistance. For example, the American Institute of Chemical Engineers has established the Center for Waste Reduction Technologies (CWRT), a program based on targeted research, technology transfer, and enhanced education.

Industry Programs

A significant pollution prevention resource may very well be found with the "competition." Several large companies have established well-known programs that have successfully incorporated pollution prevention practices into their manufacturing processes. These include, but are not limited to: 3M—Pollution Prevention Pays (3P); Dow Chemical—Waste Reduction Always Pays (WRAP); Chevron—Save Money And Reduce Toxics (SMART); and General Dynamics—Zero Discharge Program.

Smaller companies can benefit by the assistance offered by these larger corporations. It is clear that access to information is of major importance when implementing efficient pollution prevention programs. By adopting such programs, industry is affirming pollution prevention as a good business practice and not simply a noble effort.

FUTURE TRENDS

The development of waste management practices in the United States has recently moved toward securing a new pollution prevention ethic. The performance of pollution prevention assessments and their subsequent implementation will encourage increased research into methods that will further aid in the reduction of wastes and pollution.

It is evident that the majority of the present day obstacles to pollution prevention are based on either a lack of information or an anxiety associated with economic concerns. By strengthening the exchange of information among businesses, a better understanding of the unique benefits of pollution prevention will be realized in the future.

SUMMARY

1. The passage of the Pollution Prevention Act of 1990 has redirected industry's approach to environmental management; pollution prevention has now become the environmental option of this decade and the 21st century. Whereas typical waste management strategies concentrate on "end-of-pipe" pollution control, pollution prevention attempts to handle waste at the source (i.e., source reduction).

2. The EPA's policy establishes the following hierarchy of waste management:

Source Reduction
Recycling/Reuse
Treatment
Ultimate Disposal

3. In order to properly design and then implement a pollution prevention program, sources of all wastes must be fully understood and evaluated. A multimedia analysis involves a multifaceted approach. It must not only consider one waste stream but all potentially contaminant media (e.g., air, water, land).

4. The four phases of a pollution prevention assessment procedure are: planning and organization, assessment, feasibility analysis, and implementation.

5. EPA has developed a national Pollution Prevention Information Clearinghouse (PPIC) and the Pollution Prevention Information Exchange System (PIES) to facilitate the exchange of information needed to promote pollution prevention through efficient information transfer.

6. It is evident that the majority of the present-day obstacles to pollution prevention are based on either a lack of information or an anxiety associated with economic concerns. By strengthening the exchange of information among businesses, a better understanding of the unique benefits of pollution prevention will be realized in the future.

REFERENCES

ASTM. *Standard Guide for Industrial Source Reduction,* Draft Copy: New York American Society of Testing and Materials, June 16, 1992.

EPA. *The EPA Manual for Waste Minimization Opportunity Assessments.* Cincinnati, OH: August 1988.

EPA. *1987 National Biennial RCRA Hazardous Waste Report—Executive Summary.* Washington D.C.: GPO, 1991.

EPA. *Pollution Prevention Fact Sheet.* Washington, D.C., Author, March 1991.

Theodore, L., personal notes.

Theodore, L., and Allen, R. *Pollution Prevention, An ETS Theodore Tutorial.* Roanoke, VA: ETS International, Inc., 1993.

Theodore, L., and McGuinn, Y. *Pollution Prevention.* New York: Van Nostrand Reinhold, 1992.

World Wildlife Fund. *Getting at the Source.* New York, 1991.

31

Industrial Applications

Brent D. Wainwright

INTRODUCTION*

One of the key elements of the assessment phase of a pollution prevention program involves mass balance equations. These calculations are often referred to as material balances; the calculations are performed via the conservation law for mass. The details of this often-used law are described below.

The conservation law for mass can be applied to any process or system. The general form of the law follows:

$$mass\ in - mass\ out + mass\ generated = mass\ accumulated \qquad (31–1)$$

This equation can be applied to the total mass involved in a process or to a particular species, on either a mole or mass basis. The conservation law for mass can be applied to steady-state or unsteady-state processes and to batch or continuous systems. A steady-state system is one in which there is no change in conditions (e.g., temperature, pressure) or rates of flow with time at any given point in the system; the accumulation term then becomes zero. If there is no chemical reaction, the generation term is zero. All other processes are classified as unsteady-state.

To isolate a system for study, the system is separated from the surroundings by a boundary or envelope that may either be real (e.g., a reactor vessel) or imaginary. Mass crossing the boundary and entering the system is part of the mass-in term. The equation may be used for any compound whose quantity does not change by chemical reaction, or for any chemical element, regardless of whether it has participated in a chemical reaction. Furthermore, it may be written for one

*Information for this section was drawn from L. Theodore's personal notes and Theodore and Reynolds, 1989.

piece of equipment, several pieces of equipment, or around an entire process (i.e., a total material balance).

The conservation of mass law finds a major application during the performance of pollution prevention assessments. As described in the previous chapter, a pollution prevention assessment is a systematic, planned procedure with the objective of identifying methods to reduce or eliminate waste. The assessment process should characterize the selected waste streams and processes (ICF Technology, 1989)—a necessary ingredient if a material balance is to be performed. Some of the data required for the material balance calculation may be collected during the first review of site-specific data; however, in some instances, the information may not be collected until an actual site walk-through is performed.

Simplified mass balances should be developed for each of the important waste-generating operations to identify sources and gain a better understanding of the origins of each waste stream. Since a mass balance is essentially a check to make sure that what goes into a process (i.e., the total mass of all raw materials), what leaves the process (i.e., the total mass of the product(s) and by-products), the material balance should be made individually for all components that enter and leave the process. When chemical reactions take place in a system, there is an advantage to doing "elemental balances" for specific chemical elements in a system. Material balances can assist in determining concentrations of waste constituents where analytical test data are limited. They are particularly useful when there are points in the production process where it is difficult or uneconomical to collect analytical data.

Mass balance calculations are particularly useful for quantifying fugitive emissions, such as evaporative losses. Waste stream data and mass balances will enable one to track flow and characteristics of the waste streams over time. Since in most cases the accumulation equals zero (steady-state operation), it can then be assumed that any buildup is actually leaving the process through fugitive emissions or other means. This will be useful in identifying trends in waste/pollutant generation and will also be critical in the task of measuring the performance of implemented pollution prevention options.

The result of these activities is a catalog of waste streams that provides a description of each waste, including quantities, frequency of discharge, composition, and other important information useful for material balance. Of course, some assumptions or educated estimates will be needed when it is impossible to obtain specific information.

By performing a material balance in conjunction with a pollution prevention assessment, the amount of waste generated becomes known. The success of the pollution prevention program can therefore be measured by using this information on baseline generation rates (i.e., that rate at which waste is generated without pollution prevention considerations).

BARRIERS TO POLLUTION PREVENTION

As discussed previously, industry is beginning to realize that there are profound benefits associated with pollution prevention including cost effectiveness, reduced liability, enhanced public image, and regulatory compliance (these are discussed in the next section). Nevertheless, there are barriers or disincentives identified with pollution prevention. This section will briefly outline barriers that may need to be confronted or considered during the evaluation of a pollution prevention program.

There are numerous reasons why more businesses are not reducing the wastes they generate. The following "dirty dozen" are common disincentives:

1. *Technical limitations.* Given the complexity of present manufacturing processes, waste streams exist that can not be reduced with current technology. The need for continued research and development is evident.

2. *Lack of information.* In some instances, the information needed to make a pollution prevention decision may be confidential or is difficult to obtain. In addition, many decision makers are simply unaware of the potential opportunities available regarding information to aid in the implementation of a pollution prevention program.

3. *Consumer preference obstacles.* Consumer preference strongly affects the manner in which a product is produced, packaged, and marketed. If the implementation of a pollution prevention program results in the increase in the cost of a product, or decreased convenience or availability, consumers might be reluctant to use it.

4. *Concern over product quality decline.* The use of a less hazardous material in a product's manufacturing process may result in decreased life, durability, or competitiveness.

5. *Economic concerns.* Many companies are unaware of the economic advantages associated with pollution prevention. Legitimate concerns may include decreased profit margins or the lack of funds required for the initial capital investment.

6. *Resistance to change.* The unwillingness of many businesses to change is rooted in their reluctance to try technologies that may be unproven, or based on a combination of the barriers discussed in this section.

7. *Regulatory barriers.* Existing regulations that have created incentives for the control and containment of wastes, are at the same time discouraging the exploration of pollution prevention alternatives. Moreover, since regulatory enforcement is often intermittent, current legislation can weaken waste reduction incentives.

8. *Lack of markets.* The implementation of pollution prevention processes and the production of environmentally friendly products will be of no avail if markets do not exist for such goods. As an example, the recycling of newspaper in the United States has resulted in an overabundance of waste paper without markets prepared to take advantage of this "raw" material.

9. *Management apathy.* Many managers capable of making decisions to begin pollution prevention activities, do not realize the potential benefits of pollution prevention and may therefore take on a attitude of passiveness.

10. *Institutional barriers.* In an organization without a strong infrastructure to support pollution prevention plans, waste reduction programs will be difficult to implement. Similarly, if there is no mechanism in place to hold individuals accountable for their actions, the successful implementation of a pollution prevention program will be limited.

11. *Lack of awareness of pollution prevention advantages.* As mentioned in *economic concerns,* decision makers may be uninformed of the benefits associated with pollution reduction.

12. *Concern over the dissemination of confidential product information.* If a pollution prevention assessment reveals confidential data pertinent to a company's product, fear may exist that the organization will lose a competitive edge with other businesses in the industry.

POLLUTION PREVENTION ADVANTAGES

Various means exist to encourage pollution prevention through regulatory measures, economic incentives, and technical assistance programs. Since the benefits of pollution prevention undoubtedly surpass prevention barriers, a baker's dozen incentives is presented below:

1. *Economic benefits.* The most obvious economic benefits associated with pollution prevention are the savings that result from the elimination of waste storage, treatment, handling, transport, and disposal. Additionally, less tangible economic benefits are realized in terms of decreased liability, regulatory compliance costs (e.g., permits), legal and insurance costs, and improved process efficiency. Pollution prevention almost always pays for itself, particularly when the time investment required to comply with regulatory standards is considered. Several of these economic benefits are discussed separately below.

2. *Regulatory compliance.* Quite simply, when wastes are not generated, compliance issues are not a concern. Waste management costs associated with recordkeeping, reporting, and laboratory analysis are reduced or eliminated. Pollution prevention's proactive approach to waste management will better prepare industry for the future regulation of many hazardous substances and wastes that are currently unregulated. Regulations have, and will continue to be, a moving target.

3. *Liability reduction.* Facilities are responsible for their wastes from "cradle-to-grave." By eliminating or reducing waste generation, future liabilities can also be decreased. Additionally, the need for expensive pollution liability insurance requirements may be abated.

4. *Enhanced public image.* Consumers are interested in purchasing goods that are safer for the environment and this demand, depending on how they respond, can mean success or failure for many companies. Business should therefore be sensitive to consumer demands and use pollution prevention efforts to their utmost advantage by producing goods that are environmentally friendly.

5. *Federal and state grants.* Federal and State grant programs have been developed to strengthen pollution prevention programs initiated by states and private entities. The EPA's Pollution Prevention By and For Small Business Grant Program awards grants to small businesses to assist their development and demonstration of new pollution prevention technologies.

6. *Market incentives.* Public demand for environmentally preferred products has generated a market for recycled goods and related products; products can be designed with these environmental characteristics in mind, offering a competitive advantage. In addition, many private and public agencies are beginning to stimulate the market for recycled goods by writing contracts and specifications that call for the use of recycled materials.

7. *Reduced waste treatment costs.* As discussed in *economic benefits,* the increasing costs of traditional end-of-pipe waste management practices are avoided or reduced through the implementation of pollution prevention programs.

8. *Potential tax incentives.* As an effort to promote pollution prevention, taxes may eventually need to be levied to encourage waste generators to consider reduction programs. Conversely, tax breaks to corporations that utilize pollution prevention methods could similarly be developed to foster pollution prevention.

9. *Decreased worker exposure.* By reducing or eliminating chemical exposures, businesses benefit by lessening the potential for chronic workplace exposure, and serious accidents and emergencies. The burden of medical monitoring programs, personal exposure monitoring, and potential damage claims are also reduced.

10. *Decreased energy consumption.* As mentioned previously, energy conservation are often interrelated and complementary to each other. Energy expenditures associated with the treatment and transport of waste are reduced when the amount of waste generated is lessened, while at the same time the pollution associated with energy consumed by these activities is abated.

11. *Increased operating efficiencies.* A potential beneficial side effect of pollution prevention activities is a concurrent increase in operating efficiency. Through a pollution prevention assessment, the assessment team can identify sources of waste that results in hazardous waste generation *and* loss in process performance. The implementation of a waste reduction program will often rectify such problems through modernization, innovation, and the implementation of good operating practices.

12. *Competitive advantages.* By taking advantage of the many benefits associated with pollution prevention, businesses can gain a competitive edge.

13. *Reduced negative environmental impacts.* Through an evaluation of pollution prevention alternatives, which consider a total systems approach, consideration is given to the negative impact of environmental damage to natural resources and species that occur during raw material procurement and waste disposal. The performance of pollution prevention endeavors will therefore result in enhanced environmental protection.

The development of new markets by means of regulatory and economic incentives will further assist the effective implementation of waste reduction. Various combinations of the pollution prevention barriers provided above have appeared on numerous occasions in the literature, and in many different forms. However, there is one other concern that both industry and the taxpayer should be aware of. Carol Browner, EPA Administrator, has repeatedly claimed that pollution prevention is the organization's top priority. *Nothing could be further from the truth.* Despite near unlimited resources, the EPA has contributed little to furthering the pollution prevention effort. The EPA offices in Washington, Research Park Triangle, and Region II have exhibited a level of bureaucratic indifference that has surpassed even the traditional attitudes of many EPA employees. It is virtually impossible to contact any responsible pollution prevention individual at the EPA. Calls are rarely returned. Letters are rarely returned. On the rare occasion when contact is made, the regulatory individual typically passes the caller onto someone else who "really is in a better position to help you," and the cycle starts all over again (L. Theodore and B. Wainwright, personal notes).

This standard bureaucratic phenomena has been experienced by others in industry *and* the EPA (L. Theodore, personal notes; ICF Technology, 1989). Two letters of complaint to the EPA Region II Administrator resulted in a response that was somewhat cynical and suggestive of a reprimand. Ms. Browner chose not to reply to the complaints (L. Theodore and B. Wainwright, personal notes). Notwithstanding some of the above comments, pollution prevention efforts have been successful in industry because these programs have often either produced profits or reduced costs, or both. The driving force for these successes has primarily been economics and *not* the EPA. Economic considerations are considered in the next section.

ECONOMIC CONSIDERATIONS ASSOCIATED WITH POLLUTION PREVENTION PROGRAMS

The purpose of this section is to outline the basic elements of a pollution prevention cost accounting system that incorporates both traditional and less tangible economic variables. The intent is not to present a detailed discussion of economic analysis but to help identify the more important elements that must be considered to properly quantify pollution prevention options.

The greatest driving force behind any pollution prevention plan is the promise of economic opportunities and cost savings over the long term. Pollution prevention is now recognized as one of the lowest-cost options for waste/pollutant management. Hence, an understanding of the economics involved in pollution prevention programs/options is quite important in making decisions at both the engineering and management levels. Every organization should be able to execute an economic evaluation of a proposed project. If the project cannot be justified economically after *all* factors and considerations have been taken into account, it should obviously not be pursued. The earlier such a project is identified, the fewer resources will be wasted.

Before the true cost or profit of a pollution prevention program can be evaluated, the factors contributing to the economics must be recognized. There are two traditional contributing factors—capital costs and operating costs—but there are other important costs and benefits associated with pollution prevention that need to be quantified if a meaningful economic analysis is going to be performed.

The economic evaluation referred to above is usually carried out using standard measures of profitability. Each company and organization has its own economic criteria for selecting projects for implementation. In performing an economic evaluation, various costs and savings must be considered. The economic analysis presented in this section represents a preliminary, rather than a detailed, analysis. For smaller facilities with only a few (and perhaps simple) processes, the entire pollution prevention assessment procedure will tend to be much less formal. In this situation, several obvious pollution prevention options, such as the installation of flow controls and good operating practices, may be implemented with little or no economic evaluation. In these instances, no complicated analyses are necessary to demonstrate the advantages of adopting the selected pollution prevention option. A proper perspective must also be maintained between the magnitude of savings that a potential option may offer and the amount of manpower required to do the technical and economic feasibility analyses.

FUTURE TRENDS

The main problem with the traditional type of economic analysis is that it is difficult—nay, in some cases, impossible—to quantify some of the not-so-obvious economic merits of a pollution prevention program. Several considerations, in addition to those provided in the previous section, have just recently surfaced as factors that need to be taken into account in any meaningful economic analysis of a pollution prevention effort. These factors are certain to become an integral part of any pollution prevention analysis in the future. What follows is a listing of these considerations:

Decreased long-term liabilities

Regulatory compliance

Regulatory recordkeeping

Dealings with the EPA

Dealings with state and local regulatory bodies

Elimination or reduction of fines and penalties

Potential tax benefits

Customer relations

Stockholder support (corporate image)

Improved public image

Reduced technical support

Potential insurance costs and claims

Effect on borrowing power

Improved mental and physical well-being of employees

Reduced health maintenance costs

Employee morale

Other process benefits

Improved worker safety

Avoidance of rising costs of waste treatment and/or disposal

Reduced training costs

Reduced emergency response planning

Many proposed pollution prevention programs have been quenched in their early stages because a comprehensive analysis was not performed. Until the effects described above are included, the true merits of a pollution prevention program may be clouded by incorrect and/or incomplete economic data. Can something be done by industry to remedy this problem? One approach (L. Theodore & B. Wainwright, personal notes) is to use a modified version of the standard Delphi panel that the authors have modestly defined as the WTA (an acronym for the Wainwright-Theodore Approach). In order to estimate these "other" factors and/or economic benefits of pollution prevention, several knowledgeable individuals within and perhaps outside the organization are asked to independently provide estimates, with explanatory details, on these benefits. Each individual in the panel is then allowed to independently review all responses. The cycle is then repeated until the group's responses approach convergence.

Finally, pollution prevention measures can provide a company with the opportunity of looking their neighbors in the eye and truthfully saying that all that can reasonably be done to prevent pollution is being done . . . in effect, the company is doing right by the environment. Is there an advantage to this? It is not only a difficult question to answer quantitatively but also a difficult one to answer. The reader is left with pondering the answer to this question in terms of future activities.

SUMMARY

1. One of the key elements of the assessment phase of a pollution prevention program involves mass balance equations. These calculations are often referred to as material balances; the calculations are performed via the conservation law for mass.

2. Industry is beginning to realize that there are profound benefits associated with pollution prevention including cost effectiveness, reduced liability, enhanced public image, and regulatory compliance. Nevertheless, there are barriers or disincentives identified with pollution prevention.

3. Various means exist to encourage pollution prevention through regulatory measures, economic incentives, and technical assistance programs.

4. The greatest driving force behind any pollution prevention plan is the promise of economic opportunities and cost savings over the long term.

5. The main problem with the traditional type of economic analysis is that it is difficult, or in some cases, impossible, to quantify some of the not-so-obvious economic merits of a pollution prevention program.

REFERENCES

ICF Technology Incorporated, *New York State Waste Reduction Guidance Manual.* Alexandria, VA: Author, 1989.

L. Theodore: personal notes.

L. Theodore and B. Wainwright: personal notes.

Theodore L., and Reynolds, J. *Introduction to Hazardous Waste Incineration.* New York: Wiley-Interscience, 1989.

32

At Home

INTRODUCTION

Concurrent with the United States' growth as an international economic superpower during the years following World War II, a new paradigm was established whereby society became accustomed to the convenience and ease with which goods could be discarded after a relatively short useful life. Many have come to expect these everyday comforts with what may be considered an unconscious ignorance towards the ultimate effect of our throwaway lifestyle. In fact some, while fearful of environmental degradation, are not aware of the ill-effects actions have on the ecosystem. Many individuals who abide by the "not in my back yard" (NIMBY) mindset also feel pollution prevention does not have to occur "in my house."

The past two decades have seen an increased social awareness of the impact of certain lifestyles on the environment. Public environmental concerns include issues such as waste disposal, hazardous material regulations, depletion of natural resources, as well as air, water, and land pollution. Nevertheless, roughly one-half of the total quantity of waste generated each year can be attributed to domestic sources!

More recently, concern about the environment has begun to stimulate "environmentally-correct" behavior among us all. After all, the choices made today affect the environment of tomorrow. Simple decisions can be made at work and at home that conserve natural resources and lessen the burden placed on waste management systems. By eliminating waste at the source, all participate in the protection of the environment by reducing the amount of waste otherwise needed to be treated or ultimately disposed.

This chapter is a condensed, revised, and updated version of an unpublished (but copyrighted) 1992 text prepared by M. K. Theodore and L. Theodore titled *A Citizen's Guide to Pollution Prevention*.

Perhaps the most important area where the consumer can apply the pollution prevention principles is in the home. As described earlier, the average citizen generates millions of tons of waste each year in the form of wrappings, bottles, boxes, cans, grass clippings, furniture, clothing, and phone books, to name a few. Container and packaging material includes glass, aluminum, plastics, steel and other metals, paper and paperboard. The average citizen also discharges waste to water streams and the atmosphere and does not use energy efficiently and in a conservative manner.

The chapter contains individual sections devoted to the following pollution prevention areas where waste reduction activities/procedures can be implemented:

1. Solvents, paints, and pesticides
2. Recycle/reuse activities
3. Energy-related activities
4. Other general activities

Each of these topics is treated in a separate section below. Although some of the material appear earlier in the text, this chapter—as with all others in the text—was written on a stand-alone basis.

SOLVENTS, PAINTS AND PESTICIDES*

A solvent is a substance that can dissolve another substance. Water is the most common solvent; however, many solvents have an organic rather than a water base. Organic solvents are used to clean brushes and rollers, dissolve or thin paints, dilute varnishes and other oil-based products, and clean up after painting or varnishing. These can cause environmental and health impacts if used or disposed of improperly.

Organic solvents are either chlorinated or nonchlorinated. Almost all organic solvents are toxic to aquatic life, even in low concentrations. Airborne solvents can heighten smog conditions. Solvents with chlorinated hydrocarbons resist ordinary breakdown to less harmful components and are very persistent in the environment.

Solvents may cause serious health effects if they come into contact with the skin or eyes or are inhaled. Excessive solvent exposure can cause a wide range of symptoms, many quite serious. The most damaging are the halogenated solvents, which are often found in paint strippers, spot removers, and degreasers.

Waste reduction activities regarding solvents, paints and pesticides that can be implemented at home are provided below.

1. Purchase just the amount needed, and use it up. If there is any left over, offer it to friends, neighbors, or housing rehabilitation programs.

2. Take leftover solvents, paints, and pesticides to a household hazardous waste day. Nationwide, more than 1,000 programs were held in 1993. The material received is recycled or sent to a licensed hazardous waste disposer.

*Information for the next four sections was drawn from Holmes, Singh, and Theodore, 1993, and Theodore and McGuinn, 1992.

3. Store carefully. Keep solvents, paints and pesticides in well-ventilated racks, out of reach of children and animals. Store them in the original container, sealed tightly and kept dry. If the container begins to leak, place it in a larger, intact container.

4. Consider alternatives. Some suggestions are: instead of a drain cleaner, use a mechanical device; instead of furniture polish, a damp rag works well; instead of moth balls, use cedar chips; instead of oil-based paint or thinner, use water-based products, which can be dried out, then put in the trash; instead of oven cleaners, use a self-cleaning oven or baking soda, water, or a scouring pad; instead of a pesticide, use physical and biological controls.

5. Do not flush solvents, paints and pesticides down a toilet or drain. A sewage treatment plant cannot break down all toxic substances; some enter surrounding waterways. They can also disrupt the biological process on which treatment plants and septic tanks rely.

6. Do not dump them in a ditch or backyard since they can poison local plants and wildlife, contaminate soil where children play, and leach through soil into groundwater.

7. Do not discard with the trash since they can injure sanitation workers and damage equipment. Chemicals can react with other substances in household trash, leading to fires or explosions in trucks or waste-handling facilities. In a landfill, chemicals can form a poisonous brew that may find its way into groundwater. If incinerated, they can contribute to air pollution.

RECYCLE/REUSE ACTIVITIES

People feel good about recycling. It is a simple, direct, and daily way to feel one is helping the environment. "In the first week in November 1992, more adults took part in recycling than voted," says Jerry Powell, editor of *Resource Recycling* magazine and chair of the National Recycling Coalition. "We're more popular than democracy."

Some 5,400 cities and towns had curbside recycling programs in 1992—five times as many as in 1988. And forty-one states have official recycling goals, ranging from plans to recycle 25 percent of all garbage within a few years to Rhode Island's ambitious target of 70 percent (*Consumer Reports,* 1994).

Not everything can be recycled easily. Americans are currently recycling well over 30 percent of several major materials, including paper, glass containers, and steel and aluminum cans. This material, along with plastic containers, newspaper, and cardboard account for only about a third of the discards by weight. Recycling programs have barely begun to deal with much of the waste that pours daily into landfills and incinerators: food wastes, textiles, shreds of plastic wrap, baby diapers, durable plastics that cannot be remelted, and broken and obsolete products.

All forms of trash disposal, including recycling, have environmental impacts. The best thing a consumer can do is to avoid buying new things whenever possible. Think like the 19th-century New Englanders, whose motto was, "Use it up, wear it out, make it do."

Recycle/reuse activities at home that can result in waste reduction are provided below.

1. Since paper waste is estimated to be 38 percent of municipal solid waste, recycling paper saves more landfill space than recycling any other material.

2. Use both sides of the paper.

3. Have name and address removed from junk mail list. Use junk mail for scrap paper, grocery lists, and so on.

4. Use newspaper as wrapping paper. Use crumbled newspaper to clean windows.

5. When purchasing a computer printer, check for paper-saving options. Donate the old printer to a school organization.

6. Encourage local schools and village offices to follow recycling practices for environmental and economic reasons. Some experts are now recommending that cities charge households different fees according to the amount of trash they generate. Some cities, such as Seattle, have started to bill households directly, with the price rising sharply for every additional trash can. In one rural New York town that tried this program, the amount of trash buried in the local landfill decreased by more than half, and the recycling rate more than doubled within a year.

7. Spread the word at fast-food restaurants by commenting to managers about good/bad habits. Let personnel know that you appreciate environmentally conscientious franchises.

8. In any store, do not use a bag unless needed. Have different size cloth bags that can be used and reused for grocery shopping. Some grocery stores reward patrons for using their own bags and/or returning plastic bags to a common bin for cooperative use.

9. Reuse plastic bags brought home from the store as garbage bags instead of buying new garbage bags for that purpose.

10. When ordering take-out coffee, use a personal refillable mug. Some environmentally conscious coffee shops encourage this by offering a reduced price for those who bring their own mug.

11. Shop for products that have as little packaging as possible. Buy the largest-sized package or a concentrate at the store and then, at home, mix and refill in another container.

12. Invest in resealable containers for storing leftovers. Avoid the use of disposable plastic wraps and storage bags. Recycle jelly jars; they are perfect for leftovers and allow one to see what is inside. These jars also make nice drinking glasses. Or, fill a pretty jar with homemade jam or a favorite sauce and present as a house gift.

13. If family members "brown bag" their lunch, use environmentally conscious containers for this purpose. These reusable containers should be compartmentalized and insulated so that the contents are not squashed and are kept hot or cold.

14. Minimize the use of paper towels and paper napkins. Invest in cloth napkins for everyday use, and use a wiping cloth or towel rather than a new paper towel each time.

15. Buy products that use recycled materials in their manufacturing or packaging.

16. Recycle whatever one can and follow the locality's specific recycling instructions to the letter. This is particularly problematic with plastics. The most notorious lookalikes are polyethylene terephthalate (PET), the clear, shiny plastic that soda bottles are made from, and polyvinyl chloride (PVC), another clear plastic used mainly for packaging cooking oil. Because PVC starts to decompose at the temperature at which PET is just beginning to melt, one stray PVC bottle in a melt of 10,000 PET bottles can ruin the entire batch.

17. Buy nickel-cadmium batteries and recharge them. When buying rechargeable batteries is not feasible, buy alkaline batteries. They are more expensive than carbon-zinc batteries but are a better value because they last longer.

18. Do not use disposable razors. Invest in a quality razor and change the blade, or use an electric razor. Consider growing a beard.

19. Invest in electronic equipment and other durable goods that have warranties and are easy to repair. Donate old but functioning appliances to a local shelter, school, or nonprofit group instead of contributing to the solid waste problem by discarding them.

20. More than 200 million tires are discarded each year. This number can be reduced by buying high-mileage tires and by maintaining the proper air pressure in tires. Check the tire pressure every other time the gas tank is filled.

21. Consider a dairy service to have milk products delivered in refillable bottles. If family members drink bottled water, use a water service that provides large refillable bottles rather than buying individual bottles at the grocery store.

22. Yard trimmings and food scraps account for 25 percent of America's municipal solid waste. Recycling them saves landfill space and reduces the need for incineration. Composting yard waste and kitchen scraps is simple and inexpensive. The end product can be used in the lawn or garden where it aerates the soil and aids in drainage. It also gives nutrients back to the soil with less danger of contaminating local water supplies than that posed by chemical fertilizers. In addition, plants grown in compost-enriched soil need less watering than others and resist disease better.

ENERGY-RELATED ACTIVITIES

Energy-related activities that can be implemented in a home setting and result in waste reduction are provided below. The reader is again reminded that the generation of energy, for example, electrical energy, produces waste and pollution. Thus, any energy conservation activity is a pollution prevention measure.

1. The location of the house can enhance the use of natural sources of energy, which conserves other energy use.

2. The direction of the sun on the house, prevailing winds, shade and shelter from trees and terrain must be considered by the architect.

3. The design and type of materials used in the construction of the house have an impact on energy conservation. Selection of concrete, steel, wood, plastic, insulation, number of openings, doors, and windows must be made with future energy conservation in mind.

4. Construct a steel-framed house. With the shortage and high price of quality lumber, it is predicted that 25 percent of all houses built between now and the year 2000 will have steel frames. Steel-framed houses use recycled steel. Steel wall framing can be placed on 4- or 8-foot centers instead of the 16-inch centers common with standard wood framing. This reduces the thermal bridges, or gaps, in the wall insulation. The steel framing also provides room for nine inches of wall insulation, providing an insulation level of better than R-30. Another energy advantage of steel framing is that steel settles very little over time. Therefore, the house should remain airtight over its life, and windows and doors should continue to fit and operate smoothly (Dudley, 1994).

5. Ask the local utility to do a walk-through and provide suggestions on ways to conserve energy in the house.

6. All new residential-sized furnaces are required by Federal law to carry an Annual Fuel Utilization Efficiency rating (AFUE), and to achieve an AFUE of at least 78 percent.

7. Heating is the single biggest energy user in the house. A well-maintained heating system will hold down fuel costs and provide reliable comfort. The system should be checked periodically by a professional to assure efficiency.

8. During the winter, keep the thermostat at 70 degrees Fahrenheit during the day, lowering it when the family retires. For every degree over 70, one can expect to use 3 percent more heating energy.

9. Zone thermostats can help save energy by allowing the homeowner to adjust heating or cooling demands for different sections of the house. An automatic setback thermostat offers comfort and convenience since it allows the user to program different comfort and setback periods for each day of the week.

10. The hot water heater is the second largest energy consumer in the house. Using it efficiently can add up to big savings. One can save up to 10 percent on water heating costs by simply wrapping a fiberglass blanket around the water heater and securing it with duct tape, or by installing a ready-made insulation kit. Most new heaters are already insulated and do not need additional fiberglass blankets.

11. Proper maintenance assures the heater's efficiency. Drain a few gallons of water from the heater every six months to remove sediment that accumulates and reduces the heater's efficiency. Consult the owner's guide for other maintenance recommendations.

12. If the house will be vacant for two or more days, lower the temperature of the water heater.

13. The hot water heater setting can safely be lowered to 130 to 140 degrees Fahrenheit for families with an automatic dishwasher. Without a dishwasher, the setting can be lowered to 110 to 120 degrees Fahrenheit.

14. Central air conditioning is found in three of every four new houses. Even though government standards have made the equipment much more energy efficient than in years past, it is still a tremendous energy user. One can significantly reduce annual operating costs simply by raising the thermostat setting two or three degrees—from 74 to 76 degrees Fahrenheit. The homeowner can compare competing brands for efficiency by checking the Seasonal Energy Efficiency Rating (SEER).

15. The material used for the air conditioning ducts as well as how firmly the sections are connected is an energy concern. Cold air leaking from seams or migrating through the duct walls can drastically increase overall operating costs.

16. Before purchasing an air conditioner, determine how much cooling capacity is needed. Too large a model tends to cycle on and off so much that it might not properly dehumidify the room. Too small a unit may not keep the room cool enough. In the appliance store, check the bright yellow Energy Guide label that displays the Energy Efficiency Rating (EER) for an indication of how much it will cost to operate.

17. After installation, consult the owner's guide and follow maintenance recommendations for washing filters and vacuuming coils. Public utilities esimate regular changing of filters can save up to 20 percent in energy costs (Christman, 1994).

18. Under the right conditions, a whole-house fan can ventilate an entire house on the electricity an air conditioner would use to cool one room.

19. A ceiling fan can work up enough of a breeze to make one feel cooler. This wind-chill effect can make a room that is 82 degrees feel like 75 degrees Fahrenheit. Even an air-conditioned room will seem cooler if a ceiling fan stirs the air. That allows the air conditioner's thermostat to be set higher and result in a small but modest saving on utility bills.

20. Vents in the gable ends, the eaves, and along the roof ridge help let out the heat. Adequate insulation will slow heat buildup, though it may not reduce overall cooling costs. A radiant barrier (reflective foil on the attic floor) can help slow the flow of heat to the rooms below.

21. When choosing windows, the frame has a significant effect on a window's thermal performance, price, and upkeep. Wood frames, plain or clad in vinyl or aluminum, tend to be more expensive than all vinyl. Aluminum is a good heat conductor. In a temperate climate, an aluminum frame may be a practical choice but it will not offer the best thermal protection in cold New England winters.

22. The glass one chooses also affects a window's price and performance. Single glazed are best reserved for garages and other spaces that do not require heating or cooling. Most new house have double-pane. In a regular double-glazed window, air fills the gap between the panes. A step up in thermal performance and price are windows filled with an inert gas, usually argon. Low emissivity (low-e) glass has a coating that helps reduce heat loss in the winter and heat gain in the summer by blocking nearly all the long-wave infrared rays. Some low-e coatings, designed for hot climates or southern exposures, reduce the buildup of heat from the sun. Other low-e coatings, meant for cold climates, allow more of the sun's warmth into the house.

23. Weather stripping, which blocks drafts around doors and windows, will not save much energy. Recent studies have shown that such drafts actually contribute little to overall heat loss. Still, weather stripping will do a lot to make the house feel more comfortable; this may save some energy indirectly since the homeowner may not feel the necessity to turn up the thermostat as much if the room is not drafty.

24. When choosing a home appliance, consult the bright yellow Energy Guide label that displays the unit's energy efficiency rating (EER). It represents a measure of how much it costs to operate. In most cases, the higher the EER, the lower the unit's energy costs.

25. The United States Department of Energy has required all refrigerators made after January 1, 1993 to use about 30 percent less electricity than used previously. Further tightening of the standard is expected for 1998.

26. Choose a refrigerator which has the least amount of chloroflurocarbons (CFCs). Most refrigerators of this type will be phased out by 1996.

27. Take care not to place the refrigerator right next to the range, or where sunlight will fall on it; otherwise, it will have to work harder to stay cool.

28. Clean the refrigerator regularly. Periodically clean and dust the condenser coils and air vents found in the back or bottom of the refrigerator according to the instruction manual.

29. The refrigerator contents should be arranged efficiently for the purpose of good air circulation, and items should be placed logically with good visibility so that family members can open the door, make a selection, and shut the door. Contents should also be placed and replaced in the same position so that food does not go unnoticed and unconsumed, eventually spoiling and thus wasted.

30. Set the freezer thermostat at 0 degrees Fahrenheit—a lower temperature does not improve storage life much and adds to energy consumption. A tightly packed freezer keeps food colder with less energy use. When the freezer is not packed, make ice cubes, put them in bags, and fill the freezer with them.

31. Keep a bottle of drinking water in the refrigerator instead of running the tap until the water gets cool each time a drink is wanted.

32. Bathrooms should be equipped with energy conservation in mind. Install water-flow reduction devices in the showers. Faucet aerators should be used in faucets. These devices reduce hot water use by one-third without affecting water pressure.

33. When brushing teeth, shaving, soaping up or shampooing in the shower, do not waste water.

34. When leaving a room, turn off the lights.

35. Do not leave the television on unless a program is being watched.

36. Lighting controls or "timers" can help save energy dollars. Timers can be set to run lights on or off at predetermined times, while photocell controls are sensitive to light, and turn lamps on and off at sundown and sunrise.

37. Consider using task lighting (lighting directed at a specific area) instead of overhead or general lighting that may light unused areas. By limiting lighting only to areas where it is needed, savings in the cost of both the bulbs and energy can be made.

38. Light-colored walls reflect light, which can reduce the number and wattage of bulbs.

39. Arrange furniture to take advantage of natural light.

40. During warm weather, cook outside to avoid heating the kitchen with the heat from the oven which necessitates the need for air conditioning.

41. Consult recipes so that ingredients can be organized. For instance, if some ingredients will be used in several dishes, they can be chopped or minced ahead of time, divided up, even frozen, and ready when needed.

42. On the top of the range, use pots and pans that are properly sized to fit the burners. Using a small pan on a large burner wastes energy; the use of a large pan on a small burner is energy-inefficient as well.

43. Use the oven efficiently. Organize baking so that the oven is not heated and reheated unnecessarily.

44. Do not "peek" in the oven. Every time the door is opened, the temperature drops approximately 25 degrees Fahrenheit and the oven has to use more energy to raise the temperature to its original setting.

45. It is not necessary to preheat the oven when cooking dishes that require more than an hour.

46. Certain dishes can be prepared in quantity at an energy savings.

47. If quality is not affected, allow frozen dishes to defrost in the refrigerator before baking to reduce the length of time it would take to heat the dish from a frozen state to the proper temperature in the oven.

48. Use oven-to-table serving dishes rather than separate dishes when possible.

49. Conserve energy with a microwave; it cooks food more rapidly and uses 70 to 80 percent less electricity than a regular oven.

50. Conserve water with a dishwasher. More water is wasted when dishes are handwashed. If dishes must be rinsed or scrubbed beforehand, have a pot filled with water for this purpose.

51. Run a full dishwasher and save energy. Eighty percent of the energy used in automatic dishwashers goes toward heating water.

52. If the dishwasher does not have the energy-saver option, open the dishwasher door after the rinse cycle to allow the dishes to air dry.

53. Minimize the use of lights and heat-emitting appliances during the day when cooling loads are the highest. Run the appliances at night whenever possible. Rates are usually lower at off-peak hours when demand drops. A few electric utilities are set to open a high-tech communications link with customers that will allow them to program their appliances as they do a videocassette recorder, turning devices on and off to take advantage of the lowest rates and possibly reducing home electric bills by hundreds of dollars a year. In a pilot program, the American Electric Power Company of Columbus, Ohio, one of the nation's largest utilities, found that customers using the new system in Ohio, West Virginia, and Indiana cut electricity use 50 to 60 percent during peak hours. According to an assistant controller for American Electric, the resulting cut in demand could allow the utility to defer building new generating plants, helping to hold down rates (Salpukas, July 6, 1944).

The reader is referred to Chapter 27 for additional details on energy conservation measures in the home that serve as pollution prevention measures.

OTHER GENERAL ACTIVITIES

Other general waste reduction activities that can be accomplished at home are provided below. Some of these will be examined again in Chapter 34.

1. Landscaping is an important component in energy conservation. The direction of the sun, prevailing winds, shade and shelter from trees, and terrain play a part.

2. Select shrubs and trees not only for their beauty but for the year-round effect these have on energy needs of the house.

3. Deciduous trees (those that shed their leaves in winter) provide a great deal of shade during the summer months. This cooling effect decreases the need for air conditioning. In the winter months when these trees lose their leaves, sunlight is allowed to pass through, thus providing the house with solar warmth.

4. A natural shelter of shrubs at an entrance doorway can divert and minimize the effect of chilling winter winds and reduce the amount of heat loss.

5. Plant shrubs that curtail soil erosion, particularly at the foundation of the house. The soil protects the foundation and allows the structure to be more effectively maintained using less energy.

6. Allow shrubs to grow in their natural shapes rather than sculpturing to decrease the amount of energy used for maintenance.

7. Develop a habitat that encourages natural control of insects rather than resort to energy users such as electronic zappers. Make an effort to attract and protect birds. Insects form a large part of avian sustenance. Interestingly, birds are most numerous and active just at those times when harmful insects are at their height of activity (Seymour, 1970).

8. Birds consume large quantities of weed seeds. Furthermore, small rodents that are troublesome in the garden form a large part of the diet of birds of prey. This control by nature should be encouraged as opposed to a control measure that requires energy.

9. Cultivate fruit trees and a vegetable garden. Superior varieties may be grown in a home garden. The products can be freshly gathered at their peak of perfection. The homeowner will produce food energy for the family and expend only the energy used in the physical labor of planting and caring for the produce. The energy expended at the plant store is much less than that spent while shopping at the supermarket for the same yield, and is often far more satisfying.

10. Use a manual lawnmower and hand tools when possible.

11. When shopping for garden machinery or tools, check the bright yellow Energy Guide label that displays the unit's EER, or energy efficiency rating. It represents a measure of how much it costs to operate. In most cases, the higher the EER, the lower the unit's energy costs.

12. Consider whether the use of electric rather than gas-powered machines and tools are more energy efficient.

13. Machinery and tools should be maintained according to their guidebooks to insure efficient and energy conscious operation and at the same time prolong the life of the appliance.

14. Energy conservation measures can be shown to include conserving water. This and the following suggestions are related to this measure. Giving the lawn or garden too much water wastes water and money, and does not help the plants. Position sprinkler and hoses carefully. Sidewalks need not be dampened.

15. Water early or late in the day, avoiding the full sun, to minimize evaporation.

16. Apply water slowly to prevent runoff. In a garden, consider using a soaker hose. For a large plant or shrub, create a "catch basin" around its trunk.

17. Put in ground cover and plants that can survive on moderate amounts of water. Contact a local nursery or a Cooperative Extension Service to learn more about water-saving vegetation suited to a particular area (*Consumer Reports,* 1992).

18. Set out a rain barrel to create a reservoir when needed or to fill a watering can or wash a car.

19. Use mulch to help retain moisture, prevent erosion and inhibit weeds.

20. Have a paper handy during the day to jot down items that are needed. Before leaving the house to shop, make a master list. This will organize the outing in the most efficient way.

21. Only buy needed items and never shop when you are hungry. Do not allow children to convince you to buy unneeded items.

22. Shop during off-peak hours whenever possible.

23. Walk, bike or take public transportation whenever possible.

24. Coordinate shopping with friends and car pool to save energy.

25. Shop by catalog.

26. Take advantage of the telephone to comparison shop.

27. When shopping for any new appliance, look for the yellow Energy Guide label which indicates the unit's energy efficiency.

28. Buy products that are packaged with energy conservation in mind.

29. Since energy is required to produce nearly any product, buy products that make use of recycled material.

30. Carry a reusable tote rather than taking a new bag each time.

31. When planning a trip for business or pleasure, think in an environmentally conscious way. Preparation will pay dividends in enjoyment and efficient use of available hours and energy.

32. If traveling by personal car, it should be in maximum operating condition. Before embarking on a long trip, the car should be given a thorough inspection by a competent mechanic. The destination, the weather and varied type of terrain should be taken in to consideration.

33. Allowing two and one-half hours for each 100 miles provides reasonable allowance for driving time, meals, gasoline, rest stops, and has been shown to conserve energy (as well as lives).

34. Pack the car sensibly but travel as lightly as possible. An overloaded car consumes more energy and is dangerous for many reasons. It is more difficult to drive and adds stress to the car and the driver. Occupants are uncomfortable, which contributes to stress. In warm weather, the overcrowding also generates more heat requiring more air conditioning. Further, if a repair has to be made, the car may have to be unloaded.

35. When the air conditioner is first turned on, leave the car windows open so that the hot air is blown out. The air conditioner will have less overheated air to cool.

36. Conserve fuel and brakes by using smart driving techniques. Avoid jackrabbit starts and do not accelerate up to a stop.

37. Underinflated car tires can worsen fuel economy, degrade handling, and accelerate tire wear. Overinflated tires harshen the ride, wear unevenly, and sometimes contribute to blowouts. Consumers Union recommends that tires be checked at least once a month. An estimated 3 billion scrap tires dot the landscape in legal and illegal dumps.

38. Travel during off-peak time. It is more energy conscious for many reasons. Since there is less volume, there is less time and energy wasted waiting in line, on the road, in train stations, airports, and restaurants. Airlines and hotels often offer incentives to travel during off-peak hours in an effort to increase capacity and offset losses at these times.

39. When staying away from home, at a hotel or with relatives, continue to use and recommend the same energy conscious practices that you would do in your own home.

40. Coordinate trips to conserve energy. Avoid situations such as two cars traveling to the same destination when a carpool could have been utilized.

Before pollution prevention becomes a fully accepted way of life, considerable effort still needs to be expended to change the way we look at waste management. A desire to use "green" products and services will be of no avail in a market where these goods are not available. Participation in pollution prevention programs will increase through continued education, community efforts, and lobbying for change. Market incentives can be created and strengthened by tax policies, price preferences, and packaging regulations created at the federal, state, and local levels. We should all do our part by communicating with industry and expressing our concerns. For example, citizens should feel free to write letters to decision makers at both business organizations and government institutions regarding specific products or legislation. Letters can be positive demonstrating personal endorsement of a green product, or disapproving, expressing discontent and reluctance to use a particular product because of its negative environmental effect (Theodore & McGuinn, 1992).

Is all this worthwhile? Both the EPA and environmental groups have claimed that applying the pollution prevention principles into practice is likely to require some change in our daily routines, but that these changing habits will not necessarily result in a more difficult lifestyle. Although this has yet to be shown, it does appear some modest changes in lifestyle may be in order. The long-term impact on the economy of not buying the extra family car (perhaps for the kids), a TV for another room, a new dress to replace a "used" or already worn one, extra shoes, and so on has also yet to be determined, and could have a significant effect on jobs. This may very well bring about changes, perhaps dramatically, to our industrial economy.

SUMMARY

1. The past two decades have seen an increased social awareness of the impact of our lifestyles on the environment. Public environmental concerns include issues such as waste disposal, hazardous material regulations, depletion of natural resources, as well as air, water, and land pollution. Nevertheless, roughly one-half of the total quantity of waste generated each year can be attributed to domestic sources!

2. Three pollution prevention measures related to solvents, paints and pesticides that can be implemented at home include:

a. Take leftover solvents, paints and pesticides to a household hazardous waste day. Nationwide, more than 1,000 programs were held in 1993.

b. Keep solvents, paints, and pesticides in well-ventilated racks, out of reach of children and animals.

c. Do not flush solvents, paints and pesticides down a toilet or drain. A sewage treatment plant cannot break down all toxic substances; some enter surrounding waterways.

3. Three pollution prevention measures related to recycle/reuse activities that can be implemented at home include:

a. Encourage local schools and village offices to follow recycling practices for environmental and economic reasons.

b. Spread the word at fast-food restaurants by commenting to managers about good/bad habits. Let personnel know that you appreciate environmentally conscientious franchises.

c. Shop for products that have as little packaging as possible. Buy the largest-sized package or a concentrate at the store and then, at home, mix and refill in container of your choice.

4. Three pollution prevention measures related to energy activities that can be implemented at home include:

a. Ask the local utility to do a walk-through and provide suggestions on ways to conserve energy in the house.

b. Under the right conditions, a whole-house fan can ventilate an entire house on the electricity an air conditioner would use to cool one room.

c. When choosing an appliance, consult the bright yellow Energy Guide label that displays the unit's energy efficiency rating (EER); it represents a measure of how much it costs to operate. In most cases, the higher the EER, the lower the unit's energy costs.

5. Three pollution prevention measures related to other general activities that can be implemented at home include:

a. Landscaping is an important component in energy conservation. The direction of the sun, prevailing winds, shade and shelter from trees and terrain play a part.

b. Cultivate fruit trees and a vegetable garden. Superior varieties may be grown in a home garden. The products can be freshly gathered at their peak of perfection.

c. Walk, bike, or take public transportation whenever possible.

REFERENCES

Christman, L. "Air Conditioners Need Spring Service," *Newsday,* May 26, 1994.

Consumers Reports, February, 1994.

Consumers Reports, May 1992.

Dulley, J. "Steel Yourself for Big Task of Building Your Own House," *Newsday,* May 28, 1994, C7.

Holmes, G., Singh, R., and Theodore, L. *Handbook of Environmental Management and Technology.* New York: Wiley-Interscience, 1993.

Salpukas, A. "Big Hopes Put on Electric Wires." The New York Times, July 6, 1994, D1.

Seymour, E. L. D. (ed.). *The Wise Garden Encyclopedia,* New York: Grosset & Dunlap, 1970.

Theodore, L., and McGuinn, Y. *Pollution Prevention,* New York: Van Nostrand Reinhold, 1992.

33

At Work

INTRODUCTION

Many of the same comments, suggestions, and procedures provided in the previous chapter (Chapter 32, At Home) also apply to environmental measures that can be implemented in the office. There has been an attempt to eliminate raw duplication with earlier material; however, this chapter has been written in a manner that will allow it to be read on a stand-alone basis. Nevertheless, the concerned reader may choose to also read the previous chapter.

The easiest, most direct way for the office worker to make a difference is to simply become environmentally aware and to apply the pollution prevention principles presented in Chapters 30 and 31. There are many areas of environmental concern in an office setting. One of the main issues deals with the generation of waste pollution. As described earlier, Americans generate millions of tons of waste each year in the form of wrappings, bottles, boxes, cans, food scraps, furniture, and many other items. Products that are bought and thrown away can have a significant impact on the environment. Products (and packaging) designed to be thrown away after a single use can increase disposal costs, deplete natural resources, contribute to litter, and add to the nation's waste disposal problem. Another area of concern is energy conservation. This issue arose when the country was in the early stages of the first wave of national environmental awareness. The Arab oil embargo introduced the energy-economy synergy; the concept of energy conservation as an environmental protection measure emerged soon afterward. It did not take long for people to realize that when auto mileage efficiency doubled, both the gasoline cost for driving and auto emissions were halved.

This chapter attempts to address many of the these environmental problems. The use of "at work" pollution prevention principles clearly does not involve the use of high-technology equipment or major lifestyle changes; success is only dependent upon active and willing public participation. One person can make a difference. This chapter proposes some of the well documented as well as some of the not-so-well documented pollution prevention solutions. It is divided into four topics (or sections) to which the office worker is regularly exposed and to which the pollution prevention principle can be simple and readily applied. These include:

1. Minimizing waste generation
2. Recycle/reuse activities
3. Energy-related activities
4. Other general activities

A separate section is provided for each subject area.

MINIMIZING WASTE GENERATION*

Environmentalists often urge the public to "reduce, reuse, recycle." Significantly, recycling is third on the list—less desirable than reusing material or reducing the amount used in the first place. A key part of environmental planning is what is being called "source reduction"—the design or purchasing choices that reduce the amount of materials used for a given purpose. It is an area in which packaged-goods manufacturers have been particularly active in recent years. For example, non-reusuable glass containers, on average, weighed 44 percent less in 1987 than in 1972.

The manufacture of complex products consumes considerable energy—to mine and refine minerals, power the assembly plant, and transport goods from plant to store. In the office, machines become obsolete, wear out, or, are not worth repairing. Few are recycled; the metals, plastics, and such used in making them generally go up in smoke or back into the ground, and are lost for future use. Discarding durable goods not only wastes valuable materials—it can often unleash hazardous ones. Durable goods are a bit like a boomerang. They are thrown out, but the hazards they contain can return. The disposal of durable goods needs to be addressed on a national level, as Germany has. A legislative experiment in Germany, called "Dual System," was set up to cover all forms of packaging, from shipping containers to toothpaste boxes. The law required manufacturers to either meet recycling quotas (at least 60 percent of various materials must be recycled) or to take back all the packaging they put on the market. Products are now shipped to retailers in reusable plastic containers instead of cardboard boxes.

Some waste generation practices that minimize pollution in the office are:

1. Paper waste is estimated to be 38 percent of municipal solid waste. Reducing the amount of paper waste would save more landfill space than any other material.

2. Use recycled paper material. "The problem with throwing away a ton of cardboard is not that it is going to hurt somebody if you burn it or bury it," says John Schall, an environmental economist. "The problem is that you have to make the next ton of cardboard by cutting down trees, which has immensely greater environmental impact than disposing of it."

3. Collect newsprint and office paper and then sell it to paper mills. Recycled paper quality

---

*Information for the next four sections was drawn from Holmes, Singh, and Theodore, 1993, and Theodore and McGuinn, 1992.

is improving as more mills invest in new equipment as these companies sense the support they receive from consumers. Since 1989, the industry has spent nearly two billion dollars to triple the number of mills making recycled newsprint in North America.

4. In some offices, it is cost efficient to have a main filing system that avoids duplication of material. This could save on material and office space.

5. Share or rent office equipment where feasible.

6. Buy in bulk. Also buy concentrates and refill smaller containers.

7. Consider the environmental impact of new office construction. In a study of landfills, it was found that about 12 percent of what is buried is waste from construction—chunks of concrete, splintered wood, old windows, and so on. Cost-effective alternatives, such as sharing an office or partitioning into a smaller space, should be investigated before construction is undertaken.

8. In bathrooms, install water flow reduction devices. Consider installation of sensors that turn water on and off, and flush toilets by body heat.

9. Post signs to remind employees to conserve water by turning faucets off and reporting any water leaks.

10. Maintain a smoke-free work place. The atmosphere is cleaner and there is less pollution for the air filter to capture. The office windows and walls will be cleaner and easier to maintain. A smoke-free workplace also presents one less fire hazard to worry about.

11. Get employees involved in waste minimizing efforts. Post economic saving results as well as health benefits for this activity.

RECYCLE/REUSE ACTIVITIES

Many analysts have now compared the environmental impact of using virgin raw materials—both in harvesting or mining the materials, and in preparing them for use in factories—versus the environmental costs of collecting, sorting, and remanufacturing recycled materials. In almost every case, using recycled materials has substantial environmental benefits.

An unusually thorough analysis done by the Tellus Institute, a Boston environmental consulting group and think tank, found that a major benefit of using recycled materials is that it saves energy. And, energy use is responsible for major environmental impacts of production: the depletion of nonrenewable resources, air pollution, the generation of greenhouse gases that may contribute to global warming, and so on. Using recycled materials can make a huge difference in energy use in some cases. Recycling also reduces the environmental impact of obtaining raw materials in the first place.

Recycling does help to keep garbage out of landfills and incinerators, both of which may pose environmental problems. Recycling's greatest advantage may not be at the dump, but at the factory. Making new products out of recycled materials almost always produces much less air and water pollution, and uses up much less energy than making the products out of virgin raw material (*Consumer Reports,* 1993).

Recycle/reuse activities at work that can result in waste reduction are provided below.

1. Use recycled paper whenever possible.

2. Avoid practices that waste space on correspondence, for example, using wide margins, double-spaced or large printing, or using only one side of the paper.

3. For interoffice mail, circulate one copy, when feasible, instead of sending several. After the worker has read the material, he or she indicates he or she has seen it, and routes it on to the next person.

4. Reuse envelopes in the same manner.

5. Open cardboard boxes carefully so that they may be reused.

6. Do not fax unnecessarily.

7. If new machinery must be purchased, invest in equipment that has warranties or is easy to repair.

8. Consider renting or sharing office equipment when it is cost efficient.

9. Buy used equipment or furniture at a reduced rate.

10. Donate office equipment or furniture that is not needed to a school or rehabilitation center.

11. Keep a personal mug or drinking glass at work to avoid using a new container each time a beverage is refilled.

12. Follow this same idea for meals or snacks. Instead of using a "brown bag" carry a reusable container which eliminates the need for foil, plastic, etc.

13. Set up a recycling section to encourage and make it convenient for employees to recycle. Discuss the long-range health benefits as well as cost efficiency of this project.

14. Recycle whatever one can and follow the locality's specific recycling instructions to the letter. If sorting is haphazard, the pool of material collected could be unusable.

15. Set up a suggestion box for recycling ideas and reward employees whose ideas are implemented.

ENERGY-RELATED ACTIVITIES

Office equipment is the fastest growing electricity load in the commercial sector. Computer systems alone are believed to account for five percent of commercial electricity consumption, and this figure is expected to rise to ten percent by the year 2000. Research shows that the vast majority of time the nation's 30 to 35 million personal computers are turned on, and that they are not actively in use—and 30 to 40 percent are left running at night and on weekends. Some details of the Energy Star program described in Chapter 28 are presented below.

President Clinton recently announced that the federal government—the largest buyer of computers in the world—is committed to purchasing only Energy Star compliant products. Clinton's executive order directs United States agencies to acquire only desktop computers, monitors, and printers that meet EPA Energy Star requirements, provided that they are commercially available and meet the agencies' performance needs. The order took effect in October 1993.

Through corporate purchasing efforts modeled after EPA's Green Lights program, the EPA will encourage consumers to buy computers bearing the ENERGY STAR trademark logo wherever possible. Under agreements signed with EPA through Green Lights, over 1,200 organizations and government agencies have been committed to energy-efficient lighting upgrades.

By the year 2000, Energy Star Computers and other campaigns to promote energy efficient computer equipment will lead to an estimated savings of 26 billion kilowatt-hours of electricity annually, reduced from an estimated consumption of 70 billion kilowatt-hours per year. These savings will reduce emissions of the primary greenhouse gas (see Chapter 42) carbon dioxide by 20 million tons—the equivalent discharge from 5 million automobiles. Also reduced will be emissions of 140 thousand tons of sulfur dioxide and 75 thousand tons of nitrogen oxide, the two pollutants most responsible for acid rain (see Chapter 41).

Purchasing decisions for office equipment usually depend on such characteristics as price, speed, reliability, and quality. Many corporate equipment purchasers fail to account for the costs of the electricity to operate office equipment, and the energy and equipment costs of removing the heat this equipment creates in an office or building (Theodore & McGuinn, 1992). This new innovative program should provide some major energy conservation results if properly applied across-the-board to all office equipment and procedures.

Energy-related activities that can be implemented in a work setting and result in waste reduction are provided below. The reader is again reminded that the generation of energy, for example, electrical energy, produces waste and pollution. Thus, any energy conservation activity is a pollution prevention measure.

1. The location of an office site can enhance the use of natural sources of energy, thus conserving other energy use.

2. The direction of the sun on the structure, prevailing winds, shade and shelter from trees, and terrain must be considered by the architect.

3. The design and type of materials used in the construction of the building have an impact on energy conservation. Selection of concrete, steel, wood, plastic, insulation, number of openings, doors, windows, and so on must be made with future energy conservation in mind.

4. Consider a steel-framed building.

5. Ask the local utility to do a walk through and provide suggestions on ways to conserve energy in the office.

6. A well-maintained heating system will reduce fuel costs and provide reliable comfort. The system should be checked periodically by a professional to assure efficiency.

7. During the winter, maintain the thermostat at 70 degrees Fahrenheit during the work day. For every degree over 70, approximately 3 percent more heating energy is consumed.

8. Zone thermostats can help save energy by allowing the staff to adjust heating or cooling demands for different sections of the office. An automatic setback thermostat offers comfort and convenience since it allows the user to program different comfort and setback periods for each day of the week.

9. During warm weather, most people are comfortable at room temperatures ranging from 72 to 78 degrees Fahrenheit and at a relative humidity ranging from 25 to 55 percent. Central air conditioning is an expensive kind of cooling but annual operating costs can be significantly reduced by raising the thermostat setting two or three degrees, for example, from 74 to 76 degrees Fahrenheit.

10. The material used for the air conditioning ducts as well as how firmly the sections are connected is an energy concern. Cold air leaking from seams or migrating through the duct walls can drastically increase overall operating costs.

11. Before an air conditioner for an office is purchased, a determination should be made of how much cooling capacity is needed. Too large a model tends to cycle on and off so much that it might not properly dehumidify an area. Too small a unit may not keep the area cool enough. The bright yellow Energy Guide label that displays the Energy Efficiency Rating (EER) should be consulted for an indication of how much it will cost to operate.

12. Maintenance recommendations for washing filters and vacuuming coils should be followed. Filters clogged with dust from recirculating room air reduce efficiency, increase energy consumption, and is a health concern as well. Public utilities estimate regular changing of filters can save up to 20 percent in energy costs (Christman, 1994).

13. A ceiling fan can work up enough of a breeze to make the occupants of an area feel cooler. This windchill effect can make a room that is 82 degrees feel like 75 degrees Fahrenheit. Even an air-conditioned room will seem cooler if a ceiling fan stirs the air. That allows the air conditioner's thermostat to be set higher and result in a small but modest saving on utility bills.

14. A small individual fan at one's workstation has a cooling effect.

15. Shades or blinds can reduce the amount of sunlight entering the office, thus reducing the need for cooling. In cooler weather, sunlight can be used for its warming effects.

16. When choosing new windows, the frame has a significant effect on a window's thermal performance, price, and upkeep. Wood frames, plain or clad in vinyl or aluminum, tend to be more expensive than all vinyl. Aluminum is a good heat conductor. In a temperate climate, an aluminum frame may be a practical choice, but it will not offer the best thermal protection in cold New England winters.

17. The type of glass also affects a window's price and performance. Single glazed are best reserved for garages or storage areas and other spaces that do not require heating or cooling. Most new windows are double-pane. In a regular double-glazed window, air fills the gap between the panes. A step up in thermal performance and price are windows filled with an inert gas, usually argon. Low emissivity (low-e) glass has a coating that helps reduce heat loss in the winter and heat gain in the summer by blocking nearly all the long-wave infrared rays. Some low-e coatings, designed for hot climates or southern exposures, reduce the buildup of heat from the sun. Other low-e coatings, meant for cold climates, allow more of the sun's warmth into the house.

18. Weather stripping, which blocks drafts around doors and windows, will not save much energy. Recent studies have shown that such drafts actually contribute little to overall heat loss. Still, weather stripping will help make the work place feel more comfortable. That may save some energy indirectly, since the worker may not feel the necessity to turn up the thermostat as much if the room is not drafty.

19. Install water-flow reduction devices in the employee washroom and showers. Faucet aerators are small "flow control" devices that easily fit in bathroom faucets. These devices reduce hot water use by one-third without affecting water pressure.

20. Plumbing problems should be reported and repairs made promptly.

21. When leaving a room, turn off the lights. Post signs reminding employees to turn off lights when they are not needed.

22. Automatic timers can help save energy dollars. Timers can be set to turn lights or equipment on or off at predetermined times. Photocell controls are sensitive to light, and turn lamps on and off at sundown and sunrise.

23. Use durable fluorescent bulbs. Fluorescent bulbs are more expensive, but last ten times longer and use 75 percent less electricity. These bulbs also emit less heat, which is easier on the air conditioning system.

24. Consider using task lighting (lighting directed at a specific area) instead of overhead or general lighting that may light unused areas. By limiting lighting only to areas where it is needed, savings in the cost of both the bulbs and energy can be made.

25. Light-colored walls reflect light, which can reduce the number and wattage of bulbs.

26. Arrange furniture to take advantage of natural light.

27. Minimize the use of lights and heat-emitting appliances during the day when cooling loads are the highest. Run appliances and heavy machinery at night whenever possible. Rates are usually lower at off-peak hours when demand drops.

28. Since some equipment use considerable energy when powering up, determine if it is cost-effective to turn the machine on and off at scheduled times.

29. Institute summer hours where possible. Start shifts at an earlier hour to take advantage of cooler morning hours.

OTHER GENERAL ACTIVITIES

Other general waste reduction activities that can be accomplished at work are provided below.

1. Walk, bike, or use public transportation as an alternative to automobile use.

2. If an automobile must be used, consider arranging an office shuttle service.

3. Encourage carpooling.

4. If feasible, arrange shifts to avoid traveling to and from work during rush hours.

5. The company fleet should be well maintained. A well-tuned car is an energy efficient machine.

6. The personal car should be well maintained.

7. Travel should be well planned so as to be as energy conscious as possible.

8. Landscaping is an important component in energy conservation. The direction of the sun, prevailing winds, shade and shelter from trees, and terrain play a part.

9. Select shrubs and trees not only for their beauty but for the year-round effect these have on the energy needs of the building.

10. Deciduous trees (those that shed their leaves in winter) provide a great deal of shade during the summer months. This cooling effect decreases the need for air conditioning. In the winter months when these trees lose their leaves, sunlight is allowed to pass through, thus providing the building with solar warmth.

11. A natural shelter of shrubs at an entrance doorway can divert and minimize the effect of chilling winter winds and reduce the amount of heat loss.

12. Plant shrubs that curtail soil erosion, particularly at the foundation of the building. The soil protects the foundation and allows the structure to be more effectively maintained using less energy.

13. Put in ground cover and plants that can survive on moderate amounts of water.

13. Allow shrubs to grow in their natural shapes rather than sculpturing to decrease the amount of energy used for maintenance.

14. Make an effort to attract and protect birds. Develop a habitat which encourages a natural control of insects rather than resort to energy users or chemical means that may pollute the air and water supply (Seymour, 1970).

15. Consider whether the use of electric rather than gas-powered machines and tools are more energy efficient. According to the Environmental Protection Agency, small gas-powered engines create about 10 percent of all air pollution ("EPA to Limit Lawn Mower 'pollution,'" 1994).

The important point for the reader to keep in mind is that not only are all the suggestions provided above sound environmentally but they also make good economic sense. The bottom line for the office manager is to realize that these pollution prevention activities almost always either make money or save money or both.

SUMMARY

1. The easiest, most direct way for the office worker to make a difference is to simply become environmentally aware and to apply the pollution prevention principles presented in Chapters 30 and 31.

2. Three pollution prevention measures related to minimizing waste generation at work are:

a. Paper waste is estimated to be 38 percent of municipal solid waste. Reducing the amount of paper waste would save more landfill space than any other material.

b. Collect newsprint and office paper and then sell it to paper mills. Recycled paper quality is improving as more mills invest in new equipment as these companies sense the support they receive from consumers.

c. Buy in bulk. Also buy concentrates and refill smaller containers.

3. Three pollution prevention measures related to recycle/reuse activities that can be implemented at work include:

a. Open cardboard boxes carefully so that they may be reused.

b. Consider renting or sharing office equipment when it is cost efficient.

c. Set up a suggestion box for recycling ideas and reward employees whose ideas are implemented.

4. Three pollution prevention measures concerning energy related measures that can be implemented at work include:

a. The location of an office site can enhance the use of natural sources of energy, thus conserving other energy use.

b. Use durable fluorescent bulbs. Fluorescent bulbs are more expensive, but last ten times longer and use 75 percent less electricity. These bulbs also emit less heat, which is easier on the air conditioning system.

c. Institute summer hours where possible. Start shifts at an earlier hour to take advantage of cooler morning hours.

5. Three pollution prevention measures related to other general activities that can be implemented at work include:

a. Walk, bike, or use public transportation as an alternative to automobile use.

b. Deciduous trees (those that shed their leaves in winter) provide a great deal of shade during the summer months. This cooling effect decreases the need for air conditioning. In the winter months when these trees lose their leaves, sunlight is allowed to pass through, thus providing the building with solar warmth.

c. Make an effort to attract and protect birds. Develop a habitat that encourages natural control of insects rather than resort to energy users or chemical means that may pollute the air and water supply.

REFERENCES

Christman, L. "Air Conditioners Need Spring Service," *Newsday,* May 26, 1994, B43.

Consumer Reports, February, 1993.

"EPA to Limit Lawn Mower 'Pollution,' " *Newsday,* May 5, 1994, A3.

Holmes, G., Singh, R., and Theodore, L. *Handbook of Environmental Science and Technology.* New York: Wiley-Interscience, 1993.

Seymour, E. L. D. (ed.). *The Wise Garden Encyclopedia.* New York: Grosset & Dunlap, 1970.

Theodore, L., and McGuinn, Y. *Pollution Prevention.* New York: Van Nostrand Reinhold, 1992.

34

Other Waste Reduction Areas

INTRODUCTION

The outline and form of presentation for this chapter is similar to that provided in Chapters 25 and 29. It provides suggestions regarding pollution prevention measures of a waste reduction form that can be employed in the following areas:

1. Building a house
2. In the garden
3. Traveling and vacationing
4. Shopping
5. Dining and entertaining

A separate section is provided for each of the above topic areas. In addition to the two key references cited at the start of this part of the book, some material has also been drawn from other sources in the literature (M. K. Theodore, personal notes; Theodore and McGuinn, 1992; Holmes, Singh and Theodore, 1993).

BUILDING A HOUSE

1. Check references of architect and construction company.
2. Insure that all federal, state, and city codes are met.

3. Insure that building and land development will not disturb drainage, runoff, and shallow water table flows.

4. Plan construction considering natural topography of the land to prevent changing runoff patterns.

5. Avoid lot clearing (mass removal of trees) if possible.

6. Check for radon or other soil contaminants that may affect the health and safety of the dwellers.

7. Specialized jobs should be handled by qualified people so that time and material are not wasted.

8. Hire local contractors in order to cut down on transportation of workers and supplies.

9. Carefully determine required material to limit waste. Purchase only what is needed.

10. Borrow or rent machinery when feasible.

11. Use construction materials that are made from recycled materials.

12. Use precast or ready-made components when possible.

13. Use low-lead or water-base paints instead of oil.

14. Consider using plastic or vinyl siding on the house to avoid painting.

15. Avoid the use of foam-type insulation that releases chloroflurocarbons. Use non-toxic insulative materials. Investigate the use of insulation made from recycled material.

16. Avoid using asbestos as a building material.

17. Avoid the use of formaldehyde-containing building materials.

18. Use concrete instead of asphalt on driveways.

19. Use non aerosol sprays.

20. Use gas boilers, which are cleaner than oil, for heating.

21. Install air-conditioning systems that do not use Freon.

22. Install well-designed and highly efficient thermostat temperature control systems.

23. Consider skylights and solar collection devices.

24. Use proper ventilation design.

25. Install a good filter/exhaust system over the range top.

26. Install a water softener in the house to reduce the soap/detergent consumption.

27. Install flow restrictors on the shower heads.

28. Install low-flush toilets.

29. Use gray water (from showers and sinks) to flush toilets.

30. Clean up all spills.

31. Do not use drain lines for waste disposal.

32. Dust, smoke, or particulate producing operations should be carried out during calm weather conditions.

33. Build a water tank to collect rain water for irrigation purposes or to transport it to a useful area.

34. Build a storage area for recyclables.

35. Sort out material waste such as shingles and wood for recycling, reuse, or resale instead of burning.

36. Donate what is no longer needed.

37. Properly dispose of garbage and debris.

IN THE GARDEN

1. During the summer, the watering of lawns and gardens soars to the most overwhelmingly wasteful levels of the year. Experts say that too much water is unhealthy for plants, promoting weak root systems, fungal diseases, and rot.

2. Lay lawn seeds that use less water and still provide lush-looking grass.

3. Prepare soil properly, creating a humus-rich medium for plants and lawn that requires less fertilizer and less water to thrive.

4. Do not spray water into the air where it evaporates. Plan a modern in-line drip system that puts the water right into the root zone with pipes on or just below ground level.

5. Turn off the automatic feature on the sprinkler system and use the system only when needed.

6. Collect rainwater for irrigation.

7. Use cooking water to water the plants.

8. Use water from the dehumidifier for ironing or for watering plants.

9. Use a water sump pump to water the garden.

10. Replenish the organic content of the soil regularly by composting leaves, grass clippings, and any other vegetable waste.

11. Use a mulching lawnmower; the clippings get chopped finely by the special blade and quickly degrade to return nitrogen and some organic matter to the grass and soil.

12. Do not use a gas-powered mower. It has been estimated that an hour of mowing produces as much pollution as an average car produces in 11.5 hours.

13. Group plants according to their common needs. Do not plant drought-tolerant varieties and moisture-hungry plants together. To satisfy the thirstiest plants, the drought tolerant variety will be over watered (Roach, 1994).

14. Rotate plants in the garden to fertilize the soil naturally.

15. Save seeds from plants from the previous year to plant in the spring instead of buying them.

16. Use manual or semi-manual equipment and tools.

17. Use manual or mechanical, as opposed to chemical, weed control.

18. Create a habitat for birds by growing plants that offer food and shelter. Birds consume many harmful garden insects and pests (McKinley, 1994).

19. Place netting over plants as an animal deterrent.

20. Cultivate fruit trees and grow vegetables for family consumption.

21. Do not use hazardous pesticides or herbicides.

22. Use nonaerosol sprays.

23. Spray on a still day to avoid missing the target and polluting the air.

24. Buy supplies that use the least amount of packaging.

25. Buy in bulk when it is more economical.

26. Buy only what is needed.

27. Read instructions on chemicals regarding proper storage and disposal.

28. Think of ways to reuse items that would typically be discarded.

29. Borrow or rent gardening items that are used infrequently.

30. Donate tools that are no longer needed as well as surplus supplies that would otherwise become outdated.

TRAVELING AND VACATIONING

1. Walk, bike, or take public transportation to destination.

2. Visit the library, contact the American Automobile Association (AAA) or a travel agency for information and maps about area to be visited.

3. Plan best route to destination.

4. Take a walking tour or bus tour instead of sightseeing in an individual car.

5. If traveling by personal car, insure that car is conditioned for trip.

6. Pack the car lightly. A loaded car is not fuel efficient and a crowded car is uncomfortable for occupants.

7. Try not to pack things on top of the car, since wind resistance decreases fuel efficiency.

8. Carry a container for beverages that can be refilled instead of using a disposable container each time.

9. Carry a container for garbage and dispose of the contents properly.

10. Borrow or rent items that are used infrequently.

11. Buy reusable and refillable products.

12. Travel by airplane or train when going long distances.

13. Take advantage of shuttle transportation to and from airports.

14. Do not forget pollution prevention measures when away from home.

15. Abide by all local recycling programs.

16. Try to leave the areas the way one would hope to find it. Leave only footprints behind.

17. Pack environmentally conscious products since they may not be available away from home.

18. Do not patronize vacation spots that harm the environment to maximize their tourist capacity.

19. If planning to cook own meals, pack basic condiments to avoid having to purchase small quantities that are heavily packaged.

20. Use mosquito nets instead of sprays.

21. Separate clean and dirty towels so housekeeping only takes the used ones.

22. Take short showers.

SHOPPING

1. Make a list in order to organize shopping excursion efficiency.

2. Plan shopping trips during off-peak shopping hours to avoid crowds and traffic.

3. Walk, bike, take public transportation, or carpool.

4. Carry a tote to hold items rather than taking a new bag at each store.

5. Purchase only really needed items.

6. Borrow or rent items that are used infrequently.

7. Consult *Consumer Reports* for product information.

8. Avoid purchasing items that are heavily packaged.

9. Save boxes and bags from shopping for reuse.

10. Look for products that use recycled or recyclable material.

11. Purchase products in returnable containers.

12. Buy foods in bulk to avoid excess packaging.

13. Buy clothing with natural instead of synthetic fibers.

14. Buy clothing somewhat oversized for young children.

15. Donate old clothes to charity.

16. Patronize yard or garage sales.

17. Trade items with friends.

18. Consider refurbished items.

19. Store seasonal items properly to insure reuse the next year.

20. Patronize used goods stores.

21. Buy products that are environmentally conscious.

22. Buy environmentally safe cleaning agents.

23. Buy as few disposable items as possible.

24. Store goods by the first in-first out (FIFO) method.

25. Properly store goods according to instructions on the label.

26. Buy nonaerosol sprays.

27. Check expiration dates on items.

28. Buy rechargeable batteries.

DINING AND ENTERTAINING

1. Patronize restaurants that participate in a "feed the hungry" program.

2. Notify the waiter if water or bread is not wanted.

3. Minimize the number of napkins, paper products, and other utensils when dining.

4. Share food if portions are more than one can consume.

5. If one does not want an item that comes with the meal, notify the waiter so it is not brought and wasted.

6. Do not overorder.

7. Take leftovers home.

8. Patronize fast-food restaurants that have recycle bins and dispose properly.

9. Do not take a bag unless needed.

10. When entertaining, try to establish the exact number of guests who will attend in order to plan the menu to avoid waste of food.

11. Purchase in bulk when planning dinner parties, or other functions.

12. Customize the menu to the guests.

13. Encourage guests to reuse the same cups and eating utensils, particularly at a buffet table.

14. Establish no smoking areas and keep the air quality acceptable by ventilating smoking areas.

15. Entertain guests outdoors whenever possible.

16. Use a gas grill for barbecuing.

17. Use reusable containers to store leftovers and for box lunches.

18. Recycle as much as possible from a party, especially cans and bottles.

19. Buy items that are made of recycled material.

20. Provide garbage containers at convenient locations.

21. Dispose of garbage properly.

22. Carpool to the place of dining or entertainment.

SUMMARY

1. Pollution prevention measures involving waste reduction can be employed in the following areas:

Building a house
In the garden
Traveling and vacationing
Shopping
Dining and entertaining

2. Some key pollution prevention measures involving waste reduction that can be employed while building a house include:

a. Ensure that building and land development will not disturb drainage, runoff, and shallow water table flows.

b. Carefully determine required material to limit waste.

c. Consider using plastic or vinyl siding on the house to avoid painting.

3. Some key pollution prevention measures involving waste reduction that can be employed while in the garden include:

a. Do not use hazardous pesticides or herbicides.

b. Borrow or rent gardening items that are used infrequently.

c. Encourage helpful insects, birds and animals in the garden.

4. Some key pollution prevention measures involving waste reduction that can be employed while traveling and vacationing include:

a. Visit the library, contact the American Automobile Association (AAA) or a travel agency for traveling information.

b. Properly inflate tires on the car.

c. Travel by airplane or train when going long distances.

5. Some key pollution prevention measures involving waste reduction that can be employed while shopping include:

a. Buy products at farmer markets when possible.

b. Save boxes and bags from shopping for reuse.

c. Buy clothing somewhat oversized for young children.

6. Some key pollution prevention measures involving waste reduction that can be employed while dining and entertaining include:

a. Patronize restaurants that participate in a "feed the hungry" program.

b. Patronize fast-food restaurants that have recycle bins.

c. Carpool to the place of dining or entertainment.

REFERENCES

Holmes, G., Singh, R., and Theodore, L. *Handbook of Environmental Management and Technology.* New York: Wiley-Interscience, 1993.

McKinley, M. "Inviting Birds into Your Garden," *Fine Gardening,* July/August 1994, 34–37.

Roach, M. "Lusher Lawns With Less Water," *New York Newsday,* August 11, 1994, 33.

Theodore, L., and McGuinn, Y. *Pollution Prevention.* New York: Van Nostrand Reinhold, 1992.

Theodore, M. K., personal notes, 1991.

Part VIII

Environmental Risk

Part VIII, comprised of four chapters, serves as an introduction to environmental risk. Chapter 35 is concerned with the general subject of health risk assessment, while Chapter 36 examines risk evaluation of accidents. Chapter 37 focuses on the important area of public perception of risk. Part VIII concludes with Chapter 38 that addresses risk communication issues.

35

Health Risk Assessment

CONTRIBUTING AUTHOR

Elizabeth Butler

INTRODUCTION

There are many definitions for the word risk. It is a combination of uncertainty and damage; a ratio of hazards to safeguards; a triplet combination of event, probability, and consequences; or even a measure of economic loss or human injury in terms of both the incident likelihood and the magnitude of the loss or injury (AIChE, 1989). People face all kinds of risks everyday, some voluntarily and others involuntarily. Therefore, risk plays a very important role in today's world. Studies on cancer caused a turning point in the world of risk because it opened the eyes of risk scientists and health professionals to the world of risk assessments.

Since 1970 the field of risk assessment has received widespread attention within both the scientific and regulatory committees. It has also attracted the attention of the public. Properly conducted risk assessments have received fairly broad acceptance, in part because they put into perspective the terms toxic, hazard, and risk. Toxicity is an inherent property of all substances. It states that all chemical and physical agents can produce adverse health effects at some dose or under specific exposure conditions. In contrast, exposure to a chemical that has the capacity to produce a particular type of adverse effect, represents a hazard. Risk, however, is the probability or likelihood that an adverse outcome will occur in a person or a group that is exposed to a particular concentration or dose of the hazardous agent. Therefore, risk is generally a function of exposure or dose. Consequently, health risk assessment is defined as the process or procedure used to estimate the likelihood that humans or ecological systems will be adversely affected by a chemical or physical agent under a specific set of conditions (Paustenbach, 1989).

The term risk assessment is not only used to describe the likelihood of an adverse response to a chemical or physical agent, but it has also been used to describe the likelihood of any unwanted event. This subject is treated in more detail in the next chapter. These include risks such as: explosions or injuries in the workplace; natural catastrophes; injury or death due to various voluntary activities such as skiing, ski diving, flying, and bungee jumping; diseases; death due to natural causes; and many others (Paustenbach, 1989).

Risk assessment and risk management are two different processes, but they are intertwined. Risk assessment and risk management give a framework not only for setting regulatory priorities, but also for making decisions that cut across different environmental areas. Risk management refers to a decision-making process that involves such considerations as risk assessment, technology feasibility, economic information about costs and benefits, statutory requirements, public concerns, and other factors. Therefore, risk assessment supports risk management in that the choices on whether and how much to control future exposure to the suspected hazards may be determined (Holmes, Singh, & Theodore, 1993). Regarding both risk assessment and risk management, this chapter will primarily address this subject from a health perspective; Chapter 36 will primarily address this subject from a safety and accident perspective.

THE HEALTH RISK EVALUATION PROCESS

Health risk assessments provide an orderly, explicit, and consistent way to deal with scientific issues in evaluating whether a hazard exists and what the magnitude of the hazard may be. This evaluation typically involves large uncertainties because the available scientific data are limited, and the mechanisms for adverse health impacts or environmental damage are only imperfectly understood. When one examines risk, how does one decide how safe is safe, or how clean is clean? To begin with, one has to look at both sides of the risk equation—that is, both the toxicity of a pollutant and the extent of public exposure. Information is required at both the current and potential exposure, considering all possible exposure pathways. In addition to human health risks, one needs to look at potential ecological or other environmental effects. In conducting a comprehensive risk assessment, one should remember that there are always uncertainties, and these assumptions must be included in the analysis (Holmes et al., 1993).

In recent years, several guidelines and handbooks have been produced to help explain approaches for doing health risk assessments. As discussed by a special National Academy of Sciences committee convened in 1983, most human or environmental health hazards can be evaluated by dissecting the analysis into four parts: hazard identification, dose-response assessment or hazard assessment, exposure assessment, and risk characterization (see Figure 35–1). For some perceived hazards, the risk assessment might stop with the first step, hazard identification, if no adverse effect is identified or if an agency elects to take regulatory action without further analysis (Paustenbach, 1989). Regarding hazard identification, a hazard is defined as a toxic agent or a set of conditions that has the potential to cause adverse effects to human health or the environment. Hazard identification involves an evaluation of various forms of information in order to identify the different hazards. Dose-response or toxicity assessment is required in an overall assessment; responses/effects can vary widely since all chemicals and contaminants vary in their capacity to cause adverse effects. This step frequently requires that assumptions be made to relate experimental data for animals and humans. Exposure assessment is the determination of the magnitude, frequency, duration, and routes of exposure of human populations and ecosystems. Finally, in risk characterization, toxicology and exposure data/information are combined to obtain a qualitative or quantitative expression of risk.

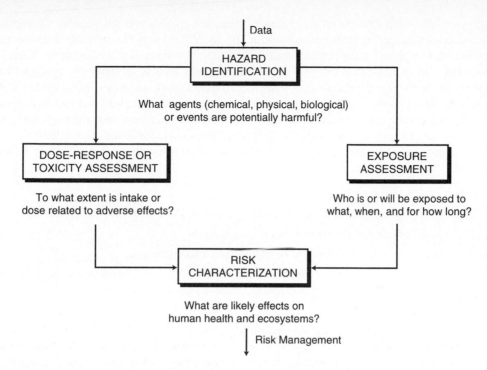

Figure 35–1.   The Health Risk Evaluation Process (Theodore and Feldman, 1992)

Risk assessment involves the integration of the information and analysis associated with the above four steps to provide a complete characterization of the nature and magnitude of risk and the degree of confidence associated with this characterization. A critical component of the assessment is a full elucidation of the uncertainties associated with each of the major steps. Under this broad concept of risk assessment are encompassed all of the essential problems of toxicology. Risk assessment takes into account all of the available dose-response data. It should treat uncertainty not by the application of arbitrary safety factors, but by stating them in quantitatively and qualitatively explicit terms, so that they are not hidden from decision makers. Risk assessment, defined in this broad way, forces an assessor to confront all the scientific uncertainties and to set forth in explicit terms the means used in specific cases to deal with these uncertainties (Rodicks & Tardiff, 1984). An expanded presentation on each of the four health risk assessment steps is provided below.

HAZARD IDENTIFICATION

Hazard identification is the most easily recognized of the actions of regulatory agencies. It is defined as the process of determining whether human exposure to an agent could cause an increase in the incidence of a health condition (cancer, birth defect, etc.) or whether exposure by a nonhuman receptor, for example, fish, birds, or other wildlife, might adversely be affected. It involves characterizing the nature and strength of the evidence of causation. Although the question of whether a substance causes cancer or other adverse health effects in humans is theoretically a yes-no question, there are few chemicals or physical agents on which the human data are definitive. Therefore, the question is often restated in terms of effects in laboratory animals or other test systems: "Does the agent induce cancer in test animals?" Positive answers to such questions are typically taken as evidence that an agent may pose a cancer risk for any exposed human. Information for short-term in vitro tests and structural similarity to known chemical hazards may, in certain circumstances, also be considered as adequate information for identifying a hazard (Paustenbach, 1989).

A hazards identification for a chemical plant or industrial application can include information about:

1. Chemical identities.
2. The location of facilities that use, produce, process, or store hazardous materials.
3. The type and design of chemical containers or vessels.
4. The quantity of material that could be involved in airborne release.
5. The nature of the hazard (e.g., airborne toxic vapors or mist, fire, explosion, large quantities stored or processed, handling conditions) most likely to accompany hazardous materials spills or releases (EPA, 1987).

An important aspect of hazards identification is a description of the pervasiveness of the hazard. For example, most environmental assessments require knowledge of the concentration of the material in the environment, weighted in some way to account for the geographical magnitude of the site affected; that is, a 1-acre or 300-acre site, a 1,000 gal/min or 1,000,000 gal/min stream. All too often environmental incidents regarding chemical emission have been described by statements like "concentrations as high as 150 ppm" of a chemical were measured at a 1,000-acre waste site. However, following closer examination, one may find that only 1 of 200 samples collected on a 20-acre portion of a 1,000-acre site showed this concentration and that 2 ppm was the geometric mean level of contamination in the 200 samples.

An appropriate sampling program is critical in the conduct of a health risk assessment. This topic could arguably be part of the exposure assessment, but it has been placed within hazard identification because, if the degree of contamination is small, no further work may be necessary. Not only is it important that samples be collected in a random or representative manner, but the number of samples must be sufficient to conduct a statistically valid analysis. The number needed to insure statistical validity will be dictated by the variability between the results. The larger the variance, the greater the number of samples needed to define the problem (Paustenbach, 1989).

The means of identifying hazards is complex. Different methods are used to collect and evaluate toxic properties (those properties that indicate the potential to cause biological injury, disease, or death under certain exposure conditions). One method is the use of epidemiological studies that deal with the incidence of disease among groups of people. Epidemiological studies attempt to correlate the incidence of cancer from an emission by an evaluation of people with a particular disease and people without the disease. Long-term animal bioassays are the most common method of hazard determination. (A bioassay as referred to here is an evaluation of disease in a laboratory animal.) Increased tumor incidence in laboratory animals is the primary health effect considered in animal bioassays. Exposure testing for a major portion of an animal's lifetime (2 to 3 years for rats and mice) provides information on disease and susceptibility, primarily for carcinogenicity (the development of cancer).

The understanding of how a substance is handled in the body, transported, changed, and excreted, and of the response of both animals and humans, has advanced remarkably. There are many questions concerning these animal tests as to what information they provide, which kinds of studies are the best, and how the animal data compares with human data. In an attempt to answer these questions, epidemiological studies and animal bioassays are compared to each other to determine if a particular chemical is likely to pose a health hazard to humans. Many assumptions are made in hazard assessments. For example, it is assumed that the chemical administered in a bioassay is in a form similar to that present in the environment. Another assumption is that animal carcinogens are also human carcinogens. An example is that there is a similarity between animal and human metabolism, and so on. With these and other assumptions, and by analyzing hazard identification procedures, lists of hazardous chemicals have been developed (Holmes et al., 1993).

DOSE-RESPONSE

Dose-response assessment is the process of characterizing the relation between the dose of an agent administered or received and the incidence of an adverse health effect in exposed populations, and estimating the incidence of the effect as a function of exposure to the agent. This process considers such important factors as intensity of exposure, age pattern of exposure, and possibly other variables that might affect response, such as sex, lifestyle, and other modifying factors. A dose-response assessment usually requires extrapolation from high to low doses and extrapolation from animals to humans, or one laboratory animal species to a wildlife species. A dose-response assessment should describe and justify the methods of extrapolation used to predict incidence, and it should characterize the statistical and biological uncertainties in these methods. When possible, the uncertainties should be described numerically rather than qualitatively.

Toxicologists tend to focus their attention primarily on extrapolations from cancer bioassays. However, there is also a need to evaluate the risks of lower doses to see how they affect the various organs and systems in the body. Many scientific papers focused on the use of a safety factor or uncertainty factor approach, since all adverse effects other than cancer and mutation-based developmental effects are believed to have a threshold—a dose below which no adverse effect should occur. Several researchers have discussed various approaches to setting acceptable daily intakes or exposure limits for developmental and reproductive toxicants. It is thought that an acceptable limit of exposure could be determined using cancer models, but today they are considered inappropriate because of thresholds (Paustenbach, 1989).

For a variety of reasons, it is difficult to precisely evaluate toxic responses caused by acute exposures to hazardous materials. First, humans experience a wide range of acute adverse health effects, including irritation, narcosis, asphyxiation, sensitization, blindness, organ system damage, and death. In addition, the severity of many of these effects varies with intensity and duration of exposure. Second, there is a high degree of variation in response among individuals in a typical population. Third, for the overwhelming majority of substances encountered in industry, there are not enough data on toxic responses of humans to permit an accurate or precise assessment of the substance's hazard potential. Fourth, many releases involve multicomponents. There are presently no rules on how these types of releases should be evaluated. Fifth, there are no toxicology testing protocols that exist for studying episodic releases on animals. In general, this has been a neglected area of toxicology research. There are many useful measures available to use as benchmarks for predicting the likelihood that a release event will result in serious injury or death. Several references (Clayson, Krewski, & Munro, 1985; Foa, Emmett, Maron, & Colombi, 1987) review various toxic effects and discuss the use of various established toxicological criteria.

Dangers are not necessarily defined by the presence of a particular chemical, but rather by the amount of that substance one is exposed to, also known as the dose. A dose is usually expressed in milligrams of chemical received per kilogram of body weight per day. For toxic substances other than carcinogens, a threshold dose must be exceeded before a health effect will occur, and for many substances, there is a dosage below which there is no harm. A health effect will occur or at least be detected at the threshold. For carcinogens, it is assumed that there is no threshold, and, therefore, any substance that produces cancer is assumed to produce cancer at any concentration. It is vital to establish the link to cancer and to determine if that risk is acceptable. Analyses of cancer risks are much more complex than non-cancer risks (Holmes et al., 1993).

Not all contaminants or chemicals are created equal in their capacity to cause adverse effects. Thus, cleanup standards or action levels are based in part on the compounds' toxicological properties. Toxicity data are derived largely from animal experiments in which the animals (primarily mice and rats) are exposed to increasingly higher concentrations or doses. Responses or effects can vary widely from no observable effect to temporary and reversible effects, to permanent injury to organs, to chronic functional impairment to ultimately, death.

EXPOSURE ASSESSMENT

Exposure assessment is the process of measuring or estimating the intensity, frequency, and duration of human or animal exposure to an agent currently present in the environment or of estimating hypothetical exposures that might arise from the release of new chemicals into the environment. In its most complete form, an exposure assessment should describe the magnitude, duration, schedule, and route of exposure; the size, nature, and classes of the human, animal, aquatic, or wildlife populations exposed; and the uncertainties in all estimates. The exposure assessment can often be used to identify feasible prospective control options and to predict the effects of available control technologies for controlling or limiting exposure (Paustenbach, 1989).

Much of the attention focused on exposure assessment has come recently. This is because many of the risk assessments done in the past used too many conservative assumptions, which caused an overestimation of the actual exposure. Without exposures there are no risks. To experience adverse effects, one must first come into contact with the toxic agent(s). Exposures to chemicals can be via inhalation of air (breathing), ingestion of water and food (eating and drinking), or absorption through the skin. These are all pathways to the human body.

Generally, the main pathways of exposure considered in this step are atmospheric transport, surface and groundwater transport, ingestion of toxic materials that have passed through the aquatic and terrestrial food chain, and dermal absorption. Once an exposure assessment determines the quantity of a chemical with which human populations may come in contact, the information can be combined with toxicity data (from the hazard identification process) to estimate potential health risks (Holmes et al., 1993). The primary purpose of an exposure assessment is to determine the concentration levels over time and space in each environmental media where human and other environmental receptors may come into contact with chemicals of concern. There are four components of an exposure assessment: potential sources, significant exposure pathways, populations potentially at risk, and exposure estimates (Paustenbach, 1989).

The two primary methods of determining the concentration of a pollutant to which target populations are exposed are direct measurement and computer analysis, also known as computer dispersion modeling. Measurement of the pollutant concentration in the environment is used for determining the risk associated with an exiting discharge source. Receptors are placed at regular intervals from the source, and the concentration of the pollutant is measured over a certain period of time (usually several months or a year). The results are then related to the size of the local population. This kind of monitoring, however, is expensive and time-consuming. Many measurements must be taken because exposure levels can vary under different atmospheric conditions or at different times of the year. Computer dispersion modeling predicts environmental concentrations of pollutants (see Chapters 10 and 15 for more information on dispersion modeling). In the prediction of exposure, computer dispersion modeling focuses on discharge of a pollutant and the dispersion of that discharge by the time it reaches the receptor. This method is primarily used for assessing risk from a proposed facility or discharge. Sophisticated techniques are employed to relate reported or measured emissions to atmospheric, climatological, demographic, geographic, and other data in order to predict a population's potential exposure to a given chemical (Holmes et al., 1993).

RISK CHARACTERIZATION

Risk characterization is the process of estimating the incidence of a health effect under the various conditions of human or animal exposure described in the exposure assessment. It is performed by combining the exposure and dose-response assessments. The summary effects of the uncertainties in the preceding steps should be described in this step. The quantitative estimate of the risk is the principal interest to the regulatory agency or risk manager making the decision. The risk manager must consider the results of the risk characterization when evaluating the economics, societal aspects, and various benefits of the risk assessment. Factors such as societal pressure, technical uncertainties, and severity of the potential hazard influence how the decision makers respond to the risk assessment. There is room for a lot of improvement in this step of the risk assessment (Paustenbach, 1989).

A risk estimate indicates the likelihood of occurrence of the different types of health or environmental effects in exposed populations. Risk assessment should include both human health and environmental evaluations (i. e., impacts on ecosystems). Ecological impacts include actual or potential effects on plants and animals (other than domesticated species). The number produced from the risk characterization, representing the probability of adverse health effects being caused, must be evaluated. This is done because certain agencies will only look at risks of specific numbers and act on them.

There are two major types of risk: maximum individual risk and population risk. Maximum individual risk is defined exactly as it implies, that is the maximum risk to an individual person. This person is considered to have a 70-year lifetime of exposure to a process or a chemical. Population risk is again the risk to a population. It is expressed as a certain number of deaths per thousand or per million people. For example, a fatal annual risk of 2×10^{-6} refers to 2 deaths per year for every million individuals. These risks are based on very conservative assumptions, which may yield too high a risk.

SUMMARY

1. Health risk assessment is defined as the process or procedure used to estimate the likelihood that humans or ecological systems will be adversely affected by a chemical or physical agent under a specific set of conditions.

2. The health risk evaluation process consists of four steps: hazard identification, dose-response assessment or hazard assessment, exposure assessment, and risk characterization.

3. In hazard identification, a hazard is a toxic agent or a set of conditions that has the potential to cause adverse effects to human health or the environment.

4. In dose-response assessment, effects are evaluated and these effects vary widely because their capacities to cause adverse effects differ.

5. Exposure assessment is the determination of the magnitude, frequency, duration, and routes of exposure to human populations and ecosystems.

6. In risk characterization, the toxicology and exposure data are combined to obtain a quantitative or qualitative expression of risk.

7. A major avenue for reducing risk will involve source reduction of hazardous materials.

REFERENCES

AIChE. "Guidelines for Chemical Process Quantitative Risk Analysis" New York: Center for Chemical Process Safety of the American Institute of Chemical Engineers, 1989.

Clayson, D. B., Krewski, D., and Munro, I. *Toxicological Risk Assessment,* Boca Raton, FL: CRC Press, Inc., 1985.

EPA. *Technical Guidance for Hazards Analysis,* December 1987.

Foa, V., Emmett, E. A., Maron, M., and Colombi, A. *Occupational and Environmental Chemical Hazards.* Chichester, England: Ellis Horwood Limited, 1987.

Holmes, G., Singh, B., and Theodore, L. *Handbook of Environmental Management and Technology.* New York: John Wiley & Sons, 1993.

Paustenbach, D. *The Risk Assessment of Environmental and Human Health Hazards: A Textbook of Case Studies.* New York: John Wiley & Sons, 1989.

Rodricks, J., and Tardiff, R. *Assessment and Management of Chemical Risks.* Washington, D.C.: American Chemical Society, 1984.

Theodore, L., and Feldman, P. *Air Pollution Control Equipment,* East Williston. NY: Theodore Tutorials, 1992.

36

Risk Evaluation of Accidents

CONTRIBUTING AUTHOR

Eleanor Capasso

INTRODUCTION

Risk evaluation of accidents serves a dual purpose. It estimates the probability that an accident will occur and also assesses the severity of the consequences of an accident. Consequences may include damage to the surrounding environment, financial loss, or injury to life. This chapter is primarily concerned with the methods used to identify hazards and the causes and consequences of accidents. Issues dealing with health risks have been explored in the previous chapter. Risk assessment of accidents provides an effective way to help ensure either that a mishap does not occur or reduces the likelihood of an accident. The result of the risk assessment allows concerned parties to take precautions to prevent an accident before it happens.

Regarding definitions, the first thing an individual needs to know is what exactly is an accident. An accident is an unexpected event that has undesirable consequences (AIChE, 1985). The causes of accidents have to be identified in order to help prevent accidents from occurring. Any situation or characteristic of a system, plant, or process that has the potential to cause damage to life, property, or the environment is considered a hazard. A hazard can also be defined as any characteristic that has the potential to cause an accident. The severity of a hazard plays a large part in the potential amount of damage a hazard can cause if it occurs. Risk is the probability that human injury, damage to property, damage to the environment, or financial loss will occur. An acceptable risk is a risk whose probability is unlikely to occur during the lifetime of the plant or process. An acceptable risk can also be defined as an accident that has a high probability of occurring, with negligible consequences. Risks can be ranked qualitatively in categories of high, medium, and low. Risk can also be ranked quantitatively as annual number of fatalities per million affected individuals. This is normally denoted as a number times one millionth that is, 3×10^{-6}; this representation indicates that on the average, for every million individuals 3 workers will die every year. Another quantitative approach that has become popular in industry is the Fatal Accident Rate (FAR) concept. This determines or estimates the number of fatalities over the lifetime of 1000 workers. The lifetime of a worker is defined as 10^5 hours, which is based on a 40-hour work week for 50 years. A reasonable FAR for a chemical plant is 3.0 with 4.0 usually taken as a maximum. The FAR for an individual at home is approximately 3.0. A FAR of 3.0 means that there are 3 deaths for every 1000 workers over a 50-year period.

RISK EVALUATION PROCESS FOR ACCIDENTS

There are several steps in evaluating the risk of an accident (see Figure 36–1). These are detailed below if the system in question is a chemical plant.

   1. A brief description of the equipment and chemicals used in the plant is needed.

   2. Any hazard in the system has to be identified. Hazards that may occur in a chemical plant include:

Fire	Explosions
Toxic vapor release	Rupture of a pressurized vessel
Slippage	Runaway reactions
Corrosion	

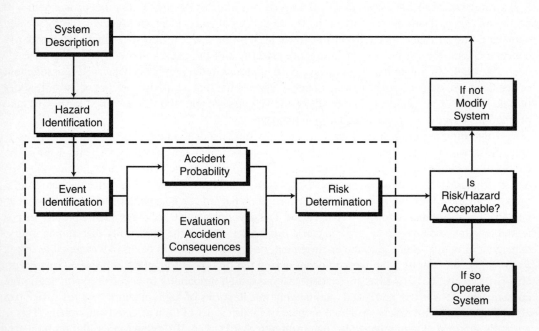

Figure 36–1.   Hazard Risk Assessment Flowchart

3. The event or series of events that will initiate an accident has to be identified. An event could be a failure to follow correct safety procedures, improperly repaired equipment, or failure of a safety mechanism.

4. The probability that the accident will occur has to be determined. For example, if a chemical plant has a 10-year life, what is the probability that the temperature in a reactor will exceed the specified temperature range? The probability can be ranked from low to high. A low probability means that it is unlikely for the event to occur in the life of the plant. A medium probability suggests that there is a possibility that the event will occur. A high probability means that the event will probably occur during the life of the plant.

5. The severity of the consequences of the accident must be determined. This will be described later in detail.

6. If the probability of the accident and the severity of its consequences are low, then the risk is usually deemed acceptable and the plant should be allowed to operate. If the probability of occurrence is too high or the damage to the surroundings is too great, then the risk is usually unacceptable and the system needs to be modified to minimize these effects.

The heart of the hazard risk assessment algorithm provided is enclosed in the dashed box (Figure 36–1). The algorithm allows for reevaluation of the process if the risk is deemed unacceptable (the process is repeated starting with either step one or two).

HAZARD IDENTIFICATION

Hazard or event identification provides information on situations or chemicals and their releases that can potentially harm the environment, life, or property. Information that is required to identify hazards includes, chemical identities, quantities and location of chemicals in question, chemical properties such as boiling points, ignition temperatures, and toxicity to humans. There are several methods used to identify hazards. The methods that will be discussed are the process checklist and the hazard and operability study (HAZOP).

A process check list evaluates equipment, materials and safety procedures (AIChE, 1985). A checklist is composed of a series of questions prepared by an engineer who knows the procedure being evaluated. It compares what is in the actual plant to a set of safety and company standards. Some questions that may be on a typical checklist are:

1. Was the equipment designed with a safety factor?
2. Does the spacing of the equipment allow for ease of maintenance?
3. Are the pressure relief valves on the equipment in question?
4. How toxic are the materials that are being used in the process and is there adequate ventilation?
5. Will any of the materials cause corrosion to the pipe(s)/reactor(s)/system?
6. What precautions are necessary for flammable material?
7. Is there an alternate exit in case of fire?

8. If there is a power failure what fail-safe procedure(s) does the process contain?

9. What hazard is created if any piece of equipment malfunctions?

These questions and others are answered and analyzed. Changes are then made to reduce the risk of an accident. Process checklists are updated and audited at regular intervals.

A hazard and operability study is a systematic approach to recognizing and identifying possible hazards that may cause failure of a piece of equipment (Theodore, Reynolds & Taylor, 1989). This method utilizes a team of diverse professional backgrounds to detect and minimize hazards for in a plant. The process in question is divided into smaller processes (subprocesses). Guide words are used to relay the degree of deviation from the subprocesses' intended operation. The guide words can be found in Table 36–1. The causes and consequences of the deviation from the process are determined. If there are any recommendations for revision they are recorded and a report is made. A summary of the basic steps of a HAZOP study is (Theodore et al., 1989):

1. Define objectives

2. Define plant limits

3. Appoint and train a team

4. Obtain complete preparative work (i.e., flow diagrams, sequence of events)

5. Conduct examination meetings that select subprocesses, agree on intention of subprocesses, state and record intentions, use guide words to find deviations from the intended purpose, determine the causes and consequences of deviation, and recommend revisions

6. Issue meeting reports

7. Follow up on revisions

There are other methods of hazard identification. A "what-if" analysis presents certain questions about a particular hazard and then tries to find the possible consequences of that hazard. The human-error analysis identifies potential human errors that will lead to an accident. They can be used in conjunction with the two previously described methods.

**Table 36–1.   Guide Words Used to Relay the Degree of Deviation
                      from Intended Subprocess Operation**

Guide Word	Meaning
No	No part of intended function is accomplished
Less	Quantitative decrease in intended activity
More	Quantitative increase in intended activity
Part of	The intention is achieved to a certain percent
As well as	The intention is accomplished along with side effects
Reverse	The opposite of the intention is achieved
Other than	A different activity replaces the intended activity

CAUSES OF ACCIDENTS

The primary causes of accidents are mechanical failure, operational failure (human error), unknown or miscellaneous, process upset, and design error. Figure 36–2 is the relative number of accidents that have occurred in the petrochemical field (Crowl & Louvar, 1990)

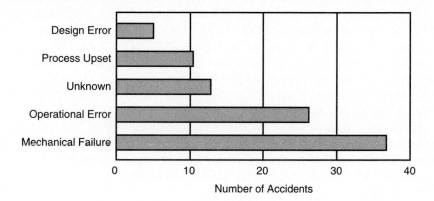

Figure 36–2.   Causes of Accidents in the Petrochemical Field

There are three steps that normally lead to an accident.

1. Initiation
2. Propagation
3. Termination

The path that an accident takes through the three steps can be determined by means of a fault tree analysis (AIChE, 1985). A fault tree is a diagram that shows the path that a specific accident takes. The first thing needed to construct a fault tree is the definition of the initial event. The initial event is a hazard or action that will cause the process to deviate from normal operation. The next step is to define the existing conditions needed to be present in order for the accident to occur. The propagation event (e.g., the mechanical failure of equipment related to the accident) is discussed. Any other equipment or components that need to be studied have to be defined. This includes safety equipment that will bring about the termination of the accident. Finally, the normal state of the system in question is determined. The termination of an accident is the event that brings the system back to its normal operation. An example of an accident would be the failure of a thermometer in a reactor. The temperature in the reactor could rise and a runaway reaction might take place. Stopping the flow to the reactor and/or cooling the contents of the reactor could terminate the accident.

Event trees are diagrams that evaluate the consequences of a specific hazard. The safety measures and the procedures designed to deal with the event are presented. The consequences of each specific event that led to the accident are also presented. An event tree is drawn (sequence of events that led up to the accident). The accident is described. This allows the path of the accident to be traced. It shows what could be done along the way to prevent the accident. It also shows other possible outcomes that could arise had a single event in the sequence been changed.

CONSEQUENCES OF ACCIDENTS

Consequences of accidents can be classified qualitatively by the degree of severity. A quantitative assessment is beyond the scope of the text; however information is available in the literature (Bellandi, 1988). Factors that help to determine the degree of severity are the concentration that the hazard is released, length of time that a person or the environment is exposed to a hazard, and the toxicity of the hazard. The worst-case consequence or scenario is defined as a conservatively high estimate of the most severe accident identified (AIChE, 1985). On this basis one can rank the consequences of accidents into low, medium, and high degrees of severity (EPA, 1978). A low degree of severity means that the hazard is nearly negligible, and the injury to person, property, or the environment is observed only after an extended period of time. The degree of severity is considered to be medium when the accident is serious, but not catastrophic, the toxicity of the chemical released is great, or the concentration of a less toxic chemical is large enough to cause injury or death to persons and damage to the environment unless immediate action is taken. There is a high degree of severity when the accident is catastrophic or the concentrations and toxicity of a hazard is large enough to cause injury or death to many persons, and there is long-term damage to the surrounding environment. Figure 36–3 provides a graphical qualitative representation of the severity of consequences (EPA, 1978).

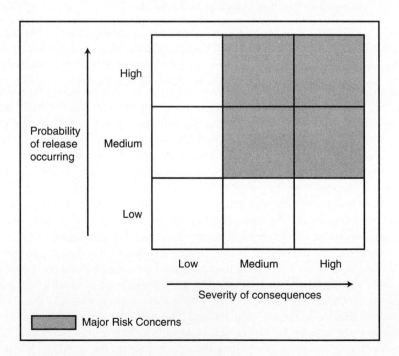

Figure 36–3.   Qualitative Probability-Consequence Analysis

CAUSE-CONSEQUENCE ANALYSIS

Cause-consequence risk evaluation combines event tree and fault tree analysis to relate specific accident consequences to causes (AIChE, 1985). The process of cause consequence evaluation usually proceeds as follows:

1. Select an event to be evaluated.
2. Describe the safety system(s)/procedure(s)/factor(s) that interfere with the path of the accident.
3. Perform an event tree analysis to find the path(s) an accident may follow.
4. Perform a fault tree analysis to determine the safety function that failed.
5. Rank the results on a basis of severity of consequences.

As its name implies cause-consequence analysis allows one to see how the possible causes of an accident and the possible consequences that result from that event interact with each other.

FUTURE TRENDS

For the most part, future trends will be found in hazard accident prevention, not hazard analysis. To help promote hazard accident prevention companies should start employee training programs. These programs should be designed to alert the technical staff and employees about the hazards they are exposed to on the job. Training should also cover company safety policies and the proper procedures to follow in case an accident does occur. A major avenue to reducing risk will involve source reduction of hazardous materials. Risk education and communication are two other areas that will need improvement.

SUMMARY

1. Risk assessment of accidents estimates the probability that hazardous materials will be released and also assesses the severity of the consequences of an accident.

2. The risk evaluation process defines the equipment, hazards, and events leading to an accident. It determines the probability that an accident will occur. The severity and acceptability of the risk are also evaluated.

3. Hazard identification provides information on situations or chemicals that can potentially harm the environment, life, or property. The processes described are process checklist, event tree, and hazard and operability study.

4. Accidents occur in three steps: initiation, propagation, and termination. The primary causes of accidents are mechanical failure, operational failure (human error), unknown or miscellaneous, process upset, and design error.

5. Consequences of accidents are classified by degree of severity into low, medium, and high.

6. Cause-consequence analysis allows one to see the possible causes of an accident and the possible accident that results from a certain event.

7. For the most part future trends can be found in hazard prevention.

REFERENCES

AIChE. *Guidelines for Hazard Evaluation Procedures,* Prepared by Batelle Columbus Division for the Center for Chemical Process Safety of the American Institute of Chemical Engineers, 1985.

Bellandi, R. *Hazardous Waste Site Remediation: The Engineer's Perspective.* New York: Van Nostrand Reinhold, 1988.

Crowl, J., and Louvar, J. *Chemical Safety Fundamentals With Applications.* Englewood, NJ: Prentice-Hall, 1990.

EPA, FEMA, USDOT. *Technical Guidance For Hazard Analysis.* Washington, DC: Author, 1978.

Theodore, L., Reynolds J., and Taylor, F. *Accident and Emergency Management.* New York: John Wiley & Sons, 1989.

37

Public Perception of Risk

CONTRIBUTING AUTHOR

Julie A. Shanahan

INTRODUCTION

Public concern about risk stems from earthquakes, fires, and hurricanes to asbestos, radon emissions, ozone depletion, toxins in our food and water, and so on. Many of the public's worries are out of proportion, with the fear being overestimated or at times underestimated. The risks given the most publicity and attention receive the greatest concern, while the ones that are more familiar and accepted are given less thought.

A large part of what the public knows about risk comes from the media. Whether it is newspapers, magazines, radio or television, the media provides information about the nature and extent of specific risks. It also helps shape the perception of the danger involved within a given risk.

Lay people and experts disagree on risk estimates for many environmental problems. This creates a problem, since the public generally does not trust the experts. This chapter concentrates on how the public views risk and what the future of public risk perception will be.

EVERYDAY RISKS

The public often worries about the largely publicized risks and thinks little about those that they face regularly. A study was recently performed that compared the responses of two groups, 15 national risk assessment experts and 40 members of the League of Women Voters on the risks of 30 activities and technologies (Goleman, 1994). This search produced striking discrepancies, as presented in Table 37–1. The League members rated nuclear power as the number 1 risk, while experts numbered it at 20 and the League ranked x-rays at 22 while the experts gave it a rank of 7.

There are various reasons for the differences in risk perception. Government regulators and industry officials look at different aspects in assessing a given risk than would members of the com-

Table 37–1.   Ranking Risks: Reality and Perception

The rankings of perceived risks for 30 activities and technologies, based on averages in a survey of a group of experts and a group of informed lay people, members of the League of Women Voters. A ranking of 1 denotes the highest level of perceived risk.

League of Women Voters	Activity or Technology	Experts
1	Nuclear power	20
2	Motor vehicles	1
3	Handguns	4
4	Smoking	2
5	Motorcycles	6
6	Alcoholic beverages	3
7	General (private) aviation	12
8	Police work	17
9	Pesticides	8
10	Surgery	5
11	Fire fighting	18
12	Large construction	13
13	Hunting	23
14	Spray cans	26
15	Mountain climbing	29
16	Bicycles	15
17	Commercial aviation	16
18	Electric power (nonnuclear)	9
19	Swimming	10
20	Contraceptives	11
21	Skiing	30
22	X rays	7
23	High school and college football	27
24	Railroads	19
25	Food preservatives	14
26	Food coloring	21
27	Power motors	28
28	Prescription antibiotics	24
29	Home appliances	22
30	Vaccinations	25

Reference: (Goleman, 1994)

munity. The "experts" will look at the mortality rates to assess risk, while the "lay people" worry about their children and the potential long-term health risks. Another reason for the difference is that people take reports of bad news more to heart than they would a report that might increase their trust.

Problems exist with risk estimates because the substance or process in question may be calculated to present too high a risk. To understand the significance of risk analyses, a list of everyday risks derived from actual statistics and reasonable estimates is presented in Table 37–2. A lifetime risk of 70×10^{-6} means that 70 out of one million people will die from that specific risk.

Risk managers in government and industry have started turning to risk communication to bridge the gap between the public and the "experts." (The next chapter treats the general subject of risk communication in more detail.) Table 37–2 enables the public to see that certain everyday risks are higher than some dreaded environmental risks. It shows that eating peanut butter possesses a greater risk than toxins in the air or water.

Table 37–2.   Lifetime Risks to Life Commonly Faced by Individuals

Cause of Risk	Lifetime (70-year) Risk per Million
Cigarette smoking	252,000
All cancers	196,000
Construction	42,700
Agriculture	42,000
Police killed in the line of duty	15,400
Air pollution (Eastern United States)	14,000
Motor vehicle accidents (traveling)	14,000
Home accidents	7,700
Frequent airplane traveler	3,500
Pedestrian hit by motor vehicle	2,940
Alcohol, light drinker	1,400
Background radiation at sea level	1,400
Peanut butter, four tablespoons per day	560
Electrocution	370
Tornado	42
Drinking water containing chloroform at allowable EPA limit	42
Lightning	35
Living 70 years in zone of maximum impact from modern municipal incinerator	1
Smoking 1.4 cigarettes	1
Drinking 0.5 liters of wine	1
Traveling 10 miles by bicycle	1
Traveling 30 miles by car	1
Traveling 1000 miles by jet plane (air crash)	1
Traveling 6000 miles by jet plane (cosmic rays)	1
Drinking water containing trichloroethylene at maximum allowable EPA limit	0.1

Adapted from: Charles T. Main, Inc., *Health Risk Assessment for Air Emissions of Metals and Organic Compounds from the PERC Municipal Waste to Energy Facility,* Prepared for Penobscot Energy Recovery Company (PERC), Boston, MA, December 1985. R. Wilson and E. A. Crouch, Risk Assessment and Comparisons: An Introduction, Science, April 1987.

ENVIRONMENTAL RISKS

In 1987, the EPA released a report titled "Unfinished Business: A Comparative Assessment of Environmental Problems" in order to apply the concepts of risk assessment to a wide array of pressing environmental problems. It is difficult to make direct comparisons of different environmental problems, because most of the data is usually insufficient to quantify risks. Also, risks associated with some problems are incomparable with risks of others. The study was based on a list of 31 environmental problems. Each was analyzed in terms of four different types of risks: cancer risks, noncancer health risks, ecological effects, and welfare effects (visibility impairment, materials damage, etc.)

The ranking of cancer was probably the most straightforward part of the study, since the EPA had already established risk assessment procedures and there are considerable data already available from which to work. Two problems were considered at the top of the list: the first was worker exposure to chemicals, which does not involve a large number of individuals but does result in high individual risks to those exposed; the other problem was radon exposure, which is causing considerable risk to a large number of people. The results from the cancer report are provided in Table 37–3.

Table 37–3.   Consensus Ranking of Environmental Problem Areas on the Basis of Population Cancer Risk

Rank	Problem Area	Selected Comments
1 (tied)	Worker exposure to chemicals	About 250 cancer cases per year estimated based on exposure to 4 chemicals; but workers face potential exposures to over 20,000 substances. Very high individual risk possible.
1 (tied)	Indoor radon	Estimated 5000–20,000 lung cancers annually from exposure in homes.
3	Pesticide residues on foods	Estimated 6000 cancers annually, based on exposure to 200 potential oncogens.
4 (tied)	Indoor air pollutants (nonradon)	Estimated 3500–6500 cancers annually, mostly due to tobacco smoke.
4 (tied)	Consumer exposure to chemicals	Risk from 4 chemicals investigated is about 100–135 cancers annually; an estimated 10,000 chemicals in consumer products. Cleaning fluids, pesticides, particleboard, and asbestos-containing products especially noted.
6	Hazardous/toxic air pollutants	Estimated 2000 cancers annually based on an assessment of 20 substances.
7	Depletion of stratospheric ozone	Ozone depletion projected to result in 10,000 additional annual deaths in the year 2100; not ranked higher because of the uncertainties in future risk.
8	Hazardous waste sites, inactive	Cancer incidence of 1000 annually from 6 chemicals assessed. Considerable uncertainty since risk based on extrapolation from 35 sites to about 25,000 sites.
9	Drinking water	Estimated 400–1000 annual cancers, mostly from radon and trihalomethanes.
10	Application of pesticides	Approximately 100 cancers annually; small population exposed but high individual risks.
11	Radiation other than radon	Estimated 360 cancers per year. Mostly from building materials. Medical exposure and natural background levels not included.
12	Other pesticide risks	Consumer and professional exterminator uses estimated cancers of 150 annually. Poor data.
13	Hazardous waste sites, active	Probably fewer than 100 cancers annually; estimates sensitive to assumptions regarding proximity of future wells to waste sites.
14	Nonhazardous waste sites, industrial	No real analysis done, ranking based on consensus of professional opinion.

Table 37–3.   (Continued)

Rank	Problem Area	Selected Comments
15	New toxic chemicals	Difficult to assess; done by consensus.
16	Nonhazardous waste sites, municipal	Estimated 40 cancers annually not including municipal surface impoundments.
17	Contaminated sludge	Preliminary results estimate 40 cancers annually, mostly from incineration and landfilling.
18	Mining waste	Estimated 10–20 cancers annually, largely due to arsenic. Remote locations and small population exposure reduce overall risk though individual risk may be high.
19	Releases from storage tanks	Preliminary analysis, based on benzene, indicates low cancer incidence (<1).
20	Non-point-source discharges to surface water	No quantitative analysis available; judgment.
21	Other groundwater contamination	Lack of information; individual risks considered less than 10^{-6}, with rough estimate of total population risk at <1.
22	Criteria air pollutants	Excluding carcinogenic particles and VOC's (included under hazardous/toxic air pollutants); ranked low because remaining criteria pollutants have not been shown to be carcinogens.
23	Direct point-source discharges to surface water	No quantitative assessment available. Only ingestion of contaminated seafood was considered.
24	Indirect point-source discharges to surface water	Same as above.
25	Accidental releases, toxics	Short duration exposure yields low cancer risk; noncancer health effects of much greater concern.
26	Accidental releases, oil spills	See above. Greater concern for welfare and ecological effects.

Not ranked: Biotechnology; global warming; other air pollutants; discharges to estuaries, coastal waters and oceans; discharges to wetlands.
Source: Based on data from USEPA (1987b).

The other working groups had greater difficulty when ranking the 31 environmental problem issues because there are no accepted guidelines for quantitatively assessing relative risks. As noted in the EPA's study, the following general results were produced for each of the four types of risks described earlier in this section (Masters, 1991).

1. No problems rank high in all four types of risk, or relatively low in all four.

2. Problems that rank relatively high in three of the four types, or at least medium in all four, include criteria air pollutants, stratospheric ozone depletion, pesticide residues on food, and other pesticide risks (runoff and air deposition of pesticides).

3. Problems that rank relatively high in cancer and noncancer health risks but low in ecological and welfare risks include hazardous air pollutants, indoor radon, indoor air pollution other than radon, pesticide application, exposure to consumer products, and worker exposures to chemicals.

4. Problems that rank relatively high in ecological and welfare risk but low in both health risks include global warming, point and nonpoint sources of surface water pollution, physical alteration of aquatic habitats (including estuaries and wetlands), and mining wastes.

5. Areas related to groundwater consistently rank medium or low.

Although there were great uncertainties involved in making these assessments, the divergence between the EPA effort and relative risks is noteworthy. From this study, areas of relatively high risk but low EPA effort/concern include indoor radon, indoor air pollution, stratospheric ozone depletion, global warming, nonpoint sources, discharges to estuaries, coastal waters and oceans, other pesticide risks, accidental releases of toxics, consumer products, and worker exposures. The EPA gives high effort but relatively medium or low risks to RCRA sites, Superfund sites, underground storage tanks, and municipal nonhazardous waste sites.

OUTRAGE FACTORS

The perception of a given risk is amplified by what are known as "outrage" factors. These factors can make people feel that even small risks are unacceptable. More than twenty outrage factors have been identified; a few of the main ones are defined below (Holmes, Singh, & Theodore, 1993).

1. Voluntariness. A voluntary risk is much more acceptable to people than an imposed risk. People will accept the risk from skiing, but not from food preservatives, although the potential for injury from skiing is 1,000 times greater than from preservatives.

2. Control. Risks that people can take steps to control are more acceptable than those they feel are beyond their control. When prevention is in the hands of the individual, the risk is perceived much lower than when it is in the hands of the government. You can choose what you eat, but you cannot control what is in your drinking water.

3. Fairness. Risks that seem to be unfairly shared are believed to be more hazardous. People who endure greater risk than their neighbors and do not attain anything from it are generally outraged by this. If I am not getting anything from it, why should others benefit?

4. Process. The public views the agency: Is it trustworthy or dishonest, concerned or arrogant? If the agency tells the community what's going on before decisions are made, the public feels more at ease. They also favor a company that listens and responds to community concerns.

5. Morality. Society has decided that pollution is not only harmful, it is evil. Talking about cost-risk tradeoffs sounds cold-hearted when the risk is morally relevant.

6. Familiarity. Risks from exotic technologies create more dread than do those involving familiar ones. "A train wreck that takes many lives has less impact on people's trust of trains than would a smaller, hypothetical accident involving recombinant DNA, which is only perceived to have catastrophic mishaps" (Goleman, 1994).

7. Memorability. An incident that remains in the public's memory makes the risk easier to imagine and is, therefore, more risky.

8. Dread. There are some illnesses that are feared more than others. Today there is greater fear given to AIDS and cancer than there is to asthma.

These outrage factors are not distortions in the public's perception of risk. They are inborn parts of what is interpreted as risk. They are explanations of why the public fears pollutants in the air and water more than they do geological radon. The problem is that many risk experts resist the use of the public's "irrational fear" in their risk management.

FUTURE TRENDS

A problem exists in the perception of risk because the experts' and lay people's views differ. The experts usually base their assessment on mortality rates, while the lay people's fears are based on "outrage" factors. In order to help solve this problem, in the future, risk managers must work to make truly serious hazards more outrageous. One example is the recent campaign for the risk involved in cigarette smoke. Another effort must be made to decrease the public's concern with low to modest hazards, that is, risk managers must diminish "outrage" in these areas. In addition, people must be treated fairly and honestly.

SUMMARY

1. Public concern of risk spans a wide range, from fires and hurricanes to radon emissions and toxins in our water and air. Most of what the public knows of risk comes from the media.

2. People often overestimate risks that are highly publicized and worry little about the familiar risks that they face every day.

3. The EPA released a study entitled "Unfinished Business: A Comparative Assessment of Environmental Problems," which compared four different types of risks for problem areas. It helped the EPA decide which problems should be given priority.

4. The public pays a great deal of attention to "outrage" factors which are all deciding factors of risk except the death rate. They are innate parts of what is meant by risk.

5. The experts need to pay more attention to the public's outrage factors. More emphasis must be placed on the higher hazardous risks and an effort is needed to decrease the public's concern on medium to light risks.

REFERENCES

Goleman, D. *Assessing Risk: Why Fear May Outweigh Harm. New York Times,* Feb. 1, 1994.

Holmes, G., Singh, B., and Theodore, L. *Handbook of Environmental Management and Technology.* New York: John Wiley & Sons, 1993.

Masters, G. *Introduction to Environmental Engineering and Science.* Englewood Cliffs, NJ: Prentice Hall, 1991.

38

Risk Communication

CONTRIBUTING AUTHOR

Patricia J. Brady

INTRODUCTION

Environmental risk communication is one of the more important problems that this country faces. Since 1987, public concerns about the environment have grown faster than concern about virtually any other national problem (Holmes, Singh, & Theodore, 1993). Some people are suffering (and in some cases dying) because they do not know when to worry and when to calm down. They do not know when to demand action to reduce risk or when to relax because risks are trivial or even nonexistent. The key, of course, is to pick the right worries and right actions. Unfortunately, when it comes to health and the environment, society does not do that well. The government and media together have failed to communicate clearly what is a risk and what is not a risk.

There are two major categories of risk: nonfixable and fixable. Nonfixable risks can never substantially be reduced, such as cancer-causing sunlight or cosmic radiation. Fixable risks can be reduced, and include those risks that are both large and small. There are so many of these fixable risks that all of them can never be successfully attacked, so choices must be made. When it comes to risk reduction, the outcome should be to obtain the most reduction possible, taking into account that people fear some risks more than others. This essentially means that the technical community should concentrate on the big fixable targets, and leave the smaller ones to later.

Risk communication comes into play because citizens ultimately determine which risks government agencies attack. On the surface, it appears practical to remedy the most severe risks first, leaving the others until later or perhaps, if the risks are small enough, never remedying the others at all. However, the behavior of individuals in everyday life often does not conform with this view. Consider now two environmental issues: gasoline that contains lead, and ocean incineration (Russell, 1989).

According to the Environmental Protection Agency (EPA), lead in gasoline poses very large risks: risks of learning disabilities, mental retardation, and worse to hundreds of thousands of children. The EPA's decision to reduce lead in gasoline is the most significant protective action the agency has undertaken in a long time. The only difference encountered on this issue was that the public acted with virtual indifference.

On the other hand, citizens threatened to lie down bodily in front of trucks and blockade harbors to stop the EPA's proposal to allow final testing of ocean incineration. The public reacted irrationally here. Every indication showed that the risk involved was small, and that the technology would be replacing more risky alternatives now in use (Russell, 1989).

Why is there such an imbalance on the perception of risk? Ironically, part of the reason lies in the fact that the people responsible for communicating this information did their job too well. They achieved their objective to get the information out to the public. Unfortunately, their objectives did not include effective communication of risk.

The professionals at the EPA are quite precise in the statements they deliver concerning risks and their apparent hazards. Their job is to present a scientifically defensible product, so they add qualifiers and use scientific terms. The problem with this is that often the public receives a misunderstanding of the actual risk (Russell, 1989).

The challenge of risk communication is to provide the information in ways that can be incorporated in the views of people who have little time or patience for arcane scientific discourse. Success in risk communication is not to be measured by whether the public chooses to set the outcomes that minimize risk as estimated by the experts; it is achieved instead when those outcomes are knowingly chosen by a well-informed public (Holmes et al., 1993).

When citizens understand a risk, and the cost of reducing it, they can determine for themselves if control actions are too lax, too stringent, or just right. The two previous cases that were used as an example demonstrate that the risk message is not getting through to people who need to know when to demand action and when to calm down. The answer is not to communicate more information, but more pertinent and understandable information. All the public needs to know is the following three pieces of information: How big is the risk? What is being done about it? What will it cost? (Russell, 1989).

This chapter will focus upon the communication of more pertinent risk information, how to get the message across in terms that are easy for an average citizen to understand, what concerned citizens can do to have a role in vital environmental solutions, and the accessibility in environmental communication to keep the public informed.

SEVEN CARDINAL RULES OF RISK COMMUNICATION

There are no easy prescriptions for successful risk communication. However, those who have studied and participated in recent debates about risk generally agree on seven cardinal rules. These rules apply equally well to the public and private sectors. Although many of these rules may seem obvious, they are continually and consistently violated in practice. Thus, a useful way to read these rules is to focus on why they are frequently not followed (EPA, 1988).

1. Accept and involve the public as a legitimate partner. A basic tenet of risk communication in democracy is that people and communities have a right to participate in decisions that affect their lives, their property, and the things they value.

Guidelines: Demonstrate your respect for the public and underscore the sincerity of your effort by involving the community early, before important decisions are made. Involve all parties that have an interest or stake in the issue under consideration. If you are a government employee, remember that you work for the public. If you do not work for the government, the public still holds you accountable.

Point to Consider: The goal in risk communication in a democracy should be to produce an informed public that is involved, interested, reasonable, thoughtful, solution-oriented, and collaborative; it should not be to diffuse public concerns or replace action.

2. Plan carefully and evaluate your efforts. Risk communication will be successful only if carefully planned.

Guidelines: Begin with clear, explicit risk communication objectives, such as providing information to the public, motivating individuals to act, stimulating response to emergencies, and contributing to the resolution of conflict. Evaluate the information you have about the risks and know its strengths and weaknesses. Classify and segment the various groups in your audience. Aim your communications at specific subgroups in your audience. Recruit spokespeople who are good at presentation and interaction. Train your staff, including technical staff, in communication skills; reward outstanding performance. Whenever possible, pretest your messages. Carefully evaluate your efforts and learn from your mistakes.

Points to Consider: There is no such entity as "the public"; instead, there are many publics, each with its own interests, needs, concerns, priorities, preferences, and organizations. Different risk communication goals, audiences, and media require different risk communication strategies.

3. Listen to the public's specific concerns. If you do not listen to the people, you cannot expect them to listen to you. Communication is a two-way activity.

Guidelines: Do not make assumptions about what people know, think, or want done about risks. Take the time to find out what people are thinking: Use techniques such as interviews, focus groups, and surveys. Let all parties that have an interest or stake in the issue be heard. Identify with your audience and try to put yourself in their place. Recognize people's emotions. Let people know that you understand what they said, addressing their concerns as well as yours. Recognize the "hidden agendas," symbolic meanings, and broader economic or political considerations that often underlie and complicate the task of risk communication.

Point to Consider: People in the community are often more concerned about such issues as trust, credibility, competence, control, voluntariness, fairness, caring, and compassion than about mortality statistics and the details of quantitative risk assessment.

4. Be honest, frank, and open. In communicating risk information, trust and credibility are your most precious assets.

Guidelines: State your credentials; but do not ask or expect to be trusted by the public. If you do not know an answer or are uncertain, say so. Get back to people with answers. Admit mistakes. Disclose risk information as soon as possible (emphasizing any reservations about reliability). Do not minimize or exaggerate the level of risk. Speculate only with great caution. If in doubt, lean toward sharing more information, not less, or people may think you are hiding something. Discuss data uncertainties, strengths and weaknesses, including the ones identified by other credible sources. Identify worst-case estimates as such, and cite ranges of risk estimates when appropriate.

Point to Consider: Trust and credibility are difficult to obtain. Once lost they are almost impossible to regain completely.

5. Coordinate and collaborate with other credible sources. Allies can be effective in helping you communicate risk information.

Guidelines: Take time to coordinate all interorganizational and intraorganizational communications. Devote effort and resources to the slow, hard work of building bridges with other organizations. Use credible and authoritative intermediates. Consult with others to determine who is best able to answer questions about risk. Try to issue communications jointly with other trustworthy sources (for example, credible university scientists and/or professors, physicians, or trusted local officials).

Point to Consider: Few things make risk communication more difficult than conflicts or public disagreements with other credible sources.

6. Meet the needs of the media. The media are a prime transmitter of information on risks; they play a critical role in setting agendas and in determining outcomes.

Guidelines: Be open and accessible to reporters. Respect their deadlines. Provide risk information tailored to the needs of each type of media (for example, graphics and other visual aids for television). Prepare in advance and provide background material on complex risk issues. Do not hesitate to follow up on stories with praise or criticism, as warranted. Try to establish long-term relationships of trust with specific editors and reporters.

Point to Consider: The media are frequently more interested in politics than in risk; more interested in simplicity than in complexity; more interested in danger than in safety.

7. Speak clearly and with compassion. Technical language and jargon are useful as professional shorthand, but they are barriers to successful communication with the public.

Guidelines: Use simple, nontechnical language. Be sensitive to local norms, such as speech and dress. Use vivid, concrete images that communicate on a personal level. Use examples and anecdotes that make technical risk data come alive. Avoid distant, abstract, unfeeling language about deaths, injuries, and illnesses. Acknowledge and respond (both in words and with action) to emotions that people express anxiety, fear, anger, outrage, helplessness. Acknowledge and respond to the distinctions that the public views as important in evaluating risks, for example, voluntariness, controllability, familiarity, dread, origin (natural or man-made), benefits, fairness, and catastrophic potential. Use risk comparisons to help put risks in perspective, but avoid comparisons that ignore distinctions which people consider important. Always try to include a discussion of actions that are under way or can be taken. Tell people what you cannot do. Promise only what you can do, and be sure to do what you promise.

Points to Consider: Regardless of how well you communicate risk information, some people will not be satisfied. Never let your efforts to inform people about risks prevent you from acknowledging and saying that any illness, injury, or death is a tragedy. And finally, if people are sufficiently motivated, they are quite capable of understanding complex risk information, even if they may not agree with you.

The preceding seven cardinal rules of risk communication only seem logical. It is when they are violated that the proper and necessary communication will fail. Because it is the public that determines which risks will be remedied first, it is important to work with them, getting them involved in the decision-making process before it is too late. When one has the cooperation of the public, carefully state the objectives. Work with these objectives to provide necessary information, and motivate the involved individuals to act. Be a listener as well as a talker. Find out what the people want to know and let their voices be heard. Be honest with the issues at hand. State the truth and do not tell people what they may want to hear; they usually only want to know the truth. Work with, not against or in competition with, other credible sources. Get the message across in all possible ways, whether it be pamphlets, radio, or television. Most importantly, speak clearly and in terms that can be understood by everyone. Take into account the concerned people, and work on a personal level. All this is necessary for communicating and being heard. Successful communication will surely follow if the seven rules are enacted.

COMMUNICATING RISK TO THE PUBLIC: GETTING THE MESSAGE ACROSS

A comprehensive community outreach program covers one or more of the following categories: information and education, the development of a receptive audience, disaster warning and emergency information, and/or mediation and conflict resolution. In developing a community outreach program, three steps must be understood and addressed (Beuby, Faye, & Newlowet, 1989):

1. Knowing the audience and its concerns. What is their "perception" of the risks involved?
2. Understanding the issue objectives. What is the "message" to get across?
3. Implementing the communication plan. How do we get the message out?

Each of these steps is vital to a successful community outreach plan. The answers to each of these questions will differ depending on the scenario at hand, and the mechanisms for communicating the risks involved will also differ.

The material below will examine four example scenarios in hazardous material/waste management that require risk communication: emergency response, remediation, facility siting, and ongoing plant operations (Beuby et al., 1989).

Emergency Response

A fire in a chemical storage warehouse is burning out of control. The fire department is on the scene, the nearby highway is closed, traffic is at a standstill, and the radio and television stations are getting up-to-date reports on the scene. Many of the local residents have heard about the fire, and few know what to do, and most are in a state of panic.

Communicating risk to this audience of potentially affected local residents and merchants means providing emergency information and guidance to a frightened public. The immediate concerns of this audience are to learn the threat to their health and safety, and to do something to protect themselves.

The central risk communication issue for an emergency response is generally to disseminate health and safety information. In conjunction with specific emergency information, the risk communicator has an even greater risk reassurance. While a company may be anxious about legal liability, it should still strive to address the community's concerns as completely as possible.

Getting the message across of reassurance, coupled with emergency directives, requires directly addressing the community's concerns. The company must work directly with health and safety personnel to immediately ascertain the risks involved, to inform the community of those risks, and present steps or actions to mitigate them.

The mechanisms for getting the message out during an emergency situation are straightforward. The news media will carry the story, and so will local radio and television stations. In the case for an extreme emergency, direct contact will be made via a mobile public address system, or through door-to-door notification.

Remediation

For years, local industrial companies had been dumping their hazardous wastes into an unlined lagoon. At the time the practice was legal, but now the lagoon is a designated Superfund site. Residents have always fretted over the smell, and now their concerns are more severe. Research indicates possible cancer risks, but no cases have been noted. Local residents are perplexed about these reports, and are worried about property value, their children, and so on. . . .

Communicating risk to individuals living or working near a hazardous waste site involves a different message, and different methods for getting the message out than that required for an emergency response situation.

The risk communicator in this case must be able to communicate health risk and offer reassurance. The problem here is that the situation does not require immediate action. Health problems can only be assessed after studying the site for some time. This gives the public time to ponder the possible negative effects it will have on them.

The process of site remediation requires site investigation, risk assessment, determination of alternate remediation methods, and subsequent selection of the best alternative. Implementation of various remediation alternatives has various levels and types of risk. The association of risk with each alternative introduces the concept of risk acceptance to the public. The message of the risk communicator must be to place these risks in perspective, while assuring the community that the safest remediation is being sought. Encouraging the community to participate in the remediation planning process may be the best way of assuring the community that the safest solution is indeed being sought.

Mechanisms for getting information on health risks out to the community could include fact sheets, newsletters, and direct contact. How each of these is an effective means for communicating the risks involved is discussed later in this chapter.

Facility Siting

A small community is concerned. Their understanding of the risks associated with hazardous wastes is limited, but they should not need to accept any risk. They see no benefits from siting a hazardous waste treatment facility in their community. They only foresee big problems. . . .

The siting of a hazardous waste treatment, storage, and disposal facility is viewed as a voluntary option to the local community. If they choose to oppose this facility, they can impose cost delays on the project, even to the point of prohibiting the new facility altogether.

Such was the case in a small town on the south shore of Long Island. Since the county's sewage treatment plant was located in East Rockaway, the county also sought to build a sludge dewatering facility in this small, budding young community. Local residents were fearful of bringing in the contaminated sludge to be treated. They opposed the trucks traveling on the main roads, past the schools and local shops. Opposition arose, various town meetings were held, and a delay was imposed on the building of this site. It is unknown at this time whether this plant will be built.

The local community will act as a friend or a foe to the siting plan, depending on its perspective risks and benefits of the new facility. The important message to get across to this audience is that the benefits of siting this new facility will outweigh the actual risks.

Risks to the community should be presented in the same way as mentioned above, except that the information should include information on the benefits of the project. Some of the possible benefits could be new jobs, and a safer, less costly method for treating sludge. The site will also bring in a profit to the town, and the money will be used to enhance the quality of the existing neighborhoods.

Education is imperative in appraising the local community of the benefits of hosting a waste facility in their area. Education includes information on wastes generated in their area, current management practices, current disposal options, and waste reduction and recycling potential.

Ongoing Plant Operations

California's Proposition 65, the OSHA "Right-to-Know" standard, SARA Title 313, and California's AB 2588 the Hot Toxics Spots bill all require companies handling hazardous materials to appraise their workers and/or the local community of the hazards present at their facilities. A consequence of these information dissemination standards may be to alienate the local community from a "risky" facility in their area. A highly publicized tragedy, such as the accidental release of a poisonous gas from a chemical manufacturing plant in Bhopal, India, could further damage the public's image of similar facilities.

The concern for facilities that handle hazardous wastes is to foster a positive image, particularly within the local community. Maintaining this positive image fosters community support for the company's activities, and helps dissuade negative public reaction in the event of an accident.

As in any risk communication effort, the primary task is to establish and maintain credibility. A facility open house is useful for introducing the public to the facility, and for building understanding and confidence in facility operations and safety precautions. Convenient public access to release and emissions data, as well as public information hotlines for disseminating that data and answering other questions are other effective measures for fostering public trust.

Regarding understanding and cooperation in risk communication, the content of the message is determined by the intention of the risk communicator. For each of the scenarios discussed above the intention of the communicator varied. The basic principle is: Whatever it is that is to be conveyed to a worried public, the risk communicator must understand the concerns of the audience and respond directly to these concerns.

SPECIFIC METHODS OF COMMUNICATING RISK

Environmental communication takes on many forms; it normally depends on the audience it is intended to serve. At times, it involves either (1) testifying in court, (2) testifying before the Congress of the United States or appearing before committees representing the Congress, (3) delivering speeches at educational facilities, ranging from kindergarten to colleges and universities, (4) addressing seminars, conferences, or workshops, (5) responding to a press release or making appearances on television, and/or (6) preparing technical documents, handbooks, guides, or pamphlets on environmental issues in both the public and private sectors. These are just a few of the activities involving environmental communications. The EPA established the Office of External Programs to assist individuals, particularly within the Agency, to accomplish this complex and critical activity (Holmes et al., 1993).

Environmental communication can also take on other significant means of communication that are not as complex. They include printed material in the form of technical documents, pamphlets, handouts, brochures, magazines, journals, issue papers, newspaper articles, editorials, and the like.

The 1990 National Environmental Education Act contains a provision that specifically calls on the EPA to work with "noncommercial educational broadcasting entities" to educate Americans on environmental problems. Educational, or public, broadcasting reaches vast numbers of Americans. Many of the public television and radio stations are locally based and independently owned. As such, they are aware of the needs and concerns of their local communities. And, because public broadcasting considers all its programs to be educational, they are reached not only in homes, but into the schools as well. Almost all public television stations provide outreach activities to supplement and support all their programming.

Spurred by growing concerns about global environmental problems, the entertainment industry is in the midst of a massive conscience raising effort on a variety of environmental issues. Although it is not the first social issue adopted by the show business industry, it just might be the catalyst for the most far-reaching public-interest campaign yet launched by the industry (Holmes et al., 1993).

Fact sheets present detailed information on the site, proposed remediation techniques, health risk analyses, and other information in a readily understandable format to be mailed to libraries, schools, business organizations, and local residents. Newsletters present information similar in content to the fact sheet, but include additional, more general information on hazardous waste management. Direct contact entails walking door-to-door to discuss the proposed remediation project and other issues related to site. This approach gives the risk communicator an opportunity to directly address local residents concerns, thereby giving residents the feeling that they do have a say. In some cases, this method is the only way to understand the opinions of the residents regarding remediation (Russell, 1989).

Largely as a result of the 1985 disaster in Bhopal, India, and the releases of other toxic chemicals in Institute, West Virginia, Congress shortly thereafter added the Emergency Planning and Community Right-to-Know Act (EPCRA) to the Superfund Amendments and Reauthorization Act of 1986 (SARA). As discussed in earlier chapters, EPCRA, often referred to as SARA Title III, establishes emergency planning districts to prepare for the appropriate response to releases of hazardous chemicals. It also suggests recommendations for communicating these risks. In addition,

EPCRA requires the annual reporting of releases of hazardous chemicals to the environment. This annual inventory has spurred action through legislation and public pressure to force companies to reduce releases to the environment (Davenport, 1992). If one believes that a business which is subject to the EPCRA requirements failed to report to the Toxics Release Inventory, they should immediately contact: Office of Compliance Monitoring (EN342), U.S. Environmental Protection Agency, Washington, D.C., 20460 (Holmes et al., 1993).

SARA Title III also contains strategies for explaining very small risks in a community context. The objectives of Title III are to improve local chemical emergency response capabilities, primarily through improved emergency planning and notification, and to provide citizens and local governments with access to information about chemicals in their localities. Title III has four major sections that aid in the development of contingency plans. They are as follows (Holmes et al., 1993):

1. Emergency Planning (Sections 301-303)
2. Emergency Notification (Section 304)
3. Community Right-to-Know Reporting Requirements (Sections 311 and 312)
4. Toxic Chemicals Release Reporting Emissions Inventory (Section 313)

Title III has also developed timeframes for the implementation of the Emergency Planning and Community Right-to-Know Act of 1986.

The relationship between Title III data and community action can best occur at the local level, through the work of the Local Emergency Planning Committee (LEPC). LEPCs are crucial to the success of the Emergency Planning and Community Right-to-Know Act. Appointed by the State Emergency Response Commissions (SERCs), local planning committees must consist of representatives of all the following groups and organizations: elected state and local officials; law enforcement, civil defense, firefighting, first aid, health, and local environmental and transportation agencies; hospitals; broadcast and print media; community groups; and, representatives of facilities subject to the Emergency Planning and Community Right-to-Know Requirements (EPA, 1988).

It was clear from the outset that the public could not put persistent and informed pressure on the EPA without a steady flow of information and guidance from the Agency. Meeting that need has been the purpose of the EPA's public participation programs. Their mission is threefold (Holmes et al., 1993):

1. To keep the public informed of important developments in the EPA's program areas.
2. To provide technical information and, if necessary, translate that information into plain English.
3. To ensure that the EPA takes community viewpoints into account in implementing these programs.

THE CITIZEN'S ROLE IN ENVIRONMENTAL ENFORCEMENT

An important part in the communication of risk is to get involved. When information is put forth, take notice and take action. No one will know of one's concerns or problems if one keeps quiet. Communication is a two-way street. It often must be crossed several times in order to be heard.

There are two important things to do when one becomes aware of a potential pollution problem: (1) make careful observations of the problem, and (2) report it to the proper authorities (EPA, 1990).

On sighting a potential problem, fully record any observations, including the date and time, where notice of the problem took place, and how information came about the problem. Try to identify the responsible parties. In the case of dumping, write down the license plate number. If the pollution aspect is visible, take pictures. In the event of no other witnesses, pictures can only tell what they saw; they do not lie.

Once this information has been gathered, call and inform the local or state authorities. When in contact with a representative, carefully give them all the information observed and ask them to look further into the problem. Follow up with phone calls to that person to be sure it has been taken into consideration, and that something is going to be done about it. If that should fail, call them back and ask to speak to the official supervisor or boss. If phone conversation is not possible, write them. If all the above fails, call the EPA regional office that covers the area of concern. If the pollution problem persists and the local, state, and regional EPA offices appear unwilling or unable to help, then contact the EPA Headquarters in Washington, DC.

Finally, if told that the pollution problem observed is legal, but one firmly believes that it should not be, feel free to suggest changes in the law by writing to the appropriate U.S. Senator or Representative in Washington, DC., or to the state governor or state legislatures to inform them of the problem. Local libraries should have the names and addresses of these elected officials.

ACCESSIBILITY IN ENVIRONMENTAL COMMUNICATION

The availability and accessibility of means to ensure environmental communication is crucial in establishing effective communications. Hotlines, toll-free numbers, and information lines provide the consumer a vital link with the EPA's environmental programs, technical capabilities, and services. The EPA is among several environmental agencies currently using these state-of-the-art means of information dissemination and service to the public (Holmes et al., 1993).

Toll-Free Numbers Offered by EPA Headquarters

RCRA/Superfund Hotline National Toll-Free 1-800-424-9346; Washington, DC Metro, 1-202-382-3000. The EPA's largest and busiest toll-free number, the RCRA/Superfund Hotline answers nearly 10,000 questions and document requests each year. The RCRA/Superfund Hotline can be reached Monday through Friday from 8:30 AM to 4:30 PM Eastern Standard Time (EST).

National Response Center Hotline, National Toll-Free 1-800-424-8802; Washington, DC Metro, 1-202-426-2675. Operated by the U.S. Coast Guard, this hotline responds to all kinds of accidental releases of oil and hazardous substances. Call this number 24 hours a day, 7 days a week, every day of the year to report chemical spills.

Chemical Emergency Preparedness Program (CEPP) Hotline, National Toll-Free 1-800-535-0202; Washington, DC Metro, and Alaska, 1-202-479-2449. Responds to questions concerning community preparedness for chemical accidents. The recent Superfund Amendments and Reauthorization Act (SARA) has increased the CEPP Hotline's responsibilities. Calls are answered Monday through Friday from 8:30 AM to 4:30 PM EST.

Asbestos Hotline, National Toll-Free 1-800-334-8571, extension 6741. The Asbestos Hotline is now available to meet the asbestos information needs of private individuals, government agencies, and regulated industry. This hotline handles about 10,000 calls each year, and it operates Monday through Friday from 8:15 AM to 5:00 PM EST.

Commercial Numbers Offered by EPA Headquarters

Public Information Center (PIC), 1-202-829-3535. Answers inquiries from the public about the EPA's programs and activities, and it offers a variety of general, nontechnical information materials. The public is encouraged to call its commercial telephone lines.

Center for Environmental Research Information, 1-513-569-7391. Central point of distribution for EPA results and reports.

National Small Flows Information Clearinghouse, 1-800-624-8301. Provides information on wastewater treatment technologies for small communities.

Pollution Prevention Information Clearinghouse, 1-703-821-4800. Provides information on reducing waste through source reduction and recycling.

Radon Information. For information about radon, call the state radon office. The Radon Office at EPA Headquarters also responds to requests for information: 1-202-260-9605.

Safe Drinking Water Hotline. Provides information on the EPA's drinking water regulations. This hotline operates Monday through Friday from 8:30 AM to 4:30 PM EST: 1-800-426-4791. In the Washington, DC area the number is 1-202-260-5534.

FUTURE TRENDS

The growing concern that risk communication was becoming a major problem led to the chartering of a National Research Council committee (May 1987–June 1988) to examine the possibilities for improving social and personal choices on technological issues by improving risk communication. The National Research Council offers advice from governments, private and nonprofit sector organizations, and concerned citizens about the process of risk communication, about the content of risk messages and ways to improve risk communication (NRC, 1989). The committee's recommendations, if followed, will significantly improve the risk communication process.

Future goals are not to make those who disseminate formal risk messages more effective by improving their credibility, understanding, and so on; it is to "improve" their techniques. "Improvement" can only occur if recipients are also enabled to solve their problems at the same time. Generally, this means obtaining relevant information for better-informed decisions (NRC, 1989). Implementation of many recommendations requires organizational resources of several kinds. One of these resources in particular is time, especially during the most difficult risk communication efforts, as when emergency conditions leave no possibility for consulting with the people concerned, or to assemble the vital information that would be necessary for them.

The committee came forward with three general conclusions that may bring to light why the task of communicating risk does not seem to be working (NRC, 1989):

Conclusion 1. Even great improvement in risk communication will not resolve the problems or end the controversy. Sometimes, they will tend to create them through poor communication. There is no ready shortcut to improving the nation's risk communication efforts. The needed improvement in performance can only come incrementally and only from constant attention to many details. For example, more interaction with the audience and the intermediaries involved is necessary to fully understand the issue at hand.

Conclusion 2. Better risk communication should not only be about improving procedures, but about improving the content of the risk message. It would be a mistake to believe that better communication is only a matter of a better message. To enhance the credibility, to ensure accuracy, to understand the concerned citizens and their worries, and to gain the insight necessary into how messages are actually perceived, the communicator must ultimately seek procedural solutions.

Conclusion 3. Communication should be more systematically oriented to specific audiences. The concept of openness is the best policy. It is true that the most effective risk messages are those that consciously address the specific audience's concerns. Similarly, the best procedures for formulating risk messages have been those that involved open interaction with the citizen's and their needs.

In the future, the communication of risk can become more effective. It should be understood that risk communication is a two-way exchange of information and opinion among individuals, groups, and organizations. The written, verbal, or visual message containing information about the risk should include advice on waste reduction or elimination, so that in the future communication efforts will no longer be necessary.

SUMMARY

1. Risk communication is one of the most important problems in environmental protection this country faces. The government and media together have failed to communicate clearly what is a risk and what is not a risk. The challenge of risk communication is to provide this information in ways that it can be incorporated in the views of people. Success in risk communication is not to be measured by whether the public chooses to set the outcomes that minimize risk as estimated by the experts; it is achieved instead when those outcomes are knowingly chosen by a well-informed public.

2. There are no easy prescriptions for successful risk communication. However, those who have studied and participated in recent debates about risk generally agree on seven cardinal rules. These rules apply equally well to the public and private sectors. Although many of these rules may seem obvious, they are continually and consistently violated in practice. Thus, a way to use these rules is to focus on why they are frequently not followed.

3. A comprehensive community outreach program covers one or more of the following categories: information and education, the development of a receptive audience, disaster warning and emergency information, and/or mediation and conflict resolution. In developing a community outreach program, three steps must be understood and addressed:

   a. Knowing the audience and its concerns. What is their "perception" of the risks involved?

   b. Understanding the issue objectives. What is the "message" to get across?

   c. Implementing the communication plan. How does one get the message out?

   4. Environmental communication can take on significant forms that are not complex; these include printed material in the form of technical documents, pamphlets, handouts, brochures, magazines, journals, issue papers, newspaper articles, editorials, and the like.

   5. There are two important things to do when one sites a potential pollution problem: (a) make careful observations of the problem, and (b) report it to the proper authorities.

   6. The availability and accessibility of means to ensure environmental dialogue is crucial in establishing effective communications. Hotlines, toll-free numbers, and information lines provide the consumer a vital link with the EPA's environmental programs, technical capabilities, and services.

   7. From May 1987 through June 1988, the National Research Council offered knowledge based on advice from governments, private and nonprofit sector organizations, and concerned citizens about the process of risk communication, the content of risk messages, and ways to improve risk communication in the service of public understanding and better-informed individual choices. The committee's recommendations, if followed, will significantly improve the risk communication process.

REFERENCES

Beuby, R., Faye, D., and Newlowet, E. *Communicating Risk to the Public: Getting the Message Across,* Fremont, CA: Ensco Environmental Services, 1989.

Davenport, G. "The ABC's of Hazardous Waste Legislation," *Chemical Engineering Progress,* May 1992.

EPA, "Chemicals in your Community: A Guide to Emergency Planning and Community Right-to-Know Act," September, 1988.

EPA. "Seven Cardinal Rules of Risk Communication," EPA OPA/8700, April 1988, including periodic updates.

EPA, Office of Enforcement, "The Public Role in Environmental Enforcement," March, 1990.

Holmes, G., Singh, B., and Theodore, L. *Handbook of Environmental Management and Technology.* New York: John Wiley & Sons, 1993.

National Research Council, Committee on Risk Perception and Communication. "Improving Risk Communication," Washington, DC: National Academy Press, 1989.

Russell, M. "Communicating Risk to a Concerned Public," *EPA Journal,* November 1989.

Part IX

Other Areas of Interest

Part IX of this book, comprised of ten chapters, examines a host of other important environmental issues. In Chapter 39, information on noise pollution is presented. Chapter 40 is concerned with highly sensitive (recently) issue of electromagnetic fields. A comprehensive examination of the acid rain problem is provided in Chapter 41, while Chapter 42 examines greenhouse effects. Chapter 43 addresses the need for environmental training. The problems arising with underground storage tanks are presented in Chapter 44. The general subject of metals is treated in Chapter 45, while the questionable concerns associated with asbestos are reviewed in Chapter 46. Chapter 47 addresses the important subject of economics. Part IX concludes with Chapter 48, which examines architectural environmental considerations.

39

Noise Pollution

CONTRIBUTING AUTHOR
Pedick Lai

INTRODUCTION

By definition, noise is a sound that is annoying and has a long-term physiological effect on an individual. Noise is a subtle pollutant. Although it can be hazardous to a person's health and well-being, noise usually leaves no visible evidence. Noise pollution has grown to be a major environmental problem today. An estimated 14.7 million Americans are exposed to noises that pose a threat to hearing on their jobs. Another 13.5 million Americans are exposed to dangerous noise levels, such as from trucks, airplanes, motorcycles, and stereos without knowing it. Moreover, noise can cause temporary stress reactions like increasing the heart-rate and blood pressure, and produce negative effects on the digestive and respiratory system.

Sound is a disturbance that propagates through a medium having the properties of inertia (mass) and elasticity. The medium by which audible sound is transmitted is air. The higher the wave, the greater its power; the greater the number of waves a sound has, the larger is its frequency or pitch. The frequency can be described as the rate of vibration that is measured in Hertz (Hz, cycles per second). The human ear does not hear all of the frequencies. The normal hearing range for humans is from 20 Hz to 20,000 Hz. And also, the human ear cannot define all sounds equally. Very low and very high notes sound more faint to the ear than do 1000 Hz sounds of equal strength; that is how the ear functions. The human voice in conversation covers a median range of 300 to 4000 Hz; and, the musical scale ranges from 30 to 4000 Hz. Hearing also varies widely between individuals.

The unit of the strength of sound is measured in decibels (dB).* Although the degree of loud-

---

*The decibel is a dimensionless unit used to describe sound intensity; it is the logarithm of the ratio of the intensity of sound to the intensity of an arbitrary chosen standard sound.

Table 39–1.   Sound Levels and Human Response

Common Sounds	Noise Level (dB)	Effect
Carrier deck jet operation	140	Painfully loud
Air raid siren	130	
Jet takeoff (200 ft)		Thunderclap
Discotheque	120	Maximum vocal effort
Auto horn (3 ft)		
Pile drivers	110	
Garbage truck	100	
Heavy truck (50 ft)	90	Very annoying
City traffic		Hearing damage (8 hr)
Alarm clock (2 ft)	80	Annoying
Hair dryer		
Noisy restaurant	70	Phone use difficult
Freeway traffic		
Man's voice (3 ft)		
Air-conditioning unit (20 ft)	60	Intrusive
Light auto traffic (100 ft)	50	Quiet
Living room		
Bedroom	40	
Quiet office		
Library	30	Very quiet
Soft whisper (15 ft)		
Broadcasting studio	20	
	10	Just audible
	0	Hearing begins

ness depends on personal judgments, precise measurement of sound is made possible by the use of the decibel scale (see Table 39–1). The decibel scale ranges from 0 (minimum) to 194 (maximum). Because the decibel scale is in logarithm form, at high levels, even a small reduction in level values can make a significant difference in noise intensity. This decibel scale measures sound pressure or energy according to international standards. By comparing some common sounds, the scale shows how they rank in potential harm. Recent scientific evidence showed that relatively continuous exposures to sound exceeding 70 dB can be harmful to hearing. Noise begins to harm hearing at 70 dB; and, each 10-dB increase seems twice as loud (Thumann & Miller, 1990).

NOISE LEGISLATION*

Because noise pollution has become such a threat to the health of so many lives, many regulations have been established to monitor and control the level of unwanted harmful sounds. The Occupational Safety and Health Act (OSHA) was signed on December 29, 1970 and went into effect April 28, 1971. The purpose of this Act is "to assure so far as possible every working man and woman in

*Information in this section and the next is drawn, in part, from Cheremisinoff and Cheremisinoff, 1977.

the nation safe and healthful working conditions and to preserve our human resources." The OSHA does not apply to working conditions that are protected by other federal occupational safety and health laws such as the Federal Coal Mine Health and Safety Act, the Atomic Energy Act, the Metal and Nonmetallic Mines Safety and Health Standards, and the Open Pit and Quarries Safety and Health Standards. This Act puts all state and federal occupational safety and health enforcement programs under federal control with the goal of establishing more uniform standards, regulations, and codes with stricter enforcement. Several of the major aspects of the Act will maintain federal supervision of state programs to obtain more uniform state inspection under federal standards. The OSHA will also make it mandatory for employers to keep accurate records of employee exposures to harmful agents that are required by safety and health standards. The law provides procedures in investigating violations by delivering citations and monetary penalties upon the request of an employee. The OSHA establishes a National Institute of Occupational Safety and Health (NIOSH) whose members have the same powers of inspection as members of the OSHA. The Act also delegates to the Secretary of Labor the power to issue safety and health regulations and standards enforccable by law. This last provision is implemented by the Occupational Safety and Health Administration.

The OSHA enforces two basic duties which must be carried out by employers. First, it provides each employee with a working environment free of recognized hazards that cause or have the potential to cause physical harm or death. Second, it fully complies with the Occupational Safety and Health Standards under the Act. To carry out the first duty, employers must have proper instrumentation for the evaluation of test data provided by an expert in the area of industrial hygiene. This instrumentation must be obtained because the presence of health hazards cannot be evaluated by visual inspection. This duty can be used by the employees to allege a hazardous working situation without any requirement of expert judgment. It also provides the employer with substantial evidence to disprove invalid complaints. This law also gives employers the right to takc full disciplinary action against those employees who violate safe practices in working methods.

Section 50–204.10 of the Act establishes acceptable noise levels and exposures for safe working conditions, and gives various means of actions which must be taken if these levels are exceeded. A 90 dBA level of exposure to sound energy absorbed is taken as the limit of exposure that will not cause any type of hearing loss in more than 20 percent of those exposed. Workers in any industry must not be exposed to sound levels greater than 115 dBA for any amount of time. Noise levels must be measured on the A scale of a standard sound level meter at slow response. The sound level meter is a measuring device that indicates sound intensity. "Slow response" is a particular setting on the meter, and when the meter is at this setting it will average out high-level noise of short-lived duration. For impact noise, a higher level of 140 dB is acceptable because the noise impulse due to impacts is over before the human ear has time to fully react to it.

Regulations of variable noise levels are covered under paragraph (c) of Section 50–204.10 in the OSHA. This paragraph states, "if the variations in noise levels involve maxima at intervals of 1 second or less, it is considered to be continuous." Therefore, when the level on the meter goes from a relatively steady reading to a higher reading, at intervals of one second or less, the higher reading is taken as the continuous sound level. Sounds of short duration occurring at intervals greater than 1 second should be measured in intensity and duration over the total work day. Such sounds may be analyzed using a sound level meter and should not be treated as impact sound.

The Federal Walsh-Healey Public Contracts Act took effect on May 20, 1969. To comply with the Walsh-Healey regulations on industrial noise exposure, industry must measure the noise level of its working environment. It provides valuable data with which an inspector can evaluate working conditions. The data may be obtained by sound survey meters with A-, B-, and C-weighted filters; and, all measurements weigh all the frequencies equally in that range.

On April 30, 1976, the Administrator of the U.S. Environmental Protection Agency (EPA) established the Noise Enforcement Division under the Deputy Assistant Administrator for Mobile Source and Noise Enforcement, Office of Enforcement. The division originally had a staff of twenty-one individuals whose responsibilities were divided into the following four general enforcement areas:

1. General products noise regulations
2. Surface transportation noise regulations
3. Noise enforcement testing
4. Regional (EPA), state, and local assistance

On December 31, 1975, the EPA set forth noise standards and regulations for the control of noise from portable air compressors. These regulations became effective on January 1, 1978. Additional regulations are currently being developed to control noise from truck-mounted solid waste compactors, truck transport, refrigeration units, wheel and track loaders, and dozers, which have been identified pursuant to Section 5 of the NCA (Noise Control Act). The surface transportation group will have similar responsibilities with respect to transportation-related products. The first such products to be regulated under Section 6 for the control of noise are new medium- and heavy-duty trucks (in excess of 10,000 lb GVWR). Regulations for trucks were set forth on April 13, 1976 and became effective on January 1, 1978. Motorcycles and buses are additional major noise sources that have been identified and for which regulations are presently being developed.

Noise enforcement testing is conducted by the EPA Noise Enforcement Facility located in Sandusky, Ohio. The facility is used to conduct enforcement testing; to monitor and correlate manufacturers' compliance testing; and, to train regional, state, and local personnel for noise enforcement. This program defines and develops the EPA enforcement responsibilities under the NCA. It also provides assistance to state and local agencies regarding enforcement of the federal noise control standards and regulations, and enforcement aspects of additional state and local noise control regulations.

To assist state and local governments in drafting noise control ordinances, EPA has published a Model Community Noise Ordinance, which is available in EPA regional offices and in the EPA headquarters in Washington, DC.

EFFECTS OF NOISE

It is estimated that between 8.7 and 11.1 million Americans suffer a permanent hearing disability (EPA, 1982). This section will examine the overall effects of noise on an industrial worker, not only in terms of hearing loss, but also in work quality.

The ear has its own defense mechanism against noise—the acoustic reflex. However, this reflex has vital weak points in its defenses. First of all, the muscles within the middle ear can become fatigued and slow if overused. A person who works in an environment with high noise levels gradually loses the strength in these muscles and thus more noise will reach the inner ear. Secondly, these muscles can be affected by chemicals within the working environment. Finally, the acoustic reflex is an ear-to-brain-to-ear circuit that takes at least nine-thousandths (0.009) of a second to perform. Individuals with poor acoustic reflex are usually subjected to temporary hearing loss when they come in contact with a loud noise. Most of the hearing loss caused by noise occurs during the first hour of exposure. Recovery of hearing can be complete several hours after the noise stops. The period of recovery depends upon individual variation and the level of noise that caused the deafness.

Noises that pose the greatest threat to the human body are those that are the highest pitched, loudest, poorest in tone, and longest lasting. Another dangerous type of sound is the sound of an explosion. Deafness due to noise usually occurs in conjunction with a fairly common hearing disorder known as recruitment of loudness. The person who has this disorder will have a smaller range of zone of hearing. However, the recruitment ear will retain its sensitivity for loud sound levels. Another problem that a person with recruited ears faces is the discomfort of using hearing aids. The hearing aid is a microphone that transmits sounds from the surrounding environment to an amplifier connected to a small loudspeaker built into an earplug and aimed at the eardrum. The major problem is that the sounds entering the hearing aid have to be amplified enough to be heard loudly, and at that level the sound may produce discomfort.

Researchers have analyzed noise and its effects on the human ear and have come up with several properties of noise that contribute to the loss of hearing. They include the "overall sound level of the noise spectrum," "the shape of the noise spectrum," and "total exposure duration." A final characteristic of noise that should be mentioned is the temporal distribution of noise. However, energy in noise is distributed across time and its final effect on the threshold shift is a function of total energy. It has been determined that partial noise exposures are related closely to the continuous A-weighted noise level (a means of correlating speech-interference level and NC (Noise Criteria) or PNC (Preferred Noise Criteria) level, and the unit of this scale is dBA) by equal energy amounts. The relation between energy and the amount of exposure is: twice the energy is acceptable for every halving of exposure time, without any increase in danger.

Noise affects the mind and changes emotions and behavior in many ways. Most of the time, individuals are unaware that noise is directly affecting their minds. It interferes with communication, disturbs sleep, and arouses a sense of fear. Psychologically, noise stimulates individuals to a nervous peak. Too much arousal makes a person overly anxious and as a result, tends to cause the person to make more mistakes. The effects of noise increase the frequency of momentary lapses in efficiency.

Noise has its effects on manual workers. From a case history from Dr. Jansen, the employees who worked in the quieter surroundings were easier to interview than the employees who worked in the noisier surroundings (Cheremisinoff & Cheremisinoff, 1977). Noise also affects a worker's behavior at home. This study revealed that the workers exposed to higher noise levels had more than twice as many family problems. Since noise affects a worker's attitude and personality, it also affects his or her output. It can interfere with communication greatly. Noise also can cause a decrease in the quality of work output when the background noise exceeds 90 dB. The effects of noise on work output depend largely on the type of work. High noise levels tend to cause a higher rate of mistakes and accidents rather than a direct slowdown of production. Results show that a worker's attention to the job at hand will tend to drift as noise levels increase.

Dr. G. Lehmann, Director of the Max Planck Institute, had determined that noise has an explicit effect on the blood vessels, especially the smaller ones known as precapillaries (Cheremisinoff & Cheremisinoff, 1977). Overall, noise makes these blood vessels narrow. It was also found that noise causes significant reductions in the blood supply to various parts of the body. Tests were also conducted employing a ballistocardiogram, which is used to measure the heart with each beat. When the test was conducted on a patient in noisy surroundings, the findings led to one conclusion: noise at all levels causes the peripheral blood vessels in the toes, fingers, skin, and abdominal organs to constrict, thereby decreasing the amount of blood normally supplied to these areas. The vaso-constriction is triggered by various body chemicals, predominantly adrenaline, which is produced when the body is under stress. Finally noise affects the nervous system. Noise wears down the nervous system, breaks down the human's natural resistance to disease and natural recovery, thus lowering the quality of general health.

SOURCES OF NOISE*

As more and more noise-generating products become available to consumers, the sources of noise pollution are extremely diverse and are constantly increasing. Commonly encountered motor vehicle noise comes from cars, trucks, buses, motorcycles, and emergency vehicles with sirens. Noise levels near major airports have become so intolerable that residents sometimes are forced to relocate, and property values sometimes depreciate because of noise pollution. Airport noise is the most common source of noise pollution that will produce an immediate effect ranging from temporary deafness to a prolonged irritation.

The noise levels a source produces can be separated into four categories. Machines, such as refrigerators and clothes dryers, are in the first group, usually produce sound levels lower than 60 dB. The second group includes clothes washers and food mixers that produce noise from 65 to 75 dB. The third group includes vacuum cleaners and noisy dishwashers, which produce a noise range from 85–95 dB. This group also includes yard-care and shop tools. The fourth group include pneumatic chippers and jet engines, which produce noise levels above 100 dB. Any amount of exposure to such equipment will probably interfere with activities, disrupt a neighbor's sleep, cause annoyance and stress, and may contribute to hearing loss.

NOISE ABATEMENT

Noise abatement measures are under the jurisdiction of local government, except for occupational noise abatement efforts. It is impossible for an active person to avoid exposure to potentially harmful sound levels in today's mechanized world. Therefore, hearing specialists now recommend that individuals get into the habit of wearing protectors to reduce the annoying effects of noise.

Muffs worn over the ears and inserts worn in the ears are two basic types of hearing protectors. Since ear canals are rarely the same size, inserts should be separately fitted for each ear. Pro-

*Information in the next two sections was drawn from Holmes, Singh, and Theodore, 1993.

tective muffs should be adjustable to provide a good seal around the ear, proper tension of the cups against the head, and comfort. Both types of protectors are well worth the small inconvenience they cause for the wearer and they are available at most sport stores and drugstores. Hearing protectors are recommended at work and during recreational and home activities such as target shooting and hunting, power tool use, lawnmowing, and snowmobile riding.

One should be aware of major noise sources near any residence, for example, airport flight paths, heavy truck routes, and high-speed freeways, when choosing a new house or apartment. When buying a house, check the area zoning master plan for projected changes. In some places, one cannot obtain Federal Housing Administration (FHA) loans for housing in noisy locations. Use the Department of Housing and Urban Development (HUD) "walkaway test." By means of this method, potential buyers can assess background noise around a house. Simply have one person stand with some reading material at chest level and begin reading in a normal voice while the other slowly backs away. If the listener cannot understand the words within 7 feet, the noise level is clearly unacceptable. At 7 to 25 feet, it is normally unacceptable; at 26 to 70 feet, normally acceptable; and over 70 feet, clearly acceptable.

Furthermore, look for wall-to-wall carpeting. Find out about the wall construction. Staggered-stud interior walls provide better noise control. Studs are vertical wooden supports located behind walls. Staggering them breaks up the pattern of sound transmission. Check the electrical outlet boxes because noise will pass through the wall if the boxes are back-to-back. Also, check the door construction; solid or core-filled doors with gaskets or weather stripping provide better noise control. Make sure sleeping areas are displaced from rooms with noise-producing equipment. Finally, insulating the heating and air-conditioning ducts help control noise.

There are some helpful hints to make a quieter home, including the use of carpeting to absorb noise. Hang heavy drapes over windows closest to outside noise sources. Put rubber or plastic treads on uncarpeted stairs. Use upholstered rather than hard-surfaced furniture to deaden noise. Use insulation and vibration mounts when installing dishwashers. When listening to a stereo, keep the volume down. Place window air conditioners where their hum can help mask objectionable noises. Use caution in buying children's toys that make intensive or explosive sounds. Also, compare the noise outputs of different makes of an appliance before making a selection.

Housing developments often are located near high-speed highways. Poor housing placement is on the increase in many communities across the country. To cope with the problem of lightweight construction and poor planning, HUD has developed "Noise Assessment Guidelines" to aid in community planning, construction, modernization, and rehabilitation of existing buildings. In addition, the Veterans Administration (VA) requires disclosure of information to prospective buyers about the exposure of existing VA-financed houses to noise from nearby airports.

The EPA is preparing a model building code for various building types. The code will spell out extensive acoustical requirements and will make it possible for cities and towns to regulate construction in a comprehensive manner to produce a quieter local environment.

The Noise Control Act of 1972 provides the EPA with the authority to require labels on all products that generate noise capable of adversely affecting public health or welfare and on those products sold wholly or in part for their effectiveness in reducing noise. The EPA also initiated a study to rate home appliances and other consumer products by the noise generated and the impact of the noise on users and other persons normally exposed to it. Results will be used to determine whether noise labeling or noise emission standards are necessary (Holmes et al., 1993).

FUTURE TRENDS

Since more and more noise generators have been developed in recent years, the chances of noise affecting individuals in this and next century will certainly increase. Many scientists and engineers are working on different plans or projects to reduce noise in the future. Two of the examples that have been developed are the electric trains and electric automobiles. In Japan and many eastern countries, electric trains are one of the most popular modes of transportation because they do not cause air pollution and produce minimum noise. The electric automobiles also reduce the noise, because they do not need to burn gasoline to run their engines. Although they are not very common today, this development is a good starting point for reducing noise. In addition, the development of new equipment and tools in the future, is certain to reduce noise. Individuals should also minimize noises surrounding or caused by them; for example, try not to use noise generators, such as vacuum cleaners, dishwashers, and high-watt stereos. If every individual does his or her level best to help reduce noise, the noise pollution will be lowered in the future and humans will hopefully live in a better environment.

SUMMARY

1. Urban noise pollution has rapidly grown to be a major environmental problem. Sound is a disturbance that propagates through a medium having the properties of inertia and elasticity.

2. The Occupational Safety and Health Act was signed on December 29, 1970 and went into effect April 28, 1971. The purpose of this Act is "to assure so far as possible every working man and woman in the nation safe and healthful working conditions and to preserve our human resources."

3. It is estimated that between 8.7 and 11.1 million Americans suffer a permanent hearing disability.

4. The sources of noise pollution are extremely diverse and are constantly increasing as more and more noise-generating products become available to consumers.

5. It is almost impossible for an active person to avoid exposure to potentially harmful sound level in today's mechanized world.

6. The environment will be better if individuals help to reduce noise in their everyday life.

REFERENCES

Cheremisinoff, P., and Cheremisinoff, P. *Industrial Noise Control Handbook,* Ann Arbor, MI: Ann Arbor Science Publishers, 1977.

EPA, Administrator of the Environmental Protection Agency, *Report to the President and Congress on Noise*, 92nd Congress Document, No. 92-63, February 1982.

Holmes, G., Singh, B., and Theodore, L. *Handbook of Environmental Management and Technology.* New York: John Wiley & Sons, 1993.

Thumann, A., and Miller, C. *Fundamental of Noise Control Engineering.* Englewood Cliffs, NJ: The Fairmont Press, 1990.

40

Electromagnetic Fields

INTRODUCTION*

Most individuals are surrounded by low-level electric and magnetic fields from electric power lines, and appliances and electronic devices. During the 1980s, the public became concerned about such fields because of media reports of cancer clusters in residences and schools near electric substations and transmission lines. In addition, a series of epidemiological studies showed a weak association between exposure to power-frequency electromagnetic fields and childhood leukemia or other forms of cancer.

The high standard of living in the United States is due in large measure to the use of electricity. Technological society developed electric power generation, distribution, and utilization with little expectation that exposure to the resultant electric and magnetic fields (EMF) might possibly be harmful beyond the obvious hazards of electric shocks and burns, for which protective measures were instituted. Today, the widespread use of electric energy is clearly evident by the number of electric power lines and electrically energized devices. Because of the extensive use of electric power, most individuals in the United States are today exposed to a wide range of EMF. It is estimated that at least 100,000 people have been exposed throughout their lives to technology-generated electric and magnetic fields.

Electrical devices act on charged and magnetic objects with electric and magnetic fields in a manner similar to how the moon influences the ocean tides through its gravitational field. Before the advent of man-made electricity, humans were exposed only to the steady magnetic field of the Earth and to the sudden occasional increases caused by lightning bolts. But since the advent of commercial electricity in the last century, individuals have been increasingly surrounded by man-

*Information for this section was drawn, in part, from Recupero (1994) and EPA (1992).

made fields generated by power grids and the appliances run by it, as well as by higher frequency fields from radio and television transmissions.

The most commonly used type of electricity in the home and work place is AC (alternating current). This type of current does not flow steadily in one direction but moves back and forth. In the United States, it reverses direction 60 times per second. The unit to denote the frequency of alternation is called a Hertz (Hz) in honor of Heinrich Hertz who discovered radio waves. The presence of electric currents gives rise to both electric and magnetic fields because of the presence of electric charges. Those electric charges with opposite signs attract each other; on the other hand, charges with the same sign repel each other. These charges, if stationary, create what has come to be defined as "electric fields." "Magnetic fields" are created when the charges are nonstationary, that is, are moving. The combination of these two forces is defined as electromagnetic fields, or simply EMF. Since types of fields alternate with alternating electric current, a 60 Hz electric power system will generate 60 Hz electric and magnetic fields.

EXPOSURE COMMENTS

Electric and magnetic fields at a power frequency of 60 Hz are generated by three main sources: production, delivery, and use of electric power. However, sources of public exposure include:

1. Power generation
2. Transmission
3. Electric circuits in homes and public buildings
4. Electric grounding systems
5. Electric appliances

Electric and magnetic fields have been measured in selected residences and outside environments to help resolve uncertainties in the interpretation of epidemiological results. Although almost all state and local governments, utilities, private firms, and individuals are currently measuring EMF, these measurements are often conducted without adequate supervision and expertise, and lack the standard QA/QC (quality assurance/quality control) requirements for research and study projects. Thus, these measurements have not been appropriate for determining public exposure in an absolute sense. In addition, no standardized procedure for EMF measurements exists. Notwithstanding this, instrument development has been responsive to the perceived needs for field measurements. In particular, a number of survey instruments that measure electric and magnetic fields that vary with time are now available, and miniaturized pocket-sized recording instruments have also been recently developed.

Mathematical models to estimate EMF exposure have been developed because measurement of fields at all locations and under all conditions of interest is not practical. Two types of models are available: theoretical and statistical. The application of theoretical models usually involves a detailed computer program. Statistical models are used to develop statistical estimates of average exposure; thus, statistical modeling does not predict individual exposures, but provides estimates for groups of the population.

EMF coupling to biological objects is another area of concern. Interestingly, an electric field immediately adjacent to a body is strongly perturbed and the intensity of the field may differ greatly from that of the unperturbed field. On the other hand, the magnetic field that penetrates the body is essentially unchanged. Both external electric and magnetic fields that vary with time induce electric fields internally and the electric current generated inside the body is proportional to the induced internal electric field.

HEALTH EFFECTS*

Since 1980, research into the possible health effects of low level electromagnetic fields has expanded greatly. Literally thousands of research papers by scientists in both the United States and Europe have been published on the subject. However, the study of potential health effects from these fields is fraught with complexities, contradictions, and what to some observers seem like impossibilities. In many studies, including human epidemiology and laboratory tests on cells and animals, the results obtained with relatively weak electromagnetic fields seem contradictory (Hileman, 1993). Nonetheless, there are many epidemiological studies that have reported an association between EMF exposure and health effects. The most frequently reported health effect is cancer. In particular, EMF exposure has been reported to be associated with elevated risks of leukemia, lymphoma, and nervous system cancer in children. Some occupational studies of adults describe an association between EMF exposure and cancer. However, as indicated above, uncertainties remain in the understanding of the potential health effects of EMF.

One should note that EMF analyses are particularly difficult for epidemiologists. The problems that have been attributed by some people to EMFs include several different kinds of cancer, birth defects, behavioral changes, slowed reflexes, and spontaneous abortions. Therefore, the process of deciding which health problems in a community belong to the "cluster" becomes exceedingly difficult. So, the answer to the question, "Can that source be the cause of my problems?" is "maybe or maybe not." The source might be the problem but trying to show that it is can be very difficult, if not impossible.

Despite the complexities and disagreements, scientific opinion has coalesced around a middle ground in recent years. In that middle ground is a great deal of evidence that electromagnetic fields do have some biological effects. They are not yet sure whether such fields can produce adverse health effects, but they believe there is some nontrivial chance that low-level fields could pose a problem, and they place a high priority on research aimed at answering that question. However, beyond the middle ground are a few scientists at one extreme who say enough evidence already exists to show that low-level fields, such as those from power lines, do have adverse health effects, in particular cancer, and therefore society should take strong measures to reduce exposures. At the other end of the spectrum is a small group of experts who say that biological effects from such fields would violate the laws of physics, and therefore low-level electromagnetic fields cannot cause cancer or any other disease. They also claim that lab studies on cells or animals that seem to show biological effects with very low-level fields are flawed in some way, for example, that there is some other explanation for the results (Hileman, 1993).

*Information for this section was drawn, in part, from Recupero (1994); EPA, 1992; Leonard, Neutra, Yost, & Lee, 1990; Department of Engineering and Public Policy, 1989; and Wilson, 1990.

For years, scientists assumed that the only harm caused by electromagnetic fields was thermal, that is, their ability to heat up an object. Even so, it was a phenomenon shown to exist only at the higher frequencies of several thousand megahertz, the range in which microwave ovens operate. In the late 1970s, scientists began to question if an association between cancer deaths in Denver children and exposure to extremely low-frequency 60 Hz fields existed. This subject has been debated in the literature since then ("Electromagnetic Fields," 1994).

Regarding breast cancer, women in electrical jobs are 38 percent more likely to die of breast cancer than other working women, according to a new study. It found an even higher death rate among female telephone installers, repairers, and line workers. "It's the strongest epidemiological evidence so far that breast cancer may be related to electromagnetic fields in some way, but it's still not very strong evidence," said University of North Carolina researcher Dana Loomis, chief author of the study published in the Journal of the National Cancer Institute (Fagin, 1994). The new study found that the breast cancer death rate was more than twice as high among female telephone installers, repairers, and line workers, compared with women who worked in nonelectrical occupations. The results were statistically adjusted to factor out income, age, race and marital status.

The above study also indicated that the risk was 70 percent higher for female electrical engineers, 28 percent higher for electrical technicians, and 75 percent higher for other electrical occupations such as electricians and power line workers. All of those jobs involve sustained exposure to electromagnetic fields, but so do some nonelectrical jobs, such as computer programmers, computer equipment operators, keyboard data enterers, telephone operators, and air traffic controllers. And for each of those five jobs, the study found that female breast cancer mortality was no higher than for the rest of the work force (Fagin, 1994).

Environmental agents that cause reproductive and developmental effects are important because they may directly influence health, lifespan, propagation, and functional and productive capacity of children. Some epidemiological studies have reported reproductive and developmental effects from exposure to EMF generated by devices in the workplace and home. Investigations of women and the outcome of their pregnancies have included operators of visual display terminals (VDTs) and users of specific home appliances (electric blankets, heated water beds, and ceiling electric heat). The reports of increased miscarriages and increased malformations suggest that maternal EMF exposure may be associated with adverse effects.

Other studies have reported an increased incidence of nervous system cancer in children whose fathers had occupations with potential EMF exposure. Regarding nervous system effects, neurotransmitters and neurohormones are substances involved in communication both within the nervous system and in the transmission of signals from the nervous system to other body organs. Neuroregulator chemicals are released in pulses with a distinct daily or circadian pattern. The few studies in which human subjects have been exposed to EMF in controlled laboratory settings describe the following effects: changes in brain activity of possibly slowed information processing, slowed reaction time, and altered cardiovascular function, including slowed heart rate and pulse that may indicate direct action on the heart.

The immune system defends against cancer and other diseases. Environmental agents that compromise the effectiveness of the immune system could potentially increase the incidence of cancer and other diseases. Studies on the effect of 60 Hz electric fields on the immune system of laboratory animals found no effect of chronic exposure of rates and mice. Thus, it may be concluded at this time that power frequencies have small or no effects on the immune systems of exposed animals.

While the hazards from these fields may or may not be significant, the fear of them is. In state after state, nervous citizens have delayed or even killed electric utilities' plans to build or expand high-voltage transmission lines. Real estate brokers report that houses next to power lines sell more slowly than others, and for lower prices. Parents with children in schools near power lines are demanding that either the schools or the lines be moved. Meanwhile, lawsuits by cancer victims against power companies are making their way through the courts in many states ("Electromagnetic Fields," 1994).

It is important to keep the overall EMF health risk in perspective. For example, there are about 2,600 new cases of childhood leukemia every year in the U.S. The chance of a given child's developing leukemia in any year is about one in 20,000, with the bulk of cases occurring by the age of five. Some epidemiologic studies have suggested that unusually strong magnetic fields may double a child's risk, raising it to one in 10,000. But even in those studies, the vast majority of leukemia cases occurred in houses calculated to have low magnetic fields. In the end, parents must make a personal decision about how much to worry—just as they routinely choose to worry about or ignore, other risks in their lives and their children's lives ("Electromagnetic Fields," 1994).

MANAGEMENT/CONTROL PROCEDURES*

As described earlier, the major source of environmental exposure to EMF is the electric power system, which includes transmission lines, the distribution system (substations, lines, and transformers), and electric circuits in residential and other buildings that provide power to appliances and machinery. Although considerable effort has been focused on the control of EMF from electric utility systems, little work has been done on controlling fields generated by electrically powered appliances, tools, and other devices.

In most circumstances, the strength of low-frequency EMF decreases with distance from the source. One simple mitigation approach is therefore to increase separation distance. There are other methods known to be effective regardless of frequency. They are:

1. Shielding
2. Design
3. Location
4. Component choice
5. Filtering

While electric fields can be easily shielded, magnetic fields are much more difficult to shield. Electric fields are shielded to some degree by almost anything such as trees, bushes, walls, and so forth. Magnetic fields can be reduced by enclosing the source in certain types of metal such as a material called Mu metal, which is a special alloy. The fields are still present, but the metal has the capability to contain them. This approach to reducing field levels may not

---

*Information for this section was drawn, in part, from Recupero (1994).

be practical for many sources, including power lines. Magnetic field intensity can also be reduced by placing wires close together so that the field from one wire cancels the field from the other. This is now being done in new designs for electric blankets. To some degree the same thing can be done for power lines, but for safety and reliability reasons power lines have minimum required spacing.

Because of the way appliances are made, they have the potential to have very high localized fields, but then the fields decrease rapidly with distance. For example, typical magnetic field strengths not near an appliance are 0.1 to 4 milligauss (mG), but the field from an electric can opener can be 20,000 mG at 3 centimeters (approximately 1 inch) from the appliance. At 30 centimeters (approximately 1 foot), appliance fields are usually around 100 times lower. For the can opener mentioned above, the level would probably be around 20 milligauss. The reader should note that the gauss is a unit for the strength of a magnetic field, also known as magnetic flux density. Magnetic flux density is measured in terms of lines of force per unit area. Remember the patterns that were generated by iron filings on a piece of paper which was placed over a magnet? These patterns are field lines. One normally speaks of magnetic fields in terms of (one) thousandths (1/1000) of a gauss or milligauss, abbreviated "mG".

When standing under a power line, one is usually at least 20 feet or more away from the line, depending on its height above ground. Under a typical 230 kilovolt transmission line the magnetic field is probably less than 120 milligauss. In contrast, if one moves about 100 feet away from the line, the magnetic field is probably about 15 milligauss, and at 300 feet away from the line, the magnetic field is probably less than 2 milligauss. From these examples, one can see that distance from the source of the magnetic or electric field can substantially reduce exposure.

Magnetic/control procedures for specific applications are discussed below. Control technology for transmission and distribution lines has been developed and could be applied if warranted. These techniques focus on compaction and shielding of transmission conductors. Compaction is based on the principle that for three-phase, balanced conductor systems, the net field (electric or magnetic) of the three phases is zero. A disadvantage of compaction is that it results in an increase in electrical arcing, which affects system reliability. For situations in which compaction was an ineffective control technology, shielding techniques have been developed that reduce the electric field at the edge of the right-of-way by approximately tenfold. Compaction techniques that have been developed include gas-insulated transmission lines, superconducting cables, and direct-current cable technologies. In cable or gas-insulated transmission technologies, conductors are inside a metallic sheath in which the electric field exists only between the conductors and the sheath; electric fields external to cable sheaths are essentially zero.

EMF inside the home and schools can be emitted from appliances, wiring systems, including the grounding, underground and overhead distribution lines, and transmission lines. A few appliances, especially electric blankets and heated water beds, have been identified as important sources of magnetic field exposure because of their close proximity to the body for long periods of time. Hair dryers and electric shavers, because they too are used close to the body, expose people to some of the strongest fields but total exposure from these is limited because they are used for only minutes per day. Manufacturers have responded by developing low magnetic field appliances. Some specific steps one can take to reduce EMF exposure at home, the office, or at school are listed below.

1. Sitting at arms length from a terminal or pulling the keyboard back still further; magnetic fields fall off rapidly with distance.

2. Switching VDTs off (not the computer necessarily) when not in use.

3. Spacing and locating terminals in the workplace, so that workstations are isolated from the fields from neighboring VDTs. Fields will penetrate partition walls, but do fall quickly with distance.

4. Using electric blankets (or water bed heaters) to warm beds, but unplugging them before sleeping. Magnetic fields disappear when the electric current is switched off. However, electric fields may exist as long as a blanket is plugged in.

5. Not standing close to sources of EMFs such as microwave ovens while in use. Standards are in place to limit microwave emissions. However, the electric power consumption by a microwave oven results in magnetic fields close to the unit that are high. The same is true of other appliances as well.

Existing mass transit systems and emerging technologies such as magnetically levitated trains, electric automobiles, and superconducting magnetic energy storage devices require special consideration. These systems can produce magnetic fields over large areas at different frequencies. Passengers on magnetically levitated trains will be exposed to static fields and to frequencies up to about 1,000 Hz. Existing engineering control technologies may not be sufficient to significantly reduce exposure.

As described earlier, another device that merits special concern is the visual display terminal. In addition to being energized by 60 Hz power, VDTs can produce EMF at frequencies of up to 250,000 Hz. VDT manufacturers, however, have begun to reduce fields by shielding techniques. Metal enclosures are used to shield electric fields, while active magnetic shielding techniques are used to reduce magnetic fields.

The reader should note that there is no simple way to completely block EMFs since the fields are generated by electrical systems and devices in the home, including the wiring and appliances. Electric fields from outside the home (power lines, etc.) are shielded to some extent by natural and building materials, but magnetic fields are not. As noted above, the further a building is from an EMF source, the weaker the fields at the building would be. Keeping fields out of the home would mean keeping any electricity from coming into or being used in the home. Often the fields from sources inside the home (e.g., appliances, wiring, etc.) will result in higher fields than from sources outside the home.

At this point, enough evidence suggests a possible health hazard to justify taking simple steps to reduce exposure to electromagnetic fields. The larger dilemma is whether the risks justify making major changes in huge, complex electric power systems that could disrupt the reliable, relatively inexpensive electric service Americans have come to take for granted ("Electromagnetic Fields," 1994).

Some questions are too large to be answered by individuals or families at this time. How much should a community spend to route transmission lines away from a school? Should a high-voltage line be put on taller towers to minimize fields at ground level even though the expense will result in higher electricity rates ("Electromagnetic Fields," 1994)?

It seems sensible to focus on simple ways of reducing exposure to electromagnetic fields rather than to make radical changes. M. Granger Morgan, a public-policy expert at Carnegie Mellon University, has proposed a strategy he calls "prudent avoidance," involving simple low-cost or no-cost measures. Although prudent avoidance can be as easy as leaning back from a computer screen, other methods of avoiding EMFs are more difficult such as moving out of a house near a power line. Whether such a move is prudent or paranoid depends largely on one's own feelings about the nature of the risk ("Electromagnetic Fields," 1994).

FUTURE TRENDS

If scientists eventually reach a consensus that low-level eletromagnetic fields do cause cancer or some other adverse health effect, then regulations defining some safe exposure level will have to be written at some later date. But so far the data are not complete enough for regulators.

Future research is also questionable at this time because much of the research into the effects of electromagnetic fields, especially that on mechanisms that could cause health effects, is cross-disciplinary, highly complicated, and has raised more questions than it has answered. It may take more than a decade to elucidate the mechanisms. It appears that the technical profession presently does not know if EMF exposure is harmful (aside from the concern for electric shocks and burns for extreme exposure). It does not know if certain levels of EMFs are safer or less safe than other levels. With most chemicals, one assumes exposure at higher levels is worse than less exposure at lower levels. This may or may not be true for EMFs. More research is required to identify dose-response relationships. There is some evidence from laboratory studies that suggest that there may be "windows" for effects. This means that biological effects are observed at some frequencies and intensities but not at others. Also, it is not known if continuous exposure to a given field intensity causes a biological effect, or if repeatedly entering and exiting of the field causes effects. There is no number to which one can point and say "that is a safe or hazardous level of EMF." Many years may pass before scientists have clear answers on cancer or on any other possible health problems that could be caused by electromagnetic fields. But over the long run, avoiding research probably will not be acceptable. It appears that the public will continue to demand research funding and answers to these questions.

Finally, the tendency to sensationalize electric and magnetic fields reporting was recently discussed by McElfresh (1994). Information on the latest 53 publications (mainly newspapers) that reviewed 5 major EMF studies was presented. Hopefully, the future will provide more objective reporting by the media on EMF issues.

SUMMARY

1. International and national organizations, industrial associations, federal and state agencies, Congress and the public have expressed concern about the potential health effects of exposure to EMF.

2. Exposure assessment research is a high priority research area because it is essential to the successful interpretation of the biological response and is critically important for risk assessment studies.

3. Research on human reproductive effects should emphasize the need to attempt replication of isolated reports of increase miscarriages and increased malformations, and reports of increased incidence of nervous system cancer in children whose fathers had occupations with potential EMF exposure.

4. The potential need for future controls to reduce risks from exposure to EMF is the rationale for control technology research. This research presently is a low priority because no firm cause-and-effect relation between human health risk and EMF exposure has been established.

5. If scientists eventually reach a consensus that low-level electromagnetic fields do cause cancer or some other adverse health effect, then regulations defining some safe exposure level will have to be written at some later date.

REFERENCES

Department of Engineering and Public Policy, "EMF from 60 Hertz Electric Power," Pittsburgh, PA, 1989.

"Electromagnetic Fields," *Consumer Reports,* May 1, 1994.

EPA. "EMF: An EPA Perspective," Washington, DC, December, 1992.

Fagin, D. *NY Newsday,* June 15, 1994.

Hileman, B. "Health Effects of Electromagnetic Fields Remain Unresolved," *Chemical and Engineering News* (C&EN), Nov. 8, 1993.

Leonard, A., Neutra, R., Yost, M., and Lee, G. "EEMF Measurements and Possible Effects," California Department of Health Services, 1990.

McElfresh, R. "Responsible Reporting of Environmental Issues by the Media," panel discussion, AWMA Annual Meeting, Cincinnati, June, 1994.

Recupero, S. "The Danger Associated with Electric and Magnetic Fields," drawn, in part, from a term paper submitted to L. Theodore, Manhattan College, 1994.

Wilson, R. "Currents of Concern." *NY Newsday,* May 1, 1990.

41

Acid Rain

CONTRIBUTING AUTHOR

Stanley Joseph

INTRODUCTION

Acid deposition, popularly known as acid rain, has long been suspected of damaging lakes, streams, forests, and soils, decreasing visibility, corroding monuments and tombstones, and potentially threatening human health in North America and Europe. The National Academy of Sciences and other leading scientific bodies first gave credence to these concerns in the early 1980s when they suggested that emissions of sulfur dioxide from electric power plants were being carried hundreds of miles by prevailing winds, being transformed in the atmosphere into sulfuric acid, falling into pristine lakes, and killing off aquatic life. The process of acid deposition also begins with emissions of nitrogen oxides (primarily from motor vehicles and coal-burning power plants). These pollutants interact with sunlight and water vapor in the upper atmosphere to form acidic compounds. During a storm, these compounds fall to earth as acid rain or snow; the compounds also may join dust or other dry airborne particles and fall as "dry deposition" (EPA, 1987). Regulations have been passed concerning the amount of SO_2 and NO_x (oxides of nitrogen) emitted in the air. These regulations have caused the power industries to find ways to cut their emissions. The three ways of lowering emissions—before combustion, during combustion, and after combustion—will be discussed.

Sulfur dioxide, the most important of the two gaseous acid pollutants, is created when the sulfur in coal is released during combustion and reacts with oxygen in the air. The amount of sulfur dioxide created depends on the amount of sulfur in the coal. All coal contains some sulfur, but the amount varies significantly depending on where the coal is mined. Over 80 percent of sulfur dioxide emissions in the United States originate in the 31 states east of or bordering the Mississippi River (EPA, 1987). Most emissions come from the states in or adjacent to the Ohio River Valley.

The extent of damage caused by acid rain depends on the total acidity deposited in a particular area and the sensitivity of the area receiving it. Areas with acid-neutralizing compounds in the soil, for example, can experience years of acid deposition without problems. Such soils are common in much of the United States. But the thin soils of the mountainous and glaciated northeast have very little acid-buffering capacity, making them vulnerable to damage from acid rain. Surface waters, soils, and bedrock that have a relatively low buffering capacity are unable to neutralize the acid effectively. Under such conditions, the deposition may increase the acidity of water, reducing much or all of its ability to sustain aquatic life. Forests and agriculture may be vulnerable because acid deposition can leach nutrients from the ground, kill nitrogen-fixing microorganisms that nourish plants, and release toxic metals.

REGULATIONS

Title IV of the 1990 Clean Air Act Amendments, Acid Deposition Control (see Chapter 4 for information on the remaining titles), which contains comprehensive provisions to control the emissions that cause acid rain, represents a legislative breakthrough in environmental protection. To begin with, it is the first law in the nation's history to directly address the problem of acid rain. The legislation calls for historic reductions in sulfur dioxide emissions from the burning of fossil fuels, the principal cause of acid rain. It also mandates significant reductions in nitrogen oxide emissions. In addition, the approach embodied in the new provisions represents a radical departure from the traditional "command-and-control" approach to environmental regulation that prevailed in this country during the 1970s and 1980s (Claussen, 1991).

During those years, environmental regulations typically required industry to achieve a particular limit on each pollutant released to the environment by installing specific pollution-control equipment. The acid rain program that the Environmental Protection Agency (EPA) is developing under the Clean Air Act Amendments takes a more flexible approach: It simply sets a national ceiling in sulfur dioxide emissions from electric power plants and allows affected utilities to determine the most cost-effective way to achieve compliance. It is estimated that this approach will result in at least a 20 percent cost savings over a traditional command-and-control program (Claussen, 1991).

The new legislation requires that, by the turn of century, sulfur dioxide emissions must be reduced 10 million tons annually from the levels emitted in 1980; this will amount to roughly a 40 percent reduction from 1980 levels. Because such reductions cannot be achieved overnight, EPA is implementing a two-phase approach that gradually tightens the restrictions placed on power plants that emit sulfur dioxide.

The first phase begins in 1995 and affects 261 units in 110 coal-burning electric utility plants located in 21 eastern and midwestern states. These plants are large and emit high levels of sulfur dioxide. Phase II, which begins in the year 2000, tightens the emissions limits imposed on these large plants and also sets restrictions on smaller, cleaner plants fired by coal, oil, and gas. Approximately 2,500 units within approximately 1,000 utility plants will be affected by Phase II. In both phases, affected utilities will be required to install systems that consciously monitor emissions in order to track progress and assure compliance.

The legislation also calls for a 2-million-ton reduction in nitrogen oxide emissions by the year 2000. A significant portion of this reduction will be achieved by utility boilers, which will be required to meet tough new emissions requirements under the acid rain provisions of the act. These requirements will also be implemented in two phases. EPA established emission limitations in mid-1992 for two types of utility boilers (tangentially fired and dry bottom, wall-fired boilers); regulations for all other types of boilers will be issued by 1997. As with the sulfur dioxide emissions, these utilities will be required to install equipment that will continuously monitor emissions.

The acid rain provisions also look to the future by placing a permanent cap on sulfur dioxide emissions and by encouraging energy conservation, the use of renewable and clean alternative technologies, and pollution-prevention practices. These ground-breaking provisions will help ensure that lasting environmental gains are made.

To help bring about the mandated sulfur dioxide emissions reductions in a cost-effective manner, EPA is implementing a market-based allowance-trading system that will provide power plants with maximum flexibility in reducing emissions. Under this system, EPA will allocate allowances to affected utilities each calendar year based upon formulas provided in the legislation. Each allowance permits a utility to emit one ton of sulfur dioxide. To be in compliance with the law, utilities may not emit more sulfur dioxide than they hold allowances for. This means that utilities will have to either reduce emissions to the level of allowances they hold or obtain additional allowances to cover their emissions.

Utilities that reduce their emissions below the number of allowances they hold may elect to trade allowances within their systems, bank allowances for future use, or sell them to other utilities for profit. Allowance trading will be conducted nationwide, so that a utility in North Carolina, for example, will be able to trade with a utility in California. Anyone may hold allowances, including affected utilities, brokers, environmental groups, and private citizens.

The legislation also establishes a permanent cap on the number of allowances EPA issues to utilities. Beginning in the year 2000, EPA will issue 8.95 million allowances to utilities annually. Although the lowest-emitting plants will be able to increase their emissions between 1990 and 2000 by roughly 20 percent, these utilities may not thereafter exceed their year-2000 emission levels.

Utilities that begin operating in 1996 and beyond will not be allocated allowances. Instead, they will have to buy into the system by purchasing allowances. This will effectively limit emissions even as more plants are built and the combustion of fossil fuels increases. These measures will help ensure that the benefits gained from the emissions reductions will not be eroded over time.

The allowance allocation for each unit affected by Phase I of the new law is listed in the legislation. An individual unit's allocation is based on standard formula: the product of a 2.5-pound sulfur dioxide per million Btu emission rate multiplied by the unit's average fuel consumption for 1985–87 (Claussen, 1991).

The allowance system provides incentives for power plants to reduce their emissions substantially more than is required since allowances freed by installing pollution-control equipment can be sold for profit.

EPA's role in allowance trading will be to receive and record allowance transfers and also to ensure at the end of the year that a utility's emissions did not exceed the number of allowances held. When two parties agree to an allowance transfer, their formally designated representatives will notify EPA in writing to make it official. EPA will record the transaction by entering it into an automated allowance tracking system, but will not otherwise participate in the trading process. The tracking system that will be developed by the Agency over the next two years will monitor compliance by keeping records of allowance holdings and the status of allowances traded. EPA will be writing regulations for such issues as calculating and allocating allowances, for the mechanics of allowance transfers, for allowance tracking, and for the operation of reserves, sales, and auctions.

EPA will maintain a reserve of 300,000 special allowances that will be allocated to utilities that develop qualifying renewable energy products or use conservation measures. The allowances will be granted to utilities on a first-come, first-served basis starting in 1995 for conservation activities initiated after 1992.

The legislation provides a strong incentive for utilities to comply with the law and not exceed their allowances. Utilities that do exceed their allowances must pay a $2000-per-ton excess emissions fee in the following year. Since the excess emissions fee will substantially exceed the expected cost of compliance through the purchases of allowances, EPA expects that the market will do much of the work of ensuring compliance with the mandated reduction requirements.

The idea behind the allowance system was to achieve significant reductions of acid-rain-causing emissions at the lowest possible cost. It happens to be a good system.

EMISSIONS REDUCTION—BEFORE COMBUSTION

In an attempt to mitigate the effects of acid rain several proposals have appeared before the U.S. Congress. Reductions in sulfur dioxide emissions, particularly from utility and industrial coal-fired boilers, is the primary target for combatting acid rain.

Several means exist to limit the amount of sulfur in the fuel prior to combustion and include the use of lower-sulfur coals and coal cleaning. Reduction of nitrogen oxides emissions cannot be accomplished at this point because it is formed after (and following) incomplete combustion. The two major reduction procedures described below include coal switching and coal cleaning. Although this development is directed toward coal (the fuel of primary concern in this nation), it may also be applied, in some instances to other fossil fuels.

Coal Switching

For many power plants, the most economical strategy for reducing sulfur dioxide emissions tends to be switching from higher-sulfur to lower-sulfur coals. Because the sulfur content in coal varies across regions, this move to consume lower-sulfur coals would result in a major shift in regional coal production from higher-sulfur supply regions, to lower-sulfur supply regions. It could also generate regional hostility by causing shifts in existing coal markets.

Existing coal-fired power plants now burning higher-sulfur coals without scrubbers would be faced with the most stringent requirements for reducing emissions. Most of these plants were initially designed to burn bituminous coals.

Under most circumstances, higher-sulfur plants would face relatively little technical difficulty in shifting to lower-sulfur coals, but there may be some additional costs, especially for upgrading electrostatic precipitators. A few plants, such as cyclone-fired boilers, are not technically well-suited for burning lower-sulfur coals because of the difference in ash-fusion temperatures.

Also, there is some question as to the type of lower-sulfur coals likely to be in demand by power plants shifting to these coals. Since most existing boilers were initially designed to burn bituminous coals, it is not clear whether these units can economically shift to lower-sulfur subbituminous coals. Some of the questions are technical, such as the potential for slagging or fouling when an off-design coal is burned in these boilers.

Consumption of subbituminous coals will entail higher heat rates, higher handling costs, and capacity derates. Together, these economic and technical considerations tend to make the use of subbituminous coals in bituminous boilers a very site-specific issue that does not provide clear economic advantages.

Coal Cleaning

Another way to control sulfur emission is to clean the coal before burning. This process can reduce sulfur dioxide emission by 20 to 90 percent. Coal cleaning can be done in three ways: physical (gravity separation), chemical (reaction or bioremediation), or electrical. Details on the principal cleaning method, by gravity, are provided below. Details on other separation techniques are available in the literature (Holmes, 1993).

Gravity separation is used by industry. This method depends on the size, shape, density and surface properties of the coal. The process first crushes the coal into small particles and then allows gravity to separate the pyritic sulfur from the coal. The gravity separation process is usually accomplished in a water medium. The coal containing impurities sink to the bottom and the usable coal stays on the top. The benefits of this process is that the coal is easy to handle and the coal can burn better. Although there are some benefits to this process, there are limitations as well.

One of the limitations of gravity separation is that it is ineffective in reducing sulfur content when the coal particles are very fine. When the particles are very fine the metals will not be attached to the sulfur enriched coal and separation will not occur. Another problem is with the medium. The coal must be dried after using water to separate the burning coal from its impurities; drying the coal is very expensive. There is also a major loss of energy release with the purified coal; this means more coal must be burned to get the same amount of energy produced.

EMISSIONS REDUCTION—DURING COMBUSTION

The second method that can be used to reduce the emissions of the precursors of acid rain is during combustion. Both NO_x and SO_2 emissions can be reduced during this stage of the combustion process.

The reduction of NO_x emissions is accomplished by primarily three methods: low-NO_x burners, overfire air, and fuel staging or reburning. These methods have the ability to reduce emissions by 80 percent and are cost-effective. The three processes are based on using combustion with stoichiometric air and controlling the temperature. The fuel staging process seems to work the best in reducing the emissions.

In a coal-fired boiler, reburning is accomplished by substituting 15 to 20 percent of the coal with natural gas or low-sulfur oil and burning it at a location downstream of the primary combustion zone of the boiler. Oxides of nitrogen formed in the primary zone are reduced to nitrogen and water vapor as they pass through the reburn zone. Additional air is injected downstream of the reburn zone to complete the combustion process at a lower temperature. In general, NO_x reductions of 50 percent or more are achievable by reburning. When combined with other low-NO_x technologies (such as low-NO_x burners), NO_x reductions of up to 90 percent may be achievable.

Reduction of sulfur dioxide emissions cannot be accomplished easily because many expensive problems occur and these methods are expensive. Two methods that are frequently used in industry are limestone injection multistage burner (LIMB) and fluidized bed combustion (FBC).

LIMB is an emerging control process that can be retrofitted on a large portion of existing coal-fired boilers. In a LIMB system, an SO_2 sorbent (limestone) is injected into a boiler equipped with low-NO_x burners. The sorbent absorbs the SO_2 and the low-NO_x burners limit the amount of NO_x formed. LIMB is capable of reducing both SO_2 and NO_x by about 50 to 60 percent.

The benefit of using the LIMB process is that it is one of the least expensive processes for reducing SO_2 emissions during combustion, but the sorbent injected into the boiler tends to increase slagging and fouling, which in turn increase operation and maintenance costs. Because boilers retrofitted with LIMB tend to produce more particulates of smaller sizes, particulate control becomes more difficult. Technical questions remain as to what sorbents are most effective in a LIMB system, and how and where to inject the sorbents.

In an FBC boiler, pulverized coal is burned while suspended over a turbulent cushion of injected air. This technique allows improved combustion efficiencies and reduced boiler fouling and corrosion. Such boilers also are capable of burning different kinds of low-grade fuels like refuse, wood bark, and sewage sludge. In addition, if the coal is mixed with limestone or some other sorbent material during combustion, the SO_2 is captured and retained in the ash.

FBC boilers have the potential to control NO_x as well as SO_2. FBC boilers must operate within a narrow temperature range (1500–1600°F) and lower combustion temperatures inherently limit the formation of NO_x. FBC boilers may be able to control NO_x by 50 to 75 percent at the same time as they control SO_2 by up to 90 percent. An FBC system does have one major flaw: It requires the construction of a new boiler. The FBC system is more of a replacement technology than a retrofit.

EMISSIONS REDUCTION—AFTER COMBUSTION

The final method of reducing emissions that cause acid rain is after combustion has occurred. This method is most frequently used by industry, although it is not preferred by environmentalists because it creates other wastes while reducing emissions.

The most popular process for reducing NO_x after combustion is selective catalyst reduction (SCR). It is mainly used in Japan. In the SCR system, a mixture of ammonia gas and air is injected upstream of a catalytic reactor chamber. The flue-gas mixture then travels in a vertical, downward-flow direction through a catalytic reactor chamber, where the ammonia gas disassociates NO_x to nitrogen gas and water vapor (EPA, 1987). This process benefits from its high removal rate (80–90 percent) and no retrofitting on the unit is necessary. Catalyst selection is very important for this process. Catalyst selection is based on the following criteria: resistance to toxic materials, abrasion resistance, mechanical strength, resistance to thermal cycling, resistance to the oxidation of SO_2, and resistance to plugging (Frankel, 1992).

Industry has mainly chosen the flue-gas desulfurization process (FGD) to combat SO_2 emissions. FGD uses sorbents such as limestone to soak up (or scrub) SO_2 from exhaust gases. This technology, which is capable of reducing SO_2 emissions by up to 95 percent, can be added to existing coal-fired boilers.

FGD has several drawbacks. The control equipment is very expensive and bulky. Smaller facilities do not always have the capital or the space needed for FGD equipment. If, however, the sorbent could be injected into existing ductwork, the cost of the reaction vessel could be eliminated, and it would be much easier to retrofit controls on a wider range of sources.

More recently ETS International, Inc. (Roanoke, VA) developed a Limestone Emission Control (LEC) system. The first ever full-scale LEC system will be applied to the control of acid gas emissions from a metal alloy production process located in Taiwan, R.O.C. The Limestone Emission Control system is a proprietary acid gas control system that has demonstrated high levels of acid gas removals (99 percent) at very competitive costs. A ten-year R&D program included scrutiny by the Ohio Coal Development Office, the U.S. EPA, and DOE as well as major U.S. industry. The system holds great promise for acid gas control from both the chemical and utility industries (Holmes, Singh, & Theodore, 1993).

NATIONAL ACID PRECIPITATION ASSESSMENT PROGRAM

In addition to enforcement and monitoring under the provisions of the Clean Air Act, the EPA is actively pursuing a major research effort with other federal agencies under the National Acid Precipitation Assessment Program (NAPAP). This ongoing research project is designed to resolve the critical uncertainties surrounding the causes and effects of acid rain. About $300 million have been spent for federal research since NAPAP was initiated in 1980. In September 1987, NAPAP published an interim assessment on the causes and effects of acid deposition.

Aquatic Effects

One of the most important acid rain research projects being conducted by EPA is the National Surface Water Survey. This survey is designed to provide data on the present and future status of lakes and streams within regions of the United States believed to be susceptible to change as a result of acid deposition. Phase I of the Eastern and Western Lakes Surveys showed that there are essentially no lakes or reservoirs in the mountainous West, northeastern Minnesota, and the Southern Blue Ridge of the Southeast that are considered acidic. The four subregions with the highest percentages of acidic lakes are: the Adirondacks of New York, where 10 percent of the lakes were found to be acidic; the Upper Peninsula of Michigan, where 10 percent of the lakes were also found to be acidic; the Okefenokee Swamp in Florida, which is naturally acidic; and, the lakes in the Florida Panhandle where the cause of acidity is unknown.

The 1988 Stream Survey determined that approximately 2.7 percent of the total stream reaches sampled in the mid-Atlantic and Southeast were acidic. About 10 percent of head waters in the forested ridges of Pennsylvania, Virginia, and West Virginia were found to be acidic. Streams in Florida found to have a low pH are naturally acidic. The study indicated that atmospheric deposition is the major cause of sulfates in streams. Atmospheric deposition was also found to be a major cause of sulfates in the lakes surveyed as part of the National Surface Water Survey.

Forest Effects

The NAPAP interim assessment reviewed research concerning the effects of acid deposition on forests. It focused on the effects of precursor pollutants (sulfur dioxide and nitrogen oxides) and Volatile Organic Compounds (VOCs) and their oxidants (including ozone and hydrogen peroxides) on eastern spruce-fir, southern pine, eastern hardwood, and western conifer. The assessment found that air pollution is a factor in the decline of both managed and natural forests. The San Bernardino National Forest in California and some types of white pine throughout the eastern United States are seriously affected by ozone.

Forests found to have unknown causes of damage included northeastern spruce-fir, northeastern sugar maple, southeastern yellow pine, and species in the New Jersey Pine Barrens. The high elevation forests such as the spruce-fir in the eastern United States were found to be exposed to severe natural stresses as well as being frequently immersed in clouds containing pollutants at higher concentrations than those observed in rain. Research has shown no direct impacts to seedlings by acidic precipitation or gaseous sulfur dioxide and nitrogen oxides at ambient levels in the United States. Ozone is the leading suspected pollutant that may stress regional forests and reduce growth. Research is underway to resolve the relative importance of physical and natural stresses.

Crop Effects

The NAPAP assessment indicated that there are no measurable consistent effects on crop yield from the direct effects of simulated acidic rain at ambient levels of acidity. This finding was based on yield measurements of grains, forage, vegetable, and fruit crops exposed to a range of simulated rain acidity levels in controlled exposure studies (EPA, 1987). Continuing research efforts will examine whether stress agents such as drought or insect pests cause crops to be more sensitive to rainfall acidity.

Average ambient concentrations of sulfur dioxide and nitrogen oxides over most agricultural areas in the United States are not high enough or elevated frequently enough to affect crop production on a regional scale. However, crops may be affected locally in areas close to emission sources. Controlled studies also indicate that ambient levels of ozone in the United States are sufficient to reduce the yield of many crops.

Materials Effects

The NAPAP Interim Report indicated that many uncertainties need to be reduced before a reliable economic assessment could be made of the effects of acid deposition on materials, such as building materials, statues, monuments, and car paint. Major areas of uncertainty include inventories of materials at risk, variability of urban air quality, effects on structures, and cost estimates for repair and replacement.

Human Health Effects

The NAPAP interim assessment reported that there are also many uncertainties associated with assessing the influence of ambient levels of atmospheric pollutants on human health. The primary factors involved are a lack of information on the levels of exposure to acidic aerosols for various population groups across North America; chronic health problems caused by short-term changes in respiratory symptoms and decrease in lung function; and, the effects of repetitive or long-term exposures to air pollutants. Studies on toxicity of drinking water have linked rain acidity to unhealthy levels of toxic metals in drinking water and fish.

FUTURE TRENDS

The EPA, in coordination with other federal agencies, is conducting wide-ranging research on the causes and effects of acid deposition. Major research efforts include determining effects on aquatic and forest ecosystems, building materials and human health. In the area of human health EPA is conducting exposure studies on acid aerosols. EPA is also conducting ongoing aquatics research projects that will continue into the future. As part of the National Surface Water Survey, seasonal variability of lakes in the Northeast will be studied.

Over the next several years, major research results are anticipated for improving the basis of decision making on acid rain issues. EPA also expects that Congress and other groups will continue to propose options to reduce acid deposition. As proposals are offered, EPA will provide analyses of costs, consequences, and the feasibility of implementation.

EPA's greatest challenge is to continue to reduce emissions of sulfur dioxide and nitrogen oxides. The Agency must also continue research to reduce the level of scientific and economic uncertainties about acid deposition and work to resolve the regional conflicts related to this problem. In addition to the research efforts, major federal research programs are being funded by the Department of Energy, the Tennessee Valley Authority, and the Argonne, Brookhaven, Lawrence Berkley, and Oak Ridge national laboratories.

SUMMARY

1. The process of acid deposition begins with emissions of nitrogen oxides and sulfur dioxide from motor vehicles and coal-burning power plants.

2. Title IV of the 1990 Clean Air Act Amendments calls for historic reductions in sulfur dioxide and nitrogen oxides emissions. EPA is implementing a market-based allowance-trading system that will provide power plants with maximum flexibility in reducing emissions.

3. Means to limit the amount of sulfur in the fuel prior to combustion include the use of lower-sulfur coals and coal cleaning. Reduction of nitrogen oxides emissions cannot be accomplished at this point because it is formed due to incomplete combustion.

4. Reduction of NO_x emissions during combustion can be accomplished by three methods:

low-NO$_x$ burners, overfire air, and fuel staging or reburning. Two methods that are frequently used in industry to reduce sulfur dioxide emissions during combustion are limestone injection multistage burning and fluidized bed combustion.

5. One of the more popular processes for reducing NO$_x$ after combustion is selective catalyst reduction. Industry has mainly employed flue gas desulfurization processes to combat against SO$_2$ emissions after combustion.

6. The National Acid Precipitation Assessment Program is an ongoing research project designed to resolve the critical uncertainties surrounding the causes and effects of acid rain.

7. EPA, along with other federal agencies, is conducting wide-ranging research on the causes and effects of acid deposition. EPA's greatest challenge is to continue to reduce emissions of sulfur dioxide and nitrogen oxides.

REFERENCES

Claussen, E. "Acid Rain: The Strategy," *EPA Journal,* January/February 1991.

EPA, "Acid Deposition," National Acid Precipitation Assessment Program Interim Report, 1987.

Frankel, K. "Acid Rain," Manhattan College Term Paper (submitted to L. Theodore), April 13, 1992.

Holmes, G., Singh, B., and Theodore, L. *Handbook of Environmental Management and Technology,* New York: John Wiley & Sons, 1993.

42

Greenhouse Effect and Global Warming

CONTRIBUTING AUTHOR
Nelayne Alvarez

INTRODUCTION

The "greenhouse effect" is a phrase popularly used to describe the increased warming of the earth due to increased levels of carbon dioxide and other atmospheric gases, called greenhouse gases. Just as the glass in a botanical greenhouse traps heat for growing plants, greenhouse gases trap heat and warm the planet. The greenhouse effect, a natural phenomenon, has been an essential part of Earth's history for billions of years. The greenhouse effect is the result of a delicate and non-fixed balance between life and the environment. Yet, the greenhouse effect may be leading the planet to the brink of disaster. Since the Industrial Revolution, the presence of additional quantities of greenhouse gases threatens to affect global climate. However, the predicted effects of this increase are still debated among scientists.

How the Greenhouse Effect Works

The energy radiated from the sun to the earth is absorbed by the atmosphere, and is balanced by a comparable amount of long-wave energy emitted back to space from the earth's surface. Carbon dioxide molecules (and greenhouse gases) absorb some of the long-wave energy radiating from the planet to the surface of the earth. Because of the greenhouse heat trapping effect, the atmosphere itself radiates a large amount of long wave-length energy downward to the surface of the earth and makes the earth twice as warm as it would have been if warmed by solar radiation alone (Thompson, 1993).

The greenhouse gases trap heat because of their chemical makeup and, in particular, their triatomic nature. They are relatively transparent to visible sunlight, but they absorb long wavelength, infrared radiation cmitted by the earth (Thompson, 1993).

Cycles of Carbon Dioxide

Carbon dioxide comprises only a very small portion of the atmosphere, a little more than 0.03% by volume ("The Ice Record of Greenhouse Gases," 1993). This colorless, odorless gas is of vital importance to life on Earth. Indeed, without it, there probably would not be any plants or animals or human beings on this planet. But too much carbon dioxide could be as harmful as too little.

There are two important natural cycles in the world that play a major part in determining the concentration of carbon dioxide in the atmosphere: terrestrial and oceanic (Thompson, 1993). The terrestrial cycle starts with photosynthetic plants, which use sunlight, water, carbon dioxide, and a pigment called chlorophyll to form glucose and oxygen. It has been estimated that plants consume 500 billion tons of carbon dioxide every year, converting it into organic compounds and oxygen. By respiration, decay, and burning hydrocarbons, carbon dioxide is returned to the atmosphere.

The oceans cover about 70 percent of the Earth's surface. All the gases that make up the atmosphere are also dissolved in the oceans. Carbon dioxide is exchanged between the atmosphere and the ocean interface until an equilibrium is reached. Carbon dioxide is then transferred to deeper water by convective transport cycles which lower the concentration at the surface, thereby allowing more of the gas from the atmosphere to diffuse in the ocean.

Greenhouse Gases: Evidence of Climatic Change

The Environmental Protection Agency (EPA) has concluded that energy consumption in general has contributed almost 70 percent to the greenhouse effect in the last 10 years (Krause, 1992). Four important trace gases are combining to amplify the natural greenhouse effect: carbon dioxide, methane, nitrous oxide, and chlorofluorocarbons (CFCs). Each of these is briefly discussed below.

The primary man-made contributor to the greenhouse effect is carbon dioxide, accounting for approximately 50 percent of the blame for global warming. Carbon dioxide levels have risen at least 25 percent in the last 150 years. For instance, from analysis of air trapped in arctic ice, it is known that pre–Industrial Revolution levels of carbon dioxide were at 280 ppm (ppm = parts per million) and by 1984 the levels had risen to 343 ppm ("The Ice Record of Greenhouse Gases," 1993). This rise of carbon dioxide in the atmosphere is largely due to the burning of such fossil fuels as natural gas, coal, and petroleum; another contributor is worldwide deforestation. Deforestation increases carbon dioxide levels in the atmosphere in two basic ways. First, when trees decay or are burned, they release carbon dioxide. Second, without the forest, carbon dioxide that would have been absorbed for photosynthesis remains in the atmosphere. For example, a rainforest can hold 1 or 2 kg of carbon per square meter per year, as compared to a field of crops, which can absorb less than 0.5 kg of carbon per square meter every year. The current annual rate of atmospheric increase in carbon dioxide is 0.4%, which is equivalent to 10^{10} metric tons per year (Lyman, 1991).

Methane is an odorless, colorless gas found in the atmosphere in traces of less than 2 ppm ("The Ice Record of Greenhouse Gases," 1993). Like carbon dioxide, methane is a natural product and is twenty times more effective at trapping heat than carbon dioxide. It is produced by anaerobic bacteria microorganisms that live without oxygen in wetlands, rice fields, cattle, termites, and ocean sediments. Methane's annual growth rate in the atmosphere is now about 2.0 percent per year (Lyman, 1991).

Nitrous oxide is produced naturally and artificially. The atmosphere is 79 percent nitrogen and although plants need nitrogen for food, they cannot use it directly from the air. It must first be converted by soil bacteria into ammonium and then into nitrates before plants can absorb it. In the process, bacteria release nitrous oxide gas. In addition, farmers add chemical fertilizers containing nitrogen to the soil. Another way of forming nitrous oxide is by combustion. When anything burns, whether it is a tree in the rainforest, natural gas in a stove, coal in a power plant, or gasoline in a car, nitrogen combines with oxygen to form nitrous oxide. Nitrous oxide also destroys the ozone layer, which filters out dangerous ultraviolet radiation from the sun and protects life on earth. The concentration of nitrous oxide is increasing at the current rate of 0.3% each year (Lyman, 1991).

Chlorofluorocarbons (CFCs) are used as coolants (CFC-12) for refrigerators and air conditioners, as blowing agents (CFC-11) in packing materials and other plastic foams, and as solvents. CFCs trap heat 20,000 times more effectively than carbon dioxide. CFCs are virtually indestructible. They are not destroyed or dissolved by any of the natural processes that normally cleanse the air. In addition, they may stay in the lower atmosphere. These high-power greenhouse gases (CFCs) also attack the ozone layer; each CFC molecule can destroy 10,000 or more molecules of ozone, a gas made up of oxygen. The current rate of atmospheric increase in CFCs is now growing by about 5 to 7 percent annually (Lyman, 1991). Due to this rapid increase in the concentration of CFCs, a worldwide phaseout of chlorofluorocarbons production is being undertaken by the year 2000 (The Montreal Protocol).

GREENHOUSE DEBATE

Although most scientists are in agreement that higher levels of trace greenhouse gases in the atmosphere are causing global warming and that there is strong evidence to show it has already begun, others feel that the planet is actually entering another ice age. The current trends in weather could be natural fluctuations or could be the result of global climate patterns that run on cycles of thousands of years. Or, on the other hand, they could lead to climatic chaos.

In 1988, James Hansen of the National Aeronautics and Space Administration (NASA) Goddard Institute for Space Studies testified before the Senate Committee on Energy and Natural Resources ("No Way to Cool the Ultimate Greenhouse," 1993). He told the committee he was 99 percent certain that a 1°F rise in world temperatures since the 1850s has been caused by increasing greenhouse effect. "It is time to stop waffling so much and say that the evidence is pretty strong that the greenhouse effect is here," he said. But others argue that the earth has a natural control mechanism that keeps the earth's climate in balance. For instance, higher temperatures due to an increasing greenhouse effect may naturally trigger events that will cool the earth (e.g., increased clouds) and hold the climate in balance.

Scientists in favor claim that the climate models have been reliable enough to conclude that the greenhouse effect is causing global warming. Dr. Hansen, the leading spokesperson on the greenhouse effect, says that "it is just inconceivable that the increase of greenhouse gases in the atmosphere is not affecting our climate" ("No Way to Cool the Ultimate Greenhouse," 1993).

Other researchers believe that the warming of the earth over the last 100 to 150 years is part of a long-term, natural cycle that has little to do with the production of greenhouse gases. They remain unconvinced that the accumulation in the atmosphere of greenhouse gases is concrete evidence of any rise in the average earth temperature. On this lack of evidence, three scientists from the G. C. Marshall Institute in Washington DC reported that any warming of the earth in the last 100 years is better explained by the variation in natural climate and solar activity (Tesar, 1990). According to this theory, the most probable source of global warming appears to be variations in solar activity. The amount of solar radiation reaching the earth is controlled by three elements that vary cyclically over time. The first element is the tilt of the earth's axis, which varies 22 to 24.5 degrees and back again every 41,000 years. The second element is the month of the year in which the earth is closest to the sun, which varies over cycles of 19,000 and 24,000 years. Finally, the third element is the shape of the orbit of the earth, which, over a period of 100,000 years, changes from being more elliptical to being almost fully circular. They stated that changes in the earth's temperature have followed changes in solar activity over the last 100 years. When solar activity increased from 1880s to the 1940s, global temperatures increased. The observed global temperature rise of 1°F was during this period, before 67 percent of global greenhouse gases emissions had even occurred. When it declined from 1940s to the 1960s, temperatures also declined. When solar activity and sunspot numbers started to move up again in the 1970s and 1980s, temperatures did the same. This is hard to explain as a greenhouse effect phenomenon because the increased emissions of greenhouse gases should have created a period of accelerated temperature rise.

EFFECTS OF GLOBAL WARMING

A rise in average global temperature is expected to have profound effects. But while scientists are uncertain on the causes of global warming and the degree of impact that it will have, the need to study future situations has led the Environmental Protection Agency (EPA) and other environmental groups to investigate what would happen to the planet after a 3–8°F warming (Boyle, 1990).

Climate changes will have a significant effect on weather patterns. There will be changes in precipitation, storms, wind direction, and so on. Rising temperatures are expected to increase tropical storm activity. The hurricane season in the Atlantic and Caribbean is expected to start earlier and last longer. Storms will be more severe. Some researchers believe the planet will be a wetter place. Global circulation models (GCM) predicted that a doubling of carbon dioxide could increase humidity 30 to 40 percent (Boyle, 1990). However, such increases will not occur uniformly around the world. Perhaps humid tropical areas will become wetter while semi-arid regions will become drier.

As the earth gets warmer, there will be a rise in the average water level of the oceans. As water is heated, it expands, or increases in volume. According to theory, global warming could cause sea levels to rise. Rising sea levels will gradually flood low lying coastal areas. Beach erosion will be an increasing problem. The EPA has estimated that if the sea level rises 3 feet (0.9 meters), the nation will lose an area the size of Massachusetts, even if it spends more than $100 billion to protect critical shorelines. In addition to lost beaches, houses and other buildings that sit close to the water's edge will be undermined and destroyed.

If polar and temperate zones become warmer, there will be a poleward shift of ecological zones. Animal and plant species that now live in a particular area will no longer be able to survive there. The EPA predicts an increase in extinction rate as well as changes in migration patterns. As the ecological zones shift polewards, there may be a decrease in the amount of area suitable for forests, with a corresponding increase in grasslands and deserts. This means a loss in productive land, both for agriculture and for habitats of a broad range of plants and animals. For example, the nation's major grain crops—corn, wheat, and soybeans—are strongly affected by precipitation and temperatures. The warming trend will cause changes in water quantity and quality in some areas. This will affect drinking supplies as well as the water needs of industry and agriculture. Rising sea levels may contaminate water supplies as seawater migrates up rivers. For example, a 2 feet (0.6 meter) rise in sea level would inundate Philadelphia's water intakes along the Delaware River, making the water too salty to drink.

Heat waves extract a physical toll on people. The heat puts a strain on the heart, as the body tries to cool itself. Studies have shown that the number of cases of heart and lung disease increases when temperature rises. Contagious diseases, such as influenza and pneumonia, and allergenic diseases, such as asthma, will also be affected by the weather and become more prolific. The lifecycles of mosquitos and other disease-carrying insects are also extended in warmer weather. Climate changes, sea level rises, and other direct effects of greenhouse warming can be expected to have major social, economic, and political effects. For example, if agricultural productivity declines, personal income will fall and jobs will decline.

COMBATTING THE GREENHOUSE EFFECTS

National Approach to the Greenhouse Effect

With only 5 percent of the world's population, the United States today produces nearly 25 percent of global carbon emissions ("Clinton Unveils New Greenhouse Policy," 1993). The past years have yielded a flurry of proposals to deal with global warming. In the United States two comprehensive global warming bills were first introduced to Congress in late 1988, followed by other related legislation. These bills would establish a national goal of cutting carbon dioxide emissions by 20 percent by the year 2000 and include programs to implement national least cost planning, improve automobile fuel economy, develop renewable energy sources, plant trees, and assist developing countries in slowing population growth and deforestation. In the ensuing years, however, the bills were split into sections, each of which will be considered by a different congressional committee. However, key elements of this legislation face severe hurdles due to budget constraints and the opposition of powerful industries. The White House has given mixed signals on its commitment to slowing climate change, but now a recent presidential proposal appears in the offing. President Clinton's plan is to discourage the use of fossil fuels by raising energy taxes ("Clinton Unveils New Greenhouse Policy," 1993). He has already proposed a tax on various forms of energy that would set the country on a path of reducing carbon dioxide emissions. Combining higher taxes with tougher auto fuel economy standards, increased use of nonfossil energy sources (such as solar and wind power), and investment in energy-efficient technologies, are some of the administration's strategies to meet the goal. However, it would be unfair to say that Congress has taken no steps on a national level to combat global warming. The new Clean Air Act (of 1990), which represents the first revisions of the original Clean Air Act, is the best American policy regarding the greenhouse effect. The bill sets forth technical standards for 191 toxic air pollutants and calls for significant

reductions in tailpipe emissions. It mandates a 10-million-ton two-phase reduction in sulfur dioxide and a two-million-ton reduction in oxides of nitrogen (NO_x) emissions, and provides a flexible
plan for the 111 affected coal-fired utility plants. The cost for all of this emission control is hefty
for industry ($25 to 35 billion per year), but the Clean Air Act is a triumph for environmentalists.

Having determined that the United States is swiftly becoming more open to taking an approach of active prevention against the greenhouse effect, the field of policy and legislation to
combat global warming can be categorized into three main divisions: (1) the reduction of the
amount of greenhouse gases emitted to the atmosphere, (2) the total elimination of fossil fuels as
energy sources, and (3) the reduction of the effects of greenhouse gas emission by reforestation or
alternate methods.

International Approach to the Greenhouse Effect

Individual efforts and domestic legislation are inadequate to deal with problems that transcend borders. The United States can spend trillions of dollars on reducing greenhouse gas emissions within
its borders, but it is wasted money unless the rest of the world follows suit. The greenhouse effect
is a global problem, and the world must consent to an international agreement. The most serious
obstacle in realizing a worldwide agreement on greenhouse gas emissions is the conflict between
developing and developed nations (Schneider, 1991). Developing nations see the problem as a result of industrialized nations' activities and do not want their fledgling economies restrained. As a
result of this, they are resistant to international legal control on industry, in which developed nations are anxious to involve them.

As nations try to agree on solutions that are equitable to all, global warming is also likely to
be a major world political issue. Some action has already been taken: In 1987, 24 nations and the
European Community signed the Montreal Protocol on Substances that Deplete the Ozone Layer
(Schneider, 1991). It called for a freeze on the production and use of CFCs. Eleven countries rati-
fied the Protocol by January 1989, when it went into force by the signatories. The Montreal Protocol is considered to be the state of the art agreement among many nations. The question is whether
an agreement of this kind can be implemented for carbon dioxide control. One problem is that
CFCs are only produced by 37 countries worldwide and that controlling their production is relatively simple compared to trying to control the infinite sources of carbon dioxide. In the case of
CFCs, a substitute can be found; but the worldwide control of carbon dioxide is going to require
major changes and innovative approaches. The existence of international cooperation on the scale
illustrated by the Montreal Protocol is indicative of what can be done between nations to solve
long-term environmental problems. An international treaty to solve this problem could include different efforts for different countries: The goal of one nation could be to decrease emissions,
whereas that of another could be an intense reforestation plan.

FUTURE TRENDS

Regarding future trends, there appears to be three approaches to the response to this problem. The
first approach is the "wait-and-see" approach, whose countermeasures may be inappropriate. The
second course of action is the "adaptation to incurable changes" approach, which is based on the

assumption that there will be plenty of time in which to decide and act on climatic change. The third approach is the "act now" approach, which is the only one that demands an immediate legislative (and industrial) response. But the problem lies in the legal and economic systems, which normally respond only to immediate and certain threats (Schneider, 1991). Which course of action the world will adopt regarding the greenhouse problem is difficult to predict at this time.

SUMMARY

1. The greenhouse effect describes the increase of "greenhouse gases" in the atmosphere and the absorption and re-emission of long-wave radiation by these gases.

2. Some scientists feel there is strong enough evidence to show that global warming has already begun, and others feel that the planet is actually entering another ice age.

3. Although the scientific world is uncertain on the causes of global warming, the need to study future situations has led the EPA to create scenarios on what would happen to the planet after a 2 to 5°C warming.

4. At present, both national and international politicians are beginning to notice the important implications of the greenhouse effect, and plans are being made to deal with the problem.

5. Which course of action the world will adopt regarding the greenhouse problem is difficult to predict at this time.

REFERENCES

Boyle, R. *Dead Heat*. New York: Basic Books, 1990.

"Clinton Unveils New Greenhouse Policy," *Science News*, October 23, 1993.

"The Ice Record of Greenhouse Gases," *Science*, February 12, 1993.

Krause, F. *Energy Policy in the Greenhouse*. New York: John Wiley & Sons, 1992.

Lyman, F. *World Resources Institute: The Greenhouse Trap*. West Palm Beach, FL: Beacon Press, 1991.

"No Way to Cool the Ultimate Greenhouse," *Science*, October 29, 1993.

Schneider, S. *Global Warming*. New York: Sierra Club Books, 1991.

Tesar, J. *Our Fragile Planet: Global Warming*. Prospect Heights, IL: Blacksmith Graphics Books, 1990.

Thompson, S. *The Greenhouse Effect*. New York: Lucent Books, 1993.

43

Environmental Training

INTRODUCTION

Employee development in the environmental area is an investment employers make in the future of their organizations. Like any other investment, the return depends upon the quality of the investment and its applicability to the organization. The goal of training is the development of the human resource—that is, to help employees reach their full potential as professionals. Employee development, sometimes referred to as human resource development, is comprised of a variety of mechanisms such as on-the-job training, internships, exchanges, full- and part-time study at educational institutions, and self-study. These activities are used to attract and retain the best employees, to build expertise in a field, to improve employee morale, and to maintain professional credibility.

Consider the situation being faced by companies that produce or use chemicals now considered hazardous. The training and retraining workload requirements produced by the Superfund Amendments and Reauthorization Act (SARA) of 1986, the Clean Act of 1990, the Pollution Prevention Act of 1990, and the proposed (at the time of preparation of this chapter in early September, 1994) water pollution legislation, are staggering (Bunner, 1991). Other important training activities fall under the domain of the Department of Transportation (DOT) and the Resource Conservation and Recovery Act (RCRA). HAZMAT training under DOT includes the handling and transportation of both hazardous and nonhazardous (e.g., gasoline) chemicals. Both tanks and drums are considered. RCRA training primarily addresses Part B (i.e., fully permitted) facilities. Any TSD (treatment, storage, and disposal) activities, for example, tank unloading or loading, op-

The material for this chapter was primarily drawn from a 1990 United States Environmental Protection Agency Manpower Training Information Branch (MTIB) report, prepared by Leo H. Stander, Jr. and Charles D. Pratt.

eration of all (including peripheral) equipment, landfills, and so on, also requires some form of training. Some of the options presented in this chapter may be useful as a means of providing additional training.

The purpose of this chapter is to provide general information concerning a few of the existing environmental training activities. These include:

Academic training

Employee exchange programs

Summer employment and cooperative training

Short-term training

Self-study training

The chapter concludes with a section on future trends in environmental training.

ACADEMIC TRAINING

Academic environmental training involves going back to school for additional education and may include both full-time and part-time attendance at colleges and universities. Many employers encourage employees to participate in these activities because it shows a willingness to obtain and maintain expertise in this field of endeavor and to improve technical and managerial capabilities. They encourage participation by allowing time off from work and by directly paying or reimbursing the employee for the tuition, fees, books, and other incidental expenses that may be incurred. Individuals can obtain training towards a baccalaureate or advanced environmental degree either through part-time study while working on the job or through long-term training.

This form of long-term training can be defined as away-from-the-job training on a full-time basis for a period covering ninety or more consecutive days. Usually, this type of training involves a concentrated academic regimen of study and coursework towards a post-graduate degree. Long-term training in the fields of environmental management can be obtained from colleges or universities that provide courses in environmental science and engineering.

Many employers allow for environmental training and provide incentives, especially where the training is job-related. However, since the number of requests for these training opportunities may exceed the resources available, employees may have to compete for approval. Usually, the employer has established eligibility requirements for candidates and has established criteria for evaluating the requests for financial assistance. Such criteria include: relevancy of the proposed environmental training to the organization; ability and motivation of the candidates; quality and cost-effectiveness of the proposed training; and the candidate's career potential. For example, in the United States Environmental Protection Agency (EPA), an approved candidate can receive full salary and benefits plus tuition, fees, and book allowance. Some state agencies offer comparable long-term training incentives.

Another type of resource available to individuals interested in securing additional environmental academic instruction in their profession is part-time study. Part-time study involves attending one or more classes during an academic term while being employed on a full-time basis. These classes may be job-related or of personal interest. As with the long-term training described above, courses can be part of a curriculum designed to assist the individual in securing an environmental degree. Many institutions have academic programs specifically designed to accommodate the student who is also a professional. Such accommodations include scheduling classes in the evenings and on weekends so there is minimal interference with the work schedules.

Another training opportunity available from some universities is the transmittal of courses by low-power television broadcast to an employer's facilities. This is particularly useful where several individuals may need to take a course at the same time. These courses are offered for academic credit and can be used to help fulfill requirements toward an advanced degree. This is described in more detail in the last section of this chapter.

EMPLOYEE EXCHANGE PROGRAMS

Though not a specific training resource for all individuals involved in environmental management, employee exchange programs are an available technique for employees to use in securing additional training and experience. Employee exchange programs are opportunities for individuals in public sector occupations to work in other public sector occupations or in academia or industry, and vice versa. In theory, such an exchange can result in better cooperation and understanding and can improve delivery of government services. Two examples of such exchange programs are: Intergovernmental Personnel Act (IPA) assignments and assignments provided by the President's Commission on Executive Exchange.

IPA assignments (EPA, 1987) involve employee exchanges between the U.S. government and a state or local governmental agency, an educational institution, or certain nonprofit organizations such as professional societies and research organizations. IPA assignments are made under the authority of the IPA of 1970. An assignment occurs when a federal or nonfederal employee temporarily leaves his or her organization to work for another organization in another sector. The assignments must be designed so that they are beneficial to both organizations and can be made on a full-time, part-time, or intermittent basis. Initially the assignments last for a period of up to two years but may be extended for a period not to exceed four years. Costs are usually shared by the participating organizations. One of the coauthors of this book, Professor Louis Theodore, a chemical engineering professor at Manhattan College, participated in an IPA program involving environmental training during the 1973–1974 academic year. Interestingly, the bulk of Dr. Theodore's outside consulting activities have primarily been in training, particularly with EPA programs.

Appointments under the President's Commission on Executive Exchange provide senior government executives with opportunities to be placed in a corporate assignment to gain fresh insights from the private sector. The program provides senior corporate executives with opportunities to take assignments in senior government positions and to become acquainted with decision-making processes in the federal government. However, these assignments can last no longer than one year. Although these assignments are usually not related to environmental management activities, the knowledge acquired from such an exchange can be of assistance in managing various environmental program operations.

SUMMER EMPLOYMENT AND COOPERATIVE TRAINING

Summer employment and cooperative (co-op) training are two techniques sometimes used by employers to evaluate potential new hires before they complete their studies. (This has become a particularly popular approach used in many government hiring programs.) It also gives students an opportunity to improve their qualifications with professional work experience before graduation. These techniques allow prospective employees to develop job skills while providing employers with low-cost ideas and fresh perspectives.

Co-op education allows a student to alternate terms of environmental study with terms of part-time or full-time employment in business, industry, or government. Students can blend classroom study with supervised employment in an area relevant to their vocational and educational goals. Co-op students usually alternate full-time employment with full-time study during their final year before receiving their baccalaureate degree. However, at most universities, students are eligible to start their co-op programs following the freshman year. During the periods of employment, co-op students receive salaries and sometimes earn credits toward a degree. Once they receive their baccalaureate degree, many of the co-op students return as permanent employees of the company where they were employed during college.

Summer employment with industry or with a federal or state agency is another way a college student can gain knowledge in the field of environmental management. For example, the U.S. Public Health Service's Commissioned Officer Student Training and Extern Program (COSTEP) is a recruiting device that offers opportunities for students in health-related fields, such as engineering or environmental science, to gain knowledge and experience during summers after their sophomore year.

SHORT-TERM TRAINING

Short-term training is intense instruction on a given technical or administrative topic. Offerings can last from a few hours to ninety days, but usually last less than a week. Short-term training utilizes a variety of group learning formats, including workshops, seminars, classes, and, to a certain extent, conferences. This type of environmental training is a staple of professional development and is the principal technique used by employers to upgrade their employees from novices to journeymen to experts in their fields.

Short-term training is, by far, the most prevalent training resource available to professionals in environmental management. Literally thousands of offerings are available each year, covering a variety of environmental topics. They are sponsored and/or taught by consultants, university faculty, government agency personnel, industrial associations, professional societies and organizations, and even trade publications. Information on such offerings can be obtained from direct-mail advertising, professional journals, and newsletters.

Some employers conduct short-term training for their own employees, whereas others offer training to interested participants at a nominal fee. Charges for such courses offered and conducted by the EPA's Air Pollution Training Institute (APTI) cost $110 per day for lecture courses and $150 per day for laboratory courses, with typical courses lasting from three to five days. There is no charge for employees of state and local agencies with responsibilities in air pollution control.

Courses offered through the Air and Waste Management Association (one of the coauthors is involved with AWMA) as part of a Specialty Conference of the Annual Meeting cost approximately $100 per two-hour session or approximately $250 to $500 for a one or two-day session, respectively. Courses or workshops offered by consultants or trade groups typically cost between $300 and $750 for one to three-day day sessions. However, these figures can be misleading because the total cost to the company, agency, or organization will be significantly higher. For example, the inclusion of travel, room and board, car rental, and so on, can increase the cost for a four-day course to approximately $2500 (Theodore, personal notes). This does not include the "cost" associated with the individual being absent from work during the course; this cost estimate ranges from $500 to $1000 per day (Theodore, personal notes).

SELF-STUDY TRAINING

Environmental self-study allows students to participate without incurring travel expenses or time away from the office. On the negative side, there is a lack of interaction with other students and no direct guidance is provided by the instructor. Some individuals consider self-study training as an imposition on their private time, and feel that it takes away from their productive work time. Despite these possible shortcomings, the majority of individuals find that a great deal of information and knowledge can be obtained through self-study training.

Self-study programs meet three objectives:

1. They are designed to reach a wide audience
2. They are relatively inexpensive
3. They encourage "learning by doing"

Economically speaking, there is little doubt of the cost-effectiveness of such a program. In many cases, the travel costs alone prevent prospective attendees from participating in other types of training. Currently, the cost of some self-study programs in environmental protection are underwritten by the federal government or public organizations. There is little or no cost to an employer to initiate an internal training program based on the self-study courses available from the EPA and other sources.

An important characteristic of the self-study format is learning-by-doing. There are two levels of learning-by-doing: The first involves the mechanics of writing answers into blocks and receiving feedback by comparing the answers. The second level arises when the student uses a course manual in a work situation and begins to apply the principles contained in the course. Also, many of the self-study materials contain worksheets and trouble-shooting guides to assist the student in his/her work.

More recently, a set of unique environmental tutorials, entitled Theodore Tutorials (ETS, 1992), has been developed (by one of the coauthors of this book) that can be used for self-study purposes. One of the key features of these tutorials is that a Theodore Tutorial is a self-instructional problem workbook. It attempts to meet the challenge of effective instruction for students with diverse backgrounds, including nontechnical education, with an approach that lies between programmed instruction and the conventional textbook. The general format for these

Theodore Tutorials is as follows. The material is divided into three parts: Basic Operations, Problems, and Solutions. The first part of each tutorial workbook provides a series of basic operations that are required when solving most engineering problems. Each basic operation refers to a particular calculation from chemistry, physics, thermodynamics, and so forth, that many individuals refer to as Basic Concepts. Each Basic Operation is presented with a title, problem statement, pertinent data, and solution in programmed instructional format. The second part of each tutorial contains problems. This section deals with individual calculations associated with the title topic in question. These problems are laid out in such a way as to develop the reader's technical understanding of the subject in question. Each problem contains a title, introduction, problem statement and data, solution in programmed-instructional format, and a concluding comment statement. The more difficult problems can be found at or near the end of each set. Various options are available to the reader in attempting to solve each problem. These include:

1. Employing the problem statement only.
2. Employing the problem statement and the introduction.
3. Employing the problem statement and the introduction, plus the right side of the solution outline in programmed-instructional format.
4. Employing the problem statement and the introduction, plus the right- and left-hand sides of the solution outline in programmed-instructional format.

If difficulty is encountered in solving the problems, the reader can refer to the solution section (in Part 3) that immediately follows the Problem section. An Appendix, consisting of a discussion of SI units, conversion constants, physical and chemical properties, glossary, and so on, is also included.

From the perspective of an organization, the self-study approach has much to offer in terms of meeting its goals by controlling training costs and by providing an ongoing information exchange and training program. From the students' perspective, self-study offers a means to learn at their own pace and to build a reference library for future use.

FUTURE TRENDS

Management support to its training staff is essential for a training program to be successful in the future. Managers must take time out to understand training standards, resource requirements, and organizational impacts. While internal experts or consultants can develop specific information for the training programs, support for the program should come from the top down, be felt by staff and employees, and result in the desired organizational change.

Satellite courses have suddenly emerged as a major actor in the training field. The EPA, in conjunction with North Carolina State University, has presented numerous environmental courses via the satellite route. Transmissions are usually accomplished to nearly fifty locations. Environmental regulatory officials not only take courses in a relaxed theater-style setting but also are provided with an opportunity to interact directly with the lecturer(s). One of the coauthors (Dr. L. Theodore) of this book, recently served as moderator/lecturer for a three-day course on hazardous waste incineration (Theodore, personal notes). This approach to training appears to be an extremely attractive option from an economic point of view. One negative feature that may be reduced or eliminated in the near future is the inability of the lecturer to interact with the student during his/her presentation.

The Future Trends section of many of the chapters contains statements related to the need for training. There is no question that the solution to nearly all of this nation's environmental problems can be achieved through training—either at the technical or domestic level; although this chapter has primarily focused on technical industrial training, domestic training also needs to be considered.

In the present day sphere of budget-cutting, training often is eyed as easy fat to trim. Oftentimes, managers become tempted to look at a cost that does not appear to reap immediate, measurable dollar benefits and begin a process of rationalization to defend the cut. This is dangerous logic that will hopefully change in the future.

SUMMARY

1. Employee development is an investment employers make in the future of their organizations.

2. Many employers encourage employees to participate in academic training activities because it shows a willingness to obtain and maintain expertise in the environmental field.

3. Employee exchange programs are opportunities for individuals in public sector occupations to work in other public sector occupations or in academia or industry, and vice versa.

4. Summer employment and co-op training are two techniques sometimes used by employers to evaluate potential new hires before they complete their studies.

5. Short-term training is intense instruction on a given technical or administrative topic. Offerings can last from a few hours to ninety days, but usually last less than a week.

6. Self-study programs meet three objectives: (a) They are designed to reach a wide audience, (b) they are relatively inexpensive, and (c) they encourage "learning by doing."

7. Management support to its training staff is essential for a training program to be successful over the long run.

REFERENCES

Bunner, W. "Regulations Dictate Training Assessment," *Environmental Protection,* January/February, 1991.

EPA. EPA Intergovernmental Personnel Act (IPA) Handbook, Special Resources Program, Personnel Management Division, Office of Administration, 1987.

ETS Theodore Tutorials. Roanoke, VA: ETS International, 1992.

Theodore, L.: Personal notes.

44

Underground Storage Tanks

CONTRIBUTING AUTHOR

James McKenna

INTRODUCTION

Leaking underground storage tanks (LUST) contribute to the contamination of the environment and pose a great risk to human health. The acronym LUST has apparently been dropped by industry and the government probably because the term is politically/socially incorrect or unacceptable. There are an estimated five to six million underground storage tanks in the United States that contain either a hazardous substance or petroleum. Of those, approximately 400,000 are believed to be leaking. Many more will begin to leak in the near future.

Under the Resource Conservation and Recovery Act (RCRA), an underground storage tank (UST) is defined as a tank with 10 percent or more of its volume underground. This 10 percent includes piping. Only about 16,000 of the 5 to 6 million UST systems are protected against corrosion. Another 200,000 are made of fiberglass, which breaks easily. Almost half of the tanks to be regulated by the Environmental Protection Agency (EPA) are petroleum storage tanks owned by gas stations. Another 47 percent store petroleum for other industries such as factories, farms, police and fire departments, and individuals. The remaining 3 percent are used by a variety of industries for chemical storage.

Many of the petroleum tanks were installed during the oil boom of the 1950s and 1960s. Two 1985 studies of tank age distribution indicate that approximately one-third of the existing motor fuel storage tanks are over 20 years old or of unknown age. Most of these tanks are constructed of bare steel not protected against corrosion. With steel tanks, corrosion is the leading cause of leakage, accounting for 92 percent of the leaks in the tank, and 64 percent of leaks in the pipes.

Substances released from leaking tanks can poison crops, damage sewer lines and buried cables, and lead to fires and explosions. The most serious concern, however, is groundwater contamination. One gallon of gasoline is enough to render one million gallons of groundwater unusable based on federal drinking water standards. Groundwater represents two-thirds of the fresh water on the planet, and if you eliminate unavailable fresh water such as glaciers and the ice caps, groundwater makes up 95 percent of available fresh water. More than half of the United States relies on groundwater as a source of drinking water. Groundwater drawn for large-scale agricultural and industrial can also be adversely affected by contamination from leaking underground storage tanks.

EARLY REGULATIONS

It had become apparent that regulations for leaking underground storage tanks were needed. In 1984 federal laws were enacted in response to increasing problems resulting from leaking USTs. These laws were provided in the RCRA amendments that formed regulations on USTs. Certain regulations required all owners and operators to register their tanks with state agencies giving tank age, location, and substance stored. They also set up design requirements for new tanks installed after May 1985. Owners were now responsible for detecting leaks and the cleanup of releases. Tank owners also had to demonstrate that they were financially capable of cleaning up leaks and compensating third parties for damages. There were some exclusions to these regulations. There were statutory exclusions, which were tank systems that Congress specifically exempted from regulations, and regulatory exclusions, which were tanks exempted after the EPA determined they did not pose a danger to human health or the environment. A listing of each group is provided below (Holmes, Singh, & Theodore, 1993).

Statutory Exclusions

1. Farm or residential tanks of 1100 gallons capacity or smaller used for storing motor fuel for noncommercial purposes
2. Tanks that store heating oil for use on the premises where they are stored
3. Septic tank systems
4. Pipeline facilities regulated under specific federal or state laws
5. Any surface impoundments, pits, ponds, or lagoons
6. Storm water or wastewater collection systems
7. Flow-through process tanks
8. Liquid traps or associated gathering lines directly related to oil or gas production and gathering operations
9. Tanks in underground areas

EPA Regulatory Exclusions

1. Tanks that store (a) hazardous wastes listed or identified under Subtitle C of the Solid Waste Disposal Act, or (b) a mixture of such hazardous wastes and regulated substances
2. Wastewater treatment tank systems regulated under section 402 or 307(b) of the Clean Water Act

3. Equipment or machinery containing regulated substances for operational purposes, such as hydraulic lift tanks

4. USTs whose capacity is 110 gallons or less

5. USTs containing de minimis concentrations of regulated substances

6. Any emergency spill or overflow containment system that is expeditiously emptied after use

A later amendment of the Comprehensive Environmental Response, Compensation and Liability Act (CERCLA) in 1986 provided $500 million dollars over the next five years for a Leaking Underground Storage Tank Trust Fund. This revenue was collected primarily through a tax on motor fuels.

FEDERAL REGULATION

Their are three main sets of federal regulations: the technical regulations, which address technical standards for corrective action requirements for owners and operators of USTs; the UST State Program Approval Regulations, which set regulations for approval of states to run UST programs in lieu of the federal program; and the financial responsibility requirements, in which owners and operators must show financial responsibility (Noonan & Curtis, 1990). All three are addressed in the EPA's Federal Register proposed on April 17, 1988. Subpart D has the greatest impact of any part of the proposal and will be discussed below in more depth (Federal Register, 1988).

Adherence to the performance and operating standards for USTs will reduce both new and existing incidents of leaks from UST systems. The regulations also include extensive requirements for release detection. EPA views release detection as an essential backup measure combined with prevention techniques. Release detection monitoring on a frequent and consistent basis is the best known method for quickly detecting a release from a UST and reducing the potential environmental damages and liability. Thus, these requirements are in keeping with the overall goal of the UST regulations.

Seven general categories of release detection methods are acceptable. These are tank tightness or precision tests, manual tank gauging systems, automatic tank gauging systems, inventory control methods, groundwater monitoring, vapor monitoring, and interstitial monitoring. The EPA believes that any of these methods can be successful if proper procedures are followed; therefore, no one method is preferred (Noonan & Curtis, 1990).

Release detection is required for all UST systems. The deadline for providing detection for existing tank systems varies with the year the tank was installed. Older tanks require release detection sooner while new tanks must include release detection upon installation. The detection system must be able to detect leaks from any part of the tank or piping that routinely contains product. The system must be installed, operated, and maintained in accordance with the instructions set forth by the manufacturer. The regulations also address performance standards for release detection. Four of the seven methods—inventory, manual and automatic tank gauging, and tank tightness tests—have specific volume or leak rate limits above which the method must be able to detect a leak with a probability of detection of at least 0.95 and a probability of a false alarm less than 0.05. The other three methods—vapor monitoring, groundwater, and interstitial monitoring—have no numerical standards to be met, only general standards.

The release detection regulations are divided into petroleum UST systems and hazardous substance UST systems. Generally, UST systems that store petroleum must conduct release detection every thirty days; however, several exceptions apply. New or upgraded USTs may use monthly inventory controls in conjunction with a tank tightness test every five years (until December 22, 1998) or until ten years after installation (for new tanks). Existing USTs that are not upgraded can use monthly inventory controls with annual tank tightness tests until December 22, 1998, by which time the tank must be upgraded or closed. Tanks of less than 550 gallons capacity may use weekly tank gauging.

The piping of petroleum UST systems must meet different standards. Pressurized piping must be equipped with an automatic line leak detector and have an annual line tightness test or monthly monitoring. Suction piping does not require release detection, provided certain conditions are met. These conditions include that the below-grade piping operates at a negative pressure and the piping is sloped so the products will flow back into the tank. Only one check valve per line is included, and that valve is located as close as practical to the suction pump. Suction piping that does not meet these requirements must have line tightness tests at least every three years or monthly monitoring.

UST systems that store hazardous substances are covered by separate regulations. All existing systems must meet the petroleum release detection requirements described above, and must be upgraded by December 22, 1998, to meet the requirements for new hazardous substance systems. Release detection for new systems must include secondary containment systems that are able to contain all substances released from the tank system until the substances are detected and removed. They also must prevent the release of any regulated substance to the environment throughout the operational life of the UST system and must be checked for leakage at least every 30 days. If a double tank is used, the outer wall must be strong enough to contain a release from the inner tank. The inner tank leak must also be detected. If the entire system is surrounded by a liner, that liner must be strong enough to contain a leak. These requirements also pertain to piping for hazardous substance systems. In addition, pressurized piping must be equipped with an automatic line leak detector, similar to petroleum systems (Noonan & Curtis, 1990).

For each of the seven specific types of release detection that can be used to meet the requirements of these regulations, a performance standard is also specified. For example, if product inventory control is used, that method must be able to detect a release of one percent of monthly flow-through, plus 130 gallons, on a monthly basis. If inventory control cannot provide this level of accuracy, it would not be considered as an acceptable release detection method.

The use of manual tank gauging is restricted to tanks of 2,000 gallons or less. This method's performance standards are specified in terms of a weekly standard and a monthly standard. For tanks of 550 gallons or less the required precision is 10 gallons weekly and 5 gallons monthly. For tanks of 550 to 1,000 gallons, the standards are 13 gallons weekly and 7 gallons monthly. Tanks of 1,000 to 2,000 gallons capacity are allowed standards of 26 weekly and 13 gallons monthly, respectively (Noonan & Curtis, 1990).

A tank tightness test must be able to detect a leak rate of 0.1 gallons per hour. These tests must also take into account the effects of thermal expansion or contraction of the product. In addition, vapor pockets, tank deformation, evaporation or condensation, and a location of the water table need to be considered.

Automatic tank gauging systems may be used if they can detect a leak rate of 0.2 gallons per hour, and if they are integrated with inventory control.

Vapor monitoring systems are a fifth available release detection method. Prior to their installation, the site must be assessed to ensure that their use is appropriate. These systems must be able to detect any significant increase in vapor level above the background concentration.

Groundwater monitoring may be used as a release detection method but again requires a site assessment. Such an assessment should show that the stored substance is immiscible in water and will float; also, that the water table is usually 20 meters or less below the ground surface, that the soil's hydraulic conductivity is at least 0.01 cm/sec, and that the monitoring wells are designed and placed properly.

Interstitial monitoring may be used for UST systems with secondary containment. Several standard requirements apply, such as the assurance that any leak from the inner tank of a double-walled tank be detected.

Any other method not listed in the regulations may be used if it can detect a leak rate of 0.2 gallons per hour with a probability of 0.95, a probability of a false alarm less than 0.05, and if such a method is approved by the implementing agency (Noonan & Curtis, 1990).

RELEASE RESPONSE AND CORRECTIVE ACTION

Following the confirmation of a release, the leak must be investigated and remedied. Emergency and corrective actions will then be implemented. Emergency actions will identify and reduce any immediate health threats, such as explosions or fire. Corrective actions will be taken to mitigate long-term threats to human health and to the environment. Immediate actions might include pumping the remaining product from a leaking tank or dispersing explosive vapors, while long-term correction could include groundwater cleanup plans using air stripping or other such measures.

Subpart F of the Federal Register details seven actions to be taken after a leak is discovered. These are provided below.

1. The initial response of any release should include three steps: notification of the release to the appropriate agency; prevention of any further release; and, mitigation of any immediate fire, explosion, or vapor hazards. These steps should occur within 24 hours of the confirmation of the release.

2. Following the initial response, the owner or operator should immediately begin initial abatement measures. First, the regulated substance to prevent further leakage should be removed. Then, any exposed portion of the release must be inspected to stop its spreading. The response should attempt to stop any fire or explosion hazards. Problems caused by polluted soil should be investigated. Finally, the removal of free product, if it is present, is to be initiated.

3. A site characterization must also be performed and a report submitted to the implementing agency within 45 days of release confirmation. This report should contain information about the nature and quantity of the release, surrounding populations, location and use of nearby wells, land use, climatological conditions, and similar factors.

4. If free product is found on the site, steps must be taken to remove the free product. Not only will this prevent spreading, but the product can still be used, saving money. Extra care should be taken when dealing with a flammable product. Another report must be submitted within 45 days detailing the removal, treatment, and disposal of the product.

5. Investigations for soil and groundwater cleanup must be conducted if needed. This is warranted in the case of contaminated groundwater, wells, or soil.

6. The owner or operator may be required to submit a corrective action plan for soil and groundwater cleanup. The plan will only be accepted if the agency finds that it adequately protects human health and the environment.

7. For all confirmed releases that require a corrective action plan, the implementing agency must take a number of steps to assure public participation and notice of corrective action procedures. These steps could include public notice in a newspaper or letters to affected parties.

CLEANUP PROCEDURES
AND ECONOMIC CONSIDERATIONS

Only a limited number of technologies to clean soil, air, and water of the contaminants principally associated with gasoline are available that have demonstrated performance records and have progressed to full-scale applications. One reason for this is there are different types of spills and each should be treated using an appropriate procedure. Whether groundwater is in jeopardy will mostly determine what method should be used for cleanup. The final cost of the project is often determined more by what method is used rather than the size of the spill.

The first type of spill is petroleum that has not yet infiltrated the water table. Removal here is essential because the toxin in the unsaturated soil can eventually enter the groundwater. The methods available for this type of removal are excavation and disposal, enhanced volatilization, incineration, venting, vitrification, and microbial degradation.

Excavation and disposal can be 100 percent effective in this situation. This method entails actually removing the dirt, many times with the use of a backhoe, and carrying it off site for disposal. The drawbacks of this procedure include difficulty for deep excavation and increased risk of exposure for the workers. Removal-off site can also be dangerous. The cost for this method runs about $200 to $300 per cubic yard if the soil is considered hazardous. This is relatively expensive and therefore only used for small spills.

Enhanced volatilization has not been widely used but has an effectiveness near 99.99 percent. This method can be enhanced through rototilling, pneumatic conveyer systems, and low temperature thermal stripping. Only low temperature thermal stripping is effective for petroleum spills. The limitations of enhanced volatility are soil characteristics, contaminant concentrations, and the need to control dust and organic vapors. The cost is $250 to $300 per cubic yard.

Incineration is widely used and is very reliable (Holmes et al., 1993; Theodore & Reynolds, 1988). It can achieve 99.99 percent effectiveness depending on what is burned. However, to burn the contaminants, they must be brought to the surface. Many substances are not safe to be burned at all and have regulations against incineration. Even when approved, location for incineration plants are hard to come by since residential areas do not want them "in their back yard." The cost will usually be between $250 and $640 per cubic yard.

Venting is not widely used but can have an effectiveness of 99 percent. An advantage to venting is that it is relatively easy to implement and causes minimal damage to structures and pavement. An example of venting is vapor stripping. Calculational details on vapor stripping are available in the literature (McKenna, Mycoch, & Theodore, 1995; Theodore & Allen, 1994; Theodore & Barden, 1995). The drawbacks include critical design requirements that often remain undefined, soil characteristics, and the possibility of explosion. The cost is only $15 to $20 per cubic yard.

Two relatively new methods are microbial degradation of contaminants and vitrification. The advantage of microbial degradation is that the soil is treated on site and contaminants are completely destroyed. For its effectiveness this technique depends on oxygen levels, nutrient levels, temperature, and moisture content of the soil. The cost is between $66 and $123 per cubic yard. A combination of soil venting and microbial degradation is often one of the least costly and most effective corrective actions.

The next type of spill to consider is one where the products have reached the water level but have not yet dissolved into the groundwater. There are two ways often used to capture the free floating spill—the trench method and the pumping well method. The trench method is most effective when the water table is no more then 15 feet deep. Excavation of the trench is easy to undertake and with this method, the entire edge of the gasoline plume can be captured. It is similar to digging a moat around a castle that is the source of the spill, and waiting for it to fill up. This method does not reverse water flow and should not be used if a drinking water well is immediately threatened. This method can cost about $100 per cubic yard of soil excavated.

For deep spills, a pumping well system is normally used. This method can reverse the direction of groundwater flow. The cost is $100 to $200 per foot of depth. Dual-pump systems and oil/water separators are typically used for deeper releases.

The final situation to examine is the most dangerous, and is the most expensive to clean up. This occurs when the contaminants get into the water table and dissolve. There are three technologies widely used with relative success: air stripping, filtration through granular activated carbon (GAC), and biorestoration (Clarke, 1989).

Air stripping is a proven effective means of removing organic chemicals from the groundwater. It works by providing intimate contact of air and water, thus allowing diffusion of volatile substances from the liquid phase to the gas phase. There are three types of air stripping: diffused aeration, which has a 70 to 90 percent effectiveness; tray aerators, which have an effectiveness of 40 to 60 percent; and packed towers, which can be almost 100 percent effective (McKenna et al., 1995; Theodore & Allen, 1994; Theodore & Barden, 1995). The limitations of air stripping are the types of chemicals that can be effectively removed and the possible air pollution impact. Also, possible high noise levels and zoning laws may restrict the maximum height of the tower. The cost will run anywhere from $50,000 to $100,000.

Next there is the use of granulated activated carbon (GAC), which is excellent for removing organic compounds dissolved in water, but is very costly. It works by adsorbing the contaminants onto the activating carbon. The design of a GAC system is very complex and requires more complete pilot testing. More judgment is needed for GAC than other methods, since a system can vary from site to site. The limitations include high solubility components that do not adsorb well, the presence of iron, manganese, and hard water will decrease effectiveness, and the dangers of fire increase due to the fact that gasoline-soaked carbon can self-ignite. The cost can run about $300,000 to $400,000 for a typical GAC unit. A combination of a GAC system and air stripping is usually the best alternative.

Biorestoration, unlike the other two methods shown, is a destructive technique. This is a distinct advantage since the pollution is not simply transformed into another media; it is completely destroyed. The end products are carbon dioxide and water. However, the degree of cleanup is highly dependent on specific environmental conditions affecting microbial growth. It does not promise to be a cost-effective alternative at this time. The system cannot be used where quick startup is needed and must remain running 24 hours a day, 7 days a week. The cost is about $30 to $40 per cubic yard.

FUTURE TRENDS

The problems caused by leakage from USTs has become too big for the EPA to handle alone and a new approach needs to be taken. Traditionally, the EPA has controlled all areas of the tank program until states demonstrated it could operate independently. Under the new "franchise concept," the EPA will help states and counties succeed in implementing and enforcing their own tank programs. The EPA initially will focus on assisting the states to establish basic tank programs and then provide a range of services to help them improve their performance. This includes providing special expertise, develop training videos, publishing handbooks, and job training. In this sense, the EPA can be viewed as a franchiser while states and counties are owners of franchises. Through education and training, the EPA, states, and local communities will do a better job of communicating the dangers of leaking tanks to their owners (Holmes et al., 1993).

SUMMARY

1. Leakage from underground storage tanks contribute to the contamination of the environment and pose a great risk to human health.

2. It had become apparent that regulations for underground storage tanks were needed. Federal laws were enacted in 1984 in response to increasing problems resulting from leaking USTs. The RCRA amendments formed regulations for USTs but left many exceptions.

3. The problems caused by leakage from USTs has become too big for the EPA to handle alone. Under the new "franchise concept" the EPA will help states and counties succeed in implementing and enforcing their own tank programs.

4. The federal regulations consist of three major sets of regulations; these technical regulations are set forth in EPA's Federal Register 40 CFR Part 280.

5. Following the confirmation of a release the leak must be investigated and remedied. Emergency and corrective actions must also be implemented.

6. Only a limited number of technologies to clean soil, air, and water of the contaminants principally associated with gasoline are available that have demonstrated performance records and have progressed to full-scale applications. One reason for this is there are different types of spills and each should be treated using an appropriate procedure.

REFERENCES

Clarke, J. "In Situ Treatment of Contaminated Soil and Rock," 1989.

Holmes, G., Singh, B., and Theodore, L. *Handbook of Environmental Management & Technology*, New York: John Wiley & Sons, 1989.

McKenna, J., Mycoch, J., and Theodore, L. *Handbook of Air Pollution Control Technology* (in publication), Boca Raton, FL, Lewis Publishers, 1995

Noonan D., and Curtis, J. *Groundwater Remediation and Petroleum*, Boca Raton, FL, Lewis Publishers, 1990.

Rules and Regulations, Federal Register, 52(185), pp. 27197–37207, Friday, September 23, 1988.

Theodore, L., and Allen, R. *ETS THEODORE TUTORIAL, Air Pollution Control Equipment*. Roanoke, VA: ETS International, Inc., 1994.

Theodore, L., and Barden, J. *ETS THEODORE TUTORIAL, Mass Transfer Operations*, (in preparation), Roanoke, VA: ETS International, Inc., 1995 (anticipated)

Theodore, L., and Reynolds, J. *Introduction to Hazardous Waste Incineration*, New York: Wiley-Interscience, 1988.

45

Metals

CONTRIBUTING AUTHOR

J. Erik Moy

INTRODUCTION

In recent years a great amount of media attention has focused on the effects of industry on the environment. While a large portion of the attention has focused on "politically correct" issues such as waste incineration, nuclear waste disposal, and rainforest destruction, the environmental and biological damage due to metal contamination has largely been ignored by the media (although not by the scientific community). Lead poisoning, long known to occur in children through the ingestion of lead-based paint chips, is also virtually ignored by the media. In addition, the disposal of large quantities of nickel-cadmium batteries and lead-acid batteries in landfills, a source of groundwater contamination, receives scant attention.

Since heavy metals are strongly attracted to biological tissues and to the environment, and remain in them for long periods of time, metal pollution is a serious issue. Overall, metals are quite abundant and persistent in the environment (Oehme, 1978). This chapter will discuss the metals posing the greatest threat to health and the environment; that is, the most toxic metals, including metals used in large quantities by industry, and metals found in common everyday products such as batteries and paint. The four major metals to be considered are lead, mercury, cadmium, and arsenic.

The scientific community has long known the dangers of metal contamination. Exposure to mercury occurred in 19th-century hat makers. They developed a shaking and slurring of speech due to exposure to large quantities of inorganic mercury during the manufacturing process (Holmes, Singh, & Theodore, 1993). In the 1930s reports of wastes containing chromium were reported in the United Kingdom. In addition, a chromium discharge onto a filter bed resulted in the termination of a biological process. These findings were reported by H. E. Monk and J. H. Spencer in the Proceedings of the Institute of Sewage Purification in the 1930s (Lester, 1987). Since the

1950s, the determination of health hazards posed by chemical and other environmental agents has received attention. However, man's *total* exposure to a chemical or metal from various sources such as water, air, food, home, and work only has been considered since the 1970s (World Health Organization, 1976).

LEAD

Lead occurs naturally in soil, air, water, and plants. However, industrial and technological uses of lead contribute the most damage to man's health. The highest exposure occurs during mining, smelting, and other manufacturing operations that produce lead. While the air concentration in large cities having dense automobile traffic (eg., New York) is about 2 to 4 g/m^3, the lead concentration in smelting and storage battery facilities usually exceeds 1000 g/m^3. Children also are exposed to lead via ingestion of lead-based paint chips and other lead-containing objects (World Health Organization, 1977).

Lead normally localizes near the points of discharge and any amount (normally about 20 percent) that does not localize usually is widely dispersed in the atmosphere. Discharges of lead do occur into soil and water but air discharges are of the most concern. Lead ore smelters, for instance, create emission pollution problems in localized areas. The height of the stack and its trapping devices, the topography of the surrounding area, and numerous local characteristics determine the exact amount of pollution caused by a lead ore smelter. Lead emissions from a lead ore smelter contribute to soil and water pollution in addition to air pollution. As emission control devices become more effective, air pollution from lead emissions should start to decrease (World Health Organization, 1977).

Drinking water becomes contaminated with lead due to corrosion of plumbing material in homes and water distribution systems. Most public water systems deliver water to households containing lead solder; in addition, materials used in faucets contribute a certain amount of lead to drinking water (Holmes et al., 1993). Homes containing lead-lined water storage tanks and lead pipes have the highest concentrations of lead. This occurs primarily in areas where the water is soft; that is, the water contains low amounts of both calcium and magnesium (World Health Organization, 1977).

Health effects of high lead ingestion are significant and may lead to brain damage, high blood pressure, premature birth, low birth weight, and nervous system disorders. Children are most affected by lead in drinking water. It is imperative to test for lead in drinking water if it is suspected the water may contain lead (Holmes et al., 1993).

Amounts of lead in gasoline have been drastically reduced due to efforts by the Environmental Protection Agency (EPA) that began in the early 1970s. The EPA's overall automotive emission control program required the use of unleaded gasoline in many cars beginning in 1975. By 1986, the lead content of leaded gasoline had been reduced to 0.1 g/gal.

During the past decade, many communities have begun to implement recycling programs to reduce the amount of waste in the municipal solid waste (MSW) stream. While recycling has had an impact on the amount of solid waste in landfills, an abundant amount of lead still is present in MSW streams. Greater amounts of lead occur in MSW streams than amounts of cadmium; lead in municipal solid waste has grown in several areas (Table 45–1). Lead-acid batteries contribute the greatest

Table 45–1.   Lead in Products Discarded in MSW, 1970–2000 (in short tons)

Products	1970	1986	2000(est)	Tonnage	Percentage
Lead-acid batteries	83,825	138,043	181,546	Increasing	Variable
Consumer electronics	12,233	58,536	85,032	Increasing	Increasing
Glass and ceramics	3,465	7,956	8,910	Increasing	Increasing;; stable after 1986
Plastics	1,613	3,577	3,288	Increasing; decreasing after 1986	Fairly stable
Soldered cans	24,117	2,052	787	Decreasing	Decreasing
Pigments	27,020	1,131	682	Decreasing	Decreasing
All others	12,567	2,537	1,701	Decreasing	Decresing
TOTALS	164,840	213,832	281,886		

amount of lead to the municipal solid waste stream along with consumer electronics, glass, ceramics, and plastics. In contrast, the amount of lead contributed by soldered cans and pigments has dropped considerably.

Lead-acid batteries contributed 65 percent of the lead in municipal solid waste in 1986 although the percentage ranged between 50 and 85 percent during the 1970 to 1986 period. However, lead-acid batteries are recycled to a large extent compared with the other categories in Table 45–1. The other main contributor of lead to the municipal solid waste stream is consumer electronics, which account for approximately 27 percent of lead discards. This includes soldered circuit boards, leaded glass in television sets, and plated-steel chassis (Holmes et al., 1993).

MERCURY

In March 1970, fish from Lake Erie and Lake St. Clair outside of Detroit were determined to contain mercury. This was the first of a series of events that has since raised public consciousness about mercury pollution. The alarming discovery that mercury could be transported so easily throughout the aqueous environment led to a high degree of concern from both the scientific community and the general public (Jones, 1971).

How is mercury distributed in the environment? Globally, land sources emit mercury vapor, which circulates throughout the atmosphere and enters the oceans. Since the ocean's mercury content is so large (approximately 70 million tons), it is difficult to determine yearly increases in the mercury content of the world's oceans (World Health Organization, 1977). Mercury pollution in the aqueous environment occurs when organic molecules from dead organisms and sewage react with mercury to form soluble organic complexes. Anaerobic bacteria in river and lake bottoms convert mercury into the organic compound methyl mercury, a highly poisonous substance. Methyl mercury dissolves in water; this results in the transport of mercury into the aquatic food chain, which ultimately leads to human consumption of mercury (Jones, 1971).

Although the aquatic environment and food chain contains a surprising amount of mercury contamination (particularly in fish), the exposure to elemental mercury vapor in the workplace still poses the greatest threat to human health. Diseases caused by mercury and its toxic compounds are numerous and in most countries qualify for worker's compensation. However, a lack of reporting of mercury poisoning occurs in most developing countries; evidence suggests a large number of workers are exposed to high mercury concentrations in these countries. Most people exposed to mercury in industry work in the mining industry or in chloralkali plants. Mercury levels in the atmosphere in these industrial settings may attain levels as high as 5 mg/m^3 (World Health Organization, 1976).

The natural degassing of the earth's crust, the major source of mercury, contributes between 20,000 and 125,000 tons per year of mercury to the atmosphere. Industrial production of mercury via mining and smelting was about 10,000 tons per year in 1973 and has been increasing 2 percent annually. Total mercury releases into the environment by man amounted to 20,000 tons per year in 1975; this includes the burning of fossil fuels, steel, cement and phosphate production, and metal smelting from sulfide ores (World Health Organization, 1976).

CADMIUM

Cadmium, a rare but toxic metal, is most commonly found in rechargeable nickel-cadmium batteries. Its color is silvery-white and it is soft and ductile; in addition, it possesses good electrical and thermal conductivity. When cadmium is exposed to moist air, it slowly oxidizes to form a thin layer of cadmium oxide, thereby protecting itself from further corrosion.

Cadmium occurs in nature most often as the mineral greenockite (CdS). Normally it is mined with zinc, but occasionally it is mined with lead and copper ores. The end uses of cadmium include batteries, pigments, and plastic stabilizers. However, the consumption of cadmium in 1986 was a small 4,800 tons (compared to 1.2 million tons of lead). The consumption in the United States decreased until 1983, but then started to increase once again.

The most prevalent use of cadmium today is in nickel-cadmium rechargeable batteries; their popularity is growing due to their rechargeable nature. Although they were invented in the early 1900s, nickel-cadmium batteries were not widely used until the mid-1940s when they came into use in industrial and military applications. Currently, military and industrial uses of cadmium include satellites, missile guidance systems, naval signaling, computer memories, television and

Table 45–2.　Cadmium in Products Discarded in MSW, 1970–2000 (in short tons)

Products	1970	1986	2000 (est)	Tonnage	Percentage
Household batteries	53	930	2,035	Increasing	Increasing
Plastics	342	520	380	Variable	Variable; decreasing after 1986
Consumer electronics	571	161	67	Decreasing	Decreasing
Appliances	107	88	57	Decreasing	Decreasing
Pigments	79	70	93	Variable	Variable
Glass and ceramics	32	29	37	Variable	Variable
All others	12	8	11	Variable	Variable
TOTALS	1,196	1,806	2,680		

camera lighting, and portable hospital equipment. Consumer use of nickel-cadmium batteries began in the early 1960s; however, their popularity grew more rapidly in the early 1970s. Their uses are endless, toys, hand-held tools, flashlights, hedge trimmers, VCRs, cameras, electric shavers, and alarm systems.

Although it occurs in much smaller quantities in municipal solid waste than does lead, the amounts of cadmium in MSW have increased due to the disposal of nickel-cadmium batteries (indicated in Table 45–2). As of 1980, nickel-cadmium batteries were the largest contributor to cadmium in MSW (Holmes et al., 1993).

ARSENIC

Arsenic is likely familiar to most people as a poison used by villains in mystery novels and movies to kill their innocent victims. Many movie buffs can relate this statement to the Oscar award-winning movie in the early 1940s titled *Arsenic and Old Lace* starring Cary Grant. But although arsenic is a poison, its more detrimental effect is its ability to cause cancer. Lead arsenate was used as a pesticide in farms and gardens but now has been replaced by synthetic pesiticides. Arsenic compounds are found in the home; typical products containing arsenic are rat poison and plant killers. However, most products now contain little or no arsenic (Holmes et al., 1993).

FUTURE TRENDS

This chapter has highlighted those metals posing the greatest threat to human health and the environment. Since increasing metal contamination is occurring through the disposal of products such as lead-acid and nickel-cadmium batteries in the municipal solid waste stream, the use of prevention and recycling methods in the future would alleviate metal contamination. In addition, as environmental regulations become more stringent, industry must focus on perhaps other less damaging materials to replace those metals causing contamination, or must attempt to integrate both pollution prevention and recycling methods into their processes.

SUMMARY

1. Recent media attention has focused on environmental issues such as nuclear waste disposal, waste incineration, and rainforest destruction. Unfortunately, only a small amount of media coverage is placed on the effect of metal contamination on health and the environment through lead poisoning and metal products in municipal solid waste.

2. Lead has virtually been eliminated from gasoline and the paint industry. However, the disposal of lead-acid batteries and other products containing lead in municipal solid waste has increased. Health effects of lead ingestion include brain damage, increased blood pressure, nervous system disorders, and premature birth.

3. The dangers of mercury poisoning were first discovered during the 19th century. Human exposure to mercury occurs through the food chain (particularly through fish) and to a greater extent in the workplace. Mercury poisoning leads to kidney damage, birth defects, and even death.

4. Cadmium is best known for its use in nickel-cadmium rechargeable batteries. Although it is a rare metal and is not used to the same extent as lead, cadmium consumption is increasing and is present in the municipal waste stream in significant amounts.

5. Although arsenic is best known as a poison, its main characteristic is its ability to cause cancer. Lead arsenate, a pesticide, is no longer used; however, some household products such as rat poison and plant killers still contain arsenic. Overall, the use of arsenic is decreasing.

6. Since metal contamination is steadily increasing through the disposal of lead-acid and nickel-cadmium batteries and the industrial use of mercury, a greater emphasis in the future will be placed on preventing health and environmental damage from metals.

REFERENCES

Holmes, G., Singh, B., and Theodore, L. *Handbook of Environmental Management and Technology*, New York: John Wiley & Sons, 1993.

Jones, H. *Mercury Pollution Control*. Park Ridge, NJ: Noyes Data Corp., 1971.

Lester, J. (ed.) *Heavy Metals in Wastewater and Sludge Treatment Processes: Treatment and Disposal (Foreword)* , Vol. II. Boca Raton, FL: CRC Press, 1987.

Oehme, F. *Toxicity of Heavy Metals in the Environment, Part 1*. New York: Marcel Dekker, Inc., 1978.

World Health Organization. *Environmental Health Criteria 1: Mercury*. Geneva: 1976.

World Health Organization. *Environmental Health Criteria 3: Lead*. Geneva: 1977.

46

Asbestos

INTRODUCTION

Asbestos fibers can cause serious health problems. If inhaled, they can cause diseases that disrupt the normal functioning of the lungs. Three specific diseases—asbestosis (a fibrous scarring of the lungs), lung cancer, and mesothelioma (a cancer of the lining of the chest or abdominal cavity)—have been linked to asbestos exposure. These diseases do not develop immediately after inhalation of asbestos fibers; it may be 20 years or more before symptoms appear.

In general, as with cigarette smoking and the inhalation of tobacco smoke, the more asbestos fibers a person inhales, the greater the risk of developing an asbestos-related disease. Most of the cases of severe health problems resulting from asbestos exposure have been experienced by workers who held jobs in industries such as shipbuilding, mining, milling, and fabricating where they were exposed to very high levels of asbestos in the air, without benefit of the worker protections now afforded by law. Many of these same workers were also smokers. These employees worked directly with asbestos materials on a regular basis, and generally for long periods of time as part of their jobs. Additionally, there is an increasing concern for the health and safety of construction, renovation, and building maintenance personnel, because of possible periodic exposure to elevated levels of asbestos fibers while performing their jobs.

Whenever one discusses the risk posed by asbestos, one must keep in mind that asbestos fibers can be found nearly everywhere in the environment (usually at very low levels). There is, at this time, insufficient information concerning health effects resulting from low-level asbestos exposure, either from exposures in buildings or from the environment. This makes it difficult to accu-

The contents of this chapter have been drawn, in part, from EPA document 20T2003, "Managing Asbestos in Place," June 1990.

rately assess the magnitude of cancer risk for building occupants, tenants, and building mainte-nance and custodial workers. Although, in general, the risk is likely to be negligible for occupants, health concerns remain, particularly for the building's custodial and maintenance workers. Their jobs are likely to bring them into close proximity to ACM (abestos-containing materials), and may sometimes require them to disturb the ACM in the performance of maintenance activities. For these workers in particular, a complete and effective O&M (operation and maintenance) program can greatly reduce asbestos exposure. This kind of O&M program can also minimize asbestos ex-posure for other building occupants as well.

The term "asbestos" describes six naturally occurring fibrous minerals found in certain types of rock formations. Of that general group, the minerals chrysotile, amosite, and crocidolite have been most commonly used in building products. When mined and processed, asbestos is typically separated into very thin fibers. When these fibers are present in the air, they are normally invisible to the naked eye. Asbestos fibers are commonly mixed during processing with a material which binds them together so that they can be used in many different products. Because these fibers are so small and light, they may remain in the air for many hours if they are released from ACM in a building. When fibers are released into the air they may be inhaled by people in the building.

Asbestos became a popular commercial product because it is strong, will not burn, resists corrosion, and insulates well. In the United States, its commercial use began in the early 1900s and peaked in the period from World War II into the 1970s.

REGULATORY CONCERNS

Over the last fifteen years, the U.S. Environmental Protection Agency (EPA) and several other fed-eral agencies have acted to prevent unnecessary exposure to asbestos by prohibiting some uses and by setting exposure standards in the workplace. Now the government is also acting to limit exposure to the public at large (EPA, 1985.) Five agencies have major authority to regulate asbestos (EPA, 1985).

1. The Occupational Safety and Health Administration (OSHA) sets limits for worker expo-sure on the job.

2. The Food and Drug Administration (FDA) is responsible for preventing asbestos contam-ination in food, drugs, and cosmetics.

3. The Consumer Product Safety Commission (CPSC) regulates asbestos in consumer prod-ucts. It already has banned the use of asbestos in drywall patching compounds, ceramic logs, and clothing. The CPSC is now studying the extent of asbestos use in consumer products generally, and is considering a ban on all nonessential product uses that can result in the release of asbestos fibers.

4. The Mine Safety and Health Administration (MSHA) regulates mining and milling of as-bestos.

5. The EPA regulates the use and disposal of toxic substances in air, water, and land, and has banned all uses of sprayed asbestos materials. The effects of cumulative exposure to asbestos have been established by dozens of epidemiological studies. In addition, EPA has issued standards for handling and disposing of asbestos-containing wastes.

EPA has a program to help abate asbestos exposure in schools. Since 1982, when EPA is-sued the Asbestos-In-Schools Identification and Notification Rule, the agency has required all local education agencies to inspect for friable asbestos materials; to notify parents and teachers if such materials are found; to place warning signs in schools where asbestos is found; and, to keep accurate records of their actions to eliminate the problem.

Congress passed the Asbestos School Hazard Abatement Act of 1984 to help those schools with the most serious hazards and the greatest financial need. The Act gives EPA the responsibility for providing both financial and technical assistance to local education agencies.

EPA offers technical assistance and guidance on asbestos. Under the TAP (Technical Assistance Program), each of the agency's ten regions has a Regional Asbestos Coordinator backed up by a staff of technical experts. These are listed in Table 46–1 (EPA, 1989).

Table 46–1. Regional Asbestos Coordinators (TAP)

Region	Address and Phone	Jurisdiction
EPA Region 1	JFK Federal Building Boston, MA 02203 (617) 565-3835	Connecticut, Massachusetts, Maine, New Hampshire, Rhode Island, Vermont
EPA Region 2	Woodbridge Avenue Edison, NJ 08837 (201) 321-6671	New Jersey, New York, Puerto Rico, Virgin Islands
EPA Region 3	841 Chestnut Street Philadelphia, PA 19107 (215) 597-3160	Delaware, District of Columbia, Maryland, Pennsylvania, Virginia, West Virginia
EPA Region 4	345 Corland Street, NE Atlanta, GA 30365 (404) 347-4727	Alabama, Florida, Georgia, Kentucky, Mississippi, North Carolina, South Carolina, Tennessee
EPA Region 5	230 S. Dearborn Street Chicago, IL 60604 (312) 886-6003	Illinois, Indiana, Michigan, Minnesota, Ohio, Wisconsin
EPA Region 6	Allied Bank Tower 1445 Ross Avenue Dallas, TX 75202-2733 (214) 655-7244	Arkansas, Louisiana, New Mexico, Oklahoma, Texas
EPA Region 7	726 Minnesota Avenue Kansas City, KS 66101 (913) 236-2835	Iowa, Kansas, Missouri, Nebraska
EPA Region 8	One Denver Place 999-18th Street Suite 500 Denver, CO 80202-2413 (303) 293-1744	Colorado, Montana, North Dakota, South Dakota, Utah, Wyoming
EPA Region 9	215 Fremont Street San Francisco, CA 94105 (415) 974-7290	Arizona, California, Hawaii, Nevada, American Samoa, Guam
EPA Region 10	1200-6th Avenue Seattle, WA 98101 (206) 442-4762	Alaska, Idaho, Oregon, Washington

The EPA has also published several documents that provide state-of-the-art guidance on how to identify and control friable asbestos-containing materials. In addition, the Agency is beginning the operation of several new programs. These include:

1. Contractor certification
2. Pilot information centers
3. Rules to provide worker protection during asbestos abatement activities
4. Expanded technical assistance materials.

In July 1989, EPA promulgated the Asbestos Ban and Phasedown Rule. The rule applies to new product manufacture, importation, and processing, and essentially bans almost all asbestos-containing products in the United States by 1997. This rule does not require removal of ACM currently in place in buildings.

SOURCES

In February 1988, the EPA released a report titled EPA Study of Asbestos-Containing Materials in Public Buildings: A Report to Congress. EPA found that "friable" (easily crumbled) ACM can be found in an estimated 700,000 public and commercial buildings. About 500,000 of those buildings are believed to contain at least some damaged asbestos, and some areas of significantly damaged ACM can be found in over half of them.

According to the EPA study, significantly damaged ACM is found primarily in building areas not generally accessible to the public, such as boiler and machinery rooms, where asbestos exposures generally would be limited to service and maintenance workers. Friable ACM, if present in air plenums, can lead to distribution of the material throughout the building, thereby possibly exposing building occupants. ACM can also be found in other building locations.

Asbestos in buildings has been commonly used for thermal insulation, fireproofing, and in various building materials, such as floor coverings and ceiling tile, cement pipe wrap, and acoustical and decorative treatment for ceilings and walls. Typically, it is found in pipe and boiler insulation and in spray-applied uses such as fireproofing or sound-deadening applications.

The amount of asbestos in these products varies widely (from approximately 1 percent to nearly 100 percent). The precise amount of asbestos in a product cannot always be accurately determined from labels or by asking the manufacturer; nor can positive identification of asbestos be ascertained merely by visual examination. Instead, a qualified laboratory must analyze representative samples of the suspect material.

HEALTH CONCERNS

Intact and undisturbed asbestos materials do not pose a health risk. The mere presence of asbestos in a building does not mean that the health of building occupants is endangered. ACM that is in good condition, and is not somehow damaged or disturbed, is not likely to release asbestos fibers into the air. When ACM is properly managed, release of asbestos fibers into the air is prevented or minimized, and the risk of asbestos-related disease can be reduced to a negligible level.

However, asbestos materials can become hazardous when, due to damage, disturbance, or deterioration over time, they release fibers into building air. Under these conditions, when ACM is damaged or disturbed—for example, by maintenance repairs conducted without proper controls— elevated airborne asbestos concentrations can create a potential hazard for workers and other building occupants.

As described above, the potential for an asbestos-containing material to release fibers depends primarily on its condition. As described earlier, if the material, when dry, can be crumbled by hand pressure—a condition known as "friable"—it is more likely to release fibers, particularly when damaged. The fluffy spray-applied asbestos fireproofing material is generally considered "friable." Pipe and boiler insulation materials can also be "friable," but they often are enclosed in a protective casing that prevents fiber release unless the casing is damaged. Some materials that are considered "nonfriable," such as vinyl-asbestos floor tile, can also release fibers when sanded, sawed, or otherwise disturbed. Materials such as asbestos cement pipe can release asbestos fibers if broken or crushed when buildings are demolished, renovated, or repaired.

CONTROL MEASURES

Most asbestos-containing material can be properly managed where it is. In fact, asbestos that is managed properly and maintained in good condition appears to pose relatively little risk.

Proper asbestos management begins with a comprehensive inspection by qualified, trained, and experienced inspectors, accredited through an EPA or state-approved training course. Inspecting the condition of asbestos materials initially with accredited inspectors and at least semiannually visits with trained custodial or maintenance staff is extremely important so that changes in the material's condition, such as damage or deterioration, can be detected and corrected before the condition worsens. Sometimes normal activities can damage asbestos material and cause fiber release, particularly if the material is "friable." A thorough initial inspection and regular surveillance can prevent accidental exposure to high levels of asbestos fibers.

The proper methods for dealing with asbestos are:

1. Developing and carrying out a special maintenance plan to insure that asbestos-containing materials are kept in good condition. This is the most common method when the materials are in good condition at the time of initial inspection.

2. Repairing damaged pipe or boiler covering, which is known as thermal system insulation.

3. Spraying the material with a sealant to prevent fiber release—a process called encapsulation.

4. Placing a barrier around the materials, known as an enclosure.

5. Removing asbestos under special procedures.

The last three methods of response actions—encapsulation, enclosure, and removal—and sometimes the second method—repair—must be done by accredited asbestos professionals.

The final response action, asbestos removal, is generally necessary only when the material damage is extensive and severe, and other actions will not control fiber release. Removal decisions should not be made lightly. An ill-conceived or poorly conducted removal can actually increase rather than eliminate risk. Consequently, all removal projects must be designed, supervised, and conducted by accredited professionals and should be performed in accordance with state-of-the-art procedures. In addition, one may wish to hire an experienced and qualified project monitor to oversee the asbestos contractor's work to make sure the removal is conducted safely.

FUTURE TRENDS

Training of custodial and maintenance workers is one of the major approaches that can be employed in a successful asbestos control program. This is the key to future activities. If building owners do not emphasize the importance of well-trained custodial and maintenance personnel, asbestos O&M tasks may not be performed properly. This could result in higher levels of asbestos fibers in the building air and an increased risk faced by both building workers and occupants.

With proper training, custodial and maintenance staffs in the future will successfully deal with ACM in place, and greatly reduce the release of asbestos fibers. Training sessions should provide basic information on how to deal with all types of maintenance activities involving ACM. However, building owners should also recognize that O&M workers in the field often encounter unusual, "nontextbook" situations. As a result, training should provide key concepts of asbestos hazard control. If these concepts are clearly understood by workers and their supervisors, workers can develop techniques to address a specific problem in the field. Building owners who need to provide O&M training to their custodial and maintenance staff should contact an EPA environmental assistance center (listed under Regulations) or an equally qualified training organization for more information.

SUMMARY

1. Asbestos fibers can cause serious health problems. If inhaled, they can cause diseases that disrupt the normal functioning of the lungs. Three specific diseases—asbestosis (a fibrous scarring of the lungs), lung cancer, and mesothelioma (a cancer of the lining of the chest or abdominal cavity)—have been linked to asbestos exposure.

2. Over the last fifteen years, the U.S. Environmental Protection Agency (EPA) and several other federal agencies have acted to prevent unnecessary exposure to asbestos by prohibiting some uses and by setting exposure standards in the workplace.

3. According to an EPA study, significantly damaged ACM is found primarily in building areas not generally accessible to the public, such as boiler and machinery rooms, where asbestos exposures generally would be limited to service and maintenance workers.

4. Intact and undisturbed asbestos materials do not pose a health risk. The mere presence of asbestos in a building does not mean that the health of building occupants is endangered. ACM that is in good condition, and is not somehow damaged or disturbed, is not likely to release asbestos fibers into the air. When ACM is properly managed, release of asbestos fibers into the air is prevented or minimized, and the risk of asbestos-related disease can be reduced to a negligible level.

5. The proper methods for dealing with asbestos are: maintenance, repairing, encapsulation, enclosure, and removal.

6. Training of custodial and maintenance workers is one of the major approaches that can be employed in a successful asbestos control program. This is the key to future activities.

REFERENCES

EPA, *The ABCs of Asbestos in Schools,* TS799, June, 1989.

EPA, Office of Public Affairs, *Asbestos Fact Book,* February, 1985.

47

Economics

An understanding of the economics involved in environmental management is important in making decisions at both the engineering and management levels. Every engineer or scientist should be able to execute an economic evaluation of a proposed environmental project. If the project is not profitable, it should obviously not be pursued; and, the earlier such a project can be identified, the fewer are the resources that will be wasted.

Economics also plays a role in setting many state and federal air pollution control regulations. The extent of this role varies with the type of regulation. For some types of regulations, cost is explicitly used in determining their stringency. This use may involve a balancing of costs and environmental impacts, costs and dollar valuation of benefits, or environmental impacts and economic consequences of control costs. For other types of regulations, cost analysis is used to choose among alternative regulations with the same level of stringency. For these regulations, the environmental goal is determined by some set of criteria that does not include costs. However, cost-effectiveness analysis is employed to determine the minimum economic way achieving the goal. For some regulations, cost influences enforcement procedures or requirements for demonstration of progress towards compliance with an environmental quality standard. For example, the size of any monetary penalty assessed for noncompliance as part of an enforcement action needs to be set with awareness of the magnitude of the control costs being postponed or bypassed by the noncomplying facility. For regulations without a fixed compliance schedule, demonstration of reasonable progress towards the goal is sometimes tied to the cost of attaining the goal on different schedules (Holmes, Singh, & Theodore, 1993).

This chapter is a condensed, revised, and updated version of the chapter "Economic Concerns," appearing in the 1985 USEPA APTI Training Manual titled *Hazardous Waste Incineration,* by T. Shen, Y. McGuinn, and L. Theodore, and the chapter "Economic Considerations" from the 1992 Van Nostrand Reinhold text titled *Pollution Prevention,* by L. Theodore and Y. McGuinn.

Before the cost of an environmental project can be evaluated, the factors contributing to the cost must be recognized. There are two major contributing factors, namely, capital costs and operating costs; these are discussed in the next two sections. Once the total cost of a project has been estimated, the engineer must determine whether the process (change) will be profitable. This often involves converting all cost contributions to an annualized basis. If more than one project proposal is under study, this method provides a basis for comparing alternate proposals and for choosing the best proposal. Project optimization is covered later in the chapter, where a brief description of a perturbation analysis is presented.

Detailed cost estimates are beyond the scope of this chapter. Such procedures are capable of producing accuracies in the neighborhood of +/- 10%; however, such estimates generally require many months of engineering work. This chapter is designed to give the reader a basis for preliminary cost analysis only.

CAPITAL COSTS

Equipment cost is a function of many variables, one of the most significant of which is capacity. Other important variables include equipment type and location, operating temperature, and degree of equipment sophistication. Preliminary estimates are often made from simple cost-capacity relationships that are valid when other variables are confined to narrow ranges of values; these relationships can be represented by the approximate linear (on log-log coordinates) cost equations of the form (McCormick & De Rosier, 1984)

$$C = \alpha(Q)^\beta$$

where C represents cost; Q represents some measure of equipment capacity; and α and β represents empirical "constants" that depend mainly on the equipment type. It should be emphasized that this procedure is suitable for rough estimation only; actual estimates (or quotes) from vendors are more preferable. Only major pieces of equipment are usually included in this analysis; smaller peripheral equipment such as pumps and compressors are not discussed.

If more accurate values are needed and if old price data are available, the use of an indexing method is better, although a bit more time-consuming. The method consists of adjusting the earlier cost data to present values using factors that correct for inflation. A number of such indices are available; one of the most commonly used is the chemical engineering fabricated equipment cost index (FECI) (McCormick & De Rosier, 1984; Matley, 1985), past values of which are listed in Table 47–1. Other indices for construction, labor, buildings, engineering and so on, are also available in the literature (McCormick & De Rosier, 1984; Matley, 1985). Generally, it is not wise to use past cost data older than 5 to 10 years, even with the use of the cost indices. Within that time span, the technologies used in the processes have changed drastically. The use of the indices could cause the estimates to be much greater than the actual costs. Such an error might lead to the choice of alternative proposals other than the least costly.

The usual technique for determining the capital costs (i.e., total capital costs, which include equipment design, purchase, and installation) for a project and/or process can be based on the factored method of establishing direct and indirect installation cost as a function of the known equip-

Table 47–1.   Fabricated Equipment Cost Index

Year	Index
1995	362.0 (estimated)
1994	361.3
1993	360.8
1992	358.2
1991	361.3
1990	357.6
1989	355.4
1988	342.5
1987	323.8
1986	318.4
1985	325.3
1984	334.1
1983	327.4
1982	326.0
1981	321.8
1980	291.6
1979	261.7
1978	238.6
1977	216.6
1976	200.8
1975	192.2

ment costs. This is basically a modified Lang method, whereby cost factors are applied to known equipment costs (Neveril, 1978; Vatavuk & Neveril, 1980).

The first step is to obtain from vendors (or, if less accuracy is acceptable, from one of the estimation techniques previously discussed) the purchase prices of primary and auxiliary equipment. The total base price, designated by X—which should include instrumentation, control, taxes, freight costs, and so on—serves as the basis for estimating the direct and indirect installation costs. The installation costs are obtained by multiplying X by the cost factors, which are available in literature (Vatavuk & Neveril, 1980; Vogel & Martin, 1983; Ulrich, 1984; Vogel & Martin, 1984; Theodore, 1993). For more refined estimates, the cost factors can be adjusted to more closely model the proposed system by using adjustment factors that take into account the complexity and sensitivity of the system (Neveril, 1978; Vatavuk & Neveril, 1980).

The second step is to estimate the direct installation costs by summing all the cost factors involved in the direct installation costs, which include piping, insulation, foundation and supports, and so on. The sum of these factors is designated as the DCF (direct installation cost factor). The direct installation costs are the product of the DCF and X.

The third step consists of estimating the indirect installation costs. The procedure here is the same as that for the direct installation cost—that is, all the costs factors for the indirect installation costs (engineering and supervision, startup, construction fees, etc.) are added. The sum is designated as the ICF (indirect installation cost factor). The indirect installation costs are then the product of ICF and X.

Once the direct and indirect installation costs have been calculated, the total capital cost (TCC) (McCormick & DeRosier, 1984) may be evaluated as:

$$TCC = X + (DCF) (X) + (ICF) (X)$$

This cost is converted to annualized capital costs with the use of the capital recovery factor (CRF), which is described later. The annualized capital cost (ACC) is the product of the CRF and the TCC and represents the total installed equipment cost distributed over the lifetime of the facility.

Some guidelines in purchasing equipment are listed below:

1. Do not buy or sign any documents unless provided with certified independent test data.
2. Previous clients of the vendor company should be contacted and their facilities visited.
3. Prior approval from the local regulatory officials should be obtained.
4. A guarantee from the vendors involved should be required. Startup assistance is usually needed, and an assurance of prompt technical assistance should be obtained in writing. A complete and coordinated operating manual should be provided.
5. Vendors should provide key replacement parts if necessary.
6. Finally, 10 to 15 percent of the cost should be withheld until the installation is completed.

OPERATING COSTS

Operating costs can vary from site to site because the costs partly reflect local conditions—for example, staffing practices, labor and utility costs. Operating costs like capital costs may be separated into two categories: direct and indirect costs. Direct costs are those that cover material and labor and are directly involved in operating the facility. These include labor, materials, maintenance and maintenance supplies, replacement parts, waste (e.g., residues after incineration) disposal fees, utilities and laboratory costs. Indirect costs are those operating costs associated with, but not directly involved in operating the facility; costs such as overhead (e.g., building-land leasing and office supplies), administrative fees, local property taxes and insurance fees fall into this category.

The major direct operating costs are usually associated with the labor and materials costs for the project, which involve the cost of the chemicals needed for operation of the process (Vogel & Martin, 1983). Labor costs differ greatly, but are a strong function of the degree of controls and/or instrumentation. Typically, there are three working shifts per day with one supervisor per shift. On the other hand, the plants may be manned by a single operator for only one-third or one-half of each shift; that is, usually only operator, supervisor, and site manager are necessary to run the facility. Salary costs vary from state to state and depend significantly on the location of the facility. The cost of utilities generally consists of that of electricity, water, fuel, and steam. The annual costs are estimated with the use of material and energy balances. Cost for waste disposal can be estimated on a per-ton-capital basis. Cost of landfilling ash can run significantly upwards of $100/ton if the material is hazardous, and can be as high as $10/ton if it is nonhazardous. The cost of handling a scrubber effluent can vary depending on the method of disposal. For example, if the conventional sewer disposal is used, the effluent probably has to be cooled and neutralized before disposal; the cost for this depends on the solids concentration. Annual maintenance costs can be estimated as a percentage of the capital equipment cost. The annual cost of replacement parts can be computed by dividing the cost of the individual part by its expected lifetime. The life expectancies can be found in the literature (Vatavuk & Neveril, 1980). Laboratory costs depend on the number of samples tested and the extent of these tests; these costs can be estimated as 10 to 20 percent of the operating labor costs.

The indirect operating costs consist of overhead, local property tax, insurance, and administration, less any credits. The overhead comprises payroll, fringe benefits, social security, unemployment insurance and other compensation that is indirectly paid to plant personnel. This cost can be estimated as 50 to 80 percent of the operating labor, supervision, and maintenance costs (Ulrich, 1984; Vogel & Martin, 1984). Local property taxes and insurance can be estimated as 1 to 2 percent of the total capital cost (TCC), while administration costs can be estimated as 2 percent of the TCC.

The total operating cost is the sum of the direct operating cost and the indirect operating costs, less any credits that may be recovered (e.g., the value of the recovered steam). Unlike capital costs, operating costs are calculated on an annual basis.

HIDDEN ECONOMIC FACTORS*

The main problem with the traditional type of economic analysis, discussed above, is that it is difficult—nay, in some cases impossible—to quantify some of the not-so-obvious economic merits of a business and/or environmental program.

Several considerations have just recently surfaced as factors that need to be taken into account in any meaningful economic analysis of a project effort. What follows is a summary of these considerations:

Long-term liabilities
Regulatory compliance
Regulatory recordkeeping
Dealings with the EPA
Dealings with the state and local regulatory bodies
Fines and penalties
Potential tax benefits
Customer relations
Stockholder support (corporate image)
Improved public image
Insurance costs and claims

*Information for this section is taken from Theodore, 1993.

Effect on borrowing power
Improved mental and physical well being of employees
Reduced health maintenance costs
Employee morale
Worker safety
Rising costs of waste treatment and/or disposal
Training costs
Emergency response planning

Many programs have been quenched in their early states because a comprehensive economic analysis was not performed. Until the effects described above are included, the true merits of a project may be clouded by incorrect and/or incomplete economic data. Can something be done by industry to remedy this problem? One approach is to used a modified version of the standard Delphi Panel. In order to estimate these "other" economic benefits, several knowledgeable individuals within and perhaps outside the organization are asked to independently provide estimates, with explanatory details, on these economic benefits. Each individual in the panel is then allowed to independently review all response. The cycle is then repeated until the groups responses approach convergence.

PROJECT EVALUATION AND OPTIMIZATION

In comparing alternate processes or different options of a particular process from an economic point of view, it is recommended that the total capital cost be converted to an annual basis by distributing it over the projected lifetime of the facility. The sum of both the annualized capital costs (ACCs) and the annual operating costs (AOCs) is known as the total annualized cost (TAC) for the facility. The economic merit of the proposed facility, process, or scheme can be examined once the total annual cost is available. Alternate facilities or options (e.g., a baghouse versus an electrostatic precipitator for particulate control, or two different processes for accomplishing the same degree of waste destruction) may also be compared. Note that a small flaw in this procedure is the assumption that the operating costs will remain constant throughout the lifetime of the facility.

Once a particular process scheme has been selected, it is common practice to optimize the process from a capital cost and O&M (operation and maintenance) standpoint. There are many optimization procedures available, most of them are too detailed for meaningful application for this chapter. These sophisticated optimization techniques, some of which are routinely used in the design of conventional chemical and petroleum plants, invariably involve computer calculations. Use of these techniques in environmental management analysis is usually not warranted, however.

One simple optimization procedure that is recommended is a perturbation study. This involves a systematic change (or perturbation) of variables, one by one, in an attempt to locate the optimum design from a cost and operation viewpoint. To be practical, this often means that the engineer must limit the number of variables by assigning constant values to those process variables that are known beforehand to play an insignificant role. Reasonable guesses and simple short-cut mathematical methods can further simplify the procedure. More information can be gathered from this type of study because it usually identifies those variables that significantly impact on the overall performance of the process and also helps identify the major contributors to the total annualized cost.

SUMMARY

1. An understanding of the economics involved in environmental management is important in making decisions at both the engineering and management levels. Every engineer or scientist should be able to execute an economic evaluation of a proposed environmental project.

2. The usual technique for determining the capital costs (i.e., total capital cost, which includes equipment design, purchase, and installation) for a project and/or process is based on the factored method of establishing direct and indirect installation costs as a function of the known equipment costs.

3. Operating costs can vary from site to site because these costs partly reflect local conditions—for example staffing practices, labor and utility costs. Operating costs like capital costs, may be separated into two categories: direct and indirect costs.

4. The main problem with the traditional type of economic analysis, discussed above, is that it is difficult—nay, in some cases impossible—to quantify some of the not-so-obvious economic merits of a business and/or environmental program. Several considerations have just recently surfaced as factors that need to be taken into account in any meaning full economic analysis of a project effort.

5. In comparing alternate processes or different options of a particular process from an economic point of view, it is recommended that the total capital cost be converted to an annual basis by distributing it over the projected lifetime of the facility.

6. One simple optimization procedure that is recommended is the perturbation study. This involves a systematic change (or perturbation) of variables, one by one, in an attempt to locate the optimum design for a cost and operation viewpoint.

REFERENCES

Holmes, G., Singh, B., and Theodore, L. *Handbook of Environmental Science and Technology,* New York: Wiley-Interscience, 1993.

Matley, J. "CE Cost Indexes Set Slower Pace," *Chem Eng.,* April 29, 1985, 75–76.

McCormick R. J., and De Rosier, R. J. *Capital and O&M Cost Relationships for Hazardous Waste Incineration,* Cincinnati, OH: Acurex Corp., EPA Report 600/2-87-175, October, 1984.

Neveril, R. B. *Capital and Operating Costs of Selected Air Pollution Control Systems,* Niles, IL: Gard, Inc., EPA Report 450/5-80-002, December 1978.

Theodore, L. *Introduction to Pollution Prevention,* ©, 1993, East Williston, NY.

Ulrich, G. D. *A Guide to Chemical Engineering Process Design and Economics,* New York: John Wiley & Sons, 1984.

Vatavuk, W. M., and Neveril, R. B. "Factors for Estimating Capital and Operating Costs," *Chem Eng.,* November 3, 1980, 157–162.

Vogel, G. A., and Martin, E. J. "Hazardous Waste Incineration, Part 3—Estimating Capital Costs of Facility Components," *Chem Eng.,* November 28, 1983, 87–90.

Vogel, G. A., and Martin, E. J. "Hazardous Waste Incineration, Part 3—Estimating Operating Costs," *Chem Eng.,* January 9, 1984, 97–100.

48

Architecture in the Environment: History, Practice, and Change

CONTRIBUTING AUTHOR
Georgeen A. Theodore

INTRODUCTION

As environmental concerns present some of the most pressing issues to the world, both professional and academic architects have begun to address how planning and built form affect the environment. While "architecture" may appear to be one of the many contributors to the current environmental state, in reality, the energy consumption and pollution affiliated with the materials, the construction, and the use of buildings contributes to most major environmental crises. In fact, architectural planning, design, and building significantly contribute to the destruction of the rain forest, the extinction of plant and animal species, the depletion of nonrenewable energy sources, the reduction of the ozone layer, the proliferation of chlorofluorocarbons (CFCs), and exposure to carcinogens and other hazardous materials. Where one chooses to build, which construction materials are selected, how a comfortable temperature is maintained, or what type of transportation is needed to reach it—each issue, decided by both architect and user, significantly impacts the overall environmental condition. Sadly, despite these opportunities to shape a healthier future, an analysis of American planning and building describes an assault on the existing ecological conditions.

HISTORICAL CONCERNS

A schematic review of the United States' architectural expansion reveals a strict adherence to the grid. While facilitating the organization of a new country, the gridding of land parcels and urban plans made few allowances for existing conditions. In fact, "slapped down anywhere," the grid imposed a man-made order on nature. From the New England town, to the first cities of Philadelphia,

New York, and Washington DC, the grid etched an order atop the country with little acknowledgment of or regard for the natural landscape. Instead, in the case of the earliest urban examples, the grid contained nature in the form of the village or town "green." Unfortunately, the green did not retain a reserve of the natural landscape. Rather, as nature controlled, it set the precedent for the simulation and subjugation of nature. Today, many housing developments raze forests only to turf and replant the area with something else. The simulation of landscapes, rather than reserving or using the existing landscapes, increases net land usage, energy consumption, and pollution. The retention of untouched and undeveloped land protects more than just trees. Each area—forest, wetland, prairie, coastal plain—sustains a complete ecosystem of plant and animal life. In examining the clearing of a forest, not only are the trees lost, but also the birds that used to live in and off of them, the plants that needed those trees' shade to survive, the animals that ate those understory plants, and so on. These losses diagram the chain reaction of ecological destruction caused by land development. With this in mind, the reports of multiple species eradication loom that much larger.

The earlier examples of architecture, in both autochthonous and colonial cultures, exhibit tremendous adaptation to both site and climate. But as buildings evolved from dwellings necessary for survival to conveyors of status and wealth, architectural planning and forms increasingly ignored the existing environment. A study of contemporary architecture, particularly housing developments, shows the mass production of styles transplanted anywhere. These styles originally became categorized because they evolved from an architectural response to climatic conditions. The Stick Style's steep roofs and projected eaves respond to climatic conditions while its diagonal "stick work" suggestively diagrams the structural frame. But when these architectural elements appear on the surface of an airtight, concrete box in a development in Dallas, they cease to have any real function. In order to convey sociocultural meaning, the architect/developer and homeowner lose the opportunity to have a building that responds to and respects the natural environment.

The quintessential American architecture—the suburban house complemented by a lawn, paved driveway, and two-car garage—evolved from a long history of anti-urban development celebrating a frontier sense of independence and isolation. Unfortunately, this evolution of American housing, combined with the mass production and purchasing of the car, led to the present day condition of major suburban and extraurban growth. Necessitating car use for practically every activity outside the home, the suburban house's auto-reliance causes massive fossil fuel consumption, road building, and parking paving. The extensive development of the American suburb has spawned other enclaved architectural forms: the mall, the retail park, the industrial park, the business park, and the leisure complex. All create a greater dependence on the car and disturb more land. The ecological repercussions are enormous. Considering net hours spent in today's home—families are smaller, more households have both partners working, more people live alone—the increase in square area of living space per person exemplifies society's tendency toward excessive expenditures of money, energy and other resources. These wastes extend to the land. Each house typically occupies a cleared lot of land, destroying an enormous portion of existing ecological environments. Because an individual normally does not need or use that much land, current efforts encourage a reduction of that private land while increasing community land in the form of public green spaces like parks and undeveloped zones.

The desire for more (land, space, money, things, and so on) seems human, but in fact identifies the most important environmental concern. Reduction represents the most significant means of addressing environmental problems. Whether it be car use, private green space, or total built square footage, less is environmentally more. Beginning with less built space starts a whole chain of environmental reductions in energy and materials consumption.

THE CURRENT DEBATE

Reviewing actions of current political, governmental, and legislative bodies reflects the desire and urgency for change. Green parties, groups, and leaders with environmental agendas aid in public awareness and implementing change. For example, both the Vice President of the United States Al Gore and the recent Presidents of the American Institute of Architects have raised many concerns to the national level. Within the government, the Environmental Protection Agency has researched and implemented change in a broad range of issues from hazardous materials found in the built environment, like asbestos, lead, radon, mercury (found in paints) to energy sources and consumption. Particularly significant and innovative are the new city ordinances, like that of Austin, which encourage energy conservation through financial incentives. The Green Builder Program, sponsored by the Environmental and Conservation Services Department of Austin, Texas, uses a rating system encouraging environmentally sensitive building practices and products in new homes. Large organizations, like the North Carolina Recycling Association and the National Audubon Society, have publicized environmental concerns and new practices through the design of their buildings. Both aim to conserve natural resources and to be as energy efficient and nontoxic as possible.

As architects have struggled to come to terms with the environmental implications of their buildings, the term "sustainability" has become the catch-word. While "sustainability" will not answer all environmental concerns, it provides a program to address current practices. With the present rates of fossil fuel consumption and ozone depletion, the earth's systems will be unable to support life. This risk of extinction necessitates examination and change. As Robert M. Solow (1991) states, " . . . it is an obligation to conduct ourselves so that we leave to the future the option or the capacity to be as well off as we are . . . Sustainability is an injunction not to satisfy ourselves by impoverishing our successors." How can the species sustain itself, that is, secure a viable environment for future generations? Through analyzing the environmental impact of architectural siting, design, construction, and use, a greater understanding can suggest ways to alter practices in order to do the least possible damage to the environment. The following discussion suggests environmentally conscious practices specifically related to architecture.

Recycling another building normally offers the most significant environmental savings. Particularly in places where there are unused and vacant buildings, to build more of the same represents one of the greatest environmental wastes. The initial energy spent in construction—through preparing the site, manufacturing the building materials, transporting them to the location, and then assembling them in construction—normally exceeds years of operational costs. Therefore, barring the least efficient structures, reuse, even with renovation, is the most sustainable choice. But if this is not possible, there are many ways in which the traditional building process can be readdressed with sustainability in mind.

SITING

As described above, the sprawl of development has threatened or destroyed many ecosystems. Therefore, one of the first site concerns is to avoid clearing previously untouched land. Once the land or place has been chosen, the existing landscape, the topography, wind movements, and context should be analyzed to inform the design. First, one should use the given resources. Retaining existing trees and other plant life does the least ecological damage, while additionally saving later expenditures for artificial landscaping. Next, topography and wind movements can be used to naturally assist in creating a more comfortable environment. Careful siting, in relation to the given landscape, reduces the building's heating and cooling loads. For example, tree groupings can provide wind barriers in the winter, while others can direct winds into the building during the summer. Along the same lines, deciduous trees offer a building summer shading, while still allowing for passive solar heating in the winter. Additional concern for solar orientation can provide the building with natural lighting. With a balance in relation to heating/cooling gains and losses, fenestration uses daylight to produce a more comfortable, healthy, and energy efficient space. The building's context must also be examined as a potential source of environmental hazards and opportunities. The surrounding buildings and structures can significantly influence siting. Like the natural elements mentioned above, built forms create shade and redirect wind. They also effect site hydrology. Buildings and nonporous surfaces (like asphalt) change how water moves through and drains from a site. In general, a site should be well drained with adequate flooding and erosion control for proper building maintenance and a healthy living environment. The best siting will not disturb the normal patterns of water flow and drainage. But if this is unavoidable, the effect of redirected water should be analyzed to avoid upsetting existing ecologies and conditions.

Another important site consideration is potential pollution sources. For the most part, industry and transportation create the greatest amounts of air, noise, and water pollution: roadways, cars, airports, oil refineries, power plants, and so on. Siting analysis of these potential sources should either suggest the use of another site or a way to avoid exposure to the hazards.

DESIGN

Environmentally conscious design offers perhaps the greatest opportunity for ecological improvement. For the most part, the current "green" trends concentrate on materials, products, and energy systems. This emphasis allows architects to ignore the environmental implications of their buildings. Responsible behavior requires more than a substitution of traditional building materials with recycled or nontoxic products. An ethical response to the environmental concerns necessitates change at the core, that is, in the architectural theory of design. Environmental concerns must be completely incorporated into architectural thinking. Then, as an integral aspect of the architectural process, sustainability can shape design decisions and form buildings.

Several key concerns shape an environmentally conscious design strategy: minimizing the building's effect on the existing ecosystem, minimizing the use of new resources, increasing the energy efficiency of the building in its form and operation, and creating a healthy environment for the users.

Minimizing the building's effect on the existing environment has been discussed above, specifically in the site analysis section. Additionally, those aspects of the designed landscape can complement and enhance the viability of the existing ecosystems. The use of the traditional turf lawn represents a seriously destructive design practice. It removes the existing, natural environment at the risk of plant and animal biodiversity. Also, lawn maintenance requires irrigation and mowing, which increases water and fossil fuel consumption. Mowing and the use of pesticides both contribute to pollution. Instead, to complement the existing landscape, drought resistant native plantings enhance an outdoor environment to the benefit of resource management and ecosystems. Native plants thrive with a minimum of watering, chemicals (pesticides and fertilizers), and cutting. They also aid in maintaining or restoring an ecosystem's biodiversity. In areas that must be cleared for parking and walkways, the substitution of pervious paving materials (gravel, crushed stone, open paving blocks, pervious paving blocks) minimizes runoff and increases infiltration and groundwater recharge.

Minimizing the use of resources, particularly new resources, can be achieved in several ways. Again, to recycle that modernist line, less is more. Smaller is better. Beginning with the preliminary design, the interior space should be kept to a minimum. This reduces land use, building materials, and operational energy expenditures.

Increasing energy efficiency through reduced operational expenditures can be achieved in several ways. Passive systems, such as solar heating, daylighting, and natural cooling (berms, shade, and ventilation), produce a more energy efficient building with minimal expenditures. As suggested above in the site considerations, a building should be designed to work with the climate and natural energy sources. A building that responds to and takes advantage of what is naturally given results in a more sustainable design. (Climate, solar energy, topology, and on-site materials all qualify as givens.) A multitude of opportunities exist. To begin, what will create a comfortable environment? Orientation, built forms (like shading devices), and window and door locations can reduce heating and cooling loads while simultaneously enhancing living conditions. Also, a more systematized address of heating and cooling loads reduces the operating energy expenses of the building. High levels of insulation, high performance windows, and a tight construction (but not at the expense of indoor air quality) create a more energy efficient building.

Considering that people generally spend about 90 percent of their time indoors, the quality of indoor air crucially impacts well being and comfort. (The reader is referred to Chapter 11 for additional details on indoor air quality.) Indoor air pollution comes from many different sources, both indoor and out. One of the more serious threats to indoor air quality and health is radon. Radon rises from subsurface uranium deposits through and into buildings. Posing a tremendous threat, radon is the nation's second cause of lung cancer (National Council on Radiation Protection and Measurements). Other outdoor pollutants—like pesticides and car exhaust—threaten many buildings' indoor air quality. All three pollutants—radon, pesticides, and car exhaust—can be significantly reduced by good planning and design. First, an adequate ventilation system prevents accumulation within the building. While the building should open up for natural ventilation, an airtight construction will avoid many problems. For example, radon usually enters a building through cracks in the foundation. In the case of pesticides, the building's envelope works doubly. Careful detailing of the building, particularly in its corners and where it meets the ground, prevents many pests from entering. As a result, toxic interior pesticides and fumigants become unnecessary. Additionally, an airtight construction through detailing prevents many pollutants, particularly exterior pesticides and car exhaust, from entering the interior. Another preventive measure, the removal or avoidance of the pollution source, improves indoor air quality. Detaching a garage or parking structure from inhabited spaces eliminates direct exhaust infiltration into the building. In the cases where the pollution sources cannot be removed, ventilation intakes should be situated to avoid contaminants: other building's exhausts, car pollution, and pesticides.

Indoor air pollutants, like outdoor pollutants, pose more serious problems when buildings have inadequate, poorly maintained, or improperly located ventilation systems. An adequate ventilation system lessens the harmful effects of pollutants like lead, formaldehyde, carcinogenic wood finishes, smoke, and biological contaminants (bacteria, molds, mildew, and viruses). Especially in the case of lead dust and biological contaminants, keeping interiors clean and dust-free improves indoor air quality. In addition to increased ventilation and maintenance, source removal eliminates many problems. Smoking, a major indoor air pollution source, should be prohibited in interiors. Exposure to other pollutants, like lead, mercury, and volatile organic compounds, can be more easily avoided through the greater availability of non-toxic building materials and finishes.

In smaller scale residential projects where there is little threat of on-site or near-site pollution sources, natural ventilation may suffice. But with larger scale projects, or those that are exposed to other sources of pollution (traffic, the exhausts of other buildings, the outgassing of building materials) conditions necessitate mechanical ventilation systems. Particularly in buildings like offices, with a large number of users, successful mechanical ventilation becomes crucial to maintaining indoor air quality. Without proper ventilation or systems maintenance, problems like outgassing or sick building syndrome can significantly affect the health and productivity of the building's users.

The building's design should incorporate recycling into the program so that it is easy and available. For example, a kitchen or an office can be designed to include recycling containers or cabinets for glass, aluminum, plastic, and paper. Composting systems for waste and sewage can be specified and located. Also, saving water can serve as a recycling opportunity. The recycled water from clothes washers, baths, showers, and non-kitchen sinks can be redirected for irrigation use. Another way to save water is through harvesting rainwater with a water catchment system.

Finally, the greatest recycling opportunity exists in the building itself. It should be designed with reuse in mind. A building should be adaptable with no or minimal renovation. As mentioned above, this may help avoid the enormous energy and material expenditures required by a new building's construction.

MATERIALS

Educated material selections greatly enhance the resource and energy savings created by an ecologically aware design. The use of each building material impacts both the global and local environments through its extraction, its manufacture, and its use. For example, the lumbering and strip mining industries have devastated ecological systems. Therefore, the selection of a material should be made only after an impact analysis of its removal or extraction. This type of thinking has led to some changes in the lumber industry. For example, to minimize the use of old growth timber, sustainably produced lumber or recycled plastic lumber products have been introduced. While this represents an improvement, the greatest ecological savings occurs through using less.

In addition to the raw material itself, the material's processing should be considered. Thinking in terms of the total environmental cost has led to the analysis of materials' embodied energy. Manufacturing a building material often requires large expenditures of water, fossil fuels for energy and transportation, and human labor. Many environmental experts suggest choosing low embodied energy materials, i.e., materials that need less energy to make them usable. As a result, the building product uses less resources and generates less pollution in its manufacture. Normally, the material is closer to its natural state. For example, natural stone has a low embodied energy, while plastics, steel, and aluminum have high embodied energies. Additionally, when available, using materials found on or near the site normally reduces energy expenditures. (This is not to suggest cutting the site's trees for lumber.) For example, using local stone in the place of brick eliminates not only the manufacturing energics and pollution but also larger transportation costs. Regarding materials with low embodied energy and from local sources, it is crucial to consider the net energy calculated with use. Always try to envision the total picture of chained actions and reactions. For example, a certain type of insulation may be completely synthetic; it requires a large amount of energy to manufacture and also must be transported from elsewhere. But the energy savings resulting from its installation may exceed the preliminary expenditures.

Many building materials outgas, that is, release harmful, airborne materials that pose a risk to the local environment's air quality. The volatile organic compounds (VOCs) most often found in floor finishes, paints, stains, adhesives, synthetic wallpapers, plywood, and chipboards should be avoided to maintain a healthy environment. In substitution, many new VOC-free products are now available. In addition to VOCs, building materials emitting CFCs and HFCs, like insulation, should not be used.

As always, recycling represents an important concern. When possible, salvaged building materials should be used. On the other end of the building process, using building materials that can eventually be recycled will eliminate further resource expenditures. Along similar lines, products and materials need to last; durability increases net energy savings.

BUILDING SYSTEMS AND EQUIPMENT

Selecting energy efficient systems and equipment greatly reduces the environmental impact of a building's operation. These systems reduce not only operational costs, but create a whole chain of environmental savings. The lower operational costs normally reflect reduced operational energies and fuel expenditures. For example, the use of low energy bulbs lowers not only the building's electricity requirement, but the power plant's load. As a result, savings occur on both the local and larger levels. Greater use of this type of equipment would reduce the number of electricity plants, saving more resources and reducing pollution. Other systems, like high efficiency heating and cooling equipment, have similar advantages. For example, a photovoltaic electric generating system creates an on-site power source with a significant reduction of pollution. Other building equipment, like high efficiency appliances, significantly reduce electricity expenditures. Water efficient equipment, such as shower heads and toilets, decrease water use. Studies in California have shown retrofitting buildings and homes with energy efficient lighting, pumps, fans, refrigerators, and so on can lcad to at least a 75 percent reduction in energy use (Ledger, 1994).

CONSTRUCTION

Construction concerns reiterate many of the points and themes discussed above. The environmental impact of the building's construction should be as minimal as possible. The existing landscape, particularly on-site trees, should be protected. The use of pesticides and other chemicals should be restricted to avoid polluting the groundwater supply. Construction debris should be minimized and recycled. As always, durability and longevity generates the greatest energy savings: Build to last. Finally, like the building itself, the construction site should never be a hazard for those who use it.

FUTURE TRENDS

A program for the future consists of the difficult obligation to implement change. A brief survey like this chapter serves to heighten awareness, but the crisis requires a more significant response. Of course, the most responsible and helpful behavior is to commit to lessening the environmental impact of general practices. From the individual, to corporations, to governmental bodies, every bit counts. Unfortunately, the only proven way to get widespread change is through economic incentives. With penalties issued for unsustainable building practices, awareness and change could possibly extend to all sectors of the building industry. Presently, resistance exists on many levels of the building process—maintaining the status quo is far easier than switching to an unknown. Using economic incentives will significantly empower the environmental cause, especially among groups without obvious reasons for changing their practices (only reason: helping the world). Already, certain programs give lower interest rates for "green" home improvements or utility rebates for high efficiency equipment use. In addition to economic incentives, governmental- and corporate-sponsored projects have the capability to mainstream environmentally conscious practices. Through showcasing sustainable design, work that perhaps would not be funded otherwise, ideas, and research turn into practice precedents.

SUMMARY

1. Architectural planning, building, and use contribute tremendously to the environmental crises; therefore, theory and practice must be analyzed to implement change.

2. Historically and presently, architecture has developed a pattern of wastefulness and indifference in relation to the natural environment.

3. As more attention has been given to architectural concerns in ecological discourse, sustainability has emerged as a program for improved practices.

4. Once a site has been chosen, the existing landscape, given resources, topography, wind movements, and context should be used to form the design.

5. Several key concerns shape an environmentally conscious design strategy: minimizing the building's effect on the existing ecosystem, minimizing the use of new resources, increasing the energy efficiency of the building in its form and operation, and creating a healthy environment for the users.

6. Educated material selections greatly enhance the resource and energy savings created by an ecologically aware design.

7. Energy-efficient systems and equipment reduce operational costs, fuel and other resource expenditures, and pollution.

8. The environmental impact of the building's construction should be as minimal as possible.

9. For the future, economic incentives and other mainstreaming practices will increase awareness and implement change.

REFERENCES

Ledger, B. "Architecture and the Environment: Where do We Stand Now?," *The Canadian Architect,* June 1994, 14.

National Council on Radiation Protection and Measurements.

Solow, R. M. "Sustainability: An Economist's Perspective," Eighteenth J. Seward Johnson Lecture in Marine Policy, Marine Policy Center, Woods Hole Oceanographic Institution. June 14, 1991.

Part X

Ethics

Part X, comprised of two chapters, serves as an introduction to the general subject of ethics. Chapter 49 is concerned with environmental ethics. A comprehensive examination of engineering ethics is also included in Chapter 49. Part X concludes with Chapter 50, which addresses a relatively new area of concern, environmental justice (sometimes referred to as environmental equity or environmental racism); this subject has been notably absent from the mainstream environmental agenda but clearly requires more attention.

49

Environmental Ethics

CONTRIBUTING AUTHOR

Ruth Richardson

INTRODUCTION

In 1854, President Franklin Pierce petitioned Chief Seattle—the leader of the Coastal Salish Indians of the Pacific Northwest—to sell his tribe's land to the United States. In his response to President Pierce and the white Europeans' pursuit to own and "subdue" the Earth, Chief Seattle penned thoughts as environmentally pensive and poignant as any uttered in the more than 140 years since: "Continue to contaminate your bed and you will one day lay in your own waste" (Fahey & Armstrong, 1987).

His message fell on the deaf ears of the U.S. government and public. Cries for respect for the Earth such as his remained few and far between for the next century. In the wake of events such as the Industrial Revolution, the First and Second World Wars, and the Cold War, a concern for the environment played little, if any, part in influencing either public policy or private endeavors.

More than a hundred and forty years later, however, Chief Seattle's words echo in every Superfund site, landfill, and oil spill. Public opinion has swung to the green side and a new ethic has evolved: an environmental ethic. As one shall soon see, however, the recent movement toward environmentalism has not created new moral codes. Instead, it has changed the emphasis and expanded the concept of the "common good" that lies at the heart of determining if an action is ethical.

This chapter will first present the variety of moral theories and philosophies that have governed ethics historically. The movement of environmentalism into an influential ethical force is then developed. Once these historical developments have been presented, today's dilemma of coordinating technology with environmental responsibility will be explored. Finally, the future trends evidenced by present and past activities will be discussed.

MORAL ISSUES

The conflict of interest between Chief Seattle (and Native Americans in general) and President Pierce (and the European American expansion) provides a perfect example of how ethics and the resulting codes of behavior they engender can differ drastically from culture to culture, religion to religion, and even person to person. This enigma, too, is noted again and again by Seattle (Martin & Schinzinger, 1989):

> I do not know. Our ways are different from your ways . . . But perhaps it is because the red man is a savage and does not understand . . . The air is precious to the red man, for all things share the same breath . . . the white man does not seem to notice the air he breathes . . . I am a savage and do not understand any other way. I have seen a thousand rotting buffaloes on the prairie, left by the white man who shot them from a passing train. I am a savage and I do not understand how the smoking iron horse can be more important than the buffalo we kill only to stay alive.

Chief Seattle sarcastically uses the European word "savage" and all its connotations throughout his address. When one finishes reading the work it becomes obvious which viewpoint (President Pierce's or his own) Chief Seattle feels is the savage one. What his culture holds dearest (the wilderness) the whites see as untamed, dangerous, and savage. What the whites hold in highest regard (utilization of the earth and technological advancement) the Native Americans see as irreverent of all other living things. Each culture maintains a distinct and conflicting standard for the welfare of the world. Opposing viewpoints and moralities such as these are prevalent throughout the world and have never ceased to present a challenge to international, national, state, community, and interpersonal peace.

It is generally accepted, however, that any historical ethic can be found to focus on one of four different underlying moral concepts:

1. *Utilitarianism* focuses on good consequences for all
2. *Duties Ethics* focus on one's duties
3. *Rights Ethics* focus on human rights
4. *Virtue Ethics* focus on virtuous behavior

(Note that Duties and Rights Ethics are often considered together as Deontological Ethics.) (Martin & Schinzinger, 1989).

Utilitarians hold that the most basic reason why actions are morally right is that they lead to the greatest good for the greatest number. "Good and bad consequences are the only relevant considerations, and, hence all moral principles reduce to one: 'We ought to maximize utility'" (Martin & Schinzinger, 1989).

Duties Ethicists concentrate on an action itself rather than the consequences of that action. To these ethicists there are certain principles of duty such as "Do not deceive" and "Protect innocent life" that should be fulfilled even if the most good does not result. The list and hierarchy of duties differs from culture to culture, religion to religion. For Judeo-Christians, the Ten Commandments provide an ordered list of duties imposed by their religion (Martin & Schinzinger, 1989).

Often considered to be linked with Duties Ethics, Rights Ethics also assesses the act itself rather than its consequences. Rights Ethicists emphasize the rights of the people affected by an act rather than the duty of the person(s) performing the act. For example, because a person has a right to life, murder is morally wrong. Rights Ethicists propose that duties actually stem from a corresponding right. Since each person has a *right* to life, it is everyone's *duty* to not kill. It is because of this link and their common emphasis on the actions themselves that Rights Ethics and Duty Ethics are often grouped under the common heading: Deontological Ethics (Barbour, 1993).

The display of virtuous behavior is the central principle governing Virtue Ethics. An action would be wrong if it expressed or developed vices—for example, bad character traits. Virtue Ethicists, therefore, focus upon becoming a morally good person.

To display the different ways that these moral theories view the same situation one can explore their approach to the following scenario that Martin and Schinzinger (1989) present:

> On a midnight shift, a botched solution of sodium cyanide, a reactant in organic synthesis, is temporarily stored in drums for reprocessing. Two weeks later, the day shift foreperson cannot find the drums. Roy, the plant manager, finds out that the batch has been illegally dumped into the sanitary sewer. He severely disciplines the night shift foreperson. Upon making discreet inquiries, he finds out that no apparent harm has resulted from the dumping. Should Roy inform government authorities, as is required by law in this kind of situation?

If a representative of each of the four different theories on ethics just mentioned were presented with this dilemma, their decision-making process would focus on different principles.

The Utilitarian Roy would assess the consequences of his options. If he told the government, his company might suffer immediately under any fines administered and later (perhaps more seriously) due to exposure of the incident by the media. If he chose not to inform authorities, he risks heavier fines (and perhaps even worse press) in the event that someone discovers the coverup. Consequences are the utilitarian Roy's only consideration in his decision-making process.

The Duties Ethicist Roy would weigh his duties and his decision would probably be more clearcut than his utilitarian counterpart. He is obliged foremost by his duty to obey the law and must inform the government.

The Rights Ethicist mindframe would lead Roy to the same course of action as the duties ethicist—not necessarily because he has a duty to obey the law but because the people in the community have the right to informed consent. Even though Roy's inquiries informed him that no harm resulted from the spill, he knows that the public around the plant has the right to be informed of how the plant is operating.

Vices and virtues would be weighed by the Virtue Ethicist Roy. The course of his thought process would be determined by his own subjective definition of what things are virtuous, what things would make him a morally good person. Most likely, he would consider both honesty and obeying the law virtuous, and withholding information from the government and public as virtueless and would, therefore, tell the authorities.

The scenario used here will be revisited later in this chapter through the eyes of environmentalism to illustrate how this movement is changing the focus of old theories about morality.

MODERN DAY MAINSTREAM ENVIRONMENTALISM

Minds like John Muir and Rachel Carson (see Chapters 1 and 2) were unique in their respective generations. Their ideas of respect for all flora and fauna were far from predominant in the American mainstream. Rachel Carson's 1962 benchmark book *Silent Spring* took environmentalism from pure naturalism into the scientific realm. The evidenced claims she made about the harm caused to wildlife by a range of pesticides (most notably DDT) were as controversial as they were ground breaking. Over the next decade the younger generation embraced a new concern for the environment. The older generation, however, generally dealt with this young movement with opposition rather than cooperation. This was due in large part to the confrontational attitude of many of the youths as well as the perceived threat that the industry-restricting movement itself caused to their economic well-being. As the younger generation grew into positions of power and learned more cooperative tactics, their environmentalist ideas moved from the fringes to the mainstream. On route, the conversion was carried out in the form of both personal growth and government legislation. There seems still to exist, however, two factions of environmentalism: pure environmentalism (environmentalism for its own sake) and environmentalism for humanity's sake. While they share a common concern for the well-being of the natural world, fundamental differences exist.

One of the most common arguments against the destruction of rainforest land is that any one of the plant or insect species destroyed in the process could contain the elusive cure for cancer or AIDS. With this argument, the ultimate concern is for humanity: We should preserve the natural world because it is best for the human race to do so. This could be considered environmentalism for humanity's sake and there are a number of other manifestations of it in today's world. The war against the destruction of ozone in the earth's stratosphere is waged largely in the interest of human welfare. While the greenhouse effect has the potential to harm wildlife also, this effect is secondary to that on humanity—both today and in future generations. This type of environmentalism displays the inherent egocentric attitude of humankind. This faction maintains "an ethic that is secondarily ecological" (Rolston, 1986). Here the natural world should be protected because of humanity's dependence on its homeostasis.

The second, more "extremist" form of environmental morality is "primarily ecological" (Rolston, 1986). As Aldo Leopold proclaimed, "A thing is right when it tends to preserve the integrity, stability, and beauty of the biotic community. It is wrong if it tends otherwise" (Leopold, 1949). Here, humanity has a binding responsibility to protect the homeostasis of the natural world. In this view humanity is considered a part of the interdependent environment rather than something above it. The Native American's adoration of the Great Spirit—which favored the human species no more than any other—is the religious embodiment of such a viewpoint.

The renewed awareness of the environment and awakened concern for its well-being has influenced the ethical world to the point that it has uprooted the focus of the moral correctness of an action. This effect on ethical theories was predicted by John Passmore in 1974: "What it needs for the most part is not so much a 'new ethic' as a more general adherence to a perfectly familiar ethic. For the major sources of our ecological disasters—apart from ignorance—are greed and shortsightedness" (Barbour, 1993).

Aldo Leopold made the following observation on personal ethics in his 1949 *A Sand County Almanac*: The scope of one's ethics is determined by the inclusiveness of the community with which one identifies oneself (Leopold, 1949). Leopold parallels the mistreatment of the earth to the mistreatment of slaves that were handled as property. The slave owners were not ethically obliged to the slaves because they considered them outside rather than part of their community. Just as the realm of community grew to include the ex-slaves, it must once again expand to incorporate the whole land community (Leopold, 1949). The incorporation of environmentalism into everyday ethics, therefore, does not require a redefinition of one's ethics, but, rather, a redefinition of one's "community." This can be applied to each of the ethical theories presented above.

For the utilitarian it requires counting the natural world among those effected by bad and good consequences. The focus of utilitarianism is broadened to include effects on future generations and the welfare of living things other than humans. For the deontological ethicists, the recognition of the environment as part of the community gives it inherent rights and, in turn, imposes on humans the duty to respect those rights. For the virtue ethicists, the virtue of respecting all members of the community would bind them to consider the environment when making decisions.

In the scenario presented earlier, Roy's moral thought process would be affected by the inclusion of the environment into his community regardless of the ethical school of thought he associated himself with. Although his discreet inquiries informed him that no apparent harm resulted from the chemical spill, an environmental impact analysis would have to be made for the utilitarian Roy to fully assess good and bad consequences. If future harm were likely, it may be essential to let the government know so that remediation techniques may be employed at the dumping site. The decision of the rights and duties ethicist Roys would be influenced by their obligation to the environment as well as the surrounding human community. During the virtue ethicist Roy's decision-making process, he would consider which option was the most virtuous with respect to the environment. In each of these cases, an ecologically ethical Roy would have to obtain a reasonable estimate, with the help of the government if necessary, of the environmental effects—immediate and long-term—of the dumping.

In each of these new twists upon old theories on ethics, there exists the fundamentals of a "land ethic." The ethical umbrella is expanding to include under its cover all living beings. Fields of conduct such as disposal and treatment of owned property and land are now becoming judged ethically rather than on the grounds of economic feasibility and personal whimsy.

The mainstreaming of environmentalism is by no means worldwide. The countries in which the greatest impact is seen are the same countries where extensive industrialization exists. Industrialization itself has been crucial to the development of the environmental movement. Not only do its environmental problems and pollution generate concern, citizens of industrialized nations enjoy lives with the luxury of free time and options necessary to be able to devote themselves to such a concern. In poorer countries and communities, the struggle of everyday survival far outweighs any aesthetic concern for the environment. Abraham Maslow's concept of a "hierarchy of needs" can be applied in explaining the difficulty of establishing the environmental movement in impoverished communities and third-world countries.

Maslow maintains that there exist the following "hierarchy of needs" for every human being. He finds *five levels of need*:

1. Survival (physiological needs): food, shelter, health.
2. Security (safety needs): protection from danger and threat.
3. Belonging (social needs): friendship, acceptance, love.

4. Self-esteem (ego needs): self-respect, recognition, status.

5. Self-actualization (fulfillment needs): creativity, realization of individual potentialities.

Maslow maintains that these levels form a hierarchy; lower levels must be satisfied before the individual can give attention to higher levels" (Barbour, 1993). Until the lower levels of need are at least partially satisfied, a person cannot commit him or herself to the pursuit of higher-leveled needs. For example, a person who is struggling to find any source of food will not be preoccupied with how environmentally conscious the farmer was in the use of fertilizers or pesticides while cultivating the food.

Consider, for example, a town such as many in the mountains of Appalachia where one industry—coal mining—provides all of the town's employment and generates most of the taxes used by the town in running schools and other municipal operations. When the coal mining company turns to strip mining—a process that essentially rips the mountains to shreds and contaminates groundwater with the heavy metals released—can the miners be expected to jeopardize the welfare of their entire families by protesting because the methods of their employer are environmentally negligent? Their survival needs for food and shelter supersede any idealistic desire they have to preserve the environment. Abuse of this natural hierarchy has been defined as environmental racism (see next chapter) and is epitomized by the disproportionately large number of landfills, chemical plants, and toxic dumps in the poorer communities and countries.

TECHNOLOGY AND ENVIRONMENTALISM

In the ethical theories presented here, established hierarchies of duties, rights, virtues, and desired consequences exist so that situations where no single course of action satisfies all of the maxims can still be resolved. The entry of environmentalism into the realm of ethics raises questions concerning where it falls in this hierarchy. Much debate continues over these questions of how much weight the natural environment should be given in ethical dilemmas, particularly in those where ecological responsibility seems to oppose economic profitability and technological advances. Those wrapped up in this technology/economy/ecology debate can generally be divided into three groups:

1. Environmental extremists

2. Technologists to whom ecology is acceptable provided it does not inhibit technological or economic growth

3. Those who feel technology should be checked with ecological responsibility

Each is briefly discussed below.

After his year-and-a-half of simple living on the shores of Walden Pond, Henry David Thoreau professed "in wildness is the preservation of the world" (Barbour, 1993). He rejected the pursuit of technology and industrialization. While most would agree with his vision of nature as being inspirational, few would choose his way of life. Even so, the movement rejecting technological advances in favor of simple, sustainable, and self-sufficient living is being embraced by more and more people who see technology as nothing but a threat to the purity and balance of nature. Often called environmental extremists by other groups, they even disregard "environmental" technologies that attempt to correct pollution and irresponsibilities, past and present. They see all technology as manipulative and uncontrollable and choose to separate themselves from it. To them, the environment is at the top of the heirarchy.

On the other extreme are the pure technologists. They view the natural world as a thing to be subdued and manipulated in the interest of progress—technological and economic. This is not to say one won't find technologists wandering in a national park admiring the scenery. They do not necessarily deny the beauty of the natural environment, but they see themselves as separate from it. They believe that technology is the key to freedom, liberation, and a higher standard of living. It is viewed, therefore, as inherently good. They see the environmental extremists as unreasonable and hold that even the undeniably negative side effects of certain technologies are best handled by more technological advance. The technologists place environmental responsibility at the bottom of their ethical heirarchy.

Somewhere in the middle of the road travels the third group. While they reap the benefits of technology, they are concerned much more deeply than the technologists with the environmental costs associated with industrialization. It is in this group that most environmental engineers find themselves. They are unlike the environmental extremists since, as engineers, they inherently study and design technological devices and have faith in the ability of such devices to have a positive effect on the condition of the environment. They also differ from the technologists. They scrutinize the effects of technologies much more closely and critically. While they may see a brief, dilute leak of a barely toxic chemical as an unacceptable side effect of the production of a consumer product, the technologists may have to observe destruction—the magnitude of that caused by Chernobyl—before they consider rethinking a technology they view as economically and socially beneficial. In general, this group sees the good in technology but stresses that it cannot be reaped if technological growth goes on unchecked.

ENGINEERING ETHICS

The ethical behavior of engineers is more important today than at any time in the history of the profession. The engineers' ability to direct and control the technologies they master has never been stronger. In the wrong hands, the scientific advances and technologies of today's engineer could become the worst form of corruption, manipulation, and exploitation. Engineers, however, *are* bound by a code of ethics that carry certain obligations associated with the profession. Some of these obligations include:

1. Support ones professional society
2. Guard privileged information
3. Accept responsibility for one's actions
4. Emply proper use of authority
5. Maintain one's expertise in a state of the art world
6. Build and maintain public confidence
7. Avoid improper gift exchange
8. Practice conservation of resources and pollution prevention

9. Avoid conflict of interest

10. Apply equal opportunity employment

11. Practice health, safety, and accident prevention

12. Maintain honesty in dealing with employers and clients

There are many codes of ethics that have appeared in the literature. The preamble for one of these codes is provided below:

> Engineers in general, in the pursuit of their profession, affect the quality of life for all people in our society. Therefore, an Engineer, in humility and with the need for Divine guidance, shall participate in none but honest enterprises. When needed, skill and knowledge shall be given without reservation for the public good. In the performance of duty and in fidelity to the profession, Engineers shall give utmost (Martin & Schinzinger, 1989).

FUTURE TRENDS

Although the environmental movement has grown and matured in recent years, its development is far from stagnant. To the contrary, change in individual behavior, corporate policy, and governmental regulations are occurring at a dizzying pace.

Because of the Federal Sentencing Guidelines, the Defense Industry Initiative, as well as a move from compliance to a values-based approach in the marketplace, corporations have inaugurated companywide ethics programs, hotlines, and senior line positions responsible for ethic training and development. (At the time of the writing of this chapter, an Ethics Officers Association was being formed.) The Sentencing Guidelines allow for mitigation of penalties if a company has taken the initiative in developing ethics training programs and codes of conduct.

In the near future, these same Guidelines will apply to infractions of environmental law (Cartusciello, 1994). As a result, the corporate community will undoubtedly welcome ethics integration in engineering and science programs generally, but more so in those that emphasize environmental issues. Newly hired employees, particularly those in the environmental arena, who have a strong background in ethics education will allay fears concerning integrity and responsibility. Particular attention will be given to the role of public policy in the environmental arena as well as in the formation of an environmental ethic.

Regulations instituted by federal, state, and local agencies continue to become more and more stringent. The deadlines and fines associated with these regulations encourage corporate and industrial compliance of companies (the letter of the law) but it is the personal conviction of the corporate individuals that lies the spirit of the law, and the heart of a true ecological ethic.

To bolster this conviction of the heart, there must be the emergence of a new *dominant social paradigm* (Barbour, 1993). This is defined as "the collection of norms, beliefs, values, habits, and survival rules that provide a framework of reference for members of a society. It is a mental image of social reality that guides behavior and expectations" (Barbour, 1993). The general trend in personal ethics is steadily "greener" and is being achieved at a sustainable pace with realistic goals.

A modern day author suggests the following: The flap of one butterfly's wings can drastically affect the weather (Gleick, 1987). While this statement sounds much like one conceptualized by a romantic ecologist, it is actually part of a mathematical theory explored by the contemporary mathematician James Gleick (1987) in his book *Chaos, Making a New Science*. The "butterfly" theory illustrates that the concept of interdependence, as Chief Seattle professed it, is emerging as more than just a purely environmental one. This embracing of the connectedness of all things joins the new respect for simplified living and the emphasis on global justice, renewable resources, and sustainable development (as opposed to unchecked technological advancement) as the new, emerging social paradigm. The concept of environmentalism is now *widely* held; its future is becoming *deeply* held.

SUMMARY

1. In 1854, Chief Seattle penned warnings as environmentally pensive and poignant as any uttered in the 140 years since: "Continue to contaminate your bed and you will one day lay in your own waste."

2. It is generally accepted that any historical ethic can be grouped into one of the following:
  a. Utilitarianism
  b. Duties Ethics
  c. Rights Ethics
  d. Virtue Ethics

3. The incorporation of environmentalism into everyday ethics does not require a redefinition of one's ethics, but, rather, a redefinition of one's "community" to include nonhuman inhabitants of the land.

4. In the traditional ethical theories, established hierarchies of duties, rights, virtues, and desired consequences exist so that situations where no single course of action satisfies all of the maxims can still be resolved. Debate continues over where the environment falls in this hierarchy.

5. "Engineers in general, in the pursuit of their profession, affect the quality of life for all people in our society. Therefore, an Engineer . . . shall participate in none but honest enterprises . . ."

6. At present, the concept of environmentalism is *widely* held; its future is becoming *deeply* held.

REFERENCES

Barbour, I. *Ethics in an Age of Technology*. San Francisco: Harper, 1993.

Presentation by Cartusciello, N. Chief, Environmental Crimes Section, U.S. Department of Justice, May 4, 1994.

Fahey, J. and Armstrong, R. (eds.). *A Peace Reader: Essential Readings on War, Justice, Non-Violence & World Order*, Mahwah, NJ: Paulist Press, 1987.

Gleick, J. *Chaos, Making a New Science*. New York: Viking, 1987.

Leopold, A. *A Sand County Almanac*. New York: Oxford University Press, 1949.

Martin, M. W., and Schinzinger, R. *Ethics in Engineering*. New York: McGraw Hill, 1989.

Rolston, H., III, *Philosophy Gone Wild*. Buffalo, NY: Prometheus Books, 1986.

50

Environmental Justice

CONTRIBUTING AUTHOR

Molleen Kate Theodore

INTRODUCTION

Capitalism divides the population into classes and distributes political, legal, and economic privileges inequitably. This system empowers the controlling class while leaving the lower class, which is disproportionately minority, with little power. An examination of the history of environmental protection emphasizes the effect of this inequitable division. Environmental protection policy has attempted to reduce environmental risks overall; however, in the process of protecting the environment, risks have been redistributed and concentrated in particular segments of society. Although federal regulations to protect the environment are not explicitly discriminatory, the environmental protection policy has not been sensitive to distributional inequalities, nor has it adequately addressed specific minority environmental concerns. Low-income minority communities are disproportionately exposed to environmental hazards such as toxic waste disposal sites, lead, pesticides, air pollution, and contaminated fish (Bryant & Mohai, 1992).

History has shown that the discriminatory tendencies of the status quo mar attempts at environmental protection. As legislation evolves through the policy process, existing inequities are reinforced. This has caused much speculation as to the efficacy and neutrality of the mainstream environmental protection agenda and has essentially enlisted minority efforts in the movement for environmental justice. Lead provides an example of successful grassroots activism through community empowerment. A related minority response charges that policy has been orchestrated with intentionally racist motives. Domestic accusations of environmental racism are echoed internationally, where third world countries, inhabited predominately by poor minorities, have become receptacles for the hazardous waste of western countries.

Environmental justice can be achieved, in part, with a concerted effort on the part of grassroots and mainstream activists. Minorities have a responsibility to exercise their rightful political and legal power. At the same time, federal protection policy needs to devote attention to specific minority environmental concerns, to monitor the implementation and enforcement of environmental regulations, and to incorporate considerations of equity into policy.

DISPROPORTIONATE ENVIRONMENTAL HAZARDS AFFECTING MINORITY COMMUNITIES

According to a U.S. General Accounting Office study examining population ethnicity and location of off-site hazardous waste landfills in the southeastern region of the United States, African Americans comprise the majority of the population of three out of every four communities with such hazardous waste landfills (EPA, 1992). While siting decisions supposedly result from technical concerns, there are no geological reasons to site environmental waste in low-income minority areas. Political and economic reasons provide a partial explanation for this concentration. Residents are often unaware of the negative effects of environmental hazards and of the available recourses to opposition. Further, they are rarely politically organized or influential, and they often lack the economic and legal resources needed to oppose such unfavorable land uses. Some specific minority-related applications are discussed below.

African American children have a higher percentage of unacceptably high blood lead levels (Agency for Toxic Substances and Disease Registry, 1988). A common route of exposure occurs in buildings with deteriorating lead-based paint through the ingestion of paint chips and inhalation of paint dust. Lead poisoning is a particularly frightening epidemic because the effects of exposure are not immediately visible. Children, more so than adults, are particularly sensitive to the physiological and neurobehavioral effects of lead poisoning at low levels. While lead poisoning is preventable with blood lead testing and abatement, this preventable toxin continues to poison low-income, minority communities where testing is not always available and lead abatement is rarely affordable. (The reader is referred to Chapter 45 for more information on lead.)

A nationwide study of selected pesticides in the milk of mothers found that Hispanic women had higher levels of certain pesticides than White women (Savage, 1976). This evidence is explained by the fact that most Hispanic women in the study were from the Southwest, where pesticide use is generally higher. Agricultural workers are exposed to many toxic substances in the workplace. Such exposure can cause cancer and a wide range of noncancer health effects (EPA, 1992). Agricultural workers are predominately minorities; Latinos, in particular, are disproportionately exposed to pesticides (EPA, 1992). These minority communities often lack health care to deal with the effects of daily toxic exposure and lack mobility to escape this hazardous situation.

A study of the distribution of total suspended particulates from 1970 to 1984 found that African Americans experience higher average exposures and higher average risk reduction benefits (from air pollution controls) (EPA, 1992). A later study also found that racial minorities, in comparison to the majority of the population, are at increased relative risk of air pollution exposure (EPA, 1992). Air pollution is a concern everywhere, but there is a more acute concern in urban areas, where pollution levels are generally higher. A higher percentage of African and Hispanic Americans, in comparison to White Americans, live in urban areas (Department of Commerce, 1990). This increased risk to minorities is dismissed by some as a product of urban life. However, discriminatory residential and labor limits have historically placed minorities in the city; they did not all freely choose where to reside.

Dietary exposure to pollutants such as PCBs and dioxins can occur through fish consumption. While it is difficult to connect dietary exposure and race, it seems that minority populations, particularly Native Americans, are disproportionately exposed to such contaminates (West, Fly, Larkin, & Marans, 1989). Native American communities tend to consume more fish for their dietary protein than the average population. Even when concentrations of chemicals in water are below detection limits, damaging levels of pollutants can bioaccumulate in fish tissues and contaminate the fish consumer with toxins. The quantity of fish eaten, the method of fish preparation, and the species of fish eaten contribute to the level of exposure to contaminants. These communities are unknowingly being contaminated because of their traditional diet.

This redistribution of and inattention to minority environmental risks have persecuted the segment of the population that has historically lacked political influence, legal access, economic stability, residential mobility, and adequate education and health-care systems. If the controlling class of the population was being directly exposed to the hazards of waste landfills, to debilitating levels of lead, and to cancer-causing pesticides to the same extent as these minority communities, federal environmental protection policy would probably be more attentive.

FEDERAL ENVIRONMENTAL PROTECTION

In response to growing environmental concerns, the Environmental Protection Agency (EPA) was created by the federal government. Its agenda has been defined by a series of legislative acts since the late 1960s. (The reader is referred to Chapters 2, 4, and 5 for more details.) The environmental policy of the EPA has historically had two main points of focus: defining an acceptable level of pollution and creating the legal rules to reduce pollution to a specified level. To some, it seems that the program has been most concerned with economic costs and efficiency (Lazarus, 1987). Consequently, policy seems to lack considerations of equity, both distributional and economic. While EPA's two main points of focus are important considerations, relying on such criteria in the formation of environmental protection policy neglects to account for the inequalities of capitalism and its effects throughout the policy process.

The history of environmental policy making illustrates the incompatibility of equity and efficiency; it seems unlikely that increases in progressive distribution will come without a loss of efficiency. Economic pressures of environmental regulation have motivated corporations to seek new ways to reduce costs. Industries have attempted to maximize profits by externalizing environmental costs (Cole, 1992). It has been suggested that this redistribution of costs is more regressive in its effects than the general sales tax (Dorfman & Snow, 1980). If this is so, then the economic costs of environmental protection would be more heavily imposed on low-income populations. To date, big corporate polluters often have more to gain financially by continuing pollution practices than in obeying regulations. In some instances, the result of increased environmental costs has paradoxically caused negative impacts on environmental regulations. As long as corporations feel unaffected by such environmental degradation, they have little incentive, other than altruism, to end debilitating practices. Only a shift of the burden from industry, local governments, and consumers to federal and state governments could ameliorate the regressive nature of total distribution. Without the fear of rising costs, this shift would unavoidably decrease the incentive to reduce polluting activities in the most cost effective manner.

An examination of the distribution of enforcement of environmental laws found that "[t]here is a racial divide in the way the U.S. government cleans up toxic waste sites and punishes polluters. White communities see faster action, better rules, and stiffer penalties than communities where Blacks, Hispanics, and other minorities live. This unequal protection often occurs whether the community is wealthy or poor." Penalties for violation of hazardous waste laws were 46 percent higher in white communities than in minority communities. "Abandoned hazardous waste sites in minority areas take twenty percent longer to be placed on the national priority action list than those in white areas" (Lavelle & Coyle, 1992). This evidence indicates that the distributional implications of environmental policy need to be considered in the decision making, implementation, and monitoring of environmental protection.

THE ENVIRONMENTAL JUSTICE MOVEMENT

Evidence of the effects and concentration of environmental pollution in minority communities has fueled a grassroots environmental movement since the early 1980s. The movement calls for grassroots, multiracial, and multicultural activism to redress the distributional inequalities that have resulted from past policy and to prevent the same inequalities from occurring in future policy. The movement advocates that minorities use historically nonexercised political and legal power to push the EPA to address minority concerns and to oppose policies that impoverish the poor.

The Environmental Justice movement is committed to political empowerment as a way to challenge inequities and injustices. Empowerment is the inclusive involvement and education of community members by equipping them with skills for self representation and defense. Organized activism at the grassroots level could circumvent the power structures that underrepresented particular communities in the first place. Community activists want to participate in the decision making that affects their communities. Further, they argue for increased pay for community members who engage in environmentally hazardous labor, for better working conditions in factories, and for the requirement of more on the job safety precautions. Activists contend that industries must contribute to community development if they are to detract from the community in other ways. For example, activists suggest industrial investment in community projects and educational systems (Marquez, 1994). The use of legal power is also encouraged. In order for court litigation to function effectively in poor and minority communities, law must be practiced in such a way that empowers people, that encourages group formation, and that understands the wider social implications of such legal activity (Cole, 1992).

A protest in Warren County, North Carolina marks the first example of such community activism. When PCBs were illegally dumped along North Carolina state roads in 1982, the state was confronted with a serious toxic waste disposal problem. Warren County, a rural, poor, and 66 percent black community, was chosen as the disposal site for the contaminate soil. This should not be dismissed as a product of rural residency; there are a proportionately higher number of White Americans living in rural areas than African or Hispanic Americans (Department of Commerce, 1990). Feeling specifically and unjustly targeted, the Warren County citizens organized a protest that attracted national attention and began a movement linking environmental issues with social justice. The protest attracted the attention of civil rights activist and United Church of Christ's Commission for Racial Justice Director, Reverend Benjamin Chavis, Jr.

Five years later, the Commission for Racial Justice released the results of a study connecting environmental assaults and racism. The study found that toxic waste dumps were disproportionately located in minority committees. It showed that three of every five African and Hispanic Americans live in areas with controlled toxic waste sites. According to the report, race plays a more significant role that poverty in the siting of environmentally dangerous facilities (UCC Commission for Racial Justice, 1987). Plagued by daily struggles for survival, politically unorganized and powerless poor communities have long been the receptacle for toxic waste disposal. The findings of this study suggested that the environmental needs of low-income, minority communities are not being justly considered (UCC Commission for Racial Justice, 1987).

In response to the growing grassroots movement, EPA created an Environmental Equity work group to review evidence that low-income and minority communities bear a disproportionate exposure to environmental risks. The work group was appropriately titled, for considerations of equity have been notably absent from the agenda of both the EPA and the mainstream environmental groups. The findings of the study indicated "a clear cause for health concerns." The report concluded that "racial minorities may have a greater *potential* for exposure to some pollutants because they tend to live in urban areas, are more likely to live near a waste site, or exhibit a greater tendency to rely on subsistence fishing." At the same time, EPA claimed that poverty is a more significant factor than race in determining which communities are at high risk. While a correlation was identified between income levels and environmental contaminants, insufficient data linking health effects among different race and income groupings left many questions unanswered. In the case of lead, however, the epidemiological data unequivocally demonstrated that "Black children have disproportionately higher blood lead levels than White children even when socioeconomic variables are factored in" (EPA, 1992).

GET THE LEAD OUT

Even though low-income, minority communities have historically lacked political, legal, and economic power, community activism and mobilization have been effective in combating certain environmental problems. Further, existing environmental legislation and the power of the state and federal bureaucracy can actually be used in achieving the goals of community activists. People United for a Better Oakland (PUEBLO), a multiracial organization centered in Oakland, California, has successfully employed community activism though political empowerment and legal and economic pressure in the pursuit of environmental justice. Alarmed by a study claiming 20 percent of Oakland children had lead blood levels high enough to cause permanent brain damage, PUEBLO activists began a campaign to "Get the Lead Out" in 1990 (Marquez, 1994). Activists demanded lead screening for low-income children, locally mandated changes of city lead ordinances, and lead cleanup in existing sites. Even though lead screening was legally mandated by the state of California, many clinics and doctors were not offering the service. Further, PUEBLO activists were concerned that many families did not realize that lead (in their children) was a problem. Activists called for the city of Oakland to change its lead ordinance to limit the use of lead in areas and to clean up lead in existing sites. Lead has both public and private sources; exposure can occur from lead paint in old homes and from automobile and industrial emissions. In some instances, public parks had to be closed down because the ground had been poisoned by a neighboring highway.

In the class-action lawsuit *Matthews v. Coye* (1991), the NAACP, ACLU, and NRDC all rallied for Medicaid to provide for the testing of lead poisoning in Californian children. The settlement required the state of California to screen about 500,000 low-income children under the age of six for lead poisoning at a cost of about $15 to $20 million (Lee, 1992). In addition, Oakland imposed a ten dollar tax levy on existing homes. This levy will be redistributed to finance projects of home abatement, park testing, and parental education to prevent and protect against lead poisoning. This is a substantial victory for a poor minority community. The example of PUEBLO in Oakland demonstrates that environmental activism can work to reduce risk and to challenge the inequitable pattern of redistribution, implementation, and enforcement.

ENVIRONMENTAL RACISM

Environmental policy evolves from a political process that has historically excluded poor people, particularly minority people. While environmental problems are an unavoidable product of industrial life, the disproportionate exposure to particular segments of society is avoidable. Some charge that environmental pollution has been consciously directed at minority communities. Rev. Benjamin Chavis defines environmental racism as "racial discrimination in environmental policy making." He further accuses the predominately white, mainstream environmental movement of excluding minority people in ideology and membership. Environmental racism activist Richard Bullard believes that the consequences of environmental racism have occurred by design rather than by accident (Bullard, 1993). He claims that "African Americans, no matter what their educational or occupational achievements or income level, are exposed to greater environmental threats in their neighborhoods because of their race" (Bullard, 1992). Because racist intentions have not been proven as clearly as Bullard's accusations suggest, many dismiss his rhetoric as propagandistic.

Environmental racism activists have organized members by claiming that the disproportionate concentration of environmental hazards in minority communities is an assault on their civil rights. Attempts to block permits (issued to allow one to operate) by claiming discrimination have historically been difficult because federal environmental laws do not directly address racial disparities. For example, the Clean Air Act did not provide grounds for racial distinction to affect placement decisions regarding waste sites and pollution sources. The Civil Rights Act prohibits state action that has the effect of discrimination, even if discrimination was not racially motivated. This new route of court litigation might be more successful, for it exempts protesters from proving intent. Recent legal challenges to the chosen location of hazardous waste sites and other pollution sources are now being investigated under the 1964 Civil Rights Act (Cushman, 1993).

The process of segregation, which involves a white exodus from the city and a black influx into the city, moved minorities into buildings that were already contaminated with lead-based paint. As the paint deteriorated, it was the minority population who is most directly afflicted by the hazardous health effects. While segregation was motivated by racism, minority exposure to the hazardous effects of lead paint was not intentionally racist. Persistent racial barriers to residential and labor opportunities further complicate accusations of racism. Minorities are more likely to live in close proximity to pollution, to be employed in environmentally hazardous jobs, and to suffer from a disproportionately higher number of environmentally related injuries (Wright, 1990).

The location of hazardous waste disposal is understandably a matter of much opposition; no one wants a garbage disposal site in their backyard. This has been described in the past by the acronym NIMBY, Not In My BackYard. Siting decisions are supposedly made according to geographical and technical feasibility; however, considerations of political and economic feasibility invariably enter into the decision-making process. Waste management companies claim that they do not specifically look for minority communities; rather, it is all a matter of business. But, when companies need cheap property to dispose of garbage and to build potentially air-contaminating incinerators, they turn to areas with cheap land and minimal opposition. Companies claim not to be exploiting racism; their actions are justified as realities of capitalism.

Many theories attempt to explain why minorities are disproportionately affected by environmental pollution. An awareness of the litigation process, the history of segregation, and the process of siting decisions sheds some light on this sensitive issue. However, the limited data available connecting environmentally caused death and disease with race makes it difficult to distinguish this victimization as a product of racism rather than one of poverty. While many question the validity of intentionally racist policy, it is difficult to deny that the environmental movement has not been affected by the social, political, and economic structure in the United States, which was racist when created. If vestiges of racism exist within that order, then truly "raceblind" policy would seem impossible. Is capitalism racist if it perpetuates racial divisions? Although there is no definitive answer, one could argue that vestiges of racism do exist within the structural framework. Unless this discriminatory tendency is explicitly circumvented, racist remnants will continue to affect the process of policy making, implementation, and enforcement.

DOMESTIC AND INTERNATIONAL ENVIRONMENTAL BLACKMAIL

The economic pressures of environmental regulations have encouraged a dangerous negotiation process involving an exchange of money for health hazards. Environmental blackmail provides an example of the environmentally unsound decisions that directly and continually confront low income and minority communities. Environmentally undesirable industries often solicit poor, segregated communities, promising to employ community members and to add money to the tax base in exchange for permission and support (Marquez, 1994).

Whether this is environmental blackmail or self exploitation is debatable. Perhaps the autonomy of these community members should be reassessed. Inadequate information of the potential environmental hazards and vulnerable economic situation has left them, arguably, unable to make self imported decisions. If the community says no, they will have refused an opportunity for increased employment and tax revenue. If the community says yes, they will be endangering the health of themselves and their children. There is rarely a unanimous response to such difficult questions.

The need to determine what is an acceptable level of risk and pollution, concerns which have preoccupied federal policy, is posed to minority communities in a direct and troubling way. Monetary compensation, even if it were fair, is not a solution to the environmental problems of minority communities. African Americans have lower life expectancy rates, higher infant mortality rates, and higher cancer mortality rates than White Americans (EPA, 1992). While there is little data proving the pollution and waste contribution to these differences, the available figures are disturbing. They clearly emphasize the need for more information and attention to the distributional inequalities and reduction of environmental risk.

The environmental justice movement is not domestically contained; the pressure of more stringent environmental regulations in the United States has extended pollution problems internationally. Third-world countries, inhabited predominately by poor minorities, have become receptacles for the hazardous waste of western countries. For example, the less developed and poorer states in Africa, Central America, and the Caribbean have been offered considerable revenue in exchange for acceptance of the hazardous waste of industrialized, western countries. An estimated one-fifth of the total annual global trade of hazardous wastes is transferred from industrialized countries to developing countries, "most of which lack the technology or administrative capacity to dispose of [the hazardous waste] safely." Further, it is claimed that this hazardous waste exchange has, on occasion, occurred "without the approval of the host states and is the result of bribery of officials to allow the wastes to enter the country covertly." This exchange, as defined by African states, is "a form of exploitation of poor and weak states by advanced countries and business firms." African states are not satisfied with regulation of international hazardous waste trade; they want to ban "waste colonialism" completely (Porter & Brown, 1991).

An exchange of financial support for the acceptance of environmental hazards is almost impossible to refuse in a state of poverty; the limited choices of poverty necessitate myopic vision. While the short-term financial benefits are viewed as a potential escape from the cycle of poverty, the long-term effects of continued exposure to health risks are the frightening repercussions of the exchange. Stopping this debilitating cycle requires a change in the political and economic power structure that created the inequalities.

FUTURE TRENDS

To date, environmental legislation has not fully addressed the inequities inherent in capitalism; economic factors predispose certain segments of the population to increased risk. The process of policy making, implementation, and enforcement of environmental protection regulations have redistributed and concentrated risks in low-income, minority communities. Even though these communities seem to lack political, legal, and economic power, community activism and mobilization have been effective in some instances in combating specific environmental problems. The example of the PUEBLO activism illustrates the possibility of success when minorities actively exercise their rightful political and legal power in combination with the power of federal and state governments and existing environmental legislation. This type of activity promises to increase in the future.

Although success incorporates mainstream participation, the environmental justice movement should be led by the voice and concerns of low-income, minority victims globally. Future eradication of the disproportionate exposure of environmental pollution will hopefully challenge wider systemic inequalities that plague minority communities.

SUMMARY

1. Capitalism divides the population into classes and distributes political, legal, and economic privileges inequitably. This system empowers the controlling class while leaving the lower class, which is disproportionately minority, with little power. An examination of the history of environmental protection emphasizes the effect of this inequitable division.

2. While siting decisions supposedly result from technical concerns, there are no geological reasons to site environmental waste in low-income minority areas. Political and economic reasons provide a partial explanation for this concentration.

3. The environmental policy of the EPA has historically had two main points of focus: defining an acceptable level of pollution and creating the legal rules to reduce pollution to a specified level.

4. Evidence of the effects and concentration of environmental pollution in minority communities has fueled a grassroots environmental movement since the early 1980s. The movement calls for grassroots, multiracial, and multicultural activism to redress the distributional inequalities that have resulted from past policy and to prevent the same inequalities from occurring in future policy.

5. People United for a Better Oakland (PUEBLO), a multiracial organization centered in Oakland, California, has successfully employed community activism though political empowerment and legal and economic pressure in the pursuit of environmental justice.

6. Environmental policy evolves from a political process that has historically excluded poor people, particularly minority people. While environmental problems are an unavoidable product of industrial life, the disproportionate exposure to particular segments of society is avoidable.

7. The environmental justice movement is not domestically contained; the pressure of more stringent environmental regulations in the United States has extended pollution problems internationally. Third-world countries, inhabited predominately by poor minorities, have become receptacles for the environmentally hazardous waste of western countries.

8. Future eradication of the disproportionate exposure of environmental pollution will hopefully challenge wider systemic inequalities that plague minority communities.

REFERENCES

Agency for Toxic Substances and Disease Registry. *The Nature and Extent of Lead Poisoning in Children in the United States: A Report to Congress*. Atlanta, GA: Centers for Disease Control, 1988.

Bryant, B., and Mohai, P. *Race and the Incidence of Environmental Hazards*, Boulder, CO: Westview Press, 1992.

Bullard, R. Jr. "In Our Backyards: Minority Communities Get Most of the Dumps," *EPA Journal: Environmental Protection—Has It Been Fair?* Washington DC: 1992.

Bullard, R. Jr. *Confronting Environmental Justice: Voices from the Grassroots*. Boston, MA: South End Press, 1993.

Cole, L. "Empowerment as the Key to Environmental Protection: The Need for Environmental Poverty Law," *Ecology Law Quarterly,* 1992.

Cushman, J. Jr. "U.S. to Weigh Blacks' Complaints About Pollution," *New York Times*, 19, No. 1993, natl. ed., A1, A9.

Department of Commerce, Bureau of the Census. *Statistical Abstract of the United States*, Washington DC: 1990.

Dorfman, N., and Snow, A. "Who Will Pay for Pollution Control? The Distribution by Income of the Burden of the National Environmental Protection Program, 1972–1980." *National Tax Journal*.

EPA, *Environmental Equity: Reducing Risk for All Communities*, Washington DC: 1992.

EPA Science Advisory Board. *Reducing Risks: Setting Priorities and Strategies for Environmental Protection.* Washington DC: 1990.

Lavelle, M., and Coyle, M. "Unequal Protection: The Racial Divide in Environmental Law, A Special Investigation." *National Tax Journal,* 1992.

Lazarus, R. "Pursuing 'Environmental Justice': The Distributional Effects of Environmental Protection." *Northwestern University Law Review,* Spring, 1987.

Lee, B. "Environmental Litigation on Behalf of Poor, Minority Children: *Matthews v. Coye*: A Case Study," Chicago, IL, 1992.

Marquez, B. Lecture, University of Wisconsin/Madison, 5 May 1994.

Porter, G., and Brown, J. *Global Environmental Politics.* Boulder, CO: Westview Press, 1991.

Savage, E. *National Study to Determine Levels of Chlorinated Hydrocarbon Insecticides in Human Milk,* Fort Collins, CO: EPA, 1976.

United Church of Christ Commission for Racial Justice. *Toxic Wastes and Race in the United States: A National Report on the Racial and SocioEconomic Characteristics of Communities with Hazardous Waste Sites,* 1987.

West, P., Fly, J., Larkin, F., and Marans, P. "Minority Anglers and Toxic Fish Consumption: Evidence of the StateWide Survey of Michigan, 1989." In B. Bryant and P. Mohai, Eds., *The Proceedings of the Michigan Conference on Race and the Incidence of Environmental Hazards,* 1989, 108–122.

Wright, B. H. *The Effects of Occupational Injury, Illness, and Disease on the Health Status of Black Americans, The Proceedings of the Michigan Conference on Race and the Incidence of Environmental Hazards,* 1990.

Index